ADULTHOOD AND AGING

ADULTHOOD AND AGING

Jeanne L. Thomas
UNIVERSITY OF WISCONSIN-PARKSIDE

ALLYN AND BACON

Boston   London   Toronto   Sydney   Tokyo   Singapore

Copyright © 1992 by Allyn & Bacon
A Division of Simon & Schuster, Inc.
160 Gould Street
Needham Heights, MA 02194

Library of Congress Cataloging-in-Publication Data

Thomas, Jeanne L.
    Adulthood and aging / Jeanne L. Thomas.
       p. cm.
    Includes bibliographical references and index.
    ISBN 0–205–13377–0
    1. Adulthood. 2. Aging. 3. Adulthood—United States. 4. Aging—
United States. I. Title.
    HQ799.95 T48   1992
305.24—dc20   91–38995
                                                        CIP

Executive Editor: Susan Badger
Series Editor: Diane McOscar
Series Editorial Assistant: Laura Lynch
Production Administrator: Deborah Brown
Production Coordinator: Elaine Ober
Editorial-Production Service: P.M. Gordon Associates
Text Designer: Glenna Collett
Cover Administrator: Linda Dickinson
Manufacturing Buyer: Louise Richardson

Printed in the United States of America

10 9 8 7 6 5 4 3 2 1   96 95 94 93 92 91

Photo Credits   Chapter 1: p. 8, © Ken Karp; p. 10, © AP/Wide World Photos, Inc.; p. 27, © Lionel J. M. Delevingne/Stock, Boston, Inc. *Chapter 2:* p. 41, © George Bellerose/Stock, Boston, Inc.; p. 45, © Peter Menzel/Stock, Boston, Inc.; p. 47, Courtesy of The Children's Defense Fund. *Chapter 3:* p. 53, © Deborah Kahn Kalas/Stock, Boston, Inc.; p. 59, © Eric Neurath/Stock, Boston, Inc.; p. 70, © Patricia Ann Schwab/Stock, Boston, Inc. *Chapter 4:* p. 90, © AP/Wide World Photos, Inc.; p. 94, © Leslie Holzer/Photo Researchers, Inc.; p. 105, © Jim Harrison/Stock, Boston, Inc. *Chapter 5:* p. 116, © Laima Druskis; p. 127, © Laima Druskis; p. 129, © Joseph Schuyler/Stock, Boston, Inc. *Chapter 6:* p. 141, © Lora E. Askinazi/The Picture Cube, Inc.; p. 162, © H.U.D. *Chapter 7:* p. 170, © Rhoda Sidney/Stock, Boston, Inc.; p. 180, © Frank Siteman/The Picture Cube, Inc.; p. 182, © Richard Sobol/Stock, Boston, Inc. *Chapter 8:* p. 190, © Hella Hammid/Photo Researchers, Inc.; p. 209, © Michael Weisbrot and Family/Stock, Boston, Inc.; p. 214, © AP/Wide World Photos, Inc. *Chapter 9:* p. 225, © Will McIntyre/Photo Researchers, Inc.; p. 239, © J. Berndt/Stock, Boston, Inc.; p. 247, © Irene Springer *Chapter 10:* p. 254, © Nancy Bates/The Picture Cube, Inc.; p. 264, © Teri Leigh Stratford/Photo Researchers, Inc.; p. 273, © Ed Lettau/Photo Researchers, Inc. *Chapter 11:* p. 281, © Jean-Claude Lejeune/Stock, Boston, Inc.; p. 292, © Elizabeth Crews/Stock, Boston, Inc.; p. 299, © Anna Kaufman Moon/Stock, Boston, Inc. *Chapter 12:* p. 307, © Stephen Capra; p. 312, © The United Nations; p. 314, © Marianne Gontarz/The Picture Cube, Inc. *Chapter 13:* p. 329, © Laima Druskis; p. 330, © Jim Anderson/Stock, Boston, Inc.; p. 333, © Cathy Cheney/Stock, Boston, Inc. *Chapter 14:* p. 351, © Gloria Karlson/The Picture Cube, Inc.; p. 353, © Betsy Cole/The Picture Cube, Inc.; p. 360, © Teri Stratford. *Chapter 15:* p. 370, © Irene Springer; p. 371, © Michael Weisbrot and Family/Stock, Boston, Inc.; p. 381, © Michael Weisbrot and Family/Stock, Boston, Inc.

For my best friends
Ann Thomas and Honey

CONTENTS

Preface   *xvii*

1 **APPROACHES TO THE STUDY OF**
ADULT DEVELOPMENT AND AGING   2

The Significance of the Study of Adult Development   3
    Why study adult development and aging?
    The "development" of the study of adult development and aging
The Study of Adulthood and Aging: A Life-span Perspective   6
    Topics and goals characterizing the life-span orientation
        Defining the field   Key assumptions of the life-span orientation
Research Methodology and Related Issues   13
    Validity
        Internal validity   External validity   Statistical conclusion
        validity   Construct validity
    Other key psychometric issues
        Reliability of measurement   Age equivalence of measurement
    Sampling considerations: Assuring that research reflects
        diversity
Developmental Research Designs   20
    Three central variables
    Three basic developmental research designs
    The sequential designs
Pertinent Ethical Issues   26
        Diversity in Adulthood: The significance and
        challenges of cross-cultural research   12
        Open Questions: Protecting research participants
        while ensuring scientific progress   28
Summary   30
Key Terms   30
Suggestions for Further Reading   31

2   THEORIES IN THE STUDY OF ADULT DEVELOPMENT   32

Models and Theories   33
   Models
      Model functions
   Theories
      Theory functions   The variety of developmental theories
      Developmental theories and research

Models of Development   39
   The mechanistic model
      Model assumptions   The mechanistic model, theory, and
      applications for aging
   The organismic model
      Model assumptions   The organismic model, theory, and
      research on aging
   The dialectical model
      Model assumptions   The dialectical model, theory, and
      research on aging
   Open Questions: **What is successful aging?   36**
   Diversity in Adulthood: **Cultural context in Erikson's developmental theory   48**

Summary   50
Key Terms   51
Suggestions for Further Reading   51

3   CHANGES IN PHYSICAL FUNCTIONING THROUGHOUT ADULTHOOD   52

Changes in Physical Appearance   53
   Changes in the skin and hair
   Changes in height and weight

Aging of the Major Organ Systems   55
   The nervous system
   The cardiovascular system, respiratory system, and basal metabolism
   The skeletal and muscular systems
   The digestive and urinary systems
   The immune system
   The reproductive system
      Sexual physiology and functioning   The climacteric: A universal experience unfolding in diverse ways   Sexual impacts of the climacteric   Physiological impacts of the climacteric: Reflections of culture   Sexual dysfunction   Infertility
   Aging: A gradual and individual process

Biological Theories of Aging   75
 Genetic theories
 Wear and tear theories
Longevity: Reflections of Heredity and Lifestyle   77
 Gender and racial differences in longevity
 Influences of longevity
 Claims of exceptional human life spans
 Open Questions: Is there a "double standard of aging"?   56
 Diversity in Adulthood: Cultural differences in Israeli
  women's reactions to menopause   68
Summary   79
Key Terms   80
Suggestions for Further Reading   81

4 **HEALTH AND HEALTH CARE THROUGHOUT ADULTHOOD**   82

General Influences of Physical Health   83
 Health in early adulthood: Variation by race and gender
 Lifestyle: Choices of young adulthood and their long-term
  impact
   *Diet and exercise Stress and personality Cigarette
   smoking The use of alcohol and other drugs Sexually
   transmitted diseases*
Health Changes in Adulthood   91
 Health impacts of the climacteric
 Other health changes: Gender and racial differences
 Causes of death in old age
Health Care and the Aged   97
 Older people and health care: Formal, informal, and self-care
 Older people and long-term care
   *Long-term care in the community Long-term care in
   nursing homes*
 Diversity in Adulthood: Health status in old age:
  Racial differences and the "crossover" effect   84
 Open Questions: How should we pay for long-term care?   102
Summary   108
Key Terms   109
Suggestions for Further Reading   109

5 **BASIC COGNITIVE PROCESSES**   110

Age-related Changes in Sensation and Perception   111
 Sensation versus perception
 Vision and hearing in early adulthood
 Normal age-related changes in vision

Pathological age-related changes in vision
Normal age-related changes in hearing
Pathological age-related changes in hearing
Normal age-related changes in taste and smell
Normal age-related changes in pain perception
Normal age-related changes in the vestibular system
    and kinesthesis

Basic Cognitive Functioning: Research on Age Differences   **122**
Age differences in attention and arousal
Age differences in reaction time and psychomotor skills
Practical implications of age differences in basic intellectual
    processes

*Interventions: Optimizing Performance and Mobility in
    Later Life*   **132**
Diversity in Adulthood: Variation in the extent of
    decreased auditory sensitivity   114
Open Questions: Should driving privileges be
    restricted in old age?   131

Summary   **133**
Key Terms   **134**
Suggestions for Further Reading   **135**

6   INTELLIGENCE, WISDOM, AND CREATIVITY   **136**

Views of Adult Intelligence   **137**
Stages of adult intellectual development
Components of adult intelligence

Psychometric Studies of Adult Intelligence   **146**
Measures of adult intelligence
Measurement problems
Psychometric research on change in adult intelligence
Explanations for age-related changes in adult intelligence

Reasoning and Problem Solving Throughout Adulthood   **152**
Research on logical reasoning and problem solving
Research on practical problem solving

Wisdom and Creativity   **157**
Diversity in Adulthood: Culture and Piaget's
    problem-solving tasks   139
Open Questions: Does intelligence decline with age?   161

Summary   **162**
Key Terms   **162**
Suggestions for Further Reading   **162**

7 *LEARNING AND MEMORY THROUGHOUT ADULTHOOD*   **164**

Learning, Memory, and Performance   **165**
    The inseparability of learning and memory
    Learning and memory versus performance
Age Differences in Memory Performance   **166**
    The information processing approach to memory
    Encoding versus retrieval deficits
    Nonability influences of performance
    Memory in everyday life
    Interventions to improve older adults' memory
Education Throughout Adulthood   **177**
    College: Diversity in colleges and their students
    Continuing education and nontraditional students
    Elderhostel
    Diversity in Adulthood: **Women's ways of knowing**   **178**
    Open Questions: **Should the "three boxes of life"**
        be redistributed?   **183**
Summary   **184**
Key Terms   **185**
Suggestions for Further Reading   **185**

8 *PERSONALITY: CHANGE AND STABILITY*   **186**

Defining Personality   **187**
Qualitative Descriptions of Adult Personality:
    Classic Stage Theories   **188**
        Freud's psychoanalytic theory
        Jung's analytic theory and cross-cultural research on the
            "parental imperative"
        Erikson's psychosocial theory
        The Chicago researchers
                Havighurst's developmental tasks   *Robert Peck*
                Bernice Neugarten
        More recent approaches
                Levinson: The life structure   *Gould: Shedding false assumptions*
Personality Measurement and Psychometric Research   **201**
    Self-report measures
    Projective measures
    Quantitative research on adult personality
Personality, Life Satisfaction, and Aging:
    Varied Paths to Contentment in Old Age   **205**
Personality Development in Women   **208**
Moral Judgment and Reasoning   **211**
        Kohlberg: Moral reasoning among Harvard students

Carol Gilligan and women's moral reasoning
Concluding Thoughts   *215*
Open Questions: **Is the concept of the "midlife crisis" useful?**   **206**
Diversity in Adulthood: **Women around the world: Mental health in the middle years of adulthood**   **212**
Summary   *215*
Key Terms   *216*
Suggestions for Further Reading   *217*

9   *P*SYCHOPATHOLOGY AND PSYCHOTHERAPY: *MENTAL HEALTH PROBLEMS IN OLD AGE*   218

Defining Mental Health: Impacts of Cultural Context and Cohort   *219*
Age and Major Functional Disorders   *221*
Depression
Diagnosing depression: Rates of depression and race, class, and gender   Causes of depression   Treating depression in the elderly
Age, gender, and racial differences in suicide rates
Schizophrenia
Alcohol abuse in old age
Dementia   *233*
Dementia symptoms
Conditions producing dementia symptoms
Alzheimer's disease (AD)
Incidence of AD   Distinguishing features   Course of AD Possible causes of AD   Diagnosis of AD   Treating AD
Mental Health Services and Elderly Adults   *243*
Older adults' use of mental health services
Treatment settings
Treatment approaches for the elderly
Diversity in Adulthood: **The "healthy adult personality": A culturally biased definition?**   **220**
Open Questions: **Schizophrenia and the nature-nurture controversy**   **230**
Summary   *247*
Key Terms   *248*
Suggestions for Further Reading   *248*

10   *L*OVE AND MARRIAGE *THROUGHOUT ADULTHOOD*   250

Before Marriage: Intimacy, Dating, and Mate Selection   *251*
Intimacy: Variation by age and gender
Dating: Age and gender differences in dating relationships

Mate selection

Marriage   *257*

Adjustment to marriage

Studying marital satisfaction: Comparing views of "happy
marriages" across the lines of gender, race, and social class

The impact of marriage

Changes over time in marital satisfaction

Alternatives to Marriage   *267*

Remaining single

Cohabitation

Homosexuality

Divorce and Remarriage   *271*

Divorce

Remarriage

Diversity in Adulthood: The many American ways of
married life   262

Open Questions: Are remarriages more successful than
first marriages?   275

Summary   *276*

Key Terms   *277*

Suggestions for Further Reading   *277*

11 *R̲ELATIONSHIPS BETWEEN GENERATIONS:*
    AFFECTION AND INTERACTION   *278*

Parenthood   *279*

Why do people have children? Cross-cultural variation
in motivations

Remaining child-free

Pregnancy and birth: Women's and men's unique experiences

The transition to parenthood

Parenting under special circumstances

Single mothers and fathers   *Stepparents*

Older parents and older children

Parents and adolescents   *The "empty nest"*

The "refilled nest"

Elderly Parents and Adult Children   *291*

Geographic proximity

Multigenerational households

Contact between the elderly and adult children: Gender, race,
and class differences

Feelings between older parents and their children

Grandparenthood and Great-grandparenthood   *297*

Grandparents

Diversity in grandparenthood

Age differences   Gender differences   Race, ethnicity, and grandparenthood
Grandparenthood and mental health
Great-grandparents
Diversity in Adulthood: **Why have children? It depends on culture!**   280
Open Questions: **Should homosexuals be allowed to rear children?**   287

Summary   301
Key Terms   301
Suggestions for Further Reading   301

12   *FAMILY RELATIONSHIPS: HELPING OLDER RELATIVES*   **302**

Family Traditions of Mutual Support   303
Long-term reciprocal support patterns
Race and class variation in support patterns
Family Caregiving for the Frail Elderly   305
Caregiving experience
Caregiver Burden: A Stress and Coping Model   306
The stressors of caregiving
Caregiving and role conflict: "Women in the middle"
Appraisals: Attitudes toward providing care
Mediators: Steps to minimize caregiver burden
Mediation through caregiving networks
Other reactions to caregiving
Variation in caregiving: Gender, relationship, and racial differences
Family Caregiving and Formal Sources of Long-term Care   316
Family caregiving and institutionalization
Concluding Thoughts   318
Diversity in Adulthood: **What should adult children do for aged parents? Answers from American and Japanese women**   312
Open Questions: **Should the family or the state be responsible for older peoples' long-term care?**   317

Summary   319
Key Terms   319
Suggestions for Further Reading   319

13   *BONDS WITH SIBLINGS, FRIENDS, AND THE COMMUNITY*   **320**

Sibling Relationships Throughout Adulthood   321
The importance of brothers and sisters

Contact, feelings, and exchanging help between adult brothers
and sisters
Friendship   *324*
Age differences in friendship
Class, race, and gender differences in friendship
Confidants in old age
Adults in the Community   *329*
Political involvement
Voluntary organizations and volunteer work
Religious involvement
Age, gender, and racial differences in religious involvement
Religion as a resource in old age
Specialized housing and communities for elderly people
Diversity in Adulthood: What is a friend? The contrasting
perspectives of men and women   328
Open Questions: Is age-segregated housing best for young
and old?   338
Summary   *340*
Key Terms   *340*
Suggestions for Further Reading   *340*

14   WORK AND RETIREMENT   *342*

Careers   *343*
Theories of career choice
Differentialist views   Developmentalist views
Career entry
Job satisfaction
Career changes
Older adults in the labor force
Stereotypes of older workers and age discrimination
Special Career Issues   *352*
Race, ethnicity, and careers
Discrimination in employment
Unemployment
Harassment in the workplace
Retirement   *359*
Early retirement
Preparing for retirement
Adjusting to retirement
Gender and racial differences
Retirement income
Diversity in Adulthood: Women and work:
Are their experiences unique?   346
Open Questions: Affirmative action:
Social justice or reverse discrimination?   356

Summary   *366*
Key Terms   *367*
Suggestions for Further Reading   *367*

15 DEATH AND DYING   *368*

Defining Death   *369*
Medical and Ethical Issues   *370*
   Euthanasia and living wills
   Hospice care
Attitudes Toward Death   *376*
   Facing death: Theoretical perspectives
   Facing death: Survey research on age, gender, and
      racial differences
   Facing death: Research on the terminally ill
        Kübler-Ross' stages   *Other research on terminal illness*
Social and Legal Issues   *381*
   Survivors' reactions to death
   Conjugal bereavement
   Death of a parent
   Funerals
   Wills and inheritance patterns
   Open Questions: **Euthanasia: Mercy or murder?**   **372**
   Diversity in Adulthood: **Racial differences in
      funeral practices**   **386**
Summary   *388*
Key Terms   *388*
Suggestions for Further Reading   *389*

APPENDIX: STATISTICAL TOOLS COMMONLY USED IN DEVELOPMENTAL RESEARCH   *390*

   Overview
Descriptive Statistics   *391*
   Measures of central tendency
   Measures of variability
Inferential Statistics   *393*
   Comparing group means
   Examining patterns of association between variables
   Causal analysis

GLOSSARY   *398*

REFERENCES   *421*

INDEX   *461*

*P*REFACE

*G*OALS AND ORIENTATION OF ADULTHOOD AND AGING

My desire to write this book stemmed primarily from the satisfaction that I find in introducing undergraduates to the scientific study of aging. In my courses, I strive to convey some of the excitement of the field of adult development, and of the processes of growing older. As many instructors can attest, that excitement is not always immediately obvious to young college students (or even to older college students). However, as students learn about the diverse ways in which aging processes unfold, about the multifaceted influences of those processes, and about areas of unanswered questions and exciting empirical developments, many find that a course about aging is much more interesting than they had anticipated. I have found that some of my students enter my course with negative stereotypes of older people, but leave it with a deep appreciation for the contributions that elderly adults make to our society and our world. I count my contribution to that change in perceptions among my most satisfying professional accomplishments.

Students who enroll in a course on adult development and aging are often majoring in psychology, sociology, social work, or nursing; these students tend to approach the course with one or more main goals. Some view the course as an important element in their preparation for graduate study in developmental psychology, gerontology, social work, or public administration; others plan to work immediately after graduation in a mental health, health care, or human services agency that serves older adults. Still other students take the course out of personal interest in the topic. Certainly, these student goals are not mutually exclusive, and most students who take the course probably have all three objectives to a greater or lesser extent.

These student goals do, however, reflect the distinct priorities and instructional needs that a text should fulfill. First, a text should provide an adequate theoretical and empirical background to serve as a foundation for further study of adult development at the graduate level, and possibly for student research (e.g., honor's thesis, B.A. or B.S. thesis) related to adult development and aging. Secondly, the text should address practical issues to an extent that prompts students to consider empirical work in terms of its potential application in their own lives or in professional settings designed to meet the needs of older adults and their families. I have prepared this book to meet those objectives.

Three themes shape the book's presentation of adult development. First, the book takes a life-span orientation. I discuss physical, psychological, and social changes that take place in middle and later adulthood as long-term consequences of the choices and circumstances surrounding earlier periods of the life cycle, and I consider events occurring in early adulthood with respect to their eventual impact later in development. A second theme is the importance of examining adult development as a multicultural phenomenon. Throughout the book, I point out ways in which race, gender, social class, and culture moderate developmental processes and outcomes. The most obvious reflections of this theme are the *Diversity in Adulthood* boxes appearing in each chapter, in which a topic addressed in the chapter is examined from a multicultural perspective. In addition, virtually all chapters include explicit attention to multicultural issues. A third, more general, theme is encouragement for students to think critically about the material. The book provides students with sufficient grounding in research methodology, measurement issues, and statistical approaches to critically consider research findings. And, the *Open Questions* boxes in each chapter introduce a controversial issue related to topics raised in the chapter and prompt students to evaluate contrasting arguments regarding that issue.

Throughout the book, I present an overview of both classic and contemporary research and theory. I have made special efforts to include the most current information available for each chapter: over 40 percent of the citations relate to work published since 1987. Many of the remaining citations are to classic work that continues to have an impact on research today. I discuss all research—both classic and contemporary—with an eye toward showing the student both the significance of the work and ways in which researchers' decisions concerning sampling, measurement, and analysis can affect the outcome of the research.

ORGANIZATION OF ADULTHOOD AND AGING

The fifteen chapters comprising the book form seven clusters of related chapters. The first two chapters present material that forms a foundation for the remainder of the text. Chapter 1 offers a brief history of the field and examines the importance of studying adult development and the elements of a life-span orientation to development. Chapter 1 also includes an extensive discussion of research methodology (including validity in research design, age equivalence in measurement, reliability, and sampling), developmental research designs, and ethical issues in research. In Chapter 2, developmental world views and theories are presented, together with in-depth examinations of selected theories and related research. The next two chapters deal with physical aspects of adult development and aging. Chapter 3 describes physical changes that occur with age, biological theories of aging, and longevity. Chapter 4 addresses health and health changes throughout adulthood; this chapter also considers health care issues with particular attention to long-term care, its funding, and its future in an aging society.

The following three chapters present information on age-related changes in basic psychological processes. In Chapter 5, changes in perception, attention, arousal, reaction time, and psychomotor functioning are described; this chapter also includes a section discussing interventions that can minimize the impact of normal and pathological age-related changes in these dimensions. Chapter 6 reviews research on adult intelligence, reasoning and problem solving, wisdom, and creativity; in these discussions, bodies of contrasting findings (e.g., cross-sectional versus longitudinal and sequential studies of intelligence; logical versus practical problem solving) are highlighted, and possible sources of these contrasts are discussed. Chapter 7 provides an overview of research on learning and memory performance throughout adulthood, as well as a discussion of education as it touches the lives of young, middle-aged, and elderly adults.

In the next two chapters, normal and pathological patterns of change in personality are described. In Chapter 8, classic and contemporary theories and research concerning normal adult personality development are presented; a chapter theme is the extent to which change and stability characterize adult personality. Chapter 9 considers psychopathology and psychotherapy in old age; dementia in general and Alzheimer's disease in particular are extensively discussed, as are depression, schizophrenia, and substance abuse. This chapter also considers ways in which the mental health needs of contemporary older Americans are met, and ways in which those needs might be more effectively addressed.

The following three chapters provide intensive coverage of family relationships in adulthood; no competing text provides such extensive coverage of the family as a context of aging. Chapter 10 addresses intimacy and dating, mate selection, marriage and divorce, and alternatives to marriage. Chapter 11 considers intergenerational relationships: research on parent-child relationships throughout adulthood, grandparenthood, and great-grandparenthood is summarized. Chapter 12 is devoted to the important topic of intergenerational support networks, with a focus on family caregiving from a stress-and-coping perspective.

The next two chapters outline broader social contexts of adult development. In Chapter 13, relationships with siblings are discussed, as well as relationships with friends and with the community. Political involvement, volunteer work, and religious involvement are all considered, as are the types of housing, neighborhoods, and community settings in which older individuals reside. Chapter 14 is devoted to work and retirement. Theories of career development are presented, as well as career-related issues particularly germane to women and minorities. This chapter also includes a discussion of preparation for retirement, adjustment to retirement, and retirement income. Chapter 15 is devoted to issues related to death and dying. Medical and ethical issues surrounding care of patients suffering from life-threatening illness are considered, together with research on attitudes toward death and on the processes of grieving and bereavement.

PEDAGOGICAL FEATURES AND SUPPLEMENTS

I have included several features to enhance the instructional value of the book. Each chapter begins with a brief narrative overview of the chapter contents, followed by a set of questions for students to consider as they read the chapter. Technical terms in each chapter are printed in boldface when they initially appear, are defined in the glossary at the end of the book, and are listed at the end of the chapter. As noted above, each chapter includes a *Diversity in Adulthood* box which stresses multicultural aspects of development and an *Open Questions* box which encourages consideration of contrasting views regarding a controversial issue. Each chapter closes with a summary and a set of suggestions for further reading. These suggestions, as well as the extensive bibliography at the end of the book, provide starting points for student papers and research. In each chapter, charts and graphs are used to illustrate important concepts and research findings, and captioned photographs visually reinforce key points.

A unique pedagogical feature is the statistical appendix appearing at the end of the book. Students who enroll in a course on adult development and aging bring a diverse set of backgrounds and goals to the course. From an instructor's viewpoint, this diversity is particularly apparent in the extent of students' familiarity with statistical techniques, and this diversity can present difficulties for the instructor. Although a detailed understanding of statistics is by no means necessary to appreciate course material, students with some awareness of the power and limitations of widely used techniques can certainly examine the course material more critically, are better prepared to read a wider range of primary source material, and are prepared to draw more soundly based inferences regarding the material. The appendix provides an overview of statistical methods; it can serve as a review for students with some statistical background, or an introduction for students lacking such a background.

The *Instructor's Manual* for the text provides film and video suggestions and a set of suggested class activities for each chapter. The *Instructor's Manual* also provides 40 to 50 multiple choice questions for each chapter. Most of these questions require the student to apply material presented in the chapter (rather than simply memorize it), and "negative" questions (e.g., which of the following is *not* a symptom of dementia?) are avoided.

ACKNOWLEDGMENTS

I am indebted to the reviewers who contributed to the development of this book. Their interest and their insightful comments and suggestions had a strong impact on the book's evolution. All of them helped to make the final product a better book than it otherwise could have been, and I am grateful to them:

Denise Barnes-Lacoste
     University of North Carolina at Chapel Hill
Elaine Blakemore
     Indiana University
     Purdue University at Fort Wayne
Cameron Camp
     University of New Orleans
Lisa Friedenberg
     University of North Carolina at Asheville
Irene Hulicka
     Buffalo State College
Jennifer Kinney
     Bowling Green State University
Victoria Molfese
     Southern Illinois University
Dana Plude
     University of Maryland
Dean Rodeheaver
     University of Wisconsin-Green Bay
Taher Zandi
     State University of New York at Plattsburgh

I also owe recognition to friends and colleagues at the University of Wisconsin-Parkside for their support and encouragement. Michael Gurtman, my department chair, was unique in his faith that my book would be a worthwhile contribution; I offer him my warmest thanks. Ron Pavalko, of the Sociology and Anthropology Department, provided wise advice concerning various "nuts and bolts" issues related to writing a textbook. I am grateful to Chancellor Sheila Kaplan and Vice Chancellor John Stockwell for their support of my sabbatical leave during part of the time that I worked on the book. And, I am indebted to my colleagues David Beach and Beecham Robinson for showing me that taking pedagogy and teaching seriously can be a rewarding source of intellectual excitement. Most of all, I thank my students for their interest in my adult development courses and the inspiration that their interest has given me.

I consider myself most fortunate to have worked with a highly capable, efficient, and supportive staff at Allyn and Bacon. I especially appreciate the efforts of Diane McOscar, senior editor. Her interest and enthusiasm kept me going at times when my own motivation ebbed. Her sage and patient advice had an inestimable impact on the final form of the book, and her efforts in coordinating the work of the reviewers and the production staff made the book a reality. I also thank Laura Lynch, editorial assistant, for her attention to countless details and for always having the answer to my sometimes obscure questions.

Finally, I am deeply grateful to my mother, Ann Thomas, and to Honey. My mother remained confident that I would meet deadlines and produce a book that I could be proud of—even during the bleaker moments when I had my doubts. And, Honey lay at my feet while I wrote the book and never seemed to doubt that I would finish it and finally take her for a walk.

Adulthood and Aging

CHAPTER ONE

APPROACHES TO THE STUDY OF ADULT DEVELOPMENT AND AGING

We are embarking on the study of the adult years of the life cycle. In this chapter, we identify issues that provide orientation for the material covered throughout the book. We begin with the history of the study of adult development and aging, and the importance of continued progress in the field. This book presents the study of adult development from a life-span perspective; we also consider, then, the unique nature of that viewpoint, and the reasons that it can be particularly enlightening. Finally, we explore issues that must be confronted in researching adult development, including ethical issues that scientists in the field face. Questions to consider in reading the chapter include:

How has the age distribution of the American population changed in recent decades, and why has it changed?

How has the study of adult development been approached in the past?

What does a life-span orientation to the study of a particular period of the life span, such as adulthood, entail?

What issues must researchers consider in gathering information that will permit interpretable, broadly applicable conclusions regarding adult development?

What ethical concerns are of special interest in conducting research on adult development and aging?

THE SIGNIFICANCE OF THE STUDY OF ADULT DEVELOPMENT

Why study adult development and aging?

Today, this question seems overly obvious. The adult years, after all, encompass the vast majority of the life span. Furthermore, it is apparent to the layperson and to professionals that these years are a time of tremendous change for the individual, and that these changes have great import for the society in which the individual develops. However, that awareness has not always colored our perspective of human development. For many years, developmental researchers confined their attention to the early years of the life span, and the processes of aging were primarily studied as social problems.

Both demographic and social forces impel scholars to turn their attention toward the adult years. Over the past century, we have witnessed the "graying of America." This phrase refers to a gradual shift in the age distribution of the population such that an increasing proportion of the population is represented by those aged 65 and over. In fact, the most rapidly growing segment of the American population at this time is the "oldest old," those aged 85 and older. Figure 1.1 illustrates the increase in the older American population during the twentieth century.

These demographic trends stem from several forces. First, birth rates have decreased during much of the twentieth century, in part reflecting in-

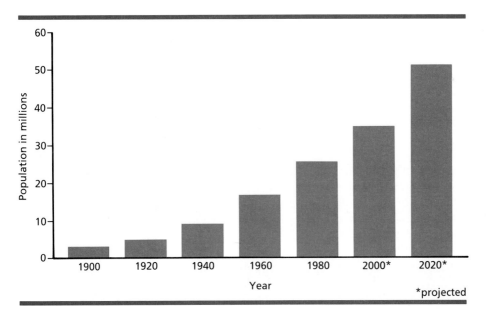

Figure 1.1
U.S. population aged 65 and older. (Source: U.S. Bureau of the Census, 1984.)

creases in medical technology (e.g., contraceptive effectiveness), shifting economic trends, and changes in men's and women's roles and aspirations. With a falling birth rate, the proportion of adults to children in the population increases.

Second, life expectancy at birth has increased during the twentieth century, most notably for Caucasians and to a lesser extent for racial minorities (e.g., Markides, 1989). Thus, more people now survive to old age. This change also undoubtedly reflects advances in medical technology, since illnesses that formerly caused death early in life are now more effectively treated. Increased life expectancy at birth may also reflect social changes, including legislation controlling food additives and labeling; regulations governing the production, use, and storage of toxic chemicals; increased health awareness on the part of the general public; and improved access to health care for wider segments of the population.

Scientists expect both the graying of America and the particularly rapid increase in the numbers of the oldest old to continue at least through the remainder of the twentieth century. In fact, as the individuals born during the "baby boom" following World War II mature, these trends will become even more pronounced. Given the sheer numbers of baby boomers, their aging could become problematic—both for those individuals and for their society—if we lack understanding of adult growth and development.

Thus, because adulthood and advanced old age are experienced by more and more people, understanding the processes of change and stability that occur during these years is of utmost importance. As a society, we must be prepared to anticipate and respond to the physical, psychological, and social needs that individuals encounter at various points in adult life. Equally important, our society can benefit tremendously from awareness of the talents and resources that adults offer at various points in their journey through adulthood.

The "development" of the study of adult development and aging

For the most part, the systematic study of adult development is a twentieth-century phenomenon. Prior to that time, there were isolated examinations of adult physical and psychological development, but not sustained study of these processes (Baltes, 1979; Baltes, Reese, & Lipsitt, 1980). Among the earliest and most important examinations of adult development was **Quetelet**'s 1842 volume entitled *A Treatise on Man and the Development of his Faculties*. In this book, Quetelet summarized demographic, anthropometric, and psychological data regarding changes occurring throughout the life span. His work is notable for the insight he provides into methodological issues and into central concepts—such as critical periods—in the study of human development.

When psychology emerged as a distinct field, the earliest psychologists also turned their attention toward changes occurring during adulthood. In

1922, **G. Stanley Hall** published *Senescence*, in which he described processes of aging on the basis of his own experience, his study of medical and physiological aspects of aging, and a survey administered to aged individuals concerning problems, attitudes, and self-perceptions (Charles, 1970). **E. L. Thorndike** studied associations between adult age and interests and ability, and the implications of these associations for adult education (Charles, 1970).

During the twentieth century, professional interest in adult development has expanded tremendously (Charles, 1970). The first research unit with a deliberate goal of studying adult development and aging was established in 1928 at Stanford University; this group was concerned with older workers' difficulty in obtaining jobs in California. The National Institutes of Health (NIH) were founded in 1946; NIH supports research in many areas of human performance and development, including adult development and aging.

The Gerontological Society of America, the largest professional society in the field of aging, was founded in 1945. Since that time, the GSA has been a forum for physicians, biologists, and behavioral and social scientists interested in aging. One of the contributions of the GSA is its sponsorship of two important journals: the *Journal of Gerontology* and *The Gerontologist*. Also in 1945, Division 20 of the American Psychological Association was established; this membership division brought together psychologists interested in adult development and aging.

In addition, major research programs dealing with social, psychological, and physiological processes of adult development and aging were instituted in the second half of the twentieth century (Charles, 1970). A committee on social adjustment in old age was established at the University of Chicago in 1943; this outstanding interdisciplinary group (later known as the Committee on Human Development) has provided fundamental contributions. Other ongoing longitudinal research programs were initiated in Framingham, Massachusetts in 1940, at the Duke University Medical Center in 1950, in Seattle in 1956, and in Boston in 1963. The Baltimore Longitudinal Study, one of the most extensive continuing programs of research on human aging, began in 1958 under the auspices of the National Institutes of Health.

The scholars associated with longitudinal research projects at the University of California's Institute of Human Development—the Oakland Growth Study, the Berkeley Growth Study, and the Guidance Study—became involved in the study of adult development (Eichorn, Clausen, Haan, Honzik, & Mussen, 1981). These longitudinal programs were started early in the twentieth century, when the research participants were young children or adolescents. However, as these subjects matured, the researchers' interests expanded to include the participants' experiences of adult life (Eichorn et al., 1981). Most recently, Erik Erikson and his colleagues (Erikson, Erikson, & Kivnick, 1986) interviewed the surviving parents of the Guidance Study participants, and interpreted interview findings in the context of psychosocial development in old age.

We see, then, that the study of adult growth and change has itself matured. Beginning with scattered pretwentieth century origins, the field has grown into a thriving, well-established multidisciplinary specialty. One feature of this specialty is its grounding in a life-span perspective of development.

THE STUDY OF ADULTHOOD AND AGING: A LIFE-SPAN PERSPECTIVE

The **life-span perspective** is not a single theory of human development. Nor does the term necessarily refer to the study of a single quality—such as intellectual growth or personality development—from conception through death. Rather, the life-span perspective is an *orientation or viewpoint* regarding the study of development, either throughout the life cycle or within a particular period of the life span such as childhood, adolescence, or adulthood. This orientation includes goals and topics of interest, and rests upon fundamental assumptions.

Topics and goals characterizing the life-span orientation

Defining the field   Life-span developmental science is commonly defined as the description, explanation, and optimization of intra-individual change and interindividual differences in behavior from birth to death (Baltes, Reese, & Nesselroade, 1977; Baltes, Reese, & Lipsitt, 1980). This definition encompasses several general topics and related goals.

First, the definition identifies two topics of primary interest to life-span developmental scientists. The first is that of ***intra*-individual change**, or ways in which any single person changes during his or her lifetime. These changes can be in many areas. Changes in physical functioning—including physical growth, changes in health, changes in motor performance and athletic abilities, increases or decreases in stamina and strength, and other aspects of physical functioning—are an area of interest. Similarly, life-span developmental scientists are interested in psychological changes, including changes in basic processes such as learning, memory, and problem solving as well as changes in personality, moral reasoning, adjustment, and morale. Finally, life-span developmental scientists are interested in age-related changes in social relationships. What kinds of relationships with other people and with society do we have at various points in our lives, and how do these relationships affect us?

The second area of interest is that of ***inter*individual differences** in development, or ways in which changes experienced over time vary from one person to the next. In this respect, we consider ways in which personal characteristics—for example, race, gender, and social class—moderate physical, psychological, and social change throughout the life cycle. A related concern is the personal and social significance of these dimensions of variation.

In considering intra-individual change and interindividual differences in development, the life-span orientation encompasses three goals. The first is that of **description**. In this capacity, the scientist gathers information providing a profile of change and stability, and of differences between persons in change and stability. This goal, then, involves answering such questions as:

What changes in health occur during adulthood, and how do these changes differ for men and women?

What aspects of moral reasoning change during old age, and what aspects remain the same? To what extent do these aspects of change and stability reflect individual differences in education, or social class?

How do relationships between parents and children change as parents grow older? How do these patterns of change vary systematically with race and ethnicity?

The second goal goes a step further. Once satisfactory descriptions of change and stability and of individual differences in these patterns have been developed, **explanations** of these patterns need to be formulated. The second goal, then, is to identify causes of change and stability throughout the life span, and of individual variability in these patterns. Thus, the scientist confronts such research questions as:

What factors influence health in old age? Why are some older individuals more vulnerable to illness than others?

Why does moral reasoning change during the adult years? Are specific (or general) adult experiences associated with these changes?

What circumstances affect parent-child relationships as parents age? Are there historical or contemporary aspects of minority-group cultures that might explain racial or ethnic variation in these relationships?

The third goal of the life-span orientation is that of **optimization**. Optimization requires applying our understanding of the ways in which people change as they grow older, individual variation in these patterns of change, and factors influencing these changes. Often, we can identify patterns of change that are more adaptive—for the individual or for society—than other patterns. Most would agree, for example, that it is more adaptive to retain robust health in old age than to experience chronic disability; few would argue that warm and supportive parent-child relationships are more desireable than hostile, cold bonds. The final goal of the life-span orientation involves finding strategies aimed at the individual or society that can foster these adaptive developmental patterns.

Through preventative optimization, such as active forms of exercise, the incidence of cardiovascular disease and other chronic illnesses can be minimized.

At least two approaches to optimization are possible. In an **alleviative** approach to optimization, some type of change has already occurred. An older woman has already experienced a decline in health, for example. The objective then is to minimize the impact that this health change has on her life. Alleviative optimization could mean educating the woman about the health problem in question and the factors that affect it; providing medication, therapy, or other forms of treatment; or providing home health care or other forms of supportive services to help the woman retain as much autonomy as she wishes.

The second approach is **preventative optimization**. Here, one takes steps to prevent maladaptive changes from occurring in the first place. For this approach, thorough understanding of the cause of the developmental process in question is critical. We know that the incidence of cardiovascular disease is influenced by lifelong health habits such as diet, exercise, and smoking. Preventing the development of cardiovascular disease might be accomplished by educating the public about healthful dietary practices; by making aerobic exercise programs convenient, inexpensive, and available; and by taking educational and legislative steps to discourage smoking.

We see, then, that life-span developmental science involves the *description, explanation, and optimization of intra-individual change from birth to death, and of interindividual differences in patterns of change.* Going beyond this definition, we can identify assumptions upon which the field's scope and objectives rest.

Key assumptions of the life-span orientation   Assumption 1: Development is a lifelong process. We assume that substantial and significant changes in behavior occur at all points in the life span from birth to death. No single period—whether it be infancy, adolescence, or old age—is of primary importance for the study of development (Baltes et al., 1980). Developmental scientists have not always made this assumption. Traditionally, the study of development was guided by the **biological growth orientation**. Following this orientation, one assumes that some state of complete maturity is attained relatively early in life. Behavioral changes occurring after that time would be considered processes of decline or aging, distinctly different from earlier processes of growth and development.

In the life-span orientation, no special state of absolute maturity is assumed. Instead, substantial and lasting age-related changes occurring at all points of the life span are considered to be developmental processes. Scholars in the field stress that "the task is to identify the form and course of these behavioral changes as they occur at various points in the life course, and to establish the pattern of their temporal order and interrelationship" (Baltes et al., 1980, p. 70). From a life-span perspective, we look at adulthood—and all periods of the life span—in order to understand how simultaneous changes in physical, psychological, and social functioning affect one another. We also try to determine how changes experienced at any age are related to both earlier and later life events.

Assumption 2: Pluralism of development. Life-span scientists assume that developmental change can occur in many forms. These changes may vary in the point of the life cycle at which they begin, in their duration, in the point in the life cycle at which they end, and in their pattern (Baltes et al., 1980). Some processes, such as physical growth, begin at conception and continue at varying rates until death. Other patterns of change, such as language development, are prominent and substantial early in the life cycle but are far less apparent at later ages. Some areas of change, such as memory performance in childhood, can be usefully described as increases in proficiency. Other types of changes, such as speed of learning unfamiliar material in old age, can be described as decreases in proficiency. Still other processes, such as moral reasoning, involve the disappearance of some modes of performance and the emergence of new modes—or the reorganization of existing skills—with the passage of time.

Just as we must remember that developmental change can take varied forms, we must also recognize plurality in the influences of development. Scholars have proposed that these influences be organized into three categories (Baltes, Cornelius, & Nesselroade, 1980; Baltes et al., 1980). **Normative age-graded events** are biological and environmental factors whose action is

Nonnormative life events have profound effects on the lives of the few people who experience them.

closely linked to chronological age. These influences act on most people, and do so at "typical" ages. Menarche, puberty, sensory changes of middle and later adulthood, beginning formal schooling in early childhood, and marrying for the first time in young adulthood are all examples of these normative age-graded influences.

The second category is **normative history-graded events.** These influences are major events and processes indexed by historical time, rather than chronological age. Because these events are occurrences of major historical importance, they affect nearly everyone alive when the events take place. For that reason, these events are considered normative. Economic depressions, wars, natural disasters, epidemics, and processes such as industrialization and urbanization are examples of these influences. All of these events undoubtedly have widespread impact, although the nature of that impact usually varies depending upon the age at which these events are experienced. For example, the outbreak of a major war will have different impacts on a young adult, his or her children, and his or her elderly parents.

The third category of influences is **nonnormative life events.** These events, unlike those in the first two categories, do not act on most people and are labeled *non*normative for that reason. But these unusual incidents have a substantial impact on the lives of those few individuals who experience them. Examples of nonnormative life events are being abused as a child, suffering permanent injury or disfigurement in an accident, winning the Nobel prize, or being elected President of the United States.

The three types of influences jointly shape the pattern of individual lives, yielding patterns of change that vary—as noted earlier—in time of onset, direction and form, and duration.

Assumption 3: Development varies with historical and cultural context. The study of development from a life-span perspective always involves deliberate consideration of the social context within which development occurs (Baltes et al., 1980; Neugarten & Datan, 1973). If we are to understand, explain, and optimize the changes that a contemporary American woman experiences during adulthood, we must consider not only the events of her own life but also the nature of the society within which those events occur. Because each society provides a unique setting for individual change—in the physical environment, the economic climate, the political system, and the character of major social institutions (e.g., the family, schools)—development will inevitably reflect these features.

Bernice Neugarten and her colleagues (e.g., Hagestad & Neugarten, 1985; Neugarten & Datan, 1973) have proposed that adult life is ordered in part by a "social clock," a set of socially-shared, generally unspoken assumptions about the appropriate timing of life events. These scholars found that participants in their research could readily identify the "best" ages for men and women to marry, to have children, to attain peak career success, to retire, and to experience other typical events of adult life (e.g., Neugarten & Peterson, 1957). Furthermore, virtually all of their respondents could describe themselves as "on-time," "early," or "late" relative to these expectations (e.g., Neugarten, Moore, & Lowe, 1965). These expectations vary according to social class within a particular culture, and between cultures (Hagestad & Neugarten, 1985).

Given these contextual factors, we should not be surprised that the physical, psychological, and social changes that an American woman confronts in the latter part of the twentieth century are dramatically different from those that a woman would have experienced in colonial America, or from those that a woman living in present-day China or South Africa might encounter. As the attention to normative history-graded events suggests, we seek to understand adult development from a life-span orientation as a process of individual change occurring *in a changing and varied world*. Cross-cultural research on adult experience and aging contributes to this insight; the *Diversity in Adulthood* box for this chapter examines cross-cultural research.

Assumption 4: The importance of an interdisciplinary approach. Because of the variety of changes considered in a life-span orientation, and because of the explicit attention to the historical and cultural context of development, an interdisciplinary approach is an essential component of the life-span orientation. This orientation, in fact, is now labeled "life-span developmental *science*," in contrast to the earlier label of "life-span developmental *psychology*" (Baltes et al., 1980). If we are to adequately implement a contextual study of physical,

BOX 1.1 $\mathbf{D}$*IVERSITY IN ADULTHOOD*

The significance and challenges of cross-cultural research

Cross-cultural research is one strategy used in the **comparative developmental approach**. In that approach, one attempts a "systematic and theory-guided analysis of developmental change in behavior as seen in various subpopulations of living organisms," (Baltes et al., 1977, p. 190). The subpopulations examined are distinct cultural groups, each representing a unique range of social and environmental circumstances. For example, one might study adaptation to death of a spouse among rural women in the American Midwest, rural women in a developing African nation, and rural women in the Soviet Union. Other examples are the study of physical growth among various racial and cultural groups, the study of language or perceptual development in different cultural settings, and the examination of ethnic differences in sex roles.

This approach offers unique insights into human development. Most generally, cross-cultural research helps us to map the "scope" of development, and vividly demonstrates the impact of the environment on development. As we consider the diversity of mourning customs across cultures we gain a new perspective on such customs in our own society. We see, too, the extent to which these practices are a reflection of the environment. In addition, cross-cultural research can help to identify universal aspects of developmental processes, and thereby enhance our understanding of those processes. For instance, identifying aspects of adaptation to death of a spouse that appear in virtually all cultures would suggest that these aspects are fundamental to the process itself. Thus, our appreciation of the nature of that adaptation can be enhanced through cross-cultural study.

Finally, cross-cultural research can extend the range of questions that we ask about development. As we appreciate the extent to which our own experiences are culturally shaped, we begin to make new inquiries about the developmental significance of that experience. As we identify unfamiliar life patterns, we correspondingly examine their developmental import.

Needless to say, cross-cultural research involves a set of unique challenges. One of the most difficult tasks is to obtain "functionally equivalent" measures (Baltes et al., 1977; Eckensberger, 1973). Suppose you were conducting a cross-cultural study of mourning, and were assessing grief (using a structured questionnaire or interview) among bereaved persons in several cultural groups. You would need to ascertain that the linguistic translations of the grief measure were adequate for all groups. Furthermore, it would be important to evaluate the extent to which the measures possessed *psychological equivalence* for all groups: the behaviors assessed must have the same meaning in all groups. And, the instrument should have similar levels of reliability and validity for all groups (Eckensberger, 1973).

Still another challenge for cross-cultural researchers lies in interpreting cultural differences. Because cross-cultural research is nonexperimental, the causes of cultural differences in development are never clearly identified. Often in cross-cultural research, genetic and environmental variation are confounded: groups differ not only in their social and physical environment but also in their genetic background. In that case, hereditary and environmental influences may (depending on the topic of the research) stand as equally plausible explanations of cultural differences (Baltes et al., 1977).

For example, some data describe unusual longevity among residents of isolated mountainous regions of Soviet Georgia (e.g., Benet, 1976), although the veracity of these reports has recently been questioned (e.g., Bennett & Garson, 1986; Palmore, 1984). To the extent that such differences in longevity do exist, however, it would be reasonable to explain them as outcomes of genetic influences, of cultural traditions regarding diet and exercise, or of some combination of these factors. Of course, cultural variation in other processes—such as courtship practices—are less readily attributed to the impact of genetic processes and more readily attributed to environmental impact.

psychological, and social development and the interrelations among these processes, the viewpoint of any single discipline—whether it be that of psychology, sociology, biology, anthropology, economics, or some other field of specialization—is likely to prove inadequate.

RESEARCH METHODOLOGY AND RELATED ISSUES

Researchers of adult development attempt to gather information that will provide clear, broadly applicable answers to questions concerning the description, explanation, and optimization of behavioral changes in adult life. Such an approach demands attention to issues of validity, measurement, sampling, and research design. To illustrate these issues, we will consider an imaginary study testing the hypothesis that *changes in the frequency of social interaction occurring in later adulthood cause changes in levels of life satisfaction during this period of the life cycle*. You can envision this study as an attempt to demonstrate that increased or stable frequency of social interaction would lead to an improved or stable outlook on one's current lot in life, the past, and the future. Decreased frequency of social interaction, however, would lead to a more negative perspective on one's life.

Validity

The term "validity" is used in at least four senses in the context of research methodology. In some cases, the term describes the interpretations that are warranted on the basis of a study or experiment. At other times, validity refers to the psychometric (or measurement) tools that a researcher selects for use in a study or experiment. You can think of validity as being roughly synonymous with the *quality* of a study or the measures used therein.

Internal validity   The **internal validity** of a study is the extent to which it can provide clear, unambiguous pictures of the relationships among the variables of interest (Campbell & Stanley, 1963; Cook & Campbell, 1979). In other words, a study that is strong in internal validity can answer the questions that the researcher set out to answer. In the context of our hypothetical study, has the study been planned so as to provide well-founded conclusions concerning the extent to which changes in frequency of social interaction cause changes in life satisfaction? If so, then the study is strong in internal validity.

Scientists identify several threats to internal validity. These "threats" are circumstances that prevent researchers from obtaining clear answers to the questions that motivated their study (Campbell & Stanley, 1963; Cook & Campbell, 1979). One threat is **history**, the effects of events outside the researcher's interests that coincide with the presumed causal events being investigated. As frequency of social interaction changes during adulthood, *what other changes or events* simultaneously occur that might explain changes in life satisfaction? For example, deteriorating health or a drop in income following retirement, may affect life satisfaction. A second type of threat is that of **maturation**, or the impact of *intra-individual changes that naturally occur* and that are distinct from the presumed causal variable. It is possible that level of life satisfaction normally changes during adulthood, without any change in the frequency of social interaction.

A third common threat to internal validity is known as the **testing** effect. When a study involves repeatedly measuring a quality or characteristic, such as level of life satisfaction, the *measures used on an earlier occasion* may themselves affect the characteristic being evaluated. These measurement effects could masquerade as influences of the presumed causal variable. In our example, completing a questionnaire that measures life satisfaction may prompt reflection on the quality of one's life. That reflection may itself increase or decrease level of life satisfaction, and these effects may be mistaken for consequences of changing frequency of social interaction.

Mortality is another threat to internal validity. In this case, ill-founded conclusions stem from *biasing loss of research participants* over the course of a study. To modify our example slightly, suppose a researcher were attempting to demonstrate that one group of research participants, who received an experimental intervention designed to increase their frequency of social interaction (e.g., social activities provided in community settings, such as churches and senior centers), showed increased life satisfaction. The researcher would simultaneously attempt to demonstrate that a control group, which did not receive the experimental intervention, showed no change in life satisfaction.

It is possible that participants from the experimental group who were initially lowest in life satisfaction—those that were exceptionally depressed or disoriented, perhaps—would be most likely to drop out of the study. These participants may lack the motivation or energy to participate in the experimental program, or may even feel threatened or demoralized by the program. There would be no reason, however, to suspect such a nonrandom pattern of mortality in the control group. In this case, the pattern of experimental mortality would result in a higher average level of life satisfaction for the experimental group following the training program simply because of the loss of experimental group participants who were initially lowest in life satisfaction.

A final threat to internal validity is the **selection** effect. These effects occur when groups to be compared in a study *differ from the outset of the study*, and those differences are *related to variables of interest*. In the modification of our example above, suppose that the experimental group (which received the program to increase the frequency of interaction) and the control group (which did not receive the program) were drawn from different neighborhoods, and differed also in average annual income. If income is related to level of life satisfaction for this sample, then the researcher would draw unsound conclusions regarding the program's actual impact on level of life satisfaction.

External validity   Any experiment involves a unique group of participants, a unique setting, and a unique approach to measuring the variables that the researcher is studying. The **external validity** of a study is the extent to which the conclusions stemming from the study can be *generalized* across experimental units (e.g., groups of participants), across settings, and across measures of the variables of interest (Campbell & Stanley, 1963; Cook & Campbell, 1979). As with internal validity, there are several threats to external validity.

External validity may be weakened by the **reactive effects of testing**. In this case, an event that is irrelevant to the purposes of a study (event X) occurs, and event X influences the relationship between the variables being examined in the study. The relationship observed between the variables of interest in the study, therefore, cannot be generalized to situations in which these variables are examined and event X has not occurred.

To return to our example, suppose the researcher questioned participants during a holiday season when higher-than-normal levels of festive social activities might be expected. It is possible that respondents would report higher levels of social interaction during that holiday season than they would at other times of the year. More important, the celebratory types of interaction that occur during a holiday might have a more beneficial effect on life satisfaction than would more routine occasions of interaction. For that reason, the researcher could not confidently generalize the findings to the relationship between frequency of social interaction and level of life satisfaction at all times of the year.

Another threat to external validity that arises from testing is a possible sensitizing effect. Simply asking older people how much social interaction they engage in may prompt them to take part in social activities from which they ordinarily would refrain. If testing thus artificially inflates the level of social interaction, the relationship between social interaction and life satisfaction may not generalize to situations in which older individuals are not being questioned about their social activities.

Another class of threats to external validity are **interactions with a treatment variable**. In these situations, the effects of an independent variable (or treatment) cannot be disentangled from the effects of a potential threat to internal validity. The problem here is that the relationship between the variables of interest may be unique to situations in which this internal validity threat is present. For example, suppose a researcher were interested in testing the effectiveness of a program designed to increase the frequency of social interaction and thereby enhance life satisfaction. If the researcher advertised the program through announcements in church bulletins and organization newsletters, the participants thus contacted might be especially friendly or community-minded, since they belong to a church or organization. The experimental program may be genuinely effective in increasing interaction frequency and levels of life satisfaction for those individuals. However, the effects of the program might be unique to such socially-oriented people; the same effects might not be observed in a group of more introverted adults. In this example, there is an interaction between *selection effects* (a threat to internal validity) and the treatment variable.

Other threats to external validity are **reactive effects**, in which the setting of a study affects the outcome, and **multiple treatment interference**, in which a researcher simultaneously tests the effects of several kinds of treatments on the same group of subjects. In the former case, the effects of a treatment—such as a support group meeting in a senior citizen's center—cannot be generalized to social interaction in other settings. In the latter case, it is impossible to determine which of the several treatments to which participants are exposed—a support group, a telephone reassurance system, social skills training, or some combination of these individual treatment components—affect life satisfaction. Furthermore, the impact of this "treatment package" cannot be generalized to individuals who received only one component of the total package (only the support group, for example).

Statistical conclusion validity   Statistical conclusion validity is the extent to which a study provides sound statistical evidence as a basis for conclusions (Cook & Campbell, 1979). In order to provide this evidence, a study must have several characteristics. The study must be sensitive enough to identify relationships between the variables in which the researcher is interested, and must be otherwise planned so as to provide evidence that the variables of interest are systematically related.

Several circumstances have been identified as potentially leading the researcher to ill-founded conclusions on the basis of statistical evidence (Cook & Campbell, 1979). A study with **low statistical power** is not sensitive enough to detect genuine relationships between variables. This problem can arise if the sample is too small or if exceedingly rigorous statistical procedures are used for data analysis. In these situations, a researcher might conclude that the variables of interest are not related, when in fact they are. Changing frequency of social interaction may actually be associated with changing levels of life satisfaction, but a researcher may conclude that they are not on the basis of a study using a very small sample or extremely conservative statistical tests.

Statistical conclusion validity may also be threatened by low **reliability** of measures, or of treatment implementation. Reliability of measurement will be discussed in greater detail in the next section. For present purposes, it is sufficient to think of reliability as synonymous with *consistency*. If a researcher uses a measure of life satisfaction that provides inconsistent scores—in the *absence of any actual change* in level of life satisfaction—then the researcher is almost certain to draw unwarranted conclusions on the basis of these measurements.

By the same token, if an experimental treatment is administered inconsistently (perhaps because different experimenters are involved in the study, or because a single experimenter fails to follow standard procedures), then it will be almost impossible to identify associations between the treatment and other variables. In our example, if several experimental support groups are organized to increase social interaction and thereby enhance life satisfaction, and if each group is organized and run differently by different facilitators, then consistent impacts of these groups on life satisfaction can hardly be expected.

Construct validity   Still another sense in which the term "validity" is used is that of **construct validity**. Construct validity is the extent to which a test, scale, questionnaire, or other measurement procedure assesses what the researcher intends it to measure (e.g., Cook & Campbell, 1979). For example, do scores on a scale that a researcher selects as her measure of life satisfaction actually reflect respondents' contentment with their current life circumstances, their perspective on their past, and their outlook on their future? Or do these scores reflect some other quality? It is possible that, instead of life satisfaction, scores reflect respondents' general intelligence, their cooperative or belligerent nature, or the extent to which they want to present themselves in a socially desirable manner. If so, then the scale in question would be weak in construct validity as a measure of life satisfaction. Using that scale would provide an inaccurate picture of the actual relationship between frequency of social interaction and level of life satisfaction. Thus, problems with construct validity can be considered another type of threat to internal validity.

Most often, one assesses the construct validity of a scale by considering its relationship to other measures of the same quality, as well as to measures of different qualities. A life satisfaction scale that is strong in construct validity should produce scores that are systematically related to scores on other, better established measures of life satisfaction. At the same time, this measure of life satisfaction should yield scores that are *not* systematically related to scores on measures that are unrelated to life satisfaction (e.g., height; manual dexterity; political liberalism).

Other key psychometric issues

Reliability of measurement   As we noted above, reliability can be considered synonymous with consistency in measurement. Under virtually all weather conditions and with virtually all drivers, you expect a reliable car to start promptly and operate just as it did on earlier occasions. Such consistency, or reliability, is also a desirable property of tests, scales, and other procedures used to assess psychological and sociological concepts. If one assumes that the quality being measured (such as an individual's level of life satisfaction) does not change, one would expect a reliable measure of life satisfaction to yield virtually the same score every time it is administered to the same individual.

Reliability is evaluated in a number of ways. One may be interested in the extent to which a test or scale yields consistent scores on different occasions. In this case, one is concerned with **test-retest reliability**. Alternatively, one may be primarily interested in the extent to which all items or questions making up a scale seem to be consistently assessing the same property (e.g., are all of the questions concerned with life satisfaction?). In this case, one would consider the **internal consistency** of the measure. Finally, one may evaluate the extent to which alternative forms of a test administered concurrently yield consistent scores, or the extent to which independent observers of an individual's behavior reach consistent judgments regarding that behavior. In the former case, one examines **alternate forms reliability**, and in the latter case one considers **interscorer reliability**.

Age equivalence of measurement   A great deal of developmental research involves examining age changes, age differences, or both age changes and age differences in behavior (see the section on *Developmental Research Designs*, pp. 20–26). For these purposes, developmentalists must consider whether measures of behavior obtained at different ages are logically comparable. For at least two reasons, it is possible that measures that may initially appear comparable actually are not. Comparing responses to the same scale, test, or questionnaire—or even comparing observations of the same behavior—that are obtained at different points in the life cycle may be like attempting to add apples and oranges.

For example, suppose a researcher compares scores on a measure of life satisfaction for young adults and older adults. It is quite possible that scores on this measure reflect slightly or substantially different qualities at these age levels. Such a measure might include questions concerning the satisfaction that one finds in work, marriage, and parenting; the meaning of these questions probably differs for young and older adults. Most young adults are intensely involved in their careers, marriages, and childrearing responsibilities. However, many older adults are far less involved in these activities. Responses to the same questions may reflect entirely different qualities for a 30-year-old wife and mother who is busy advancing her career and for a 70-year-old retired widow whose adult children live far away.

A related question concerns possible age differences in the significance of the behavior being measured. Even if one is fairly confident that a particular test, observation, or other assessment procedure reflects the same qualities at different ages, it is possible that these qualities have different meanings at different points in the life cycle. For example, one might devise procedures for measuring "personal autonomy," the extent to which an individual relies on herself (rather than others) for dealing with personal, social, and practical problems. Ideally, one would have evidence—such as correlations between the scores on this measure and on other measures of similar and dissimilar qualities—that the assessment procedure seemed to be measuring something that was reasonable to label as "personal autonomy."

However, one must still consider the possibility that personal autonomy has unique meanings at different points in the life cycle. This quality probably has one type of significance for a young woman entering a career and establishing economic independence, but a different type of significance altogether for an elderly woman who is bedridden and impoverished. For the young woman, high scores on a personal autonomy measure would likely reflect psychological integrity and would be maturationally appropriate. For the elderly woman, however, high scores on the personal autonomy measure could be reflections of defensiveness, denial, or incoherence. Given the circumstances of her life, it would be more adaptive for the older woman to be able to comfortably depend on others than to strive for autonomy.

Sampling considerations: Assuring that research reflects diversity

As the discussion of internal and external validity suggests, the nature of the sample has a critical impact on the conclusions that are warranted on the basis of a study. Much of the research that we will consider throughout the book was conducted with white, middle-class samples; on that basis, we can characterize this work as weak in external validity. Furthermore, many of the statistical tests commonly used in developmental research (see the Appendix, pp. 390–397, for a more thorough discussion of these tests) are based upon the assumption that the data were obtained from a random sample drawn from a clearly-specified population. Since relatively little research on aging is conducted with such samples, we can also criticize the statistical conclusion validity of much gerontological research. Because of these ties between the nature of the sample and validity of a study, it is important that researchers provide a clear, detailed description of their samples. It is equally important, of course, that readers consider these descriptions as they critically evaluate the study's findings and conclusions.

A **random sample** is one in which each member of a population has an equal chance of being included; the selection of one population member does not influence the likelihood of any other member being selected for the sample. In a random sample of the American elderly, each older person in the United States would be equally likely to be included. Such a sample might be obtained using Census records to identify and locate all elderly Americans, and then independently selecting participants from that roster using a random numbers table.

Random samples, such as this one, are the type of sample most likely to also be representative samples of the population of interest. A sample may, however, be a nonrandom sample but still be representative. In a **representative sample**, variation in important characteristics in the sample are proportional to variation in the same characteristics for the population. For example, if we know that approximately 90 percent of the elderly American population is Caucasian, that approximately 60 percent is female, and that approximately 30% lives alone, then a representative sample of older Americans would have similar percentages with these characteristics.

The characteristics considered in evaluating the representativeness of a sample depend upon the nature of each study. A researcher interested in family caregiving for the frail elderly would probably be concerned that the sample of elderly participants be representative of older Americans with regard to age, overall health status, types of health problems, family size, and geographic proximity of family members. In contrast, a researcher studying older men's adjustment to retirement would be concerned that the sample be representative of male retirees nationwide with respect to former occupation, annual household income, time since retirement, marital status, and overall general health.

DEVELOPMENTAL RESEARCH DESIGNS

Three central variables

For the study of development in a dynamic physical and social environment, three variables—age, cohort, and time of measurement—form a framework for research design (e.g., Baltes et al., 1977; Schaie, 1965). **Age** is the chronological age of research participants when the study is conducted. A **cohort** is a population of individuals born at a particular point or interval in time. For example, in a 1990 study of health status among the "oldest old" aged 85 and older the participants might be selected from the cohort of Americans born 1880 to 1900. Finally, **time of measurement** is the overall condition of the sociocultural and physical environment affecting participants when the study is conducted.

Obviously, the three dimensions are interdependent. If a study includes participants of particular ages (e.g., ages 20, 40, and 60) and is conducted at a particular point in historical time (e.g., 1990), then the cohorts included in the study (e.g., 1970, 1950, and 1930 cohorts) are determined by the intersection of age and time of measurement. Similarly, if a study includes members of a particular cohort (e.g., individuals born in 1930) and these individuals are studied at a particular age or ages (e.g, ages 40, 50, and 60), then the times of measurement (e.g., 1970, 1980, and 1990) are determined by the intersection of age and cohort.

Three basic developmental research designs

Research on human development attempts to describe behavior as a function of age. Three research designs are used in most developmental research, although developmental scientists recognize that these designs are not ideally suited to the goal of studying age functions. Figure 1.2 provides a graphic representation of these designs.

By far the most commonly used developmental research design is the **cross-sectional** design. In this approach, individuals representing different age groups are compared at a single point in time. An example of a cross-sectional study would be one in which a researcher compared IQ test scores for a group of 20-year-olds, a group of 40-year-olds, and a group of 60-year-olds; all age groups would be tested at the same time (e.g., all tested in 1990). A second design is the **longitudinal** design, in which repeated observations are made of the same individuals at successive ages. In this case, a researcher would obtain

Cross-sectional design:
All subjects tested in 1990.

Age
groups:
$\begin{cases} 60 \longrightarrow 1930 \text{ cohort} \\ 40 \longrightarrow 1950 \text{ cohort} \\ 20 \longrightarrow 1970 \text{ cohort} \end{cases}$

Age and cohort confounded.

Longitudinal design:
All subjects born in 1920.

Time
of
measurement:
$\begin{cases} 1940 \longrightarrow \text{Age } 20 \\ 1960 \longrightarrow \text{Age } 40 \\ 1980 \longrightarrow \text{Age } 60 \end{cases}$

Age, time of measurement confounded.

Time-lag design:
All subjects aged 20.

Time
of
measurement:
$\begin{cases} 1990 \longrightarrow 1970 \text{ cohort} \\ 2010 \longrightarrow 1990 \text{ cohort} \\ 2030 \longrightarrow 2010 \text{ cohort} \end{cases}$

Time of measurement and cohort confounded.

Figure 1.2
Basic develop-
mental designs.

IQ test scores for a group of 20-year-olds, then retest the same individuals 20 years later at age 40, and 20 years later still at age 60.

The cross-sectional and longitudinal designs differ in many respects. One of the most important differences is in the types of inferences that each design permits. Recall that the three critical variables in developmental research are age, cohort, and time of measurement. In a cross-sectional comparison of individuals of different ages, each age group also represents a different cohort since all participants are observed at a single time. The cross-sectional design thus **confounds** age and cohort. This means that if differences between the 20-year-olds and the 40-year-olds are identified, it is impossible to determine whether these differences reflect maturational (age) differences or differences between members of different generations, or cohorts.

Age groups might differ in IQ scores because of universal processes of development occurring in the sensory and nervous systems. Alternatively, the groups might differ in IQ scores because of generational differences in educational experience, or because of an evolutionary trend that is apparent across generations. Thus, one cannot assume that significant age *differences* identified in a cross-sectional study are necessarily indicative of age *changes*—the *intra-* individual change specified earlier as a central focus of life-span developmental science.

Nonetheless, the cross-sectional design is a widely used strategy for developmental research. The design is efficient, since differences in behavior can be compared over broad age ranges (a 40-year range, in the example above) in a relatively short time. A cross-sectional study, then, might be conducted as a preliminary step to a longitudinal study of intra-individual change. In that preliminary step, the researcher could make sure that the measures and procedures were appropriate for all of the ages of interest.

Furthermore, there are situations in which a researcher is interested in identifying age differences per se. A scientist with applied research interests might want to describe age differences in older individuals' use of home health care services; she could get that information by conducting a cross-sectional study of subjects in their seventies, eighties, and nineties. Such a study would not identify ways in which needs for these services change as an individual ages, but could be useful for making short-term projections of a population's service needs.

The longitudinal design, which does provide direct evidence of age changes in behavior, would seem an ideal choice for the study of intra-individual change. However, practical and methodological considerations discourage widespread use of this design. Particularly in the study of adult development, researchers often want to study broad age spans; longitudinal research is correspondingly heavy in the demands for time and money. In the example described above, 40 years would be needed to describe age changes in IQ test scores. Several events become increasingly likely over that time span, and these events can complicate the interpretation of the study findings.

The study may outlive the researcher, or the measures selected as the best available at the outset of the study may no longer be well-regarded by the time the study is completed. Participants may move away, lose interest in the study, or die before the study is completed, so that comparisons of the "same" sample at different time points may be misleading. Furthermore, the loss of subjects may be nonrandom. Riegel and his colleagues (Riegel, Riegel, & Meyer, 1967) showed that the participants remaining at the conclusion of a longitudinal study were those who had been initially the most intellectually able. Thus, mortality (see earlier discussion of internal validity, pp. 13–14) can threaten the interpretation of longitudinal results.

There are other problems in the interpretation of longitudinal data. Since the same individuals are studied on several occasions, testing effects pose a threat to the validity of these studies. Taking an initial IQ test may prompt a 20-year-old to read about topics that she otherwise would not; if so, later test scores could be affected. History may also pose a validity threat in interpreting longitudinal data. Since members of a single cohort are observed at several times of measurement, the researcher must question the extent to which age changes observed in that cohort can be generalized to other cohorts. If the cohort studied shows an increase in average IQ scores between the ages of 20 and 60, it is possible that this increase reflects the consequences of living during an unusually enriching historical period. A similar age change might not appear for cohorts living during a less stimulating era. Thus, a longitudinal design—

while potentially providing evidence of age changes in behavior—is not necessarily the best choice for developmental research.

A third, less frequently used, design is the **time lag**. In the time-lag design, individuals of a single age are observed at several points in time. An example would be a study in which a researcher obtained IQ test scores for a group of 20-year-olds in 1990, for a second group of 20-year-olds in 2010, and for a third group of 20-year-olds in 2030. At each time of measurement, of course, the 20-year-old participants are drawn from a different cohort.

The practical constraints of time and money in this case are similar to those of the longitudinal design. One would conduct a time-lag study if the goal were to examine the ways in which social or cultural change affected the behavior of individuals at a particular point in development. However, this design does not permit the researcher to distinguish cohort from time of measurement effects. For example, a researcher might conduct a time-lag study of young adults' IQ test scores in an effort to learn how changes in educational practices affected IQ. Unfortunately, she would not be able to rule out the possibility that any significant differences between cohorts stemmed from differences in the social and cultural climates on the occasions that each cohort was tested.

None of these three basic developmental designs can readily provide straightforward answers to the types of questions of greatest interest to life-span developmental scientists—questions concerning intra-individual changes in behavior and interindividual differences in these processes of change. The cross-sectional design can describe only age differences in behavior, and these age differences are confounded with differences between cohorts. The longitudinal design provides evidence of age changes, but these changes may be unique to a specific cohort and may reflect the effects of testing or history. The time-lag design can identify differences associated with time of measurement, but these differences are confounded with cohort differences.

The sequential designs

Because the three basic developmental designs alone cannot provide completely satisfactory answers to questions concerning human development, three more complex designs were devised (Adam, 1978; Schaie, 1965). In each of the sequential designs, two or more sequences of age differences, cohort differences, or time of measurement differences are examined. In a sense, the sequential designs each are different combinations of two of the more basic cross-sectional, longitudinal, and time-lag designs. Figure 1.3 illustrates the general strategies of the sequential designs.

In the **cohort-sequential** design, two or more cohorts are measured at two or more ages. In other words, a longitudinal sequence is observed for at least two cohorts. A researcher conducting a cohort sequential study of IQ in adulthood might test a group of 20-year-old participants in 1990, and retest the

Cohort sequential:
Two cohorts measured at two ages

Time of measurement:

1990	2010	2030
Test 1970 cohort (Age 20)	Test 1970 cohort (Age 40)	
	Test 1990 cohort (Age 20)	Test 1990 cohort (Age 40)

Time sequential:
Two age groups compared at
two times of measurement

Time of measurement:

1990	2000
20 year olds (1970 cohort)	20 year olds (1990 cohort)
vs.	vs.
40 year olds (1950 cohort)	40 year olds (1960 cohort)

Cross sequential:
Two cohorts observed at two times
of measurement

Time of measurement:

1990	2000
1920 cohort (Age 70)	1920 cohort (Age 80)
vs.	vs.
1940 cohort (Age 50)	1940 cohort (Age 60)

Figure 1.3
Sequential
designs.

same participants in 2010 when they were age 40.[1] In addition, the researcher would test a second group of 20-year-old participants (representing a second cohort) in 2010, and retest these participants in 2030 when they were age 40. You can think of this design as a repeated sequence of longitudinal studies. The design allows the researcher to examine age changes and evaluate the generality of these changes across cohorts; the design also allows the researcher to independently examine age differences and cohort differences.

However, the cohort-sequential design does not allow the researcher to examine the effects of time of measurement, since each time of measurement in this design represents a unique combination of participants' ages and cohorts. Thus, this design is recommended only for instances in which the researcher is

---

1. Rather than retesting the same individuals, the researcher could test a second sample from the same cohort. One would take this approach if repeated testing were likely to affect the results of the study.

confident that the behavior being studied is subject to little, if any, influence of sociocultural change (Schaie, 1965). Because few aspects of human behavior can be assumed to be independent of cultural influences, this design is not often the method of choice for the study of human development. However, this design could be useful in studying development in nonhuman species. As we note later in the chapter (see Box 1.2, p. 28–29), important questions concerning aging can be effectively addressed through animal research.

The **time-sequential** design involves comparing two or more age groups at two or more times of measurement. Here, a researcher would examine IQ test scores for a group of 20-year-olds and a group of 40-year-olds tested in 1990, and examine scores for 20-year-olds and 40-year-olds tested in 2010 as well. You can think of this design as a repeated sequence of cross-sectional studies: the researcher can describe age differences in behavior, and differences related to time of measurement.

In the time-sequential design, it is impossible to evaluate the extent to which cohort is related to behavior, since each unique combination of age and time of measurement represents a unique cohort. The time-sequential is the best design to use, then, only if a researcher can reasonably assume that the behavior being studied is not influenced by cohort (Schaie, 1965). One would not be likely to select this design for the study of intelligence, since it is likely that both evolutionary processes and generational differences in education are related to intellectual performance. However, the time-sequential design could be a wise choice for other variables of interest to developmental scientists, such as personality.

Finally, the **cross-sequential** design involves comparing members of two or more cohorts at two or more times of measurement. In this design, a researcher could begin in 1990 by obtaining IQ scores for individuals born in 1920 (age 70) and individuals born in 1940 (age 50). Again in 2000, the researcher would obtain a second set of IQ scores for individuals born in 1920 (age 80) and in 1940 (age 60). In a sense, the cross-sequential is also like a repeated sequence of cross-sectional studies; here, though, the age groups differ at the different times of measurement. The cross-sequential design allows the researcher to examine differences related to cohort and differences related to time of measurement.

In the cross-sequential design, the researcher cannot determine whether age is related to the behavior being studied, since each combination of cohort and time of measurement represents a unique age level. Since developmental researchers are particularly interested in studying how behavior varies with age, it would seem that this design would rarely be a wise choice. However, Schaie (1965) notes that the cross-sequential design *is* often a design of choice for the study of adult development. In this area, it often is reasonable to assume that the behavior being studied is stable over relatively long age spans. One is then more interested in examining the effects of cohort or time of measurement. Areas of performance such as vocabulary and verbal fluency, for example, are fairly stable throughout much of adulthood. However, one could reasonably question whether these qualities vary across generations or across points of historical time.

Clearly, all three of the sequential designs have the potential to provide more informative answers to questions of interest to developmental scientists. It is also clear, though, that these designs require a great deal of time to implement, at least for the study of adult development. For that reason, these designs are not frequently used in the study of human aging. The time demands of these designs are, however, less severe in the study of human infancy and childhood and in the study of aging in species with short life spans.

PERTINENT ETHICAL ISSUES

Planning developmental research involves not only addressing methodological issues, such as those pertaining to validity, reliability, sampling, and design. It is equally important that the scientist give careful thought to ethical questions surrounding a study. There are at least two ethical issues confronting researchers.

First, the scientist should contemplate ways in which her findings could be used—or misused. For example, a scientist who reports that abilities critical for safe driving regularly decline in old age must realize that her findings could be used to bolster arguments that older people should not be allowed to drive. Research reporting that psychomotor skills become slower in old age and that capacity for sustained attention decreases with age could be used to justify employment discrimination against middle-aged and elderly adults. Findings that older adults, compared to younger people, need more time to learn and remember could provide a rationale for reducing or eliminating continuing education programs. Clearly, there are few areas of research in which findings do not have the potential for misapplication.

Second, the researcher must ensure that research participants are treated in an ethically acceptable manner. Researchers of human development are bound by at least two sets of standards in their treatment of research participants. First, these scientists are obligated by legal standards regulating all types of human interaction. In addition, government agencies (which provide financial support for a great deal of developmental research), universities and other institutional research settings, and professional societies have established guidelines regarding the ethical treatment of both human and animal research participants. For much research on adult development, the ethical standards developed by the American Psychological Association (APA) are a relevant set of guidelines.

Most generally, these guidelines direct the researcher to weigh the potential benefits of his or her research (for the participants themselves, for others like the participant, or for society and science in general) against any potential risks associated with participation. The *Open Questions* box (see pp. 28–29) in

Despite pressure from animal rights activists, scientists assert that they are morally obligated to conduct research that may improve the quality of human life.

this chapter explores this issue. The APA guidelines specify ten considerations in planning a study (APA, 1982). The guidelines cover such issues as the type of information that should be provided to potential subjects prior to their participation, as well as the conditions under which deception of participants may be justified. The guidelines also specify the participants' freedom to withdraw from a study or to decline to participate at all, the researcher's obligation to protect participants from unnecessary discomfort or danger during participation, the researcher's obligation to identify and alleviate any unanticipated negative consequences of participation, and the confidentiality of information obtained about subjects during their participation.

Although researchers should seriously consider *all* of these guidelines in planning a project, some merit particularly careful attention in designing research on aging. One of the APA guidelines states that researchers are obliged to inform potential participants "about all aspects of the research that might reasonably be expected to influence willingness to participate and explain all other aspects of the research about which participants inquire" (APA, 1982). In other words, researchers are expected to obtain **informed consent** from subjects prior to their participation.

BOX 1.2   *OPEN QUESTIONS*

Protecting research participants while ensuring scientific progress

Research on aging involves studying the behavior of living organisms—either humans or other animals—under various circumstances. At times, the circumstances under which behavior is studied are physically stressful, psychologically distressing, or both. However, understanding reactions to these circumstances can often lead to valuable practical applications and scientific progress. Most would argue, for example, that there is enormous practical and scientific merit in studying the impact of the environment upon longevity, the relative efficacy of various pain-relief medications, or the effects of chemical dependency on individuals of various ages. It is just as clear, though, that the experimental study of topics such as these may pose risks to the humans or animals involved. A recurring dilemma facing investigators of adult development and aging—as well as scientists in other fields—is the best approach to take in ensuring that research participants' rights are respected while scientific progress is made.

Most citizens and scientists alike would agree that some set of ethical guidelines for conducting research are essential. As noted in the text, many developmental researchers follow the guidelines developed by the American Psychological Association (APA) regarding the ethical treatment of human research participants. APA has developed a similar set of guidelines describing the ethical treatment of laboratory animals. Both sets of guidelines exhort researchers to thoroughly weigh the potential value of their research against any actual or potential risks to participants, to refrain from subjecting participants to physical or psychological risks that are not essential to the conduct of a study, and to generally treat participants with courtesy, consideration, and dignity. Certainly, all are sound prescriptions for conducting research in an ethically acceptable manner.

Scientists welcome ethical guidelines for their work, and most endorse the APA guidelines in particular. Nonetheless, some have also voiced concerns about the consequences of these guidelines for research findings. Some have suggested that individuals who agree to participate in research under conditions of informed consent constitute an inherently biased sample (e.g., Agnew & Pike, 1987; Cozby, Worden, & Kee, 1989), and that findings from such samples may not apply to most people. For example, individuals who agree to participate in a study of the effectiveness of a retirement planning workshop may have a unique view of a desirable retirement lifestyle and the importance of planning for retirement. The study might be quite informative concerning the effect of these workshops on workers who provide informed consent and agree to participate in research, but might not provide much information at all about retirees in general. In effect, obtaining informed consent may undermine the external validity of a study.

Recently, controversy has also arisen over the use of laboratory animals in research. Animal rights activist organizations assert that much medical and

---

Occasionally, it is difficult to ensure that this guideline has been adequately observed in research on aging. In the study of older individuals suffering from Alzheimer's disease or other forms of dementia, for example, one may not be able to obtain informed consent from the participants themselves; consent from a guardian must be sought.[2] Other situations in which securing truly

---

2. In that event, as with research in which young children are the participants, one should still attempt to explain the project to the participants and ascertain that they are willing to participate.

psychological research imposes needless suffering on animals in order to produce findings of dubious value. These activists have attempted to delay construction of new animal research facilities and to increase the cost of construction through existing zoning laws and property use laws; have conducted grossly deceptive media campaigns; have destroyed laboratory property and been involved in the theft of laboratory animals; have made animal research needlessly expensive because of the cost of security systems and equipment replacement; and have intimidated researchers with threats of harm to the researchers' families and personal property (Johnson, 1990). In response to this type of pressure, Cornell University recently refused a substantial federal grant that would have provided support for a highly successful research program involving animal experimentation (Landers, 1989).

Researchers counter the animal rights activists' arguments by pointing to the tremendous importance that this research has for optimizing the quality of human life. More and more, scientists are willing to assert that they have a moral imperative to conduct research that can improve the quality of human life, even if this work necessitates the study and eventual sacrifice of laboratory animals (Landers, 1989). This assertion is particularly well justified in the study of aging: animal research makes it possible to study topics of importance for understanding aging and the factors that affect aging. The species often used in laboratory research (e.g, rats, nonhuman primates)

have relatively short life spans. Furthermore, it is possible to conduct experimental research—involving deliberate manipulation of a treatment variable(s)— that is simply not feasible with human samples. It would be virtually impossible, for example, to conduct a well-controlled study of the effect of following a particular diet throughout adulthood with a human sample. The time required for such a study would be prohibitive, and the practical problems entailed in making sure that all participants in a treatment group actually followed the experimental diet would be overwhelming. This study would be quite possible to carry out using laboratory animals, however.

Perhaps the most certain statement regarding the tension between the ethical treatment of research participants and the need for scientific progress is that there are no clear-cut, easy answers to these dilemmas. The dilemma must be confronted anew in planning each research project, so that this tension is destined to remain an "open question." Balancing the potential value of planned research against risks that the research might pose for participants is a complex task, and thus is not best left to the individual researcher. Fortunately, most universities and other research settings have formed Institutional Review Boards (IRBs) which assist the researcher in making this judgement. At most institutions, the IRB is comprised of scientists, nonscientists, attorneys, and members of the community.

informed consent may be challenging are in the study of individuals who have visual or auditory impairments, and in cross-cultural research. The sensory, language, and cultural barriers can make it difficult for the researcher to feel confident that she has adequately explained the purposes and procedures of the study.

APA guidelines also state that researchers must respect participants' freedom to terminate their participation in an experiment at any point. As the guidelines explain, "the obligation to protect this freedom requires careful thought and consideration when the investigator is in a position of authority or influence over the participant" (APA, 1982). Insuring **freedom from co-**

ercion, too, can occasionally pose unique challenges for researchers of aging. An investigator studying institutionalization, for example, must ensure that potential subjects understand that their participation in the research is not required for their continued residence in the institution, and that refusal to participate will not affect their care in any way. By the same token, researchers studying the benefits of supportive services (e.g., home health care, housekeeping services, transportation services, etc.) for the frail elderly must make certain that potential subjects understand that their services will not be terminated if they choose not to participate or if they decide to withdraw from the research at any time.

SUMMARY

Much of the impetus for systematic attention to processes of adult development stems from demographic forces, as the age distribution of the American population has shifted upward throughout this century. With the emergence of psychology as a distinct field, scientific interest in adulthood and aging increased. Still greater progress has continued since World War II, with the formation of professional societies and the establishment of major research programs.

Today, much research on adulthood and aging is conducted from a life-span orientation. The goal of this orientation is to describe, explain, and optimize intra-individual change in behavior and interindividual differences in patterns of change. The life-span orientation further rests on a set of assumptions.

The chapter reviewed six developmental research designs. Basic designs provide ambiguous findings. The complex sequential designs are both more informative and more difficult to implement. In addition to methodological concerns, the researcher confronts ethical challenges in planning developmental research.

KEY TERMS

Age	History
Alleviative optimization	Informed consent
Alternate forms reliability	Interactions with treatment variable
Biological growth orientation	Interindividual differences
Cohort	Internal consistency
Cohort-sequential design	Internal validity
Comparative developmental approach	Interscorer reliability
Confound	Intra-individual change
Construct validity	Life-span perspective
Cross-sectional design	Longitudinal design
Cross-sequential design	Low statistical power
Description	Maturation
Explanation	Mortality
External validity	Multiple treatment interference
Freedom from coercion	Nonnormative life event
G. Stanley Hall	Normative age-graded event

Normative history-graded event

Optimization

Preventative optimization

Quetelet

Random sample

Reactive effects

Reactive effects of testing

Reliability

Representative sample

Selection

Test-retest reliability

Testing

E. L. Thorndike

Time of measurement

Time-lag design

Time-sequential design

SUGGESTIONS FOR FURTHER READING

Baltes, P. B., Reese, H. W., & Nesselroade, J. (1977). *Life Span Developmental Psychology: Introduction to Research Methods*. Monterey, CA: Brooks/Cole.

Fischer, D. H. (1977). *Growing Old in America*. New York: Oxford University Press.

Hareven, T. K. & Adams, K. J. (Eds.) (1982). *Aging and Life Course Transitions: An Interdisciplinary Perspective*. New York: The Guilford Press.

Kane, R. A. & Kane, R. L. (1981). Assessing the Elderly: *A Practical Guide to Measurement*. Lexington, MA: Lexington Books.

Munnichs, J. M. A., Mussen, P., Olbrich, E., & Coleman, P. G. (Eds.). (1985). *Life-span and Change in a Gerontological Perspective*. New York: Academic Press.

Sinnott, J. D., Harris, C. S., Block, M. R., Collesano, S., & Jacobson, S. G. (1983). *Applied Research in Aging: A Guide to Methods and Resources*. Boston: Little, Brown & Co.

CHAPTER TWO

*T*HEORIES IN THE STUDY OF ADULT DEVELOPMENT

This chapter examines philosophical issues related to the study of adulthood and aging. Scientists planning research on adult development, and practitioners applying the results of that research, are guided by assumptions that are often unspoken. These assumptions concern the nature of human beings, the ways in which people change with age, and the reasons these changes occur. We consider three sets of assumptions that have shaped theories of adult development.

The chapter also explores several developmental theories. There is a dazzling array of theories that provide a foundation for research in adulthood and aging; this chapter includes a relatively brief presentation of selected theories and research related to these theories. We examine theories and related research in greater depth throughout the book, as we consider physical, psychological, and social changes occurring in adulthood.

Questions to consider in reading the chapter include:

What are theories and what functions do they serve?

How are theories evaluated?

What kinds of assumptions do developmental scientists make about human beings, changes that occur within people, and the causes of these changes?

How are these assumptions related to theories?

MODELS AND THEORIES

Chapter One reviewed methodological and ethical issues that scientists consider when planning research; this chapter addresses philosophical issues providing a background for research. Many people assume that the scientist's primary goal is to accumulate new knowledge. This assumption has some validity, but it both overlooks the source of that goal and oversimplifies the process of research. Although scientists are fundamentally concerned with extending the scope of knowledge, research findings have little meaning without a theoretical perspective from which they can be interpreted. Scientific theories, in turn, rest on a foundation of assumptions—notions which the scientist takes as "givens."

Models

Any scientist begins with assumptions about the existence and functioning of basic entities. For the developmental scientist, these entities are human beings and their development; the scientist's basic assumptions about these entities are **models** (or "world views"). There are three widely recognized models of human development; each is described more fully in the second section of this chapter. At this point, we consider the functions that models serve, and how models are related to theories.

Model functions   Perhaps the most important model function is to provide a metaphor to enhance understanding. Just as a scale model of an automobile can clarify its operation, models of development are intended to clarify human development. The three models of human development each provide a unique metaphor (e.g., a machine, a living organism, a process of conflict) that highlight critical features of age-related change and help us to understand that process.

A second model function is to provide a foundation for theory development. As the model helps the scientist understand behavior and development, the scientist gains a better basis for formulating theories. Finally, models serve a "limiting" function when the scientist interprets research findings. Model assumptions provide boundaries for the kinds of explanations that are logical (Overton & Reese, 1973; Pepper, 1942; Reese & Overton, 1970). These boundaries, and illustrative questions related to their application in a hypothetical study of childrearing, include:

Unidirectional versus *reciprocal* causation. Do environmental influences lead to behavior changes only, or can the individual influence the environment as well? For example, are childrearing choices determined by parents' cultural backgrounds, or do parents' decisions about childrearing also influence the culture?

Elementarism versus *holism*. Does it make sense to study individual aspects of behavior, or must these discrete behaviors always be understood in a broader context? For example, can we understand childrearing decisions by asking questions concerned solely with childrearing, or must we also question parents about other goals in their lives to understand their behavior as parents?

Structure-function *versus* ***antecedent-consequent***. Can we best understand behavior by identifying its purpose and ways in which behavior is related to that function, or does an analysis of behavior in terms of preceding events and subsequent consequences provide greater insight? To understand childrearing behaviors, is it necessary to understand parents' goals in childrearing and how their behaviors are related to these goals? Can we understand parenting just as well by studying simply what parents do, when and where they do these things, and what happens as a result?

Structural *versus* ***behavioral change***. What changes with development? Is it the function (and corresponding structure) of behavior, or simply the behavior itself? Do parents' goals in raising children change as they and their children mature? Or do parents simply behave differently as they and their children get older?

Discontinuity *versus* ***continuity***. As the individual develops, do new behaviors that are fundamentally different from earlier ones emerge, or are new behaviors predictable outgrowths of earlier behaviors? Do parents experience distinct stages of parenting, in which they do distinctly different things as parents? Do parents simply do some things with their children more frequently—and other things less frequently—as they and their children mature?

Theories

Whereas models are sets of *assumptions*, theories are collections of statements subject to confirmation or disconfirmation. One definition of a scientific **theory** is "a set of statements including (1) laws and (2) definitions of terms" (Baltes et al., 1977, p. 16). The terms defined in a theory identify concepts that must be considered to adequately understand a phenomenon. For example, in defining such terms as "successful aging," and "disengagement," theorists single out these concepts as critical for understanding adjustment in old age. The laws included in a theory explain relationships among these concepts, and may specify the circumstances under which these relationships apply. As the *Open Questions* box for this chapter describes, one theory of personal functioning in old age proposes that aging successfully is related to a process of disengagement (see p. 36).

Theory functions   Theories serve two functions. First, theories summarize existing knowledge and highlight associations among currently known facts. A theory of adjustment to parenthood, for example, should bring together scientifically-based information concerning that process, and circumstances related to satisfactory and unsatisfactory levels of adjustment. The theory should also specify ways in which empirical findings concerning parenthood are related to one another. Without this integration, it would be nearly impossible to identify the significance of any individual study.

In addition, theories suggest new questions to guide further research. Thus, theories not only give meaning to current knowledge, but also suggest areas about which more *should* be known. As an example, Piaget's theory of cognitive development brings together observations of infants', children's, and adolescents' intellectual performance and highlights interrelationships among these findings. Equally important, the theory has prompted scientists to question the applicability of Piaget's concepts to intellectual performance in old age; research designed to answer these questions has extended our understanding of adult cognitive development (e.g., Labouvie-Vief, 1985; Papalia & Bielby, 1974).

How are theories evaluated? One criterion is the extent to which a theory fulfills its intended functions. Does the theory bring together what is known about an area, integrate this information, and also suggest new areas for exploration? In addition, P. H. Miller (1983) notes that a useful theory should be logically sound (e.g., propositions should not contradict one another), should be testable (e.g., the terms defined in the theory should have some relationship to observable events), should be parsimonious (e.g., should include as few concepts as possible), and should cover a reasonably broad area of science. Finally, a useful theory must be falsifiable: it must be possible to derive predictions from the theory that one could demonstrate to be false (Popper, 1961).

The variety of developmental theories   There are many theories of development; these theories differ from one another in three ways. Developmental theories vary, first, in the aspect of development addressed. Some theories, such as the biological theories of aging (see Chapter Three), are concerned with age-related changes in single cells, organs, or organ systems. Other theories, such as the disengagement and activity theories of aging, address changes in the individual's relationship to society, and the impacts of these changes (see Box 2.1). There are developmental theories concerned solely with changes in personality, and others which address only cognitive changes. Thus, theories of development provide different perspectives on just what develops.

Theories also vary in the models that provide their foundations. Each model of development (see below) comprises a unique set of assumptions about humans and development. Any single developmental theory stems from one, but *only* one, of these sets of assumptions. Each of the three models, however, provides a foundation for several developmental theories.

A group of theories that are all consistent with a single model is a "family of theories." Just as members of human families resemble one another but each have a unique appearance, members of a family of theories share general assumptions but also include different concepts and laws. For example, both Piaget's theory of intellectual development and Kohlberg's theory of moral development are consistent with the same model, but one theory addresses change in cognitive functioning and the other describes change in the grounds

BOX 2.1   *OPEN QUESTIONS*

What is successful aging?

Much gerontological research concerns "successful aging." In this work, scholars attempt to define aging successfully, and the circumstances that contribute to that process. Disengagement theory and activity theory guided much of the initial work in this area. The theories share some conceptual features, even though each proposes a unique path toward successful aging.

A challenge for both theories was to define "successful aging." As Sheila Chown (1968) observed, investigators have considered several alternatives. One possible criterion is public opinion regarding appropriate behaviors for elderly individuals, so that aging successfully would be behaving as an elderly person "should." Another possibility is the older person's satisfaction with her current social roles and activities, so that a contented elderly person would be aging successfully. The most frequently used criteria are "experienced feelings of satisfaction with the present and the past" (Chown, 1968, p. 139). Thus, older individuals who express comfort and pleasure with both their current lot in life and the events of their past are those who have aged successfully.

Both disengagement theory and activity theory include the notion of engagement, or involvement, as a central variable. These theories stem from observations that, in old age, engagement with society—social

activities and social interactions—is typically curtailed. The theories then diverge in their accounts of the source of this process and in the relationship between engagement and successful aging.

According to disengagement theory, aging is naturally characterized by a process in which both society and the aging person withdraw from one another (Cumming & Henry, 1961). The aging individual is not excluded involuntarily from opportunities for social engagement, but she accepts (and perhaps even seeks) decreased social involvement. At the same time, the older individual grows increasingly preoccupied with herself. Disengagement theory posits that "the older person who has a sense of psychological well-being will usually be the person who has reached a new equilibrium characterized by a greater psychological distance, altered types of relationships, and decreased social interaction with the persons around him" (Havighurst, Neugarten, & Tobin, 1968, p. 161).

Activity theory proposes a different picture of the antecedents of successful aging. According to this theory, elderly people have the same needs for engagement as do younger adults. When decreased social involvement occurs in old age, it is not because of the internally-driven, maturational process posited by disengagement theory. Such decreased involvement

used for making moral judgments. These theories are based on the same assumptions but, not surprisingly, each incorporates totally different concepts stemming from those assumptions.

Finally, theories vary in emphasis given to hereditary and environmental influences of development. The "nature-nurture" controversy actually predates the field of psychology and the scientific study of human development. Philosophers and theologians have debated the question for centuries. Today, most scholars of human development agree that hereditary and environmental factors interact to mold behavior and development: neither factor alone can account for behavior or its systematic change with age. Theorists do, however, vary in the relative emphasis ascribed to hereditary and environmental influences, as well as in the processes through which these factors affect the individual.

For example, some theories, such as social learning theory, stress environmental influences leading to age-related behavior change. Hereditary influ-

would reflect, instead, *society's* withdrawal from the aging individual. According to this theory, "the older person who ages optimally is the person who stays active and who manages to resist the shrinkage of his social world" (Havighurst et al., 1968, p. 161). This theory, then, is one of many social theories of aging which propose that *continuity* optimally characterizes later life (e.g., Atchley, 1989).

Both theories have some empirical support. According to Bernice Neugarten (1968b), disengagement theory was based upon initial analysis of data from a major longitudinal study, the Kansas City Study of Adult Life. Further examination of these data, however, revealed that while the *process* of disengagement was undeniable, the extent to which that process served as a condition of optimal aging was questionable. In other longitudinal research, feelings of life satisfaction were positively related to activity: more engaged older individuals were more satisfied (Maddox, 1965).

Upon further examination of the Kansas City data—this time taking participants' personality characteristics into consideration—the investigators concluded that neither disengagement theory nor activity theory alone could sufficiently explain successful aging. Personality is a critical variable mediating the relationship between social engagement and satisfaction in later life. As Neugarten, Havighurst, & Tobin (1968) explain, aging individuals choose among lifestyle options presented by the social environment. The older person, then, is dominated neither by inexorable social pressure to disengage or remain active nor by rigid maturational forces. Personality predicts which older people will disengage and which will remain involved.

Certainly, the circumstances that promote successful aging are still an open question, and are likely to remain so. Some theorists even argue that the very concept of "successful aging" requires substantial revision. Ryff (1982), for example, argues that early conceptions of successful aging were not sufficiently developmental and were isolated from major theories such as Erikson's. Consequently, research guided by these formulations lacked explanatory power. According to Ryff (1986), successful aging should be examined as a multidimensional phenomenon reflecting current and previous life experiences and the individual's interpretation of those experiences.

Even if one grants that the concept of successful aging is potentially useful, it is safe to say that its nature and antecedents will remain elusive. Particularly in light of a dialectical perspective on development, continual social and historical changes result in continually changing possibilities for adaptation in old age.

ences are given relatively little emphasis in these theories. However, these theorists propose a variety of mechanisms through which environmental influences affect the individual. As Wohlwill (1973) explains, there are at least four means through which these factors are believed to influence us. In the "hospital bed" model, the individual is completely passive and the environment "operates" on her as though she were a hospital patient. In the "amusement-park" model, the individual selectively exposes herself to certain environmental influences, but has no control over the way these experiences affect her. The "swim meet" model proposes that the environment is a setting for development: specific environmental stimuli, like specific features of an individual swimming pool, have relatively little impact on the individual. Finally, in the "tennis match" model, there is an interaction between environmental and personal influences: one is affected by a tennis partner's behavior, but one also affects the partner's tennis game.

Despite their variety, developmental theories share an implicit definition of "development." One might think that any behavioral or physical change might be described as development. However, this definition would incorporate countless trivial and temporary changes. Taking a shower, eating until full, and dropping a semester course would all fit this broad definition. As M. Green (1989) explains, theorists reserve the term "development" for changes that have two characteristics. First, developmental changes have **temporality**. These changes extend over a relatively long period of time (e.g., weeks, months, or years as opposed to seconds, minutes, or hours). By this criterion, puberty and senescence are developmental changes; taking a nap is not.

Of course, the passage of time alone does not mean that development has occurred. Time must pass before one can prepare for retirement. However, that preparation will not occur simply because time has elapsed. Other events and processes (e.g., gathering information about retirement and pensions, developing hobbies, etc.) must take place before retirement preparation can occur. Age and time, then, are not causal variables (Wohlwill, 1970).

Developmental changes also have **directionality** (Green, 1989). As we noted in the last chapter, developmental changes take varied forms (e.g., increases in proficiency, decreases in proficiency, reorganization of existing skills). However, developmental changes are cumulative and relatively irreversible—or at least not easily undone. Thus, changes in height and the formation of a personality are developmental events. However, changing one's hair color is not developmental because it is not cumulative; opening a checking account is not developmental because the experience is easily reversed.

Developmental theories and research   As the functions of scientific theories suggest, useful theories are both based on research and provide an impetus for future research. Thus, theories are always tentative structures in a continual process of formation and reformation. Scientists integrate research-based information into a theory, and then conduct new research in an attempt to answer new questions stemming from the theory. These questions are often stated as predictions and are usually referred to as **hypotheses**.

It is possible that the extent to which the theoretically-based hypothesis is or is not supported will identify ways in which the theory needs to be modified. The theory as originally formulated may only apply to certain kinds of people, or may only apply in specific circumstances. Or, new concepts may have to be incorporated in order to account for new findings. Figure 2.1 illustrates these reciprocal relationships between research and theory.

Theories have still another relationship to research. The concepts defined in a theory are highlighted for the scientist's attention. According to the theory, one must consider these concepts to understand the process of development in question. Other concepts, those that are not defined in the theory, are presumably not important for understanding that developmental process. Thus, theoretically-based research will reflect the scientist's concern to adequately measure and examine the concepts included in the theory, and her

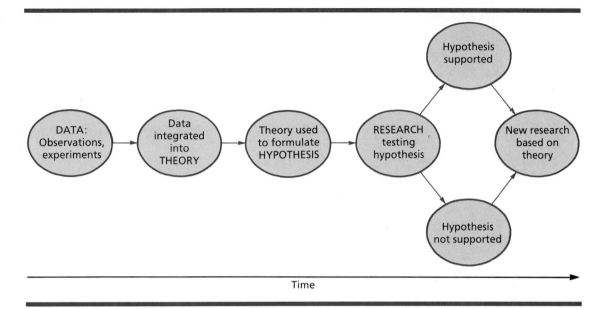

Figure 2.1
Theory and research.

implicit decision not to assess concepts that are irrelevant from the perspective of that theory.

For example, according to the activity and disengagement theories of aging, it is critical to know about an older individual's level of social involvement in order to understand her level of adjustment to aging (see Box 2.1, p. 36). Both theories highlight social involvement as a central concept, and the researcher using either theory as a framework will include several reliable and valid measures of social involvement in her research design. However, neither theory includes proficiency in memory tasks or level of income as relevant to understanding adjustment in old age. Scientists who use either theory as their basis for research, then, will devote great care to assessing social involvement, but little or no effort to evaluating cognitive performance or income level.

MODELS OF DEVELOPMENT

There are currently three major models of development—the **mechanistic**, the **organismic**, and the **dialectical**. Each comprises assumptions about human nature, human development, and the causes of human development. Each is the foundation for a "family" of developmental theories. This section examines the assumptions of each model; Table 2.1 summarizes these assumptions. We also briefly describe a theory that is consistent with each of the three models, and examples of research based upon the theory. Remember, though, that the theory we consider in the context of each model is only one example of that family of theories. Extended discussion of other developmental theories and related research continue throughout the book.

The mechanistic model

Model assumptions   Recall that each model of development uses a unique metaphor for understanding human behavior and development. In the mechanistic model, the metaphor is the machine (Overton & Reese, 1973; Reese & Overton, 1970). Human beings are viewed as **reactive**—or passive and machine-like—in this model. Machines do not operate spontaneously: they must be plugged in, turned on, fed coins, or in some way acted upon before they will operate. Furthermore, the parts of the machine have a great deal to do with the nature of the machine's operation. An iron cannot operate as a coffeepot or a clock no matter what environmental action impinges on it.

The mechanistic model portrays humans in a similar vein. We do nothing spontaneously, but behave in response to environmental influences. The physical structures composing humans have an irrefutable influence on our behavior. Humans cannot fly unaided, for example, regardless of the environmental events to which we are exposed.

The mechanistic model describes development as a process of **quantitative change** (Overton & Reese, 1973; Reese & Overton, 1970). A machine performs the same kinds of operations (e.g., ironing clothes, making coffee, keeping time) throughout its operational life, although it may operate more quickly, more slowly, with greater or less magnitude, and so forth, depending on envi-

Table 2.1

Assumptions of developmental models

	Human nature	Type of change	Cause of change
Mechanistic Model	Reactive, passive (e.g., like a machine)	Quantitative only	Changes in physical structures; Environmental influences
Organismic Model	Active, organized (e.g., like a living organism)	Qualitative only	Movement toward a "highest" form of organization; Changes in functions served by organized forms or structures
Dialectical Model	Both active and reactive (e.g., like a process of conflict or competition)	Both quantitative and qualitative	Interactions between the individual and the context of her behavior

Theories based on the mechanistic model propose that people engage in essentially the same behaviors throughout their lives.

ronmental input. In the same way, mechanistically-based developmental theories propose that new behaviors do not appear over the course of development.

As the individual develops, she increases or decreases her use of the same behaviors, and combines these behaviors in new ways. For example, a mechanistically-based theory of language acquisition would describe language development in terms of changes in the *amount or quantity* of certain behaviors. The theory might describe age-related *increases* in vocabulary, length of utterance, and proficiency in articulation, as well as *decreases* in behaviors such as crying and babbling. Apparently new behaviors can actually be reduced to new combinations of earlier, simpler behaviors (Overton & Reese, 1973; Reese & Overton, 1970). Conversing (a relatively mature behavior) could be reduced to such component behaviors as articulating individual words, using a fairly extensive vocabulary, attending to a partner's speech, being sensitive to "turn-taking" in verbal interactions, and so forth.

The quantitative changes that comprise development result from two kinds of influences in mechanistically-based developmental theories (Overton & Reese, 1973; Reese & Overton, 1970). **Material causes** are the effects of the individual's physical make-up. Again, a theory of language development based on this model would include genetic, neurological, and muscular human characteristics as influences; a mechanistically-based theory of adjustment to motherhood might stress hormonal influences and related physiological changes associated with childbirth. In addition, theories based on this model include **efficient causes**, or the influence of the physical and social environment.

Again considering the machine as a metaphor for human behavior and development, this family of theories calls our attention to the parts of the machine and the forces impinging on it to understand the machine's operation and how that operation changes. The behaviors involved in conversing would, according to a mechanistically-based theory of language acquisition, be behaviors acquired from the individual's physical characteristics (e.g., neurological structures associated with language use; musculature of the lips, tongue, etc.) as acted upon by environmental influences (e.g., parental attention for mastering vocabulary and articulation; efficiency of communicating through words as opposed to babbling or crying).

According to the mechanistic model, if we have complete information about the characteristics of the machine and the forces acting on it, we can make thorough predictions about the machine's future operation. Similarly, if we have a complete understanding of relevant human physical structures and environmental influences, then we should be able to make precise predictions of future behavior.

The mechanistic model, theory, and applications for aging   The theories most closely associated with the mechanistic model are behaviorism (e.g., Skinner, 1953; 1974) and social learning theory (e.g., Bandura, 1977). P. H. Miller (1983) summarizes the general orientation of these theories as:

- *An emphasis on learned behavior*. Although these theorists recognize that there are biological limits on any organism's behavior, their interest is in learned behaviors. Thus, primary attention is devoted to relatively permanent behavior changes resulting from experience.
- *An emphasis on environmental control of behavior*. The physical and social environments are a complex set of stimuli. Some stimuli cue behavior, while others are consequences of behavior. In both instances, the stimuli determine behavior.
- *Breakdown of behavior into simple units*. These theorists recognize the vast complexity of most human behavior, and they believe that behavior can be best understood by reducing its complexity. The strategy is to break a complex behavior (e.g., carrying on a conversation) into relatively simple units (e.g., speaking words and sentences, listening to the partner) and identify the ways in which environmental stimuli are related to these simple behaviors. When these relationships are understood, the simple behaviors can be recombined into the original complex behavior, now with insight into its environmental determinants.
- *A focus on observable behavior*. A common misconception of behaviorism is that the very existence of unobservable processes—such as thinking, feeling, remembering—is denied. Skinner (1974) did not deny that these covert processes (that he labeled "private events") exist. He did assert, however, that our understanding of behavior cannot be advanced by studying private events. Rather, we will best understand behavior and its causes by studying the observable, environmental stimuli that provide cues and consequences for behavior.

Behaviorism and social learning theory use a common set of principles to guide their analysis of behavior. These principles include reinforcement, discriminative stimuli, generalization, shaping, and extinction. Explanations of these principles appear in all general psychology texts, and we will not repeat them here. For our purposes, it is more important to examine one way in which these theories have been used to manage pathological behavior in old age.

Behavior modification is a set of techniques that apply these learning principles in order to change behavior. When behavior modification is used with humans, it is usually in a clinical context. The goal is to reduce the frequency of problematic behaviors (e.g., aggression, self-mutilation, overeating, smoking) and/or to increase the frequency of more adaptive behaviors (e.g., smiling, speaking).

As Baer (1973) notes, behavior modification is often an attempt to bring about behaviors that normally emerge over the course of development, but that have not in a particular case. The effort then is to provide an efficiently programmed set of environmental cues and consequences that will lead to the desired behaviors, rather than waiting for nature to provide cues and consequences according to a less efficient schedule. From this perspective, one could say that normal development—like any process of behavior change—requires time, but that deliberate environmental programming could reduce the time required from years to days or hours.

Behavior modification has been used with children for over two decades, but has only recently gained broad application in gerontological contexts. As with children, it appears that these techniques can change older adults' behaviors. For example, one group of researchers demonstrated that an institutionalized elderly woman's paranoid behaviors could be virtually eliminated through a behavioral treatment program (Carstensen & Fremouw, 1981). Another researcher reported that caregivers for dementia victims used behavior modification to reduce the frequency of troublesome behaviors (e.g., loud protests against being left alone, frequent telephone calls), or to increase the frequency of adaptive behaviors (e.g., socializing with the family) (Haley, 1983).

The organismic model

Model assumptions   The metaphor in the organismic model is the living organism—an organized, integrated entity (Overton & Reese, 1973; Reese & Overton, 1970). Unlike the machine metaphor of the mechanistic model, the individual parts of the organism in this metaphor have little meaning in isolation. Only in the context of the total organism do these components function. The metaphor also suggests that this totality is in a continual process of change. Thus, the organism progresses from one state of organization to a new state until some final, most sophisticated level of organization is reached (Overton & Reese, 1973).

The metaphor shapes the model's assumptions about humans and their development. First, it is assumed that humans are fundamentally **active**: "the organism is the source of acts, rather than being activated by external or peripheral forces" (Overton & Reese, 1973, pp. 70). Clearly, this is a different perspective of human nature from that offered by the mechanistic model. The organismic model proposes that internal processes (e.g., talents, goals, desires, etc.) can explain behavior, but the mechanistic model proposes that these internal processes themselves must be explained in terms of material and efficient causes.

In the organismic model, development is comprised of **qualitative changes**. Again, the organization of parts into a whole is a critical aspect of the metaphor. As the individual develops, the organization of component parts changes, and new properties of the individual emerge. The new properties differ from earlier properties not in amount or quantity, but in their basic nature or quality. In Piaget's theory, for example, development is not portrayed as a process of acquiring more and more of the same intellectual skills. Rather, Piaget describes development as a process through which the nature and configuration of intellectual skills change as the individual matures. Theories consistent with the organismic model, then, generally describe development as a process comprised of distinct **stages** or eras.

Behavior and development are explained in terms of the organism's inherent organization and activity; two causes are used in explanations. A **formal cause** is the pattern or organization of a phenomenon. For example, Piaget might explain an adolescent's response to a conservation of volume problem with reference to the unique configuration of formal operational cognitive abilities. Kohlberg (e.g., 1970) would explain an individual's response to a moral dilemma by citing the constellation of moral beliefs at her level of development.

In addition, the organismic model includes the notion of **final cause**. These explanations refer to some *end state* toward which change is directed; theories in this family all propose a final stage of development. Following the final stage, no further changes in organization occur. Freud's theory of personality development provides an example. Freud proposed a final stage of genital sexuality. Changes in personality occurring prior to this final stage could be understood, according to Freud, as necessary steps toward the ultimate goal of achieving genital sexuality. Freud did not recognize important personality changes occurring in adulthood after one had attained genital sexuality.

The organismic model, theory, and research on aging   Piaget's theory of intellectual development is one of the best known and most widely researched theories consistent with the organismic model. According to the theory (e.g., Flavell, 1963; Piaget, 1970), cognitive development proceeds as a sequence of stages. Each stage—the sensorimotor, the preoperational, the concrete operational, and the formal operational—is characterized by a unique configuration of processes through which the individual acquires and uses information. One individual may differ from another in the rate at which these stages are traversed, but not in the order in which the stages are experienced.

The final stage of cognitive development, formal operations, is normally reached in early adolescence. Piaget devoted little attention to the possibility of cognitive changes in adulthood. He did suggest, however, that this final stage may be reached at different ages by different individuals, depending on their aptitudes and the nature of their educational and occupational training (Piaget,

1972). He did not believe that the nature of intellectual functioning continued to change after formal operations had been attained.

Researchers of adult cognitive development have questioned this belief, and attempted to determine whether adult intelligence reflects the properties of formal operations; we examine this work further in Chapter Six. Diane Papalia (e.g., 1972; Papalia & Bielby, 1974) was among the first scientists to address these questions. Her work encompasses the study of conservation and classification performance across the life span, levels of moral reasoning across adulthood, and animism in the reasoning of young and older adults. On the basis of her research, and her examination of related work, she suggests that some adults experience qualitative change in cognitive functioning after the advent of formal operations. Papalia also concluded, however, that other adults seem never to attain formal operations at all.

Papalia offered several possible interpretations of these findings (Papalia & Bielby, 1974). Most of the research on which her conclusions were based were cross-sectional studies, so it is possible that there were cohort differences, rather than age changes, in levels of cognitive performance. It is also possible, however, that actual age changes in intellectual functioning do occur as a result of neurological changes occurring in old age, or because the social environments of many elderly people are less stimulating than the social environments of many younger people. It is also possible that "terminal drop," a process of profound cognitive decline occurring shortly before death, affected the performance of elderly participants in Piagetian-based research. Finally, other scholars suggest that older adults' apparent "regression" to earlier levels of cognitive functioning are actually adaptations to the circumstances of adult life (Labouvie-Vief, 1985; see pp. 154–155).

Some propose that older adults' relatively poor cognitive performance in many cross-sectional studies may reflect lack of intellectual stimulation in their environments.

In any case, Piaget's theory has clearly stimulated research. This work, in turn, has expanded our understanding of intellectual development in old age. It is also clear that the findings of this work do not entirely conform to Piaget's assertions. As we see in subsequent chapters addressing cognitive functioning, these discrepancies between the theory and research findings have prompted new theoretical propositions and research testing these propositions.

The dialectical model

Model assumptions   The dialectical model is the most recently constructed model of development, and some scholars believe that it may be the most useful one (Baltes et al., 1977). The basic metaphor of the dialectical model has not yet been precisely described, but is most often identified as the process of conflict. In this model, change is a basic process, and it is assumed that change will occur in unpredictable ways.

The dialectical model seems to embrace the conflicting assumptions of the mechanistic and organismic models. In this model, it is assumed that humans are both reactive and active. Klaus Riegel (1975), one of the most prominent scholars discussing the model, explained that "man not only transforms the outer world in which he lives, but is himself transformed by the world which he and others have created" (p. 51). The individual and the environment, then, are interdependent: each influences the other, and is influenced by the other.

According to Riegel, development reflects synchronies and asynchronies among events in four dimensions: the inner-biological, the individual-psychological, the cultural-sociological, and the outer-physical. Because humans are assumed to influence the environment and to be influenced by the environment, this model implies that scientists should devote as much attention to examining the cultural and physical setting of development as the people developing within that setting. As the *Diversity in Adulthood* box explains, Erik Erikson's theory[1] is an outstanding example of a theory in which the cultural, historical, and physical contexts of development are thoroughly examined.

The dialectical model also includes the assumption that development embraces both quantitative and qualitative change. In this model, quantitative changes provide useful descriptions of development, but only within limits. When quantitative change exceeds these limits, the developing individual is transformed, and a description in terms of qualitative change becomes more useful. For example, one might describe changes in memory proficiency occur-

---

1. Erikson's theory is often classified as consistent with the organismic model of development, since the process of development is described as a universal sequence of stages and a final stage of development is posited. The theory is also, however, outstanding in its treatment of the cultural context of development, and does stress processes of conflict as key sources of developmental change. In these respects, the theory is more consistent with the dialectical model of development.

The one on the left will finish high school before the one on the right.

Adolescent pregnancy isn't just a problem in America, it's a crisis. To learn more about a social issue that concerns all of us, write: *Children's Defense Fund, 122 C Street, N.W., Washington, D.C. 20001.*

The Children's Defense Fund.

The dialectical model emphasizes asynchronies between the individual's biological and psychological maturity and the physical and social challenges that the environment presents.

ring in old age as decreases in quantitative indices of memory performance (e.g., recalling fewer items from a list, needing more time to remember, decreased accuracy in recall). If these decreases in memory proficiency progress to an extreme level, however, the process is better described as a transformation of the person. The impact of Alzheimer's disease is an example.

The dialectical model emphasizes interactions between people and the environment in explaining development. More specifically, conflict between the individual—a biological and psychological entity—and the physical and social environment is a source of change. Conflict *within* the person—between the individual's biological and psychological processes, for example—also prompts change. In discussing adult life events, Riegel (1975) explains that there may be asynchronies between the individual's level of biological or psychological maturity and the challenges in the physical and social environment. These asynchronies present crises for the individual, and it is precisely these crises that trigger further growth.

In the dialectical model, finally, it is assumed that we cannot make complete or accurate predictions of future behavior. Change is a given in this model,

BOX 2.2   *DIVERSITY IN ADULTHOOD*

Cultural context in Erikson's developmental theory

Erik Erikson is among the most prominent contemporary theorists of development. In two respects, Erikson's theory is unusual, if not unique. Erikson portrays personality development as a life-span process; few other theorists offer such a description. Erikson describes development as a process grounded in the individual's culture at a particular period of history.

Erikson describes personality development as a process through which the individual confronts age-related psychosocial crises spanning the life cycle. In confronting each crisis, the individual incorporates a dynamic balance between a set of opposing tendencies. As an infant, for example, it is necessary to integrate varied interactions with the caregiver and others in order to balance tendencies toward *trust* and *mistrust*.

The last three crises of Erikson's model occur in adulthood (Erikson, 1950; 1982). In young adulthood, the individual confronts the psychosocial crisis of balancing intimacy with isolation. The task of the young adult, then, is to synthesize her capability for emotional intimacy with her capacity to function apart from intimate relationships. Middle adult-

hood is characterized by opposing tendencies toward generativity and stagnation. At this point, one must balance the capacity to provide for others and society with the ability to care for oneself. Finally, the individual confronts the crisis of ego integrity versus despair in later adulthood. The elderly person, according to Erikson, ideally balances satisfaction with the past against regrets and fear of death.

Some discussions of Erikson's theory omit the notion of "preworking and reworking." Through this concept, Erikson proposes that each of the age-related psychosocial crises has a period of particular urgency, such as young adulthood for the crisis of intimacy versus isolation. Each crisis is nonetheless present in some form throughout the life cycle (e.g., Erikson et al., 1986). In other words, infants and elderly men and women must also balance intimacy and isolation, although not in the same way that a young adult faces this challenge.

Though Erikson proposes that the sequence of psychosocial crises comprising personality development is universal, he also asserts that the nature of the confrontations with these crises are unique

and **incidental causes** are assumed to operate. In other words, this model proposes that unpredictable, accidental combinations of causes will occur and will have unanticipated outcomes (Baltes et al., 1977).

The dialectical model, theory, and research on aging   As we noted earlier, the dialectical model is the most recently formulated model of development. Although the model is often described as the most useful perspective on development, few theories have been elaborated using dialectical assumptions as their foundation. The model has, however, provided a perspective for reexamining research on life-span development in general and adult development in particular (e.g., Gergen, 1977). For example, scholars have discussed research on reasoning, memory, discriminative learning, and operant behavior from a dialectical standpoint (Datan & Reese, 1977; Sinnott, 1984, 1989a, b).

Rebecca's (1975) examination of sex-role socialization is an example of a dialectical analysis. Rebecca proposed that neither mechanistically-based learning theories nor organismically-based cognitive theories could account for

in each culture. Childrearing traditions, expectations regarding marital relationships, norms regulating interactions between individuals of different ages, and other aspects of the culture will affect the manner in which we meet these crises. Similarly, the social, political, economic, and environmental circumstances of any particular historical period influence the development of individuals living during that era.

In the course of his long and productive career, Erikson has gathered many kinds of evidence illustrating the impact of culture upon development. Erikson differs from most personality theorists in the extent to which his work has drawn upon anthropological methods and data. In his best known work, *Childhood and Society* (1950), Erikson described child development in the Sioux and Yurok Indian tribes, as well as the developmental implications of racial discrimination experienced by African American children. More recently, Erikson has considered the impact of historical context and social change on the lives of contemporary American elders (Erikson et al., 1986).

Erikson took still another unique approach to the study of the dynamic relationship between individual development and social context. In his "psychohistories," Erikson examined the development of well-known historical figures using their writings, public statements and activities, and others' reports of their conversations and behaviors. The individuals that Erikson "analyzed" in this manner included Adolf Hitler, Martin Luther, Maxim Gorky, George Bernard Shaw, and Mohandas Gandhi. Through this approach, Erikson further illustrated the dynamic interplay between an individual's developmental needs, the crises facing the individual's society, and the opportunities and challenges that society and the developing individual present to one another.

Erikson, then, stands out as a developmental theorist keenly aware of the cultural context of development. By drawing on both cross-cultural information and the method of psychohistory, the theory is unparalleled in its stress on the cultural diversity of development. We will return to this theory and related research in Chapter Eight.

sex-role socialization. Her dialectical theory encompasses three stages of sex-role development; however, the transitions between stages are more important than the stages themselves. These transitions are prompted by asynchronies between the four developmental dimensions described by Riegel (1975): the inner-biological, the individual-psychological, the cultural-sociological, and the outer-physical.

In Rebecca's (1975) Stage 1, the infant has an undifferentiated concept of sex-roles. Infants, in other words, are not aware of differences between men and women. It is only with biological and psychological growth and interaction with the social and physical environment that the child becomes aware that there is a male-female distinction and that many behaviors are viewed as appropriate or inappropriate in the context of that dichotomy. Stage 2 involves a polarized notion of sex roles. In this stage, traditional definitions of masculinity and femininity are accepted. The child embraces behaviors consistent with the stereotype of his or her gender, while avoiding behaviors characteristic of the opposite gender.

Although the child does not strive to master the behaviors characteristic of the opposite gender, the child nonetheless has "latent knowledge" of these behaviors. A girl, for example, may not attempt to become proficient at athletic or mechanical pursuits but may still acquire skills in these areas. This latent knowledge is a source of movement toward Stage 3, the stage of sex-role transcendence.

Another necessary impetus for this movement is confrontation with asynchronies between Riegel's (1975) four dimensions. For example, a man who has received training for a traditionally-female occupation (e.g., preschool teacher, nurse) might encounter discrimination when he attempts to work in that field. Thus, asynchrony between the man's individual-psychological development (the skills that he has acquired) and his cultural-sociological context (current ideas about who "should" perform certain types of jobs) has occurred. Given at least some support, the man may move from Stage 2 to the sex-role transcendence of Stage 3. (One could argue, of course, that only a man who has already experienced some sex-role transcendence would prepare for a traditionally-female occupation.)

In Stage 3, traditional notions of "masculine" and "feminine" no longer influence behavior (Rebecca, 1975). Rather, one attains situational and personal flexibility. Depending on situational demands, one may behave in a manner that is traditionally feminine (e.g., comforting a distressed friend) or traditionally masculine (e.g., aggressively confronting a belligerent stranger). Or, one may change the situation in order to deal with it comfortably and effectively. For example, a social worker may interact with clients more empathetically than his agency expects in order to work in a manner most appropriate for his personality, skills, and values.

SUMMARY

Theories, sets of laws, and definitions serve similar functions in virtually all sciences. Theories both integrate information gleaned from prior research and guide ongoing research; the extent to which theories fulfill these functions are among the criteria used in evaluating theories. There is great diversity among theories of development. These theories vary in their perspective of *what* develops, in their outlook on the "nature-nurture" issue, and in the assumptions forming their foundation.

Theories are related to research in several ways. Many hypotheses tested in developmental research are theoretically-based, and theories may be modified when its hypotheses are not supported by research results. Furthermore, the terms defined in a theory are central variables in research based on the theory. The scientist will take great care in measuring these variables and examining their interrelationships.

Any single theory of development reflects a unique model of development. Models are sets of assumptions that describe the nature and causes of development. Each of three models of development provides a unique metaphor for human beings and human development, and each model is the foundation for a "family" of developmental theories.

KEY TERMS

Active	Material cause
Antecedent-consequent	Mechanistic
Continuity	Model
Dialectical	Organismic
Directionality	Qualitative change
Discontinuity	Quantitative change
Efficient cause	Reactive
Elementarism	Reciprocal causation
Final cause	Stage
Formal cause	Structure-function
Holism	Temporality
Hypothesis	Theory
Incidental cause	Unidirectional causation

SUGGESTIONS FOR FURTHER READING

Baltes, P. B., Reese, H. W., & Nesselroade, J. R. (1977). *Life-span Developmental Psychology: Introduction to Research Methods*. Monterey, CA: Brooks/Cole Publishing Co.

Crain, W. C. (1985). *Theories of Development: Concepts and Applications*. Englewood Cliffs, NJ: Prentice Hall.

Green, M. (1989). *Theories of Human Development: A Comparative Approach*. Englewood Cliffs, NJ: Prentice Hall.

Kuhn, T. S. (1962). *The Structure of Scientific Revolutions*. Chicago: University of Chicago Press.

Lerner, R. M. (1976). *Concepts and Theories of Human Development*. Reading, MA: Addison-Wesley Publishing Co.

Miller, P. H. (1983). *Theories of Developmental Psychology*. San Francisco: W. H. Freeman & Co.

CHAPTER THREE

*C*HANGES IN PHYSICAL FUNCTIONING THROUGHOUT ADULTHOOD

What is aging? On one level, the question concerns ways in which we change physically during adulthood. Some changes—such as those in stature and the vital functions—are rarely apparent until late adulthood. But others are obvious relatively early—changes in appearance, for example. Correspondingly, one theme of this chapter is the extent to which physical aging is a long-term, gradual process. In considering these physical changes, we identify not only ways in which the body changes with age but also the extent to which different people experience these changes at different rates and to different extents. Thus, a second theme is the significance of individual differences in physical aging, and the importance of adults' choices regarding health and lifestyle as influences of aging.

Questions to consider in reading the chapter include:

How does appearance change during adulthood?
What age-related changes occur in the major organ systems as one gets older?
What individual differences in these processes are apparent?

How does the functioning of the reproductive system change for women and for men? What are the psychological impacts of these changes?

What options are currently available for infertile men and women?

How do biological theories of aging explain the physical changes that occur with age?

What circumstances seem to prolong longevity, and what factors seem to shorten it?

CHANGES IN PHYSICAL APPEARANCE

Many people in their forties and fifties find the physical changes of age all too apparent. Wrinkles adorn the face, the hair is thinned and grayed, and a "middle-aged spread" has appeared. These familiar (and usually unwelcome) changes reflect processes at the cellular and intracellular levels. These processes begin in early adulthood—even though their consequences are rarely noticed before middle adulthood. And the extent and impact of these processes reflect individual differences in both hereditary factors and exposure to environmental influences. Although everyone's appearance changes with age,

Alterations in physical appearance are among the most obvious ways in which we change with age.

then, these physical differences are more dramatic for some people than for others.

Changes in the skin and hair

The **integumentary system** includes the skin, hair, and nails. Obviously, this system is critically important for appearance. Other functions are less obvious but no less consequential. The skin provides a protective covering that retains water in body tissues and prevents the entry of foreign substances. Sweat glands, fat, and a rich network of blood vessels in the skin help to maintain a stable body temperature. Pigments in the skin protect internal tissues against excessive radiation from the sun. Sensory receptors for touch, temperature, and pain provide information about the world.

The skin itself includes an outer layer (the **epidermis**) and an inner layer of connective tissue (the **dermis**); changes in both layers result in a changed appearance. With age, the epidermis becomes thinner, and pigment cells in the epidermis are larger and clustered together to form dark **aging spots**. In the dermis, cells generally become less resilient and flexible, as fibers are **cross-linked** (attached to one another). In addition, the number of sweat and oil-secreting glands in the skin decreases with age (Rockstein & Sussman, 1979; Spence, 1989). As a result, elderly people typically have drier skin than younger adults, and older people sweat less than younger people. The latter change is one reason that the elderly are more susceptible to heat exhaustion than are younger people.

In the tissue immediately beneath the skin, the **hypodermis**, subcutaneous fat is stored. With age, much of the fat in the hypodermis is lost. One result of this loss of fat is wrinkled skin—most prominent in the face and limbs. Another consequence is diminished padding and insulation. Because of the loss of padding, bedridden older individuals may develop pressure sores without conscientious nursing care. And, because of lost insulation, older people may feel chilled when younger people are comfortable.

The hair changes with age as well. The number of hair follicles and their rate of growth decrease with age, so that hair becomes thinner all over the body (but particularly on the head). In addition, there are fewer cells producing hair pigment as one grows older. With less pigment, hair color is less vibrant; eventually, the hair becomes gray or white. In some families it is common for hair to become prematurely gray, whereas in other families hair color is retained until quite late in life (Spence, 1989).

A final change is reduced blood flow to the skin, which causes an older person's skin to feel cooler to the touch than a younger person's skin (Spence, 1989). Another consequence is slowed growth of the fingernails and toenails (Rockstein & Sussman, 1979; Spence, 1989). With age, nails may also become yellowed, curved, and rigid (Spence, 1989).

Changes in height and weight

Both men and women have a tendency to gain weight through their fifties or sixties, but to lose weight after that age (Shock et al., 1984; Spence, 1989). Most people also find (usually, to their dismay!) that their weight is redistributed in middle and later adulthood: the limbs grow thinner, while the trunk becomes thicker (Shock et al., 1984). The composition of the body changes in less obvious ways as well, including a reduction in the percentage of weight composed of water (Spence, 1989). And, height shows a slow, gradual, and slight decrease beginning in the forties (Rockstein & Sussman, 1979; Shock et al., 1984; Spence, 1989).

There are wide individual differences in the rate and the extent of all of these changes (Rockstein & Sussman, 1979; Spence, 1989). The aging of the skin, for example, is affected by both internal factors (such as heredity) as well as environmental influences (such as diet and exposure to the sun and wind). Similarly, weight gain in middle adulthood is related not only to changes in body composition and metabolism but also to diet and exercise.

Although few people welcome wrinkles, gray hair, or extra weight, there is some consolation in recognizing that these changes are typical. Even taking solace on that basis, however, a changed appearance usually has some psychological consequences. For example, those who evaluate themselves on the basis of physical appearance may suffer blows to their self-concept.

Some suggest that women suffer more than men do from the psychological impact of these changes. In an early essay, Susan Sontag (1972) posited that America has a "double standard of aging." Because traditional social roles of men and women have been challenged since Sontag developed her argument, it is reasonable to question the extent to which a double standard of aging still exists. We explore this issue in the *Open Questions* box.

AGING OF THE MAJOR ORGAN SYSTEMS

Most young adults are at their peak of physical functioning. The major organ systems function efficiently and, usually, without complications. Paradoxically, though, many of the physical changes associated with old age make their first appearance in the twenties and thirties. Aging in that sense is truly a life-span process.

All organs of the body change with age. Many of these changes are an inevitable and universal part of aging, composing the process of **primary aging** (Perlmutter & Hall, 1985). Other changes stem more from disease, disuse, or abuse than from aging itself; these changes are **secondary aging** (Perlmutter & Hall, 1985).

The distinction between primary and secondary aging is continually refined, as scientists identify ways in which what was once considered normal

BOX 3.1   *OPEN QUESTIONS*

Is there a "double standard of aging?"

In 1972, Susan Sontag published a thought-provoking article. She argued that, according to convention, normal aging is socially devastating for a woman, but enhances a man's social position. According to Sontag, aging begins earlier for women than for men, and is a more painful process for women than for men.

Not the least of the demoralizing aspects of a woman's aging is its effect on her sexual attractiveness. Because the qualities that may make men attractive to women—fame, money, and power—do not depend on a youthful appearance, men may find that growing older in itself does not detract from their attractiveness. In fact, aging (at least up to a point) may make a man more attractive.

For women, however, a youthful appearance is central to sexual allure. According to Sontag, men are valued for their accomplishments and women are valued for their decorative nature. Because aging includes inevitable changes in appearance, "for most women, aging means a humiliating process of gradual sexual disqualification" (Sontag, 1972, p. 32).

Is this portrayal still accurate today, over twenty years later? In closing her article, Sontag (1972) stated that:

> Women have another option. They can aspire to be wise, not merely nice; to be competent, not merely helpful; to be strong, not merely graceful; to be ambitious for themselves, not merely for themselves in relation to men and children. They can let themselves age naturally and without embarrassment, actively protesting and disobeying the conventions that stem from

this society's double standard about aging. (p. 38)

The past two decades have witnessed enormous changes in women's roles. Higher percentages of women in all age groups are now employed; more women are entering fields traditionally occupied by men; and, in most fields, more women today achieve positions of greater visibility and responsibility than before. In these respects, one could say that women have sought wisdom, competence, strength, and ambition—and have, with increasing frequency, attained these goals.

Nonetheless, we cannot be too optimistic about the demise of the double standard of aging. Although it may be fair to say that women today are judged more on the basis of accomplishments than in the past, women's accomplishments are probably still not valued as highly as men's are. Average salaries, for example, are consistently lower for women than for men in a wide variety of occupations. Given data such as these, we cannot reject the notion that women are still evaluated—more than men are—on the basis of their appearance.

Certainly, the cosmetic industries continue to flourish, with a myriad of products aimed at preserving a woman's youthful appearance. Advertising for these products assures us that, in order to be desirable, a woman must be young—or at least look young. Men do not receive this warning. Perhaps we must wait for the first "Oil of Olay" commercial featuring a man to proclaim that men and women have achieved equality in aging.

---

aging may instead stem from unwise choices and unfortunate circumstances. For example, many people used to believe that intellectual functioning in general and memory in particular always become seriously impaired in old age. Although some cognitive changes are a part of normal aging, many can be minimized by remaining mentally and physically active and by making wise choices regarding diet, exercise, and the use of alcohol and other drugs during early and middle adulthood.

The nervous system

Changes in the nervous system affect the functioning of virtually all organs and organ systems. The nervous system comprises the **central nervous system**, the brain and spinal cord, and the **peripheral nervous system**, nerves connecting the central nervous system with other body structures. In both divisions, the **neuron**, or nerve cell, is a fundamental unit; Figure 3.1 illustrates a typical neuron and its major structures. Unlike most body cells, neurons are postmitotic—they do not divide after birth. Therefore, neurons which are destroyed cannot be replaced; like all other body cells, many neurons die each day simply as a part of normal development. As a result, there is a gradual loss of brain mass beginning at about age 30 (Spence, 1989).

This loss of brain mass has negligible impact before old age. In fact, the vast numbers of older adults who enjoy high levels of intellectual performance shows that this change never has much practical significance for many people. The brain has many more neurons and **synapses** (connections between neurons) than are needed to function normally. The gradual loss of brain tissue becomes problematic only when so many cells are lost that the brain's reserve capacity of neurons and synapses is compromised. Furthermore, at least some neurons establish new synapses with other neurons and thereby compensate for lost neurons (Spence, 1989). It is undeniable, however, that there is less plasticity in the aged brain than in infants' and children's brains; neuro-

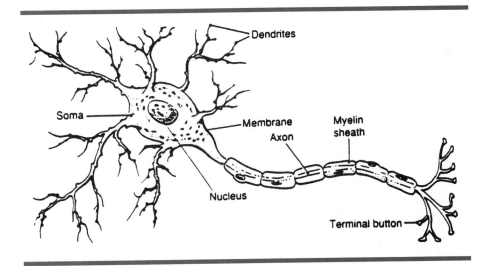

Figure 3.1
Typical neuron. (Source: Carlson, 1988.) Reprinted by permission.

logical injuries resulting from accidents or illnesses generally carry more permanent and serious consequences in old age than early in the life span.

There are other normal age-related changes in the nervous system. The outer covering of the brain, the **cortex**, accumulates yellowish pigments throughout the life span; however, this process has little significance in terms of mental functioning (Rockstein & Sussman, 1979; Spence, 1989). Within the neuron, there is an accumulation of fatty substances and of fluid-filled cavities (Rockstein & Sussman, 1979; Spence, 1989); again, the practical impact of these changes may be negligible.

In the cortex and the **hippocampus** (a brain region associated with memory functioning), two structures typically develop in healthy, alert older people. These structures are **neurofibrillary tangles** (an abnormal mass within the neuron) and **neuritic plaques** (abnormal formations between neurons). Both structures are far more prominent in the brains of older people suffering from Alzheimer's Disease, the most commonly diagnosed source of dementia.[1]

Finally, advancing age brings a decrease in the number of nerve fibers, a slowed rate of conducting impulses along nerve fibers, and slower transmission of nerve impulses across synapses (Rockstein & Sussman, 1979; Spence, 1989). In old people, some reflexes—jerk reflexes in the knees, ankles, biceps, and triceps—are diminished, inconsistent, or absent altogether (Spence, 1989).

The cardiovascular system, respiratory system, and basal metabolism

Although the cardiac system functions well for most young adults, it does change during the twenties and thirties. Research on World War II draftees revealed that the time required to return to resting heart rate (approximately 72 beats per minute for healthy young adults) increased substantially between the twenties and forties (Goldstein, 1951). This trend, unfortunately, is even more striking for contemporary young adults—probably because of increasingly sedentary lifestyles (Buskirk, 1985). Another change is a gradual decline in the power of the left ventricle of the heart (Spence, 1989; Whitbourne, 1985). Like all body tissues, this muscle becomes less flexible with age, and therefore has less power to pump blood. As a result, **cardiac output**, the amount of blood pumped per minute, decreases throughout adulthood.

Changes in the cardiovascular system continue in middle and later adulthood. However, recent research in which individuals with known or suspected diseases affecting the system were excluded reveals that these changes occur to a lesser extent than previously suspected (Shock et al., 1984). The number and size of cardiac muscle cells decrease with age. In addition, fewer capillaries supply the walls of the heart with increasing age; the resulting decrease in

---

1. Dementia refers to severe cognitive impairment most often appearing in old age. We consider Alzheimer's Disease and other forms of dementia in greater depth in Chapter 9.

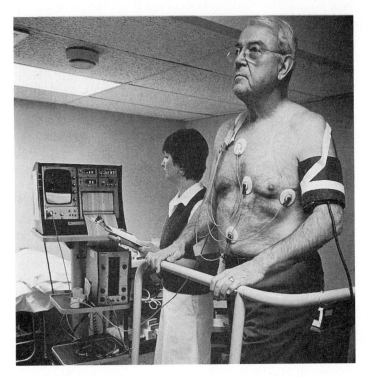

Changes in the cardiovascular system begin in youth and continue throughout adulthood.

oxygen reaching the cardiac muscle affects its ability to contract. There are increases in fat deposits on the heart surface, and accumulations of pigment in cardiac muscle cells. Finally, the lining of the heart thickens.

The blood vessels, particularly the larger arteries that carry oxygen-rich blood, become less elastic with age. As with other body tissues, the cells in the walls of these vessels contain more connective tissue and less elastin with increasing age. This condition is known as **arteriosclerosis**, or "hardening of the arteries" (Spence, 1989). Another common change is **atherosclerosis**, a gradual accumulation of lipids (fatty substances) in blood vessel walls; the result is a narrowed diameter of the blood vessels (Spence, 1989). This accumulation is more rapid for sedentary individuals and those who consume high levels of fat.

The functioning of the cardiovascular system changes with these anatomical changes. The pulse slows with advancing age. This change, together with the age-related reduction in cardiac output, means that less oxygen can be delivered to working muscles within a given period of time. Muscular activity, including cardiac activity, can be limited by this reduced **maximum oxygen consumption**. Some suggest that the increasing frequency of heart attacks in middle and later adulthood can be partially attributed to the decrease in the flow of blood and oxygen to the heart (Rockstein & Sussman, 1979). On a less extreme level, abnormalities in electrocardiograph patterns become more common in middle and later adulthood.

With age, there is also a decrease in **cardiac reserve**, the heart's ability to increase output under stress and exercise. This change, however, depends on overall health and history of physical activity (Rockstein & Sussman, 1979; Shock et al., 1984). Cardiac reserve is greater among elderly people who were athletes when they were younger, and among those who begin a program of regular aerobic exercise in later life, as compared to inactive older adults.

Although this list of anatomical and physiological changes in the cardiovascular system may sound frightening, these processes force few middle-aged adults to limit their activities. In later adulthood, however, these changes may reach a **clinical threshold** at which symptoms appear (Fries & Crapo, 1981). Chronic disease of the cardiovascular system, which can limit behavior and be life-threatening, becomes more frequent in old age.

Like the cardiac system, the respiratory system begins to change as early as the twenties. Normal age-related changes in the respiratory system, however, are particularly difficult to distinguish from changes due to continuous environmental insults such as air pollution and cigarette smoke—including "second-hand smoke" (Rockstein & Sussman, 1979). If Americans become more successful in implementing legislation that minimizes environmental pollution, then your children and grandchildren may experience far less change in the respiratory system than currently available data would suggest.

In middle and later adulthood, the overall picture in the respiratory system is of increased stiffening and rigidity (Rockstein & Sussman, 1979; Spence, 1989). Most older people show some forward curvature of the spine—sometimes because of poor posture throughout their lives and sometimes because of weakened neck and back muscles. At the same time, the rib cage becomes less expandable, both because cartilage is calcified and because there is a decrease in the number and size of muscle fibers. Cartilage in the airways of the respiratory system is progressively calcified, and thus these passages gradually become less flexible. Within the lungs, the alveoli ("air sacs") themselves become less flexible, and the walls separating adjacent alveoli gradually deteriorate. Thus, the amount of total functional respiratory surface in the lungs decreases throughout adulthood (Spence, 1989).

The difference between the amount inhaled during a normal breath and during a deep, maximum breath is the inspiratory reserve of the lungs. Conversely, the amount that can still be exhaled following a normal exhalation is the expiratory reserve. The sum of these two reserves is the **vital capacity**, a quantity which decreases throughout adulthood (Hershey, 1974). A related change in respiratory functioning is a gradual decrease in **compliance**, the maximum amount of air that can be moved in and out of the lungs during forced voluntary breathing within a fixed period of time (Rockstein & Sussman, 1979). A net impact of these changes is a decrease in the amount of oxygen delivered to the arteries, and thus to body cells.

Fortunately, these changes in the structure and functioning of the respiratory system do not trouble most adults. The system allows most young and middle-aged people to do most things; however, middle-aged adults might notice shortness of breath following less exertion than when they were younger. Even healthy older adults find that changes in the respiratory system have little effect on their everyday activities, although it is common for expirations to be noticeably more pronounced than inhalations among very elderly people. Of course, people who smoke or are exposed to high levels of pollution in their communities or workplaces may notice more substantial changes in their breathing in early or middle adulthood. One study found that there were greater age differences in respiratory functioning among a group of indigent individuals than among more affluent people (Shock et al., 1984).

Beginning in the twenties, there are also regular declines in other indicators of physiological functioning. These indicators include **basal metabolic rate**, the rate at which your body uses oxygen at rest (Shock et al., 1984). Processes of **homeostasis**, or self-regulation, also become less efficient with age (Spence, 1989). The ability to tolerate extreme temperatures, for example, begins to decrease in young adulthood (Bromley, 1974).

The skeletal and muscular systems

The skeletal system, which includes the bones and cartilage, is the locus of important physiological functions. The most obvious functions, of course, are to protect and support the soft tissues of the body and to provide points of attachment for muscles. In addition, the red bone marrow of certain bones produces blood cells.

The formation, destruction, and reformation of bones is a lifelong process. Before birth, a collagen fiber or cartilage framework for bones is formed. Next, the bone itself develops as some of the fibers or cartilage are replaced by calcium and phosphate salts. The fibers, which can undergo stretching and twisting, keep bones from being brittle. Conversely, the salts give strength to the bones. Throughout the lifespan, old bone is broken down and resorbed, and replaced by newly-formed bone.

Beginning in the thirties, bone destruction outpaces bone reformation. At that point, there is a gradual decrease in the calcium content of bones and a gradual loss of bone mass. These decreases are more extreme for women than for men, and more extreme for Caucasians than for African-Americans or Asians. As these processes continue during middle and later adulthood, **osteoporosis**, a condition in which the bones are brittle and vulnerable to fractures, may develop.

Osteoporosis is sometimes called the "silent disease," because it has no symptoms during its early stages. Most victims do not know that they have osteoporosis until it has reached an advanced stage, when bones fracture easily; fractures most often occur in the spine, wrists, and hips. In extreme cases of osteoporosis, these bones become so brittle that they fracture prior to a fall or other trauma—simply from the combined effects of weight and gravity.

Although the exact causes of osteoporosis are unknown, the rate and extent of lost bone mass is related not only to race and gender, but also to health habits throughout the lifespan. In particular, eating a diet rich in calcium and vitamin D, avoiding excessive sodium, caffeine, and alcohol, and engaging in regular weight-bearing exercise can minimize the loss of bone mass (National Institute on Aging, 1987; Spence, 1989). In addition, hormones influence bone development. Because osteoporosis appears most frequently among post-menopausal women, the hormonal changes associated with menopause (see pp. 65–66) are also believed to contribute to osteoporosis (e.g., Spence, 1989). Table 3.1 lists sources of additional information about osteoporosis.

The skeletal system changes in other ways, too. Some bone growth continues through middle adulthood as limb bones become wider (Rockstein & Sussman, 1979). By middle age, most people experience some degeneration of the intervertebral discs, which separate adjacent vertebrae (Spence, 1989); this degeneration may lead to back pain. Some estimate that nearly everyone over the age of 40 suffers from some degree of **osteoarthritis**, a chronic inflammation that eventually causes joints to degenerate (Spence, 1989). In most cases, however, the extent of joint degeneration is not great enough to cause symptoms until much later in adulthood.

Young adulthood is a period of peak muscular strength, although there are gradual declines throughout adulthood in the power of selected muscles. As with skeletal tissue, a gradual decrease in muscle mass begins in the thirties and continues throughout adulthood. This process apparently results from atrophy of muscle fibers. Because muscle fibers, like neurons, are postmitotic, they cannot be replaced when they have atrophied; lost muscle fibers are replaced by fat tissue (Spence, 1989). This process is a normal part of adult development, although it occurs more rapidly and to a greater extent for inactive individuals and those who eat a high-fat diet.

The digestive and urinary systems

If the mass media are to be believed, most people suffer from chronic digestive complaints—especially as they get older. Happily, this is not the case. The digestive system includes a long, convoluted, and differentiated tube, the gastrointestinal (GI) tract. The tract extends from the mouth to the anus, and includes the pharynx, esophagus, stomach, liver, pancreas, and the small and large intestines. As food passes through these structures, it is broken down by secretions from glands along the way (e.g., Spence, 1989).

The digestive system changes little during adulthood (e.g., Bhanthumnavin & Schuster, 1977; Spence, 1989). Muscles in various walls of the tract, particularly the esophagus, weaken with advancing age. Even the less intense muscular contractions of the esophagus, though, are strong enough to move food into the stomach. However, some older people experience swallowing prob-

Table 3.1
Sources of information about osteoporosis

American Academy of Orthopaedic Surgeons, 222 South Prospect Ave., Park Ridge,
IL 60068   (312) 823-7186
This professional organization of orthopaedic surgeons offers an educational
brochure, *Osteoporosis,* to the public.

National Osteoporosis Foundation, 1625 Eye St., N.W., Suite 1011, Washington,
DC 20006   (202) 223-2226
This voluntary organization offers programs nationwide to educate the public and
professionals about osteoporosis and related research.

---

lems and esophageal pain because the sphincter between esophagus and
the stomach does not relax as reliably in old age as in young adulthood (Spence,
1989).

The linings of the stomach and intestines thin with age and, consequently, secretions produced in these regions of the tract are reduced. Diges-
tion and the absorption of some nutrients (proteins, calcium, B vitamins) may
be impaired by these changes. Because reduced ability to absorb vitamin B-12
can lead to symptoms of dementia (see Chapter Nine, pp. 233–243), some older
people require vitamin B-12 injections even though their diet is healthy. In the
large intestine, the thinned lining makes older people susceptible to **diverticulosis**, a condition in which small pockets develop in the intestinal wall. Although diverticulosis often produces no symptoms, it sometimes causes ab-
dominal pain. Physicians recommend a diet high in fiber and liquids to prevent
diverticulosis (Heckheimer, 1989).

Finally, the liver, an important source of digestive enzymes and one of the
sites at which medications are metabolized, decreases in weight during adulthood. The liver continues to function as effectively in old age as in youth for the
most part. However, the liver's ability to process certain drugs does decline
with age, and older people may therefore react to some medications differently
than young adults do. Older people must be treated with lower levels of medications than is the case for younger adults, and there is greater danger of
medications building up to toxic levels in older adults. Often, physicians must
treat elderly patients by beginning with very low dosages, monitoring the effects
of these dosages carefully, and gradually increasing dosage until a therapeutic
level is achieved.

The most noticeable age-related changes in the urinary system are in the
bladder (Rockstein & Sussman, 1979; Spence, 1989). Bladder capacity decreases,
due to weakened muscles and increased connective tissue in the bladder wall.
Older people need to urinate more frequently than younger adults as a result.
Another change is in the awareness of the need to urinate. Young people
usually notice this sensation when the bladder is about half full, while an older
adult may not notice it until the bladder is completely full. The resulting
urgency of the need to urinate (together with a weakened urinary sphincter)

are sources of urinary incontinence, which occasionally plagues some older people.

Throughout adulthood, less noticeable changes occur in the kidneys. These organs filter waste products from the bloodstream, regulate the chemical balance of the blood, and maintain the fluid balance of the body. Beginning in early adulthood, the kidneys gradually grow smaller and there are fewer vessels supplying them with blood (Goldman, 1977). The rate at which the kidneys filter the blood also begins to decline in early adulthood (Rockstein & Sussman, 1979; Spence, 1989). Despite these changes, the kidneys continue to function effectively in healthy older people (Spence, 1989).

The immune system

Unlike the other systems that we have discussed, the immune system is not a distinct collection of organs. Rather, this system comprises cells in various tissues throughout the body and cells that travel through the bloodstream and affect other tissues (e.g., Spence, 1989). Immune responses generally become less efficient with age: susceptibility to disease increases as one grows older (Rockstein & Sussman, 1979; Spence, 1989).

Paradoxically, **autoimmune responses**, in which immune responses are directed against one's own body tissue, also become more frequent in old age. Such responses, in fact, have been offered as an explanation for rheumatoid arthritis, a chronic inflammation of the joints. Some scientists accord autoimmune responses a central role in biological theories of aging (see page 76).

The reproductive system

The reproductive system is critically important throughout the life span. In early adulthood, important issues include sexual functioning, sexual dysfunction, and infertility. In middle age, the climacteric (when functioning of the reproductive organs gradually declines) affects sexuality for many men and women. There are sexual issues of unique importance for elderly adults, such as social constraints on sexual expression and the effects of age-related health changes on sexual pleasure.

Sexual physiology and functioning   The female reproductive system includes the ovaries, where eggs (ova) are produced; the two fallopian tubes, through which ova are transported to the uterus; the uterus, which provides an optimal environment for growth of an embryo; and the vagina, which both receives sperm from the penis and serves as the birth canal. The male reproductive system includes the two testes, where sperm are produced; a system of ducts, which store and transport sperm during intercourse; glands, which produce fluids involved in the development of semen; and the penis, which transports semen to the woman's vagina.

William Masters' and Virginia Johnson's (1966; 1970) research has provided tremendous insight into human sexual functioning. Among their most important—and, at the time, surprising—findings are the similarities between the process of sexual arousal for men and women. For both, this process includes the stages of **excitation, plateau, orgasm,** and **resolution**.

The stage of excitation is triggered by a wide variety of sexual stimuli. Depending on the person and the situation, these stimuli may include sights, sounds, smells, touch, thoughts, and even dreams. Excitation is characterized by two processes: **vasocongestion** and **myotonia**. In vasocongestion, blood vessels near the surface of the body are engorged. This process results in a man's erection; for women, vasocongestion is most prominent in the genitals and the breasts. Myotonia, the second process marking the excitation stage, is a series of involuntary muscular contractions. In addition to these two processes, the stage of excitation includes lubrication of the genitals.

Vasocongestion, myotonia, and lubrication continue in the plateau stage. For both sexes, this is a stage of high arousal. Due to vasocongestion, the outer portion of the woman's vagina is engorged, resulting in an orgasmic platform that tightly grasps the penis during intercourse. At the same time, the man's testes are elevated. The result is that intercourse becomes more rewarding. Immediately before the next stage, orgasm, genital lubrication and vasocongestion reach their peak.

For both men and women, orgasm is a series of three to five rhythmic contractions of the pelvic muscles which result in intensely pleasurable physical sensations. Most men perceive orgasm in terms of ejaculation, when semen is released. However, orgasm can occur without ejaculation and ejaculation can occur without orgasm (Masters, Johnson, & Kolodny, 1985).

In the resolution stage, the body returns to its prearoused state. Men (but not women) experience a **refractory period** during resolution, when they cannot have another orgasm. For a young man, the refractory period may be only a few minutes long. The refractory period grows longer during middle and later adulthood, however (Spence, 1989).

The climacteric: A universal human experience unfolding in diverse ways   For women, changes in reproductive physiology are among the most obvious and psychologically important transformations of age. Parallel changes are less obvious for men, but are equally important. In middle adulthood men and women experience the climacteric, a period of several years during which the functioning of the reproductive organs gradually changes.

Changes in a woman's reproductive system begin in the ovaries and normally take place during the forties and fifties. At that time, the levels of estrogens and progesterone that the ovaries produce decrease. The most obvious effect of reduced hormone levels is **menopause**, the cessation of the menstrual cycle. When hormone secretion begins to drop, menstrual flow declines and intervals between menstrual periods increase for most women. A woman has experienced menopause when a full year has elapsed since her last menstrual period. After menopause, some estrogens are still produced, but now these hormones are produced primarily in the adrenal glands rather than in the ovaries. The concentration of estrogens in the blood is then lower than before menopause.

Several physical symptoms are associated with the onset of menopause, although many women experience no symptoms at all. Some data suggest that women who are troubled by these symptoms are more anxious, and more prone to express problems somatically, than other women (Strickland, 1988). Common symptoms include **hot flashes**, during which a woman experiences a brief feeling of intense heat and sweating, and red patches may appear on the chest, neck, and face; insomnia; depression or irritability; and headaches. In addition, declining hormone levels lead to changes in the ovaries, uterus, and vagina (e.g., Buchsbaum, 1983; Spence, 1989). Both the ovaries and uterus decrease in weight, and in both organs there is increased fibrous tissue. The cervical canal becomes narrower, and the vagina becomes narrower and shorter.

In addition, the walls of the vagina become thinner and less elastic, and glands which had secreted fluids lubricating the vagina atrophy. The vagina is generally drier in postmenopausal women as a result, and remaining vaginal secretions are less acidic than those of premenopausal women. Because of these changes, some postmenopausal women experience pain during intercourse (see p. 62) and vaginal infections are more common after menopause than before.

The climacteric is less obvious for men than for women, since there is no clear counterpart to menopause. The testes become smaller and less firm, and they secrete less testosterone as a man grows older. The number and motility of sperm decrease with age, although men can father children until quite late in life. The penis becomes smaller, and the blood vessels and erectile tissue of the penis become less flexible. These changes may make it more difficult to attain an erection.

The **prostate gland**, which produces secretions contributing to semen formation, also begins to atrophy in middle adulthood. Some men develop hard masses in the prostate gland, and fibrous tissue gradually replaces muscle tissue in the wall of the gland. Because of these changes, less fluid is produced by the prostate gland, and the fluid which is produced is emitted less forcefully during orgasm. In addition, portions of the prostate gland which surround the urethra may become enlarged, a condition which makes urination painful or difficult.

Sexual impacts of the climacteric.   The climacteric almost inevitably affects sexual functioning, although sexual expression often is an important part of life well into old age. Frequency of intercourse does decrease throughout adulthood for married couples, but most of this decrease (from about 13 to about 7 monthly occasions of intercourse) occurs in the first three years of marriage (Broderick, 1982). After that point, there is little change in frequency of intercourse through 30 years of marriage; the climacteric may, then, have a relatively minor impact on sexuality. In fact, sexual pleasure may increase in midlife, since there is no longer any need to be concerned about pregnancy. Because of the physiological changes of the climacteric, though, men and women may need to adapt their approach to sexual activity.

For women, the hormonal changes associated with the climacteric often mean that lubrication of the vagina during sexual arousal occurs more slowly (e.g., Buchsbaum, 1983; Spence, 1989). Women who have experienced extreme thinning of the vaginal walls may need to use water-soluble gels (not petroleum jelly) to prevent pain during intercourse. In addition, vasocongestion and myotonia unfold differently for postmenopausal women than for younger women (e.g., Spence, 1989). The outer folds of the vagina do not become as fully engorged during arousal as they do in younger women, so that the vagina does not grip the penis as tightly during intercourse.

During orgasm, middle-aged women generally experience fewer contractions of the uterus and vagina; orgasms therefore are less intense than in early adulthood. Some women find that Kegel exercises, which strengthen the pelvic muscles, help to maintain the intensity of orgasm after the climacteric[2] (Lauersen & Whitney, 1977). Occasionally, middle-aged women experience painful muscle spasms in addition to uterine contractions during orgasm. Also, middle-aged and older women return to an unaroused state after orgasm sooner than do younger women.

As men reach middle adulthood, they often find that it takes longer to attain an erection, and that their erection is not as firm as when they were younger. A change that may be more welcome for middle-aged men and their partners is that a prolonged period of sexual stimulation is needed before ejaculation. Ejaculations are generally less forceful, and—like middle-aged women—middle-aged and older men return to an unaroused state more rapidly than do younger men.

Psychological impacts of the climacteric: Reflections of culture   More information is available concerning women's reactions to the climacteric than men's reactions. For women, the psychological consequences of menopause are partly dependent on culture. Whereas women in some cultures greet menopause with dismay, women in other settings experience the change of life with relief. We examine the relationship between culture and women's experience of the climacteric in the *Diversity in Adulthood* box.

Traditionally, both physicians and the lay public have assumed that menopause is associated with suffering. Even today, advertising in clinical journals portrays menopausal women as depressed, irritable, worried, forgetful, confused, and frustrated (Voda & Eliasson, 1983). It is true that some women—as well as some men—become depressed or anxious at this point in life.

---

2. These exercises can also minimize urinary incontinence (Heckheimer, 1989).

BOX 3.2   *DIVERSITY IN ADULTHOOD*

Cultural differences in Israeli women's reactions to menopause

Among the events comprising the climacteric for women, menopause is undoubtedly one of the most salient. Both physicians and women themselves have traditionally assumed that menopause is the source of a wide variety of afflictions—everything from depression to insomnia to psychosis. We have also seen, though, that these traditional assumptions are unwarranted for many contemporary American women.

What about women representing other cultural backgrounds? Do societies fostering different traditions concerning women's roles and aspirations produce different reactions to the close of reproductive life? Cross-cultural research conducted in Israel in the late 1960s gives us some tentative answers.

This research examined ethnic group differences in Israeli women's rates of **involutional psychosis** (e.g., Datan, Antonovsky, & Maoz, 1984). The directors of this research, Aaron Antonovsky and Benjamin Maoz, noted that involutional psychosis, a unipolar depression appearing for the first time in middle age, was almost never seen among women who had grown up in traditional Near Eastern cultures. These researchers suggested that women from more youth-centered modern cultures felt that aging brought declining social status. However, women from the more traditional cultures could look forward to achieving a matriarchal status in middle and old age.

A third researcher, Nancy Datan, advanced an alternative hypothesis. She argued that women in traditional cultures gained status by bearing sons, and that menopause was threatening because of the loss of this potential. Modern women, in contrast, could aspire to nonprocreative roles after menopause; they should therefore experience the least distress related to menopause.

Middle-aged Israeli women reared in five cultures were interviewed. At the most modern end of the spectrum were Central European women who had come to Israel as young adults near the time of World War II. These women had borne relatively

---

However, the climacteric is not the only change that one experiences in middle adulthood. In addition to these physiological changes, a middle-aged woman may be struggling with her adaptation to the "empty nest," her need to support her husband as he confronts work-related stress, and her own career-related pressures. Also, because middle-aged women are traditionally the primary caregivers for frail elderly people (see Chapter Twelve, pages 308–309), aging parents' increasing needs for care may prompt distress. Any or all of these circumstances could give a middle-aged woman sound cause for anxiety or depression.

Women often experience little or no psychological distress related specifically to menopause. Strickland (1988) notes that a woman's expectations of menopause affect her likelihood of experiencing psychological symptoms of menopause; those most likely to be distressed are women with a history of depression or excessive dependency and those who stress traditional standards of femininity. In her classic study of women's attitudes toward menopause, Bernice Neugarten and her colleagues (Neugarten, Wood, Kraines, & Loomis, 1968) found that postmenopausal women expressed more positive attitudes toward the change of life than did younger women. Post-

few children, and had been relatively well-educated in their native countries. Turkish women represented an intermediate level of modernity. Born into a society in which women were veiled and polygyny was accepted, these women witnessed a tremendous expansion of women's roles during their lifetimes. However, these women had borne more children, and were generally less educated, than the Central European women.

The Persian women had been reared in a still more traditional culture: most were illiterate, many married a man chosen by their families, and most spent much of their adult life bearing and rearing children. Among the North African women, family roles were similar to those of the Persian women. Again, many had married in early adolescence, often to a man that they had not chosen, and had borne children almost continually ever since. Finally, the Moslem Arabs represented the most traditional culture. Nearly all of these women were illiterate, almost all married men chosen by their families, and childbearing spanned most of their lives.

How did these women fare in their adaptation to middle age? The women from the cultures at the intermediate points in the continuum—the Turks, Persians, and North Africans—expressed the greatest difficulty in adjusting to the climacteric. Perhaps these women had moved away from traditional assumptions about the rhythms of women's lives, but had not yet encountered the expanded set of options that women in some modern societies enjoy. In contrast, women from the most modern and the most traditional cultures apparently experienced the climacteric more smoothly.

For these women, the character of middle adulthood stemmed in part from the cultures into which they had been born. The culture's assumptions about women, in particular, had tremendous influence. More broadly, this research reminds us of the themes of the universal and the distinct in human development. All of these women reacted to a universal experience; however, the nature of their reaction was distinct, in part because of cultural differences.

menopausal women recognized benefits of menopause, such as increased feelings of tranquility and freedom; young women rarely cited such impacts. In addition, postmenopausal women asserted that menopause need not create essential discontinuity in a woman's life, and that most women can manage menopausal symptoms without difficulty. As Neugarten et al. (1968) suggested, these views imply that many middle-aged women welcome menopause and the loss of childbearing capacity, whereas younger women may regard menopause as a distant, vague, and frightening part of aging.

Sexual dysfunction   Some men and women of all ages experience sporadic problems with the sexual response cycle. Occasional lack of inclination for sexual activity, inability to become sexually aroused, or inability to attain orgasm is generally not considered problematic. However, if these episodes recur, and do not have a solely physiological basis, the individual may suffer from **psychosexual dysfunction** (DSM-III-R, 1987).

Among the more common types of psychosexual dysfunction are **inhibited sexual desire** and **inhibited sexual excitement**. Inhibited sexual desire is a problem only if the individual is concerned about his or her lack

For many women, menopause has more positive than negative psychological consequences.

of interest in sex, or if this disinterest causes problems in the relationship with the sexual partner.

The processes of vasocongestion, myotonia, and lubrication—all beginning in the excitement stage of sexual response—are under little, if any, conscious control. If these processes do not occur when one wants to have sex, the problem may be inhibited sexual excitement. For a woman, inhibited sexual excitement consists of failure to attain sufficient vaginal lubrication; there is also diminished vasocongestion, resulting in little vaginal swelling.[3] For a man, inhibited sexual excitement is a partial or total failure to attain an erection.[4]

---

3. Frigidity, an earlier term for this condition, is rarely used by contemporary physicians and sex therapists; the term is more often used—and misused—by the layperson.

4. This condition is sometimes also labeled impotence or erectile dysfunction.

For both women and men, inhibited sexual excitement may stem from either physiological problems, emotional difficulties, or both. Erectile dysfunction, for example, may result from impaired blood supply to the penis (as in the case of diseased arteries), a hormonal imbalance, neurological malfunctioning, overuse of alcohol or other drugs, side effects of some medications, fatigue, or anxiety (Bennett, Goldfinger, & Johnson, 1987; Lauerson & Whitney, 1977).

In old age, most complaints involve diminished ability to perform sexually; such complaints are more common among older men than older women (e.g., Spence, 1989). As in early adulthood, diminished sexual performance can stem from a wide variety of factors. Recall that the climacteric changes the structure and functioning of the male and female reproductive systems; some may find the necessary adaptation to these changes difficult, and may experience less sexual pleasure for that reason. Throughout the life span, good health is fundamental to sexual interest and satisfying sexual activity (Turner & Adams, 1983). If an older person or her partner are in poor health, sexual activity may be curtailed.

Older people who associate sex with procreation and youth may feel that their sexual desires are unnatural or inappropriate. Some older adults, too, fail to recognize sexual activity that does not include intercourse or orgasm as potentially satisfying, a tendency that can block sexual pleasure in old age (Turner & Adams, 1983). Particularly for older women, lack of a sexual partner[5] and prohibitions against masturbation that were instilled during childhood can also inhibit sexual expression. Older people who live in nursing homes (even married people) may have little privacy for sexual demonstrations of any kind, and may even be punished for expressing their sexuality.

Infertility Normally, young adulthood is the time of peak fertility. Just as problems may arise with sexual functioning, however, some young adults face disappointment in their efforts to conceive. **Infertility** is an inability to conceive after 12 to 18 months of unprotected sexual activity, or an inability to carry a pregnancy to term (National Center for Health Statistics, 1984). Researchers report that approximately 15 percent of American married couples are infertile (Andrews, 1984). However, most scientists believe that the actual incidence of infertility is higher. Survey figures identify only married couples who have attempted to conceive over the past year and been unsuccessful. Thus, these figures do not include married couples who have not yet tried to conceive, or unmarried people who have tried unsuccessfully to have children.

For conception to occur, both the man's and the woman's reproductive structures must be normal in structure and function, and an elaborate system of hormonal signals must be properly synchronized. Infertility is traced to a problem with the man's and with the woman's reproductive physiology about

---

5. As older and older cohorts include proportionately more women, lack of a sexual partner potentially inhibits older women's sexual activity to an increasing extent with increasing age.

equally often (approximately 40 percent of identified cases for each gender). For about 20 percent of identified cases of infertility, there are problems with both partners' reproductive physiology, or no cause is ever determined.

For a man, infertility most often stems from problems with sperm production and delivery (Andrews, 1984; Bennett et al., 1987). Microscopic examination of semen may reveal that there are too few sperm, that the sperm are atypical in shape, or that they do not swim normally. These conditions may themselves be consequences of abnormal hormone levels, injuries or infections affecting the testes, the temperature of the testes,[6] or side effects of medication.

Compared to men, women's problems with fertility stem from a more varied set of circumstances. Hormonal imbalances may disrupt the development of the ovum, the uterine lining, or the mucus covering the cervix. A woman's ovaries, fallopian tubes, or uterus may have an abnormal structure, or have been damaged by scar tissue (usually from earlier pelvic infections, sexually transmitted diseases [see Chapter Four, pp. 89–91] or surgery) or by fibroid tumors or polyps.

For both men and women, infertility may also result from exposure to certain pollutants or environmental hazards (e.g., herbicides, fertilizers), or to hazards in the workplace (Andrews, 1984; Herpel & Straube, 1988). Workers who handle substances such as lead, pesticides, polystyrene, xylene, benzene, mercury, radioactive materials, or anesthetic gases, for example, may suffer from low sperm counts, irregular ovulation, or chromosomal abnormalities. Recent evidence also suggests that both men's and women's fertility may be impaired by abuse of alcohol or marijuana (Powell & Fuller, 1983; Valimaki & Ylikahri, 1983).

Whatever the cause, a diagnosis of infertility can be emotionally devastating. Some clinicians who counsel infertile couples believe that the reaction is similar to the emotional processes leading to acceptance of death (Andrews, 1984). At one time, infertile couples who desperately wanted to have children had few options other than adoption. Today, however, many more alternatives exist, and new possibilities are explored continually.

Figure 3.2 illustrates some of the new technology available to infertile couples. Among the best known are ***in-vitro* fertilization** (IVF) and **artificial insemination by donor** (AID). In IVF, a physician removes an ovum from the woman's ovary; the ovum is placed in a shallow dish with her partner's sperm and a nourishing medium. If the ovum is fertilized, the physician implants the embryo in the woman's uterus after several days of cell division. This approach might be used if the woman ovulates regularly and has a normal uterus, but has blocked fallopian tubes (or has been surgically sterilized). The social parents are also the genetic parents of the child; however, this is not the case for most of the new "high tech" means of conception.

---

6. For example, the testes may be "overheated" if a man wears tight-fitting underwear or trousers that keep the testes too close to the body. Sperm production can be adversely affected as a result.

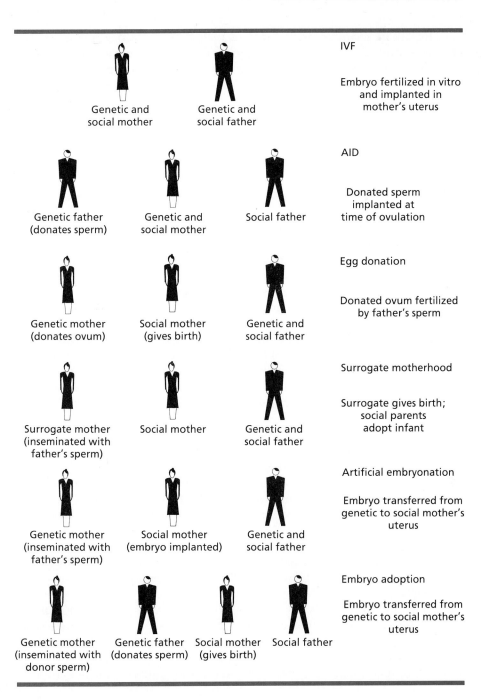

Figure 3.2
"High technology" means of conception.

In AID, for example, an anonymous male donor provides sperm which a physician implants in the woman's vagina at the time of ovulation. This alternative is most often used when the woman's reproductive system functions normally but her partner has a low sperm count, abnormal sperm, or has had a vasectomy. **Egg donation** is a similar approach. In this case, an anonymous female donor provides an ovum to be implanted for a woman who does not ovulate or whose fallopian tubes are blocked. Hopefully, the donated egg will be fertilized by the partner's sperm. **Surrogate motherhood** takes this process still further. In this case, a woman (the "surrogate") agrees to be inseminated with sperm from a man whose own partner cannot conceive or carry a pregnancy to term. The surrogate bears the child, which the couple adopts after birth.

Surrogate motherhood can be emotionally demanding for both the "adoptive" parents and the surrogate. In the "Baby M" case, for example, a surrogate wanted to keep the infant after giving birth.[7] **Artificial embryonation** is an approach avoiding some of this trauma. As with surrogate motherhood, a female donor is inseminated with sperm from the partner of a woman with ovulation or tubal problems. A few days after fertilization, a physician flushes the embryo from the donor's uterus and implants it in the social mother's uterus. In a variation of this procedure, **embryo adoption**, a female donor is inseminated with sperm from a male donor. The fertilized embryo in this case is flushed from the donor's uterus several days after fertilization and implanted in the uterus of the woman who will bear the embryo. With embryo adoption, neither of the parents who give birth and raise the child are its genetic parents (see Figure 3.2).

Many of these emerging alternatives force reconsideration of what it means to be a parent. With the possibility of donating, implanting, and adopting ova, sperm, and even embryos, one can no longer assume that the parents who raise an infant to maturity are the same individuals who provide the embryo's genetic inheritance or who give birth to the child. Some contend that these new options offer more ill than good (Andrews, 1984). These individuals argue that overpopulation and scarce funding for medical research compel a more cautious approach to designing new means of conception. Furthermore, these new alternatives could usher in undesirable social changes, including increased discrimination against the handicapped, and efforts to create "superkids" (Andrews, 1984).

Nonetheless, infertility is a much more hopeful diagnosis for would-be parents today than was the case just a generation ago. Perhaps even more important than the rapidly expanding options is the increased insight and support available for those confronting infertility. Now, most large cities offer physicians specializing in fertility treatments and counselors experienced in

---

7. Eventually, the court awarded custody of the child to the "adoptive" parents, but also awarded the surrogate liberal visitation arrangements.

work with infertile couples. In addition, there is at least one nationwide self-help group for infertile couples (Resolve, Inc., P. O. Box 474, Belmont, MA 02178-0474) which provides information and education, medical referrals, and counseling.

Aging: a gradual and individual process

Two characteristics of physical aging should be apparent. First, aging is not something that begins in middle or late adulthood. Most of the changes reviewed above begin in early adulthood—if not even earlier in the life span. Second, aging does not occur uniformly for all people. Ways in which diet, exercise, and lifestyle can promote or retard age-related physical changes have been identified repeatedly. The cultural setting in which one ages can also affect one's reaction to these changes.

BIOLOGICAL THEORIES OF AGING

Although this chapter has described physical aging in humans, aging occurs in all species. Indeed, much of the research attempting to explain why aging occurs is carried out using nonhuman species. This research—and observations about humans—forms the basis for theories of aging. Some theorists propose that the physical changes of age have a genetic basis. Others explain these changes as the long-term result of continued damage to the system throughout the lifespan.

Genetic theories

Several theories begin with the notion that aging is genetically programmed, each theory proposing a different set of mechanisms by which this programming is accomplished. In **neuroendocrine theory** (e.g., Cristofalo, 1988; Spence, 1989), the **hypothalamus** is posited as a master timekeeper that directs the production of hormones regulating growth and development. Aging is the result of the hypothalamus' diminished ability to effectively direct the production and transmission of critical hormones. Although this theory might explain aging in species that have complex nervous systems, it cannot explain aging in simpler organisms whose nervous system lacks a hypothalamus (Cristofalo, 1988).

Other programmed theories locate the source of aging within individual cells rather than in the nervous system. **Gene theory** proposes that the organism carries genes that are activated near the end of the life span; their action causes the physical changes of age (Spence, 1989). Identical twins (who are genetically identical) often die at more similar ages than fraternal twins (who are no more similar genetically than ordinary siblings), and thus this genetic theory has some support (Spence, 1989). **Gene mutation theory** points to the fact that genetic mutations occur throughout the lifespan in cells composing body tissues, and that most mutations alter cell functioning negatively. According to this theory, the long-term impact of continual mutations is physical breakdown and eventually death (Cristofalo, 1988; Danner & Holbrook, 1990; Rockstein & Sussman, 1979; Spence, 1989).

Finally, we know that normal cells cultured in the laboratory divide a species-specific number of times, called the **Hayflick limit** after the scientist who identified this cellular property (Cristofalo, 1988; Rockstein & Sussman, 1979; Spence, 1989). The Hayflick limit is the basis of the notion that death is an inherited property of individual body cells. However, scientists question the extent to which this limit can explain aging in the living body, as opposed to tissue cultures in the laboratory (Spence, 1989).

Wear and tear theories

Other scientists claim that the process of living is physically destructive; these theories differ in the type of damage specified as the cause of aging. As with the programmed theories, some wear-and-tear theories locate the critical destruction in individual cells. According to **cross-linkage theory**, stable bonds (cross-links) between molecules in body cells form continually. These bonds cannot be repaired, and they alter cell functioning. Eventually, this process impairs the way in which tissues and organs comprised of the cross-linked cells operate (Lee & Cerami, 1990; Rockstein & Sussman, 1979; Spence, 1989).

Free radical theory proposes that unstable chemical compounds, called free radicals, are continually produced by body metabolism. These free radicals readily bond with other molecules, including membranes of body cells, and aid the cross-linkage process (Cristofalo, 1988; Rockstein & Sussman, 1979; Spence, 1989). Again, cell operation is impaired by this process, and the eventual result is handicapped organ functioning. In still another cellular wear-and-tear theory, scientists point out that nonfunctional substances constantly accumulate within cells as a result of their normal metabolism. These substances have been called "cellular garbage" (Spence, 1989); they are believed to hamper cell functioning, and eventually to impair tissue and organ operation.

Autoimmune theories are a different approach to the wear and tear concept. These theories propose that the immune system loses the ability to distinguish the body's own proteins from "invaders." Therefore the system begins to attack its own tissues (Rockstein & Sussman, 1979; Spence, 1989).

At this point, it may seem as though there are more than enough answers to our question of why the body ages—and we have by no means examined all existing theories of aging! Clearly, scientists do not agree about why aging occurs. Scientists do agree on one related point, however, and that is that no *single* theory of aging is likely to prove sufficient to explain all known age-related changes in all species.

LONGEVITY: REFLECTIONS OF HEREDITY AND LIFESTYLE

How does length of life differ from one person to the next? What factors are associated with these individual differences? Two terms are commonly used in discussions of longevity. **Mean longevity** is the average life expectancy of a population. Mean longevity in humans has increased dramatically during the twentieth century. An infant born at the turn of the century could expect to live only about forty-seven years, whereas newborns today have a life expectancy of more than seventy. In other words, more people today survive to old age, thanks primarily to improved nutrition, health care, and sanitation. **Maximum longevity** is the longest recorded life span for a species; for humans, it is 114 years (Fries & Crapo, 1981). Unlike mean longevity, there is little evidence that maximum longevity has or is likely to increase.

Gender and racial differences in longevity

Mean longevity is not the same for all people. Women live longer on the average than men do, generally by about seven years. Although some readily attribute this sex difference to the greater hazards that men may encounter throughout the life cycle, this explanation is almost certainly incorrect. Women live longer than men in most cultures, despite the striking differences in men's and women's lifestyles throughout the world. More important, females outlive males in virtually all species (from fruit flies and grasshoppers up the evolutionary scale) (e.g., Rockstein & Sussman, 1979). It is unlikely that male insects live more stressful lives than their female counterparts. Most scientists believe, instead, that there is some as yet unspecified genetic basis for this sex difference in mean longevity.

There are also other dimensions of individual differences in mean longevity. Race is important, with Caucasians living longer on the average than African-Americans, Hispanic Americans, or Native Americans. And, the socio-economic development of a nation also plays a part. As Figure 3.3 illustrates, greater numbers of Scandinavians survive to old age than citizens of developing nations (Fries & Crapo, 1981). Taken together, these data point to both genetic and environmental influences of longevity.

Influences of longevity

Rockstein and Sussman (1979) believe that longevity is affected by *intrinsic factors*, the individual's genetic inheritance, and *extrinsic factors* arising in the environment. Evidence from genealogical studies (in which the life spans of all known members of a family are examined), from research conducted by life insurance companies, and from studies of identical and fraternal twins all point to a genetic basis of longevity (Rockstein & Sussman, 1979). In addition, species

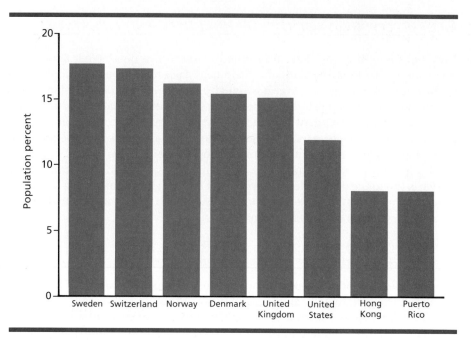

Figure 3.3
Percent of population aged 65 and over: selected countries. (Source: USDHHS, 1987.)

differences in life expectancy—as well as the sex and race differences described above—indicate that longevity has, in part, a hereditary basis.

However, environmental factors are also important—and these factors, in contrast to heredity, are ones that we can do something about. We have noted throughout the chapter that such things as diet and exercise habits, and the types of environmental influences to which one is exposed, are associated with the magnitude of age-related changes in appearance and physiological functioning. Similarly, choices concerning lifestyle may affect longevity, above and beyond one's genetic endowment.

For decades, physicians have warned that cigarette smoking and obesity shorten the life span. Marital status is also associated with longevity, although we cannot be sure why this is so. Married people typically live longer than those who remain single, who in turn outlive those who are divorced or widowed (e.g., Rockstein & Sussman, 1979). But we do not know whether getting married improves health and thereby increases life expectancy, or whether unhealthy people are unable or unwilling to get married or stay married. The association between marital status and longevity may not reflect a cause-effect relationship at all.

Experimental research conducted with animals identifies still other environmental influences. In studies with rats, eating a nutritious but very low-calorie diet almost doubles the life span; however, this diet also increases infant mortality and curtails physical and behavioral development (e.g., Cutler, 1981; Sacher, 1977). Research with fruit flies and fish demonstrates that lowering body temperature can extend the life span (e.g., Walford, 1983). Just why these manipulations of diet and body temperature increase longevity has not yet been firmly established, though. Body metabolism may be reduced, or the formation of cross-linkages or free radical bonds (see page 76) may be curtailed (e.g., Walford, 1983). Furthermore, the extent to which we can generalize these phenomena to the extension of the human life span remains to be demonstrated.

Claims of exceptional human life spans

Claims are sometimes made that extraordinary life spans are typical of geographically isolated groups. People living in Vilcabamba in Ecuador, the Abkhasian region of Soviet Georgia, and the Hunza region of Pakistan have all claimed that members of their communities often live to be well over 100. Usually, these groups attribute their longevity to hard work, a healthful environment, and dietary practices. Intriguing though these claims may be, none has stood up to rigorous scrutiny (Benet, 1976; Bennett & Garson, 1986; Mazess & Forman, 1979; Medvedev, 1974; Palmore, 1984).

In the Pakistani group, investigators concluded that these erroneous claims reflect the absence of a written language, which obviously precludes birth records (Hayflick, 1975). Lack of written records is implicated in the other instances as well. In Ecuador, many of the relevant birth records were destroyed by fire; when other documents (e.g., marriage records, census data) were examined, claims of living past the 100-mark were discredited (Mazess & Forman, 1979). In Soviet Georgia, absence of records and practical incentives to exaggerate one's age explain most of the reports. In the Soviet Union, many men at the time of World War I and the Russian Revolution apparently used their fathers' birth records to support their claims that they were too old for military service (Medvedev, 1974).

SUMMARY

Physical appearance changes throughout adulthood. Particularly for those who take great pride in their physical appearance, these changes can affect self-esteem. Some claim that changes in appearance with age have more detrimental impacts for women than for men, although we might question the extent to which this remains true in the 1990s.

The nervous system, cardiovascular system, respiratory system, skeletal system, muscular system, digestive system, urinary system, and immune system all function optimally in early adulthood. All of these systems undergo gradual, continuing changes throughout adulthood. The rate and extent of these changes vary from one person to another, sometimes on the basis of race or gender and often on the basis of health and lifestyle.

The reproductive system, too, changes in structure and function during adulthood. In middle age, the climacteric changes sexual functioning as reproductive organs decrease in size and weight. Contrary to popular stereotype, women's reaction to the climacteric seems to be positive more often than negative. Reaction to menopause, though, depends on culture.

Inability to conceive or to carry a pregnancy to term can stem from abnormalities in the structure or function of a man's or a woman's reproductive organs, although a cause cannot always be identified. Although infertility can be psychologically devastating, the ongoing development of new methods of conception provides hope for infertile individuals.

Some scientists propose that the process of aging is programmed into the individual at birth, whereas others assert that aging is a gradual long-term process of destruction inherent in life itself. Longevity, or length of the life span, is influenced by both intrinsic and extrinsic factors. It is unlikely that maximum human longevity will ever be extended much past 114 years.

KEY TERMS

Aging spots	Hypothalamus
Arteriosclerosis	Infertility
Artificial embryonation	Inhibited sexual desire
Artificial insemination by donor	Inhibited sexual excitement
Atherosclerosis	Integumentary system
Autoimmune responses	*In-vitro* fertilization
Autoimmune theories	Involutional psychosis
Basal metabolic rate	Maximum longevity
Cardiac output	Maximum oxygen consumption
Cardiac reserve	Mean longevity
Central nervous system	Menopause
Climacteric	Myotonia
Clinical threshold	Neuritic plaque
Compliance	Neuroendocrine theories
Cortex	Neurofibrillary tangle
Cross-linkage theory	Neuron
Cross-linked	Orgasm
Dermis	Osteoarthritis
Diverticulosis	Osteoporosis
Egg donation	Peripheral nervous system
Embryo adoption	Plateau
Epidermis	Primary aging
Excitation	Prostate gland
Free radical theory	Psychosexual dysfunction
Gene mutation theory	Refractory period
Gene theory	Resolution
Hayflick limit	Secondary aging
Hippocampus	Surrogate motherhood
Homeostasis	Synapse
Hot flashes	Vasocongestion
Hypodermis	Vital capacity

Suggestions for Further Reading

Notelovitz, M. & Ware, M. (1985). *Stand Tall! Every Woman's Guide to Preventing Osteoporosis*. New York: Bantam Books.

Schneider, E. L., & Rowe, J. W. (Eds.) (1990). *Handbook of the Biology of Aging*. San Diego: Academic Press.

Shock, N. W., Greulich, R. C., Andres, R., Arenberg, D., Costa, P. T., Lakatta, E. G., & Tobin, J. D. (1984). *Normal Human Aging: The Baltimore Longitudinal Study of Aging*. NIH Publication No. 84-2450. Bethesda, MD: National Institutes of Health.

Spence, A. P. (1989). *The Biology of Human Aging*. Englewood Cliffs, NJ: Prentice Hall.

Whitbourne, S. K. (1985). *The Aging Body: Physiological Changes and Psychological Consequences*. New York: Springer-Verlag.

CHAPTER FOUR

HEALTH AND HEALTH CARE THROUGHOUT ADULTHOOD

The last chapter provided an overview of changes in physiology throughout adulthood. This chapter addresses the related topic of how physical health changes; mental health issues are considered in Chapter Nine. The chapter opens with a discussion of ways in which young adults' decisions about life-style can have a long-term impact on physical health. Next, we consider how health changes with age, including changes in types of illnesses and changes in causes of death. In the last chapter, the distinction between normal aging and the impacts of disease was a theme; that theme reappears in this chapter. Older peoples' health care needs are the final issues addressed in this chapter. This discussion revolves around a second theme of the chapter—ways in which health, especially that of elderly adults, is shaped by social and political policy.

Questions to consider in reading the chapter include:

What circumstances threaten health in early adulthood, and how do these threats vary by race or gender? How does health change in middle and later adulthood?

What racial differences in causes of death are apparent? What is the "racial mortality crossover phenomenon?"

What kinds of programs provide long-term care to frail older people in the community?

What factors are related to ease of adjustment to a nursing home?

What kinds of health care services does Medicare cover, and what kinds of
services does it fail to cover?

GENERAL INFLUENCES OF PHYSICAL HEALTH

Although most people have an intuitive notion of what it means to be healthy,
health is surprisingly difficult to define. At a bare minimum, it is the absence of
disease or pathology. This definition, however, merely specifies what health is
not. Health is more positively defined as overall well-being in mental, physical,
and social functioning (Danish, 1983).

Health in early adulthood: Variation
by race and gender

Health in early adulthood is a logical point of departure not only chrono-
logically, but also qualitatively. Most young adults enjoy the best health of
their lifetime. Almost none suffer from chronic illnesses, and many have out-
grown childhood allergies and illnesses. Not surprisingly, nearly all young
adults describe their general health as good, very good, or excellent (USDHHS,
1986b).

Illnesses during early adulthood are usually acute, short-term problems—
most often respiratory problems (e.g., colds, bronchitis) or injuries. When young
adults are hospitalized, it is usually because of an accident, childbirth, or a
disease of the digestive or genitourinary systems (USDHHS, 1985). Correspondingly, the most frequent causes of death in early adulthood are accidents
(USDHHS, 1985).

Health status in young adulthood is associated with race. African-Americans suffer from hypertension in young adulthood more often than Caucasians
do, and African-Americans have a higher death rate in young adulthood—primarily because of higher homicide rates (USDHHS, 1986b). Unfortunately, there
are similar patterns of racial differences in health throughout most of adulthood. The *Diversity in Adulthood* box takes a closer look at differences in the life
expectancies of older Caucasians and older African Americans.

In early adulthood, health status is also associated with gender, educational background, and income. Young men have higher death rates than young
women, and young men and women typically die under different circumstances. Most deaths among young men stem from automobile accidents,
whereas the leading cause of death for young women is cancer (USDHHS,
1986b). Better educated adults and affluent adults enjoy better health, and
maintain their health into old age, more than their less educated and poorer
counterparts (Heinemann, 1985).

Health, like longevity (see Chapter Three), is influenced by heredity. Susceptibility to some diseases (e.g., cardiovascular disease, diabetes, cancer) runs
in families, as does a propensity for alcoholism (Schuckit, 1984; Goodwin, 1988).

BOX 4.1   **D**IVERSITY IN ADULTHOOD

Health status in old age: Racial differences and the "crossover" effect

This chapter documents racial differences in health throughout adulthood. Using a broad spectrum of health status indicators (e.g., self-ratings of health, activity impairments, etc.), African-Americans are generally in poorer health than Caucasians (Jackson & Perry, 1989). Given these statistics, it is not surprising that Caucasians have greater life expectancy than African-Americans do for most of adulthood.

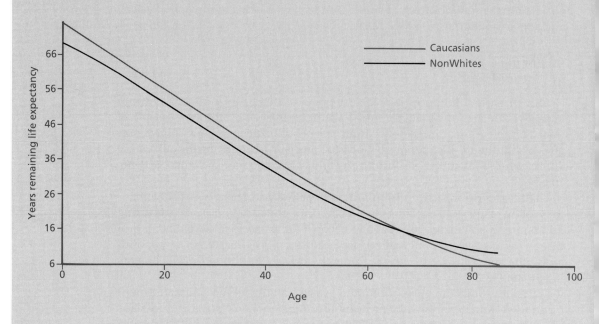

Figure 4.1
Life expectancy at various ages by race. (Source: National Center for Health Statistics, 1980.)

Fortunately, lifestyle is also closely associated with health status throughout adulthood, and to that extent one can take deliberate steps to optimize health.

Lifestyle: Choices of young adulthood and their long-term impact

In a large-scale survey of health habits, Nedra Belloc (1973; Belloc & Breslow, 1972) gathered information concerning diet, exercise, weight, and drinking and smoking practices from over 6000 adults. Several years later, she used county records to identify deaths within the initial sample, and measured associations between the number of health-promoting practices that participants had ini-

What *is* surprising is that this pattern of racial differences reverses in old age, a circumstance known as the **racial mortality crossover phenomenon**. Figure 4.1 illustrates life expectancy at various ages for "nonwhites" (95 percent of whom are African-Americans) and for Caucasians. As Figure 4.1 shows, African-American life expectancy lags behind that of Caucasians from birth through age 65. After that age, however, African-American life expectancy draws ahead of Caucasian life expectancy by an increasing margin. The same kind of crossover has been documented for Mexican-Americans (Jackson et al., 1990) and for Navajo Indians (Kunitz & Levy, 1989).

How can the racial mortality crossover phenomenon be explained? Initially, demographers believed that it reflected enumeration errors and age misreporting (Jackson et al., 1990; Kunitz & Levy, 1989; Markides & Mindel, 1987). However, when further research was conducted to control for these factors, the crossover was still apparent (Jackson et al., 1990; Markides & Mindel, 1987).

Today, most scientists explain the pattern in terms of a "selective survival" process operating throughout the life span for racial minorities. In these populations, the least "hardy" individuals die relatively early—often as a result of the social disadvantages to which they are subject—leaving the unusually robust members of the populations to survive to advanced old age. As Jackson and his colleagues (1990) explain:

> Cohorts of racial and ethnic minorities born today are still at considerable risk. Large numbers are likely to spend childhoods in low-income, single female-headed households. Children in these families will undoubtedly have inadequate diets and be exposed to inadequate educational opportunities. Job prospects will be poor in young adulthood, and a large proportion will not reach middle adulthood. . . . Dental visits, preventative health maintenance, well-baby examinations, sensory adjustments for poor hearing and vision, among other health-promoting tasks, will be largely unavailable . . . (p. 109)

Thus, the members of these groups who survive, despite these lifelong disadvantages, may be constitutionally more fit than others.

More generally, the racial mortality crossover phenomenon illustrates the variety with which aging occurs. Markides & Mindel (1987) observe that this phenomenon raises a question concerning the meaning of "old age," and suggest that the crossover implies that African-Americans and Caucasians age at different rates. If this is the case, we truly have an instance of diversity in development at the physiological level.

tially reported and their probability of death. The critical health practices were (1) eating breakfast, (2) eating regular meals rather than snacking, (3) eating moderate amounts in order to maintain normal weight, (4) not smoking, (5) drinking alcohol moderately if at all, (6) exercising moderately, and (7) sleeping 7 to 8 hours a night. For both men and women, the lowest death rates appeared for those who practiced six or seven of these habits; there were higher death rates for those practicing four or five, and still higher rates for those practicing three or fewer good health habits.

Diet and exercise   Belloc's (1973; Belloc & Breslow, 1972) research highlights the importance of diet for maintaining good health. A healthful diet is critical for maintaining proper weight, maximizing energy and vitality, and minimizing susceptibility to diseases such as gout. Even more than diet, regular exercise is crucial in order to maintain an appropriate weight; exercise also benefits the cardiovascular system by strengthening the heart and lungs and lowering blood pressure (Bennett, Goldfinger, & Johnson, 1987). As we saw in the last chapter, regular weight-bearing exercise (e.g., walking, jogging, aerobic exercise) can help to prevent osteoporosis. Some researchers claim that exercise is an excellent way to relieve depression and tension (McCann & Holmes, 1984).

Stress and personality   The stress that one experiences, and the means used to cope with stress, are also important health influences. **Stress** is the psychophysiological reaction to demands, and is as much a part of life as death and taxes. When an individual is under stress, the nervous system responds with energizing messages. In effect, the physiological reaction prepares the body to combat or to flee from a threat—whether the threat be a mugger in a dark alley or an upcoming final exam. Psychological reactions to stress include feelings of nervousness, anger, and depression.

Medical research links stress with health. In a study that is now a classic, Holmes and Rahe (1976) examined recent life events necessitating change and the illnesses experienced by hospital patients. These physicians found that individuals who had recently experienced a great deal of change were particularly likely to have health problems. Even changes that most people would welcome, such as getting a promotion or getting married, force adaptation to new circumstances and thus are stressful.

Furthermore, it is not only major life changes that are related to health. In one study, participants' "daily hassles" (e.g., a parking ticket, an unexpected bill, "setbacks" in housebreaking a puppy) were closely associated with their physical and mental well-being (Lazarus, 1981). Stress seems inherent in situations over which people feel that they lack control (e.g., Cohen, 1980)—things like the neighbor's barking dog, or the course of a loved one's dementing illness. Not only the situation itself, then, but also the extent to which people feel that they can do something about the situation is important.

Perception of control has special significance for health in old age, since older adults, like people of all ages, sometimes encounter situations over which they feel that they have little control. Chronic illnesses and institutionalization are both health-related issues of old age addressed later in the chapter. Both are also transitions following which one might realistically conclude that there are few personal actions that can change the situation. Experimental research tells us that an older person who reaches that conclusion might actually worsen her health, resulting in a vicious circle of declining health.

Rodin & Langer (1977) found, in a classic study, that nursing home residents who were encouraged to take responsibility for seeing that they received satisfactory care, for deciding how they wanted to spend time rather than delegating those decisions, and for speaking up about things that they did not like in the home fared better than a comparable group of patients who were not encouraged to take such steps. Compared to residents who were encouraged to let the staff take full responsibility for their care and contentment, the first group of residents were more active, more alert, and happier. Furthermore, the residents who were encouraged to feel in control lived longer than the residents who were encouraged to let the staff take control.

This body of research implies that people simply *react* to both major changes and daily hassles, sometimes in ways that are dangerous for health. However, other evidence accords a greater role to the individual. The tendency to experience stress and the means used to cope with stress may reflect personality factors, and these factors themselves are associated with the incidence of cardiovascular disease. Physicians Friedman and Rosenman (1974), in a study of patients suffering heart attacks at various ages, found that many of these attacks could not be explained on the basis of diet, exercise, smoking, and other health habits. Instead, personality provided some clues.

Some of the patients in Friedman and Rosenman's research had a **Type "A" behavior pattern**. These individuals were impatient, competitive, aggressive, and hostile—constantly attempting to get the most done in the least amount of time, to be the best, and to be on guard against threats. In particular, the perpetual hostility is a disposition through which Type A's actually *create* stress in their lives (e.g., Ivancevich & Matteson, 1988). Other patients had a **Type "B" behavior pattern**. These people were much more relaxed, easygoing, and benevolent in their outlook. In Friedman and Rosenman's work, the Type "A's" were unusually likely to suffer heart attacks in their thirties or forties. However, the Type "B's" rarely suffered heart attacks before their seventies—even if they smoked, did not exercise, and ate a fatty diet!

Concluding that a Type A behavior pattern is always harmful, and that a Type B pattern is always adaptive, oversimplifies things, though. Most people do not fit neatly into one category or another, but have some characteristics of both the Type A and the Type B patterns. Furthermore, the strength of the association between behavior pattern and cardiovascular functioning varies with age and gender (Harbin & Blumenthal, 1985). And one study found that, although Type A's were more likely to suffer heart attacks at relatively early ages than Type B's, Type A's made better recoveries from heart attacks than Type B's did (Ragland & Brand, 1988). Typically, Type A individuals express stronger motivation to follow diet and exercise regimens than Type B individuals do: recovery is a new project at which the Type A's strive for excellence.

Even though stress can be hazardous to health, people are free from all stress only upon death; even living with minimal stress (and the resulting boredom) could be maladaptive. Since stress is an inevitable part of life, the important thing is to learn to manage it adaptively. Psychologists have developed effective programs for stress management, including relaxation training, hypnosis, and cognitive restructuring. Many people—including die-hard Type "A's"—have successfully modified their means of handling stress through these approaches.

Age differences in perceptions of stress are also encouraging. Generally, older adults deem most life events as less disruptive than young adults do (Chiriboga & Cutler, 1980); perhaps experience is an effective teacher of how much one should worry about life changes. The news on age differences in perceptions of stress is not all good, though. Older adults identify fewer positive stressors (e.g., birth of a child, purchase of a home), and more negative stressors (e.g., death of the spouse or friends, financial problems) than do young adults (Chiriboga & Cutler, 1980).

Cigarette smoking   Of all lifestyle choices, there is none with greater or more clear health implications than the decision about the use of tobacco. Recall that some of the ways in which the respiratory system changes with age may well reflect the effects of tobacco rather than normal aging (see Chapter Three, p. 60). Over 20 years of research provides a long list of the dangers of cigarette smoking: smokers put themselves at increased risk of many diseases, including cancer, heart disease, gastrointestinal problems, bronchitis, and emphysema. Even sharing a household with a regular smoker is dangerous, as there are heightened cancer rates among nonsmoking spouses, children, and pets of smokers (Correa, Pickle, Fontham, Lin, & Haenszel, 1983).

It is disappointing, with all of the evidence regarding these dangers, that many people still choose to smoke and that the tobacco industry continues to flourish. However, recent surveys show that fewer young adults (approximately one-third of those aged 25 to 44) smoke today than in the past (USDHHS, 1987). Both recent legislation regulating smoking in public places, as well as increasing assertiveness on the part of nonsmokers, suggest that future cohorts will continue to include dwindling numbers of smokers—and possibly fewer age-related changes overall in the structure and functioning of the respiratory system.

The use of alcohol and other drugs   Both the media and contemporary norms accord alcohol a welcome place in society. Most adults drink at least occasionally; most report that they are light or moderate drinkers who consume no more than three drinks (or glasses of wine or beer) per day (Prevention Research Center, 1986). Drinking at this level is probably not harmful. Some claim, in fact, that light or moderate drinking offers protection against heart disease (Haskell et al., 1984).

At the same time, it is clear that immoderate use of alcohol is associated with direct and indirect health threats. Relatively direct effects include cirrhosis of the liver, cancer, heart failure, ulcers, and damage to the nervous system. Less directly, alcohol abuse is a contributing cause of death from automobile accidents, fires, drownings, falls, and suicide. Alcohol abuse can undermine not only one's health but also one's marriage, family life, and ability to function on the job.

To be sure, alcohol is not the only recreational drug used in the United States today. Because of their illegal status, however, it is difficult to estimate the numbers of individuals who use other drugs occasionally or regularly, and there is less reliable information available concerning the impact that these substances have on health. Scattered information is available. For example, long-term use of marijuana can damage the lungs at least as much as cigarette smoking; marijuana can also be dangerous for those who have heart disease, since the drug increases heart rate (Bennett et al., 1987). As discussed in the last chapter, marijuana can lead to decreased fertility.

In the late 1980s, cocaine abuse emerged as a major concern among legislators and law enforcement officials, health experts, and the general public. Because cocaine is both addictive and expensive, it can be socially and financially devastating. In addition, the drug produces negative physical effects, including exhaustion, headaches, tremors, blurred vision, nausea, seizures, loss of consciousness, malnutrition, impotence, irregular heartbeat, angina, and myocardial infarction (e.g., Bennett et al., 1987). When cocaine is "snorted," there can also be damage to the nasal septum; when this or any drug is used intravenously, there is the danger of skin infections, hepatitis, internal fungus infections, infection of the lining of the heart, and inflamed arteries (e.g., Bennett et al, 1987). The most serious threat from intravenous drug use, though, is the possibility of contracting acquired immunodeficiency syndrome (AIDS) through the use of a contaminated needle.

Certainly, alcohol, marijuana, and cocaine are only a few of the recreational drugs that can affect health. They are, though, among the most widely used drugs at this time, and merit special consideration for that reason. Furthermore, it is realistic to expect that all three will continue to be available (even if illegal) for those who choose to indulge. On that basis, it is critically important that adults of all ages be aware of the consequences that using these drugs can have on their health.

Sexually transmitted diseases   Up through the 1960s, **sexually transmitted diseases** (STDs) presented a fairly straightforward medical picture (Bennett et al., 1987). At that time, syphilis and gonorrhea were the two major STDs, and only five STDs had been identified altogether. Treating an STD might have been difficult because of the stigma associated with these illnesses, but reliable treatments were readily available. During the 1970s, however, medical research identified over 20 germs associated with sexually transmitted diseases, not all of which are as easily treated as syphilis or gonorrhea. Left untreated, an STD can lead to infertility, disability, or death.

Without a doubt, **acquired immunodeficiency syndrome** (AIDS) is the STD currently arousing the greatest concern, and with good reason. There was no known cure for AIDS as of 1991, the disease is fatal, and the spread of AIDS has reached epidemic proportions. As the numbers of AIDS victims continue to mount, experts predict that the health care system in many places will become

AIDS cannot be cured at this time, but can easily be prevented. This woman need not fear contracting the disease through casual contact with an AIDS patient.

overburdened—as it is now in urban areas with large numbers of AIDS patients (USDHHS, 1986c).

Although AIDS cannot be cured at this time, it can easily be prevented. AIDS is transmitted through body fluids such as semen, blood, and (possibly) vaginal fluid and breast milk. In addition, an infant can contract AIDS during a vaginal birth if her mother is infected. Mere physical contact that might occur in the home, in the workplace, or in public places—touching, hugging, kissing, and so forth—cannot transmit the virus. Nor can the virus be transmitted by sharing household objects, office equipment, swimming pools, public transportation, or toilet seats. It is also impossible to be infected simply by being near someone who has AIDS.

AIDS was initially identified among homosexual men who reported many sexual partners. The most important steps to take, then, in avoiding exposure to AIDS are to minimize the number of sexual contacts, and to use a condom during intercourse unless you are absolutely certain that your partner has not been exposed to the virus.[1] And, someone who chooses to use drugs intravenously should never share needles (see above). Finally, AIDS has in the past occasionally been transmitted through blood transfusions. Blood and blood

---

1. Blood tests can determine whether or not an individual has been exposed to the AIDS virus. There are problems with these blood tests, however. The antibody for HIV, which indicates infection, may not initially be produced when the virus first enters the system.

products used for transfusions today, though, are thoroughly checked for the presence of the AIDS virus.

We have seen that most young adults enjoy extremely good health. Health throughout adulthood is related to heredity, but is also strongly associated with diet, exercise, stress and stress management, the use of alcohol and other drugs, and sexual habits. Clearly, young adults can make a number of choices that are likely to optimize health—not only today, but for years to come. And to the extent that social opportunities and policies encourage healthful choices, not only the individual but also her society can take positive steps to optimize health throughout adulthood.

HEALTH CHANGES IN ADULTHOOD

The last chapter provided an overview of ways in which the body changes with age; those changes of normal aging are ones that virtually anyone who lives long enough will experience. Although these consequences of normal aging are a departure from the optimal physical functioning that most young adults enjoy, they are not disease states. The changes considered here, however, are pathological ones. Illness in general becomes more frequent as people get older. And some diseases—if they appear—typically develop in old age. Aging itself, however, does not lead to disease.

The health habits that are beneficial in early adulthood become even more important with advancing age. In particular, good nutrition (e.g., Ausman & Russell, 1990) and regular aerobic exercise (e.g., Emery & Blumenthal, 1990; Goldberg & Hagberg, 1990) can have pronounced mental and physical health advantages for older adults, just as they can for the young. So, in middle and old age—as in early adulthood—choices regarding lifestyle can continue to maximize chances of a healthful old age.

Health impacts of the climacteric

Cancers of the reproductive system become more frequent in middle and later adulthood. For men, cancer of the prostate gland becomes a health concern; the incidences of breast, uterine, and ovarian cancers also increase. After menopause, women's rates of cardiovascular disease increase, and approach the rate for men in the same age group (e.g., Siegler, 1989). And, recall that many scientists link the development of osteoporosis to the hormonal changes of menopause.

Preventative health care, therefore, becomes even more important in middle adulthood. During general physical examinations, men should have their prostate gland palpated and women should have pelvic examinations and mammograms. Screening tests are also available to assess diminished bone mass for women at high risk of developing osteoporosis. And, like young women, middle-aged and older women should also perform regular self-examinations of their breasts; men should regularly examine the testes as a check for testicular cancer. With the early detection that self-examinations make possible, these forms of cancer are among the most curable (American Cancer Society, 1984; USDHHS, 1982).

Hormonal replacement therapy (HRT) is sometimes used to treat women's menopausal symptoms (e.g., Buchsbaum, 1983). HRT may also prevent or slow the development of osteoporosis, and is often effective in minimizing hot flashes and drying or thinning of vaginal tissue (see Chapter Three, pages 66–67). Early studies indicated that HRT was associated with increased rates of uterine cancer; at that time, HRT involved administration of synthetic estrogens alone. Today, HRT involves administration of a mixture of synthetic estrogens and progesterone so as to mimic a woman's natural menstrual cycle. Research evaluating this approach shows that HRT is safe and beneficial; in fact, women undergoing HRT today have lower rates of uterine cancer than do untreated women (Weg, 1989).

Other health changes: Gender and racial differences

Although most middle-aged and older people consider themselves healthy, longitudinal data show that health changes during middle and later adulthood. Bayer and her colleagues (Bayer, Whissel-Bvechy, & Honzik, 1981) described health in the middle years for participants in the Berkeley Growth Studies (in which participants were studied from birth through the mid-thirties), the Oakland Growth Studies (in which participants were studied from early adolescence through the fifties), and the Guidance Study (in which participants were studied from birth through the early forties). In these studies, participants were nonrandom samples from the San Francisco Bay area; most were Caucasian and middle class, and there were approximately equal numbers of males and females.

Bayer et al. (1981) reported that most of these middle-aged adults, like those in large national surveys, described their general health as excellent or good. Most had, however, experienced health changes typical of middle adulthood. First, increasing percentages of men and women in all three samples reported illnesses of virtually all kinds. In addition, the most frequent health complaints changed. As young adults, most health problems were acute illnesses—things like the flu or broken bones. In middle age, however, most medical problems were ongoing disorders such as hypertension, persistent pain or stiffness of the joints, or metabolic diseases.

This shift from primarily short-term to primarily long-term illnesses is by no means unique to this longitudinal sample. National health surveys show that **chronic illnesses**—those that are long-term, progressive, not currently curable, and often without a readily specifiable external cause—are the predominant health complaints of middle-aged and older adults (e.g., AARP, 1988; USDHHS, 1989). In both middle adulthood (ages 45–64) and later adulthood (ages 65 and older), the most frequent chronic conditions are arthritis, hypertension, sinusitis, orthopedic impairments, hearing impairments, and heart conditions (U. S. Senate Special Committee on Aging, 1987). Other frequent chronic conditions in later adulthood include varicose veins, diabetes, cancer, and—as we have already noted—osteoporosis (USDHHS, 1989).

The frequencies of virtually all of these chronic conditions increase with age: nearly all older adults suffer from at least one of these illnesses. Many older people suffer from more than one chronic illness; this situation is known as **comorbidity** (e.g., USDHHS, 1989). As Figure 4.2 illustrates, the frequency of comorbidity increases with age. Among the oldest old (those aged 80 and over), over half of the men and nearly three-quarters of the women report two or more chronic conditions.

With these multiple health problems, the number of medications that an older person must take increases; this situation is of concern for two reasons. The possibility of adverse drug interactions increases with the number of medications taken, especially if an older person is under the care of several different specialists who communicate infrequently—or not at all (Vestal & Crusack, 1990). Also, understanding and remembering one's medical regimen becomes more difficult as the number of medications increases. Because older people have more difficulty than young adults comprehending and remembering prescription information (Morrell, Park, & Poon, 1990), the likelihood that even the best-intentioned older patient will not comply with medical treatment as her physician intended is substantial.

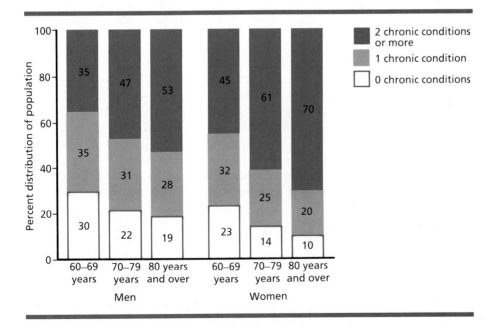

Figure 4.2
Percent distribution of population 60 years of age and over by number of chronic conditions, according to age group and sex: United States, 1984. (Source, USDHHS, 1989.)

As a result of comorbidity, the number of medications that an older person must take increases.

In considering the frequencies of chronic illness and comorbidity, two points are important. First, there are individual differences in these frequencies. Gender differences are apparent, as Figure 4.2 illustrates with regard to the frequency of comorbidity. In addition, men and women suffer from different kinds of chronic illnesses: arthritis is more often a problem for older women, whereas older men are more likely to suffer from heart disease (e.g., Verbrugge, 1989). In general, older women typically have nonfatal chronic conditions, whereas older men more often experience life-threatening chronic illnesses (Verbrugge, 1989).

There are also racial differences. Older African-Americans more often die from hypertension and heart disease than older non-Hispanic Caucasians do (Jackson, Antonucci, & Gibson, 1990; Jackson & Perry, 1989; Markides & Mindel, 1987). Older Hispanic Americans and Native Americans suffer from diabetes and from infectious and parasitic diseases at higher rates than do elderly non-Hispanic Caucasians (Kunitz & Levy, 1989; Markides, Coreil, & Rogers, 1989; Markides & Mindel, 1987). Scholars most often attribute these differences to racial, ethnic, and class differences in access to health care, and to group differences in diet and rates of obesity (e.g., Jackson & Perry, 1989; Kunitz & Levy, 1989; Markides & Mindel, 1987).

A second point is that the frequency with which any health condition is identified depends not only on the actual frequency with which it occurs, but also on the steps taken to identify it. Ilene Siegler (1989), for example, recounts data from the **Baltimore Longitudinal Study**, an ongoing examination of aging in healthy adults. Traditional medical screening identified merely half of the cases of heart disease that were later detected at autopsy. It was only when participants in this extensive study were examined under the stress of physical exercise—and using more "high tech" and costly screening tools—that the remaining cases of impaired cardiac functioning were detected. As Siegler observes, "our definition of disease may depend on technological innovation, available funds, and the willingness of apparently 'healthy' persons to undergo detailed diagnostic procedures" (pp. 121–122).

How does the increased frequency of chronic illnesses and comorbidity affect older people on an everyday basis? Surprisingly, most older individuals rate their health favorably well into old age, despite these health problems. As Figure 4.3 illustrates, only about 30 percent of people age 65 or older rate their health as fair or poor; the rest consider themselves to be in good, very good, or excellent health (AARP, 1988; USDHHS, 1987). As in the incidence

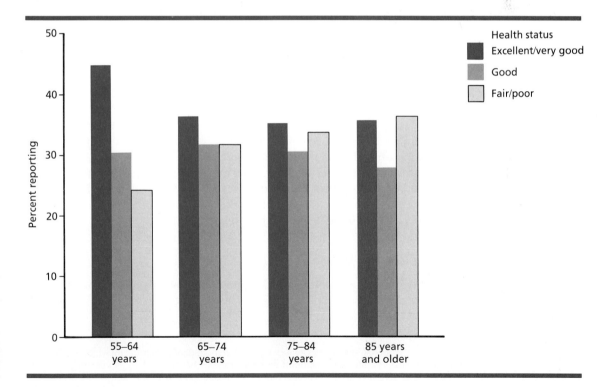

Figure 4.3
Self-reported health, by age group. (Source: USDHHS, 1986a).

of chronic disease, there are racial differences in these health ratings. Nearly half (45%) of elderly African-Americans describe their health as fair or poor (AARP, 1988).

There are clear impacts of chronic illness and comorbidity, though, despite favorable self-ratings of health. Perhaps most concretely, chronic illnesses extract a substantial financial burden (e.g., AARP, 1988). Even with Medicare and other health insurance, out-of-pocket medical expenses can be a major concern for those on a fixed income. Also, the course of acute illnesses may be complicated by the presence of chronic illness, so that an older person takes longer to recover from the flu or a cold than a young or middle-aged adult does (Hickey, 1980).

Some older people must restrict their usual activities as a result of chronic illnesses. For example, one recent survey found that 23 percent of older people had health-related difficulty with personal care activities such as bathing, dressing, transferring from a bed or chair, using the toilet, or going outside (AARP, 1988). The same survey revealed that 27 percent of respondents had health-related difficulty with home management activities such as cooking, shopping, doing housework, and managing money. Women more often encounter these problems than men do (Verbrugge, 1989), and elderly African-Americans may be less likely to suffer from activity impairments because of their health (Jackson et al., 1990).

A final consequence of chronic illnesses and comorbidity is in the area of cognitive functioning. Subsequent chapters review research comparing older and younger people's performance on various measures of intelligence, learning, and memory. Much of that work shows that older adults rarely perform as well as younger people; scholars in the area of developmental health psychology would suggest that some of these age differences should be attributed to age differences in health. Self-rated physical health is substantially related to performance on a short-term memory task and on a measure of fluid intelligence,[2] although not to performance on a measure of crystallized intelligence[3] (Perlmutter & Nyquist, 1990). Other research shows that intellectual functioning is related to hypertension (Elias, Robbins, Schultz, & Pierce, 1990), diabetes, and Parkinson's Disease (Elias, Elias, & Elias, 1990).

Causes of death in old age

The leading causes of death for older people generally parallel the most frequent chronic illnesses. The leading causes of death for the age 65 and older

---

2. This aspect of intelligence includes the capacity to deal with novel information, does not seem to depend on cultural background or education, and is believed to reflect integrity of the central nervous system. We will discuss it more fully in Chapter Six.

3. This aspect of intelligence includes the extent of one's general information, and knowledge and understanding of one's culture; it is related to educational background. We will discuss this aspect of intelligence more fully in Chapter Six.

population are (in rank order) heart diseases, cancers, strokes, influenza and pneumonia, arteriosclerosis, diabetes, accidents, respiratory diseases (bronchitis, emphysema, asthma), cirrhosis of the liver, and kidney problems (e.g., U.S. Public Health Service, 1981). Note that, for older people, accidents are a relatively infrequent cause of death, whereas accidents are the leading cause of death for young men. Not only do the relative frequencies of causes of death vary by age group, they also vary by race and ethnicity. Older Hispanic Americans and older Native Americans are more likely than non-Hispanic Caucasians to die from infectious and parasitic diseases, influenza, diabetes, pneumonia, and accidents or violence (Kunitz & Levy, 1989; Markides et al., 1989).

HEALTH CARE AND THE AGED

Given the health changes typical of adulthood, it is easy to see why health care constitutes an important set of issues for elderly individuals. Older people tend to suffer from more illnesses than younger people do, and the illnesses plaguing older adults more often require ongoing care than do acute problems that are quickly cured. This final section reviews ways in which older people use health care services, and examines issues related to **long-term care**, the ongoing medical and social care provided to those with severe impairments.

Older people and health care: Formal, informal, and self-care

In view of the frequency of chronic illnesses among elderly adults, it is not surprising that older adults use a variety of health care services. Many of these services are **formal health care** (physicians and other health-care professionals); probably, these services are the ones that first come to mind when one thinks of health care. But older people also rely on **informal care** (health care provided by family, friends, or neighbors) and on **self-care** (activities that the individual engages in to promote or restore health, prevent disease, or limit illness).

Clearly, older adults are an important clientele for the formal health care system. Elderly people are, in fact, the largest single group of consumers of formal health care services, accounting for 31 percent of all hospital stays and 42 percent of all days of care in hospitals as well as approximately 20 percent of all visits to the doctor (AARP, 1988; Krause, 1990; U. S. Senate Special Committee on Aging, 1987). As Figure 4.4 illustrates, however, not all older people make heavy use of formal health care services. A relatively small percentage of the elderly (less than 33 percent, in one study) account for a high percentage of inpatient and outpatient health care (Krause, 1990). In contrast, between 13 percent and 20 percent of the aged use no traditional medical services at all (Branch & Nemeth, 1985 cited in Krause, 1990).

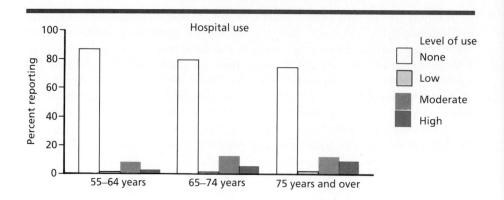

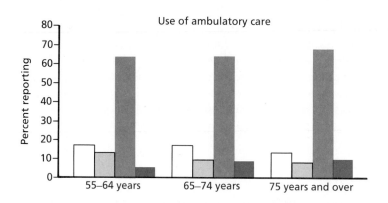

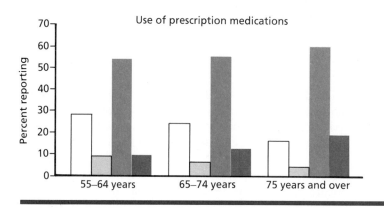

Figure 4.4
Older adults' use of health care services. (Source: USDHHS, 1986a.)

If substantial numbers of older adults do not use formal health care services when they are ill, what do they do? Self-care and informal care are common responses (Krause, 1990). On the days when her chronic arthritis is especially troublesome, an older woman might self-medicate with over-the-counter pain relievers, and take it easy. She might ask her grown children to help her with tasks that are difficult because of stiffness (including opening pain relievers packaged in child-resistant containers!), and to loan her a heating pad. Or, she might ask her friends or neighbors for advice about how they have dealt with similar symptoms.

Informal care and self-care are important resources for older adults. For an older individual, using formal health care services can entail a variety of costs. It may be time consuming or inconvenient (particularly for rural elderly people who do not have a doctor, hospital, or clinic in their community), and the cost not covered by Medicare may be burdensome (e.g., Wilson, 1989).[4] Furthermore, the ways that many physicians deal with older patients (see below), may make going to the doctor intimidating. Also, research on the self-care practices of rural elderly African-American women suggests that self-care is often effective—at least in terms of self-ratings of health—and psychologically important (Wilson, 1989). To these women, managing illnesses without using formal health care was a mark of courage and a measure of good health.

Not only can self-care and informal care be valuable components of older peoples' overall health care in and of themselves, they also have an important relationship to formal health care. Self-care and informal care can expedite the eventual use of formal health care services (Krause, 1990). Self-care requires an older adult to pay attention to symptoms and monitor their severity; these steps can be an asset if and when the person seeks advice from a health care professional. An elderly person's children, grandchildren, or friends (components of his informal care system) might provide critical links to formal health care by giving him a ride to the doctor's office or clinic, by picking up prescriptions, and/or by helping him to remember and follow the doctor or nurse's instructions.

When older people use formal health care services, what kind of reception can they expect? Scientists have given most attention to the interaction between physicians and aged patients, although nurses and speech therapists, physical therapists, and medical social workers are also important components of the formal health care system. Early studies showed that physicians generally had negative perceptions of the aged (e.g., Miller, Lowenstein, & Winston, 1976; Gruber, 1977): many admitted that they would exert less effort to treat an elderly person than a young one, for example. In all fairness, physicians at that

---

4. Many people are surprised to learn how many common medical expenses for older people are not covered by Medicare. Medicare does not cover, for example, the costs of dental care, eyeglasses, or hearing aids.

time probably had little training that would interest or prepare them for effective work with the elderly. The specialty of **geriatric medicine** has emerged only over the last three decades, and has only had a licensing examination since 1987.

Now that courses on aging and the needs of older patients are becoming increasingly common in medical school curricula (e.g., Kane, Solomon, Beck, Keeler, & Kane, 1981), one might hope that physicians would express more positive attitudes toward the aged. Unfortunately, this is not the case. In videotaped interviews between doctors and patients, physicians spent nearly all of the time discussing physical symptoms—and almost no time talking about ways in which the patient's illness might affect her life, concerns she had about those impacts, or whether or not she was anxious or depressed (Greene, Hoffman, Charon, & Adelman, 1987). Generally, doctors still spend less time with older patients than with younger ones (Radecki, Kane, Solomon, Mendenhall, & Beck, 1988) and express less inclination to provide vigorous treatment to older than to younger patients (Greenfield, Blanco, Elashoff, & Ganz, 1987). The doctor's office, then, probably still presents an unfriendly climate for the elderly patient.

At the same time, the elderly patient also contributes to her interaction with her physician. Some suggest that older people get less attention from their doctors partly because they *demand* less. In the videotaped interviews described above, older patients—as well as the doctors—kept the conversation closely focused on physical symptoms; the older patients were less likely than younger ones to ask questions about how their illness might affect their lives (Greene et al., 1987). In a cross-sectional survey, older respondents expressed less desire to have control of their health care than did younger adults, and were less likely to want health-related information (Woodward & Wallston, 1987). These older adults preferred to have professionals make decisions about their health care, and expressed less confidence than younger adults did about their ability to effectively deal with health care information and decisions.

What are the implications of these data on older patients and their doctors? We might speculate that, if physicians continue to express disinterest in the needs of older patients, they are likely to face a professional life fraught with frustration—given the growth of the aged segment of the population in general and of the oldest old (who are most likely to require extensive medical care) in particular. Hopefully, subsequent cohorts (especially the assertive "baby boomers") reaching old age will demand the most careful attention that health care professionals can provide.

Older people and long-term care

Long-term care in the community   Many people think immediately of nursing homes when they think of long-term care for the elderly. However, most long-term care is actually provided in the community, and much of this care is given by the older individual's family and friends (Kane & Kane, 1990). This pattern fits the preferences of most older adults and their families, and may well be of concrete benefit to the older adult. In one study, older people receiving care in their communities had higher morale and regained greater ability to function independently than did a comparable group receiving care in a nursing home (Braun & Rose, 1987).

Furthermore, nursing homes are an expensive way to provide long-term care. In the late 1980s, the average annual cost of nursing home care was $22,000, and that figure was expected to rise to $55,000 by the year 2018 (Who can afford, 1988). Although many people assume that these costs are covered by **Medicare** (the federal health insurance program for the aged and disabled), they could not be more wrong. Medicare actually provides very little coverage for nursing home care—or community-based long-term care. The best way of financing long-term care—in a nursing home or in the community—is an issue eliciting sharply contrasting opinions. We examine these perspectives in the *Open Questions* box.

For some older people, all necessary help with mobility, homemaking, and health care comes from family and friends. Others, though, rely on formal programs to provide these services. What kinds of programs exist to provide

Table 4.1
Common types of community-based long-term care

Home Care: an array of services that may include nursing care at home and/or assistance with housework.

Adult Day Care: centers at which rehabilitative services and/or social activities are provided during the day.

Nutrition Services: inexpensive and nutritious meals are provided either in communal settings such as churches or synagogues (transportation is usually provided as well) or delivered to the home.

Friendly Visiting: regular visits are provided to older people who are lonely. The visitor may run errands, write letters, or provide other kinds of assistance, in addition to giving companionship.

Emergency Response Systems: an automated system using the telephone, an alarm device worn around the neck, and the cooperation of family, neighbors and local emergency medical services. The systems are activated in the event of a medical emergency at home.

Telephone Reassurance: daily telephone calls made (at a prearranged time) to older people living alone. The caller may also provide news about community activities and help the older person to arrange for other services.

Respite Care: short-term relief provided to family members caring for an older person at home. The care may be given in the home, or at a day care center or health-care facility; the length of service can range from a few hours to a few weeks.

Senior Citizen's Centers: community centers providing educational, recreational, and sometimes health and/or nutritional programs for elderly people.

Sources: AARP (1985); Kane & Kane (1990)

BOX 4.2 *OPEN QUESTIONS*

How should we pay for long-term care?

Financing for long-term care presents an array of contradictions. We know that most older people prefer to receive long-term care in their communities rather than in an institution, that it is now possible to deliver all but the most technical health care in the community, and that most long-term care actually is provided in the community (e.g., Kane & Kane, 1990). Nonetheless, there is much more public funding available to cover institutional than community-based long-term care (Kane & Kane, 1990). We know that Medicare is a publically-funded health insurance program intended primarily to meet the needs of the elderly. However, Medicare provides only the most minimal coverage for long-term care (e.g., Who can afford, 1988; Kane & Kane, 1990).

A large proportion of the costs of nursing home care (and of many kinds of community-based long-term care) is paid for by Medicaid (see Figure 4.5), the federally-funded health insurance program for the poor. In order to qualify for Medicaid coverage, however, older people must exhaust their own financial assets until they meet a state-defined eligibility criterion (e.g., Liu et al., 1990). Perhaps because more long-term care is provided in the community than in nursing homes, and because most nursing home stays are brief, this process of "spending down" to poverty occurs more often in the community than in a nursing home (Liu et al., 1990).

This situation can create tragic scenarios. A woman who has worked all her life, earned a pension, saved money, perhaps bought a home, and taken pride in being financially responsible may be forced into poverty before any public funds are available to

pay for her home health aide. An elderly married couple might face the same situation if the husband falls victim to Alzheimer's disease and must spend years in a nursing home. The couple could consider an even less appealing alternative, of course—divorce as a means of providing financial security for the wife while allowing the husband to qualify for Medicaid (Liu et al., 1990).

Some experts argue that the level of concern over Medicaid spend-down is out of proportion to the scope of the problem. Stephen Moses (1990) recounts the "fallacy of impoverishment:" substantial numbers of nursing home residents receiving Medicaid have actually been able to retain sizeable assets to pass on to their heirs. The late 1980s witnessed the growth of a network of "elder law" experts (attorneys, social workers, and even Medicaid staff) who advise about ways to shelter assets while qualifying for Medicaid. Moses argues that "financially sophisticated people who are accustomed to dealing with attorneys, accountants, and financial planners can find ways to protect their assets and still qualify for Medicaid. Others, with less financial savvy, often lose what little they have before they learn how the system works" (p. 23).

Most would agree that forcing elderly people into poverty so that they can receive financial assistance for long-term care is not fair. Many might also argue that it is not fair for wealthy older people, who can well afford to pay for their own long-term care, to take advantage of public funds intended to cover health care costs for the poor. Perhaps the basic question is the extent to which the government

long-term care in the community? Unfortunately, the answer varies tremendously from one community to another. The spectrum of services seems to be limited only by the imaginations of community planners and service providers—and the availability of local, state, and federal funds (see Box 4.2). Social and political priorities thus have a direct and substantial impact on older peoples' opportunities to maintain independent living despite disabilities. Table 4.1 lists and briefly describes some of the services most often offered.

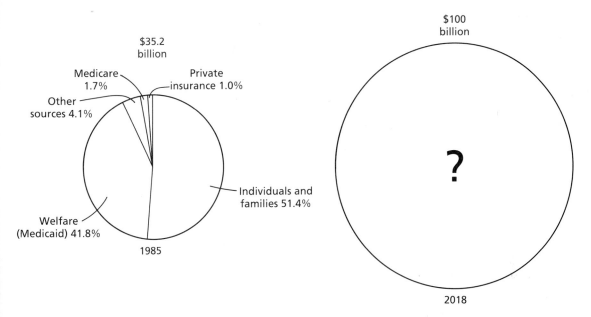

Figure 4.5
Who can afford a nursing home? (Source: "Who can afford a nursing home?", 1988. Copyright 1988 by Consumers Union of United States, Inc., Yonkers, NY 10703. Excerpt by permission from *Consumer Reports*, May 1988.)

should assume financial responsibility for the health care needs of all of its citizens, rather than only the poor.

Several countries—Canada, the United Kingdom, and most of the Scandinavian countries—have answered this challenge with universal coverage for health care, including long-term care (e.g., Kane & Kane, 1990). Such a response, however, contradicts the prevailing sentiment in the United States. With the aging of the "baby boom" generation, the debate over the best way to pay for long-term care will only become more heated.

Despite the growing spectrum of community-based long-term care services, most are not widely used (Kane & Kane, 1990). Steven Wallace (1990) suggests that these services go unused for three reasons. First, any kind of long-term care service obviously has to be *available* before it can be used: an elderly woman cannot use a home-delivered meal service that does not exist in her community. Second, services that are available in the community must be truly *accessible* before older people will use them. If home health services are too costly, or if older people in the community do not know that they exist, then those services will probably not be used.

Finally, the services must be *acceptable* to potential clients before they will be used: there must be at least a minimal match between older adults' preferences for services and the services that a community provides. Wallace (1990) describes problems with the acceptability of homemaker/home health aid services in one community as an example. Some clients were afraid that the aides would steal from them, and others worried about becoming too dependent on the aides. Still others complained of frequent employee turnover, which resulted in constant changes in the aides providing their care. Racial prejudice too was a problem in this program. Some Caucasian older people did not want to have African-American aides, and some African-American aides were harassed by Caucasian clients' neighbors.

Long-term care in nursing homes   Although most long-term care goes on in the community, nursing homes are a critical component of the array of long-term care services. Nursing homes vary from one another in many ways; one of the most important distinctions is in the level of care provided. **Skilled nursing care facilities** offer the most sophisticated level of care. Daily medical records are kept on each resident, round-the-clock nursing is provided, and a collection of medically-related services (e.g., speech therapy, occupational therapy, physical therapy) is available. Although relatively few older people reside in skilled nursing care facilities, this is the only level of nursing home care for which Medicare provides any coverage at all.

Intermediate nursing care facilities are the type of nursing homes in which most institutionalized older people receive care. These facilities are for older people who do not need continual nursing care, but who are unable to live alone. In these facilities, there may be more emphasis on meeting residents' needs for social and intellectual stimulation than their medical needs.

A common misconception is that most older people live in nursing homes. In fact, only about 5 percent of all people over the age of 65 reside in a nursing home at any one time. However, nursing homes touch the lives of far more older people than that statistic would suggest: people over age 65 have about a 40 percent chance of spending some time in a nursing home (Kane & Kane, 1990). Another common misconception is that most people who enter a nursing home never return home. Actually, most nursing home stays are relatively short—usually two or three months (Liu, Doty, & Manton, 1990; Kane & Kane, 1990). About one person out of three is discharged to the community, although some eventually return to a nursing home (Lewis, Cretin, & Kane, 1985).

Which older people are most likely to be in a nursing home? Most nursing home residents are quite old—age 85 or older (Kane & Kane, 1990). Given gender differences in longevity (see Chapter Three), it is not surprising that most residents are women. Older people who have never married, and those who are widowed or divorced, are more likely than married older peo-

In many nursing homes, nurse's aides provide most care to residents.

ple to live in nursing homes. Finally, most nursing home residents are Caucasians.

From the residents' viewpoint, nursing home staff are probably one of the most important features affecting the quality of their lives. Most nursing homes employ RNs, LPNs and nurse's aides; nurse's aides may be the most critical staff members. Usually, nurse's aides are the most numerous members of nursing staff (Kane & Kane, 1990) and usually they provide the most intimate care (Tellis-Nayak & Tellis-Nayak, 1989). Unfortunately, most nurse's aides have little education in general and minimal training for work with the elderly in particular (Kane & Kane, 1990; Tellis-Nayak & Tellis-Nayak, 1989).

Residents are unlikely to be disturbed by nurse's aides' level of training: to the resident, the attitudes that staff members express toward them is far more important than the extent of their training, skills, or knowledge (Tellis-Nayak & Tellis-Nayak, 1989). That attitude may not be as warm or caring as most would hope, however. Tellis-Nayak & Tellis-Nayak (1989) reported a sensitive ethnographic study of nurse's aides, in which they documented the discouraging life circumstances of these women. Most were from low-income families, many were the heads of their own struggling households, and few had many marketable skills or employment options. Like most nurse's aides, these women earned salaries barely above the minimum wage—about the same salary as a fast-food worker.

Given these circumstances, it is easy to imagine that even the best-intentioned nurse's aide might not always express compassion or affection for the frail elderly people under her care. Here again, social context (e.g., the life circumstances of the nurses aides) affects quality of health care for elderly people. It is also not surprising that nationally there is a 100 percent employment turnover in nurse's aides each year (Kane & Kane, 1990). This high turnover rate limits the personal continuity in residents' lives and the quality of care that they receive (Tellis-Nayak & Tellis-Nayak, 1989).

The high staff turnover rate may also make it more difficult for residents to adjust to life in a nursing home. In one study, interpersonal relationships that residents had with someone inside the home (but *not* relationships with family members or friends outside the home) were positively associated with levels of residents' participation in nursing home activities, their satisfaction with the nursing home, and their life satisfaction (Bitzan & Kruzic, 1990). Residents reporting intrainstitutional relationships had formed bonds with a roommate, another resident, a nurse or nurse's aide, or some other member of the staff; those who were ambulatory and who could hear without difficulty were most likely to have formed such relationships after six months in the home.

Certainly, there are many other factors that influence adjustment to a nursing home. Recall that the extent to which residents feel that they have control over their circumstances in a nursing home is associated with adjustment (Rodin & Langer, 1977). Many states have adopted a Bill of Rights for nursing home residents. These documents ensure that residents are not deprived of constitutional civil or legal rights solely because of admission to a nursing home, and give residents personal rights such as the freedom to manage their own finances, to wear their own clothing, to retain and use personal property in their immediate living quarters, to receive and send unopened correspondence, to have unmonitored access to a telephone, to retain a physician's services, to refuse treatment, and to discharge themselves.

Experts advise those in the process of selecting a nursing home to evaluate possible facilities on a wide variety of factors (AARP, 1985). To a large extent, these factors—like many provisions of Residents' Bill of Rights—center around the extent to which the nursing home allows the residents to express their individual preferences and to control their lives. Table 4.2 summarizes the factors that one should evaluate in selecting a nursing home.

Nursing homes that are satisfactory in terms of the criteria listed in Table 4.2 are almost always costly. Although many people assume that Medicare will cover these costs, it is highly unlikely that Medicare will. In the early 1990s, Medicare covered only the cost of care in approved skilled nursing care facilities (rather than the intermediate care facilities in which many more elderly people reside), and then only for a limited number of days (Who Can Afford, 1988; Kane & Kane, 1990). Ironically, Medicare is a health insurance program best suited for acute health care needs, since it provides mainly hospitalization and major medical benefits.

Medicaid, the federal health insurance plan for low-income people of all ages, provides more extensive coverage for care in both skilled and intermediate care facilities, as well as for long-term care services in the community (Who Can Afford, 1988; Kane & Kane, 1990). However, one must have an income less than

Table 4.2
What should you look for in a good nursing home?

Nursing homes are regulated by state and federal authorities, but their general atmosphere, policies, and programs vary. The best ones welcome visits, and employ staff members who are willing to answer questions. The following checklist provides guidelines for comparing facilities when the choice has been narrowed down to a few homes.

Licensing and Certification:

Is the nursing home licensed by the state and a member of the American Health Care Association or the American Association of Homes for the Aging?

Is the home certified for Medicare/Medicaid reimbursement?

Services and Fees:

Does the home offer the level of care (e.g., intermediate, skilled) needed?

Does the home provide complete information on its fees and a sample list of services offered and their costs?

Does the contract clearly specify what services are included in the basic fee?

Does the contract state what action (if any) the home will take if personal finances are depleted and the patient becomes eligible for Medicaid?

Living Environment:

Are the buildings in good repair and the grounds well-kept? Are there places to walk and sit outside? Is the home tastefully decorated? Are residents' rooms well-lighted and comfortably furnished? Are there adequate storage space, and bathing and toilet facilities?

Is the kitchen well-equipped? Are menus varied? Are individual food preferences considered?

Is there a warm atmosphere in the dining room?

Are nurses and attendants visible, treating residents with affection and respect?

Is good custodial care provided to residents who need it?

Resident Activities:

Is there an active social director and a varied program of recreational and social activities?

Are residents neat, comfortably dressed, and active?

Are there planned trips to concerts, exhibits, etc? Is there transportation for residents who want to attend religious services or go shopping?

Are there religious services of the resident's choice, and opportunities for contact with clergy?

Emergency Care:

Are nurses on hand at all times?

Is a physician available in an emergency?

Residents' Rights:

Is the "Residents' Bill of Rights" prominently displayed?

Is there an active resident council to represent the residents' interests?

Staff and Training:

Does the home have (in addition to an administrator) a director of nursing, a full-time social worker, and an activities director?

Does the home require nurses' aides to be trained, and provide on-the-job training?

Source: AARP (1985)

a state-defined eligibility level before Medicaid benefits are available. Box 4.2 (see pp. 102–103) discusses the stresses and indignities that this situation can present. In addition to Medicaid, some funding for community-based long-term care is available through Title XX of the Social Security Act, through Supplemental Security Income (SSI) Program Supplements, and through Title III of the Older Americans Act (Kane & Kane, 1990).

Without a national health insurance system for people of all income levels, a primary option that middle-income elderly people have to prepare for the high cost of long-term care is **private long-term care insurance**. Private insurance companies began offering these plans in the 1980s, and by 1992 dozens of plans were available. Unfortunately, policies varied widely in price and quality (Who Can Afford, 1988). Benefits were sometimes quite limited (both in terms of the amount paid for care per day and the number of days of care), some excluded coverage for victims of Alzheimer's disease and related dementing illnesses, and many did not have built-in protection for inflation. However, some policies are well-planned and can be a good choice for the middle-income older person.

*S*UMMARY

Most young adults enjoy the best health of their lifetimes, although health in early adulthood varies according to race and gender. Although health is influenced by heredity, choices that young adults make concerning diet, exercise, stress management, sexual behavior, and the use of alcohol and other drugs can have long-term health consequences.

In middle and later adulthood, the most common kinds of illness shift from acute problems to chronic conditions. Causes of death in later adulthood parallel the more common chronic illnesses, varying by race and ethnicity. Although Caucasians have greater life expectancy throughout most of the life span than do African-Americans and most other minority groups, this pattern reverses in old age.

Many physicians express negative attitudes toward older patients. But compared to younger patients, older patients may ask less of their physicians. Most long-term care is provided in the community; the kinds of programs available vary from one community to the next. Accessibility and acceptability, in addition to availability, affect the likelihood of program use.

Long-term care may also be provided in a nursing home. Generally, most nursing home residents are quite old, female, unmarried, and Caucasian. The relationships that residents may form with staff members and others in the home, affect residents' adjustment to the home. Other factors affecting adjustment are the extent of control that residents believe they have over the circumstances of their daily life, as well as such things as the quality of the physical plant, recreational and social activities, opportunities for participation in the community, and the existence of an active resident council.

Medicare provides hospitalization and major medical benefits but limited coverage for long-term care (either in a nursing home or in the community). Medicaid provides far more extensive coverage for nursing home care and for long-term care in the community. Currently, the best way to finance long-term care is being debated at the federal level.

KEY TERMS

Acquired immunodeficiency syndrome (AIDS)
Adult day care
Baltimore Longitudinal Study
Chronic diseases
Comorbidity
Emergency response systems
Formal health care
Friendly visiting
Geriatric medicine
Home care
Informal care
Intermediate nursing care facilities
Long-term care
Medicaid

Medicare
Nutrition services
Private long-term care insurance
Racial mortality crossover phenomenon
Respite care
Self-care
Senior citizen's centers
Sexually transmitted diseases (STDs)
Skilled nursing care facilities
Stress
Telephone reassurance
Type "A" behavior pattern
Type "B" behavior pattern

SUGGESTIONS FOR FURTHER READING

Bennett, W. I., Goldfinger, S. E., & Johnson, G. T. (Eds.). (1987). *Your Good Health: How to Stay Well and What to Do When You're Not*. Cambridge, MA: Harvard University Press.

Birren, J. E., & Livingston, J. (Eds.) (1985). *Cognition, Stress, and Aging*. Englewood Cliffs, NJ: Prentice Hall.

Markides, K. S. (Ed.). (1989). *Aging and Health: Perspectives on Gender, Race, Ethnicity, and Class*. Newbury Park, CA: Sage Publications.

Riley, M. W., Matarazzo, J. D., & Baum, A. (1987). *Perspectives in Behavioral Medicine: The Aging Dimension*. Hillsdale, NJ: Lawrence Erlbaum Associates.

U.S. Department of Health and Human Services. (n.d.). *Age Words: A Glossary on Health and Aging*. Bethesda, MD: National Institutes of Health.

CHAPTER FIVE

BASIC COGNITIVE PROCESSES

Does the world seem "different" as you get older? Do things look, sound, and feel different? Do capacities for attention and response change? This chapter addresses these fundamental aspects of cognitive functioning, and how these processes change with age. Themes emphasized throughout the chapter are the practical consequences of these changes and the ways in which interventions can minimize their impacts. The chapter opens with an overview of sensation and perception—the psychophysiological means of gathering information about the world. Changes in vision and hearing are emphasized, although we also examine age-related changes in taste and smell, pain perception, and the sense of balance.

Next, we examine basic cognitive processes such as attention, arousal, reaction time, and psychomotor performance. Much of the research on age differences in these areas may initially seem dry; however, the chapter identifies ways in which age differences in these processes can have important consequences for adults' experiences at work and in educational settings, and for mobility and everyday life in old age.

Finally, we consider possible responses to these age-related changes. Because the ways in which these basic processes change with age are generally in the direction of less effective or less rapid functioning, it is important to identify ways in which the consequences of these changes can be minimized.

Possible interventions range from prosthetic devices to redesign of the home, workplace, and highways.

Questions to consider while reading the chapter include:

How do vision and hearing normally change in middle and later adulthood? What are practical consequences of these changes?

How do the senses of taste and smell change in old age? What age differences are apparent in the perception of pain, and in the kinesthetic and vestibular senses?

How do various measures of attention change with age? How do reaction time and psychomotor performance change with age? What factors in addition to age affect speed of reaction time and psychomotor performance?

How can age differences in perception and basic intellectual processes influence occupational and educational performance? How can these age differences affect mobility and everyday life in old age? In what ways can the environment be adapted to minimize the impact of age changes in perception and basic intellectual processes?

AGE-RELATED CHANGES IN SENSATION AND PERCEPTION

Sensation versus perception

Throughout the lifespan, **sensation** and **perception** serve as vital bridges to the world around us. Sensation is the physical stimulation of sensory organs and the transmission of that stimulation through the nervous system. Perception, on the other hand, is the interpretation and attribution of meaning to these neural messages. In reading this book, the mechanisms through which the eye detects the dark lines on the white page and transmits this information to appropriate centers in the brain are sensory processes. Perception occurs as you recognize these patterns as letters and words. Thus, both sensation and perception provide information about the world, and thereby supply a basis for survival and adaptation.

Vision and hearing in early adulthood

As is the case for health, young adulthood is a period of optimal sensory and perceptual functioning. The organs involved in vision and hearing do show measurable changes by early adulthood, but few young adults notice these changes. In middle childhood, the lens of the eye begins to stiffen and become less able to precisely focus images on the visual sensory cells of the retina. Although most young adults do not notice this stiffening, it continues throughout adulthood and generally is discernible by the forties or fifties.

Similarly, there is a very gradual loss of hearing sensitivity during adulthood, perhaps reflecting atrophy of nervous tissue at the basal turn of the inner ear (Bromley, 1974; Corso, 1977; Fozard, 1990; Olsho, Harkins, & Lenhardt, 1985). This diminished hearing, too, is rarely noticeable until much later in adult-hood—usually the sixties or later. Men usually have a larger and more rapid loss of hearing sensitivity than do women, and city dwellers and industrial workers generally experience a greater loss than have individuals living and working in rural settings (McFarland, 1968; Olsho et al., 1985). More generally, this age-related decrease in hearing sensitivity varies from one society to an-other, apparently reflecting cultural differences in levels of "noise pollution." The *Diversity in Adulthood* box (see pp. 114–115) examines these differences in greater detail.

In light of the minimal changes in sensory organs that occur in early adulthood, it is not surprising that this period of the life span is a time of peak performance on many perceptual tasks (Kline & Scheiber, 1985). Young adults do well on tasks requiring them to recognize incomplete forms (perceptual closure), and on tasks in which they must recognize pictures of objects presented for fractions of a second (speed of recognition). There are, however, slight decreases after adolescence in performance on tasks requiring discrimination of parts or items from their context (part-whole differentiation) and on tasks requiring judgments about the orientation of objects without the aid of contextual cues (spatial orientation) (Comalli, 1970; Comalli, Wapner, & Werner, 1959).

Normal age-related changes in vision

Both the structure and the functioning of the eye change throughout adult-hood; most people first notice these changes during their forties or fifties. Major structures that change with age include the **lens**, the **ciliary body,** the **iris**, and the **pupil**; these structures are illustrated in Figure 5.1. The lens is a curved structure located near the front of the eye. Like a camera lens, the lens in the eye focuses images on sensory cells in the **retina**, the innermost layer of the eye. The ciliary body includes muscles, connective tissue, and blood vessels, and is attached to the lens. Through the action of muscles in the ciliary body, the lens becomes thicker or thinner in order to focus images on the retina.

Comprised of concentric layers of transparent fibers, the lens grows with age (e.g., Spence, 1989; Whitbourne, 1985). New fibers are continually formed around the outer layer of the lens, while older fibers are pushed toward the center. Instead of replacing old cells, then, new cells are added to the existing structure of the lens. Consequently, the lens becomes thicker, flatter, heavier, and larger with age. These changes also make the lens stiffer and less able to change shape in order to focus images on the retina. Finally, the lens yellows as it ages.

At the same time, the ciliary body changes. The muscles of the ciliary body increase in mass in the thirties, but begin to lose mass in the mid-forties (Spence, 1989; Whitbourne, 1985). Some believe that the initial increase in mass stems from the greater effort needed to change the shape of the stiffening lens. The later loss of ciliary muscle mass reflects atrophy from disuse, when the lens

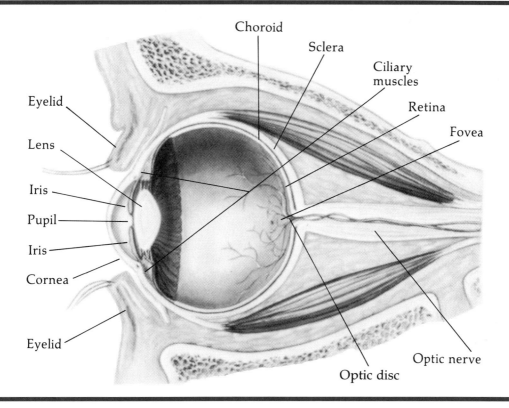

Figure 5.1
Major structures of the eye. (Source: Margaret W. Matlin, *Sensation and Perception*,
2nd edition. Copyright © 1988, by Allyn and Bacon. Reprinted with permission.)

becomes so stiff that its shape can barely be transformed at all (Whitbourne,
1985).

There are also changes in the iris (the round, pigmented muscular diaphragm of the eye) and the pupil (the round opening in the center of the eye
through which light enters). These structures react reflexively to changes in
lighting. In bright light, the iris contracts and the pupil becomes smaller so that
less surrounding light enters the eye. Conversely, the iris expands and the pupil
becomes larger in dim light, so that more available light enters the eye. Beginning in adolescence and continuing throughout adulthood, the iris dilator
muscles atrophy and the maximum size of the pupil therefore decreases. These
changes reduce the amount of light entering the eye and reaching the retina.
Finally, the fluid inside the eye, the **vitreous humor**, becomes more opaque
with aging; this change also reduces the amount of light reaching the retina
(Spence, 1989).

BOX 5.1 **Diversity in Adulthood**

Variation in the extent of decreased auditory sensitivity

This chapter describes one of the consequences of normal aging—a gradual loss of auditory sensitivity. This loss is most apparent for sounds of relatively high pitch, including sounds in the range of most conversational speech. Even though this decrease in hearing sensitivity is a universal part of the aging process, there are individual differences in its rate and extent.

One dimension of these differences, as we have noted, is gender. On the average, American women experience a less marked loss of hearing than American men do. There are also cultural differences in the extent of diminished auditory sensitivity in old age; these differences are illustrated in Figure 5.2.

As you can see in Figure 5.2, Africans retain much more of their hearing in old age than Americans; these older Africans were members

of a Sudan tribe (the Mabaans) who had spent their lives in an environment exceptionally free of noise (McFarland, 1968). Figure 5.2 also reveals that older Americans who had a life history of low exposure to noise (e.g., rural dwellers) retained more of their hearing in old age than did older Americans with a life history of extensive noise exposure (e.g., factory workers) (Baltes, Reese, & Nesselroade, 1977; Corso, 1977).

Thus, this universal age-related trend does not unfold uniformly in all individuals. Depending on life history (in particular, one's history of noise exposure), hearing may diminish quite a lot or very little in old age. It is also possible that culture affects the extent of other age-related perceptual changes. For example, we may eventually find that widespread use of microcomputers at

---

These changes in the structure and functioning of the eye lead to changes in vision. As the lens becomes stiffer and flatter, and as the muscles in the ciliary body weaken, the lens loses its capacity to focus nearby objects on the retina. Consequently, nearly everyone becomes farsighted after about age 40. This age-related change in vision is called **presbyopia**. Sadly, even young adults who are nearsighted acquire presbyopia as they get older. The increased density of the lens also leads to increased susceptibility to glare after about age 40 (Whitbourne, 1985). Because of the changes in the iris, pupil, and vitreous humor, middle-aged and older adults need more light than young adults for comfortable reading or close work.

Changes in the eye and vision continue in later adulthood. Some changes are apparent to the observer: fat and elastic tissue is lost from around the eyes, and the skin in the eyelids grows thinner in old age (Spence, 1989). These changes give some older people's eyes a sunken appearance, and they contribute to the formation of wrinkles around the eyes. Typically, a white or yellowish ring forms on the outer circumference of the cornea of older people (Spence, 1989); this ring is called the **arcus senilis**.

Most changes, though, are in the functioning of the eye rather than in its appearance. Compared to younger adults, older people have a higher **absolute**

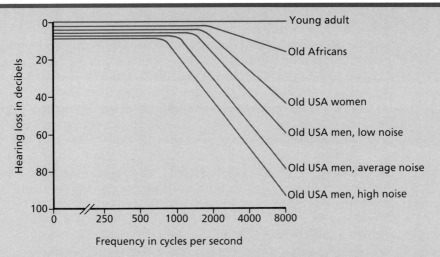

Figure 5.2

Group differences in hearing loss in old age. (Source: P. B. Baltes, H. W. Reese, & J. R. Nesselroade, *Life-Span Developmental Psychology: Introduction to Research Methods.* Copyright © 1977 by Wadsworth Publishing Company, Inc. Reprinted by permission of Brooks/Cole Publishing Company, Pacific Grove, CA 93950.)

home and at work may result in earlier appearance of presbyopia, or in the emergence of other problems. Clearly, culture leaves its imprint on normal, universal aspects of aging through the types of occupations, communities, and lifestyles that the culture fosters.

threshold: they need more light than younger people do in order to see well (e.g., Fozard, 1990; McFarland, 1968). **Dark adaptation**, the process through which the eye adapts to decreased light and allows you to see in the dark, occurs more slowly for older than for younger adults (Fozard, 1990; Kline & Scheiber, 1985). **Contrast sensitivity**, the ability to discriminate alternating light and dark bars of a test pattern, decreases with age; so, too, the ability to detect details in what we see, **visual acuity**, declines with age (Fozard, 1990). Similarly, **dynamic visual acuity (DVA)**, the ability to detect features of moving targets (such as cars moving on a highway), also decreases as one grows older (Long & Crambert, 1990).

Finally, older people have a more restricted field of view than younger adults do (Scailfa, Kline, & Lyman, 1987). Thus, it is more difficult for older adults to detect an object when it is on the periphery of their field of vision (as compared to when they are looking directly at the target), particularly if the visual display is cluttered. Putting it less technically, older adults are at a disadvantage when they have to see something out of the "corner of their eye" when they are looking at a spectacle crowded with many people and objects.

What do these age-related changes mean on a concrete level? One recent survey identified common visual demands that are particularly troublesome for older adults. These demands include reading scrolling TV displays (difficult primarily because of the decrease in DVA), driving in twilight or darkness (difficult because of slowed dark adaptation and susceptibility to glare), and reading small print (difficult because of decreased visual acuity) (Kosnik, Winslow, Kline, Rasinski, & Sekuler, 1988). Other research shows that older adults sometimes have difficulty distinguishing faces from one another, as well as signs and objects, under low levels of light; these problems stem primarily from decreased contrast sensitivity (e.g., Owsley & Sloane, 1987; Sekuler, Owsley, & Hukman, 1982).

Certainly, these impairments would frustrate an older person who has always enjoyed a high level of mobility and social interaction, or avid reading and television viewing. Some of these tasks can be made easier with relatively little effort on the individual level: providing better lighting in the home and workplace is a straightforward and economical intervention that anyone can take in her home and office. Other steps needed to ease these demands, though, call for action on a broader level. Providing better lighting on highways would make night driving easier for elderly people (as well as for younger adults), but would be a costly step on a national level. If newspapers and telephone books were printed in larger type, they would be easier for middle-aged and older people to read, but also bulkier and more expensive. If

Because of normal age-related changes in the eye, reading small print becomes increasingly difficult with age.

television producers and advertisers avoided the use of scrolling displays, they would be forced to identify new ways of presenting information—but might be rewarded if older viewers were better able to absorb the information thus presented.

Pathological age-related changes in vision

Still other changes in vision, although not a part of normal aging, occur more often in old age than earlier in life. Figure 5.3 illustrates the relative frequency of some of these impairments at various ages. The incidence of blindness increases with age: in over half of the cases in one study, the onset of blindness occurred after the age of 65 (Spence, 1989). One of the more frequent causes of blindness in old age is **glaucoma**, an eye disease that most often strikes after age 40 (Spence, 1989). Glaucoma occurs when pressure builds up within the eye

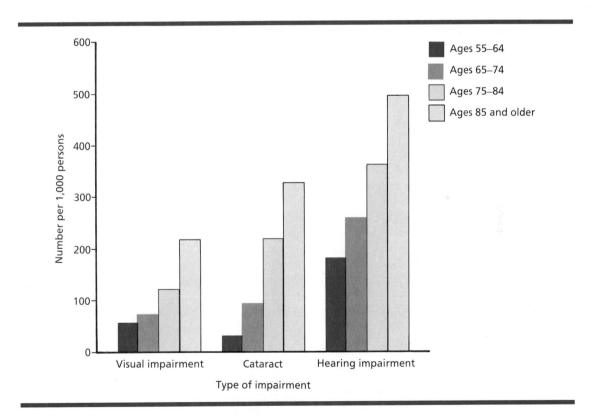

Figure 5.3
Average annual rates of selected sensory impairments among elderly adults.
(Source: USDHHS, 1986a.)

as a result of insufficient drainage of fluid from within the eye. This pressure can squeeze blood vessels within the eye and eventually cause the retina to degenerate. Glaucoma can be treated, but can lead to blindness if untreated; thus, glaucoma screening tests are a critical preventative health measure for middle-aged and older adults.

A more common, but still pathological, change in vision in old age is the development of **cataracts**. Cataracts occur when the lens becomes clouded to the point that vision is impaired, and about 90 percent of those over age 70 are believed to have some degree of cataract formation (Spence, 1989). Cataracts are fairly easily treated through outpatient surgery to remove the opaque lens, followed by a lens implant (or use of special contact lenses or glasses).

Diabetic retinopathy is a complication of diabetes whose incidence increases with age (e.g., Heckheimer, 1989). In this disease, the capillaries and blood vessels supplying the retina are damaged, and hemorrhages may occur in the eye. Scar tissue can then form on the retina, causing detachment and subsequent blindness.

Normal age-related changes in hearing

When you hear, structures in the ear have transformed sound waves into nerve impulses that the brain interprets as sound. Figure 5.4 illustrates major structures in the ear involved in this process. The outer ear collects sound waves and directs them toward the **tympanic membrane** (eardrum), which forms a boundary of the middle ear. Sound waves cause the tympanic membrane to vibrate, which in turn causes small bones in the middle ear to push against the **oval window**, a boundary of the inner ear. This pressure produces waves in fluids contained in the inner ear, and these waves activate regions of a structure called the **spiral organ** within the cochlea; the region of the spiral organ activated depends upon the frequency of the sound. Activation of the spiral organ, finally, causes nerve impulses to be transmitted to the brain via the **vestibulocochlear nerve**, or auditory nerve.

The structures of the ear change in several ways with age. Most middle-aged adults show some degeneration of cells in the spiral organ and associated nerve cells. This degeneration stems from thickening of the walls of the capillaries supplying the area, which diminishes the nutrients supplied to the organ (Spence, 1989). In addition, most people show some degeneration of the vestibulocochlear nerve after age 45; both hearing and balance are affected (Spence, 1989).

These changes result in a measurable hearing loss called **presbycusis**; there are four forms of presbycusis (Whitbourne, 1985). In *sensory presbycusis*, greatest hearing loss occurs in high frequencies, but speech understanding remains undisturbed; sensory presbycusis stems from damage to the spiral organ. *Neural presbycusis*, which more often occurs in old age than in middle adulthood, is characterized by difficulty with speech discrimination; this form of presbycusis is attributed to degeneration of neural fibers. Individuals suffer-

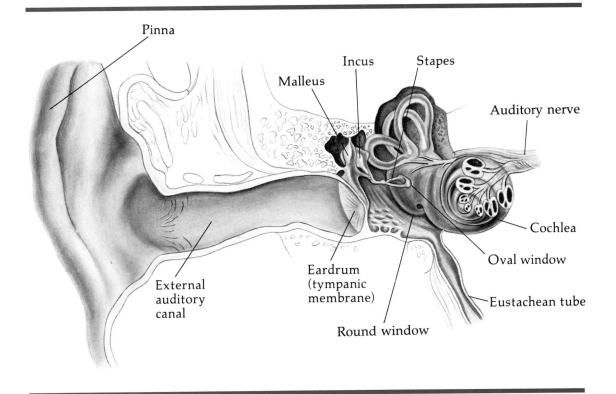

Figure 5.4
Major structures of the ear. (Source:Margaret W. Matlin, *Sensation and Perception*,
2nd edition. Copyright © 1988, by Allyn and Bacon. Reprinted with permission.)

ing from *strial presbycusis* have reduced sensitivity to sounds of all frequencies;
this form of hearing loss results from atrophy of the vessels supplying blood to
inner ear structures. Finally, in *mechanical presbycusis*, which scientists believe
is a consequence of inadequate vibration of the tympanic membrane, hearing
sensitivity gradually decreases as sound frequency increases. After age 50, most
people (approximately 70 percent) have some form of presbycusis to a greater
or lesser extent (Fozard, 1990; Olsho, Harkins, & Lenhardt, 1985).

Although the hearing loss that occurs by middle adulthood is measurable,
few people notice this change until later in adulthood. Speech understanding,
for example, remains largely intact under normal listening conditions. Under
adverse conditions (e.g., interruptions in the speech, rapid speech, competition
from background noises), however, middle-aged adults may have difficulty
understanding speech (Whitbourne, 1985). And older adults even more often
experience difficulty hearing and understanding speech—again, especially

when the speech is interrupted or competing with background noise (as in a room full of people, or when a noisy appliance is operating) or when the speaker talks quickly (e.g., Fozard, 1990).

Perhaps the most serious consequence of presbycusis is its potential impact on social interaction in old age. If an older woman constantly has to ask her family and friends to speak more loudly, or to repeat what they have said, she may begin to feel embarrassed. Her companions may become frustrated at the effort required for even a simple conversation. The woman may begin to avoid social gatherings and conversations altogether; eventually, her self-concept and psychological adjustment could be affected (Whitbourne, 1985). Hearing loss can also have other practical effects. Most people probably take for granted the extent to which sounds alert us to a malfunctioning appliance (is the refrigerator running constantly?) or to safety hazards (the sound of approaching cars at an intersection).

Pathological age-related changes in hearing

Like blindness, deafness is not a normal consequence of aging but does occur more often in old age than earlier in the life span (see Figure 5.2). Spence (1989) distinguishes two types of deafness: **conductive deafness** and **nerve deafness**. When the transmission of sound waves through the external or middle ear is impaired, an individual suffers from conductive deafness. This blockage may be due to hardened earwax or some other foreign object, an inflamed eardrum, calcified joints in the small bones in the middle ear, or a thickened oval window. In this type of deafness, the sensory receptor cells in the spiral organ are not damaged; thus, hearing aids that modify the path through which sound waves reach these receptor cells can help.

In nerve deafness, however, the receptor cells themselves or the cells that transmit their messages to the central nervous system are damaged. Most hearing aids cannot help in these cases, but a procedure called a **cochlear implant** can help (Spence, 1989). A cochlear implant fits the individual with a small microphone that acts as an "artificial ear;" the microphone transmits signals to a stimulator unit, usually worn on the belt. These signals are then converted to electrical signals that are transmitted to an implanted electrode; the electrode stimulates activity in the vestibulocochlear nerve. This activity is interpreted as sound, although the sounds are different from those perceived by an individual with normal hearing.

Normal age-related changes in taste and smell

Sometimes older people remark that food just doesn't taste as good as it used to. Although the evidence is not as consistent as with vision and hearing, there are decreases in both taste and olfactory sensitivity with increasing age. Some researchers report a gradual and continuous decrease in the number of taste buds beginning in early adulthood, although others report little if any decrease prior to age 75 (Spence, 1989). It is clear, though, that older adults do have less sensitivity to taste than do young adults (e.g., Spence, 1989; Whitbourne, 1985). This age difference probably reflects fewer taste buds, as well as decreased saliva secretion, the formation of fissures on the tongue, and age-related changes in the processing of taste sensations in the central nervous system (Spence, 1989).

Age-related changes in the sense of smell probably also contribute to older individuals' complaints that tastes are dulled. You have probably noticed that food has less flavor when you have a bad cold—or that a tempting aroma enhances the taste of food. Some studies show that olfactory sensory receptor cells decrease in number with increasing age (e.g., Spence, 1989). Older people, compared to young adults, have a higher threshold for detecting odors and have greater difficulty identifying specific odors (Stevens & Crain, 1987).

Normal age-related changes in pain perception

It is difficult to pinpoint the extent to which aging changes pain sensitivity, because there are many sources of individual differences in pain perception throughout the life span. The experience of pain depends not only on the kind of stimulation experienced, and the part of the body stimulated, but on the situation in which pain is experienced and on culturally-based orientations to pain (Kenshalo, 1977). And, experimental research on pain sensitivity with humans is difficult to conduct for ethical reasons. The evidence that we do have suggests that people normally become less sensitive to pain as they get older (e.g., Kenshalo, 1977; Whitbourne, 1985). Nonetheless, clinical researchers maintain that such an age difference has little practical impact for the management of chronic pain in young and elderly patients (Sorkin, Rudy, Hanlon, Turn, & Stieg, 1990).

Normal age-related changes in the vestibular system and kinesthesis

The **vestibular system** is a collection of organs, located primarily in the inner ear and cerebellum, providing the sense of balance and spatial orientation. **Kinesthesis** is the capacity to sense the position of various parts of the body, and movement of the limbs and other body parts. Both the vestibular system and kinesthesis show some changes with age, and these changes may interfere with balance and mobility in old age.

In the vestibular system, degenerative changes occur both in the sensory systems of the inner ear as well as in the associated areas of the central nervous system (Ochs, Newberry, Lenhardt, & Harkins, 1985). **Presbystasis**, a loss of equilibrium in old age, is the result. Research on age differences in kinesthesis reveals that older subjects make more errors in detecting "passive movement" of the knee and hip joints (Ochs et al., 1985); in passive movement, the individual does not move, but is in a moving vehicle or apparatus. There is little evidence of age differences in "active movement," in which the individual moves her limbs or body, prior to age 85 (Ochs et al., 1985).

The most important effect of age-related changes in vestibular and kinesthetic functioning is on mobility. Ochs and his colleagues (1985) report that "with advancing age, falls occur with increased frequency and are life-threatening events, especially for those 75 and older. In many cases, falls and their consequences result in limited functional mobility, dependence on family members for assistance, and possible institutionalization" (p. 379). These scholars further explain that most falls in old age can be traced to either extrinsic factors—environmental hazards such as poorly lit terrain, loose rugs, slippery floors, and so forth—or to intrinsic factors such as physical changes—including those in the vestibular system or kinesthesis. Of course, the intrinsic changes in the vestibular system and kinesthesis magnify the hazards of extrinsic factors.

BASIC COGNITIVE FUNCTIONING: RESEARCH ON AGE DIFFERENCES

Age differences in attention and arousal

The next two chapters review research documenting age differences and age changes in various aspects of intellectual performance—such tasks as learning new material, remembering what you have learned, and solving problems. In much of this research, the older participants do not perform as well as the younger subjects. A wide variety of explanations for these age differences have been offered; among these explanations are age differences in attention and arousal (e.g. Plude, in press; Plude & Murphy, in press).

We are constantly bombarded with stimuli—some coming from the environment (the sound of a lawn mower outside the window, the scent of dinner cooking, etc.) and others originating within us (feeling hungry, a mosquito bite in an unreachable spot, etc.). Attention is the psychophysiological process that governs which of these many stimuli are processed. To the extent that you can concentrate on reading this book, and not on your neighbor's stereo, you can thank your capacity for attention. Many psychologists believe that attention is a limited commodity that supports other cognitive processes, such as learning, thinking, and reasoning (e.g., McDowd & Birren, 1990).

Research examining age differences in attention has generally focused on four aspects of attention. In studies of **selective attention**, the goal is to learn whether older and younger adults differ in their ability to ignore information that is irrelevant for completing a task, and to only attend to the relevant information. One task requires subjects to sort cards containing information both relevant and irrelevant to the sorting criteria. Another is a **dichotic listening task**, in which an individual hears two different, simultaneous recordings played to the right and left ear. For example, a sequence of letters might be played to the left ear and a sequence of numbers played to the right ear. The listener must repeat a portion of the information that the experimenter designates as a target (e.g., all the vowels). On most selective attention tasks, older adults' performance is hampered more than younger adults by the presence of the irrelevant information (Rabbitt, 1965).

Researchers also study age differences in **divided attention**, the processes through which attention is controlled to carry out two tasks simultaneously. You draw upon this process when you attempt to write a check while conversing with a sales clerk, or to talk on the telephone while reading mail. Evidence in this area is consistent: for all but the simplest of tasks, older people's task performance suffers more than young adults' does under conditions of divided attention (McDowd & Birren, 1990). Aging apparently is associated with an increase in distractibility.

In studies of **attention switching**, scientists examine the consequences of alternately monitoring two or more sources of input. This process occurs when you attempt to maintain two or more streams of thought; one might be at the forefront of your attention momentarily, but the other is also in mind. When you walk into the den to get your glasses, you draw on this capacity: you are thinking about both the intention of retrieving an object and the goal of reaching a location. (If you have ever walked into a room and forgotten why you went there in the first place, you have witnessed a failure of attention switching). In contrast to the other aspects of attention, there seem to be few if any age-related changes in capacity for attention switching (McDowd & Birren, 1990).

Finally, **sustained attention**, or vigilance, is the capacity to maintain concentration on a task over an extended period of time. When you drive across the country or when you proofread a paper for typos, you are drawing on sustained attention. The tasks that researchers typically use to study sustained attention require participants to continually monitor a source of information (e.g., a computer screen, a tape recording) in order to report critical target items (e.g., the letter "q," the number 3) that occur infrequently and unpredictably. When anyone performs such a task, their attention wanes as time goes by; this phenomenon is called *vigilance decrement*. The rate and extent of the vigilance decrement do not differ for young and older adults, although older adults show less accurate performance from the outset of the task (McDowd & Birren, 1990; Parasuraman, Nestor, & Greenwood, 1989).

Furthermore, older people may be less able than young adults to use sustained attention effectively. Molander & Backman (1989) compared young and older miniature golfers' performance under both low-stress training conditions and higher-stress competition conditions. In addition to comparing the number of golf strokes under both conditions, the researchers measured participants' heart rates (an index of attention) during the critical phase when the golfers were preparing for and concentrating on striking the ball and asked them to report the mental strategies that they had used during play.

The young and older golfers apparently used different attentional strategies, as reflected in heart rate. Young golfers (whose heart rates decelerated) said that they had minimized their conscious internal activity: they had noted the obstacles on the green and the angle of the club, but otherwise used a "blank mind" strategy and struck the ball when it "felt right." In contrast, older golfers (whose heart rates accelerated) reported an internal attention strategy: they consciously thought through all steps needed to make a good shot, and did not strike the ball until they had completed this review. The young golfers used fewer shots, especially in the competition condition. Molander & Backman (1989) suggested that the older golfers' means of sustaining attention was more effortful, and therefore less effective, under the stress of competition. Because age and strategy type were confounded in this study, however, we do not know whether older golfers would have benefited from using the younger golfers' strategy.

In attempting to explain why older adults do not perform as well under circumstances requiring sustained attention, some scholars have referred to age differences in arousal level. According to the **arousal hypothesis**, older adults may be less aroused than young adults during much of the day. When researchers compare **electroencephalograms (EEGs)** measuring brain wave activity for young and older adults, the older adults' recordings show features that are characteristic of less alert mental states (e.g., Prinz, Dustman, & Emmerson, 1990). That lower level of arousal may be why older adults do not do as well on vigilance tasks (Prinz et al., 1990).

Why would older people be less alert than younger people? Age differences in sleep patterns might provide an answer. Older people generally do not sleep as well as young adults. Although the total amount of nighttime sleep and of REM sleep (when dreaming is believed to occur) do not differ for young and older adults, older people experience less deep sleep and more episodes of waking each night (Prinz et al., 1990). Perhaps, then, the episodes of nighttime waking that most older people experience impair alertness during the day.

In an extreme case, Jacobs, Ancoli-Israel, Parker, & Kripke (1989) found that nursing home residents experienced both sleep and wakefulness during *each* hour of a 24-hour period of continuous recording. They suggested that the daytime sleeping could be an effort to compensate for an interrupted night's sleep. It is also possible that the residents' sleep patterns were due to overmedication or inadequate stimulation in the environment.

A related hypothesis holds that older adults, like young children, are *over*aroused in a sense: they may be less able to inhibit excessive or irrelevant central nervous system excitation (Prinz et al., 1990). If that is the case, then older people would be less capable of maintaining an optimal balance of neural excitation and inhibition. EEGs also provide evidence of an age-related weakening of inhibitory control (Woodruff, 1985). The net impact could be greater difficulty in concentrating and sustaining attention in old age.

Taking these consequences a step further, age differences in attention and concentration themselves may explain some of the age differences in problem solving and learning and memory performance that are examined in the next two chapters (e.g., Plude, in press; Plude & Murphy, in press). You are not likely to remember information or actions that you do not pay attention to in the first place; for example, you probably do not remember putting away your toothbrush this morning. So, older people's performances on learning and memory tasks may differ from younger adults' performances because of age differences in attention and arousal.

Age differences in reaction time and psychomotor skills

One of the most reliable and well-documented age-related changes is a general slowing of behavior, including lengthened reaction time and slowed psychomotor performance (Birren, 1964; Salthouse, 1985). When psychologists study **reaction time**, they are interested in determining how long it takes an individual to respond to some kind of stimulus. The tasks used are sometimes quite simple, as when a participant must press a key as soon as a light comes on. Here, there is only one possible stimulus to be detected and only one possible response to be made. Other times, the tasks are more complex. Choice reaction time tasks, for example, require the individual to make one response when one stimulus appears but another response when another stimulus appears. Typing is a familiar example of a choice reaction time task.

Average reaction time lengthens with increasing age for even simple reaction time tasks (e.g., Spirduso & Macrae, 1990; Wilkinson & Allison, 1989). However, there are substantial individual differences within age groups in simple reaction time, so that an individual 70-year-old might respond more quickly than an individual 30-year-old (e.g., Wilkinson & Allison, 1989). And, many factors other than age are associated with reaction time. Reaction time is influenced by the type of response to the stimulus that is required. Most research shows that people of all ages make verbal responses more rapidly than manual responses (e.g., Salthouse, 1985; Spirduso & MacRae, 1990), although there are exceptions (e.g., Baron & Journey, 1989).

Not surprisingly, reaction time increases as the complexity of the task increases; the difference between young and older peoples' reaction times, too, increase with task complexity (Cerella, 1985; Spirduso & MacRae, 1990). Reaction time—and the extent of age differences in reaction time—are also affected by stimulus-response compatibility (Spirduso & MacRae, 1990). The less "natural" a required response seems for a stimulus, the longer reaction time will be and the greater the age difference in reaction time will be. In the Stroop (1935) effect, for example, subjects who are required to read color names that are printed in colors *other than* the name (e.g., "red" printed in blue, "blue" printed in green, "yellow" printed in red, etc.), respond more slowly than if the color names are printed in their own color, or in black ink.

Why do people respond more slowly as they get older? Although we might be quick to assume that age-related changes in sensation, perception, and motor capacities (e.g., presbyopia, increased stiffness, reduced muscular strength) provide an answer, this is not the case. Compared to the time required for the mental processes of interpretation, association, and decision, the time required for sensory/perceptual processes and the actual motor response is quite small (e.g., Botwinick & Thompson, 1966). The slowing, then, is apparently related to changes in the "central" mental aspect of reaction time rather than in the "peripheral" sensory and motor aspects. At this time, though, scientists cannot pinpoint exactly how these central aspects are affected.

There are some promising clues, however. Aerobic exercise can decrease reaction time, and physically fit older people may have shorter reaction times than less fit young adults (e.g., Spirduso & MacRae, 1990). Because exercise increases blood flow to the brain, this information suggests that lengthened reaction time may be a consequence of neural "malnutrition." It is also possible that the age differences in arousal (see above) can account for age differences in reaction time, since reaction time tasks demand an optimal level of arousal for a quick response (Marsh & Thompson, 1977). And, motivation may be important: in one study, researchers shortened young and older subjects' reaction times—and decreased the age difference in reaction time—by making payment for participation partially contingent on speed of response (Baron & Mattila, 1989).

An area of performance closely related to reaction time is that of psychomotor skills. **Psychomotor skills** are a broad category of actions, all of which require dexterity and which usually improve with practice. Examples include sorting cards, dialing a telephone, chopping onions, and buttoning a shirt. Like reaction time, performance of psychomotor skills slows with increasing age (e.g. Salthouse, 1985; Spirduso & MacRae, 1990). Although virtually all psychologists agree that this slowing occurs, several competing explanations have been proposed (Salthouse, 1985).

As Salthouse (1985) explained in a recent review, some believe that there are age differences in the approach to psychomotor tasks, while others maintain that young and older adults differ in the way in which psychomotor skills are mentally represented and regulated. Another possibility is that young adults' working memory capacity (i.e., ability to access and use task-relevant information) exceeds that of older adults, or that young adults are more adept at managing psychomotor tasks in the face of conflicting cognitive demands. Finally, some assert that age-related changes in neurological structures (e.g., the gradual loss of brain mass described in Chapter Three, see p. 57) can explain psychomotor slowing with age.

Although the explanation for psychomotor slowing can be debated, it is clear that young adults outperform older adults on virtually all psychomotor tasks that have been studied in the laboratory (e.g., Salthouse, 1985). Because this slowing has been demonstrated so broadly, the unusual situations in which a difference in young and older adults' speed of psychomotor performance does *not* appear may clarify the nature of psychomotor slowing.

In 1985, Salthouse identified three situations in which no age differences in speed of psychomotor performance had been identified. First, when healthy, active middle-aged or older adults are compared with less healthy, less fit young adults, age differences in speed of psychomotor performance are minimal. Second, when psychomotor performance is measured so that subjects respond vocally, rather than manually, age differences are minimized.

Third, and perhaps most important, age differences are reduced dramatically when young, middle-aged, and older adults are compared on a psychomotor task with which all have had extensive practice (Salthouse, 1985). For example, Salthouse (1984) points out that a stenographer who types 60 words per minute would execute nearly 5000 keystrokes in approximately 15 minutes of typing. Salthouse (1984) found, in fact, that older experienced typists' longer response times were offset by their greater efficiency in processing larger chunks of information to be typed. However, practice and experience do not always completely eliminate age differences in performance (e.g., Cerella, 1990). In a study of age differences in a visual/memory search task, for example, young adults benefitted from extensive practice by developing an "automatic detection" strategy; older subjects in this study did not construct such a strat-

On well-practiced tasks, age differences in speed of psychomotor performance are often minimal.

egy and continued to respond more slowly than the younger subjects even after practice (Fisk, McGee, & Giambra, 1988).

What is the importance of these exceptions? They suggest that slowed psychomotor performance in middle and later adulthood is a reliable phenomenon, but not a process that is inevitable or that always interferes with productivity. Remaining physically healthy and active throughout adulthood may minimize the extent to which behavior slows with age. When slowing does occur, it may be possible to offset that change by adopting a new style of behavior (e.g., vocal versus manual responding) when alternative behaviors are equally acceptable. In situations for which the behavior is prescribed and alternatives are not acceptable, one may compensate for psychomotor slowing by becoming familiar and well-practiced with the task at hand. And of course, productivity does not always demand speed. Depending on the task, seasoned judgement, mature experience, and insight may be much more critical than speed.

Practical implications of age differences in basic intellectual processes

Age differences in perception, attention, arousal, reaction time, and psychomotor skills carry implications for middle-aged and older adults' experiences at work, in education and training settings, and in their homes and communities. Researchers in the emerging field of **industrial gerontology** (the study of the older worker) have addressed two questions of particular relevance: the extent to which job performance changes with age, and the extent to which involvement in industrial accidents changes with age.

Because negative stereotypes of older workers have been documented for nearly four decades (for a review of this research, see Stagner, 1985), we must be suspicious of research on age differences in job performance that are based solely on supervisors' ratings. Supervisors' ratings of older workers may be negatively biased if the supervisor accepts the stereotype that older workers are less capable, less efficient, and less productive than younger workers. Fortunately, some studies have compared older and younger workers' job performance according to more objective criteria. Using this approach, no age differences were found in clerical workers' performance (Stagner, 1985); workers over age 60 were slightly less productive than younger workers in a printing establishment, but proofreaders over age 60 were more accurate than younger proofreaders (Stagner, 1985).

The objective information that is available, then, suggests that age differences in perception and in basic cognitive processes are often offset by other factors—perhaps motivation or experience. Attrition probably also moderates the impact of age differences in these basic processes. Older workers who find that they cannot work as quickly as their job demands may retire early—or they may change the type of work that they do. For example, Welford (1977) noted that factory studies showed that older workers prefer (and more often have) jobs in which speed is not critical (e.g., lifting and carrying, as compared to assembly line work).

Although one might suppose that age changes in perception, reaction time, and psychomotor skills would make the workplace more hazardous for older workers than for younger ones, this is not the case. In an unusually extensive study of industrial accidents, Root (1981) examined over one million workers' compensation records for accidents. Older workers (those over age 35) were involved in fewer accidents than younger workers (ages 18 through 34), controlling for age differences in numbers of workers.

Experience on the job is more important than age in relation to probability of accident involvement: as length of time on the job increased in Root's (1981) study, frequency of accidents decreased. Of course, the latter association could reflect the effects of selective survival as well as experience, since young workers who are accident-prone or incautious may not live to become older and more experienced workers. When older workers are involved in accidents, the injuries are generally more serious and result in more time lost from work than is the case for younger workers (Stagner, 1985).

Thus, industrial gerontologists provide an outlook of guarded optimism regarding the impact of age differences in basic cognitive processes. The same picture emerges from discussions of middle-aged and older adults' experiences in educational settings. Certainly, age differences in perception, attention, and arousal imply that learning may be more difficult for older than for younger students. As Hayslip and Kennelly (1985) point out, "if an older person cannot

Although learning may be more challenging for some elderly adults than for young people, many older students compensate for age-related changes in basic cognitive processes through motivation.

read printed material because of failing eyesight, cannot hear what is said in class because of hearing loss, or cannot copy notes or diagrams because he or she is arthritic, learning is going to be a frustrating, difficult experience. Further, the older learner may be unable to process the information quickly enough for later retention, especially when the material is complex" (p. 80).

However, older students may well compensate for these obstacles through motivation. Willis (1985) identifies a broad spectrum of personally meaningful goals that prompt older adults' participation in educational programs. These goals include comprehending one's own aging, understanding social change, combatting technological and sociocultural obsolescence, acquiring second career education, and generating satisfactory retirement roles. And, educators' creative efforts to design modes of teaching suited to older learners' needs can be beneficial. On the basis of Hayslip & Kennelly's (1985) discussion, we could suggest that changing the means and the rate of presenting information might assist older students.

How do the age differences that we have considered in this chapter affect older individuals' experiences in their homes and communities? People age 65 and older are the age group most affected by home accidents (Stearns, Barrett, & Alexander, 1985); falls, as we noted earlier, are a type of accident arousing particular concern. Age-related changes in balance, as well as attention and reaction time, undoubtedly contribute to older adults' vulnerability to falling. However, careful attention to the design and furnishing of an older individual's home can often identify hazards that contribute to this vulnerability, so that these hazards can be minimized.

Outside the home, the threat of pedestrian accidents and traffic accidents merit special concern for older people. Because of age-related changes in vision, hearing, balance, and reaction time, older people may be at greater risk of pedestrian accidents than younger adults. Stearns and his colleagues (1985) suggest that the intervals set for traffic lights and cross-walk signals may be too short for older people to safely cross an intersection.

Perhaps you think of driving as only a little less essential to life than breathing; the inadequacy of public transportation in many communities would certainly justify that opinion. However, driving, too, may be hazardous for older people. For safe driving, accurate sensory and perceptual functioning, optimal attention and arousal, short reaction time, and rapid psychomotor performance all are critical capacities (e.g., Barrett, Alexander, & Forbes, 1977; Panek, Barrett, Sterns, & Alexander, 1977). Given the information reviewed in this chapter, it is not surprising that drivers age 60 and older (like drivers in their teens and early twenties) have high accident rates, controlling for numbers of miles driven (e.g., Stearns et al., 1985). Since unsafe drivers pose a threat not only to themselves but also to other motorists and pedestrians, some believe that driving privileges should be restricted in old age. Arguments on both sides of this proposition are presented in the *Open Questions* box.

Clearly, age changes in these basic cognitive processes can make a big difference in an older individual's quality of life. It is critical, then, to explore

Should driving privileges be restricted in old age?

When appropriate statistical controls for numbers of miles driven are used, older drivers (over age 55 for men, over age 60 for women) have high accident rates (Stearns et al., 1985). Also, when an older driver is involved in an accident, he or she is more likely to be found at fault than is a younger driver (Stearns et al., 1985). The kinds of traffic violations for which people are convicted also differ for age groups: drivers over age 70 are more often convicted of sign, right-of-way, and turning violations than other age groups (Stearns et al., 1985). These kinds of driving problems may stem from the driver's failure to selectively attend to critical cues (e.g., stop signs, traffic signals), or to use this information to make a rapid decision.

This information paints a frightening picture for anyone who drives or rides in cars. However, overly broad generalizations are unwarranted. As Stearns and his colleagues (1985) point out, "many older adults have always had excellent driving skills and continue to perform well; others may have declining abilities but are able to compensate for this loss by driving more cautiously, at slower speeds, for fewer miles, and over less demanding routes of travel. Still others may have declining capacities but do not recognize or compensate for them, leading to violations and/or accidents" (pp. 708–709).

Reacting with justifiable concern about the latter group of older driver, some people suggest that driving privileges be restricted in one way or another in old age. After all, a teenager who is learning to drive is subject to the restrictions of her temporary license. Perhaps it is equally reasonable to restrict the driving of the elderly, as another high-risk group. The specific approach to restriction might be simply a more rigorous testing procedure for driver's license renewals after one has passed a certain age, such as 65 or 70. Taking a more extreme approach, various types of restrictions might be noted on older drivers' licenses. For example, the license may not permit the individual to drive at night, to drive more than 50 miles from home, or to drive on interstate highways. Or, in the most extreme case, drivers' licenses might be nonrenewable after a critical age.

Although one might be able to make a case for some approach to restricting older peoples' driving on the basis of public safety, there are also strong arguments against using age alone as a determinant of driving privileges. As noted above, older drivers vary in their driving skill—as do younger drivers. In that respect, restricted driving on the basis of age per se would be unfair.

Restricting driving on the basis of tests identifying critical deficits (e.g., poor vision or hearing, slow reaction time, distractibility) on an individual basis would make much more sense. Unfortunately, the kinds of license renewal examinations currently used are not extensive enough to serve this purpose; currently, visual acuity is one of the primary criteria for renewal, although it may be less important for actual driving performance than other skills (e.g., Panek et al., 1977). However, the cost of expanding current testing procedures to detect these deficits might well be prohibitive. Of course, any approach to restricting driving for the aged is likely to be costly, since public transportation and transportation programs for elderly adults would then require expansion.

Furthermore, arguments in favor of restricting older drivers' privileges ignore the personal and psychological importance of driving—not only for elderly people, but for adults of all ages. For many people, being able to drive provides not only mobility and convenience but also a sense of self-sufficiency. Removing that privilege might constitute a substantial blow to an older person's self-esteem, as well as to her ability to maintain interpersonal and community ties.

Rather than simply restricting driving privileges in old age, education offers a more constructive approach. Driver training tailored to the kinds of difficulties that older people most often encounter have been developed and are available in some communities. Research evaluating one of these programs indicated that it was effective and provided long-lasting benefits (Stearns & Sanders, 1980). Making such courses available nationally might be the best answer to questions concerning the safety of older motorists.

ways to minimize the consequences of these changes. The next section introduces examples of such interventions.

INTERVENTIONS: OPTIMIZING PERFORMANCE AND MOBILITY IN LATER LIFE

Most interventions designed to minimize the impacts of age changes in sensory and basic intellectual capacities fall into two categories. Some are means through which the environment—the home, the workplace, or the highway—can be transformed to become more hospitable to the older individual. Actually, these modifications make the environment more supportive for people of all ages. Young people can function well in a setting that sustains an older person's activities, although older adults cannot always function comfortably in settings designed for the needs and capacities of younger people. A second approach to intervention involves prosthetic devices which enhance or support the individual's capacities.

Human factors is the field that provides optimal designs for the conditions under which people live and work. As the population ages, professionals in this field give increased attention to ways in which these designs must be sensitive to the needs of older adults. Charness & Bosman (1990) recently summarized ways in which the home or workplace can be adapted to provide middle-aged and older people the greatest safety and comfort.

Many of these changes concern the visual and auditory features of the environment (Charness & Bosman, 1990). For example, lighting levels should generally be increased, and sudden shifts in lighting level should be avoided. Strong color contrasts should be used to highlight steps and curbs. Furniture should be positioned away from potential sources of glare, and nonreflecting, sound-absorbing material should be used on walls, floors, and ceilings. Constant sources of background noise (e.g., heating; air conditioning; piped-in music) should be minimized or eliminated. When furniture is arranged so that people face one another while conversing, a listener who is hard-of-hearing has the advantage of visual cues from the speaker's face to supplement the sound of her voice.

Other changes involve the physical design of the environment. Charness & Bosman (1990) note, as an example, that the height of standard kitchen cabinets makes a stepstool a virtual necessity for people less than 6 feet tall. Yet, age changes in the sense of balance can lead to accidents when using a stepstool. Designing kitchens so that cabinets are at a height suitable for older individuals (who are generally shorter in stature than younger people) would eliminate this particular problem. Installing grab bars and handrailings in the home is a relatively simple and inexpensive means of accommodating the home to an older resident's presbystasis. Replacing door knobs with door handles makes it easier for an arthritic person to open doors.

In the workplace and in many homes, computers have become an ubiquitous piece of equipment. Human factors researchers have also considered ways in which computers can be designed to suit the characteristics of middle-aged and older users. Systems in which the monitor position can be easily adjusted (so that users can avoid glare and neck strain), dot matrix printers that are shielded to minimize background noise, and self-paced training programs might offer greater comfort and productivity for middle-aged and older employees (Charness & Bosman, 1990).

Still further environmental modifications are possible on the roadways. Remember that dynamic visual acuity (DVA) is reduced in older people; however, when level of lighting is increased, older adults exhibit DVA at nearly the same level as young adults (Long & Crambert, 1990). Thus, providing better lighting on highways could make driving safer and easier for older motorists. Insuring that the lettering on roadside signs is of adequate size and that the signs are positioned so that older drivers have sufficient time to respond to them are other recommended changes (Charness & Bosman, 1990).

A different approach to intervention is the enhancement of the individual's capacities through prosthetic devices, rather than changing the environment. Many of these devices are ones with which we are all familiar—things like eyeglasses and hearing aids. Even here, though, there are promising innovations. Digital hearing aids, for example, are a relatively new development through which specified elements of the speech signal can be selectively amplified. This feature provides greater clarity of speech because consonants typically have less energy in the speech signal than do vowels (Fozard, 1990). Another relatively new approach is the use of "hearing dogs" to assist the individual who is hearing impaired—much like the way that guide dogs assist people who are blind (Eames & Eames, 1990). These dogs alert their hearing-impaired partners to sounds that require a response, such as a knock at the door, a ringing telephone, an alarm clock, or a smoke detector.

Certainly, this is far from an exhaustive list of interventions that can compensate for the age-related changes considered in this chapter. But because of the increasing attention given to the needs of the aged by human factors researchers, it would probably be impossible to give an exhaustive, up-to-date list of these interventions. Thus, if the prospect of diminished functioning in sensory, perceptual, and basic intellectual functioning is too daunting, the exciting advances in means of offsetting these normal changes of aging provide encouragement.

SUMMARY

By middle adulthood—and to an even greater extent in later adulthood—changes in sensation and perception are apparent. Presbyopia (farsightedness) is almost universal among middle-aged and older people. In addition, the absolute threshold, the extent of dark adaptation, contrast sensitivity, visual acuity, and dynamic visual acuity all decline with age, and the field of view becomes increasingly restricted.

Although the hearing loss that occurs by middle adulthood is measurable, few people notice this change in hearing until later in adulthood. However, older adults more often experience difficulty hearing and understanding speech—especially under adverse listening conditions. These changes in vision and hearing may interfere with an older person's mobility in the home and community, and with social interaction.

Although there is less extensive information available than is the case for vision and hearing, the senses of taste and smell also seem to diminish in old age. Similarly, older individuals are less sensitive to pain. Finally, both the vestibular system and kinesthesis show some changes with age, and these changes may interfere with balance and mobility in old age.

Compared to young adults, older adults show less capacity for selective attention, divided attention, and sustained attention; however, no age differences in attention switching have been identified. Age differences in arousal level may account for some of these age differences in attention.

One of the most reliable and well-documented age-related changes is a general slowing of behavior, including increased reaction time and slowed psychomotor performance. However, age is far from the only predictor of reaction time or speed of psychomotor performance. Other influences include mode of responding, task complexity, health and fitness, and task familiarity.

In practical situations, age differences in perception and in basic intellectual processes are often offset by other factors—perhaps motivation, experience, and attrition. Human factors researchers have identified ways in which the home, workplace, and highway can be redesigned to allow middle-aged and older individuals to function with the greatest safety and comfort.

KEY TERMS

Absolute threshold	Industrial gerontology
Arcus senilis	Iris
Arousal hypothesis	Kinesthesis
Attention switching	Lens
Cataracts	Nerve deafness
Ciliary body	Oval window
Cochlear implant	Perception
Conductive deafness	Presbycusis
Contrast sensitivity	Presbyopia
Dark adaptation	Presbystasis
Diabetic retinopathy	Psychomotor skills
Dichotic listening task	Pupil
Divided attention	Reaction time
Dynamic visual acuity (DVA)	Retina
Electroencephalogram (EEG)	Selective attention
Glaucoma	Sensation
Human factors	Spiral organ

Sustained attention
Tympanic membrane
Vestibular system

Vestibulocochlear nerve
Visual acuity
Vitreous humor

SUGGESTIONS FOR FURTHER READING

Shock, N. W., Greulich, R. C., Andres, R., Arenberg, D., Costa, P. T., Lakatta, E. G., & Tobin, J. D. (1984). *Normal Human Aging: The Baltimore Longitudinal Study of Aging*. Bethesda, MD: National Institutes of Health.

Spence, A. P. (1989). *Biology of Human Aging*. Englewood Cliffs, NJ: Prentice Hall.

Whitbourne, S. K. (1985). *The Aging Body: Physiological Changes and Psychological Consequences*. New York: Springer-Verlag.

CHAPTER SIX

INTELLIGENCE, WISDOM, AND CREATIVITY

Does age bring wisdom? Or do most people lose whatever intellectual prowess they ever had as they get older? This chapter considers intelligence and its changes with age. Although these issues are some of the oldest and most active areas of research on adult development, new questions abound. Much of the chapter examines differing views of adult intelligence and research on age differences, cohort differences, and age changes in intellectual performance. A theme recurring throughout that discussion is the extent to which growth and stability characterize adult intellectual development, and the extent to which decline occurs.

We examine some of the most widely-used measures of adult intelligence. Although these measures are the "state of the art" in this area of psychometrics, they should still arouse concern: the nature of the tests may provide a misleading picture of the ways that older people are intelligent in their everyday lives. Similarly, in cross-sectional problem-solving research, the nature of the problem to be solved may influence the conclusions drawn regarding the relationship between age and capacity. A second chapter theme, then, is the impact of research design in general and measurement approaches in particular on the picture of adult intellectual development.

The chapter closes with a discussion of qualities that are, perhaps, even less well-defined than intelligence—wisdom and creativity. We examine various definitions of "wisdom" and seek their common threads. We also review research on age differences in creative productivity.

Questions to consider in reading the chapter include:

What approaches have been taken to describing adult intelligence? In what respects does intellectual proficiency decline in old age? In what respects does it remain stable or improve with age?

How does performance on abstract, logical problems differ for young, middle-aged, and older adults? How do young, middle-aged, and elderly people differ in performance on practical problem-solving tasks?

Are there age differences in wisdom? What age differences appear in various areas of creative productivity?

VIEWS OF ADULT INTELLIGENCE

Perhaps you have a working definition of intelligence. Maybe you think that intelligent people are well-educated, articulate, and well-read; or, you may think of intelligent people as those who deal effectively with the unexpected curve balls of life. Some define intelligent individuals as those who have made

Some define intelligent people as those who have made outstanding scientific, literary, or artistic contributions.

notable literary, artistic, or scientific contributions. Despite the number and variety of intuitive definitions, intelligence has proven one of the most difficult concepts for psychologists to specify.

The chapter opens with an examination of some of the most influential efforts to define adult intelligence. Some propose that adulthood spans a sequence of stages in the growth of intelligence: at different points in adult life, people are intelligent in different ways. Other theorists, however, attempt to specify various components of adult intelligence rather than different seasons of intellectual development.

Stages of adult intellectual development

Recall from Chapter Two (see pp. 44–46) that Jean Piaget made unparalleled contributions to the understanding of cognitive development early in the lifespan. Piaget's theory describes intellectual development from birth to maturity as a universal sequence of four stages (the sensorimotor stage, the preoperational stage, the concrete operational stage, and the formal operational stage). Each stage, according to Piaget, is qualitatively different: intelligence changes in its basic nature with development. Each subsequent stage also incorporates and extends the intellectual capacities of earlier stages.

Piaget believed initially that adults think, reason, and solve problems in the same ways that teenagers do—using formal logic to reason about propositions, identifying and evaluating all possible solutions to problems, contemplating problems and questions on an abstract level, thinking about thought, and considering hypothetical and counterfactual situations (Flavell, 1963; Piaget, 1970). However, research of the 1960s and 1970s revealed that many adults did not use formal operations—and that others had progressed to a still more sophisticated level (e.g., Papalia & Bielby, 1974; see Chapter Two, pages 44–46). Other research of the same vintage identified cross-cultural differences in performance on Piagetian problems; the *Diversity in Adulthood* box presents this research and its implications for Piaget's theory.

In light of this evidence, Piaget (1972) suggested that adults may not use formal operations in all situations. Rather, people may use formal operational thinking for dealing with some kinds of problems but not others, depending on their interests and areas of expertise. An architect, for example, would probably use formal operations to solve problems related to the design of a building, but might not use these skills to improve a recipe for Hollandaise sauce. In dealing with the design problem, the architect would be familiar with the important problem elements and would thus be prepared to exhaustively consider all their complex relationships. However, she would be far less capable of such sophisticated reasoning when confronted with a culinary problem (unless gourmet cooking were her hobby).

Piaget's description of adult intelligence has been labeled a "differentiation model," since he proposed that cognitive functioning in adulthood is differentiated according to individual background (Rybash, Hoyer, & Roodin,

BOX 6.1   *DIVERSITY IN ADULTHOOD*

Culture and Piaget's problem-solving tasks

Piaget's theory has been described as embodying a "psychological universalist" position that a general theory of cognition is possible (e.g., Buck-Morss, 1975). Remember that Piaget described cognitive development as progress through a sequence of stages leading to a universally-attained end state of formal operations. His theory has been of enormous value in integrating observations about Western children's reasoning and problem solving.

However, when Piagetian researchers examined reasoning and problem solving among non-Western children, they were sometimes surprised. For example, Greenfield (1966) found that un-schooled Wolof children in Senegal were unable to solve conservation-of-amount tasks by age eight, although one would predict that the children would experience no difficulty with such problems. Such variations calls for explanation in the face of a theory of universal cognitive development.

One intriguing explanation was offered by Susan Buck-Morss (1975). She proposed that the Piagetian view of cognitive development reflects a socio-economic bias. As she explained:

> The structure of cognition with which he [Piaget] is concerned reflects the structure of an industrialized society with abstract, formal relations of production and exchange. The potential for such cognition and its sequential development is no doubt latent in all human beings, but its actual development may reflect the demands of assimilating and accommodating to a particular social reality. (p. 45)

Thus, it may be that Piaget's model accounts well for Western children's development because the theory was formulated in the social and eco-nomic context within which these children grow to maturity. For children in modern industrial and technological societies, being able to reason logically at an abstract level—a hallmark of cognitive maturity in Piaget's theory—is a valuable, if not necessary, skill. Thus, experiences from birth onward may channel intellectual development toward that end state of the "ideal Western scientist."

Different cultures, however, may demand different forms of intellectual maturity—end states different from that embodied in formal operations. Greenfield (1976) suggested that cognitive researchers could profit more by attempting to determine the characteristics of an "ideal type" in non-Western societies than by measuring non-Western individuals' intellectual proficiency against the ideal of the Western scientist.

P. M. Greenfield (1976) used this approach in research in southern Mexico. In that project, she identified weaving as a highly developed skill among mature women of the culture, and she videotaped weaving as it was carried out by skilled weavers as well as by young girls who had attained varying levels of weaving proficiency. These data could provide a basis for identifying steps along the way to expertise within this culture, and the kinds of instruction and experience that are critical in imparting skill.

Greenfield's (1976) work is an ideal illustration of a relativist approach to understanding intelligence. Instead of assuming that members of a group reason defectively because they do not solve the same kinds of problems that Westerners solve, she identified the problems that these individuals do solve and used that information as her starting point.

1986). Other theorists have used Piaget's theory as their starting point for describing postformal modes of thought. Generally, these styles of thought differ from formal operational thinking in their assumptions about logic and knowledge, causality, and contradiction; Table 6.1 summarizes contrasts between formal and postformal thought.

Table 6.1
Contrasts between formal and postformal assumptions

Formal assumptions	Postformal assumptions
Knowledge is absolute and not dependent upon situational context. Absolute laws and principles that govern the elements comprising reality can be discovered through logical analysis.	Knowledge is a constructed product of the mind, and is necessarily dependent on context rather than absolute. Logical analysis is similarly a construction and is thus a limited tool.
Reality is a set of closed, static systems. These systems are independent of one another and can be understood independently, without consideration of one another.	Reality is a whole comprised of many integrated, dynamic systems. These systems are interdependent, and thus none can be understood without consideration of the others
There is a one-way relationship between causal variables and outcome variables.	There are reciprocal relationships between variables: "causes" can be distinguished from "outcomes" only arbitrarily.
Parts of a whole are distinct from the whole itself, and have an independent existence apart from the whole.	Parts of a whole are constituted by their relationship to the whole and to one another; the parts have no independent existence.
Contradiction is to be avoided and resolved.	Contradiction is to be accepted and, if possible, synthesized into a more integrative whole.
The hypothetical and abstract are emphasized in thinking and problem solving.	Real events characterizing real life are emphasized in thinking and problem solving.

Source: Adapted from Rybash et al., 1986. Reprinted by permission of Pergamon Press.

One of the first descriptions of postformal thinking was Arlin's (1975) discussion of **problem finding**. Arlin described formal operations as a stage in which one excels at solving well-defined problems. She further believed that mature thinking went beyond that capacity, and included the ability to identify new problems in ambiguous situations. In her research, college freshmen and seniors completed traditional formal operational tasks and a "problem-finding" task. The latter task required students to think of questions about 12 common objects. Arlin evaluated students' problem-finding capacity on the basis of the generality and abstraction of their questions; relatively general and abstract questions reflected a problem-finding style of thought. As she expected, success on the formal operational tasks was a necessary condition for success on the problem-finding measure.

More recently, Commons, Richards, and Kuhn (1982) proposed **metasystematic reasoning** as a style of postformal thinking. According to these theorists, formal operations involve logical operations *within* a system (or situation), whereas adult thinking is more often directed toward a collection of diverse systems and their interrelationships. In testing this supposition, Commons and his colleagues presented college and graduate students with concrete and formal operational tasks. They also asked the students to analyze similarities and differences between four stories; the stories were written such that the similarities and differences could be interpreted in a concrete operational, a formal operational, or a postformal manner. As in Arlin's (1975) study, being able to successfully complete the formal operational tasks was needed for analysis at the postformal level.

Another stage-based approach to describing adult intelligence does not directly stem from Piaget's ideas. K. Warner Schaie (1977–1978) proposed a sequence of five stages distinguished by the individual's orientation toward knowledge. Children and teenagers are in an **acquisitive stage**, when they gather information to prepare for adult roles. At this point, one can perform quite well on general knowledge tests, even if the test items have little to do with one's interests and concerns.

Schaie (1977–1978) described young adulthood as an **achieving stage**. In this stage, the individual is less concerned with acquiring knowledge than with using it to establish independence, competence, and credibility. Young adults are at their best working on tasks relevant to their own goals and priorities.

Beginning in the thirties, individuals enter the **responsible stage**. Now, knowledge is used in the solution of practical problems related to family and career responsibilities. Some individuals in their thirties and forties attain positions of leadership in their communities or professions; Schaie believed that these individuals become skilled at integrating complex relationships, and labeled this stage the **executive stage**.

Middle-aged people who are leaders in their communities or professions may enter the executive stage of intellectual development.

The final stage in Schaie's sequence is the **reintegrative stage**, and occurs in later adulthood. In this stage, the individual is primarily concerned with identifying meaning and purpose in knowledge. Schaie described this stage as one of mature wisdom.

Components of adult intelligence

Other approaches identify unique skills that make up adult intelligence. Among the most important contemporary approaches is **information processing theory**. Developmental psychologists following the information processing approach attempt to identify age changes in the rate and efficiency of encoding information, storing that information, and retrieving and using the stored information. These scientists believe that these *component processes* of encoding, storing, and accessing information are universal, but that they may occur more rapidly or more slowly, or with more or less efficiency, for different individuals (Rybash et al., 1986). A general conclusion stemming from this work is that young adults process information more quickly and more efficiently than do older adults (Poon, 1985; Rybash et al., 1986).

This general conclusion integrates findings from several more specific areas of research within the information processing approach. One of these areas is the study of age-related changes in the attention processes determining which of the many bits of information bombarding the senses reach conscious awareness. Recall from the last chapter that young adults enjoy more rapid and effective attention processes than do older adults (Kline & Schieber, 1985).

A related area is the distinction between two general modes of information processing—**automatic** and **effortful**—and the examination of age-related changes in these modes. Automatic processing occurs rapidly, accurately, and without effort. Effortful processing, on the other hand, requires active, conscious control and may be affected by such factors as the complexity of the task or the presence of competing cognitive demands (e.g., Hasher & Zacks, 1979). Recognizing the relative locations of objects, trees, buildings, and people as you look across your campus is an example of automatic processing; you would use effortful processing to decipher a written set of directions to an unfamiliar location. Research findings in this area are generally consistent: young adults and older adults perform at the same level on tasks calling for automatic processing, but young adults' performance is superior to that of older adults on tasks that require effortful processing (Rybash et al., 1986; for an exception see Kausler, 1989).

Another approach to identifying components of adult intelligence is the **encapsulation model** (Rybash et al., 1986). This model emphasizes the emergence and growth of domain-ordered knowledge during adulthood. In other words, a central aspect of adult cognition is the acquisition, organization, and access of knowledge regarding different topics (or domains).

Proponents of the encapsulation model maintain that it is impossible to specify a universal mature form of human intelligence, because the configuration of intellectual domains depends upon individual motivations, interests, and experiences. Mature knowledge for a mechanic might include information related to the parts and operation of machines, types and causes of mechanical breakdowns, strategies for managing a profitable business, means of dealing with customers—and cognitive processes through which this information is used. In contrast, mature knowledge for an academic psychologist would include information related to the individual's professional specialization (e.g., child development, social psychology), research and statistical techniques, teaching strategies, ways of negotiating academic politics, and again the mental processes through which this information is employed.

The encapsulation model accords a prominent role to the individual in cognitive development. As the proponents of this approach explain:

> People seem to build their own knowledge systems for forms (or foundations) that represent how they use their mental resources. In this sense, domains are representations of different areas of cognitive involvement on the part of individuals. . . . The developing individual actively organizes and monitors what is known, what needs to be known, and intentionally determines how to utilize what is known. (Rybash et al., 1986, p. 4)

Other psychologists who describe adult intelligence in terms of its components do make *a priori* specifications of those components. Howard Gardner (1985), for example, proposes a **multiple-intelligences theory**. According to this theory, humans possess seven distinct "intelligences," each with neurological underpinnings. The seven intelligences are (1) linguistic intelligence, used for reading, speaking, and writing; (2) logico-mathematical intelligence, used for working with numbers and logical problems; (3) spatial intelligence, used for negotiating the physical environment; (4) musical intelligence, used for perceiving and creating rhythms; (5) bodily-kinesthetic intelligence, used for executing skilled movements; (6) interpersonal intelligence, used for understanding others; and (7) intrapersonal intelligence, used for understanding oneself.

Robert Sternberg (1985) proposes a different set of components altogether in his **triarchic theory**. According to Sternberg, intelligence comprises three interrelated aspects. There is a componential element used for analysis and information processing, an experiential element through which insight is used to integrate information and develop creative solutions to problems, and a contextual element through which one draws on personal experience to determine the best way to tackle an unfamiliar situation. According to Sternberg, you would rely primarily on the componential element of intelligence in taking an IQ test, on the experiential element in creating a dress pattern, and on the contextual element in figuring out how to safely travel across a large city if you had lost your wallet and had no money.

These efforts to specify components of adult intelligence are intriguing, but there has been only minimal progress in developing reliable, valid measures of these components. A definition of intellectual components that does have a firm foundation in measurement is Horn and Cattell's (1966; 1967) model of **fluid intelligence** and **crystallized intelligence**. Horn and Cattell maintain that human cognitive skills can be grouped into two broad categories. The first, fluid intelligence, includes such abilities as forming concepts, identifying similarities, and reasoning. Tasks calling on fluid intelligence would include extending a logical sequence of letters, numbers, or other symbols. Figure 6.1 presents a sample item from the Raven Progressive Matrices test, a nonverbal measure of intelligence that is believed to assess fluid intelligence. The test requires the examinee to select the pattern that would logically fit into the indicated space. The second component, crystallized intelligence, involves drawing on learned information to make decisions and solve problems. Situations calling on crystallized intelligence include vocabulary tests, most classroom tests, and many social situations.

Horn and Cattell (1967) asserted further that the two types of intelligence have different foundations and different developmental courses. Fluid intelligence reflects neurological health, and shows little cultural influence. This aspect of intelligence, then, is not much affected by educational background or

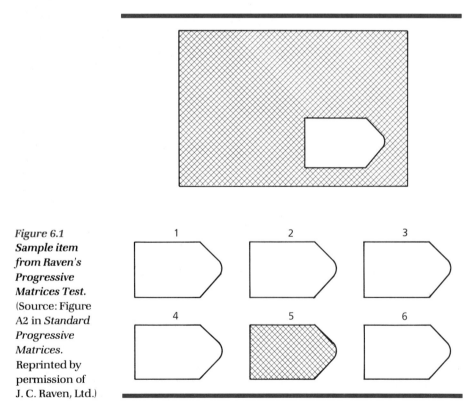

Figure 6.1 Sample item from Raven's Progressive Matrices Test. (Source: Figure A2 in *Standard Progressive Matrices.* Reprinted by permission of J. C. Raven, Ltd.)

occupational specialization. As its definition implies, crystallized intelligence is comprised of learned material, and thus does depend upon educational, occupational, and cultural experiences.

Crystallized intelligence typically increases throughout the life span, or at least until the period immediately preceding death. Fluid intelligence normally peaks in the late teens or early twenties and gradually declines throughout adulthood; age-related changes in attention processes (see Chapter Five, pages 122–125) may account for much of this decline (Stankov, 1988). Figure 6.2 illustrates the developmental trends for fluid intelligence and crystallized intelligence, as well as for neural structures, accumulation of educational experience, and general ability.

For many years, scholars believed that the age-related decline in fluid intelligence was immutable. However, researchers have recently succeeded in training older individuals to improve their performance on measures of fluid intelligence. Using a variety of measures and training approaches, scientists have found that older adults can substantially improve the accuracy of their solutions to problems drawing on fluid intelligence and to increase the difficulty of problems that they can solve (Baltes, Dittmann-Kohli, & Kliegl, 1986; Baltes & Willis, 1982; Blackburn, Papalia-Finlay, Foye, & Serlin, 1988; Denney & Heidrich, 1990; Hayslip, 1989; Lerner, 1990; Willis & Nesselroade, 1990). One group of researchers found that a training program in which older participants essentially taught themselves was as effective as training programs administered by the researchers (Baltes, Sowarka, & Kliegl, 1989).

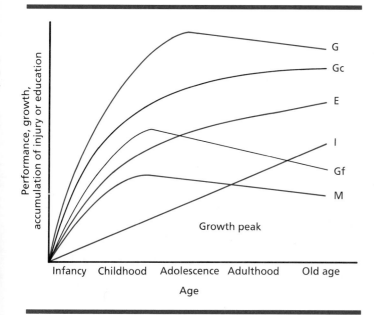

Figure 6.2
Development of fluid intelligence (Gf) and Crystallized intelligence (Gc) in relation to maturational growth and decline of neural structures (M), accumulation of injury to neural structures (I), accumulation of educational exposures (E), and overall ability (G).
(Source: Horn, 1970. Reprinted by permission)

PSYCHOMETRIC STUDIES OF ADULT INTELLIGENCE

The research reviewed next identifies ways in which intelligence shows change and stability with age; this work relies on standardized measures of intelligence that assess proficiency in several areas. We begin by examining two of the most widely used individual tests of intelligence for adults, and then note problems inherent in the use of these instruments. With that basis, we look at what researchers have learned about age differences, age changes, and cohort differences in intellectual performance throughout adulthood.

Measures of adult intelligence

Although there are many standardized measures of intelligence for adults (for an overview, see Cohen, Montague, Nathanson, & Swerdik, 1988), clinicians and researchers most often use either the **Wechsler Adult Intelligence Scale—Revised (WAIS–R)** or the **Primary Mental Abilities Test (PMA)**. Both include a variety of tasks that evaluate fluid and crystallized intelligence. The WAIS–R probably enjoys more widespread clinical use than the PMA, whereas the PMA has been used in some of the most important research programs examining adult intellectual development.

The WAIS–R (and its predecessor, the WAIS) includes eleven subtests divided into two scales, the verbal scale and the performance scale; Table 6.2 lists and briefly describes the subtests. As Table 6.2 suggests, items on the verbal scale require a vocal response and, generally, assess one's fund of learned knowledge. Most items on the performance scale call for a nonverbal response and evaluate the ability to grapple with an unfamiliar problem. Generally, the verbal scale taps mostly crystallized intelligence and the performance scale evaluates mostly fluid intelligence.

In each subtest, items are arranged in order of increasing difficulty. An examiner begins with the verbal scale, presenting the relatively easy items for a subtest first and administering more difficult items until the examinee gives several successive incorrect answers. At that point, the examiner moves on to the next subtest. Scoring depends on the number of items solved correctly within each subtest. On the performance scale (and the arithmetic subtest of the verbal scale), speed is important: bonus points are awarded for an especially rapid solution. The final score (the "IQ") is based on one's level of performance *relative to one's age group.* In successively older age groups, a lower absolute level of performance yields a higher IQ.

The PMA, like the WAIS–R, evaluates several areas of performance. In this case, though, the five subtests are not divided into a verbal and performance scale; there are time limits for all subtests. Like the WAIS–R, the subtests composing the PMA draw on both fluid and crystallized intelligence.

Table 6.2
The WAIS–R subtests

Scale	Description
Verbal scale:	
1. Information	Assesses fund of general, learned knowledge
2. Comprehension	Assesses knowledge of appropriate behavior, ability to deal with the social and physical environment
3. Arithmetic	Assesses reasoning ability, concentration, alertness, and memory
4. Similarities	Assesses verbal reasoning ability, ability to identify and integrate common elements
5. Digit span	Assesses memory ability. Requires repeating a sequence of digits in the same or reverse order
6. Vocabulary	Assesses knowledge of word definitions
Performance scale:	
1. Digit symbol	Assesses ability to copy abstract symbols paired with digits
2. Picture completion	Individual must identify a missing element from pictures of common objects
3. Block design	Individual uses colored blocks to reproduce an abstract design shown in a picture
4. Picture arrangement	Individual arranges a set of "cartoon-like" pictures in an order depicting a logical sequence of events
5. Object assembly	Individual puts together cardboard puzzles depicting common objects

Source: Based on Matarazzo, 1972. Reprinted by permission.

Measurement problems

Although both the WAIS–R and the PMA are well-regarded and widely used, both can be problematic when employed to evaluate an older adult's intellectual proficiency. When either measure is used—whether it be for a clinical evaluation or for research purposes—the intent is to assess the individual's level of intellectual *ability* by examining her test *performance*. However, most students can identify situations in which their performance on a classroom test did not accurately reflect their mastery of the course material. If students are distracted by construction outside the classroom, or by thoughts of an upcoming date, their performance can be affected. Students who are tired from a night-long study session, those who are suffering from bad colds, or those who are drowsy because of medication will probably not do their best.

Performance may similarly underestimate ability when intelligence tests are used to evaluate older adults. Older people, on the average, have less extensive educational backgrounds than contemporary young adults do; recall that performance on measures of crystallized intelligence is positively associated with education. An older woman's performance on the PMA or the WAIS–R, then, may reflect the quality, quantity, and recency of her schooling as well as her intellectual ability. Also, because many of the questions making up an intelligence test draw on "school-like" information (see Table 6.2), these items may strike the older woman as trivial, irrelevant, or uninteresting. Her reaction would probably not lead to optimal performance.

Perhaps the greatest problem in using the WAIS–R or the PMA with elderly adults, though, is the inclusion of time limits. We saw in Chapter Five (see pp. 125–128) that normal aging includes a slowing of psychomotor skills and reaction time. Obviously, an older person is at a disadvantage when responding quickly is important. In a recent cross-sectional study, one researcher found that much of the age difference in PMA test performance was eliminated when age differences in perceptual speed and speed in working with test answer sheets were statistically controlled (Hertzog, 1989).

The pressure of time may also arouse anxiety for an elderly man or woman taking an IQ test. In one study, researchers compared not only test performance but also anxiety levels for young and older adults; the older people had higher levels of **debilitating anxiety** (anxiety that interfered with performance), and these anxiety levels were associated with lower test scores (Whitbourne, 1976).

Perhaps out of anxiety, an older person may approach the testing situation too cautiously to do well. On the WAIS–R and the PMA, there are no penalties for wrong answers; it is to your advantage to guess when you are unsure. Older adults may not be inclined to risk a wrong answer by guessing, though. In a classic study, researchers administered the PMA to older adults under two conditions: some were encouraged to guess if they were uncertain whereas others were encouraged to answer only those items of which they were sure. On most scales, those who had been encouraged to guess attained higher scores (Birkhill & Schaie, 1975).

The current state of the psychometric art in intellectual assessment is, then, far from ideal for achieving a clear picture of how intelligence changes with age. However, instruments such as the WAIS–R and the PMA can provide valuable information on the relative performances of young and older adults in standardized situations. We turn next to what psychologists have learned by examining these relative performances.

Psychometric research on change in adult intelligence

For over three decades, researchers have used standardized intelligence tests in cross-sectional, longitudinal, and sequential studies of age-related changes in intelligence. Early cross-sectional studies showed that young adults performed best on standard intelligence tests; middle-aged and elderly adults' performances were substantially worse (e.g., Doppelt & Wallace, 1955). Age differences were generally greater for the performance scale of the WAIS than the verbal scale, and most older people attained higher scores on the verbal scale than on the performance scale (e.g., Botwinick, 1977; Doppelt & Wallace, 1955). This tendency for older peoples' verbal scale scores to exceed their performance scale scores is so reliable that it has been termed the **classic aging pattern**.

These cross-sectional findings suggest that intelligence begins to decline early in adulthood. However, such a conclusion would probably be ill-founded, at least in some respects. Recall that in a cross-sectional study adults of different ages are tested at a single time of measurement. Thus, the different age groups also represent different cohorts, who have had different cultural experiences in general and different educational experiences in particular. This aspect of the database is particularly important in the study of intelligence, since contemporary young adults are generally better educated than contemporary middle-aged and older adults and since crystallized intelligence is positively associated with educational background. Longitudinal and sequential research, then, provide a better perspective from which to consider age-related trends in intelligence.

Longitudinal research presents a more optimistic picture. Although fluid intelligence decreases throughout adulthood, crystallized intelligence—those learned aspects of intelligence that depend on experience and education—remains stable or improves through late adulthood (e.g., Horn, 1970; 1982). One set of longitudinal studies in which age changes in intelligence were examined is the Berkeley Growth Study, the Oakland Growth Study, and the Guidance Study (Eichorn, Hunt, & Honzik, 1981); recall that we considered this body of research in discussing health changes in adulthood. Participants in these studies were assessed using the WAIS in their thirties or forties, and these assessments were compared with intelligence tests conducted throughout the participants' infancy and adolescence.

Test performance remained stable between late adolescence and middle adulthood, as evidenced by substantial positive correlations across these age periods (Eichorn et al., 1981). These correlations show that the rank-ordering of scores changed little over the years; at the same time, the researchers found that many subjects had gained 10 or more points in IQ scores by their forties. Subsequent analyses of these samples showed that performance continued to improve in the forties and fifties on the Information, Comprehension, and Vocabulary subtests (see Table 6.2), but declined on the Digit Symbol and Block Design subtests (Sands, Terry, & Meredith, 1989).

The optimistic picture of age changes in crystallized intelligence is not unique to this particular set of longitudinal data, but is typical of the findings of longitudinal research on adult intelligence (e.g., Owens, 1966; Schaie, 1983a; Schaie, 1983b). Remember, however, that longitudinal data can reflect the impact of practice and selective attrition as well as maturation (see Chapter One, pages 22–23). For these reasons, we also need to consider sequential studies of adult intelligence.

K. Warner Schaie has directed one of the most extensive sequential research programs on intellectual functioning in adulthood (e.g., Hertzog &
Schaie, 1986; 1988; Schaie, 1983a; Schaie, 1983b; 1990; Schaie & Labouvie-Vief,
1974). In his Seattle Longitudinal Study, the PMA was administered to adults
ranging in age from 25 to 81, who were retested at seven-year intervals. Schaie
and his colleagues found that participants gained in proficiency through the
early forties, and then functioned at the same level through the late fifties or
early sixties. As Figure 6.3 illustrates, most of the participants actually maintained stable levels of performance on most abilities well into old age.

In addition to retesting as many of the original participants as possible,
Schaie added new random samples from the original cohorts at each time of
measurement. Although the repeated testing for the longitudinal sequences in
this study had little impact upon performance (Schaie, 1983a), there were
cohort differences in test scores. Later-born cohorts attained and maintained
higher levels of performance than had their earlier-born counterparts; similar
cohort differences have been identified in other studies as well (e.g., Rybash
et al., 1986; Schaie, 1990). As Schaie (1990) explains, these cohort differences
probably reflect increased educational opportunities and improvements in
nutrition and health care.

Schaie (e.g., 1983a, 1983b; 1990) concluded overall that the course of adult
cognitive development is variable, multidirectional, and subject to cultural
influence. In other words, there are wide individual differences in the age

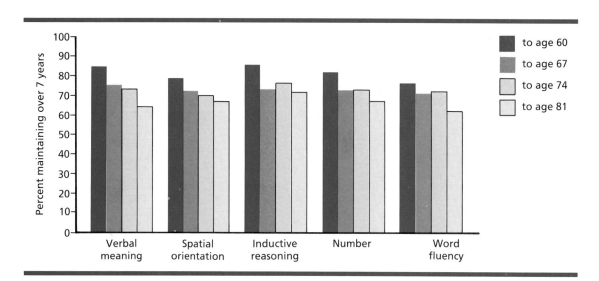

Figure 6.3
*Proportion of individuals who maintain stable levels of performance over seven years
on five primary mental abilities.* (Source: Schaie, 1990. Reprinted by permission.)

at which intellectual decline appears—this may occur for one person in his fifties but not until the eighties for another. Furthermore, different abilities (e.g., fluid versus crystallized abilities) age in different directions, with decreased performance occurring for some abilities but not others. Perhaps most important, in light of the conflicting cross-sectional and longitudinal findings, more recent cohorts exhibit a later and less pronounced decrement in performance.

Explanations for age-related changes in intelligence

Scholars offer several explanations for the declines in fluid intelligence and stable or improved performance in crystallized intelligence. Explanations for decline cite biological and health changes of adulthood, the effects of terminal drop (see below), and age differences in information processing. Biological explanations focus on age changes in the nervous system (see Chapter Three, pp. 57–58). Recall that neurons are lost throughout adulthood, that neural metabolism changes, and that there is a general slowing of behavior. These changes may affect cognitive performance through their impact on such basic processes as attention and arousal, or the ability to employ effective cognitive strategies (Poon, 1985).

Another biologically-based explanation takes changes in physical health as its starting point. Recent research shows that self-reported health is associated with intelligence test performance, especially in advanced old age (Field, Schaie, & Leino, 1988; Perlmutter & Nyquist, 1990). Willis (1989) noted that chronic illnesses, which become more common in middle adulthood, may affect cognitive functioning. Cardiovascular disease, for example, can restrict blood flow to the brain, and thus produce temporary or permanent neural "malnutrition." She also suggested that health problems may interfere with cognitive test performance because the discomfort and financial worries that they entail disrupt the concentration needed to do well.

Some suggest that poorer intellectual performance in successively older age groups reflects **terminal drop**. In an early longitudinal study, Kleemeier (1962) found that men who died soon after a time of measurement had worse scores than those who lived longer. He proposed that a deterioration in intellectual functioning precedes death, and labeled this phenomenon terminal drop.

Later, Riegel and Riegel (1972) suggested that terminal drop preceded death by as much as five years, and that it might account for age-related declines found in cross-sectional studies. Their reasoning was that successively older age groups would logically include more individuals in the critical five-year period of terminal drop; the older age groups, then, would have lower average levels of cognitive performance. Recent research suggests that terminal drop may only affect cognitive abilities that show little change with normal aging (e.g., vocabulary, verbal fluency) and that its effects are limited to two, rather than five, years preceding death (White & Cunningham, 1988).

Still other explanations for cognitive decline focus on age differences in information processing. Poon (1985) suggested that the processes of encoding and retrieving stored information operate less effectively in middle and later adulthood than earlier in adulthood. These differences, in turn, may stem from less "deep processing" of incoming information by using such techniques as elaboration, imagery, and organization. Similarly, age differences in attention processes (see Chapter Five, pages 122–124; Plude, in press; Plude & Doussard-Roosevelt, 1989; Plude & Murphy, in press) might account for some of the age differences in psychometric studies of intelligence.

How do researchers account for stable or improved performance on measures of crystallized intelligence as people get older? One approach has focused on correlates of improved performance. Eichorn et al. (1981) identified several characteristics associated with increased IQ scores between adolescence and middle adulthood. Enriching personal experiences such as traveling outside of the United States or being married to a highly intelligent person were also associated with IQ gains. Adolescent personality characteristics were also associated with extreme gains in IQ. Teenagers who were "balanced"—moderately socialized, independent, adaptable, and self-confident—were most likely to gain 13 or more IQ points by middle adulthood.

Other longitudinal research points to similar correlates of improved intellectual functioning. Willis (1989) noted a relationship between intellectual performance and work complexity. Work that requires dealing with ideas and making independent judgments calls for an above-average level of intelligence. In this research, men who filled such demanding jobs gained intellectual flexibility throughout adulthood. Related research suggests that such work has the same benefits for women (Willis, 1989).

REASONING AND PROBLEM SOLVING THROUGHOUT ADULTHOOD

One arena in which people deploy intelligence in their everyday lives is in solving problems. At work, at school, and at home, most confront more or less challenging problems nearly every day. Researchers have compared young, middle-aged, and older adults' approaches to various situations—both abstract problems that require efficient use of logic and practical, everyday problems that draw on reasoning, experience, and common sense.

Research on logical reasoning and problem solving

Piaget's theory predicts that mature adults should function at the level of formal operations, at least for solving problems within their domain of familiarity and expertise. Piaget himself did not actually examine adult cognitive performance. However, research considering adult age differences on Piagetian problems flourished in the 1970s.

In one of the first such studies, Papalia (1972) examined young, middle-aged, and elderly adults' performance on conservation of substance, weight, and volume problems. Fewer middle-aged adults than young adults solved the conservation of substance and weight problems, although these age differences were relatively small. The age differences in conservation of volume were larger, but also less consistent. The highest percentage of subjects who successfully solved the conservation of volume problem, which is believed to draw on formal operations, was in the 55 to 64 age group. Young adult college students, adults between the ages of 30 and 54, and adults age 65 and older solved this problem less frequently. Thus, the elderly adults in Papalia's (1972) research did not function at the formal operational level. In other cross-sectional studies, older adults have similarly reasoned at immature levels on classification tasks and spatial egocentrism tasks. The latter problems require imagining how a spatial array would appear from a vantage point other than one's own (for reviews, see Hooper & Sheehan, 1977 and Papalia & Bielby, 1974).

Middle-aged and older adults also find other kinds of logical problems more difficult than young adults do. Denney and Palmer (1981), for example, compared young, middle-aged, and older adults' performances on a Twenty Questions Task. In this task, the goal was to determine as quickly as possible which of 42 pictures of common objects the experimenter had designated as a target; the subject identified the target by asking questions that could be answered "yes" or "no." The most efficient strategy is to ask "constraint-seeking" questions which eliminate several items at once (e.g., is it alive?); a more laborious approach is to ask "hypothesis testing" questions which eliminate only one object at a time (e.g., is it the umbrella?). The middle-aged and older subjects asked fewer constraint-seeking questions, and consequently more questions overall, than did the youngest subjects. Reviews of research on age differences in logical problem solving and decision making show that most studies reveal the same pattern of age differences (e.g., Rabbitt, 1977; Reese & Rodeheaver, 1985).

In the face of these findings, some suggest that aging is accompanied by regression to immature levels of cognitive functioning, perhaps because of neurological degeneration or because of social isolation (e.g., Hooper, Fitzgerald, & Papalia, 1971; Hooper & Sheehan, 1977). Such regression is apparently neither universal nor unchangeable, however. Reese and Rodeheaver (1985) note that the percentages of middle-aged and older adults who conserve in cross-sectional comparisons varies from one study to another, reflecting sample differences in subjects' educational and occupational background. Relatively well-educated older people often solve conservation, classification, and other logical problems quite well.

For example, Sabatini and Labouvie-Vief (1979) compared young and older scientists' and nonscientists' solutions to formal operations problems. Because solving these problems requires taking a systematic, analytical approach similar to that used in much scientific work, both theory and common sense would predict that occupation would have at least as much to do with performance as age. That prediction was confirmed. The older scientists were actually better than their younger counterparts in solving these problems, whereas the young nonscientists solved the problems more effectively than the older nonscientists.

Furthermore, any cognitive regression that does take place may be reversible. Several types of cognitive training—including feedback about problem solution (Hornblum & Overton, 1976; Schultz & Hoyer, 1976), modeling (Denney & Denney, 1974), explanation of problem-solving strategies (Tomlinson-Keasey, 1972), and social interaction and practice in role taking (Zaks & Labouvie-Vief, 1980)—can enhance older adults' performance on Piagetian problems.

Finally, Labouvie-Vief and her colleagues (1980; 1982; 1985; Labouvie-Vief & Hakim-Larson, 1989) suggest that middle-aged and older adults' inability to solve formal operational problems may not reflect cognitive regression at all. Instead, middle-aged and older adults' performance on these problems may reflect use of reasoning modes that are better adapted to their life context than formal logic. When the tasks used to evaluate cognitive functioning require formal logic and abstract thinking—such as Piagetian tasks drawing on formal operations—middle-aged and older people may be at a disadvantage relative to younger adults.

One formal operational task requires the examinee to determine which of several possible combinations of colorless chemicals produces a certain reaction; another requires predicting which factor or combination of factors determines the speed of a pendulum swing. Both can be efficiently solved through the use of logic alone, but neither has much to do with most peoples' everyday lives. Young adult college students, however, may be accustomed to solving problems that have no obvious connection to their lives outside the classroom or laboratory. Some students may even feel that their academic responsibilities primarily involve mastering tasks with no practical or personal value. Thus, college students may be exceptionally able and willing to use formal, abstract reasoning in solving Piagetian problems.

For middle-aged and older adults, on the other hand, most opportunities for problem solving arise in dealing with concrete, practical problems at home or at work. How should one deal with an unwanted pregnancy? What should you do if you are cheated when making a major purchase? What is the most adaptive reaction to a job performance evaluation that seems unreasonable and biased? These problems cannot always be best solved on a formal, abstract level alone. It is often necessary to temper those approaches with more intuitive, subjective modes of reasoning: combining reason with emotion may lead to the best solutions. Formal logic divorced from consideration of the social or emotional issues related to a problem, then, may be strategies that middle-aged and older adults rarely exercise. Such approaches may even seem oversimplified to mature adults who are accustomed to reasoning with their hearts as well as their heads.

Research on practical problem solving

Although middle-aged and elderly adults have more difficulty than young adults with abstract problems, middle adulthood is a period of peak performance in practical problem solving. In Denney and Palmer's (1981) study, a series of "real life" problems was presented in addition to the Twenty Questions Task. These problems required subjects to propose solutions to such situations as discovering a malfunctioning refrigerator, dealing with a flooded basement, and receiving threatening phone calls. The researchers rated the quality of answers, with ratings depending on the number of solutions proposed and the extent to which solutions involved personal action rather than reliance on others. In contrast to the pattern of age differences on the Twenty Questions Task, scores on this task increased through the 40 to 50-year-old group and decreased thereafter.

Although the older adults in this study did not do as well in solving these practical problems as the middle-aged adults did, other research tells us that older people believe that their practical problem-solving ability increases with age (Williams, Denney, & Schadler, 1983). Nancy Denney and her colleagues have suggested that this contradiction may reflect young researchers' tendencies to pose practical problems that are unfamiliar or uninteresting to the elderly—and that thus demand the use of unexercised abilities (e.g., Denney & Palmer, 1981; Denney & Pearce, 1989; Denney, Pearce, & Palmer, 1982). Thus, these researchers devised practical problems relevant to the everyday experience of older adults, and used those problems as a basis for examining age differences in problem solving. Even when the problems were germane to older peoples' lives, however, Denney and her collaborators found that middle-aged adults' performances exceeded the older adults' performances (Denney & Pearce, 1989; Denney, Pearce, & Palmer, 1982).

Other research does support Denney's contention that well-chosen problems can elicit better solutions from older adults than either young or middle-aged people, though. S. W. Cornelius and Caspi (1987) designed an Everyday Problem Solving Inventory that included problems an adult might encounter in six domains: in consumer affairs, in dealing with technical information, in home management, in resolving family conflicts, in resolving conflicts with friends, and in resolving conflicts with coworkers. They administered the Inventory, along with measures of verbal ability and a traditional problem solving test, to adults aged 20 to 78. Whereas performance on the traditional problem-solving task peaked in middle adulthood, performance on the Everyday Problem Solving Inventory and verbal ability increased throughout adulthood.

It is possible that these results differ from those of Denney's work (see above) because of differences in the researchers' approaches to scoring.

Denney's scoring system rewarded participants who proposed more solutions overall and solutions involving personal action rather than cooperation or reliance on others. However, in Cornelius and Caspi's (1987) study, the most desireable solution depended on the type of problem to be solved. As these researchers explained, "everyday problem solving skills or abilities may be characterized by an individual's sensitivity to situational differences and flexibility in responding to situational nuances" (p. 147). Older adults have the experience that may be necessary to develop this sensitivity and flexibility.

A practical problem that most people encounter frequently is resolving interpersonal conflicts. Blanchard-Fields (1986) compared the performances of adolescents, young adults, and middle-aged adults on three problems in which such conflicts had to be resolved. Each problem presented discrepant accounts of a single event; the events varied in the extent to which emotions were salient. The first (the "Livia task") presented two accounts of a fictional war, each supposedly written by a historian from one of the warring nations; the second (the "visit" story) presented a teenager's and his parents' descriptions of a visit to the grandparents; and the third (the pregnancy dilemma) presented a man's and a woman's differing perspectives on an unplanned pregnancy.

After the events were presented, subjects discussed their interpretations of the discrepant accounts, how the discrepancies had arisen, whether a "right" account could exist, and whether or not the conflict could be resolved. Figure 6.4 presents Blanchard-Fields' (1986) results. As you can see, the middle-aged adults showed the most sophisticated reasoning in discussing all three events, although their performance did not differ significantly from that of the young adults. Both adult groups were more capable than the adolescents of display-

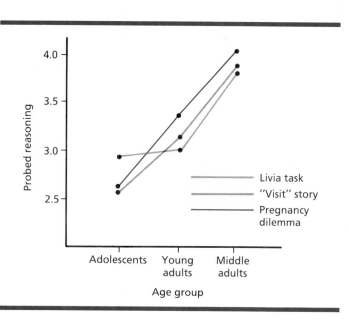

Figure 6.4
Probed reasoning scores for adolescents, young adults, and middle aged adults.
(Source: Blanchard-Fields, 1986. Copyright 1986 by the American Psychological Association. Reprinted by permission.)

ing "an increased ability to differentiate a person's interpretation of an account from the account itself" (p. 331), although most subjects (including the adolescents) were capable of formal operational reasoning. The adults proposed resolutions that centered on improved communication and increased mutual respect for ideas and values—not necessarily on determining who was "right."

As noted earlier, Labouvie-Vief and her colleagues (1980; 1985; Labouvie-Vief & Hakim-Larson, 1989) respond to findings like these by proposing that new standards of intellectual proficiency are needed to evaluate middle-aged and older adults' performances. The hallmark of cognitive proficiency in early adulthood may be the ability to employ formal logic in order to resolve conflicts and contradictions. Cognitive proficiency later in adulthood, however, may center around the wisdom to recognize some conflicts as inevitable, and the ability to reason effectively about the implications of that conflict. The adults in Blanchard-Fields' (1986) study exemplify this perspective.

WISDOM AND CREATIVITY

In addition to intelligence and reasoning, wisdom and creativity are central to adult cognitive functioning. Wisdom defies precise definition, although the quality has been discussed since ancient times. Clayton and Birren (1980) note that the definition varies from one culture to another. In ancient Greece, wisdom entailed understanding not only the nature of the world but also moral understanding; Eastern definitions often stress direct experience of the meaning of life, rather than rational skills; and most Western societies embrace a definition of wisdom as a constellation of cognition, emotion, and intuition (Clayton & Birren, 1980).

Although these definitions differ in particulars, most imply that developing wisdom requires time and experience. Psychologists have also generally discussed time and age as necessary, but by no means sufficient, conditions for the development of wisdom. Erikson (e.g., 1963; 1982), for example, describes wisdom as growing from a dynamic balance between feelings about the integrity of one's life and feelings of despair in the face of death. In Erikson's theory of personality development (see Chapter Eight, pp. 192–193), achieving this balance is a task of later adulthood. Remember that Schaie's (1977–1978) stage theory of adult intellectual development locates wisdom in the final reintegrative stage, during which one acquires a sense of the meaning of knowledge.

Does wisdom come with age, at least for some? Research addressing this question is only beginning—but already has provided some surprising answers. In one of the first systematic studies of age differences in wisdom, Smith and Baltes (1990) defined wisdom as an expert knowledge system devoted to the practicalities of life. Thus, wisdom includes exceptional insight and good judgment regarding humans and their development; rich factual knowledge about life matters and ways of dealing with life problems; understanding of past, current, and future circumstances surrounding life problems; sensitivity to alternative values and goals; and awareness of the inherent uncertainty and unpredictability of life.

Smith and Baltes (1990) used this definition as a framework for evaluating young, middle-aged, and elderly adults' proposed solutions to hypothetical life-planning problems. They presented four hypothetical problems (see Table 6.3) to their participants and asked each to "think aloud" about how the target person should deal with the problem. As Table 6.3 displays, some problems featured a young character, some featured an old character, some featured a normative problem, and others featured a nonnormative problem.

The researchers expected that only a few responses would fit their definition of wisdom; that expectation was supported, with only 5 percent of the proposed solutions considered wise (Smith & Baltes, 1990). Surprisingly, in light of the popular notion that the old are more likely to be wise than the young, Smith and Baltes found that wise responses (those given ratings of 5 or above on a 7-point scale) were evenly distributed across the age range that they studied. The older participants, in general, were no more likely to produce wise solutions than the middle-aged or younger participants. In fact, on most problems, the young and middle-aged participants' solutions were rated significantly higher (but generally not high enough to be considered wise) than the older participants' solutions. Only in proposing solutions to the nonnormative problem featuring an old character were the older participants' solutions rated higher than the younger participants' solutions.

Simonton (1990) notes that popular thinking dictates that age brings wisdom, but at the expense of creativity. If research does not support the idea that wisdom is associated with old age, is popular thinking similarly inaccurate with respect to creativity? Psychologists have examined developmental trends in creativity using two approaches. Some have taken a **psychometric approach**, comparing young and older adults' performances on standardized measures of creativity. Most such measures assess divergent thinking—the capacity to generate many novel responses to a stimulus.

Psychometric studies consistently point to an age-related decline in performance (Simonton, 1990)—just as one would expect on the basis of popular thinking. However, most of this research is cross-sectional (and thus may not reflect maturational changes), and some question the construct validity of the measures used (Simonton, 1990). Psychometric findings, then, only provide weak support for the notion that creativity decreases with age.

In the **historiometric approach**, researchers examine age-related trends in actual creative achievement rather than in standardized test performance. In other words, scientists consider whether or not age is related to the numbers of paintings, publications, poems, books, and so forth that individuals produce per time unit. The findings of this research, too, generally support the notion of an age-related decline in creativity.

Harvey Lehman (1953) published one of the first, and still the best known, historiometric studies of creative achievement. Using textbooks and histories of

Table 6.3
Life-planning problems: A fictitious person faces a decision about future options

Young target	Older target
Type of life decision: Normative	

1. Elizabeth, 33 years old and a successful professional for 8 years, was recently offered a major promotion. Her new responsibilities would require an increased time commitment. She and her husband would also like to have children before it is too late. Elizabeth is considering the following options: She could plan to accept the promotion, or she could plan to start a family.

2. Up to now, Jack, 63 years old and married, has approached compulsory retirement at 65 with some anxiety. Recently, his company was taken over. The new management has decided to close the outer suburban branch where Jack is employed. Jack is considering the following options: He can plan to take early retirement with full pay as compensation for 2 years, or he can plan to move to work in the company head office for 2 to 3 more years.

Type of life decision: Nonnormative

3. Michael, a 28-year-old mechanic with two preschool-aged children, has just learned that the factory in which he is working will close in 3 months. At present, there is no possibility for further employment in this area. His wife has recently returned to her well-paid nursing career. Michael is considering the following options: He can plan to move to another city to seek employment, or he can plan to take full responsibility for child-care and household tasks.

4. Joyce, a 60-year-old widow, recently completed a degree in business management and opened her own business. She has been looking forward to this new challenge. She has just heard that her son has been left with two small children to care for. Joyce is considering the following options: She could plan to give up her business and live with her son, or she could plan to arrange for financial assistance for her son to cover child-care costs.

Note. The specific instruction following each problem is: "Formulate a plan that covers what ___ should do and consider in the next 3 to 5 years? What extra pieces of information are needed?" Subjects were trained to think aloud.

Source: Smith and Baltes, 1990. Copyright 1990 by the American Psychological Association. Reprinted by permission.

various fields, Lehman identified the ages at which individuals made notable contributions. He concluded that the twenties and thirties were the ages of maximum creativity.

Lehman's work was criticized in at least three respects when it initially appeared (e.g., Dennis, 1956; 1958; 1966). Textbooks may present a biased view of when key contributions are made, emphasizing an individual's initial "pioneering" work at the expense of her later, equally important contributions. Furthermore, most fields become more competitive with the passage of time; thus work produced relatively early in one's career has a better chance of attracting notice than that produced later on. Finally, Lehman's analysis included the creative contributions of some who died quite early; this approach might have produced an artificially early average peak age of maximum creativity.

What have more recent historiometric studies told us about aging and creativity? Criticisms notwithstanding, Lehman's initial picture remains accurate: creative productivity in adulthood rises to a peak relatively early and declines thereafter (Simonton, 1990). The age at which peak productivity is attained varies from one field to another, though. Greatest creativity appears as early as the late twenties or early thirties in fields such as pure mathematics and theoretical physics, but not until the forties or fifties for history, philosophy, and psychology (Horner, Rushton, & Vernon, 1986; Simonton, 1990).

Furthermore, the *number* of creative accomplishments may decrease with time, but their quality may still remain high. In a study of the scholarly impact of young and older research psychologists, Over (1989) found that older scientists' articles—although fewer in number than younger scientists' articles—had as much impact as the work of their younger counterparts. Simonton (1989) too found that the last works of classical composers were rated higher in several aesthetic attributes. He explained this "swan song phenomenon" with the suggestion that "composers in their final years seem to concentrate on producing masterworks that will permanently establish their reputation" (p. 45).

Although the number of creative accomplishments may decrease with age, the quality of creative products may remain high.

Research on age-related trends in wisdom and creativity, then, both supports and refutes common beliefs about adult development. Just as many people have long believed, creativity may be a quality that flowers in youth—at least in some fields and using some standards of creativity. Wisdom, however, does not seem to be a province of the aged in particular.

This mixed picture fits well with the other research examined in this chapter. Findings in the areas of intelligence and logical reasoning include some data providing an optimistic picture of cognitive changes in middle and later adulthood—and others casting a bleak perspective. In light of all of this work, the *Open Questions* box presents a general summarizing question: does intelligence decline with age?

OPEN QUESTIONS   **BOX 6.2**

Does intelligence decline with age?

How intelligence changes with age, and particularly whether or not intellectual decline universally occurs in old age, is a longstanding controversy. Given the work that we have reviewed in this chapter, it is easy to see why this question should elicit strikingly different answers from different scholars. If there are different perspectives on just what constitutes adult intelligence, then how can there be agreement on changes in intelligence during adulthood?

The issue of intellectual decline in old age was addressed most vigorously in a series of articles by Baltes and Schaie (1974; 1976; Schaie, 1974; Schaie & Baltes, 1977), on the one hand, and Horn and Donaldson (1976; 1977) on the other. Briefly, Baltes and Schaie interpreted data from the Seattle Longitudinal Study as evidence that intellectual decline in old age is by no means universal; in fact, the study provided impressive evidence of stability for many intellectual abilities. Horn and Donaldson countered that this position was far too optimistic, glossing over reliable age-related declines in fluid intelligence.

On the basis of the work that we reviewed in this chapter, which position seems better supported? The psychometric data—including Schaie's Seattle Longitudinal Study, but also other longitudinal data—reveal both important individual differences in intellectual performance among the aged and stability in many kinds of intellectual performance until advanced old age. The literature on problem solving tells us that abstract, logical reasoning may be more difficult for older than for younger adults—but also that adults may grow more adept at solving practical problems as they get older. Current research suggests that wisdom may not come with age, and that creativity may decrease with age.

Probably, one could muster sufficient data to support an argument on either side of this debate. But the question of whether or not an age-related decline in intelligence universally occurs may not be the most important question to pursue, from a practical standpoint. As Schaie & Baltes (1977) asserted, the critical issue may be how we can enhance older peoples' intellectual functioning on tasks that they find difficult. Research reviewed in this chapter shows that researchers pursuing this direction have succeeded in improving elderly adults' performance on measures of fluid intelligence and on logical problem-solving tasks.

Rather than asking whether or not intellectual decline universally occurs in old age, then, we should probably ask how learning and intellectual growth coexist with decline in old age. This question provides a starting point for the next chapter, in which age-related change in learning and memory is addressed.

SUMMARY

Some theorists propose that adulthood spans a sequence of stages in intellectual growth, whereas others describe unique components of adult intelligence. Among the best known of the latter approaches is Horn and Cattell's model of fluid and crystallized intelligence. Crystallized intelligence typically increases throughout the life span, whereas fluid intelligence normally peaks in the late teens or early twenties. Recently, researchers have succeeded in training older individuals to improve their performance on fluid intelligence tasks.

Early cross-sectional studies showed that young adults performed best on standard intelligence tests. Longitudinal research presents a much more optimistic picture. On the basis of one of the most extensive longitudinal research programs, Schaie concluded that the course of adult cognitive development is variable, multidirectional, and subject to cultural influence.

In studies of abstract reasoning, elderly adults generally do not function at the formal operational level; middle-aged and older adults also find other kinds of logical problems (e.g., a Twenty Questions task) more difficult than do young adults. Some suggest, however, that middle-aged and older adults' performances may reflect reasoning modes well-adapted to their life context.

In addition to intelligence and reasoning, wisdom and creativity are central to adult cognitive functioning. Smith and Baltes found that the wise responses to hypothetical problems were evenly distributed across a wide adult age range. Psychometric studies consistently point to an age-related decline in creativity, as do historiometric studies.

KEY TERMS

Achieving stage
Acquisitive stage
Automatic processing
Classic aging pattern
Crystallized intelligence
Debilitating anxiety
Effortful processing
Encapsulation model
Executive stage
Fluid intelligence
Historiometric approach

Information processing theory
Metasystematic reasoning
Multiple intelligences theory
Primary Mental Abilities Test (PMA)
Problem finding
Psychometric approach
Reintegrative stage
Responsible stage
Terminal drop
Triarchic theory
Wechsler Adult Intelligence Scale—Revised (WAIS–R)

SUGGESTIONS FOR FURTHER READING

Commons, M. L., Sinnott, J. D., Richards, F. A., & Armon, C. (Eds.). (1989). *Beyond Formal Operations: Volume 2. Comparisons and Applications of Adolescent and Adult Developmental Models*. New York: Praeger.

Commons, M. L., Richards, F. A., & Armon, S. (1984). *Beyond Formal Operations: Volume 1. Late Adolescent and Adult Cognitive Development*. New York: Praeger Publishing.

Rybash, J. M., Hoyer, W. J., & Roodin, P. A. (1986). *Adult Cognition and Aging: Developmental Changes in Processing, Knowing, and Thinking*. New York: Pergamon Press.

Schaie, K. W. (1983). *Longitudinal Studies of Adult Psychological Development*. New York: The Guilford Press.

Sternberg, R. J. (Ed.) *Wisdom: Its Nature, Origins, and Development*. New York: Cambridge.

CHAPTER SEVEN

LEARNING AND MEMORY THROUGHOUT ADULTHOOD

Is it true that "you can't teach an old dog new tricks?" Some of the most widespread and distressing stereotypes of aging and the aged concern learning and memory. Many people, including many older people, believe that aging destroys the capacities to learn and remember. This chapter examines learning and memory, and changes with age in these processes.

We begin with a discussion of the interdependence of learning and memory, and the relationship of both processes to performance. The chapter reviews the ways that psychologists describe memory, age differences in learning and memory performance, and some of the explanations offered for these age differences. Much of this evidence stems from experimental studies taking place in the artificial setting of the psychology laboratory. Other work describes older adults' memory skills in everyday life, and ways to enhance older peoples' memory performance. The chapter closes with a discussion of education for young, middle-aged, and elderly adults.

Questions to consider in reading the chapter include:

How are learning and memory related to one another, and to performance?

How does the information processing approach describe memory stores and their vulnerability to the effects of aging?

How do young and older adults' performances typically differ in laboratory studies of memory performances? What nonability influences of performance probably contribute to these age differences?

How effectively do the elderly deal with memory demands of everyday life? What kinds of memory training is effective for older adults?

How does going to college affect young people? What unique strengths and weaknesses do older students bring to the classroom?

LEARNING, MEMORY, AND PERFORMANCE

The inseparability of learning and memory

Many people think of learning and memory as entirely separate processes. Students often attempt to learn new information and to remember things that they already know under different circumstances. Many times, the two processes are discussed in different chapters of psychology textbooks—or even in different psychology courses. However, further reflection reveals that learning and memory can be distinguished only in the most arbitrary way.

Psychologists have offered countless definitions of learning and memory. In this chapter, **learning** refers to the acquisition of a new skill or new knowledge as a result of practice, study, or experience. **Memory**, on the other hand, refers to the retrieval of information or skills that have previously been learned.

Now the inseparability of learning and memory becomes apparent. As Jack Botwinick (1978) explains, someone cannot remember information that she has never learned, and the extent to which an individual has learned material is typically evaluated by determining how much she can remember. In practice, it is impossible to study learning without also studying memory. All of the research reviewed in this chapter, then, concerns age differences in both processes.

Learning and memory versus performance

Although learning and memory cannot be meaningfully distinguished, both must be differentiated from performance. Learning and memory are internal processes that cannot be observed. When a professor gives a test over three textbook chapters, or when a researcher conducts a cross-sectional study of learning, the goal is to determine how much students or research participants learned by observing how much they remember. What the professor or researcher actually observes, though, is neither learning nor memory itself, but performance on a memory test. That performance is used as an index of how much the students or participants originally learned and now can remember.

Test performance is an imperfect index of learning and remembering, though. Certainly, the students' and participants' abilities to learn and remember influence their memory test performance. But their performance is also affected by a wide variety of other factors.

If a cross-sectional study shows that elderly participants remember fewer items from a list than young adults, it may be because the older people were able to learn as many items as the younger people did, but could remember less of what they learned. Or, it may be because the older adults were able to learn fewer items in the first place but could remember as much of what they learned as the younger people. The older adults' relatively poor performance may be further traced to things like anxiety in the laboratory situation, lack of motivation to learn what the experimenter presents, failure to use effective learning strategies, or being too rushed in the experiment to study the material and search through memory during the test. In other words, the older adults may be much more *capable* of learning and remembering than their observable performance might suggest.

This point provides important context for examining the literature on aging as it impacts learning and memory performance. Age differences in performance favoring young adults are the typical results in this area. However, one should not necessarily conclude that the *abilities* to learn and remember universally and irreversibly decline in old age. There are wide individual differences in older adults' learning and memory performances. More important, it is often possible to train older people to use techniques that improve learning and memory performances; these results suggest that learning and memory are less affected by age than we might otherwise suspect.

*A*GE DIFFERENCES IN MEMORY PERFORMANCE

The information processing approach to memory

Recall from the last chapter that the information processing approach is one of the most important contemporary perspectives on adult cognitive functioning. The study of memory is a major area of inquiry in the psychology of adult cognition in general and in the information processing approach in particular. This approach includes the distinctions between sensory memory, primary memory, working memory, secondary memory, and tertiary memory.

One of the basic premises of the information processing approach is that the flow of information can be traced through several hypothetical memory stores (e.g., Craik & Lockhart, 1972); Figure 7.1 illustrates these memory stores. The first is **sensory memory**. Sensory memory is the stage at which new information is initially registered (e.g., Craik, 1977; Poon, 1985). This, then, corresponds to the instant that you perceive a visual or auditory sensation; sensory memory for visual information is called **iconic memory** and sensory memory for auditory information is called **echoic memory**.

Sensory memory is fleeting. Unless deliberate attention is given to these incoming signals, they decay in less than a second. Those sensory signals that do win attention are passed along to the next memory store, primary memory (see below). Given age-related declines in sensation and perception (see Chapter Five, pp. 111–122), one might expect that there would be reliable age differences favoring young adults in sensory memory. However, research fails to identify any but the smallest differences in sensory memory (Poon, 1985).

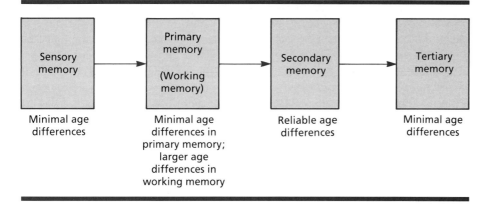

Figure 7.1
Information-processing model of memory

Primary memory is akin to current consciousness, and has a limited storage capacity and duration. If you look up a zip code and think about the number while addressing an envelope, the zip code is in primary memory at that time. Because primary memory is of limited capacity, thinking about other things as you address the envelope will cause you to forget the zip code. If you make a special effort to learn and remember the zip code so that you will never have to look it up again, it is transferred to secondary memory.

Like sensory memory, primary memory shows little change with age (e.g., Craik, 1977; Poon, 1985). Cross-sectional research has identified few differences in the capacity of primary memory: adults of all ages are able to store approximately seven items (Craik, 1968). Adults of all ages are equally efficient in retrieving information from primary memory (e.g., Poon & Fozard, 1980); older adults are somewhat slower in retrieving such information, however (Waugh, Thomas, & Fozard, 1978).

There is an exception to this general statement that primary memory is relatively invulnerable to aging. When information in primary memory must be actively manipulated or reorganized in some way, then age differences favoring young adults do appear (e.g., Craik, 1977; Dobbs & Rule, 1989; Hultsch & Dixon, 1990). **Working memory** is the term usually applied to these processes.

According to Baddeley (1986), working memory comprises at least two distinct storage regions (one for auditory-verbal information and one for visual-spatial information), as well as a single central executive system within which information is processed and manipulated. Memory tasks that involve primarily storage (e.g., remembering a zip code long enough to address an envelope) rely mostly on the capacities of the storage regions. Memory tasks that rely more heavily on processing as well as storage (e.g., solving anagrams in your head), however, depend on the capacities of the central executive system. Some researchers believe that older adults experience greater difficulty with working memory tasks primarily because of the processing demands and not the storage demands (e.g., Craik, Morris, & Gick, 1989). However, others assert that both the storage and the processing demands of working memory tasks strain the capacities of older adults (Babcock & Salthouse, 1990; Foos, 1989).

Secondary memory corresponds to what most people think of as memory capacities that they use on an everyday basis. When you take an exam, match names with faces at a party, remember birthdays or anniversaries, or tell a friend about a book that you read recently, you are using information stored in secondary memory. Most psychologists believe that secondary memory is a permanent storage of virtually unlimited capacity.

When researchers study age differences in secondary memory performance, participants learn a list of items—words, phrases, or nonsense syllables—and then recall or recognize the items. When the participants **recall** the items, they must reproduce what they learned. A familiar example of a recall task is an essay test, in which you must restate what you have learned. When a **recognition** task is used, participants must distinguish the items that they learned from a group including the learned items together with new ones. Multiple choice exams, in which you must select a correct (learned) answer from several possible answers, are recognition tasks.

There have been thousands of studies of adult age differences in recalling and recognizing material stored in secondary memory. Although these studies vary in the precise ages of the participants and in the type and amount of material to be learned and remembered, the findings are remarkably consistent. Older adults recall substantially less information from secondary memory than do younger adults, but age differences are minimal or absent altogether in recognition performance (e.g., Craik, 1977; Hultsch & Dixon, 1990; Poon, 1985). Figure 7.2 illustrates the distinct patterns of age differences in recall and recognition performance.

There are individual differences in the extent to which recall from secondary memory declines with age. Elderly people of high verbal ability—those who have extensive vocabularies, or who speak and write fluently—often remember information stored in secondary memory nearly as well as young adults (e.g., Hultsch & Dixon, 1990; Hultsch, Hertzog, & Dixon, 1990; Poon, 1985). Older people with a high level of expertise in a particular area may be nearly as proficient as young adults in remembering information related to that area (Hultsch & Dixon, 1990). For example, elderly chess players remember configurations of chess pieces on a board about as well as younger players (e.g., Charness, 1989). This effect is domain-specific, however; older chess players would probably have much more difficulty than younger ones remembering a list of words.

The final memory store is **tertiary memory**, the repository for information stored for very long periods. Memories of your early childhood friends or your grade school teachers are stored in tertiary memory. Anecdotal evidence holds that tertiary memory remains largely intact in old age, even though secondary memory does not. Students often ask, for example, why great-grandmother can recall her wedding day with startling detail even though she cannot

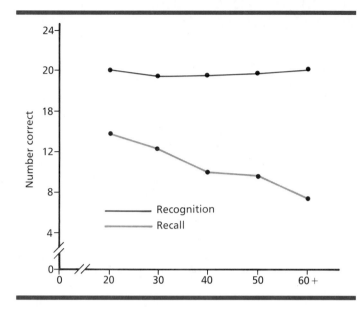

Figure 7.2
Adult age differences in recall and recognition scores. (Source: Schonfield and Robertson, "Memory Storage and Aging," Canadian Journal of Psychology, 1966, *20*, 228–236. Copyright 1966. Canadian Psychological Association. Reprinted with permission.

remember what she did last Tuesday. This anecdotal evidence conforms to **Ribot's Law** (Ribot, 1882), the proposition that information is forgotten in the reverse order from which it was acquired

Research provides only partial support for Ribot's Law as a phenomenon of normal aging. Tertiary memory does remain intact in old age: questionnaire studies assessing memory for long-past public events generally show few age differences (e.g., Howes & Katz, 1988; Poon, Fozard, Paulshock, & Thomas, 1979). In other studies, participants have demonstrated near-perfect memory of their high school classmates (recognized from yearbook photographs), proficiency in matching classmates' faces with names decades after graduation (Bahrick, Bahrick, & Wittlinger, 1975), and good recall of geographic knowledge of one's college town after many years (Bahrick, 1979). However, older peoples' memory for these remote events is no better than their recollection of recent events (e.g., Erber, 1981).

Encoding versus retrieval deficits

Researchers debate about whether age differences in secondary memory performance reflect young adults' superiority in transferring information from primary to secondary memory (encoding the information), in accessing information stored in secondary memory (retrieving the information), or in both encoding and retrieving information. Why is it important to locate the source of age differences in performance? After all, if you cannot remember material that you studied for an exam, you may feel that it does not matter whether the problem lies in how you studied the material or in how you attempt to remem-

Tertiary memory remains largely intact in old age.

ber the material. However, if you want to perform better on your next exam, locating the source of the problem is important—you need to know whether to change your study habits, your test-taking strategies, or both. In the same way, identifying the source of older adults' difficulties with secondary memory tasks provides a foundation for interventions aimed at enhancing memory performance in later life.

There is evidence that older adults experience an **encoding deficit** (e.g., Smith, 1980). In some studies, researchers use instructions to control the means through which participants encode material, and compare patterns of age differences resulting from different instructions (and thus different encoding strategies). In a classic study of this kind, Hultsch (1969) instructed some participants to organize a list of words to be learned, but instructed the others to simply learn the words. There were substantial age differences in memory performance when participants were not instructed to organize the words, but much smaller age differences when they were told to organize the words during learning.

Results such as these suggest that most young adults spontaneously take a strategic approach to learning: they organize new material, actively attempt to relate it to things that they already know, use visual imagery, or in other ways elaborate the material. Older adults, though, do not seem to use these strategies unless the researcher specifically tells them to do so, as Hultsch (1969) did.

At the same time, older adults experience a **retrieval deficit**. Remember that older adults often recognize information stored in secondary memory that they cannot recall (see Figure 7.2). Similarly, older adults' memory performance is much closer to that of young adults when a **cued recall** task is used instead of a **free recall** task (e.g., Craik, 1977; Poon, 1985). In a cued recall task, cues (or clues) are provided at the time of recall. Suppose you had learned a list of flower names, dog breeds, and state names. You would take a free recall test if you were simply told "list all the items that you learned"; you would take a cued recall test if you were told, "list the flowers, dogs, and states that you learned." Both cued recall and recognition tasks present less strenuous retrieval demands than free recall tasks.

Nonability influences of performance

Remember that it is important to distinguish between age differences in memory performance and age differences in the ability to learn and remember. Older adults may be as proficient in learning and remembering as young adults, but their performance may be affected by the situations in which performances are compared. Classic research identifies at least five factors that seem to hamper the memory performance of older adults more than the performances of younger adults.

We found in the last chapter that time pressure can impair older adults' performances on standardized measures of intelligence. Here, we find that **task pacing** similarly affects older peoples' performances in laboratory studies of learning and memory (e.g., Arenberg & Robertson-Tchabo, 1977; Poon, 1985). For example, Canestrari (1963) compared young and older adults' performances on a **paired associate** learning task. In this task, participants must learn pairs of words (e.g., DOG–HAT; BED–APPLE; YARN–TREE) so that when the first member is presented during a memory test the participant can supply the second member.

In Canestrari's (1963) study, young and older adults learned and remembered the pairs under three conditions: some had 1.5 seconds, some had 3 seconds, and some had as much time as they wanted to remember the paired associates. When time to respond was limited, the older participants remembered far fewer paired associates than younger participants. In the self-paced condition, the older participants took more time to remember, and actually did remember more pairs, than under the time limits. The age difference in performance was substantially smaller.

Not only task pacing, but also **task content** affects older adults' learning and memory performance. Many experimental studies of age differences in cognitive performance require participants to learn and remember material that has no inherent meaning: lists of nonsense syllables or unrelated words are typical materials. The intention is to make this material equally unfamiliar for all participants, rather than using material that might be more familiar (and thus easier to remember) for some people than for others. Familiarity with the material to be remembered is important. Barrett and Wright (1981) showed that older adults had higher recall scores than young adults for a list of words that were more familiar to elderly adults than to young people (e.g., poultice, counterpin, fedora, flivver), although the older subjects' recall for words more familiar to young people than to elderly adults (e.g., afro, disco, readout, narc) was poorer than the young adults' recall of those words.

Using material that is meaningless—and thus equally unfamiliar—to subjects of all ages may undermine older adults' motivation to take the time and effort to learn. Irene Hulicka's (1967) study illustrates this possibility. Hulicka recruited young adult college students and older adults for a cross-sectional study of paired associate learning; the paired associates, as usual, were comprised of unrelated words such as WINDOW–NAIL, TABLE–CAR, KITTEN–ROSE. The college students willingly learned these paired associates, and did quite well. However, the older participants reacted differently: 80 percent refused to complete the task and explained that they could see no point in learning "such nonsense." When Hulicka changed the task to incorporate some practical value, the older people were willing to participate. Instead of using unrelated words for the paired associates, Hulicka formed word pairs of occupations and surnames (e.g., BANKER–SMITH, LAWYER–JONES, PLUMBER–WRIGHT) and presented the task as one that might be confronted upon moving to a new city.

Some believe that older adults' learning and memory performances are hampered by anxiety in the experimental situation. Most people find it more difficult to learn and remember when they are nervous. You have probably been unable to remember material during an important, anxiety-arousing exam, only to recall all of the material perfectly later when you were more relaxed. Older people participating in research may confront some of the same frustration.

College students rarely find participation in psychology experiments nerve-racking. The setting and personnel are familiar; and, of course, college students are quite accustomed to the general demand to learn a specified body of material in preparation for a test. For many older adults, though, taking part in a psychology experiment is an unfamiliar experience that may arouse stress. They must come to an unfamiliar and confusing setting, and interact with unfamiliar younger people. In their everyday routines, older adults may encounter few situations in which they must study unfamiliar material under time pressure in preparation for a test. The stress that this situation elicits may prevent the older person from learning and remembering as well as she could under more relaxed conditions. In fact, one study found that older adults who were given a drug that blocked physiological arousal performed better in a learning task than a control group that received a placebo (Eisdorfer, Nowlin, & Wilkie, 1970).

It is also possible that older adults do not perform as well as younger adults because they fail to use effective approaches to the learning task. Remember that an encoding deficit is one component of older adults' difficulties with secondary memory tasks. Researchers who ask young and older adults how they attempted to learn and remember material in cross-sectional studies often find that the young adults report spontaneously using some sort of **mediator** (visual images, verbal labels, organizational strategy, etc.) but that the older adults do not (e.g., Arenberg & Robertson-Tchabo, 1977; Hulicka & Grossman, 1967; Murphy, Schmitt, Caruso, & Sanders, 1987; Poon, 1985; Thomas, 1985b).

Perhaps in their youth older people were taught to learn by rote memory and continue to fall back on that approach. Even though using mediators does not seem to occur to older adults in learning and memory studies, researchers have also found that older people are quite capable of using these strategies. When researchers have suggested that older participants use mediators, and trained them in effective mediator use, age differences in learning and memory performance are often reduced dramatically (e.g., Canestrari, 1968; Hulicka & Grossman, 1967; Murphy, et al., 1987; Robertson-Tchabo, Hausman, & Arenberg, 1976).

Explicit training in mediating is crucial for the elderly, however. When "optimal study conditions" (e.g., unlimited study time, note taking permitted, encouragement of mediator use) were provided for young and older adults, young adults' performance improved more than older adults' performance did (Rabinowitz, 1989). This study suggests that younger adults may need only encouragement and the opportunity to study effectively, but that older people may further need specific instructions in *how* to study in order to benefit.

Thus, the extent of age differences in learning and memory performance that cross-sectional research documents may reflect the impact of task pacing, task content, anxiety in the experimental situation, and older participants' failure to spontaneously use mediators. Although these conditions can certainly hamper learning for anyone, they weigh more heavily on older than on younger research participants. For that reason, the age differences in performance seen in cross-sectional studies may overestimate the extent of age differences in the abilities to learn and remember.

At least one other factor may also contribute to the age differences found in most cross-sectional studies of learning and memory. In these studies, age groups differ in many respects that might contribute to the extent of age differences in performance. Perhaps the most serious cohort difference in this context is in educational background. On the average, contemporary older adults have had fewer years of schooling than young adult college students; certainly, their educational experience is more remote than college students' experience. When cohort differences in educational background are statistically controlled, age differences in cognitive performance are reduced dramatically (Krauss, Poon, Gilewski, & Schaie, 1982).

Memory in everyday life

The research examined so far describes age differences in learning and memory performance in the laboratory. However, the laboratory setting and the experimental materials of most studies have little to do with the everyday experiences of most older adults. What do we know about "real-life" memory tasks faced in old age, and the successes and failures that older people have with these tasks?

In one study, Cavanaugh, Grady, and Perlmutter (1983) asked young and older adults to keep diaries of their memory failures. Not surprisingly, older participants recorded more instances of forgetting than the younger adults did; most forgetting was for names and faces, appointments and routines, locations, and addresses and telephone numbers. The older adults were more distressed by their memory failures than the younger adults, as were the older subjects in similar studies (e.g., Erber, Szuchman, & Rothberg, 1990; Zarit, Cole, & Guider, 1981). However, other work suggests that older adults may be more lenient in evaluating memory performance in everyday activities than are younger adults (Erber, 1989).

Sinnott (1986) examined both intentional and incidental memory for everyday experience among participants in the Baltimore Longitudinal Study of Aging (BLSA). **Intentional memory** is used to remember information that you know you will need later on, such as appointments, bus schedules, due dates for bills, and so on. **Incidental memory** is used when you remember information that you learned unintentionally and made no effort to commit to memory (such as the color of the walls in your psychology classroom, titles of magazines in a doctor's waiting room).

Sinnott (1986) contacted BLSA participants three times following one of their periodic testing sessions at the Gerontology Research Center; on each occasion, she asked them to recognize or recall information from their testing session. Some of the information represented intentional memory tasks, such as the date of the participant's next appointment at the Center, directions from the participant's hospital room at the Center to the testing area, and hours during which the hospital cafeteria served dinner. Other items on the memory tests represented incidental memory, such as objects on a table while participants worked on problem-solving tasks.

Although incidental memory declined with age, intentional memory did not (Sinnott, 1986). When the need to remember was clear and practical, older adults were just as capable as the younger adults. As Sinnott explained, "selecting to remember salient, contextually meaningful information rather than less meaningful information may be a compensatory mechanism useful in older age . . . the person (and frequently an old person) with limited memory ability may choose to use that ability to keep his or her commitments as a social being, above all" (p. 114).

Prospective memory—remembering to perform an action—is an area in which elderly adults excel relative to younger people. Researchers have asked participants to call a designated telephone number according to a schedule; in these studies, older adults call in more reliably than younger people do (e.g., West, 1984). The older adults in these studies usually report that they made notes of the times of their scheduled calls, whereas the younger people typically say that they relied on internal strategies.

A task that most people confront many times daily is remembering **discourse**; discourse is spoken language or written passages—conversations, news broadcasts, newspaper or magazine articles, letters, books, stories, and the like. Research describing age differences in memory for discourse flourished in the 1980s; most of this work concerned age differences in memory for prose and other reading tasks. The literature in this area is voluminous, complex, and therefore difficult to summarize in a concise and straightforward manner. Perhaps the best generalization is that cross-sectional research identifies age differences in performance favoring young adults (e.g., Hultsch & Dixon, 1990).

However, that pattern is moderated by characteristics of the participants, of the specific discourse processing task, and of the material to be remembered. The participant characteristic most often examined as a moderator of age differences is verbal ability. Among adults of average or below-average verbal ability, younger people nearly always remember substantially more prose than older adults (e.g., Cavanaugh, 1983; 1984; Cohen, 1979). However, when young and elderly adults of high verbal ability are compared, age differences are sometimes smaller or absent altogether (e.g., Hartley, 1986; Mandel & Johnson, 1984; Meyer & Rice, 1981). One study suggested that participants' verbal ability may reflect their overall approach to reading: use of reading practices promoting comprehension and recall are associated with high levels of verbal ability among adults of all ages (Rice & Meyer, 1985).

Task pacing affects the extent of age differences in performance, just as it does with intelligence test performance and laboratory studies of learning and memory. Usually, reading is a self-paced task: you can read as slowly as you need to, and go back over passages as necessary. Sometimes the pace at which text is presented is not under your control, however. Examples are when scrolling text appears on television or on a computer monitor, or when you listen to someone else reading prose rather than reading it yourself. When the pace of text presentation is rapid, older adults' text retention suffers more than young adults' retention (e.g., Cohen, 1979; Stine & Wingfield, 1987).

The characteristics of the material also affect the pattern of age differences in memory for discourse. When reading text that is "information dense" (that is, a relatively large number of ideas or propositions per sentence), older adults are less capable than young adults of distinguishing between ideas of greater and lesser importance. However, there is no such age difference for less "information dense" text (Stine & Wingfield, 1988).

In addition to age differences in the amount of material remembered, there are also age differences in discourse recall style. Older adults are more likely than young adults to include meaning-enhancing elaborations, interpretations, or reconstructions when recalling text that they have read or heard (Adams, Labouvie-Vief, Hobart, & Dorosz, 1990; Stine & Wingfield, 1987). However, young and older adults do not differ in the extent to which they integrate text-presented information with prior knowledge (Hultsch & Dixon, 1990; Zelinski & Miura, 1988).

Interventions to improve older adults' memory

To what extent are older people sensitive to the nature and extent of their difficulties in remembering? To what extent is it possible to minimize these difficulties through training or interventions? In the 1980s, psychologists gave increasing attention to **metamemory**, knowledge about memory, in the aged. This work identified the accuracy with which older adults evaluate their own memory capacities.

Elderly people are, in general, well aware of their memory capacity. Older adults in laboratory studies generally predict that they will perform poorly on memory tasks, relative to younger adults (Cavanaugh & Poon, 1989; Hertzog, Dixon, & Hultsch, 1990; Zelinski, Gilewski, & Anthony-Bergstone, 1990). In an unusual approach to examining age differences in memory and metamemory, adults taking part in a cross-sectional survey concerning social issues provided both objective and subjective evaluations of their memory (Herzog & Rodgers, 1989). Survey interviews included recall and recognition measures of memory for topics discussed in the interview, as well as participants' own evaluations of their memory, the interviewer's assessment of the participant's memory, and spouses' evaluations of participants' memory. Both recall and recognition memory declined with age, as did the subjective evaluations of memory.

One of the most exciting research approaches in cognitive aging is the effort to identify means through which older adults can improve their memory performance. This work not only has obvious practical value, but may provide insight into the precise nature of memory deficits in old age. Most scientists have evaluated training programs in which older adults are taught to use mnemonic strategies, although there has also been some work attempting pharmacological interventions into memory problems in later life. For example, one group of researchers found that oral administration of glucose enhanced older adults' memory performance (Manning, Hall, & Gold, 1990). Poon (1985) provides a review of pharmacological interventions for memory problems among elderly people.

Several studies demonstrate the effectiveness of teaching older people to use visual imagery to enhance their memory performance. One early study (Treat & Reese, 1976), for instance, compared young and elderly adults' paired associate memory performance under three conditions. Some were told to think of a specified visual image linking pair members, some were told to construct their own visual image linking the pair members, and some were given no imagery training or instructions at all. The imagery helped the older adults in particular; in fact, when the memory task was self-paced, there were no age differences in performance for the participants using imagery. Other studies similarly show that older people can use imagery-based mnemonics quite effectively (e.g., Anschutz, Camp, Markley, & Kramer, 1985; Rebok & Balcerak, 1989; Yesavage, 1983; Yesavage, Sheikh, Friedman, & Tanke, 1990), although—as we noted earlier—older adults are less likely than younger people to report spontaneously using mnemonics.

Training in mnemonics is unlikely to provide an answer for all problems with memory that older people experience, however. Researchers caution that not all older adults can benefit from such training, and that there is no single mnemonic approach suitable for all people and all memory tasks (Poon, 1985; Yesavage et al., 1990). There is little published information available describing the extent to which the benefits of mnemonic training are long-lasting or generalized to new situations. The information that is available is not encouraging. Studies in which participants in memory training studies are contacted three years later show that few participants are still using the mnemonics by that time (Anschutz, Camp, Markley, & Kramer, 1987) and that training benefits are no longer apparent (Scogin & Bienias, 1988).

EDUCATION THROUGHOUT ADULTHOOD

College: Diversity in colleges and their students

Most young adults continue their education after high school graduation. Some seek further education through training offered in the workplace, others receive military training, and still others attend technical schools. For many young adults, higher education occurs on a college campus. College settings nationwide are remarkably varied. One student may attend a highly selective private liberal arts college; another may go to a large state university with graduate as well as undergraduate programs; and still another student may choose a community college offering two-year programs in specific vocational areas.

Just as there is diversity in colleges, there is also heterogeneity in college students—perhaps more today than ever before. At one time, American colleges were the domain of young, wealthy, white men. That situation has changed dramatically, however. Particularly since the 1960s, a spirit of egalitarianism has infused higher education. Today, a greater percentage of young (and older) adults are attending college than ever before. The greatest increases in college attendance have been for women and minority students, for students over the age of 25, part-time students, and students attending two-year colleges (Boyer, 1987; U.S. Department of Education, 1987). With this influx of relative newcomers to higher education, college professors and administrators need more information about unique approaches that these students bring to learning. Research in this area is growing; the *Diversity in Adulthood* box reviews work describing "women's ways of knowing."

Today's college students are vocationally-oriented. In a recent survey of college-bound high school seniors, virtually all students cited factors related to career preparation as their primary goal in attending college (Boyer, 1987). These students believed that a college degree would help them to have a more satisfying career, to prepare for a specific occupation (e.g., teaching, nursing), or to get a better job. However, these students' parents voiced different goals. Parents hoped that college would provide opportunities for their sons and

---

BOX 7.1   *DIVERSITY IN ADULTHOOD*

Women's ways of knowing

The study of gender has been a thriving psychological specialization for decades. Whereas much of the work in this field during the 1960s and 1970s was designed to demonstrate the essential similarities between men and women, some contemporary scholars have made exciting contributions by describing modes of functioning unique to women. Carol Gilligan (1982), for example, developed a model of women's moral reasoning (see Chapter Eight, pages 214–215). In a similar approach, Mary Belenkey and her colleagues (1986) proposed "ways of knowing" that are more characteristic of women than of men. These scholars believe that women have an outlook on knowledge, truth, learning, and themselves as learners that are distinctly different from men's perspectives on these issues.

Belenkey et al. began their work, as did Gilligan, by recognizing women's virtual absence from the construction of major developmental theories. These women also drew on their experiences as academicians, which revealed that many women felt alienated and uncertain in educational settings. The researchers then proceeded to interview 135 women, representing a wide range of ages and social backgrounds. Some of the women were students or alumni of colleges varying in academic prestige and rigor; others were members of what

Belenkey et al. termed "invisible colleges"—human service agencies working with children and families.

The researchers identified five distinct perspectives from which women know the world and themselves. An initial way of knowing was **silence**. Women holding this perspective were generally younger and more impoverished than the other women. These women saw themselves as mindless, ever subject to the whims of external authority. Though intelligent, these women seemed unaware of their cognitive resources. For example, they were not aware of their potential to learn from others' written or spoken words. Words, in fact, were weapons to these women: words could belittle or demean, but not empower.

Other women held a perspective of **received knowledge**, in which they felt confident in taking and reproducing information provided by authorities but not in creating ideas or information on their own. These women, in contrast to the silent women, were in virtual awe of the power of words. They considered listening, taking in others' words, to be central aspects of their learning process. These women did not feel confident, however, to go beyond an authority's words and elaborate or modify received information on the basis of their own experience. These women believed that all

---

daughters to become more interesting and well-rounded, and to clarify their values (Boyer, 1987).

Both college students and their parents might reasonably ask whether attending college actually has any demonstrable impact. Happily, the answer is yes. Because most colleges and universities include developing students' intellectual potential among their primary goals, it is not surprising that the greatest and most consistent evidence identifies cognitive benefits of attending college. When college freshmen are compared with seniors, when college students are compared with similar young adults not attending college, and when college alumni are compared with similar individuals who did not attend college, clear differences emerge. Those who are or have been college students have greater substantive knowledge, greater verbal skills, and a greater intellectual disposition than individuals without college experience (Boyer, 1987; Gardner & Jeweler, 1985).

questions had a single right answer, and that alternative approaches to the question must be incorrect.

A third perspective was that of **subjective knowledge**. Women holding this perspective ranged widely in age and represented diverse educational and social backgrounds as well. They considered knowledge and truth intensely personal entities which could only be reached through experience and intuition. These women, too, had a deep trust in authority as a source of knowledge; to these women, however, the authority was within themselves.

With **procedural knowledge**, women learn and use accepted procedures for gathering and communicating information. These women believed that the processes and techniques through which knowledge was acquired were nearly as important as the content of knowledge. They used deliberate, systematic means of reasoning, and they strived for an objective standpoint with which to confront issues.

Constructed knowledge probably represents the most sophisticated perspective. In this viewpoint, women welcome both intuitive knowledge and that reached through more conventional paths. More importantly, these women recognize themselves as creators of knowledge and therefore an essential part of what they know. Compared to the women holding other perspectives, these women were far more accepting of uncertainty, ambiguity, and contradiction.

What circumstances can foster development of constructed knowledge? The researchers offered a number of suggestions for women's education. Perhaps the most important element, they felt, was that women experience confirmation of themselves as knowers. Women students must confront clear messages that they are capable of not only learning but also of creating knowledge. Men, Belenkey and her colleagues believed, receive this message many times and in many ways over the course of their education.

Perhaps the most important contribution of Belenkey's work is in providing a model of yet another approach to considering adult cognition. As Belenkey and her colleagues acknowledged, much more information is needed before we will know whether the five perspectives described represent a universal developmental sequence, what circumstances set the tempo for any such sequence, or even whether the sequence is unique to women. Clearly, though, this approach is an outstanding example of work which emphasizes the diversity in adult life.

Some believe that college goes beyond providing students with breadth and depth of information, and transforms students' very orientation toward knowledge and learning. In Belenkey's (1986) research, college was often a setting in which women moved toward relatively sophisticated "ways of knowing" (see Box 7.1). Similar evidence emerges from William Perry's (1970) longitudinal study of Harvard and Radcliffe students. On the basis of that study, Perry traced a progression from rigidity to flexibility in students' thinking.

Initially, students in Perry's (1970) research regarded knowledge as absolute. At this point, students believed that all questions had one right answer. To these students, professors were authorities who could reveal these answers. Even as students became more accepting of different points of view, they initially remained certain that eventually they would be able to identify the *one* best viewpoint. Later students took a relativistic perspective on knowledge and values, recognizing that each individual and each society constructs a system of

American colleges were once the domain of young, wealthy, Caucasian men; however, today there is more diversity among college students than ever before.

values and beliefs. The most advanced level of functioning for these students was achieved when they made a personal commitment to a set of values and beliefs, while recognizing the existence and legitimacy of other perspectives.

Clearly, then, college can have profound intellectual effects upon students; college's impact goes beyond the cognitive area, however. Despite problems of unemployment and underemployment among college graduates, statistics describing career opportunities and income levels consistently favor college graduates over those with less extensive educations (Boyer, 1987; Gardner & Jeweler, 1985).

Attending college enhances practical competence as well (Boyer, 1987; Gardner & Jeweler, 1985). College graduates marry and have children at later ages, are more likely to report planning the births of their children, and invest more time, effort, and money in childrearing than do noncollege-educated adults. College graduates also deal more effectively with financial matters than do individuals without a college education. Attending college is associated with saving a greater percentage of income, making relatively sound investments, and confronting false or misleading advertising with healthy skepticism. Also, highly educated young adults are generally better informed and motivated regarding preventative health practices such as diet, exercise, and stress management.

Although attending college can be an important and clearly beneficial experience, American higher education has come under recent criticism. One critic bemoans the extent to which contemporary college students lack "cultural literacy"—an appreciation of our heritage in areas such as history, literature, sciences, and the arts (Hirsch, 1987). According to this scholar, efforts of the 1960s and 1970s to make education at all levels relevant have undermined the substance of curricula. Another expert believes that recent efforts to foster acceptance of diverse viewpoints have created graduates who are unprepared to weigh the relative merits of opposing arguments and beliefs (Bloom, 1987).

Continuing education and nontraditional students

Many middle-aged and older adults are involved in learning. "Learning" may, however, mean something different for a middle-aged or elderly person than it does for children, adolescents, or even young adults. Sometimes, older adults learn through formal coursework occurring in a classroom, with a designated professional directing the program and evaluating performance. Even more often, though, learning in middle and later adulthood takes place in the home, in a community or social setting, or in the workplace. Middle-aged and elderly adults' "teachers" are often the media, friends and relatives, coworkers, a computer, or themselves. The processes contributing to learning may be different. Now, learning may entail not only the acquisition of new information or skills, but also the discovery of how to apply knowledge, how to integrate new and old knowledge, and how to forget information that has become obsolete or irrelevant.

Why do middle-aged and older adults seek out opportunities for learning—whether these opportunities involve taking courses at a community college or extension service, a program of self-directed study, or some other arrangement? Researchers have identified at least three motivations. Work-related pressures are important for many (e.g., Bean & Metzner, 1985). Education may be a vehicle for creating an expanded or upgraded set of job opportunities. For example, several educational programs have been developed to assist displaced homemakers in acquiring marketable skills and documenting skills already attained through years of unpaid work in the home (e.g., Balding & DeBalssie, 1983; Roy, 1986; Scannell & Petrich, 1987).

Education may also be a means through which workers insure that they remain abreast of new developments in their fields. Some professions, in fact, require continuing education credits in order to renew licensure. In this vein, Willis (1989) notes that the threat of "**professional obsolescence**" provides intellectual challenges particularly compelling in middle adulthood. "Professional obsolescence" is the use of knowledge or skills that are less effective in solving problems than other types of knowledge or skills currently available in one's field. Since middle-aged workers may have terminated their formal education many years earlier, since the average length of working life has now increased to more than 30 years, and since our highly technological society confronts an ongoing knowledge explosion, continuing job-related education is essential for many in their middle years.

Opportunities for personal growth and development are a second set of motivations for learning in the middle and later years. Mature adults taking courses on college campuses often list these goals among the factors leading to their decision to enroll (e.g., Bean & Metzner, 1985; Brookfield, 1985; Roy, 1986; Wacks, 1987; Willis, 1985). Sometimes, educational programs for middle-aged and elderly adults take normative events of this period of the life cycle as their focus. For example, one program helps grandparents adapt to their new family role (Strom & Strom, 1987). Similarly, retirement planning workshops provide opportunities for advance consideration of the personal and financial implications of retirement.

Finally, some middle-aged and elderly individuals take on a program of learning in response to new options stemming from social change. Bean and Metzner (1985) note, for example, that more adult women of all ages are seeking education in order to take advantage of expanded role opportunities. These scholars also point out that the changing structure of the American household—including the economic pressure for many families to have two incomes, and decreased family size—have provided incentives for many individuals to turn to education in their forties or fifties.

Is being a student a different experience at midlife or old age than in youth? In some respects, it is. Middle-aged adults often confront obstacles to participating in formal coursework that rarely present problems for younger adults. The demands of family and work may interfere with one's role as a student, to the extent that completing a degree program or even a single course may be virtually impossible (Bean & Metzner, 1985; Weidman & White, 1985). The scheduling of formal coursework may also create barriers, again depending on the exigencies of one's responsibilities in the home and workplace. Educational administrators, to their credit, have shown increasing responsiveness to these problems, and have begun to offer courses and programs according to innovative schedules and settings (Thompson, 1985). It is becoming possible to

Continuing job-related education is a necessity for many middle-aged employees.

take courses and even complete a degree by attending school at night, on the weekends, or between conventional academic semesters.

Middle-aged and elderly adults typically bring unique strengths to the learning program. Recall from the last chapter that some aspects of intelligence improve throughout adulthood, and that middle-aged adults are especially adept at solving practical problems. Both capacities are valuable resources for the mature student. In addition, the experience gained through years of living and working are an intellectual foundation gaining increased recognition from those involved in implementing curricula (Usher, 1986). In light of the benefits that lifelong learning can have, and of the special resources that older learners possess, some have suggested that our society should move toward more flexible scheduling of education, work, and leisure over the life cycle (Bolles, 1978). The arguments surrounding this proposition are presented in the *Open Questions* box for this chapter.

OPEN QUESTIONS   **BOX 7.2**

Should the "three boxes of life" be redistributed?

Education, work, and leisure have been described as the "three boxes of life." For most people, these "boxes" demarcate different periods of life. Education is the focus of the early years, the next few decades are centered around work, and leisure comes to the forefront only in the later years of life. Richard Bolles (1978), a psychologist, questions the extent to which this distribution of the three activities is adaptive.

One problem with this distribution, Bolles claims, is that the activities in each "box" are isolated from those in the other boxes. In other words, education in childhood and adolescence often progresses with little or no consciousness of the nature of working life in adulthood or lifestyle options for retirement. Few people have the good fortune to encounter effective means of transition from one epoch to the next, at least on the formal level (e.g., career counseling, preparation for retirement programs).

Bolles proposed that people would live more adaptively with a more even balance between the activities of learning, working, and playing throughout the life cycle. People of all ages, according to Bolles, should be actively engaged in learning, should have some contact with the world of work, and should deliberately engage in leisure. Achieving this rebalance, of course, would require change.

Bolles proposed that this change could be accomplished on an individual level, if we each had such an ongoing balance between learning, working, and playing as a goal in planning our lives. He also acknowledged, however, that social change—that is, in the institutions of education, industry and the economy, and leisure—might also be needed.

Of course, there is no guarantee that redistributing the "three boxes" of life would provide the fulfillment that Bolles claims. It is even possible that such an approach to life planning would increase stress levels for some, because people would repeatedly encounter off-time life transitions (see Chapter One, p. 11). The fundamental activities of education, work, and leisure might not unfold well at all under this plan, either. For example, it is difficult to imagine how one could implement an ambition to enter a highly specialized and technical career such as medicine according to Bolles' plan.

In any case, the wisdom of Bolles' proposal remains an open question. Although his ideas attracted attention in the late 1970s and early 1980s, it did not provide a driving force for policy planning at the close of the 1980s (Best, 1989).

Elderhostel

One of the most successful continuing education programs targeted specifically at older adults is **Elderhostel**. In this summer program, older people live in
college dormitories and take one-, two-, or three-week courses taught by regular
university faculty. In addition to participating in courses, Elderhostelers take
part in extracurricular activities and use campus recreational facilities during
their stay.

Elderhostel courses provide a stimulating and challenging experience for
students and faculty alike. These courses have no prerequisites, and assume no
prior knowledge of their topic. Although no credits, grades, exams, or assignments are given, instructors often make suggestions for outside readings and
sometimes organize field trips related to course topics. Course offerings are
diverse, including such topics as Appalachian culture, Middle Eastern politics,
perspectives on poetry, geology of the Southwest, computers and you, and
holistic health. Elderhostelers typically respond to courses with all the interest,
enthusiasm, and involvement of any professor's dreams. In fact, one
Elderhostel faculty member recently suggested (partly in jest) that these class
sessions should be videotaped and shown to young adult college students as a
model of what liberal education can and should be.

Since its inception in 1975, Elderhostel has grown tremendously. Initially,
Elderhostel was offered on five New England campuses; today, there are
Elderhostels in every state—as well as in Great Britain, Scandinavia, and Europe. Some Elderhostelers are true veterans, travelling from one campus to
another throughout the summer to combine the educational and social benefits of the program with vacations and family visits. Clearly, this program provides testimony to older adults' continued pleasure in learning.

Summary

The information processing approach proposes that the flow of information can be
traced through sensory memory, primary memory, secondary memory, and tertiary
memory. Research fails to identify substantial differences in sensory memory or primary
memory. However, when information in primary memory must be actively manipulated,
organized, or reorganized in some way, then age differences favoring young adults do
appear.

Older adults recall substantially less information from secondary memory than do
younger adults, but age differences are minimal or absent altogether in recognition
performance. The age differences in recall performance probably reflect both an encoding and a retrieval deficit. Tertiary memory remains intact in old age.

The age differences in learning and memory performance that cross-sectional
research typically documents may reflect the impacts of task pacing, task content,
anxiety in the experimental situation, and older participants' failure to spontaneously
use mediators. Furthermore, contemporary older adults have had fewer years of schooling than young adult college students; when cohort differences in educational background are statistically controlled, age differences in cognitive performance are reduced

dramatically. Several studies demonstrate the effectiveness of teaching older people to use visual imagery to enhance their memory performance.

Research examining age differences in "real-life" memory tasks shows that elderly people have higher rates of forgetting names and faces, appointments and routines, locations, and addresses and telephone numbers. Older people are as capable as younger adults at intentional and prospective memory tasks, although there are age differences in incidental memory for everyday events. In studies of memory for discourse, age differences favoring young adults are typical findings.

Most people continue their education after high school graduation. Motivations for learning among middle-aged and older adults include work-related pressures, opportunities for personal growth and development, and consequences of social change. Middle-aged and older adults may confront obstacles to participating in formal coursework that rarely present problems for younger adults. However, middle-aged and elderly adults typically bring unique strengths to the learning program.

KEY TERMS

Constructed knowledge
Cued recall
Discourse
Echoic memory
Elderhostel
Encoding deficit
Free recall
Iconic memory
Incidental memory
Intentional memory
Learning
Mediator
Memory
Metamemory
Paired associate
Primary memory

Procedural knowledge
Professional obsolescence
Prospective memory
Recall
Received knowledge
Recognition
Retrieval deficit
Ribot's law
Secondary memory
Sensory memory
Silence
Subjective knowledge
Task content
Task pacing
Tertiary memory
Working memory

SUGGESTIONS FOR FURTHER READING

Belenkey, M. F., Clinchy, B. M., Goldberger, N. R., & Tarule, J. M. (1986). *Women's Ways of Knowing: The Development of Self, Voice, and Mind*. New York: Basic Books.

Boyer, E. L. (1987). *College: The Undergraduate Experience in America*. New York: Harper & Row, Publishers.

Lumsden, D. B. (1985). *The Older Adult as Learner: Aspects of Educational Gerontology*. New York: Hemisphere Publishing.

Perry, W. G. (1970). *Forms of Intellectual and Ethical Development in the College Years*. New York: Holt, Rinehart, & Winston, Inc.

Rybash, J. M., Hoyer, W. J., & Roodin, P. A. (1986). *Adult Cognition and Aging: Developmental Changes in Processing, Knowing, and Thinking*. New York: Pergammon Press.

CHAPTER EIGHT

PERSONALITY: CHANGE AND STABILITY

Do most people have a midlife crisis? Do people become more and more set in their ways as they get older? This chapter addresses personality development, and changes in moral judgement.

Both the layperson and the psychologist use the term "personality" freely. Nonetheless, the study of personality is a field fraught with controversy. The chapter explores some of these areas of dissension: we consider theories and research describing adult personality and approaches to measuring personality.

Some scholars emphasize the emergence of new aspects of the personality in adulthood; some even maintain that middle adulthood is a period of turmoil much like adolescence. On the other hand, others point to an impressive body of research documenting stability of adult personality. A theme of this chapter is the need to identify ways in which a perspective of change as opposed to a perspective of constancy adds to our understanding of adult personality.

Questions to consider in reading the chapter include:

How do classic stage theorists—Freud, Erikson, and Jung—describe adult personality development? What changes in adult personality do the Chicago researchers identify? How have more recent scholars portrayed qualitative change in adult personality?

On what basis do McCrae and Costa maintain that there is more stability than change in adult personality?

How do disengagement theory and activity theory portray "successful aging?" In what respect must personality be incorporated into models of successful aging?

How do researchers describe women's personality growth in adulthood?

How does moral judgement change during adulthood?

DEFINING PERSONALITY

Most people have an intuitive definition of personality. You might remark that a good friend has a wonderful personality. Or, you might use a single outstanding characteristic—such as friendliness or selfishness—to describe someone's personality. Psychologists strive for more precise definitions, and many definitions have been developed. Some define personality as an all-encompassing description of the individual (e.g., Menninger, 1953). Others single out discrete aspects of the person; one theorist, for example, feels that personality is reflected in an individual's social relationships (Sullivan, 1953).

Still other psychologists feel that personality can never be adequately defined. Indeed, B. F. Skinner (e.g., 1953; 1974) maintained that the concept of personality is of limited value, although his work is generally included in personality theory texts (e.g., Hall & Lindzey, 1978). This chapter uses a definition proposed by scholars primarily concerned with personality measurement. These authors define personality as "an individual's unique constellation of psychological traits and states" (Cohen, Montague, Nathanson, & Swerdlik, 1988, pp. 286–287). An important strength of this definition is that it neither presupposes nor proscribes personality change during adulthood. The extent to which personality changes or remains stable is better addressed through theory and research than through definition.

This definition, however, does stress traits and states as personality components—a view that some psychologists would challenge. Traits are stable, internal influences on an individual's behavior. Gordon Allport (e.g., 1961), the psychologist most closely associated with the notion of traits, maintains that some **cardinal traits** are such pervasive influences that they color virtually everything that a person does. If an individual has a cardinal trait of generosity, she would display that characteristic at all times: she would never pass up an opportunity to donate to charity, to give a compliment, to share her time with someone in need, or to lend help in a community project. Some psychologists would challenge the notion that this woman was directed by a trait, however. A behavioral theorist, for example, would probably maintain that explanations for the woman's generous behavior lie in the environmental cues and consequences for that behavior (see Chapter Two, pp. 42–43).

Less prominent traits have a more circumscribed influence on an individual's behavior—one might be funny only some of the time, or critical only on occasion. Similarly, states are internal directors of behavior that are similar to traits, but states are fleeting rather than stable influences. If Susan is not characteristically a nervous person, but acts extremely nervous one day, then she is driven by state anxiety as opposed to a trait of anxiety.

QUALITATIVE DESCRIPTIONS OF ADULT PERSONALITY: CLASSIC STAGE THEORIES

Freud's psychoanalytic theory

Freud's is one of several "early formation theories" (Wrightsman, 1988), in which the foundations of adult personality are believed to be grounded in childhood experience. According to Freud, the personality comprises three components that are formed during the first years of life. The **id** is an irrational set of demanding instincts; the **superego** is an equally irrational set of moral principles; and the **ego** provides a rational capacity for coping with reality. Freud believed that intrapsychic conflict constituted a fundamental force in personality dynamics, and that interplay among the id, ego, and superego often occurs unconsciously.

Freud also believed that the personality included a fixed amount of psychic energy, or **libido**. Because there is a finite quantity of libido, psychic energy devoted to one activity cannot be used for other undertakings. During the first few years of life, libido is directed toward a biologically-determined sequence of needs. Ideally, these needs are satisfied as the child matures. If not, some libido will remain forever directed toward these infantile goals; such **fixation** leaves a life-long imprint on personality. Only through psychoanalysis, Freud believed, could fixations be overcome and libido be freed for the demands of adult life; Freud, then, portrayed adult personality as stable. Barring fixations, the healthy adult personality includes sufficient libido for loving, concerned relationships with others and for productive work.

Freudian theory has been criticized on at least two counts. Feminists assert that Freud portrays women's personality as inherently deficient and immature. Others believe that Freud's concepts are intriguing, but also distressingly vague and difficult to verify. Nonetheless, psychoanalytic theory has had a profound impact on psychology and society. Furthermore, Freud provided inspiration for some later efforts to describe adult personality, including the work of Carl Jung and Erik Erikson.

Jung's analytic theory of personality development and cross-cultural research on the "parental imperative"

Like Freud, Jung stressed unconscious aspects of the personality. Jung, however, proposed that important personality change occurs during middle and later adulthood. Jung also shared Freud's belief that conscious and unconscious personality structures form a system of distinct, interacting components. The principle personality structures are the **ego**, the conscious mind; the **personal unconscious**, experiences which were once conscious but which have been forgotten, repressed, or ignored; and the **collective unconscious**, the inherited foundation of personality which includes memories of experiences repeated with each generation.

The collective unconscious is organized around **archetypes**. Archetypes are universal ideas with a strong emotional component; Jung believed that archetypes are based on experiences that have been repeated for generations. Among these archetypes are the **anima** in men and the **animus** in women. Because men and women have lived together through the ages, man has acquired a feminine aspect (the anima) and woman has acquired a masculine aspect (the animus). The anima and animus, according to Jung, provide a foundation for men and women to understand one another.

Furthermore, these archetypes shift in prominence during adulthood. Whereas young men are dominated by the animus and young women by the anima, middle-aged men are more influenced by the anima and middle-aged women are more influenced by the animus. Consistent with this notion, Gutmann (e.g., 1975; 1977; 1985; Neugarten & Gutmann, 1964) found that older men more freely express sensual and nurturing impulses than they once did, whereas older women become more assertive and instrumental than they were in youth.

Gutmann (e.g., 1985; 1977) explains these shifts with reference to the ebb and flow of parental responsibilities. The dependency of human infants demands that parents provide both physical and emotional nurturance, and physical sex differences make gender-based specialization in providing these qualities an efficient solution. Thus, the years of active parenting—which Gutmann (1977) describes as the "chronic emergency of parenthood"—are a period in which gender differences in behavior are sharpened.

Gutmann (1977; 1985) notes that women's ability to nurse infants results, in most societies, in mothers specializing in nurturing their children. Men's greater physical strength results, in most societies, in fathers taking charge of providing physical and economic security for the family. As children reach maturity and the impetus for specialization recedes, these gender distinctions fade. Men are now free to act out their "feminine" side, and women can more freely express their "masculine" attributes. This work, then, lends support to Jung's notion of the anima and animus.

Perhaps the most important archetype in Jung's formulation is the **self**. The self is the human striving for total unity, and Jung believed that it provided a point around which all other systems of the personality were organized (e.g., Hall & Lindzey, 1978). Jung asserted that people constantly attempt to move from an incomplete stage of functioning to **self-realization**. When one attains self-realization, all aspects of the personality are fully developed and blended into a balanced whole (e.g., Hall & Lindzey, 1978). The self, rather than the ego, is the center of the personality.

Older men may express sensual and nurturing feelings more freely than they did in their youth.

Jung singled out the middle and later years of adulthood as critical for self-realization. Because all systems of the personality must be fully developed before they can be integrated into the self, self-realization is virtually impossible before one reaches middle age. Unlike Freud, then, Jung would have argued vigorously that there is qualitative change in personality during adulthood.

Erikson's psychosocial theory

Erikson would share Jung's argument. Erikson is one of a few psychologists to propose a life-span theory of personality development. Erikson portrayed personality development as an age-related sequence of eight psychosocial crises; Table 8.1 lists these crises and the approximate ages at which each is of primary importance.

During each crisis, the individual incorporates a balance between two opposing tendencies; this balance is dynamic, however. Prior to its time of primary importance, each crisis is **prework**ed along with the current focal crisis. For example, young children are in a process of developing a sense of identity, although the crisis of identity versus diffusion is not focal until adolescence. Similarly, each crisis is **rework**ed following its time of primary importance, now in the context of new focal crises. Identity development, then, continues to be a developmental issue after adolescence although that issue never again is the central developmental focus.

Erikson proposed three psychosocial crises of adulthood. The first—the need to balance intimacy with isolation (see Table 8.1)—is the focal crisis of young adulthood. For Erikson, **intimacy** should include "(1) mutuality of orgasm (2) with a loved partner (3) of the other sex (4) with whom one is able and willing to share a mutual trust (5) and with whom one is able and willing to

Table 8.1
The eight Eriksonian psychosocial crises

Trust and Mistrust	Birth to approximately 18 months
Autonomy and Shame, Doubt	18 months to approximately 3 years
Initiative and Guilt	Approximately age 3 to age 5
Industry and Inferiority	Approximately age 5 to 12
Identity and Role Confusion	Approximately ages 12 to 20
Intimacy and Isolation	Approximately the twenties
Generativity and Stagnation	Approximately the thirties and forties
Ego Integrity and Despair	Old age

Source: Erikson, 1963. Reprinted by permission.

regulate the cycles of (a) work, (b) procreation, [and] (c) recreation (6) so as to secure to the offspring . . . all the stages of a satisfactory development" (Erikson, 1950, p. 266). Although most would agree with many points of this definition, some may find it difficult to accept the notion that intimacy cannot be achieved in platonic relationships, homosexual relationships, or other relationships that do not produce offspring.

The opposing tendency, **isolation**, is avoidance of relationships leading to commitment (Erikson, 1950). As with all of the psychosocial crises, capacities for both intimacy and isolation must be incorporated. Achieving such an adaptive balance between intimacy and isolation is more likely if one has already attained a clear sense of identity.

In a classic study involving interviews with male college students, one group of researchers identified five levels of intimacy (Orlofsky, Marcia, & Lesser, 1973). Individuals rated as **intimate** had close friends and a satisfying sexual relationship. **Preintimate** individuals dated and had some understanding of intimacy, but had not established an intimate relationship. Those in **stereotyped relationships** had several friends whom they genuinely enjoyed, but those relationships were without emotional depth. Students rated as **pseudointimate** were like those with stereotyped relationships, but had made a commitment to a girlfriend. Finally, the **isolate** students did not have enduring personal relationships, and rarely initiated social contacts.

In addition to rating each student's intimacy status, the researchers also classified each student's identity status as either **identity achievement** (having made a commitment to an ideology and occupation), **moratorium** (currently undergoing a search for commitment), **foreclosure** (having a commitment to an ideology and/or occupation that they had not personally chosen), **identity diffusion** (lacking commitment to ideology and occupation), or **alienated achievement** (lacking commitment, but on the basis of a compelling rationale for avoiding commitment). Consistent with Eriksonian theory, young men with a relatively strong sense of identity (identity achieved, moratorium, and alienated achievement) had intimate relationships with both men and women.

Young men with a relatively weak sense of identity (foreclosure, identity diffusion) more often experienced stereotyped relationships and pseudointimacy.

In middle adulthood, one is primarily concerned with offsetting tendencies toward **generativity** and **stagnation**. Erikson describes generativity as "the concern in establishing and guiding the next generation" (1950, p. 267). The opposing tendency, stagnation, includes obsessive self-indulgence. Ideally, a middle-aged person is concerned both with fulfilling her own needs and with contributing to the broader welfare now and in the future.

How does one achieve a prevailing tendency toward generativity? Although he singles out parenting as an important opportunity, Erikson acknowledges that having children is neither necessary nor sufficient. Erikson discusses generativity more generally as the need to leave a lasting legacy, whether the legacy be offspring, well-trained occupational successors, a scientific discovery, or a literary masterpiece (e.g., 1950, 1982).

Others have described the process of attaining generativity in more detail. McAdams and his colleagues (McAdams, Ruetzel, & Foley, 1986) proposed that there are two steps. First, one must create something that represents self-extension, and then offer the product as a legacy—to the community, the society, or the species. Resolutions of earlier psychosocial crises are also important. Logan (1986) argued that some earlier stages have greater bearing on balancing generativity and stagnation than others. According to Logan, the psychosocial stages are a twice-repeating cycle of four stages each. The adolescent crisis of identity versus confusion is pivotal, and the crisis of intimacy versus isolation recapitulates the conflicts between trust versus mistrust and between autonomy versus shame and doubt. Generativity versus stagnation is a reworking of earlier conflicts between initiative versus guilt and between industry versus inferiority. Logan (1986) explained that middle-aged men and women are concerned with "making their mark" on the world—as is the child in the stage of initiative versus guilt—and with creating something of lasting worth—as is the older child attempting to balance industry and inferiority.

Available research supports Erikson's (1950) portrait of middle adulthood. Generativity scores are positively associated with motivations to achieve power and intimacy (McAdams, Ruetzel, & Foley, 1986), with chronological age (Darling-Fisher & Leidy, 1988; Peterson & Stewart, 1990; Ryff & Migdal, 1984; Viney, 1987), and with psychological well-being (Domino & Hannah, 1989). In addition, young adults in one study expected that generativity impulses would become more important as they got older; middle-aged adults, in contrast, found that generativity motives were more important to them now than they had been earlier (Ryff & Migdal, 1984).

In old age, the final psychosocial crisis—**ego integrity** versus **despair**—is focal. Growing awareness of mortality triggers this crisis, and Erikson (1982) suggests that few people actually achieve an ideal balance. The task is to balance feelings that one has lived a meaningful life against regrets about the past. Elderly people strive for this balance by reminiscing with friends and family to gain assurance that their life has been well-lived. If regrets outweigh feelings of satisfaction with the past, Erikson believes that the individual confronts death with despair and fear.

Erikson and his colleagues (Erikson, Erikson, & Kivnick, 1986) illustrate how the crises are reworked in old age through their analysis of the lives and recollections of the parents of participants in the Berkeley Growth Study. These elderly people have taken part in longitudinal research for over sixty years, providing a wealth of life history data. In balancing ego integrity and despair, and in reworking earlier crises, continued social and psychological involvement are critical (Erikson et al., 1986). Participants' involvement include relationships with friends, family, and neighbors. And many of these older individuals' vital involvements are symbolic, as they reflect on their parents and grandparents, their values, and current social issues and problems.

This research, like most Eriksonian research, has involved white, upper-middle class respondents representing a handful of cohorts. As with much of the work that we review in this chapter, then, we must question the generality of these findings. Some argue that Erikson presents a judgmental picture of development. For example, Cornett and Hudson (1987) recently questioned the usefulness of Erikson's theory for understanding gay men's personality development; recall that the definition of intimacy specifies that these relationships must be procreative. More generally, Erikson's theory can be portrayed in an oversimplified manner as an age-related achievement scale. One might regard the theory as a set of prescriptions that one *must* attain intimacy in early adulthood, generativity in middle adulthood, and integrity in old age.

The Chicago researchers

Havighurst's developmental tasks   Robert Havighurst proposed that personality development occurs through mastering a series of **developmental tasks**. A developmental task is "a task which arises at or about a certain period in the life of the individual, successful achievement of which leads to his [sic] happiness and to success with later tasks, while failure leads to unhappiness in the individual, disapproval by the society, and difficulty with later tasks" (Havighurst, 1952, p. 2). For each of six age periods—infancy and early childhood, middle childhood, adolescence, early adulthood, middle age, and later maturity—Havighurst identified a set of developmental tasks; those of adulthood are listed in Table 8.2.

Developmental tasks stem from three sources. Some arise from physical change and growth, such as learning to walk or adapting to menopause. Some are based on social demands, such as learning to read or acquiring the skills of responsible citizenship. Others reflect individual values and goals, such as selecting a career or developing a sense of ethics. Clearly, these sources are interdependent. In fact, Havighurst (1952) notes that most tasks reflect combined impacts of all three influences.

Like Freud's, Jung's, and Erikson's theories, Havighurst's sequence of developmental tasks is certainly subject to criticism. Some claim that this ap-

Table 8.2
Robert Havighurst: Developmental Tasks of Adulthood

Tasks of Early Adulthood:

   Finding a mate

   Learning to live with a marriage partner

   Starting a family

   Rearing children

   Managing a home

   Getting started in an occupation

   Taking on civic responsibility

   Finding a congenial social group

Tasks of Middle Age:

   Achieving social and civic responsibility

   Establishing and maintaining an economic standard of living

   Developing adult leisure-time activities

   Relating to one's spouse as a person

   Accepting and adjusting to the physiological changes of middle age

   Adjusting to aging parents

Tasks of Later Maturity:

   Adjusting to decreasing physical strength and health

   Adjusting to retirement and reduced income

   Adjusting to death of a spouse

   Establishing an explicit affiliation with one's age group

   Meeting social and civic obligations

   Establishing satisfactory physical living arrangements

Source: Havighurst, 1952. Reprinted by permission.

proach, too, is judgmental (e.g., Wrightsman, 1988) as there is no explicit consideration of tasks confronted by those who do not marry and have children. To these critics, Havighurst's model implies that establishing a traditional nuclear family is the only acceptable pattern of adult growth. Another criticism is that Havighurst overemphasizes the importance of chronological age; indeed, this is a frequent criticism of stage theories (Wrightsman, 1988). Nonetheless, there is evidence that adult life is regulated by "social clocks" (see Chapter One, p. 11), and some of Havighurst's developmental tasks match common-sense notions of sequential challenges of childhood, adolescence, and adulthood.

Robert Peck   Robert Peck (1968) takes Erikson's description of adult development as his starting point. As Peck—and Erikson (1950)—note, Erikson provides much greater detail in his descriptions of the crises of childhood and adolescence than those of adulthood. Peck suggests that middle and later adulthood encompass several challenges; everyone confronts these challenges in her own sequence.

According to Peck (1968), middle age requires coming to terms with *valuing wisdom versus valuing physical powers*. Because physical changes of aging become apparent in middle adulthood, one whose self-worth is anchored to her attractiveness is well-advised to value the judgement and experience that may come with age. Peck also suggests that the climacteric may open up possibilities for platonic relationships that might have been overlooked earlier in adulthood. Thus, middle age brings opportunities for *socializing in human relationships*.

Peck (1968) notes that middle-aged adults face two changes in their social world, and thus require emotional (or *cathectic*) *flexibility*. First, many find that important relationships are disrupted at this time: parents die and grown children leave home. A second change, however, is that many people take on new roles in the community and workplace at this point in life. To the degree that middle-aged adults are prepared to reinvest emotional energy in new outlets when earlier ones are foreclosed, one can optimize adjustment.

Peck's final issue of middle age is that of *mental flexibility versus mental rigidity*. While acknowledging that wisdom can compensate for decreased strength and attractiveness, Peck warns that wisdom does not come automatically from experience. One must draw on experience in new situations, but also have the good judgement to recognize that unique aspects of new situations may dictate a new approach.

In later adulthood, Peck identifies *ego differentiation versus work-role preoccupation* as a challenge of adapting to changing social roles. On retirement, one must develop a varied set of activities and interests. The challenge of *body transcendence versus body preoccupation* continues the process of adjusting to the physical changes of age. And, in identifying *ego transcendence versus ego preoccupation* as a task of later life, Peck—like Erikson (1950)—maintains that a satisfying old age requires knowing that one has provided a lasting social legacy.

Bernice Neugarten   Drawing on interviews conducted with a small, select sample of Chicagoans, Neugarten (1968a) provides a vivid picture of personality change in adulthood. She asked participants to describe the outstanding characteristics of middle adulthood; their responses convinced her that the forties and fifties are aptly labeled the prime of life. Qualities that Neugarten termed the "**executive processes of the personality**"—self-awareness, feelings of mastery, problem solving strategies—come into their own at this time.

While some of Neugarten's respondents expressed regret at the lost vigor of youth, virtually all took pride and pleasure in newfound feelings of competence. Most felt that they had a broader array of strategies to deal with problems, and that they exercised better judgement than they had when they were younger. There was also increased **interiority**, as respondents grew more reflective and took stock of their accomplishments relative to their goals.

These men and women described new feelings toward younger and older adults. Cultural change and life experience created boundaries between the respondents and younger people, but these individuals also identified new significance in their relationships with younger adults. As Erikson (e.g., 1950) and Havighurst (1952) would predict, these men and women were concerned about being role models for younger people and being able to provide good advice. Many, at the same time, felt a new closeness to older adults. Older people were uniquely capable of understanding dilemmas with which the respondents were struggling, since older adults had confronted and resolved the same issues years before.

Men and women described middle adulthood differently; you might wonder whether the same pattern of gender differences would appear today. Whereas the women demarcated middle age by events in their families, the men looked to events in the workplace as delineaters of middle age. Even the single women in Neugarten's sample used a "mythical family life cycle" in identifying themselves as middle-aged. These women thought of their friends' families, or the families that they might have had.

Physical changes of middle adulthood were more important to men than to women. Men noted decreased vigor and health concerns more often than women did; women, in fact, were often more worried about changes in their husbands' health than in their own. Finally, women characterized middle adulthood as a period of increased freedom, whereas many men felt new constraints. The women in this generation had devoted their youth to homemaking and childrearing; with children's departure from home, they felt free to turn their energy in new directions. For men, however, middle age brought increased pressure at work, and sometimes job burnout or boredom.

Although this study remains a classic and provides a unique view of middle adulthood, we must be cautious generalizing these findings. Neugarten's respondents were an elite sample: they had been selected from University of Chicago alumni lists, *Who's Who in America*, *American Men of Science*, and Chicago professional directories. These individuals were reflective and fluent, and thus able and willing to describe their perceptions of middle adulthood. However, the extent to which their views are shared by other middle-aged people—the poor, the homeless, or the illiterate, for example—is an empirical question. Also, the extent to which middle-aged people today and in the future would provide similar descriptions of middle age remains to be seen.

More recent approaches

The classic stage theorists and the Chicago researchers all portray adulthood as a period in which personality changes in important ways. Some research conducted in the past two decades provides new perspectives on adult personality but preserves the notion that adults experience personality changes. The samples and methods of this work depart from conventional developmental research approaches (see Chapter One, pp. 13–26). The samples have included psychiatric outpatients and middle-aged men; methods have included survey research and intensive analysis of biographical material. These contemporary approaches have strong intuitive appeal, as do the classic approaches. However, we must—as always—be cautious about the generality of these researchers' conclusions.

Levinson: The life structure Daniel Levinson's (1986; Levinson, Darrow, Klein, Levinson, & McKee, 1978) theory describes the formation and reformation of **life structure**. Levinson defines life structure as the underlying pattern of one's life at any particular time; the pattern reflects relationships with others. The "others" are often other people—spouses, friends, children, parents, coworkers, and so forth. But these others may also be symbolic or fictional characters, an institution, a nation, a social cause, nature, an ideal, or an artistic piece. Your life structure, then, reflects the people and things important to you at any time.

Levinson (1986; Levinson, Darrow, Klein, Levinson, & McKee, 1978) based his notion of the life structure on an intensive study of 40 men aged 35 to 45. These men were biologists, novelists, factory workers, or business executives; each was studied over a three-year period. Levinson and his colleagues interviewed each man for 15 to 20 hours (spread over several occasions), and used this information to construct a biography for each. In addition, each man completed the **Thematic Apperception Test (TAT)** (see pp. 202–203), a widely used personality measure. On the basis of their intensive examination of this material, Levinson and his staff described change and stability in adult life structure.

Since the publication of the findings of this study of middle-aged men, Levinson has conducted similar research involving women. There have also been several unpublished dissertations exploring the applicability of Levinson's ideas to women's adult development (e.g., Adams, 1983; Droege, 1982; Furst, 1983; Stewart, 1977). This work suggests that Levinson's ideas describe women's development as well as men's. We consider women's personality development, including studies conducted from a Levinsonian perspective, later in the chapter.

According to Levinson (1986; Levinson et al., 1978), the life structure evolves through a sequence of age-related periods spanning adulthood. Throughout the sequence, relatively stable *structure-building* periods alternate with transitional *structure-changing* periods. During the structure-building periods, a life structure is formed as one makes choices providing a framework for activities and goals. The structure building periods usually last five to seven years. Structure-changing periods bring the end of the existing life structure and create the potential for a new structure. In that process, one evaluates the current life structure and the possibilities for change; this evaluation leads to new commitments, and thus a new life structure. Figure 8.1 depicts the sequence of structure-building and structure-changing periods for early, middle, and late adulthood.

Levinson (1986; Levinson et al., 1978) asserts that middle adulthood is a time of crisis. He gives special attention to the **midlife transition**, a structure-

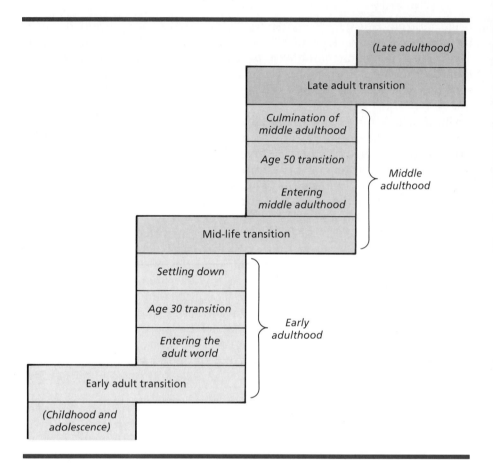

Figure 8.1
Developmental periods of adulthood. (Source: Levinson et al., *The Seasons of a Man's Life.* Copyright © 1978 by Daniel J. Levinson. Reprinted by permission of Alfred A. Knopf, Inc.)

changing period of the early forties; three processes should occur during this period. One brings the era of early adulthood to an end by reexamining the early adult life structure; next, one begins building a new structure by making new choices. Most important, the middle-aged adult resolves four polarities of motivation and self-concept.

Like Erikson and the Chicago researchers, Levinson (1986; Levinson et al., 1978) believes that many people become aware of their mortality at this point, and that this awareness prompts a reevaluation of the choices made in youth. The men in Levinson's sample expressed urgency that their remaining years be used wisely, and attempted to form an effective life structure for middle adulthood. Thus, a new life structure emerges as one changes external aspects of life (e.g., divorce, career change) or makes less obvious changes (e.g., changing the nature of the marital relationship, changing one's perspective on work).

At the same time, the middle-aged adult undergoes a process of **individuation** as he[1] attempts to "reintegrate a polarity—that is, a pair of tendencies or states that are usually experienced as polar opposites, as if a person must be one or the other and cannot be both" (Levinson et al., 1978, pp. 196–197). Levinson believes that both aspects of these polarities are part of personality throughout life. With individuation, a middle-aged person more freely recognizes and expresses both tendencies.

One polarity is that of **young/old**, as middle-aged adults strive to integrate the energy and spontaneity of youth with the maturity and wisdom of age. A second polarity is **destruction/creation**: men in Levinson's sample had a poignant awareness of mortality, and their own destructive potential. Coming to terms with that potential, however, also alerted men to their power to create and generate.

There is a polarity of **masculine/feminine**, reminiscent of Jung's notion of the anima/animus archetype. Like Jung, Levinson asserts that it is only at mid-life that a man can feel sure enough of his masculinity to comfortably express feminine qualities. The final polarity is that of **attachment/separateness**. Younger adults are concerned with attachment, as they establish families and careers. These tendencies are increasingly tempered with a pull toward separateness in mid-life: one becomes more inwardly oriented, more concerned with self-examination and reflection.

Levinson's portrayal of adult development conforms to many people's intuitive notions. However, his theory has been criticized. Wrightsman (1988) expressed concern over Levinson's methodology. Although some might argue that intensive study of selected cases is an ideal means of constructing developmental theory, others have objected that Levinson's examination of the interview and biographical material was not intensive enough (Sears, 1979).

Perhaps the most serious criticism, though, concerns the narrow age range within which data were collected. Remember that the participants in Levinson's research were aged 35 to 45, and were studied over a three-year period. Given that basis, it is best to be cautious in accepting his propositions concerning early adult life structures and transitional periods, as well as the life structures and transitions of later adulthood.

Gould: Shedding false assumptions Roger Gould, a psychiatrist holding a psychoanalytic perspective, proposes that personality matures through a recurring process of shedding **false assumptions** about oneself, the world, and life. These false assumptions may be constructed early in life, as children

---

1. Recall that most of Levinson's published work (e.g., 1978) reports research on men's development, although the little information that is available suggests that his model applies to women's development also.

contemplate the apparent power and security of adulthood. Like Erikson, Havighurst, and Levinson, Gould (1972; 1978) presents a stage theory: he proposes that people shed different false assumptions at different points in adulthood.

Gould (1978) based his ideas on research with psychiatric outpatients and a large-scale questionnaire study. First, Gould tape-recorded group therapy sessions. He asked medical students to review the tapes and identify statements of personal feelings that were outstanding for the group. These statements were the basis for a questionnaire that was presented to over 500 white, middle-class adults aged 16 to 60.

On the questionnaire, respondents rated the extent to which each statement applied to their current lives. Gould reviewed these responses to identify the number of people in each of seven age groups endorsing each statement. On the basis of the relative frequency with which the statements were endorsed in each age group, Gould proposed an age-linked sequence of six major periods of adult development. In each period, individuals challenge false, usually unspoken, assumptions; these assumptions and their corresponding developmental periods are listed in Table 8.3.

Even relative to other stage theorists, Gould (1978) stresses the significance of chronological age. He asserts that age provides a universal, reliable timetable for passage through the sequence of developmental periods. In this theory, then, not only the sequence of stages but also the *precise time* in the life cycle when these stages appear are specified.

We should be cautious in wholeheartedly accepting Gould's claims of a universal sequence of development linked closely to chronological age. Remember that Gould's ideas are based on cross-sectional data; these data cannot provide compelling evidence of age changes (see Chapter One, pages 20–22). In

Table 8.3
Roger Gould: Themes of adult periods

Ages 16–22:	Renouncing the assumption that "I'll always belong to my parents and believe in their world."
Ages 22–28:	Renouncing the assumption that "doing things my parents' way, with will power and perseverance, will bring results. But if I become too frustrated, confused, or tired, or am simply unable to cope, they will step in and show me the right way."
Ages 28–34:	Renouncing the assumption that "life is simple and controllable. There are no significant coexisting contradictory forces within me."
Ages 34–45:	Renouncing the assumption that "there is no evil or death in the world; the sinister has been destroyed."
Ages 45–53:	The die is cast.
Ages 53–60:	Years of warming and mellowing.

Source: Gould, 1978. Copyright © 1978 by Robert Gould, M.D. Reprinted by permission of Simon & Schuster, Inc.

addition, Gould did not carry out statistical tests to determine the reliability of age differences in frequencies of endorsing different statements. Finally, Gould's research involved only white, middle-class participants. As is the case for most of the other theories considered in this chapter, it is reasonable to suppose that a different model of adult personality development might emerge from research involving nonwhites and non-Westerners. Gould's—and Levinson's—work may be of value in identifying some of the dynamics of adult personality, rather than in offering a strict prescription of a developmental timetable.

PERSONALITY MEASUREMENT AND PSYCHOMETRIC RESEARCH

Generally, researchers interested in personality development use a cross-sectional or longitudinal design, and employ widely accepted measures of personality and interviews. Before examining the fruits of these efforts, we will consider some common approaches to assessing personality, and the strengths and weaknesses of these methods. Most personality measures can be classified as either **self-report measures** or **projective measures**.

Self-report measures

These measures gather an individual's report of her characteristics, needs, tendencies, or values. On some, examinees are asked to indicate the extent to which certain traits (e.g., friendliness, intelligence) characterize them. On others, examinees report whether or not each of a number of statements (e.g., I like to read sports magazines; I am afraid of a lot of things) describe them. Three of the more widely used self-report measures of personality are the **Minnesota Multiphasic Personality Inventory (MMPI)**, the **California Personality Inventory (CPI)**, and the **Sixteen Personality Factor Questionnaire (16-PF)**.

The MMPI is the single most widely used self-report measure of personality (Lubin, Larsen, & Mattarazzo, 1984). This test was developed in the 1930s as a tool for psychiatric diagnosis; the developers created hundreds of test items, each of which presented a self-descriptive statement and asked for a response of "true" or "false." When this item pool had been compiled, the test was administered to two groups of adults: psychiatric inpatients at the University of Minnesota hospital and control subjects (e.g., hospital visitors, healthy clients at a testing center in Minnesota, general medical patients at the University hospital, WPA workers). Next, the developers identified the items to which the inpatients and the control subjects had responded differently. Those 550 items were retained for the final version of the test. A revised version of the test, sharing the original format but with updated norms, has recently been published.

Items are distributed among three validity scales and ten clinical scales. In a sense, the validity scales are built-in checks that an examinee's responses provide an honest and accurate self-description. Responses on the clinical scales are used to develop an interpretation of the individual's personality.

Although the MMPI was originally developed as a diagnostic tool, it is used today for a wide variety of purposes, including research, educational screening, and personnel selection. Some psychologists have objected to such widespread use of an instrument designed for diagnostic purposes. One response to these objections was the development of the California Personality Inventory, or CPI. The CPI was developed through a process like that used for the MMPI, and also presents self-descriptive statements requiring a true/false response. However, the CPI is shorter than the MMPI, and its content is more oriented toward positive personality strengths than toward psychiatric disorder.

The 16-PF, a third self-report measure, was developed through factor analysis. In this method, developers examined responses to many items in order to identify clusters of items that examinees answered similarly. If you were taking the 16-PF, you would be presented with 171 personality traits and asked to rate the extent to which each describes you. Your ratings would provide a basis for characterizing you in terms of 16 broad personality traits, such as maturity, persistence, shyness, and self-sufficiency.

Self-report personality measures have at least two weaknesses. First, individuals may attempt to distort the impression that they present, although some self-report measures (e.g., the MMPI) have safeguards against this tendency. Second, some people respond more on the basis of a general response set than on the basis of their view of themselves. Some people, for example, may agree with virtually all items; some may rate themselves as having a moderate level of nearly all traits. Nonetheless, self-report measures enjoy high levels of reliability and validity, and—because of their widespread use—there is a rich literature describing correlates of test responses.

Projective measures

If you were assessed using a projective measure, an examiner would present an ambiguous stimulus and ask you to react to it. Depending on which projective measure were used, the stimulus might be an inkblot, a picture, a word, or an incomplete sentence. Because these stimuli are relatively unstructured, different people respond to them in different ways. The assumption is that the examinee's response reflects her needs, goals, desires, fears, and conflicts rather than the nature of the stimulus itself.

Among the widely used projective measures are the **Rorschach**, the **Holtzman Inkblot Technique (HIT)**, and the Thematic Apperception Test (TAT). In both the Rorschach and the Holtzman, the projective stimuli are inkblots, some black and white and some with color. The examinee describes what each blot might be. The TAT stimuli are a set of 30 black and white pictures, some nearly as realistic as photographs and some much more fanciful. On the TAT, the examinee tells a story about what is happening in the picture, what led up to the scene, and how it is likely to be resolved.

These measures, too, have strengths and weaknesses. Projective tests are good icebreakers: most people find the tasks interesting and the valuative nature of the situation is thereby downplayed. Another advantage is that projective tests demand less verbal fluency than do many objective measures, since no reading is required. Finally, some claim that projective measures are less culturally biased than objective measures, and TAT-like materials have been successfully used in cross-cultural research on adult development (e.g., Gutmann, 1977).

Certainly, projective measures have problems as well. Although it is difficult to evaluate the reliability and validity of projective measures, available evidence suggests that the tests are less adequate in these respects than self-report measures. To a greater extent than self-report tests, interpretation of responses depend on the skill and theoretical orientation of the examiner. Finally, although the assumption behind the use of these measures is that responses reflect personality components, responses are also influenced by situational factors (e.g., characteristics and behavior of the examiner) and can be affected by the desire to create a particular impression (e.g., Weisskopf & Dieppa, 1951; Hamscher & Farina, 1967).

In surveying theory and research on adult personality development, we have already seen that some work provides compelling evidence that personality changes fundamentally during adulthood. The theories reviewed earlier in the chapter, and Gould's and Levinson's research relying on projective measures and interviews, support this viewpoint. Other research, however, supports the notion that there is more stability than change in adult personality. Much of the latter evidence is based on the use of self-report personality measures; we turn to this work next.

Quantitative research on adult personality

Robert McCrae and Paul Costa (1984) advance the strongest argument that personality remains stable across adulthood. They base this assertion primarily on their analysis of data from the Baltimore Longitudinal Study of Aging (BLSA), an ongoing study of adult development that began in 1958; recall that we initially examined findings from the BLSA in Chapter Four (see p. 95). In addition, Costa and McCrae identify findings from other research that bolster their contention that there is little change in personality during adulthood.

The psychological measures used in the BLSA include two self-report measures of personality, the 16-PF (see p. 202) and the Guilford-Zimmerman Temperament Survey. Using these data, McCrae and Costa (e.g., 1984; Costa, et al., 1986; McCrae, Costa, & Arenberg, 1980) initially identified three independent domains of personality—neuroticism, extraversion, and openness to experience—that together comprised 18 separate traits; they termed this representation the NEO model. Further analysis lead to augmentation of the NEO model with two additional factors—Agreeableness and Conscientiousness; the resulting representation is the **five-factor model** (e.g., Costa, 1989; Costa & McCrae, 1988; Digman & Inouye, 1986).

According to McCrae and Costa (1984; Costa, 1989; Costa & McCrae, 1988; Costa, McCrae, & Arenberg, 1980; McCrae, Costa, & Arenberg, 1980), the BLSA data provide compelling evidence of stability in personality after approximately age 30. When the researchers examined correlations between trait scores obtained several years apart, these correlations were high and positive. Nor were there substantial changes in mean levels of personality traits. Thus, men[2] who attained relatively high scores on extraversion as young adults remained more outgoing than their peers when they were middle-aged; those who expressed relatively little openness to experience when they were young rarely became more open as they aged.

Data supporting the contention of personality stability do not reside in the BLSA alone, however. McCrae and Costa (1984; Costa, 1989) review similar findings obtained in other longitudinal studies. Across a variety of samples and self-report measures, there is little evidence of change in subjects' descriptions of their personalities over thirty years or more. In addition, the evidence for stability is not based only on self-reports. Costa and McCrae (1988; Costa, 1989) also found that spouses' ratings of BLSA participants' personalities similarly reflected stability.

One longitudinal study puts these findings in a broader perspective, however. Haan (1989) also reports significant positive correlations between personality assessments made in early, middle, and later adulthood; however, she notes that there were far stronger correlations between personality scores obtained throughout participants' childhood. In that set of longitudinal data spanning most of the life cycle, then, childhood was a period of greater personality stability than adulthood. Haan (1989; Haan, Millsap, & Hartka, 1986) suggests that personality changes are partly the result of confrontation with life experiences of tremendous consequence. Because most are sheltered from such experiences during youth, it is reasonable to view adulthood—when we are no longer protected from these experiences—as a time when personality change is more likely.

One might wonder whether participants in longitudinal research attempt to answer personality measures in the same way each time they are tested, and thereby create an illusion of greater stability than actually exists. That possibility seems unlikely. In one longitudinal study, researchers asked middle-aged participants to complete a personality measure that they had initially completed twenty-five years earlier as college students (Woodruff & Birren, 1972). These middle-aged people completed the measure twice: first, to describe themselves at the current time, and then to *attempt to reproduce the responses*

---

2. Although the BLSA originated in 1958 as a longitudinal study of aging in men, a sample of women was added to the study beginning in 1978. However, most of McCrae and Costa's discussions have focused on the male subjects.

that they remembered giving as college students. The middle-aged and actual college-age responses were quite similar, as McCrae and Costa (1984) would have predicted. In fact, those two sets of responses were more similar than were the actual college-age responses and the remembered college-age responses.

McCrae and Costa (1984) recognize that their assertion of personality stability flies in the face of classic theory and some current thinking about adulthood as a time of fundamental change. Their argument casts particular doubt on the popular idea of the "midlife crisis." Partly for that reason, they developed a Midlife Crisis Scale; items inquired about dissatisfaction with family and career, a sense of meaningless, feelings of mortality, and sensations of conflict. They administered the scale to over 300 men aged thirty to sixty, and found no evidence of high scores among the middle-aged men (using various ages as cutoff points for middle age). Scores were, however, somewhat higher for individuals rating themselves relatively high in Neuroticism (e.g., Costa, 1989).

How do McCrae and Costa (1984) explain their findings? They suggest that personality stability is the result of the individual's deliberate and nondeliberate efforts, and social pressure. Most people try to maintain a consistent view of themselves (e.g., Atchley, 1989). Life would indeed be chaotic if we could never predict how we might feel and react in the future. By engaging in familiar activities, remaining involved in stable relationships, and maintaining commitments to careers and goals, people take steps to shape their worlds so as to preserve stability. Friends, coworkers, and family members have a stake in keeping our behavior within predictable limits, so we may also encounter subtle (or not so subtle) social pressure to maintain a stable personality.

This overview of classic and current thinking about adult personality presents contrasting perspectives. Some maintain that adulthood is a period of qualitative change in personality, while others assert that personality remains stable in adulthood. The *Open Questions* box for this chapter attempts a synthesis of these positions.

PERSONALITY, LIFE SATISFACTION, AND AGING: VARIED PATHS TO CONTENTMENT IN OLD AGE

Research examining the correlates of **life satisfaction** in old age has a long tradition in the study of adult personality; life satisfaction (also often referred to as morale or psychological well-being) is the older individual's contentment with her current life circumstances, her perspectives on her past, and her outlook on the future. Much of the early work on life satisfaction was conducted from the perspective of either **disengagement theory** or **activity theory**. These theories were initially examined in Chapter Two (see pp. 36–37), in the context of the nature of successful aging. Now we review these theories, and take a closer look at the importance of personality in the relationship between life satisfaction and social involvement in old age.

BOX 8.1 *OPEN QUESTIONS*

Is the concept of the "midlife crisis" useful?

"Leave me alone—I'm having a crisis!" Some assume that this plea is sung almost universally by those in their forties and fifties. There is no shortage of popular images illustrating the "midlife crisis": the stodgy executive who suddenly adopts youthful attire and takes a nubile young lover, the professional who abandons a successful career to do unskilled work, the 50-year-old tortured by existential doubts about the strivings of her youth. This chapter shows us that there is some evidence consistent with a crisis period in middle adulthood, particularly in Levinson's (Levinson et al., 1978) work.

Should the popular images and the evidence be questioned? Perhaps; characterizing middle adulthood as a time of unusual stress and turmoil may obscure rather than clarify understanding. Developmental psychologists view the entire life cycle as a sequence of multifaceted changes (see Chapter One, pp. 9–13), and most changes entail stress. On that basis, singling out middle adulthood as a crisis period seems unwarranted. We might, with just as much justification, speak of a "childhood crisis," an "adolescent crisis," a "young adult crisis," and an "aging crisis," since individuals also adapt to physical, psychological, and social change at these times.

Furthermore, the evidence that a period of crisis is universal and inevitable in middle adulthood is far from overwhelming. Although Levinson (Levinson et al., 1978) found that virtually all in his sample experienced such a crisis, other research presents a different picture. For example, women do not experience a midlife crisis—at least not when and how men do.

Not even all men fit the pattern that Levinson describes. In Farrell and Rosenberg's (1981) large-scale study of men at midlife, social class was related to the experience of crisis. Men in unskilled occupations experienced greater stress in middle age than did professional or middle-class men, although the lower-class men often used denial or avoidance as coping mechanisms. The BLSA evidence documenting stability of personality casts strong doubt on the likelihood that most go through a crisis period in the middle years.

How helpful, then, is the concept of a midlife crisis? The concept does have value in calling attention to the middle years as a time of profound change in the body, in psychological functioning, and in social roles. For the clinician who works with middle-aged adults, a crisis perspective may help to identify ways in which these changes create distress and turmoil for some. It remains to be demonstrated, though, that experiencing a time of crisis is either normal, inevitable, or beneficial.

Recall that disengagement theory posits that aging is characterized by mutual withdrawal on the part of society and the aging person (Cumming & Henry, 1961). The older individual is not excluded involuntarily from social involvement; instead, she accepts, and perhaps even seeks, decreased involvement. Life satisfaction results from disengagement, according to this theory. Activity theory (e.g., Maddox, 1963), in contrast, proposes that older adults have the same needs for involvement as younger adults, and that remaining socially involved leads to life satisfaction in old age.

Remember, too, that neither theory provided an adequate picture of the relationship between social engagement and life satisfaction. For some older people, disengagement provided a satisfying style of life, but for others activity and involvement were just as satisfying. As we saw earlier, Neugarten, Havighurst, & Tobin (1968) identified personality as a mediator of the relationship between activity level and life satisfaction. Which personalities sought disengagement in old age, and which found social involvement more satisfying?

Altogether, Neugarten et al. (1968) identified four personality types in their examination of the Kansas City Study data; by examining these types in relation to levels of activity and life satisfaction, they further specified eight patterns of aging. The first personality type was the **integrated** individual; these older people were cognitively and emotionally healthy, self-accepting, and moderately controlled. All had high levels of life satisfaction, but they varied in activity levels. Some, the "reorganizers," were quite involved: when one activity was lost (e.g., retirement), these people substituted new activities (e.g., volunteer work). Other integrated people had moderate levels of activity: these "focused" individuals invested themselves in a few, carefully selected activities rather than attempting to maintain all areas of involvement as they aged. Still other integrated personalities (the "disengaged") had low levels of activity. These individuals were content to shed social involvement as they aged, and chose a "rocking chair" lifestyle.

Neugarten et al. (1968) labeled the second personality type the **armored-defended**. All of these individuals were striving, ambitious, and achievement-oriented; all maintained strong controls over their own impulses. All, too, aggressively defended against anxiety, including anxiety evoked by their own aging, and exhibited high or moderate levels of life satisfaction. Some fit a "holding on" pattern, in which they defended against aging by remaining active and involved. Others, the "constricted," used curtailed involvement as their defense.

The **passive-dependent** personality type comprised two patterns of aging. In the "succorance-seeking" pattern, older adults with strong dependency needs maintained high or medium levels of activity and life satisfaction. As long as these older people had close relationships that they could depend on to satisfy emotional needs, all was well. Others, the "apathetic," exhibited both low levels of activity and moderate or low levels of life satisfaction. In their activity level, these individuals were like the "disengaged"; however, these older people had not actively sought decreased involvement, but simply expressed lifelong patterns of passivity and apathy.

The final personality type was the **unintegrated**. Individuals of this type had a "disorganized" pattern of aging, exhibiting impaired cognitive or emotional functioning. Although these individuals lived independently in the community, they did so with minimal social involvement and expressed little life satisfaction.

As Neugarten (1977) explained, "the aging individual not only plays an active role in adapting to the biological and social changes that occur with the passage of time but in *creating* patterns of life that will give him [sic] greatest ego involvement and life satisfaction" (p. 643). More recent research leads us to the same conclusion. In a unique approach to examining correlates of life satisfaction, Ogilvie (1987) constructed "identity matrices" of meaningful involvements and the extent to which each involvement allowed his participants to express desired personality features or characteristics. Integrating these matrices with measures of time spent in each involvement provided an index of personal style; spending time in meaningful pursuits predicted life satisfaction for these older people. Similarly, Holahan (1988) found that engagement in activities related to life goals contributed to life satisfaction for intellectually-advantaged older adults. As in the Kansas City Study, then, being able to choose a life pattern providing self-expression was important to adjustment in old age.

PERSONALITY DEVELOPMENT IN WOMEN

The past three decades witnessed a virtual explosion of interest in women's lives and development. A central research question was whether women's personalities develop through unique paths. Much of this work suggests that early adult personality development may take on a special character for women. Helson and Moane (1987) reported an extensive study of over 100 young women who were questioned when they graduated from college, again in their late twenties, and a third time in their early forties. On all three occasions, the women completed the CPI. In addition, the researchers used several other self-report personality measures and assessed the women's involvement in work and family.

In their twenties, these women gained self-control and social maturity, a more realistic perception of life and the world, insight into significant others, and a deeper sense of femininity. In their thirties, femininity and openness to change decreased. At the same time, confidence, independence, nurturance, affability, organization, commitment, and work orientation all increased. Other changes occurring in the thirties were increased coping skills and self-acceptance.

As is the case with any longitudinal study, these researchers described changes occurring in a single cohort studied during one period of history. However, Helson and Moane (1987) carefully considered external validity (see Chapter One, pp. 15–16) in discussing their results. The researchers pointed out that all of their participants were white upper-middle class women who had experienced young adulthood during the germination of the women's movement and the blossoming of feminism. Certainly, these social trends—as well as concurrent political, economic, and demographic changes—could be reflected in the sample's pattern of personality growth.

However, Helson and Moane (1987) also noted parallels between the changes reflected in their data and those seen in earlier longitudinal studies in which young adult women were included (e.g., Block, 1971; Freedman & Bereiter, 1963; Haan, 1981; Kelly, 1955). These similarities suggest that this pattern of personality growth is not unique to this cohort. In addition, the researchers noted that the changes that they described were common to women in their sample who reported different levels of involvement in family and work. This finding, too, suggests that Helson and Moane's findings have generality beyond this sample of women.

What about women's personality development during middle and later adulthood? Several unpublished studies have been conducted from a Levinsonian perspective. After reviewing this work, P. Roberts and P. M. Newton (1987) concluded that Levinson's theory of building and rebuilding life structures applied well to women. The 39 women interviewed for these studies experienced the same kinds of developmental milestones that Levinson described for men, and encountered these events at approximately the same ages that men did. However, women and men dealt with these milestones differently. In particular, women entered and progressed through adulthood guided by more complex **Dreams**—senses of themselves and their potential—than men did.

For men (e.g., Levinson et al., 1978), the Dream centered around an independent achiever in an occupational role. Women, however, sometimes formed Dreams focused on relationships to others, sometimes developed occupationally-centered Dreams, and sometimes formed no Dream at all (Roberts & Newton, 1987). Most often, though, the women in these studies described a **split Dream** that included equal attention to career and relationships.

Other scholars have taken a different approach to examining older women's personality development. Grace Baruch and Rosalind Barnett (e.g., Baruch, Barnett, & Rivers, 1983; Baruch, 1984) studied psychological well-being among middle-aged women. Unlike the other research considered in this chapter, the 238 participants were a random sample of women aged 35 to 55. Even more important, the researchers selected employed married women with children, employed married women without children, employed divorced women with children, employed never-married women, married women who were not working outside of the home but who had children, and married women who

For women, a "split Dream" that includes goals related to both career and family may be a guiding principle in life.

were not working outside of the home and who did not have children. This research, then, allows consideration of well-being for women with different lifestyles. The use of a random sample (see Chapter One, p. 19) gives some confidence that the findings can be generalized beyond the women who actually participated in the research.

"Psychological well-being" is a frequently-used concept in the study of adult personality and adjustment; like "personality", different researchers define and measure this concept differently. Baruch and Barnett (e.g., Baruch et al., 1983; Baruch, 1984) identified two independent aspects of psychological well-being for the women in their research. The first aspect was **mastery**, the extent to which a woman felt in control of her life; the second was **pleasure**, the extent to which a woman felt happiness and optimism.

Women in the six subgroups differed in levels of mastery and pleasure (e.g., Baruch et al., 1983; Baruch, 1984). As Figure 8.2 illustrates, women expressing greatest mastery were those working outside of the home, whether married, never married, or divorced. Married women—regardless of employment or

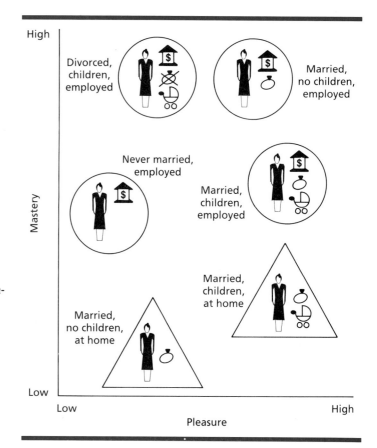

Figure 8.2
Mastery and pleasure for women in the six subgroups. (Source: Baruch et al., *Lifeprints*, 1983. Copyright 1983 by McGraw-Hill. Reprinted by permission of McGraw-Hill.)

parental status—expressed the most pleasure. The women judged highest in well-being overall were the employed married women with children—those that might be expected to be under the most stress. This study shows that middle-aged women can thrive on a challenging mixture of roles.

Still another conclusion from Baruch and Barnett's work is that these women expressed no sense of a midlife crisis (e.g., Baruch et al., 1983; Baruch, 1984). Other recent research contradicts this finding, however. In an intensive study of women aged 45 to 60, most had experienced a major change in status and self-concept (Harris, Ellicott, & Holmes, 1986; Reinke, Ellicott, Harris, & Hancock, 1985), although usually not around age 40 as Levinson and his colleagues (1978) would predict. The turning points for these women were linked to events in the family life cycle—much like the women that Neugarten had studied a generation earlier.

Baruch and Barnett's work is reviewed with care for two reasons. First, it is one of a handful of studies taking a deliberate focus on women's personality development. Second, Baruch and Barnett's methods provide a statistical basis for generalizing their findings to contemporary, metropolitan American women—a characteristic that sets this project apart from most. However, the issue of women's psychological well-being in middle and later adulthood should also be examined still more broadly. Cross-cultural research provides some glimpses into sources of well-being for women in a wide variety of cultures. The *Diversity in Adulthood* box briefly reviews this work.

MORAL JUDGMENT AND REASONING

Thus far we have considered views of adult personality, and particularly the extent to which personality changes or remains stable during adulthood. Now, we address a related issue: the grounds on which adults base moral decisions. In this area, gender—as much as age—distinguishes approaches to making moral decisions.

Kohlberg: Moral reasoning among Harvard students

Lawrence Kohlberg (e.g., 1963; 1970; Colby, Kohlberg, Gibbs, & Lieberman, 1983; Kohlberg, Levine, & Hewer, 1983; Levine, Kohlberg, & Hewer, 1985) made some of the most important contributions to the understanding of moral reasoning. Kohlberg presented vignettes describing moral dilemmas to his participants. In one vignette, for example, a man must obtain a costly medication to save his wife; a druggist refuses to make payment arrangements, even though the medication is the only hope for the wife's survival and the man cannot afford the total payment. The participant must decide whether or not the man would be justified in stealing the medication, and why.

BOX 8.2   *DIVERSITY IN ADULTHOOD*

Women around the world: Mental health in the middle years of adulthood

In a review of ethnographic literature on adulthood and aging, Jennie Keith (1990) observed that women in most social settings experience less psychological difficulty than men do as they age. Why should this be so? Many think of women as a disadvantaged group, at least in terms of social status and role options. Keith suggests that these very differences may, paradoxically, work to women's advantage in middle and later adulthood.

Keith reminds us that women in most societies devote their lives to responsibility for home and children. In that context, the transitions of middle and later adulthood are less dramatic than role changes that men experience. This interpretation provides an interesting contrast to Baruch and Barnett's (e.g., Baruch et al., 1983) finding that metropolitan American women who had devoted themselves to homemaking did not express particularly high levels of psychological well-being. Perhaps women in traditional cultures whose lives are immersed in the domestic realm benefit from following a culturally prescribed life pattern, whereas American women today receive far less approval for choosing such a lifestyle.

Keith also offers other explanations for women's psychological advantage in adjustment to aging. Women, she suggests, have more experience than men do with discontinuity and change throughout their lives. In patrilocal societies, a woman experiences a dramatic transition when she leaves her parents' household to take up residence with her husband's family. Women, too, gain experience in adapting to changes in their bodies—menstruation, pregnancy, nursing— well before middle adulthood. Perhaps these experiences prepare women to adapt to the

inevitable physical and social changes that come with age.

The social changes of aging can benefit women more concretely in some societies. Keith notes that "in many societies . . . [women's] social position improves with age. The shift from timid, dominated bride to powerful household head provides not only experience of discontinuity but also a clear-cut increase in power and status" (p. 93). Social opportunities open up for women in these contexts. In the family, she may gain authority over younger kinswomen, authority to which she was once subject. In the broader society, she may become eligible for positions of power and ceremony only available to older women.

The possibility of age removing constraints on a woman's life is reminiscent of the ways in which the women in Neugarten's (1968) study of middle age described this period of the life cycle. With the easing of child-care responsibilities, many felt free to pursue new interests and seek new positions of authority and responsibility outside of the home. Like the women in more traditional societies, these women viewed middle adulthood as a time in which new opportunities had only begun to present themselves.

Keith's (1990) discussion helps to place notions of personality, mental health, and adult development in broader context. There are both similarities and differences as we compare these anthropological findings with the results of research on middle-aged and older Americans. Clearly, the pleasures and strains of growing older reflect a strong influence of culture. By the same token, experience of one's culture may change with the tempo of the life cycle.

Kohlberg (1963) evaluated responses in terms of the grounds used for making a decision, and identified three stages of moral development spanning childhood and adolescence. Each stage has two levels, so Kohlberg postulated

Table 8.4
Kohlberg's stages of moral development

Preconventional Moral Reasoning

The individual makes moral decisions on the basis of concrete consequences of an
action, such as reward or punishment.

Stage 1 **Punishment and obedience orientation**: Judgments are made in
order to avoid punishment and conform to the wishes of an authority,
such as parents or teachers.

Stage 2 **Instrumental-relativist orientation**: Moral, good actions are those
which satisfy one's own needs (or occasionally others' needs).

Conventional Moral Reasoning

The individual makes moral decisions so as to conform to the expectations of
others—the family, the peer group, or the nation.

Stage 3 **"Good boy/nice girl" orientation**: Judgments are made in terms of
conforming to cultural expectations. For example, actions which help
others or win others' approval are considered good. In addition, individuals now begin to consider not only an action and its physical consequences, but also the intention behind the action, in evaluating the
moral status of the action.

Stage 4 **Law and order orientation**: Showing respect for authority and fulfilling
one's duty are considered prime moral obligations. Judgments about the
moral status of an action are made on the basis of the extent to which
the action conforms to expectations and maintains the status quo.

Postconventional Moral Reasoning

The individual now attempts to define moral principles independently, apart from the
influences of other people or of designated authority.

Stage 5 **Social contract orientation**: Moral actions are those which enhance
the common good. This orientation also involves a view of rules not as
fixed and absolute, but as socially constructed products which can be
changed by mutual agreement. Such agreements should be sought if
they would optimize the general welfare.

Stage 6 **Universal ethical principle orientation**: The individual judges actions
according to personally-constructed moral standards. One may make
judgments that deviate markedly from conventional notions of right and
wrong if the circumstances of the judgment so dictate.

Source: Adapted from Stevens-Long, *Adult Life*, published by Mayfield Publishing Co., © 1988.
Reprinted by permission.

six levels of moral reasoning altogether. The characteristics of these stages are
briefly summarized in Table 8.4.

In an intensive longitudinal study of Harvard University students,
Kohlberg (1970) further explored adult moral development. Examining these
students' responses to the vignettes convinced him that postconventional
moral reasoning (stages 5 and 6—see Table 8.4) is reached in adulthood, rather
than adolescence. Furthermore, he asserted that attaining postconventional
reasoning hinged on experiences predominant in adult life; he had tied the

emergence of earlier levels of reasoning to cognitive development. The experiences prompting movement toward postconventional reasoning include membership in a college community in which one encounters diverse values, and experiences such as marriage and parenthood in which one undertakes sustained responsibility for others.

Kohlberg's view of moral development has been criticized on at least two counts. First, cross-cultural research casts doubt on the extent to which this sequence of stages appears universally (e.g., Edwards, 1980). Thus, Kohlberg's theory may reflect the cultural context of his research rather than a universal maturational process. Second, Carol Gilligan (1982) asserted that Kohlberg's theory does not accurately portray women's moral development.

Carol Gilligan and women's moral reasoning

Gilligan (1982) noted that women in Kohlberg's research responded in ways that were consistently judged less mature than men's responses. She argued that women responded in this manner because the standard vignettes failed to confront them with issues relevant to their lives. According to Gilligan, the conflict between one's own and others' welfare is the most central moral dilemma with which adult women contend.

Gilligan examined reactions to this dilemma in a study of women contemplating abortion. All were interviewed initially during the first trimester of a confirmed pregnancy, and then a year later. Gilligan asked each woman to discuss her perspective of the decision that she faced, how she was confronting the decision, what alternatives she was considering, reasons for and against each alternative, other people involved in her decision, conflicts entailed in the

Gilligan contends that conflict between one's own welfare and the well-being of others is the most important moral dilemma that women face.

decision, and how the woman believed that her decision would affect her self-concept and relationships.

Gilligan (1982) concluded that women experience a set of moral transitions distinct from those that Kohlberg described. She proposed a sequence of three moral perspectives through which women progress; each represents a successively more complex understanding of the relationship between self and others. Initially, a woman evaluates moral dilemmas from the perspective of concern for her own survival. Later, the woman equates goodness with self-sacrifice. Finally, in the most advanced perspective, the woman identifies care—toward both herself and others—as the best guide to resolving moral conflicts.

Concluding Thoughts

As the chapter closes, we find that there is valid empirical evidence supporting two contrasting perspectives of the adult personality. On the one hand, there is documentation for qualitative change in personality during adulthood; on the other hand, there is a sound basis for asserting that adult personality remains stable. Recall that which of these portrayals are drawn often depends on the approach to measurement that one adopts. Scholars using interview and projective methods tend to emphasize change, whereas those depending on self-report measures more often stress stability.

The issue of the influence of design and measurement on research findings arose in earlier chapters. For example, whether one claims that intelligence declines or remains relatively stable with age depends partly on whether a cross-sectional or longitudinal design is used, and what aspects of intelligence one chooses to assess. The general lesson is that conclusions based on research cannot be evaluated without also considering the way in which the research was conducted.

In the case of describing adult personality, it is unlikely that any single, universal description of either change or stability is likely to prove adequate. There are simply too many significant sources of diversity in personality development for any one model to be useful. This chapter highlights gender and cultural background as particularly important sources of diversity.

Summary

A theme of this chapter is ways in which a perspective of change as opposed to a perspective of stability adds to our understanding of adult personality. Classic stage theories (e.g., Jung, Erikson) and the work of the Chicago researchers emphasize qualitative change in adult personality. Similarly, Levinson's theory describes the formation and reformation of life structure, whereas Roger Gould proposes that adult personality changes through a recurring process of shedding false assumptions about oneself, the world, and life. Other research, however, supports the notion that there is more stability than change in adult personality.

Longitudinal research following women from college graduation through mid-life suggests that early adult personality development may take on a special character for women. Other research shows that middle-aged women can thrive on a challenging mixture of roles.

Bernice Neugarten and her colleagues identified personality as a mediator of the relationship between activity level and life satisfaction in old age. Altogether, these scholars identified four personality types in their examination of the Kansas City Study data. By examining these types in relation to levels of activity and life satisfaction, they further specified eight patterns of aging.

An overview of work on adult moral judgement and reasoning reveals that gender provides as reliable a basis as age for distinguishing approaches to moral decisions.

KEY TERMS

Activity theory
Alienated achievement
Anima
Animus
Archetypes
Armored-defended
Attachment/separateness
California Personality Inventory (CPI)
Cardinal trait
Collective unconscious
Despair
Destruction/creation
Developmental tasks
Disengagement theory
Dream
Ego
Ego integrity
Executive processes of the personality
False assumptions
Five factor model
Fixation
Foreclosure
Generativity
Holtzman Inkblot Technique (HIT)
Id
Identity achievement
Identity diffusion
Individuation
Integrated
Interiority
Intimacy
Intimate

Isolate
Isolation
Libido
Life satisfaction
Life structure
Masculine/feminine
Mastery
Midlife transition
Minnesota Multiphasic Personality
    Inventory (MMPI)
Moratorium
Passive-dependent
Personal unconscious
Pleasure
Preintimate
Prework
Projective measures
Pseudointimate
Rework
Rorschach
Self
Self-realization
Self-report measures
Sixteen Personality Factor Questionnaire
    (16-PF)
Split Dream
Stagnation
Stereotyped relationships
Superego
Thematic Apperception Test (TAT)
Unintegrated
Young/old

SUGGESTIONS FOR FURTHER READING

Erikson, E. H. (1963). *Childhood and Society*. New York: W. W. Norton & Co.

Erikson, E. H., Erikson, J. M., & Kivnick, H. Q. (1986). *Vital Involvement in Old Age*. New York: W. W. Norton & Co.

Gould, R. (1978). *Transformations: Growth and Change in Adult Life*. New York: Simon & Schuster.

Hall, C. S., & Lindzey, G. (1978). *Theories of Personality*. 3rd Edition. New York: Wiley.

Levinson, D. J., Darrow, C. N., Klein, E. B., Levinson, M. H., & McKee, B. (1978). *The Seasons of a Man's Life*. New York: Knopf.

Wrightsman, L. S. (1988). *Personality Development in Adulthood*. Newbury Park: Sage Publications.

CHAPTER NINE

PSYCHOPATHOLOGY AND PSYCHOTHERAPY: MENTAL HEALTH PROBLEMS IN OLD AGE

Do most people develop dementia as they grow old? When someone develops a mental disorder in old age, is there any hope for improvement? We seek answers to these questions, as this chapter examines psychopathology as it affects elderly adults.

The chapter also reviews mental health services for older adults. Older adults, compared to younger people, are underserved by mental health professionals; we identify possible reasons for this disparity. The chapter also surveys treatment approaches that are successful with older people.

Questions to consider in reading the chapter include:

Are older adults more vulnerable to depression than younger people? What treatments for depression are successful in later life?

What are the signs of schizophrenia? What treatments for schizophrenia are currently used?

Why are professionals concerned about alcohol abuse among the aged?

What is dementia? Why is the distinction between primary and secondary dementia critical? How is Alzheimer's disease currently diagnosed?

Why do older adults use mental health services at unusually low rates? In what settings are mental health services provided to the aged?

DEFINING MENTAL HEALTH: IMPACTS OF CULTURAL CONTEXT AND COHORT

Defining mental health is a surprisingly difficult problem. Experts have more often concentrated on specifying what mental health is *not*: comprehensive taxonomies of psychological disturbance exist. Part of the problem is that nearly any definition reflects the cultural context in which it is developed. What one society deems normal and appropriate may be considered profoundly disturbed in another; what one group sees as a rational means of coping may be judged a pathological reaction by others (e.g., Turner & Turner, 1982). The *Diversity in Adulthood* box explores this issue.

This point is particularly important in an examination of psychopathology among the aged. Different age groups, or cohorts, represent different (though overlapping) cultural histories (see Chapter One, p. 20). Thus, standards spelling out mental health may well differ in their suitability for adults of different ages. On a practical level, professionals may need to define their treatment goals differently when working with elderly clients as opposed to younger adults. For example, Smyer, Zarit, and Qualls (1990) point out that clinicians working with clients who suffer from irreversible dementia may define success in terms of minimizing *excessive* disability, rather than in terms of eliminating any impairment whatsoever.

Birren & Renner (1980), while recognizing that what constitutes normality varies by culture, identify general characteristics of mental health. They describe mentally healthy individuals as having a positive attitude toward themselves, an accurate view of reality, the capacity to master their environment, autonomy, balance in personality, and an orientation toward growth. Although this definition does specify important assets, even these criteria could be problematic when used to evaluate elderly adults. Mastery of the environment and autonomy, for example, may occur differently for a frail or impoverished elderly person than for a young adult.

How do older people themselves define mental health? Older men and women clearly distinguish between normal aging and psychopathology. Elderly research participants rate depression, paranoia, and hypochondriasis in hypothetical older people as evidence of moderate to severe disturbance, quite different from normal, healthy old age (e.g., Hochman, Storandt, & Rosenberg, 1986; Roy & Storandt, 1989).

Adults of different ages include different characteristics in their portraits of mental health and pathology. When asked how they would describe someone their age who was well-adjusted, middle-aged and elderly participants offered different descriptions (Ryff, 1989); Figure 9.1 summarizes these responses. Both groups stressed positive relationships, caring for others, continued growth, enjoyment of life, and a sense of humor. But the older participants mentioned acceptance of change more often than the middle-aged partici-

BOX 9.1   **D**IVERSITY IN ADULTHOOD

The "healthy adult personality": A culturally biased definition?

Remember that psychologists disagree about the best way to define "mental health." In some cases, dissension centers on the possibility of sexist bias in these specifications. This argument is not new. Feminists have long deplored Freudian views of normal and abnormal personality. However, the advent of DSM-III, and its revision DSM III-R, lent a new cast to these objections. Both DSM III and DSM III-R attempt to provide reasonably clear and objective guidelines for identifying and classifying psychopathology.

Some have charged, however, that applying these standards can almost inevitably lead a psychologist or psychiatrist to conclude that a woman is disturbed (Broverman, Broverman, & Clarkson, 1970; Kaplan, 1983a, 1983b). These critics maintain that a woman who conforms closely to traditional standards of femininity—one who is extremely passive, extremely dependent, or even just overly slim—could be diagnosed as suffering from mental disorder. Unfortunately, a woman who firmly rejects traditional femininity—for example, a woman who is unusually aggressive, exceptionally competitive, or extremely independent—might be classified as suffering from still other disorders.

Some women also object to the inclusion of **premenstrual syndrome (PMS)** in DSM III and DSM III-R. PMS is relatively common, at least at a mild level, and includes such symptoms as irritation, anxiety, and depression; increased appetite or food cravings; sleep disturbances; fatigue; and breast tenderness, headaches, bloating, and weight gain. Some women feel that a problem with clear physiological origin should not be included in this taxonomy of psychiatric problems. In effect, some argue that currently accepted definitions of mental health and mental illness damn nearly all women to be judged as disturbed.

For our purposes, the more important question that follows from this argument is the extent to which it might be raised more broadly. In other words, do contemporary standards of mental health incorporate cultural bias? Do we unwittingly assume that adjustment to modern American culture represents adjustment in all times and in all places?

Although professionals argue about the boundaries between mental health and mental illness, there are some generally accepted criteria. One recent text, for example, specifies several distinguishing characteristics; for example, mental illness includes dysfunctional behavior and the inability to distinguish reality from fantasy (Papalia & Olds, 1988). Although both criteria are probably reasonable inclusions, both could also be applied in a culturally-biased manner.

For example, in applying the criterion of ability to distinguish reality and fantasy, one might look for such behaviors as hallucinating or claiming to be a deity or the personal representative of a deity. Most modern Americans would have little difficulty in labeling these behaviors as disturbed. In some cultures and some religious groups, however, the same behaviors might be taken as signs that an individual actually has spiritual gifts or a holy destiny.

Similarly, behaving in a dysfunctional manner might be concretely signaled by suicide attempts. Again, few modern Americans would hesitate to classify these behaviors as signs of pathology. In some Eastern cultures, however, suicide may be respected as an ultimate sacrifice. The Japanese Kamikaze pilots of World War II are, perhaps, the most compelling example of this perspective.

The point is neither to condemn any and all standards of mental health and mental illness, nor to accuse mental health professionals of sexism and cultural bias. Rather, the lesson to be learned is that any standards for judging mental health must be applied in context. As adult life unfolds in widely differing contexts, it is unlikely that any single definition of the "normal, healthy adult" will suffice for all purposes. Perhaps the best goal for students of adult development is to be aware of the cultural context within which definitions are developed, and the restrictions that the context implies.

pants; middle-aged subjects cited confidence and assertiveness, and self-knowledge and self-acceptance more often than older subjects (see Figure 9.1). In describing a poorly adjusted person of their own age, both groups emphasized crankiness and complaining. The middle-aged adults further stressed being overly critical of oneself and intolerant to a greater extent than the older subjects did (see Figure 9.1).

Clearly, mental health and disturbance may manifest themselves differently at different points in adulthood. The next section reviews age-related trends in depression, schizophrenia, and alcohol abuse, some of the most frequently diagnosed and most disabling forms of psychopathology. Diagnosis of these conditions is more challenging in the case of an older adult than of a younger person.

AGE AND MAJOR FUNCTIONAL DISORDERS

The psychiatric problems considered in this section—depression, schizophrenia, and substance abuse—are **functional disorders** with primarily psychological (as opposed to physical, or organic) origins. However, one may suffer from one of these problems and also have an organic disorder. We examine the symptoms of these diseases, their prevalence, and their causes in this section.

Depression

Although the focus of this chapter is on mental health problems in old age, depression is by no means a psychological disorder that appears only in later life. Nearly everyone, whatever their age, feels down at times. However, sometimes these feelings go beyond simply "having the blues," but are instead oppressive and disabling. When do such feelings constitute a psychiatric problem, and not just a passing mood? Who is most likely to suffer from depression? What causes these problems? What treatments for depression work well with older clients?

Diagnosing depression: Rates of depression and race, class, and gender   Depression is one of the most commonly diagnosed psychiatric disorders in old age (e.g., Cohen, 1990; LaRue, Dessonville, & Jarvik, 1985). In a sense, a diagnosis of depression is a relatively optimistic outcome of a psychiatric evaluation, since older depressed patients often respond well to treatment (e.g., LaRue et al., 1985). Although many older adults report some symptoms of depression (e.g., Gallagher & Thompson, 1983; see below), a diagnosis of **major depression** is only made when an individual exhibits a cluster of symptoms.

A psychologist or psychiatrist might use either of two sets of criteria in arriving at a diagnosis of major depression: the Research Diagnostic Criteria

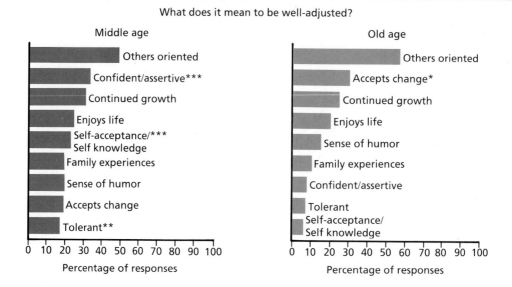

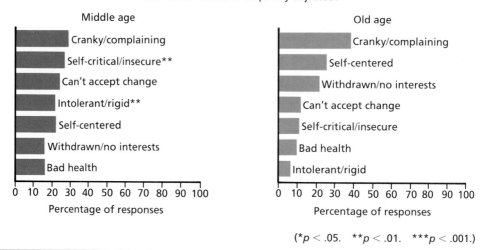

Figure 9.1
Views of adjustment by age group. (Source: Ryff, 1989. Copyright 1989 by the American Psychological Association. Reprinted by permission.)

(RDC) (Spitzer, Endicott, & Robins, 1978) or the DSM III-R (Diagnostic and Statistical Manual of Mental Disorders, 3rd Edition—Revised) of the American Psychiatric Association (1987). In both systems, the signs of major depression are:

Persistent mood disturbance, or **dysphoria**: feeling depressed, sad, down, blue, hopeless, or low.

At least four (DSM III-R) or five (RDC) of the following symptoms, present for at least two weeks: changes in appetite and weight, sleep disturbance, psychomotor agitation or retardation, loss of energy or fatiguability, loss of interest or pleasure in usual activities and/or sexual activity, feelings of worthlessness or guilt, impaired concentration or thought, suicidal thoughts or behavior.

No evidence of schizophrenia.

For RDC: Impaired functioning (e.g., at work or school, with family, taking medication in response to above symptoms).

For DSM III-R: Dysphoria not due to organic disorder or uncomplicated bereavement.

Although geropsychiatrists generally agree that depression is one of the more common disorders afflicting the aged, there is disagreement as to whether elderly people are more vulnerable to major depression than are younger adults. Certainly, older adults are more likely than younger people to encounter events and circumstances (such as health changes, decreased income) that could give rise to dysphoria. Some surveys identify depressive symptoms in as many as two-thirds of the community-dwelling elderly (e.g., LaRue et al, 1985). However, only about 1 percent of the aged in the community meet the criteria for major depression (e.g., Blazer, Hughes, & George, 1987), whereas approximately 4 percent of younger adults exhibit that level of symptoms (Nolen-Hoeksema, 1988).

In one recent survey of the community aged, adults aged 70 to 98 had significantly higher scores than did younger adults on a standard depression measure (Gatz & Hurwicz, 1990). However, young, middle-aged, and elderly people in that study did not differ in their frequencies of attaining scores suggesting a serious level of depression. Newman (1989) suggests that findings such as these illustrate problems that arise when professionals apply standard depression measures and diagnostic criteria in work with older adults.

According to Newman (1989), both surveys in which depression scale scores are compared across age groups and more probing efforts to detect depression in clinical practice may suffer from inherent sources of bias. The bias stems from failure to take normal age-related changes into account. In reviewing the above list of the physical symptoms of major depression, notice that some may appear as part of the normal aging process (see Chapter Three). For example, it is common for people to experience changes in appetite, sleep, and weight as they grow older. Using standard depression scales that inquire about such changes, then, may overestimate rates of depression among elderly adults because nondepressed older people would probably also report these symptoms (Downes, Davies, & Copeland, 1988; Newman, 1989).

On the other hand, a clinician evaluating an elderly client may fail to diagnose depression if she adheres closely to criteria such as the RDC or DSM

III-R (Newman, 1989). Notice, for example, that RDC specifies that the dysphoria and physical symptoms of depression must prevent an individual from carrying out her usual responsibilities at home or at work. Such impairment is much more likely to be detected if one has a full-time job and responsibility for a spouse and small children than if one is retired and living alone.

Furthermore, older adults are more likely to seek help for psychiatric problems from their family doctor or other primary health care provider than from a mental health specialist (e.g., Schurman, Kramer, & Mitchell, 1985). Unfortunately medical residents (particularly nonpsychiatric residents) may know few of the diagnostic criteria for depression and rarely screen elderly patients for depression (Rapp & Davis, 1989). Thus, physicians, too, may fail to identify depression in the aged. Elderly women may be especially at risk of misdiagnosis: physicians who lack specific training in geriatrics may attribute symptoms of depression to menopause or bereavement. In that event, tranquilizers or sedatives may be prescribed rather than medications that are more effective treatments for depression (see below).

Apart from age, what other characteristics are associated with rates of depression? The findings are contradictory. Women are more likely to receive a diagnosis of severe depression than men are, but only in early and later adulthood; in middle age, men outnumber women in receiving that diagnosis (Leaf, et al., 1988). Some researchers find no gender difference in rates of depression among the elderly (e.g., Smallegan, 1989).

Race and class are also associated with rates of depression. Not surprisingly, depression is more prevalent among lower- than higher-income groups (Smallegan, 1989). African-Americans have similar rates of depression as do Caucasians (e.g., Markides & Mindel, 1987), although one study found that depression was less common among relatively affluent African-Americans than among Caucasians (Smallegan, 1989). Mexican-Americans report depressive symptoms less frequently than non-Hispanic Caucasians do in community surveys, whereas Asian-Americans exhibit slightly higher rates of depression than do Caucasians (Markides & Mindel, 1987).

Causes of depression   Biologically-based explanations focus on the functioning of the central nervous system (CNS) and on physical health problems. Some scientists believe that depression results from inadequate amounts of certain **neurotransmitters** (chemical substances accomplishing communication between neurons) or from an imbalance of neurotransmitters in the CNS (e.g., LaRue et al., 1985; Maas, 1978). Depression in the elderly, in particular, may stem from neurotransmitter irregularities, since levels of neurotransmitters decline with age (Gerner & Jarvik, 1984).

There is also a reliable association between physical illness and depression in the aged (e.g., Jarvik & Perl, 1981). Several diseases—such as dementia, brain tumors, metabolic disorders, infections, and cardiovascular disease—share symptoms of depression (Fry, 1986; Lehmann, 1982). Dysphoria could be a rational reaction to awareness of illness, pain and disability, and the financial burden of illness. Furthermore, depression can be a side effect of many medications, including antihypertensives, nonnarcotic analgesics, anti-parkinsonian drugs, and steroids (Ouslander, 1982).

Others propose that depression is caused by psychological or social factors. Some believe that experiencing loss triggers depression (e.g., Gaylord & Zung, 1987). Actual, potential, and even imagined loss of such things as a loved one, health or attractiveness, a job or a role, personal possessions or a pet, or lifestyle and group membership have been cited as sources of depression. Many older adults, of course, encounter many of these losses.

Treating depression in the elderly   Although many mental health professionals have pessimistic expectations for work with elderly clients (e.g., Gatz, Popkin, Pino, & VandenBos, 1985; see below), depression appearing in later life is actually no more long-lasting than younger adults' episodes of depression (Lewinsohn, Fenn, Stanton, & Franklin, 1986). A variety of treatment approaches are used with patients suffering from depression, and often combinations of treatments are used.

Pharmacotherapy is treatment with psychoactive drugs; two families of drugs are used in treating major depression. Among the most widely used and most effective are **heterocyclic antidepressants (HCAs).** There are problems in using HCAs with elderly clients, however; some medical conditions and medications proscribe their use, and side effects are more pronounced in elderly patients (Epstein, 1978). **MAO inhibitors** are the second family of drugs

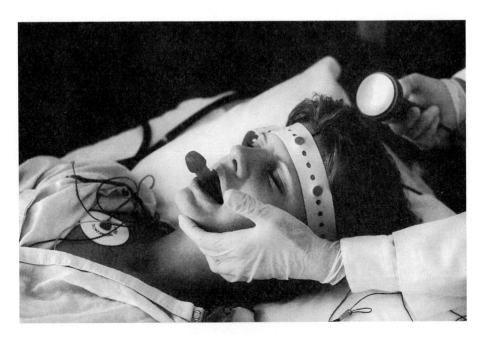

Electroconvulsive therapy (ECT) is an effective treatment for major depression.

used to treat depression, but these substances are generally less effective than the HCAs and produce more side effects.

Hollywood screenwriters and novelists have portrayed **electroconvulsive therapy (ECT)** as a frightening approach more oriented toward controlling unruly patients than toward treatment. However, ECT is actually an effective treatment for major depression; it is most likely to be used with suicidal patients and those for whom pharmacotherapy has proven ineffective (e.g., Weiner, 1979). In ECT, a brief current of electricity is passed between the patient's temples; the current causes a convulsion similar to an epileptic seizure.[1] Following the treatment, the patient may suffer temporary memory loss for recent events (including the ECT). However, ECT usually lifts the patient's depression immediately; pharmacotherapy, in contrast, may require up to a week to take effect.

The basic notion behind **psychotherapy** is that patients can benefit by talking about their problems to a professional. Psychotherapy alone may be used to treat depression, or it may be combined with pharmacotherapy or ECT. Even a quick scanning of clinical journals and textbooks reveals hundreds of approaches to psychotherapy. Among those frequently used in treating depression are **behavior therapy** and **cognitive therapy**.

A behavior therapist attempts to change a patient's behavior (and thus ease the depression) by altering the consequences that the patient encounters in daily life (e.g., Lewinsohn, 1975; Gallagher & Thompson, 1983). The patient might be rewarded for increasing social activities, for example, and thereby developing interests and friendships that are themselves uplifting. Any self-deprecating or pessimistic statements that the patient makes would be ignored, whereas the therapist (as well as family, friends, and others with whom the patient is in regular contact) would react attentively to positive statements. As we saw in Chapter Two (see pp. 42–43), behavior therapy has been used with older patients suffering from a wide variety of disorders, and it is effective in treating depression in the aged (e.g., Gatz et al., 1985).

Cognitive therapy for depression is based on the view that self-defeating patterns of thought lead the patient to view herself, her experiences, and her future in an irrational and pessimistic manner (e.g., Beck, 1967). The thrust of therapy is toward changing these thought patterns through a multistep process (Storandt, 1983). A first step is to review the history of the patient's problem; during this review, the therapist would point out instances in which the patient had previously interpreted her experiences inappropriately and negatively. A second step is to identify "automatic thoughts" that lead to depression; an example would be thinking "I'm a worthless person" following a disagreement with an acquaintance. Finally, the patient learns to use rational thinking and

---

1. Muscle relaxants are administered when ECT is used, to protect the patient from injury during the seizure.

logic to distinguish facts (e.g., a disagreement with an acquaintance) from ideas (e.g., "I'm a worthless person"). Researchers have documented substantial improvements among depressed elderly patients treated with cognitive therapy (e.g., Gatz et al., 1985).

Age, gender, and racial differences in suicide rates

Suicide has an obvious relationship to depression, although not everyone who commits suicide is depressed and—fortunately—most depressed individuals do not commit suicide. Documenting the suicide rate is difficult, because many deaths that appear accidental (automobile accidents, for example) may actually be suicides. However, the approximately 25,000 confirmed cases per year justifies the designation of suicide as a serious public health threat (e.g., Manton, Blazer, & Woodbury, 1987; National Center for Health Statistics [NCHS], 1985).

Relative to younger adults, elderly people are disproportionately likely to commit suicide. Although people over age 65 constitute roughly 13 percent of the population, they account for 17 percent of reported suicides (NCHS, 1985). Compared to adults aged 18 to 24, suicide is 25 percent more common among those aged 65 to 74 and *70 percent* more common among adults aged 75 to 84 (Cohen, 1990).

Young adults make far more unsuccessful efforts to commit suicide than older people do, though. Among young adults, there are approximately seven attempted suicides for every "successful" effort, whereas there is only one unsuccessful attempt for every eight accomplished suicides among elderly people (Sendbeuhler & Goldstein, 1977; Stenback, 1980). Some believe that such a dramatic difference in effort-to-success ratios reflects an age difference in motivations for suicide attempts. Clinical work and analysis of suicide notes suggests that younger people attempting suicide may be attempting to express hostility or self-deprecation, whereas older adults are more often reacting to serious health problems or isolation (Darbonne, 1969; Osgood, 1985).

Suicide rates vary by gender and race, as well as by age (Manton et al., 1987; NCHS, 1985); Figure 9.2 illustrates these patterns. Men have higher suicide rates than women throughout adulthood, and the rate is much higher for Caucasian men than for non-Caucasian men. Caucasian women have higher suicide rates than non-Caucasian women, particularly in middle adulthood.

Some propose that older Caucasian men have higher suicide rates than older women and non-Caucasian men in reaction to diminished social power (Osgood, 1985). Because Caucasian men are a dominant group in contemporary America, it may be especially traumatic for these individuals when age-related events such as retirement and decreased income curtail their social power.

Scholars also note that suicide rates among non-Caucasian men have increased over the past decade (e.g., Manton et al., 1987), and Figure 9.2 shows

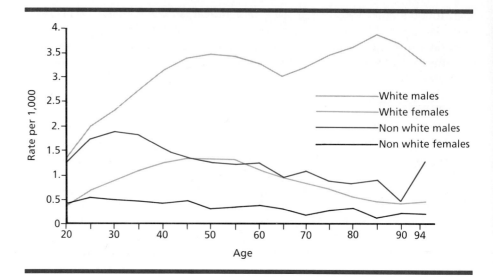

Figure 9.2
Suicide rates by age, race, and gender.
(Source: Manton et al. 1987, based on analysis of NCHS data for 1962 to 1981. "Suicide in Middle and Later Life," *Journal of Gerontology, 42:* 219–227. Copyright © The Gerontological Society of America. Reprinted by permission.)

that there is a surge in suicide rates in advanced old age for non-Caucasian men. Perhaps this increase signals changing social and psychological circumstances for extremely old non-Caucasian men. For example, changing family structure in minority groups may place these men at increased risk of isolation (e.g., Manton et al., 1987).

Schizophrenia

Schizophrenia is one of the most puzzling functional mental disorders. Perhaps the most disturbing aspects of schizophrenia is that it typically strikes in adolescence and young adulthood—periods of the life cycle that are usually characterized by peak functioning in nearly all capacities. In fact, the diagnostic criteria for schizophrenia specify that the disturbance usually appears in these periods of the life span (DSM III-R, 1987). Reported rates of schizophrenia in the elderly vary, but the median rate is 1 percent (Cohen, 1990).

The symptoms of schizophrenia vary from one individual to another. Nonetheless, DSM III-R (1987) does specify a set of typical symptoms. Thought content is disturbed, as is the form of thinking. Schizophrenics report bizarre, delusionary ideas with no basis in reality, and often jump from one idea to a completely unrelated one. Many schizophrenics suffer from hallucinations, and report hearing voices, feeling tingling or burning sensations, or experiencing other sensations with no apparent basis in reality. Emotions may be inappropriate to the situation, or simply blunted and flattened. The sense of self may be disturbed, and goal-directed activity may be impaired. Some schizophrenics withdraw from the external world, and some show bizarre psychomotor behaviors (e.g., reduced or absent movement and activity, a rigid posture, repeated or stereotyped movements).

Experts disagree as to whether elderly schizophrenics manifest different symptoms as compared to younger schizophrenics; there is also disagreement concerning distinctions between the consequences of growing old as a chronic schizophrenic as opposed to developing schizophrenia initially in old age. Some maintain that the symptoms do not vary systematically with age (e.g., Blazer, George, & Hughes, 1988), although others believe that schizophrenic symptoms become less severe as patients grow older (LaRue et al., 1985). Still others have reported that young and elderly schizophrenics experience different kinds of delusions (e.g., Post, 1987).

The cause or causes of schizophrenia are open to debate. Beliefs about the cause have changed historically; today, most contention centers on the extent to which schizophrenia stems from hereditary and environmental factors. We examine views of the origins of schizophrenia in the *Open Questions* box.

Just as the symptoms of schizophrenia vary from one person to the next, so does the course of the disease. About 20 percent of schizophrenics make a lasting recovery following their initial psychotic episode (LaRue et al., 1985). However, between 10 percent and 23 percent continue to exhibit symptoms and spend most of their lives in institutions, and the remainder have intermittent periods of adequate functioning in the community and episodic attacks during which they are hospitalized (LaRue et al., 1985).

Because of the schizophrenic's disturbed thinking and hallucinations, it is difficult to treat these patients using psychotherapy. Treatment for schizophrenia, therefore, centers on the use of **antipsychotic medications** which attempt to normalize the action of neurotransmitters in the CNS. Unfortunately, these medications have unpleasant side effects, and it is difficult to insure that schizophrenic patients treated in an outpatient setting follow their medication regimen.

Since the 1960s, American mental health professionals have attempted to **deinstitutionalize** patients and provide treatment outside of psychiatric hospitals whenever possible. Elderly schizophrenics—both those who have spent most of their lives in institutions and those who develop the disorder in old age—have generally not benefitted from this trend. Prior to the 1990s many such older people were in nursing homes rather than in psychiatric facilities (e.g., Gatz et al., 1985; Kermis, 1986). Although the care that older adults receive in psychiatric hospitals may not be as specialized or attentive as one might wish, nursing homes were even less prepared—in terms of the number or the training of their staffs—to provide treatment for aged schizophrenics beyond simply administering medication.

BOX 9.2 **OPEN QUESTIONS**

Schizophrenia and the nature-nurture controversy

In searching for the cause of schizophrenia, varied paths have been pursued. In the Middle Ages and Colonial America, schizophrenics were believed to be possessed by the devil; later, moral weakness or personal failings were held as the answer (Restak, 1984). Twentieth-century approaches may seem more scientific, but unfortunately they have failed to provide generally-accepted answers about the origin of schizophrenia.

Many psychologists and psychiatrists, particularly early in this century, held that schizophrenia resulted from early trauma (Restak, 1984). Following this approach, parents—particularly the mother —were often blamed for children's pathology. Occasionally, the search for early trauma was broader, focusing on the individual's experiences at school, in the peer group, or in the neighborhood. In a related approach, some experts asserted that schizophrenia was caused by current life stresses.

Contemporary thinking focuses on more biologically- than environmentally-based causes (Restak, 1984). Some researchers search for biochemical differences between the neurological functioning of schizophrenics and nonschizophrenics, and several such differences have been identified. Others have gathered impressive evidence of a genetic basis for schizophrenia. There is a high concordance rate: when one identical twin has schizophrenia, there is a good chance that the other twin will be similarly diagnosed (e.g., Gottesman, 1979). Studies of the incidence of schizophrenia in Denmark (where exceptionally detailed population health records are kept) reveal that adopted children are likely to develop schizophrenia if a biological parent suffers from the disorder, but not if an adoptive parent is schizophrenic (e.g., Restak, 1984).

Today, many experts believe that schizophrenia, like many other characteristics, may stem from both genetic and environmental factors (Restak, 1984). One may inherit a genetic predisposition to develop the illness, but whether or not that predisposition is actualized may depend on the environment. In a stressful setting lacking in social support, a vulnerable individual may indeed develop severe schizophrenic symptoms. But such an individual living in a more relaxed and supportive setting may be entirely normal, or perhaps a bit eccentric.

Thus, the source of this particular disturbance is an open question. Although scientists hope to gain greater insight into the origins of schizophrenia, it is likely that there will always be unanswered questions in the area. As Restak (1984) points out, most complex questions cannot be answered beyond a certain level. It is unlikely, for example, that a *single* cause of such phenomena as racism or poverty will ever be identified. Similarly, it may be that many avenues to understanding, and many questions, will always surround disturbances of psychological functioning.

Legislation was passed in the early 1990s with the intention of screening individuals with a primary diagnosis of mental illness out of nursing homes.[2] Since most nursing homes are unprepared to provide psychiatric services, such a policy should work to the advantage of both nursing homes and aged individuals who need those services. However, elderly schizophrenics are caught between this goal and that of deinstitutionalization: the implication is that neither setting is considered appropriate for these patients. This legislation has

---

2. Alzheimer's disease (see below) is treated as an exception in this legislation, so patients suffering from Alzheimer's disease can be admitted to nursing homes.

also created problems for nursing homes, including how individuals applying for admission should be screened for mental illness and which members of the staff are qualified to perform that screening.

Alcohol abuse in old age

Identifying the misuse of alcohol as a major public health problem in contemporary America is a common, if not a trite, observation. Of course, alcohol abuse is a problem that is by no means unique to older adults; rates of problem drinking are lower among elderly people than among young and middle-aged adults, in fact. In the 1980s, America instituted massive efforts to prevent, detect, and treat these problems among adolescents and young adults. There has been far less attention, however, to drinking problems in later life.

It is difficult to determine how many older people experience problems with alcohol, although these problems almost certainly occur less frequently among the aged than among younger adults. Recent reviewers estimate that between 4 percent and 8 percent of the elderly suffer from alcohol abuse, and that rates of other forms of substance abuse are far lower (Cohen, 1990). Studies in which older medical or psychiatric patients are included show a greater incidence of alcohol abuse: these estimates range from 10–58 percent of the patients surveyed (Mishara & Kastenbaum, 1980). Approximately 10 percent of alcoholics in treatment are over age 60 (Brody, 1982; Gomberg, 1982; Schuckit, 1977).

Experts express concern about problem drinking in later life for four reasons. First, the sheer number of older individuals, and expectations that their number will increase (see Chapter One, p. 3) justify concern. Second, characteristics of older cohorts, including their likelihood to use mental health services, are changing. To date, elderly people in need of these services have been woefully underserved (see below). Scholars expect future older cohorts to make greater use of available mental health services than do contemporary elders, as older peoples' attitudes toward psychiatric services become more positive.

A third source of concern is the pattern of cohort differences in drinking. General population surveys indicate that the percentage of abstainers increases, and the percentage of problem drinkers decreases, with increasing age (Clark & Midanik, 1982). Scholars thus predict increased numbers of older problem drinkers in the future, particularly since the drinking practices of contemporary older people reflect experience with Prohibition (Brody, 1982; Gomberg, 1982; Williams, Stinson, Parker, Harford, & Noble, 1987). Finally, physicians may mistake the effects of alcohol abuse in older patients for irreversible dementia (Brody, 1982). The impact of such mislabeling can be devastating, since custodial care may be provided rather than treatment.

A related concern is that the consequences of alcohol misuse for mental and physical health are far more serious for older adults as compared to younger adults. The combined effects of alcohol misuse and aging can result in decreased resilience in all body systems (Williams, 1984). In addition, elderly adults are a high risk group with respect to drug and alcohol interaction. Because older people consume more medications than do younger adults (see Chapter Four, p. 93), drinking—whether problematic or not—is more likely to result in these interactions than is the case with younger people (Lamy, 1988; Williams, 1984).

With increasing age, individual differences in virtually all characteristics increase; drinking history is no exception. Researchers have compared older problem drinkers who began drinking in young adulthood—the **Early Onset** drinkers—with those whose drinking problems began in later life—the **Late Onset** drinkers (e.g., Dunham, 1981; Schuckit & Miller, 1975). Late Onset men, compared to Early Onset men, are younger, more likely to be separated or divorced but less likely to be widowed, more likely to live alone, more likely to show organic brain syndrome, and more likely to report drinking-related problems (i.e., driving difficulties, health problems, marital problems, etc.) (Schuckit & Miller, 1975).

Early Onset problem drinking may stem from personality characteristics, while Late Onset problem drinking may more often be a response to stresses associated with aging (e.g., Hochhausser, 1982). Other scholars, however, have found no relationship between normal age-related stresses and Late Onset problem drinking (e.g., Borgatta, Montgomery, & Borgatta, 1982; La Greca, Akers, & Dwyer, 1988). Still other work reveals that older adults with drinking problems differ from older nonproblem drinkers in their characteristic means of coping with life stresses (Moos, Brennan, Fondacaro, & Moos, 1990). Older problem drinkers, compared to older nonproblem drinkers, are more likely to cope with problems through resigned acceptance, pursuit of alternative rewards, or emotional discharge. Older nonproblem drinkers more often rely on logical analysis, positive reappraisal, or seeking guidance and support to deal with problems.

Hochhausser (1982) proposed that problem drinking is a reaction to events that are perceived as unpredictable and uncontrollable. According to Hochhausser (1982), an elderly person's decision to use alcohol may stem from the perception of control that the substance affords. As the older individual confronts both internal changes (e.g., changes in health status, sleep patterns, and metabolism) and external changes (e.g, death of a spouse or relative, relocation, and changes in financial status)—over which he or she has virtually no control—use of alcohol or drugs may appear to be a response that is, at least initially, under personal control.

Discussions of treatment for older alcoholics are optimistic. "Social therapy" or "socialization" has been identified as an effective treatment, particularly in combination with antidepressant medication (Zimberg, 1974). Administrators of agencies serving the aged have recommended a variety of community responses to problem drinking in later life; community education, treatment programs designed specifically for older abusers, enhanced social services for the aged, and control of alcohol and drug distribution to elderly people have been suggested (Brown, 1982). Effective treatment, however, relies on effective methods of diagnosing drinking problems in later life.

Effective assessment of problem drinking in old age requires consideration of age differences in lifestyle and of the ways in which others perceive elderly people. Since older adults are more likely to be retired and to be widowed than are younger people, problems at work or marital problems—both indicators of pathological patterns of alcohol use—are not as useful in diagnosis as they are with younger adults. Furthermore, the impact of alcohol on occupational functioning may not be as reliable a signal of drinking problems among middle-aged and older adults who have not yet retired as it is with younger adults. Negative (and inaccurate) stereotypes of older workers are common: older workers are believed to be less efficient, more frequently absent from work, less productive, and less reliable than younger workers (see Chapter Fourteen, p. 351). Thus, changes in performance that would arouse concern in the case of a young employee may be dismissed in the case of an older worker.

Recall from Chapter Four (see pp. 97–99) that older people more often visit physicians than do young adults; one might therefore expect that alcohol abuse would be detected promptly. However, health care practitioners who have not been specifically trained for geriatric work may attribute confusion, forgetfulness, slurred speech, and similar behaviors to normal aging or dementia rather than exploring drinking as explanations (Williams, 1984). Experts on substance abuse in the aged suggest that professionals should be alert to different indicators of possible alcohol abuse than they would consider in assessing a younger person. These indicators include decreased effectiveness of medication, falls and unusual accidents, forgetfulness and/or apathy, changed eating habits, and changed housekeeping standards (Williams, 1984).

DEMENTIA

Many of the fears that people express about aging focus on the possibility of **dementia**, a progressive and sometimes irreversible impairment of cognitive functioning. Dementia is not a specific disease, but a collection of symptoms that may stem from any of several conditions (Crook, 1987). **Alzheimer's disease (AD)** is the best known and most frequently diagnosed condition producing these symptoms in old age, and is the fourth leading cause of death in old age (Veterans Health Services and Research Administration [VHSRA], 1989). Tragically, causes and cures for Alzheimer's disease have not been identified, although answering these questions is one of the most active areas of research today. After an overview of the symptoms of dementia and other conditions that can produce these symptoms, Alzheimer's disease is considered in depth.

Dementia symptoms

The outstanding symptoms of dementia are progressive cognitive and behavioral impairment that interfere with work or social functioning (Aronson, 1988; DSM III-R, 1987; Heston & White, 1983). Memory, attention and concentration, and judgement deteriorate: while the victim may initially be able to handle routine tasks at work or at home, any change in routine proves baffling. A woman may report to work at her usual time, forgetting that her shift has changed; a man may forget that he invited guests for dinner. Capacity for abstract thinking declines; a woman may no longer be able to distinguish main points from details when she reads the newspaper, or be able to understand the significance of folk sayings and proverbs.

The afflicted individual behaves inappropriately in social situations and may show personality changes; an elderly executive may be verbally abusive and profane to her secretary for no apparent reason. The victim's grooming deteriorates: he forgets that he has worn the same soiled outfit for several days, and forgets to shave. Eventually, the victim grows disoriented and has difficulty finding words and names for familiar things and people. At that point, he may not know who he is, the current day, month, or year, or where he is. He may not remember the names of his neighbors, friends, or even wife and children.

As the disease progresses, there are often emotional and mood disturbances: patients may be agitated and aggressive (e.g., Cohen-Mansfield, Marx, & Rosenthal, 1990). A victim may spend hours pacing or wandering, and may shout or strike out at others. In the latest stages, many are incontinent and unable to perform basic self-care functions such as bathing, dressing, and feeding (Aronson, 1988).

Conditions producing dementia symptoms

The conditions leading to dementia compose three categories (Heston & White, 1983). **Primary undifferentiated dementias** are diseases affecting brain tissue and thus exerting effects on cognition and behavior. Because these diseases produce minute changes in brain tissue that are similar to one another, and because their cognitive and behavioral symptoms do not differ from one another, they can only be diagnosed with certainty upon direct examination of brain tissue. Alzheimer's Disease is a form of primary undifferentiated dementia.

Primary differentiated dementias similarly affect brain tissue and produce the characteristic dementia symptoms. However, these diseases also have unique symptoms that allow clinicians to make fairly certain diagnoses without examining brain tissue (Heston & White, 1983). For example, **Parkinson's disease,**[3] **Huntington's disease,** and **normal-pressure hydrocephalus** pro-

---

3. Although Parkinson's Disease can produce dementia symptoms, it does not always do so.

duce characteristic motor disturbances that are not typical of other forms of dementia (Crook, 1987).

Secondary dementia (or **pseudodementia**) refers to a collection of diseases and circumstances that do not directly attack brain tissue but still yield the usual symptoms of dementia (Crook, 1987; Heston & White, 1983). Unlike the primary dementias, many of these conditions are at least partially reversible (e.g., Crook, 1987; Heston & White, 1983). Thus, the diagnostic process when any form of dementia is suspected must be exhaustive so as to rule out the possibility of reversible conditions. Diseases or infections, and many medications, are sources of secondary dementia. Secondary dementia may also stem from malnutrition or severe nutritional imbalance, alcohol abuse, or depression.

Depression is the most common cause of secondary dementia, afflicting as many as 13 percent of the community-dwelling elderly and as many as 30 percent of older adults seen in hospitals and nursing homes (Crook, 1987; O'Boyle, Amadeo, & Self, 1990). Because depression can often be treated effectively (see above), it is tragic for a physician to mistake this form of pseudodementia for Alzheimer's disease. Often, a thorough patient history will provide clues distinguishing depression from dementia; Table 9.1 lists some of these clues.

Recall that Alzheimer's disease is the most frequently diagnosed form of primary undifferentiated dementia. What other diseases fit into this category? **Multi-infarct dementia (MID)** refers to dementia symptoms resulting from multiple small strokes, and accounts for approximately 8 percent to 29 percent of all cases of dementia in the elderly (VHSRA, 1989).[4] Although MID produces the same dementia symptoms as Alzheimer's disease and other dementias, the symptoms appear suddenly and progress in a "stairstep" fashion with periodic marked deteriorations of functioning. In Alzheimer's disease, symptoms appear and intensify so gradually that it is often difficult to say exactly when the disease began. African-Americans may be more vulnerable to MID than Caucasians are because of relatively high rates of hypertension among African-Americans (Baker, 1988).

Other forms of primary dementias are less common than MID and Alzheimer's disease. **Pick's Disease** is a rare form of dementia sharing many of the symptoms of Alzheimer's disease, but producing different changes in brain tissue. Early in the course of Pick's Disease, memory impairment may be less prominent and disturbed social behavior and personality change may be more apparent than is typical of Alzheimer's disease. Another uncommon form of primary dementia is **Jakob-Creutzfeldt Disease**; this disease has a much more rapid course than Alzheimer's disease (Crook, 1987; VHSRA, 1989). Finally, recent reports identify AIDS patients at high risk of developing dementia either

---

4. By comparison, AD accounts for 50 percent or more of dementia cases, and AD and MID combined produce dementia symptoms in 10–20 percent of cases.

Table 9.1
Symptoms distinguishing depression from dementia

Depression	Dementia
Uneven progression over weeks	Even progression over months or years
Complains of memory loss	Attempts to hide memory loss
Often worse in morning, better as day goes on	Worse later in day or when fatigued
Aware of, exaggerates disability	Unaware of or minimizes disability
May abuse alcohol or other drugs	Rarely abuses drugs

Source: Heston & White (1983). Reprinted by permission.

as a consequence of the AIDS virus itself or because the immune system is unable to resist other infections that may produce dementia (VHSRA, 1989).

Alzheimer's disease (AD)

Incidence of AD   At the close of the 1980s approximately two-thirds of the aged suffering from dementia were believed to have AD, accounting for over a million cases in the United States alone (Crook, 1987). Although there are few data available documenting the incidence of Alzheimer's Disease internationally, one group of researchers concluded that rates of AD in China are similar to those in the United States (Jin et al., 1989).

AD is characterized by an insidious onset of cognitive and behavioral symptoms: impairments begin as minor difficulties that are easy to rationalize and deny, and only gradually become incapacitating. For that reason, it is often difficult to pinpoint the age of onset for AD. By convention, the age of onset is defined as the age at which memory deficits are irreversibly established (Heston & White, 1983). The woman who forgot that her work shift had been changed, as described above, would have reached that point.

With increasing age, the probability of developing AD increases, as illustrated in Figure 9.3. This trend, paired with the rapid growth in the oldest segments of the population, leads to the prediction that the number of AD victims may double within the next 50 years (Crook, 1987).

Distinguishing features   As a form of primary undifferentiated dementia, AD produces both the behavioral and cognitive impairments common to other dementias as well as unique changes in the brain. Two changes occur; both also occur in the brains of nonaffected elderly people (see Chapter Three, p. 58), but to a far lesser extent. Senile plaques and neurofibrillary tangles are distributed throughout the cortex and hippocampus, a brain structure centrally involved in memory. The tangles are collections of pairs of neuronal filaments wrapped around one another; the plaques are spherical lesions with a core of a

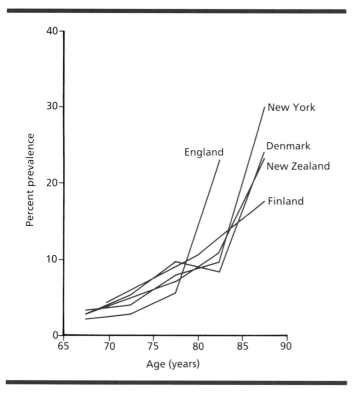

*Figure 9.3
Age-specific prevalence of dementia.* (Source: VHSRA, 1989.)

protein called **amyloid** surrounded by degenerated fragments of neurons (Crook, 1987). The density with which plaques and tangles are distributed is directly related to the severity of symptoms. In addition to these tissue changes, there are also abnormalities in the neurochemistry of AD patients. The most significant is a decrease in an enzyme involved in producing **acetylcholine**, a neurotransmitter that is important in learning and memory (Crook, 1987).

Until high numbers of plaques and tangles are identified in the brain of a dementia patient, a diagnosis of AD based on behavioral and cognitive symptoms is "probable" rather than definite. Much of the diagnostic process (see below) currently revolves around efforts to identify a cause of the dementia symptoms *other than* AD; if no such cause can be found, then a diagnosis of probable AD is made. Plaques and tangles, at present, can only be detected by directly examining the tissue of the brain, not by X-rays or other electronic means of examination. Although the tissue examination could theoretically be accomplished with a biopsy of brain tissue, this procedure entails considerable risks for the patient. Thus, a diagnosis of probable AD is only confirmed via autopsy.

Course of AD   The course of AD varies from one afflicted individual to another; those suffering from other health and behavioral problems in addition to AD show more rapid declines than others (Teri, Hughes, & Larson, 1990). Clinicians recognize seven stages of deterioration altogether; the stages are listed and briefly described in Table 9.2. As public awareness of AD has grown, so has fear of the disorder. It is not uncommon for older adults to mistake normal age-related changes in learning and memory (see Chapter Seven) for the first signs of AD, or for younger people to conclude that grandmother has AD because she occasionally forgets names or appointments. Crook (1987) points out that many such individuals can be reassured that AD is probably not the problem, as fewer than 10 percent of those at Stage 2 (see Table 9.2) progress to more severe levels of impairment over the next several years.

Possible causes of AD   As of 1990, no cause of AD had been identified. However, scientists continue to explore several possible causes. Many believe that the disease has a genetic basis, because the incidence of AD is considerably higher among close relatives of victims than among the general population (e.g., Crook, 1987; Heston & White, 1983). At least two other forms of dementia, Pick's Disease and Huntington's Disease, have a hereditary basis; these facts lend strength to the argument that AD, too, may stem from genetic factors.

Other suggestive evidence is an established link between AD and Down's Syndrome, a genetically-based form of mental retardation (Aronson, 1988). Individuals suffering from Down's Syndrome who survive to middle and later adulthood develop the symptoms of dementia as well as the plaques and tangles characteristic of AD (Wisniewski, Wisniewski, & Wen, 1983). However, a specific mechanism of genetic transmission has not been identified, and close relatives of AD victims often do not develop the disease.

Others contend that AD is caused by viral infection. Some "slow viruses," which may lie dormant in cells for many years before having any observable effect, produce dementia symptoms (Heston & White, 1983). Jakob-Creutzfeldt disease is caused by such a virus. The AIDS virus too can produce dementia symptoms, as we saw earlier (VHSRA, 1989).

Some people believe that exposure to high levels of aluminum may lead to AD: unusually high levels of aluminum have been detected in brains of AD victims and aluminum can produce lesions similar to plaques and tangles in laboratory animals' brains (Aronson, 1988; Heston & White, 1983). Most experts believe, however, that this cause is unlikely. Producing lesions *similar* to plaques and tangles, not *identical* to them, is only weak evidence (Heston & White, 1983). Because aluminum is abundant in nature, people are constantly exposed to large amounts—in most cases, without developing AD. Conceivably, a metabolic disorder (possibly with a genetic basis) that impairs the processing of aluminum might be a cause of AD (Heston & White, 1983). There is no need, however, to avoid using cookware, deodorants, or antacids that contain aluminum.

Diagnosis of AD   Recall that AD can only be definitively diagnosed upon autopsy, and that any prior diagnosis is a probable one reached by excluding other causes of the dementia symptoms. What steps should a physician follow before making a diagnosis of probable AD? Much of her effort is directed toward attempting to identify a source of dementia symptoms other than AD. Because some of the conditions producing these symptoms can be effectively treated, it is critical that this search be exhaustive; family members should be skeptical of a diagnosis of AD following a brief interview and examination.

The major elements of the diagnostic process are a detailed patient history, a comprehensive physical examination with special attention to neurological aspects of the patient's functioning, a mental status examination, a psychiatric evaluation, and an array of laboratory tests (VHSRA, 1989). Because some medications can produce dementia symptoms, the patient should refrain from taking medications (to the extent that health permits) prior to the examination.

The patient history should document the patient's entire health background as completely as possible (VHSRA, 1989). The history should include details of the dementia symptoms (e.g., when they began, how they have changed), and should document any environmental hazards to which the patient has been exposed, any medications that she regularly takes, and any previous episodes of psychiatric illness such as depression. Since dementia symptoms can stem from physical illness or infection, a thorough physical examination is critical (VHSRA, 1989). The physician should carefully evaluate neurological functioning, noting such features as reflexes, coordination, gait, and sensory functioning.

During the mental status examination, the doctor examines the patient's attention, orientation, immediate and delayed memory, language ability, ability to draw or copy, calculating ability, abstract thinking capacity, thought content, and judgement (VHSRA, 1989). Much of this evaluation can be accomplished during an unstructured interview with the patient, or while taking the patient

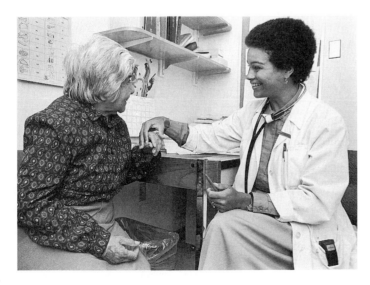

Taking a detailed patient history is a critical step in diagnosing Alzheimer's disease.

Table 9.2
Stages of dementia: The global deterioration scale

GDS stage	Clinical phase	Clinical characteristics
1. No cognitive decline	Normal	No subjective complaints of memory deficit. No memory deficit evident on clinical interview.
2. Very mild cognitive decline	Forgetfulness	Subjective complaints of memory deficit, most frequently in following areas: (a) forgetting where one has placed familiar objects; (b) forgetting names one formerly knew well. No objective evidence of memory deficit on clinical interview. No objective deficits in employment or social situations. Appropriate concern with respect to symptomatology.
3. Mild cognitive decline	Early confusional	Earliest clear-cut deficits. Manifestations in more than one of the following areas: (a) patient may have gotten lost when traveling to an unfamiliar location; (b) co-workers become aware of patient's relatively poor performance; (c) word and name-finding deficit become evident to intimates; (d) patient may read a passage or a book and retain relatively little material; (e) patient may demonstrate decreased facility in remembering names upon introduction to new people; (f) patient may have lost or misplaced an object of value; (g) concentration deficit may be evident on clinical testing.
		Objective evidence of memory deficit obtained only with an intensive interview conducted by a trained geriatric psychiatrist. Decreased performance in demanding employment and social settings. Denial begins to become manifest in patient. Mild to moderate anxiety accompanies symptoms.
4. Moderate cognitive decline	Late confusional	Clear-cut deficit on careful interview. Deficit manifest in following areas: (a) decreased knowledge of current and recent events; (b) may exhibit some deficit in memory of one's personal history; (c) concentration deficit elicited on serial subtractions; (d) decreased ability to travel, handle finances, etc.
		Frequently no deficit in following areas: (a) orientation to time and person; (b) recognition of familiar persons and faces; (c) ability to travel to familiar locations.
		Inability to perform complex tasks. Denial is dominant defense mechanism. Flattening of affect and withdrawal from challenging situations occur
5. Moderately severe cognitive decline	Early dementia	Patient can no longer survive without some assistance. Patients are unable during interview to recall a major relevant aspect of current lives: e.g., their address or telephone number of many years, the names of close members of their family (such as grandchildren), the name of the high school or college from which they graduated.

(Continued)

Table 9.2
Stages of dementia: The global deterioration scale   *(Continued)*

GD stage	Clinical phase	Clinical characteristics
5. *(Continued)*		Frequently some disorientation to time (date, day of week, season, etc.) or to place. An educated person may have difficulty counting back from 40 by 4s or from 20 by 2s.
		Persons at this stage retain knowledge of many major facts regarding themselves and others. They invariably know their own names and generally know their spouses and children's names. They require no assistance with toileting or eating, but may have some difficulty choosing the proper clothing to wear and may occasionally clothe themselves improperly (e.g., put shoes on the wrong feet, etc.)
6. Severe cognitive decline	Middle dementia	May occasionally forget the name of the spouse upon whom they are entirely dependent for survival. Will be largely unaware of all recent events and experiences in their lives. Retain some knowledge of their past lives but this is very sketchy. Generally unaware of their surroundings, the year, the season, etc. May have difficulty counting from 10, both backward and, sometimes, forward. Will require some assistance with activities of daily living, e.g., may become incontinent, will require travel assistance but occasionally will display ability to travel to familiar locations. Diurnal rhythm frequently disturbed. Almost always recall their own name. Frequently continue to be able to distinguish familiar from unfamiliar persons in their environment.
		Personality and emotional changes occur. These are quite variable and include: (a) delusional behavior (e.g., patients may accuse their spouse of being an imposter; may talk to imaginary figures in the environment, or to their own reflection in the mirror); (b) obsessive symptoms (e.g.,person may continually repeat simple cleaning activities);(c) anxiety symptoms, agitation, and even previously nonexistent violent behavior may occur; (d) cognitive abulia (i.e., loss of willpower because an individual cannot carry a thought long enough to determine a purposeful course of action).
7. Very severe cognitive decline	Late dementia	All verbal abilities are lost. Frequently there is no speech at all—only grunting. Incontinent of urine; requires assistance toileting and feeding. Lose basic psychomotor skills (e.g., ability to walk). The brain appears to be no longer able to tell the body what to do. Generalized and cortical neurological signs and symptoms are frequently present.

Source: Reisberg, Ferris, deLeon, & Crook (1982). "The Global Deterioration Scale for Assessment of Primary Degenerative Dementia." *American Psychiatric Association*, 1982, *139*, 1136–1139. Copyright 1982. Reprinted by permission.

history. However, a standardized instrument should also be used; several instruments are available.

In the psychiatric evaluation, the physician attempts to determine whether the dementia symptoms might be caused by depression or some other condition producing reversible symptoms. Finally, an array of laboratory tests should be performed. The tests typically ordered include blood tests, urine examination, chest X-rays, an electrocardiogram, an electroencephalogram, neuroimaging examinations to evaluate brain structure, examination of cerebrospinal fluid, and skull X-rays. Although the plaques and tangles of AD cannot be detected with currently available neuroimaging methods, these tests can identify some of the other conditions producing dementia symptoms.

Treating AD   Although a cure for AD does not yet exist, several treatments aimed at minimizing impairment are available. Any of several drugs might be prescribed for an AD patient; these drugs rarely improve the patient's cognitive performance, but they typically do elevate the patient's mood and thus improve her overall functioning (Crook, 1987). Psychoactive drugs primarily used in treating other psychiatric disorders are often helpful for AD patients; antidepressants and antipsychotic medications, for example, may prove beneficial (Crook, 1987). Experimental drug treatments are also available. Many are based on the finding that AD patients have deficient amounts of an enzyme involved in producing acetylcholine, and possibly other irregularities in neurochemistry (Crook, 1987; Heston & White, 1983). The success of these efforts has been mixed, and research in this area continues.

A broad array of psychological interventions are used with AD patients and their families. Behavioral interventions are often effective. Teaching concrete skills such as note taking to make everyday memory tasks less demanding may help patients in the early stages of AD (VHSRA, 1989). Similarly, nighttime wandering (a common behavioral problem in AD) can often be managed by appropriate scheduling of meals and exercise, and control of noise and lighting at night (e.g., Crook, 1987; VHSRA, 1989). More generally, eliminating hazards in the patient's environment (e.g., keeping matches and car keys hidden or locked up; installing double cylinder dead bolt locks on doors; increasing the level of lighting; adjusting water heaters to prevent scalds from hot water; removing artificial fruits that can be mistaken for food) and minimizing change in the environment (e.g., avoid rearranging furniture or pictures, or replacing carpet) are important (VHSRA, 1989).

Reality orientation is a widely used form of psychotherapy aimed at enhancing dementia patients' functioning. The theory behind reality orientation is that impaired cognition can often be compensated for by strengthening previously unused capacities (Folsom, 1985). Ideally, reality orientation involves systematic review of the patient's identity, the current time and place, and significant events; in practice, however, reality orientation often amounts to brief group sessions during which patients recite the day of the week, the name of the institution, and the like (VHSRA, 1989). Although reality orientation may have little actual effect on patient functioning, it does boost the morale of staff members working with patients (VHSRA, 1989).

Other psychological interventions are more promising. Hill, Evankovich, Sheikh, and Yesavage (1987) reported that an AD patient improved his memory for name-face pairs by learning an imagery mnemonic system. A program in which patients learned skills for remembering personal information, managing spatial orientation and way-finding tasks, communicating pleasure and displeasure, and mastering activities of daily living improved the functioning of dementia patients in a short-term residential facility (McEvoy & Patterson, 1986). Also, a cognitive stimulation program in which family members worked with patients on conversation skills, memory exercises, and problem-solving techniques stabilized patients' behavior and improved their emotional outlook (Quayhagen & Quayhagen, 1989).

Therapeutic efforts should be directed not only at the AD patient, but also at the family. Most dementia patients are cared for in the community by family members, at least during the early stages of their illness. Gerontological research exhaustively documents the **caregiver burden** that these relatives (typically the patient's spouse or adult children) experience (e.g., Zarit, Orr, & Zarit, 1985). One of the most positive outcomes of heightened awareness of AD and other forms of dementia in the 1980s was the emergence of strategies aimed at ameliorating this burden.

Chapter Twelve is devoted to the topic of family caregiving. At this point, we briefly survey some of the means through which caregiver burden is eased. These efforts can involve individual counseling for the caregiver and her[5] family, work with organizations,[6] use of adult day care or respite care services (see Chapter Four, p. 101), and involvement in a caregiver support group. Whatever the specific approach, the goals are to minimize stress for caregivers by providing information about AD and other forms of dementia (including information about the nature and course of dementia, legal and financial issues, and nursing homes), giving advice about managing practical care-giving problems (e.g., safety hazards, personal hygiene, incontinence), and managing anger, stress, anxiety, and depression (Mace & Rabins, 1981; Oliver & Bock, 1987; Zarit et al., 1985).

MENTAL HEALTH SERVICES AND ELDERLY ADULTS

We have already discussed mental health services for the aged in the context of treatment for depression, schizophrenia, substance abuse, and dementia. This

---

5. Most family caregiving is carried out by women, although researchers are beginning to examine the unique stresses that male caregivers confront (see Chapter Twelve).

6. One of the largest and most active self-help groups is the Alzheimer's Association. Their national office is located at 360 N. Michigan Ave., Chicago, IL 60601; many communities have local chapters. The association can be reached at 1–800–922–2413.

section addresses more general issues concerning older adults' use of mental health services, including settings in which these services are provided to elderly people and ways in which treatment approaches may need to be modified for effective work with older adults.

Older adults' use of mental health services

Experts agree that the elderly are an underserved population for mental health professionals. Statistics documenting this phenomenon abound. Of all services provided at community mental health centers (CMHCs), only 6 percent are provided to older adults, and approximately 3 percent of the mental health services provided by private practitioners are delivered to elderly individuals (Gatz, 1989). Although older adults seen in a medical setting were as likely as younger adults to receive a diagnosis of mental disorder, they were less likely than younger adults to be treated by a mental health specialist (Goldstrom et al., 1987). Furthermore, older adults' use of mental health services (both inpatient and outpatient) declined over the period 1950 to 1975, a period during which all other age groups increased their use of such services (Kahn, 1975; Meeks et al., 1990).

Why do mental health services fail to reach older adults? Explanations have pointed toward older peoples' inclinations, mental health professionals' preferences, and the systems through which mental health services are made available. Some posit that elderly people have a negative perception of mental health services, and that they believe that seeking such services is tantamount to an admission of psychosis (for a review see Gatz et al., 1985). Lasoski and Thelen (1987), for example, found that older participants were as likely as middle-aged participants to rate individuals described in vignettes as needing professional help, but were less likely to believe that outpatient services would be appropriate. Other research reveals that older women find psychotherapy more acceptable when the problem to be addressed is relatively low in intimacy (e.g., meaningful use of time) as opposed to highly intimate problems (e.g., marital difficulties) (Hayslip, Schneider, & Bryant, 1989).

Others argue, however, that the elderly do not show such a bias against the use of psychiatric services (Gatz & Pearson, 1988; Gatz et al., 1985). In Lasoski and Thelen's (1987) study described above, the older adults recommended outpatient therapy more often than inpatient treatment for the disorders described in vignettes, and they rarely suggested that the individuals described should deal with their problems on their own or with help from friends or a member of the clergy. Furthermore, these participants (both middle-aged and elderly) believed that older people use mental health services less often than younger people primarily because they were not aware that the services were available; they only rarely cited embarrassment about the need for treatment.

Mental health professionals are believed to harbor negative perceptions of elderly people in general and pessimistic views of treatment outcomes for the aged (e.g., Smyer et al., 1990). For example, one group of researchers found that clinical psychologists rated older hypothetical clients as less desireable to work with than younger hypothetical clients who had identical histories; these psychologists also expected less improvement from the older than the younger hypothetical clients. Gatz and Pearson (1988), however, caution that this supposed ageism on the part of mental health professionals may be overestimated.

The ways in which mental health services are delivered have also been cited as an explanation for older adults' low rate of use. Nurses, other health care professionals, and community service agencies rarely refer older adults for mental health services, and services targeted specifically for elderly patients may receive low priority at mental health facilities (e.g., Smyer et al., 1990). Medicare policies clearly provide a disincentive for older people to seek mental health services, or for professionals to provide them. Medicare coverage for both inpatient and outpatient psychiatric services is severely restricted in terms of number of days of coverage, copayment requirements and dollar caps on coverage, and the types of professionals who can be reimbursed for services (e.g., Meeks et al., 1990; Roybal, 1988).

Treatment settings

Nonetheless, mental health services are effectively provided to older adults in a variety of settings. Although CMHCs have traditionally underserved the elderly (see above), formal affiliations between CMHCs and Area Agencies on Aging are associated with higher rates of service to the aged (Lebowitz, 1987; Lebowitz, Light, & Bailey, 1988; Smyer et al., 1990). Outreach mental health programs have been instituted in nontraditional settings such as senior centers and older adult nutrition sites in the hope of reaching greater numbers of older people (Smyer et al., 1990). Services are sometimes provided via telephone sessions or home visits in an attempt to overcome problems of physical access (Gatz et al., 1985).

Recall that deinstitutionalization has, until quite recently, moved the chronically mentally ill elderly from psychiatric facilities to nursing homes. Unfortunately, mental health professionals are rarely readily available in nursing homes (e.g., Meeks et al., 1990; Tourigny-Rivard & Drury, 1987). However, nurses and nurses' aides have welcomed continuing education focused on the mental health needs of the elderly, and residents have apparently benefitted from such efforts (Tourigny-Rivard & Drury, 1987).

Treatment approaches for the elderly

Remember that many of the means used to treat such problems as depression and schizophrenia in young adults are effective with older people as well. Both psychoactive medication and individual psychotherapy hold promise for the mentally ill aged. However, both approaches may need to be implemented differently in the case of an older person as opposed to a young adult.

Because of physical and health changes of normal aging (see Chapters Three and Four), there is greater danger of accidental drug overdose and of drug interactions for older patients. Therefore, a physician must monitor medication effects much more carefully for older as compared to younger patients. Individual psychotherapy, too, must be tailored to elderly patients. Some necessary changes in approach include using large print materials, developing a shorter and/or more structured treatment plan, making more extensive use of life review and reminiscence techniques, terminating treatment more gradually, and coordinating efforts with community resources such as telephone reassurance or Friendly Visitor programs (e.g., Gatz, 1989).

Therapeutic approaches that involve other people are also helpful to elderly patients. **Group therapy** has enjoyed widespread application for decades, and its specific application to the mental health needs of aged clients is increasing. Psychotherapy groups (focused on a particular kind of problem or on personal growth), psychoeducational groups designed to develop skills for coping with emotions such as depression and anger, and self-help groups aimed at normalizing problematic experiences (e.g., caring for a demented spouse) are all effective with the aged (e.g., Smyer et al., 1990).

A specialized form of group therapy, **family therapy**, also has important promise for the mentally-ill elderly. Because family relationships maintain or increase in importance during later life (see Chapters Ten, Eleven, Twelve), the family can potentially exacerbate or ameliorate psychological problems of the aged. In family therapy, the goal is to evaluate interactions among family members, identify problematic patterns, and hopefully replace them with more adaptive practices (Herr & Weakland, 1979).

Herr and Weakland (1979) identify problems that can arise in older adults' family relationships. Difficult family situations include blaming the older person for all problems in the family, believing (accurately or inaccurately) that the older person demands unreasonable levels of support, and forming or maintaining symbiotic relationships that permit neither aging parents nor adult children to express individuality or independence. In addition to enhancing patterns of family interaction, family therapy may help the older person and her family to meet age-related challenges such as the need for physical rehabilitation or institutionalization (Herr & Weakland, 1979).

Finally, a creative (and possibly cost-effective) means of addressing feelings of isolation, loneliness, and uselessness is **pet therapy** (e.g., Brickel, 1984; Gatz et al., 1985). Providing pets in both institutional settings (e.g., Brickel, 1979; Winkler, Fairnie, Gericevich, & Long, 1989) and in the community (e.g., Lago, Connell, & Knight, 1983) has been effective, perhaps because of the companionship and physical contact that pets provide and the responsibility and activity that they demand. Pet therapy can yield not only psychological benefits but also may reduce blood pressure (Holden, 1981). Like all forms of therapy, of course, pet therapy is not the answer for every depressed or lonely older

For older adults who enjoy animals, pet therapy can offer both mental and physical health benefits.

individual. Pet therapy would be of little help for an elderly person who has never liked animals.

This chapter has shown, then, that older adults are as vulnerable to many forms of psychopathology as younger people are. One may grow old with a chronic mental disorder such as depression, alcohol abuse, or schizophrenia. Or, one may develop an illness in old age, after a lifetime of effective functioning. In either case, the appropriate response is one of guarded optimism. Although not all mental disorders afflicting older people can be cured at this time, many kinds of mental health problems can be effectively treated in later life.

SUMMARY

Experts describe mentally healthy individuals as having a positive attitude toward themselves, an accurate view of reality, capacity to master their environment, autonomy, balance in personality, and an orientation toward growth. When asked how they would describe someone their age who was well-adjusted, middle-aged and elderly adults offered different descriptions.

Although geropsychiatrists agree that depression is one of the more common disorders afflicting the aged, there is disagreement as to whether the elderly are more vulnerable to major depression than are younger adults. A variety of treatment approaches are used with patients suffering from depression, and often combinations of treatments are used. Relative to younger adults, elderly people are disproportionately likely to commit suicide.

Experts disagree as to whether elderly schizophrenics manifest different symptoms as compared to younger schizophrenics. Treatment for schizophrenia centers around the use of antipsychotic medications that attempt to normalize the action of neurotransmitters in the CNS. Unfortunately, these medications have unpleasant side effects.

Recent reviewers estimate that between 4 percent and 8 percent of the elderly suffer from alcohol abuse, and that rates of other forms of substance abuse are far lower among the aged. Experts suggest that professionals should be alert to different indicators of possible alcohol abuse than they would consider in assessing a younger person.

Dementia is not a specific disease, but a collection of symptoms that may stem from any of several conditions singly or in combination. Alzheimer's disease (AD) is the best known and most frequently diagnosed condition producing these symptoms in old age. Currently, a diagnosis of AD is probable (rather than definite) prior to autopsy, and is based on behavioral and cognitive symptoms. Although a cure for AD does not yet exist, several treatments aimed at minimizing symptoms are available.

Experts agree that the elderly are an underserved population by mental health professionals. Mental health services can, however, effectively be provided to older adults in a variety of settings.

KEY TERMS

Acetylcholine
Alzheimer's disease (AD)
Amyloid
Antipsychotic medication
Behavior therapy
Caregiver burden
Cognitive therapy
Deinstitutionalize
Dementia
Dysphoria
Early onset
Electroconvulsive therapy (ECT)
Family therapy
Functional disorders
Group therapy
Heterocyclic antidepressants (HCA's)
Huntington's disease

Jakob-Creutzfeldt disease
Late onset
Major depression
MAO inhibitors
Multi-Infarct Dementia (MID)
Neurotransmitter
Parkinson's disease
Pet therapy
Pharmacotherapy
Pick's disease
Premenstrual syndrome (PMS)
Primary differentiated dementia
Primary undifferentiated dementia
Pseudodementia
Psychotherapy
Reality orientation
Secondary dementia

SUGGESTIONS FOR FURTHER READING

Blazer, D. (1990). *Emotional Problems in Later Life: Intervention Strategies for Professional Caregivers.* New York: Springer.

Costa, P. T., Whitfield, J. R., & Stewart, D. (1989). *Alzheimer's Disease: Abstracts of the Psychological and Behavioral Literature.* Washington, DC: American Psychological Association.

Heston, L. L., & White, J. A. (1983). *Dementia: A Practical Guide to Alzheimer's Disease and Related Illnesses.* New York: W. H. Freeman.

Kalish, R. A. (1989). *Midlife Loss: Coping Strategies*. Newbury Park, CA: Sage Publications.

Knight, B. (1986). *Psychotherapy with Older Adults*. Newbury Park, CA: Sage Publications.

Mace, N. L., & Rabins, P. V. (1991). *The 36-hour Day*, 2nd ed. Baltimore: Johns Hopkins University Press.

Thomas, R. M. (1989). *Counseling and Life-span Development*. Newbury Park, CA: Sage Publications.

Zarit, S. H., Orr, N. K., & Zarit, J. M. (1985). *The Hidden Victims of Alzheimer's Disease: Families Under Stress*. New York: New York University Press.

CHAPTER TEN

*L*OVE AND MARRIAGE THROUGHOUT ADULTHOOD

How do people find a husband or wife? What are the ingredients of a happy marriage? What causes marriages to break up? This chapter addresses these issues, as we consider marriage and other love relationships. A theme running throughout our consideration is the extent to which men and women experience these intimate relationships in distinct ways.

The chapter begins with intimacy in romantic relationships, the process of selecting a marital partner, and lifestyles that some choose instead of marriage. In examining marriage, we identify circumstances associated with marital satisfaction, changes in marital satisfaction over time, and marital satisfaction in later life.

Of course, many marriages do not survive for "the long haul." Divorce and remarriage are also considered in this chapter. We review divorce rates, some of the challenges of adjusting to divorce, and differences in the experience of divorce at different ages.

Questions to consider in reading the chapter include:

What qualities are important in dating relationships? How do theorists explain the process of mate selection?

What variables are associated with levels of marital satisfaction? What does research tell us about satisfaction with marriage in the middle and later years?

What types of satisfactions and stresses do remaining single, cohabitation, and homosexuality offer?

How do people react to divorce? What issues are unique to middle-aged and older people who divorce? How do first marriages differ from subsequent marriages?

BEFORE MARRIAGE: INTIMACY, DATING, AND MATE SELECTION

Intimacy: Variation by age and gender

Intimacy can refer to many kinds of experiences. Wong (1981) offered a typology in which intimate relationships could involve brief or extended duration, situation-specific or more generalized contact, and varying levels of self-disclosure. Using Wong's (1981) typology, you could have an intimate relationship with a friend that you have known for many years, that you see nearly every day, and with whom you share your most personal feelings. You could also have an intimate relationship with someone that you meet on a transcontinental plane trip and with whom you have an extended conversation, but that you never see again. Or, you might have an intimate relationship with a colleague that you see a great deal at work (but nowhere else) and with whom you talk about work-related issues. This approach, then, emphasizes the variety with which adults experience intimacy.

Is intimacy different for men and women, or for people of different ages? Research suggests that it is. In a cross-sectional study involving young, middle-aged, and older married couples, Reedy, Birren, and Schaie (1981) identified six components of love: emotional security, respect, help and play behaviors, communication, sexual intimacy, and loyalty; they also asked respondents how important each of these components were to their relationship. Figure 10.1 illustrates the age differences. Across all age groups, women stressed emotional security more—but loyalty less—than did men. Young adult lovers stressed the importance of communication in their relationships more than did the older couples, but the young adults placed less emphasis on emotional security and loyalty than did older lovers.

Dating: Age and gender differences in dating relationships

Some intimate relationships are romantic relationships, and dating is one context within which these relationships are established and maintained. Questions concerning dating abound—not only for dating couples, but also for social scientists. Researchers have examined the factors associated with satisfaction in dating relationships, circumstances predicting which relationships

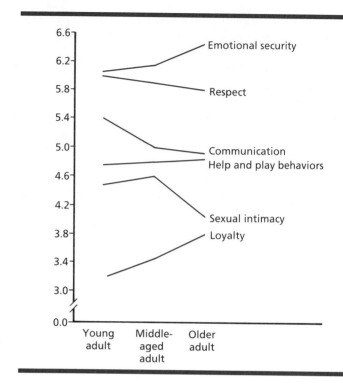

Figure 10.1
Age differences
in love relation-
*ships. (*Source:
Reedy et al., 1981.
Reprinted by per-
mission of S. Kar-
ger AG, Basel.)

will last, and age differences in dating practices. As new trends in dating emerge, scientists explore these options as well.

Most college students would probably predict that the extent to which dating partners are satisfied with their relationship has a great deal to do with the duration of the relationship, and they would be right (e.g., Hendrick, Hendrick, & Adler, 1988). What, then, makes for a satisfying dating relationship? Intimacy is one factor, but by no means the only one. Furthermore, men and women apparently weigh intimacy differently as they evaluate dating relation-ships.

R. K. Thomas, T. M. Miller, and J. E. Karsko (1989) examined college students' satisfaction with dating relationships. Students reporting greatest satisfaction had relatively high self-esteem, relatively low levels of interpersonal dominance, and relatively low feelings of inequity in the relationships. In addi-tion, a relatively high rating of intimacy in the relationship predicted high levels of satisfaction for men, but not for women.

Intimacy is associated with the duration of dating relationships in still another way. According to one group of researchers, it is not simply the actual or perceived level of intimacy that is important. Rather, the extent to which dating partners *agree* about their level of intimacy reliably predicts the proba-bility that the relationship will endure (Hill, Peplau, & Rubin, 1981).

Others take a different approach to examining satisfaction with dating relationships. Cate, Lloyd, and Long (1988) considered couples' perceptions of rewards and fairness in their relationship. College students in this study rated their own and their partner's contributions to their relationship, the outcome of the relationship for themselves and their partner, their satisfaction with the relationship, and how rewarding they found the relationship. Perceived rewards in the relationship were important predictors of satisfaction; in contrast to Thomas et al.'s (1989) findings, equity (perceived contributions and outcomes for self and partner) was less important in predicting satisfaction.

Have you ever been disappointed the first (or only) time that you went out with someone? One innovation in matchmaking is designed to minimize those unpleasant surprises. Videodating allows clients to examine a dossier illustrated with photographs and a videotaped interview in order to select potential dating partners. When a client selects a possible date on the basis of this information, the man or woman is then contacted and given the opportunity to review the same information about the client. On that basis, the man or woman can either accept or reject the client's offer of a date.

As you might suspect, videodating is fairly costly and thus attracts affluent single adults. Clients of a West Coast videodating service said that they put a great deal of planning and work into preparing their dossier (Woll & Young, 1989). Although most believed that they had succeeded in projecting a desired image, most were not pleased with the clients who responded. But these clients gave the service favorable marks for providing an opportunity to "screen" potential dates before meeting them.

Thus, scientists have clarified some of the ways in which intimacy is important in dating and in which dating evolves in our increasingly technological society. Unfortunately, research in this area is plagued with methodological problems. Virtually all studies rely on dating couples' own reports of their relationship. Perhaps studies that depended on friends or observers' ratings of the relationships would provide an entirely different picture.

Furthermore, participants in most dating research are college students—usually Caucasian, upper-middle class young adults living on a college campus. This, obviously, is a very narrow segment of the population. As a result, we know very little about dating among young adults not attending college, among minority groups, or among middle-aged or older adults.

Some have explored dating in later life. Drawing on the membership list of a metropolitan singles club, K. Bulcroft and M. O'Conner-Roden (1986) interviewed dating couples aged 60 to 90, and compared their experiences to those of college students. Young and older daters alike were interested in romance: both old and young thrilled to the awkward excitement of falling in love, and both cherished romantic dinners and gifts.

There were age differences in dating, however (Bulcroft & O'Connor-Roden, 1986). Compared to the college students, the older daters' relationships intensified more quickly: few were interested in "playing the field" in their sixties, seventies, or eighties. But the elderly couples rarely expected to marry

*Like young
adults, elderly
daters cherish
romantic gifts
and gestures.*

the person they were dating. Older women were especially reluctant to marry. These women said that there seemed to be little point in getting married, since there was no possibility of starting a family. Many had cared for their late husbands during a fatal illness, and they did not want to regain the caregiver role.

The older couples also had more mixed feelings about sexual aspects of their relationship (Bulcroft & O'Conner-Roden, 1986). These older people, of course, had grown up with traditional prohibitions against sexual relations outside of marriage, and now confronted more permissive dating customs. Despite their ambivalence, most of the couples were sexually intimate and took great pleasure in this aspect of their relationships.

Mate selection

Often, the desired, logical, and actual outcome of dating is to select a husband or wife. Are there any regularities in that mysterious process? There is ample evidence of **assortativeness** (or homogamy), the tendency to marry someone similar to oneself. This process operates with respect to age, educational background, socioeconomic status, physical attractiveness, and intelligence. However, assortativeness has decreased with respect to race and religion (Murstein, 1980).

To a lesser extent, personality is also a dimension along which assortativeness occurs. Remember, though, that measuring personality in a reliable and valid manner can be a Herculean feat (see Chapter Eight, pp. 201–203). Partly for that reason, scientists have had less success in demonstrating assortativeness in the realm of personality than with respect to more objectively measured characteristics such as age and education.

Furthermore, Murstein (1980) notes that self-esteem may affect the extent of assortativeness in personality. He concluded that individuals with high self-esteem believed that their personalities were similar to their spouse's personalities—and actually gave similar responses on objective personality measures. Individuals with low self-esteem, however, perceived less similarity between their own and their spouse's personalities; personality measures also revealed less similarity for low self-esteem individuals.

Another way to understand how spouses are selected is through **exchange theories** of mate selection. These theories propose that both parties in a relationship attempt to make their interaction as "profitable" as possible (Murstein, 1982). In determining whether or not a relationship is likely to be profitable, one would consider the rewards as well as the costs that would be encountered in the relationship.

In contemplating a relationship with Kevin, for example, Ginger would consider Kevin's physical attractiveness, his future earning capacity, and his warm personality to be clear rewards. Other possible rewards might be the companionship, sexual gratification, security, and social status that the relationship provides to her. However, most relationships also entail costs. In that respect, Ginger would be concerned about the need to give up privacy, freedom, and flexibility in her use of time. Other costs might be that Kevin spends money irresponsibly or disagrees about the desirability of having children. Ginger's decision about the relationship would reflect her overall perspective of the balance between the rewards and costs that the relationship offers.

One of the most important exchange approaches is **Stimulus-Value-Role theory (SVR)** (Murstein, 1976; 1980; 1982). Figure 10.2 illustrates the process of mate selection as it is described in this theory. According to this theory, mate selection is a process encompassing a **stimulus stage**, a **value comparison stage**, and a **role compatibility stage**. In each stage, one emphasizes different qualities in evaluating the reward/cost balance of a possible relationship.

The stimulus stage encompasses a couple's initial encounter and formation of mutual first impressions. During the first few dates, then, your judgement about a potential partner would reflect your own perceptions (e.g., how attractive is he? What kind of temperament does he have? Is he sexy?), and second-hand information. If you have been told that Josephine College has realistic aspirations of becoming President of the United States, or that she has a drug problem, then your initial judgement of her will be influenced by that knowledge as well as by your opinion of her appearance and personality.

If both members of a couple have positive impressions during the stimulus stage, they may reach the value comparison stage. Now, a partner's appearance and reputation are less important. You are more concerned about whether or not your partner shares your interests, attitudes, and beliefs. This stage involves a great deal of self-disclosure, as partners share their feelings and

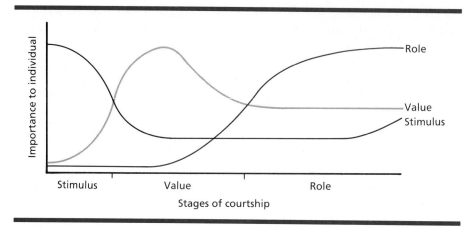

Figure 10.2
Stimulus-value-role theory of mate selection. (Source: Murstein, *Who Will Marry Whom?* Copyright 1976 by Springer Publishing Co. Inc. Used by permission.)

observe the impact of these revelations upon one another. Couples who spend hours talking together, who feel that they must see one another each day, and who take pleasure in introducing one another to their friends, interests, and hobbies are probably in this stage.

Couples who successfully navigate both the stimulus and the value comparison stages may marry. More often, though, the couple progresses to the third stage of evaluating how well they function as a couple. You would now be concerned with the match between the roles that you fulfill now (and expect to play in the future) and your partner's roles and aspirations. For example, you would consider the compatibility of your educational and career goals and those of your partner.

Murstein (1982), the sociologist proposing SVR theory, concluded that the theory was well supported by research, but also noted that this research had not been longitudinal. Mate selection probably does involve evaluations along the dimensions of stimulus, value comparison, and role compatibility, but individuals may not consider these dimensions in the sequence that Murstein describes.

Other influences of mate selection include timing, critical incidents, and the social network (Murstein, 1982). Timing often plays a critical role in determining who marries—or does not marry—whom. Many people have met someone to whom they were strongly attracted at an inopportune time (e.g., when already married, when being shipped overseas by the armed forces), when they were unable to marry. Unexpected critical events may either push a couple into marriage (as in the case of an unplanned pregnancy) or rule out the possibility of marriage altogether (as in the case of a job transfer). And, the social network—parents, friends, coworkers—may, through their reaction to the couple, either encourage or discourage marriage.

Clearly, the process of selecting a husband or wife is a topic of great scientific interest. But to most people, what is psychologically most important is the eventual outcome of the process. We turn next to that outcome, and examine the transition to married life.

MARRIAGE

Adjustment to marriage

Is being a newlywed entirely blissful, or is it also stressful? Does getting married change a person? Do the answers to these questions differ for men and women? In a classic study, Lowenthal, Thurnher, Chiriboga, and their colleagues (1975) identified critical issues facing recently-married young men and women. These young adults were struggling to achieve a satisfactory balance between their roles at work and their roles in the marriage; some were also concerned with the prospect of integrating children into the family.

At least for some, adjusting to married life was stressful (Lowenthal et al., 1975). About half had experienced emotional problems. Across all four age groups included in this study,[1] newlywed women were among those most frequently contemplating suicide and newlywed men most often experienced feelings of despair and meaninglessness. Perhaps these reactions stemmed from the challenge of restructuring one's life around another person, and even facing a "death" of one's former social self.

Studying marital satisfaction: Comparing views of "happy marriages" across the lines of gender, race, and social class

Lowenthal et al.'s (1975) classic study paints a pessimistic portrait of satisfaction with the early years of marriage. More recent research provides a brighter outlook: investigators have identified components of marital satisfaction during the early years and variables associated with satisfaction. However, satisfaction with marriage is a complex phenomenon that is not easily studied. Measuring marital satisfaction is challenging partly because the concept is abstract. Like many concepts in which researchers are interested, there is no single, straightforward characteristic that scientists can easily agree on and observe as an indicator of the quality of a marriage. As a result, many measures of marital quality are widely used and it is therefore difficult to compare findings in this area.

Most often, research on marital satisfaction relies on one spouse's (or sometimes both spouses') reports of the quality of the marriage. This approach

---

1. The other age groups were high school seniors, middle-aged adults, and preretirement couples.

makes sense, since a husband and wife are experts on the quality of their marriage. However, the dangers of relying solely on self-reports (even from both spouses) are great. How much should we trust Suzie's assertion that her marriage is flawless? Isn't it possible that she is unwilling to admit—to us, if not to herself—that she and Jay have real problems in their marriage?

Furthermore, newly married couples may not have had time to discover problems in their relationship. When one has invested 20 years or more in a relationship, on the other hand, it may be nearly impossible to evaluate it critically and give an objective report. Even the most cooperative research participant may be unable to resist looking at her marriage through rose-colored glasses.

Despite these measurement problems, the study of marital satisfaction flourishes. Psychoanalytic theory links satisfaction in marriage to the husband's and wife's levels of adjustment (Doherty & Jacobson, 1982)—which, in turn, reflect the long-term impact of early experience (see Chapter Eight, p. 188). In contrast, **behavior exchange theory (BET)** proposes that marital satisfaction stems from the way that the husband and wife behave toward one another (Doherty & Jacobson, 1982). According to this theory, the balance between rewards and punishments in spouses' interaction determines their level of satisfaction. If one can make that interaction more rewarding than punishing—perhaps through training in communication and other relationship skills—then one can often improve the couple's satisfaction with their marriage (Jacobson & Martin, 1976).

Empirical work identifies components and correlates of marital satisfaction. In a longitudinal study, 373 couples (199 African-American couples, 174 Caucasian couples) were interviewed initially during the first year of their marriage and one year later (Crohan & Veroff, 1989; Ruvolo & Veroff, 1989). One of the questions that these researchers pursued concerned dimensions of **marital well-being**. In other words, when a woman says that she is happily married, just what is she saying about her relationship with her husband? These researchers were especially interested in exploring the extent to which the dimensions of marital well-being identified among newlyweds were unique to the early years of marriage.

For these couples, there were four components of marital well-being (Crohan & Veroff, 1989). A *happiness* component reflected couples' positive feelings about the spouse, the marriage, and its future. There was also an *equity* component; in that respect, feeling that you and your spouse benefit equally from the relationship—and believing that your spouse feels the same way—is important. A third aspect was a feeling of personal *competence* in the role of husband or wife. The final component was the perception of *control* in the marriage: part of these newlyweds' satisfaction with their marriage was feeling that they could do things to make the marriage better.

Are these components of marital well-being unique to the early years of marriage? Crohan and Veroff (1989) believe that they are, at least in one respect. Earlier studies of marital satisfaction had suggested that there might be still another component of marital well-being—confidence in the *stability* of the relationship. However, these newlyweds' confidence that their marriage would last were inseparable from their general feelings of happiness in the relationship. Perhaps stability is rarely a concern during the first year of marriage, but becomes more important as the relationship endures. In any case, satisfaction with marriage—even during the first couple of years—is closely related to husbands' and wives' general feelings of well-being (Ruvolo & Veroff, 1989).

A related approach to understanding marriage is to identify characteristics associated with marital satisfaction. Taking this perspective, individual differences along several dimensions—gender, class, and race—emerge. Generally, husbands express higher levels of marital satisfaction than do wives (Bernard, 1972; Wrightsman, 1988). Women and men differ not only in levels but also in sources of marital satisfaction. In a study of African-American couples, husbands' marital satisfaction was most closely associated with the extent of support and commitment in their relationship, whereas wives' marital satisfaction was most closely associated with the degree of openness and flexibility in their communication (Thomas, 1990). However, husbands who are dissatisfied with their marriages make more errors in interpreting their wives' verbal and nonverbal messages, and give their wives more unintended messages, than husbands who are satisfied with their marriages (Thompson & Walker, 1989). Quality of communication is important for both husbands' and wives' satisfaction, but is apparently related to satisfaction in different ways for men and women.

Expectations regarding marriage are also important. According to Wrightsman (1988), highly educated people have different expectations for their marriages than do less educated individuals. Highly educated people may be disappointed if their marriage fails to provide personal growth, romantic expression, or self-actualization. To the extent that less well-educated couples do not expect these things from their relationship, they will not be disappointed if the relationship fails to provide them.

Some examine correlates of marital satisfaction on a more detailed level. In their study of African-American and Caucasian newlyweds, Crohan and Veroff (1989) identified not only components of marital well-being but also how each of these dimensions were associated with individual and couple characteristics. Income, for example, was positively associated with feelings of competence in the marital role for African-Americans but was negatively associated with Caucasian newlyweds' feelings of competence. Crohan and Veroff (1989) suggested that high-earning Caucasian newlyweds were so involved in demanding careers that they did not devote adequate time and effort to mastering the role of husband or wife.

On the other hand, relatively high-earning African-American newlyweds may run a lesser risk of being overinvolved in a career. Discrimination still bars many African-Americans from entering the most demanding and prestigious occupations. High income may therefore be related to high feelings of competence for African-Americans because the income provides greater confidence, greater self-esteem, or simply greater resources for mastering the husband or wife role. There may be a critical level of affluence that contributes to feelings of competence in the marital role; either too much or too little income may preclude these feelings.

The impact of marriage

How does getting married affect men and women as individuals? Doherty and Jacobson (1982) suggest that getting married may have positive consequences, particularly for young adults who were poorly adjusted before marriage. Such individuals show enhanced levels of self-esteem and vocational aspirations and decreased levels of aggression and substance abuse following marriage. It is not clear why that pattern of association exists, though. It may be that marriage actually is conducive to mental well-being. On the other hand, it is also possible that poorly adjusted individuals are unable to marry, or that marriage and mental health are joint outcomes of other circumstances.

Perhaps, too, the relationship between marital status and well-being varies from one person to the next. Jessie Bernard (1972), for example, asserts that marriage has far more health benefits to offer husbands than wives. Also, the timing of marriage can moderate its impact. Marrying at an exceptionally early age—such as during high school—is associated with negative consequences, including lower levels of educational attainment and higher rates of divorce (Doherty & Jacobson, 1982). One cannot assume that marriage will necessarily provide an opportunity for personal growth and development: marriage may only be a beneficial experience if it occurs at an optimal point in an individual's maturation.

Changes over time in marital satisfaction

The difficulties in studying marital quality are multiplied when scholars attempt to chart changes over time in marital satisfaction. If researchers compare younger and older married couples' reports, there are the problems inherent in cross-sectional comparisons (see Chapter One, pp. 20–22). Furthermore, some of the individuals will be in their first marriage, while others will have been divorced or widowed and then remarried.

If scientists limit their consideration to intact first marriages, the sample becomes more and more biased with increasing length of marriage (e.g., Bengtson, Rosenthal, & Burton, 1990; Blieszner, 1986; Huyck, 1982). The youngest couples in the sample include some who will eventually divorce. The middle-aged and elderly couples, however, have managed to stay together much longer. If the older couples report greater satisfaction on the average than the younger couples, it may be because the individuals of their cohort who were dissatisfied with their marriages divorced long ago, and thereby disqualified themselves from the study.

With these caveats in mind, what is a satisfying marriage like in the middle years of adulthood? The Berkeley Growth Studies, the Oakland Growth Studies, and the Guidance Study (these longitudinal data were discussed in earlier chapters) provide an "insider's view" of married life for middle-aged couples, and identify ways in which happy marriages differ from less happy ones at this point in the life cycle. Skolnick (1981) separated the marriages in this sample into two broad groups—those rated by professional observers as satisfying and those rated as unsatisfying. She then asked both spouses to select statements that characterized their marriage. The statements concerned expectations and assumptions about marriage, satisfactions and dissatisfactions with the marriage, the spouse's performance as a husband or wife, the quality of their personal relationship, their divisions of labor, and their relationships with friends and others outside of the marriage.

For these Caucasian, predominantly middle-class married couples, the outstanding characteristic of the satisfying marriages at midlife was an enjoyable and affectionate relationship with the spouse (Skolnick, 1981). These husbands and wives said that they liked one another, admired and respected one another, and enjoyed each other's company. The couples with less satisfying marriages were prone to describe their marriage as a utilitarian arrangement, rather than a bond based on affection and commitment.

The satisfying marriages were by no means conflict-free (Skolnick, 1981). These happily married couples believed that conflict was a normal part of married life. In marriages rated as less satisfying, couples much more often selected statements suggesting that they dealt with conflict either by avoiding it altogether or in ways that only led to more hostility and tension. More recent research supports Skolnick's (1981) portrayal of conflict management. In dissatisfying marriages, there were vicious cycles of withdrawal on the part of the husband followed by hostility on the part of the wife (Roberts & Krokoff, 1990). In satisfying marriages, however, interaction patterns were more symmetrical and adaptive (Roberts & Krokoff, 1990).

Skolnick's (1981) data do not justify an oversimplified picture of either the satisfying or less satisfying midlife marriages, however. Skolnick (1981) found variability in relationships within both groups. Some with a satisfying marriage spent a great deal of time together and shared virtually all activities; others, just as satisfied with their relationship, were content for each partner to "do their own thing." Some who were dissatisfied with the marriage clung to traditionally-defined roles for husband and wife, while others reported far more egalitarian relationships—but no more satisfaction with the marriage. Some couples spent little time with friends or community involvements, whereas others were active members of their social circle; these patterns, however, did not distinguish middle-aged couples reporting greater and lesser satisfaction with their marriages. As we see in the *Diversity in Adulthood* box, variability in marital relationships is the rule rather than the exception.

BOX 10.1   **D**IVERSITY IN ADULTHOOD

The many American ways of married life

Married life, of course, is unique for every married couple. How have scientists described this variety? Some distinguish marriages on the basis of the distribution of power between husband and wife (Scanzoni & Scanzoni, 1976). Others take a more concrete approach to identifying distinctive marriage styles, including **marital noncohabitation** in which the husband and wife live apart—most often during military service or incarceration (Rindfuss & Stephen, 1990).

As with people, differences between marriages become more pronounced as time goes by. One of the earliest and still the best-known efforts to document variety in long-term marriages is that of Cuber & Harroff (1965). These researchers studied middle-aged men and women who had achieved success in their professions and financial comfort. Within this privileged group, Cuber and Harroff identified five types of enduring relationships.

Most would consider three patterns relatively low-quality relationships. In the *conflict-habituated marriage,* couples experienced almost constant conflict, although it was often concealed (Cuber & Harroff, 1965). In the *devitalized marriage,* couples were deeply in love as young adults. However, in middle adulthood they shared fewer activities, spent less time together, had less frequent and less enjoyable sexual relations, and generally found their relationship less meaningful. The third type of marriage, the *passive-congenial marriage,* is similar to the devitalized marriage. In both cases, husband and wife spent little time together and shared few interests, took little pleasure in their sexual relationship, and found their marriages less satisfying than other parts of their lives. However, the passive-congenial marriages had this character from the outset, whereas the devitalized marriages began as more intense and involving relationships.

Cuber and Harroff's (1965) remaining two types of marriages are higher quality "*intrinsic marriages.*" For couples in a *vital marriage,* being together and sharing important—and even unimportant—matters is the central thing in life. Shared activities are enjoyable *because* they are shared, not because of the activity itself. The partners in these relationships, however, maintain a strong sense of individual identity. In the *total marriage,* virtually all aspects of life are completely shared. The wife's career, for example, may be an undertaking in which the husband is as involved as the wife. Although conflict arises in these marriages, the important thing is not how the disagreement is resolved but that *some* resolution be reached without tarnishing the couple's complete involvement.

More recent scholars have criticized Cuber and Harroff's (1965) portrayal of high-quality marriages. According to Marks (1989), intrinsic marriages imply that spouses are near-perfect companions, that they make heroic sacrifices for the sake of the relationship, and that they are virtuosos in providing empathy no matter what circumstances (including extramarital affairs) come to pass. The unfortunate result, Marks claims, is that Cuber and Harroff's work suggests that high-quality marriages are a rarified type.

Marks (1989) provides a more differentiated view of high-quality marriages and how such marriages might change—while maintaining their high quality—with time. According to Marks, all marriages are partnerships in which husband and wife mesh their involvements in three areas of their lives (see Figure 10.3). The first area is inner ("I") strivings and impulses that are important to the husband *or* wife as an individual; the second is the relationship ("P") with the spouse. The third area is the individual's outward focus ("3rd") on such things as a career, children, friends, relatives, and the community. These outward foci of attention are not necessarily also important to the individual's spouse, although couples in some marriages may share outward focuses ("joint 3rd"), such as involvement in childrearing, churchwork, or a family business.

In his analysis, Marks (1989) describes four possible types of high-quality marriages (see Figure 10.3). In a **balanced connection** marriage, couples have an even balance between joint undertakings and privacy. Both are in touch with their

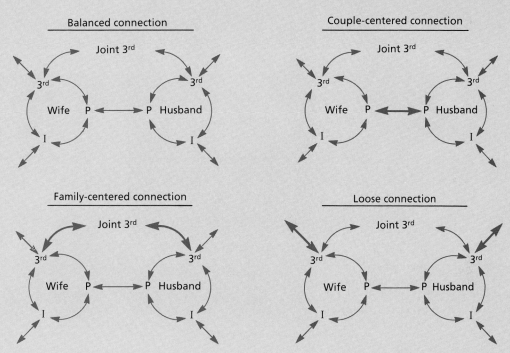

Figure 10.3
Types of high-quality marriage relationships. (Source: Marks, "Toward a Systems Theory of Marital Quality," *Journal of Marriage and Family, 51* (1): 15–26. Copyright 1989 by the National Council on Family Relations, 3989 Central Ave. N.E., Suite #550, Minneapolis, MN 55421. Reprinted by permission.)

inner strivings and are able to share these impulses as part of their relationship, both have active individual outward focuses, and both are involved in shared outward focuses. A **couple-centered connection** is similar to this first pattern, but husband and wife concentrate more energy on their relationship than on their individual inward focuses, or on their individual or shared outward focuses. A **family-centered connection** is a marriage in which husband and wife invest more energy in their shared outward focus (e.g., childrearing) than in their relationship, their individual inward focus, or their individual outward focus. Finally, in a **loose connection**, both spouses concentrate energy on their individual outward focuses; a dual-career couple, for example, might have such a relationship.

Marks (1989) suggests that high quality marriages may shift from one type to another over the family life cycle. In the early years of marriage, a couple-centered connection is often prominent. When children arrive, the wife often shifts to a family-centered connection. The husband may make the same shift (yielding a child-centered connection), or may shift to a loose connection as he confronts increasing career pressures. As children grow more self-sufficient, both husband and wife may adopt a loose connection if both now have involving careers. In the postparental years, the loose connection may endure, the couple may again have a couple-centered connection, or they may use grandparenting as a vehicle for establishing a family-centered connection.

Many happily married people consider conflict a normal part of married life.

Remember that feelings of happiness, equity, competence, and control are important dimensions of marital satisfaction during the first few years of marriage (Crohan & Veroff, 1989). As noted earlier, it is difficult to compare findings in this area because of the varied approaches to evaluating marital quality. Nonetheless, there are some common themes in marital satisfaction early and later on in marriage. Enjoyment of the partner and relationship are important at both times, as is the ability to confront disagreements constructively so as to improve the marriage.

Are there no changes, then, in marital satisfaction as the years go by? At this point, we turn to the large body of research attempting to identify and explain changes in levels of marital satisfaction over the life cycle. Some of the earliest research suggested that husbands and wives grow disenchanted with their relationship as the years pass (e.g., Pineo, 1961). More recent work has a more optimistic message, however. Gilford and Bengtson (1979) found that negative sentiments between spouses (e.g., sarcasm, disagreements, anger, and the like) decreased with age, and that young and old spouses expressed more positive sentiments (e.g., cooperation, stimulation) toward their partners than their middle-aged counterparts.

Indeed, the most frequently reported pattern is a **"U-shaped curve"** of marital satisfaction (e.g., Anderson, Russell, & Schumm, 1983; Burr, 1970;

Menaghan, 1983; Rollins & Cannon, 1974; Rollins & Feldman, 1970). Satisfaction with marriage is high during the first few years, and then declines throughout the childrearing years. Married couples report the least satisfaction when their children reach adolescence. As children reach maturity and begin to empty the nest, their parents' satisfaction with their marriage generally improves and becomes nearly as high as in the initial years of marriage.

What accounts for this pattern? Changes in the extent to which husbands and wives can spend time as a couple are probably important. In one instance, low levels of satisfaction in the middle years reflected extreme stress on the part of a small group of mothers—those with preschool children and low incomes who were working full-time (Schumm & Bugaighis, 1986). These women found little time to discuss daily matters with their husbands; their satisfaction with marriage declined, apparently as a result. Similarly, further analysis of one of the classic cross-sectional studies documenting the U-shaped pattern (Rollins & Feldman, 1970) shows that as parents become more involved in childrearing they often experience less companionship as a couple; when children leave home, the parents have more time to do things together (Rollins, 1989). When statistical techniques are used to compare levels of satisfaction at different stages of the family life cycle, holding companionship between spouses constant, differences in levels of marital satisfaction across stages of the family life cycle disappear (Rollins, 1989).

There are other reasons that marital satisfaction may decline during the childrearing years and then improve. As many parents are quick to suggest, the stresses of parenting teenagers are probably one reason. A recent study identified that factor, together with middle-aged mothers' identity questioning (see Chapter Eight, pp. 208–210), as sources of dissatisfaction with marriage (Steinberg & Silverberg, 1987). With the passing of the stormy teenage years, and resolutions of parents' identity questions, the marriage may improve. The next two chapters focus on these transitions in parent-child relationships.

More concretely, children's maturity and departure from the home lessen the amount of work around the house for both parents, but especially the mother (Rexroat & Shehan, 1987). Wives devote more time to housework than husbands do throughout their marriage. However, husbands and wives in the postparental years spend less time—and more nearly equal amounts of time—working in or around the house than they have for years (Rexroat & Shehan, 1987). Perhaps the decrease in the amount of housework to be done, and the increased equity in its sharing, improves the marital climate.

Skolnick's (1981) longitudinal data suggest still another reason for changes over time in marital satisfaction. Comparing average ratings of marital quality when these couples were young adults with their ratings in middle adulthood, Skolnick found no evidence of change. This finding, then, failed to support the U-shaped curve pattern of marital satisfaction. Despite the stability of average scores, however, nearly half of the marriages in the sample had changed markedly in satisfaction ratings. Of these, approximately two-thirds of the couples found that their marriage had improved, whereas one-third had marriages that worsened.

Skolnick (1981) examined the extensive case histories for these couples in an effort to identify the sources of these changes, and concluded that situational factors most often provided an explanation. As she described:

> Money starts coming in after hard times or becomes more of a problem; difficulties in the years of diapers and bottles smooth out as the child grows older, or an easy parental career runs into difficulties when the children become teenagers; health problems go and come; in-law problems ease as the couple grows into middle age, or grandparents become a problem as they advance into old age. (Skolnick, 1981, p. 295)

More recent research also suggests that situational factors have a great deal to do with ratings of marital satisfaction. For example, a longitudinal survey of farm families revealed that downturns in the rural economy during the 1980s were closely associated with ratings of marital satisfaction and frequency of considering divorce (Johnson & Booth, 1990).

What about marriage in old age? In some ways, contemporary elderly couples are charting new territory. Because of increased life expectancy, marriages today can potentially endure for an unprecedented length of time. And, because the twentieth century has witnessed a decrease in family size, older couples have an extended **postparental phase** of married life when they do not have children living with them.

As the U-shaped curve of marital satisfaction implies, most older couples report high levels of marital satisfaction (e.g., Atchley & Miller, 1983; Bengtson et al., 1990). Remember, though, that such findings may reflect a "survivor" bias: individuals who were unhappy in marriage may have divorced before reaching old age. Certainly, not all researchers find high levels of satisfaction among elderly couples. For example, Depner and Ingersoll-Dayton (1985) found that unhappy marriages were more typical than happy ones in a random nationwide sample of adults aged 50 to 75 and over.

It is difficult to say how age-related transitions such as retirement and health changes affect older peoples' marriages. Some report that marital satisfaction increases following retirement (e.g., Gilford, 1984), although retirement may have a negative impact on marital satisfaction if the husband but not the wife is retired (Lee, 1988). In some studies, the onset of health problems in old age is associated with decreased marital satisfaction (Gilford, 1984). Others find that health problems have little impact on the quality of marriage (e.g., Johnson, 1985), or that taking care of a frail spouse intensifies feelings of commitment, closeness, and love (Fitting, Rabins, Lucas, & Eastham, 1986).

Examining marriage and satisfaction with marriage, then, leads to two general conclusions. First, marital satisfaction is often different (in both levels and sources) for husbands and wives; that conclusion presents a paradox, since gender differences appear in this situation of, perhaps, greatest intimacy between men and women. Second, most (though not all) work points to changes in satisfaction with marriage as the marriage endures, and those changes are apparently linked to factors outside of the marital relationship itself—changes in parenting responsibilities, husbands' and wives' individual development, and situational influences such as finances, retirement, and health.

ALTERNATIVES TO MARRIAGE

We have devoted so much attention to marriage because it is a normative experience. However, alternatives to marriage became much more visible in the 1970s, 1980s, and 1990s. These alternatives include remaining single, nonmarital cohabitation, and homosexual relationships.

Remaining single

Perhaps the most basic questions about those who remain single are how many people choose this option and what kinds of people most often make this choice. The numbers of unmarried people increased in the 1970s and 1980s, but still, the choice not to marry is atypical (Shostak, 1987). Recent statistics show that approximately 23 percent of men and 17 percent of women over age 18 are never married (Shostak, 1987). Not surprisingly, the number of never-married individuals decreases with age.

Women with high levels of intelligence, education, and occupational achievement are disproportionately likely to remain single, whereas the opposite is true for men (Macklin, 1980; 1987). Rates of remaining single also vary by race. African-Americans are remaining unmarried at increasing rates; in fact, demographers predict that if current trends continue through the remainder of the century most African-Americans will then stay single (Shostak, 1987).

How do other people react to singles? As the numbers and visibility of never-married adults have grown, their public image has improved. Shostak (1987) notes that lifelong single adults have historically been viewed as self-centered, neurotic, irresponsible, unfortunate, lonely, immoral, and deviant. However, by the mid-1970s very few people accepted these negative stereotypes; most contemporary Americans believed that remaining single was a legitimate alternative lifestyle.

Any one image of single people—whether it be the "swinging single" or the lonely spinster—is likely to be an oversimplification, and some have formulated typologies of never married people. Stein (1981) proposed that single individuals could be distinguished on the basis of whether they were single on a voluntary or involuntary basis, and whether they viewed their status as temporary or permanent. Elaborating on that typology, Shostak (1987) described as **ambivalent** unmarried individuals who were voluntarily but temporarily single; young adults pursuing advanced education or careers would probably fall into this category. **Resolved** singles are voluntarily single and expect to remain unmarried; some (e.g., priests, nuns) have lifestyles precluding marriage, and others simply prefer unmarried life (Shostak, 1987). **Wishfuls** are involuntarily and temporarily single (Shostak, 1987); clients of computer or videodating services would best fit into this category. Finally, Shostak (1987) describes **regretful** singles as those who are involuntarily single but expect to remain unmarried.

What are long-term consequences of remaining unmarried? Unfortunately, relatively little information is available describing quality of life for unmarried middle-aged and older adults. Cockrum and White (1985) found that, for middle-aged unmarried women, life satisfaction was predicted by the availability of attachment relationships and the extent of loneliness experienced. For middle-aged never married men, self-esteem and social integration predicted life satisfaction.

Approximately 5 percent of men and women aged 65 to 74 have remained single all their lives; among adults age 75 and older, the figures are 3.5 percent of the men and 6.2 percent of the women (Keith, 1986). In an early review of research on never-married older adults, Gubrium (1975) concluded that these individuals were lifelong isolates, that they were not particularly lonely in old age, that being single offers advantages in old age (since one does not experience bereavement), that few have any thoughts of marriage in old age, and that, consequently, elderly never-married people make up a special "social type."

More recent work contradicts most of Gubrium's (1975) conclusions. Rubenstein (1987) questioned married, widowed, and never-married elderly men and women and found that few of the never-married could be described as "lifelong isolates." Although some had lived alone throughout adulthood, others were currently living with family members or had lived with relatives for a substantial portion of their adult lives. Never-married individuals were lonely more often than the married people, but less often than the widowed respondents. Other research also shows that lifelong singles are socially active rather than isolated and that they enjoy satisfying relationships with family and friends (Bengtson et al., 1990; Stull & Scarisbrick-Hauser, 1989).

Of course, people who never marry are sheltered from the trauma of the death of a spouse, as Gubrium (1975) concluded. Nonetheless, the lifelong single older people in Rubenstein's (1987) study did confront loss with the deaths of parents, siblings, and friends, so they were not spared the experience of bereavement. Finally, Rubenstein found that some of the never-married men were thinking about marriage, and that some regreted that they had never married.

Cohabitation

Another option increasing in visibility in recent years is **cohabitation**. Most research on cohabitation—like most research on dating—has been conducted with college student samples (Atwater, 1985; Macklin, 1978). We know that cohabitation is a common experience for contemporary undergraduates, but we know far less about how often people not attending college live together. Census figures show that, while most cohabitors are relatively young (74 percent of women and 66 percent of men under age 35), cohabiting couples represent a wide age range, with 6 percent over age 65 (Macklin, 1987). There are sometimes financial incentives for middle-aged men and women to cohabit, since widows who remarry prior to age 60 can no longer collect their late husbands' Social Security benefits.

As cohabitation became more popular in the 1970s and 1980s, it became increasingly clear that this experience unfolds in different ways for different couples—much like marriage. Some distinguish these relationships according to level of commitment (e.g., Macklin, 1978; 1980). One could distinguish a temporary arrangement of convenience, an affectionate dating relationship involving shared living arrangements, a trial marriage arrangement, and cohabitation as a temporary or permanent alternative to marriage. Across these relationship types, one would see increasing commitment to the partner and to the relationship. In fact, for individuals living in permanent, committed cohabitation relationships, there are few differences between the partners' perceptions of their relationship and married couples' views of their relationships (Atwater, 1985; Macklin, 1978).

Cohabitation may be an important developmental experience. Virtually all cohabitants feel that the experience was tremendously valuable for their personal growth (Macklin, 1978). As Macklin (1978) points out, however, these self-report data must be taken with a grain of salt, particularly since there are no longitudinal studies on the developmental impact of cohabitation.

Researchers have compared the marital quality for couples who did and did not live together before marriage. Early studies revealed few differences between the two types of couples in marital satisfaction, conflict, egalitarianism, or emotional closeness (e.g., Macklin, 1987). However, more recent studies identified differences favoring married couples who had not cohabited prior to marriage (Macklin, 1987). These findings may reflect a "honeymoon effect" in the reports of the couples who had not cohabited, differences in expectations regarding marriage for those who did and did not cohabit, or the absence of structured, formal ways of assisting cohabiting couples to use their premarital experience to assess and enhance their relationship (Macklin, 1987).

Homosexuality

Homosexuality is another alternative to marriage. Although many people stereotype homosexuals, there is at least as much diversity in homosexual lifestyles as there is among married or cohabiting couples. A. P. Bell and M. S. Weinberg (1978) identified five kinds of lifestyles among male and female homosexuals in the San Francisco area.

In Bell and Weinberg's (1978) sample, the **close-coupled** homosexuals were involved in enduring monogamous relationships. These individuals reported few sexual problems and were happy and self-accepting. The **open-coupled** homosexuals lived with a lover, but were less satisfied with the relationship than were the close-coupled homosexuals. Many of the open-coupled individuals were interested in sexual contacts outside of their cohabitant relationship.

Functional homosexuals were not involved in an exclusive relationship, but had several sexual partners. Many were active in the gay liberation movement, and many had experienced difficulties (e.g., arrests, convictions) related to their sexual orientation. Nonetheless, few expressed regret or discomfort regarding their sexual orientation. These individuals were "functional" in the sense of being energetic, self-reliant, cheerful, optimistic, and self-accepting.

In contrast, the **dysfunctionals** were troubled, poorly adjusted individuals. Many regretted being homosexual and reported sexual problems. Of all of the groups identified in this study, these homosexuals were the most likely to have experienced legal problems or job difficulties related to their sexuality. Finally, the **asexuals** were generally uninvolved with others: they had few sexual contacts, and reported sexual problems.

Recall from Chapter Four (see pp. 89–91) that the 1980s witnessed growing awareness of acquired immunodeficiency syndrome (AIDS). Although it is certain that this awareness will have a continuing impact on homosexual life styles, it is difficult to say what the long-term impact will be. It is reasonable to speculate that some of the lifestyles that Bell and Weinberg (1978) described might become less frequent. In particular, the "functional" and "open-coupled" relationships might place one at an especially high risk of being infected.

More recent work highlighting the diversity of homosexual lifestyles contrasts gay and lesbian relationships. Although gay and lesbian couples living together in long-term relationships do not differ in their levels of commitment, lesbians do things together and confide in one another more often than gay men do (Macklin, 1987). Lesbian couples are more likely to be monogamous than are gay men, they have sex less frequently than gay couples do (at least early in their relationships), and they are more likely to stay together than are gay men (Blumenstein & Schwartz, 1983). Other researchers have contrasted lesbians' and heterosexual couples' relationships. The two types of couples do not differ in scores on measures of relationship quality; however, lesbians report that lovemaking leads to orgasm more often than women in heterosexual relationships and lesbians express less concern about unequal power in their relationships than women in heterosexual relationships do (Macklin, 1987).

For virtually all homosexuals in contemporary America, discrimination and the threat of discrimination are serious problems. Goodman, Lakey, Lashof, and Thorne (1983) explain that because of the "heterosexual assumption" that everyone is and should be heterosexual, homosexuals live in an alien world in which their most personal feelings are deemed illegitimate. More concretely, these authors describe laws forbidding homosexuality, discrimination in the workplace, physical threats and assaults against homosexuals, little acceptance by most religious bodies, neglect of homosexuality in many sex education programs, and many physicians' inadequate awareness of homosexuals' needs.

Homosexuals also face problems in their family relationships (Goodman et al., 1983). Parents are sometimes unable or unwilling to accept their children's homosexuality, so that a homosexual son or daughter may never have their lover welcomed into the family as a daughter- or son-in-law would be. Even homosexual relationships of many years' duration cannot be legally sanctioned as marriages, and formerly married homosexuals may lose access to their children as a result of their sexual orientation.

DIVORCE AND REMARRIAGE

Divorce

Divorce rates, like many other demographic statistics, show both historical period effects and cohort effects; the coming of age of the "Baby Boom" generation has been associated with particularly high divorce rates (e.g., Norton & Moorman, 1987). Further, divorce rates vary according to region of the country, race, and age. Divorce occurs more frequently in the Western regions of the United States than in other parts of the country, among African-Americans and non-Hispanic Caucasians than among Hispanic groups, and among young adults than among middle-aged and older adults (e.g., Bengtson et al., 1990; Frisbie, 1986; Uhlenberg, Cooney, & Boyd, 1990). Although divorce rates have risen for older adults, the increase has been much lower than for younger adults (Treas & Bengtson, 1987). Scholars predict, however, that if current trends continue there will be a dramatic increase in the proportion of middle-aged and older women who are divorced (Uhlenberg et al., 1990).

Often, the decision to seek a divorce evolves over a long period—months or even years—and one spouse (often the wife) is much more in favor of the divorce than the other (Wallerstein & Kelly, 1980). Not surprisingly, the spouse who expresses more reluctance to divorce usually experiences greater emotional stress than his or her partner. No matter how much in favor of a divorce one is, however, the event typically is traumatic.

J. B. Kelly (1982), in a recent overview of research on divorce, outlined six typical patterns of emotional reaction. She also pointed out that these patterns are by no means mutually exclusive. Indeed, one might experience several of these emotions at once.

Anger is the most common emotional reaction to divorce. For most couples, separation involves conflict and bitterness. When children are involved, it is even more likely that the couple will experience prolonged conflict. Another common emotional reaction is *depression*; men and women find divorce depressing for different reasons. For men, custody decisions and visitation arrangements are often a source of distress. Women are more likely to be depressed as a consequence of the financial impact and loneliness.

Some divorced people report feelings of *disequilibrium*: these individuals find their own behavior unpredictable and disturbing. Some might engage in violence, even though they would normally never behave that way. Despite the negative emotions leading up to divorce, many divorced people find that they still have feelings of *attachment* to their former spouse; these feelings are probably maladaptive, since researchers report that reducing attachment to the ex-spouse is central to post-divorce adjustment (Tschann, Johnston, & Wallerstein, 1989). Feelings of *relief* also occur, especially for women who may now feel free from tension, fear, conflict, and ambivalence. Divorced women also commonly report feeling that they have a *new chance in life*. The divorce may be a turning point prompting them to explore new educational or career opportunities.

Partly because it is a less common experience, the breakup of marriage in the middle and later years can be more trying and complex than it is earlier in adulthood. What kinds of circumstances prompt couples to end a marriage of many years duration? What unique stresses do these men and women confront?

Research focused specifically on divorce in middle and later adulthood is scarce, and thus there is little information on the circumstances leading to divorce in later life. In one study, middle-aged formerly married couples said that disagreements had not been a problem, but that some "crisis event" had forced them to recognize that much of the earlier shared pleasure and communication in their relationship had diminished (Hayes, Stinnett, & DeFrain, 1980). The devitalized marriage (Cuber & Harroff, 1965; see Box 10.1, pp. 262–263), then, cannot always be counted on as an enduring pattern.

Clinicians who work with middle-aged couples suggest other stressors that can lead to divorce. According to N. W. Turner (1980), divorce may be a reaction to personal growth or change in oneself or the spouse. If Margarita experiences substantial change in her own values, goals, or talents, then she forces her husband Leon to adapt in order for the marriage to endure. If Leon is unable or unwilling to adjust, their marriage may not survive. Turner also points out that most middle-aged married couples have been together long enough to make extensive comparisons between their own marriage and the marriages of their friends, neighbors, and relatives. When these comparisons reflect unfavorably on the marriage, some couples divorce.

Of course, divorce is traumatic at any age. The available information clearly suggests, though, that it is more difficult for middle-aged and older couples ending a long-term marriage than for younger people who have been married a shorter time. In one of the few studies comparing young, middle-aged, and older individuals' psychological reactions to divorce, Chiriboga (1982) found that recently separated middle-aged and older individuals reported greater unhappiness, fewer positive emotional experiences, more difficulty dealing with social situations, more personal discomfort, and a more pessimistic outlook on the past and future than did younger adults. Men and women in their fifties, sixties, or seventies experienced the greatest difficulty, whereas those in their forties reacted more like adults in their twenties and thirties.

All divorced people must make radical changes in their patterns of social interaction and sexual relationships. As a newly single person, one must reformulate relationships with friends, family, and acquaintances. According to Kitson and Raschke (1981), many middle-aged divorced people feel especially insecure about re-establishing a single lifestyle after years of marriage. For women, at least, this insecurity probably has a realistic basis. Reviewers report that middle-aged and older women often have few social ties and lack satisfying sexual relationships (e.g., Kelly, 1982).

There are other kinds of adjustments that are unique to the older divorcing couple. Relationships with adult children and aging parents pose challenges, but may also offer resources. Hagestad, Smyer, and Stierman (1984) found that middle-aged women often turned to their adult children and their parents for support during the crisis of divorce, whereas middle-aged men reported that their children and parents reacted negatively to their divorce. For both men and women, relationships with parents rarely changed in quality as a result of their divorce (Hagestad et al., 1984). When these relationships did change, they were more likely to improve than worsen. Ironically, some

The financial impact of divorce can be devastating, especially for women.

middle-aged respondents confided that fear of their parents' disapproval had led them to delay the divorce.

More concretely, the economic implications of dissolving a marriage of long duration are more imposing than they are for shorter-term marriages. Middle-aged and older couples, in general, have more extensive joint assets (e.g., homes, investments, savings, business holdings) to be divided than younger couples do. The necessary legal and economic arrangements can be complex, prolonged, and traumatic for all involved (Turner, 1980; Raschke, 1987).

Middle-aged and elderly women may face special financial jeopardy when they divorce, especially women who devoted their youth to full-time homemaking and supporting their husbands' climb up the corporate or professional ladder (e.g., Raschke, 1987; Uhlenberg et al., 1990). These displaced homemakers may find that they have little legal claim to the fruits of the husband's career (including Social Security or pension benefits), despite the substantial contribution they made to establishing that career. Because of gender differences in career patterns and earnings, of course, men are far less likely to suffer similar financial losses from divorce. For many men, the main financial consequence of divorce is child support.

One recent analysis further suggests that part of the devastating financial impact of divorce stems from its effect on patterns of saving throughout the life cycle (Fethke, 1989). Most people have earnings that parallel expenses up to about age 45, and they consequently do little saving as young adults. Between 45 and 60, most are able to save, and then draw on their savings after age 60, when expenses generally outpace earnings (Kotlikoff & Summers, 1981). When divorce interrupts the savings cycle or destroys assets, however, few are able to make up for this effect by saving more later on (Fethke, 1989). Given the high divorce rates of contemporary married couples, more older adults in the future will have experienced a divorce. There may be, then, a new class of elderly poor who have experienced the breakup of their marriage.

What circumstances are associated with the extent to which one adjusts following divorce? Not surprisingly, the level of personal resources that one enjoyed prior to divorce positively affects adjustment, whereas conflict with the ex-spouse during the separation period interferes with adjustment (Tschann et al., 1989). Personal resources important to adjustment include socioeconomic status, stable psychological functioning, and a strong kinship and friendship network (Bengtson et al., 1990; Tschann et al., 1989).

Remarriage

Many divorced people eventually remarry, although the rate of remarriage following divorce has decreased in recent years (Norton & Moorman, 1987). According to one estimate, nearly 40 percent of married couples include a previously married partner (National Center for Health Statistics, 1980). Men are more likely than women to remarry throughout adulthood (Spanier &

Furstenberg, 1987), and this gender difference increases with age (Bengtson et al., 1990; Norton & Moorman, 1987).

Remarriage relationships undoubtedly differ from initial marriages in many ways. One or both partners may be adapting to stepchildren and the ambiguities of stepfamily roles (see Chapter Eleven, pp. 282–288) (Crosbie-Burnett, 1989). Finances typically present greater challenges for remarried than first-married couples, often because of child support arrangements (Crosbie-Burnett, 1989; Lown, McFadden, & Crossman, 1989). A formerly married man or woman inevitably views the subsequent marriage through a psychological "lens" created by experience in the initial marriage (e.g., Moss & Moss, 1980a; Spanier & Furstenberg, 1987). Experience in the initial marriage creates expectations and habits that, deliberately or not, will affect the new marriage.

OPEN QUESTIONS   BOX 10.2

Are remarriages more successful than first marriages?

If getting married is an expression of hope and faith in the future, then getting remarried must be a triumph of optimism over painful experience. Most remarried individuals probably anticipate that their new marriage will be better than their former one. After all, experience surely brings skill in judging potential partners and dealing with the stresses of married life. Is this optimism well-founded? How do remarriages compare to initial ones?

Divorce rates are higher for remarriages than for initial marriages, although the difference is slight (Spanier & Furstenberg, 1987). The higher divorce rate for remarriages may be because there are few norms guiding behavior for remarried couples and for stepparent-stepchild relationships (e.g., Cherlin, 1978). It may also be that someone who has experienced divorce in the past is less reluctant to end an unsatisfying second marriage with a second divorce (Spanier & Furstenberg, 1987). Despite the stigma attached to multiple divorces, there is the knowledge that one has survived the emotional and legal turmoil of divorce before and can do so again.

Although researchers have compared satisfaction with initial marriages and remarriages, the findings are contradictory. Some find higher quality in initial marriages, others find that remarriages are more successful, and still others report no differences (Vemer, Coleman, Ganong, & Cooper, 1989). Vemer

et al. (1989) used meta-analysis to review studies examining marital satisfaction in remarriage. Meta-analysis allows a researcher to examine the findings of previous studies and statistically measure the consistency and strength of differences (such as those between first marriages and remarriages) that are identified.

Vemer et al. (1989) found that meta-analysis pointed to greater marital satisfaction among couples in their first marriage than among remarried couples. However, they noted that the difference in levels of satisfaction was so small that it probably lacked any practical significance. The difference was much too small to justify warning divorced individuals to have second thoughts about getting married again, for example.

Although research gives us a tentative "no" to the question of whether remarriages are more successful than initial marriages, the further question of why this is so remains open. As we have noted, some remarriages confront strains that do not arise in initial marriages (e.g., stepfamily relations) and some problems that come up in any marriage (e.g., finances) are particularly troubling for remarried couples. Perhaps as professionals in the future give more attention to helping remarried couples to deal with such issues, a more definitive answer to questions concerning the relative quality of first marriages and subsequent marriages will emerge.

Further, someone who remarries becomes a member of a second "marriage cohort" (e.g., Spanier & Furstenberg, 1987). If Jay married for the first time as a young man in the 1960s, and then again as a middle-aged man in the 1980s, he has been subject to two sets of cultural standards regarding marriage and the roles of husbands and wives. In the process, he has been forced to reevaluate his own notions of married life.

Common sense and optimism would suggest that people who remarry express greater satisfaction with their later marriage than their first marriage. It is reasonable to hope that we learn from experience, even the bitter experiences of a failed marriage and divorce. That may not be the case, though. The *Open Questions* box reviews evidence regarding the relative success of first marriages as compared to remarriages.

There has been little study of remarriage in old age. Motivations prompting remarriage in old age include companionship and, for women, concerns with finances and home maintenance (Bengtson et al., 1990; Gentry & Shulman, 1989). Since divorce rates are still lower in middle and later adulthood than in early adulthood (see above), elderly couples who remarry are more likely to have lost a former spouse to death than to divorce. Widowed older people who remarry usually knew one another prior to the death of their former spouse (Bengtson et al., 1990). Older individuals in good health, those with adequate finances, those who had had successful initial marriages, and those with support for the remarriage from their friends and relatives are the ones most likely to remarry (Bengtson et al., 1990).

SUMMARY

Predictors of satisfaction with dating relationships include personality factors, feelings of equity in the relationship, intimacy in the relationship (for men), perceived rewards in the relationship, and dating partners' agreement about their level of intimacy. Scientists have provided ample evidence of assortativeness in mate selection, and family sociologists have proposed several exchange theories of mate selection. One of the most important exchange approaches is Stimulus-Value-Role theory.

Among newly married couples, there are four components of marital satisfaction: happiness, equity, personal competence, and perceived control. Generally, husbands express higher levels of marital satisfaction than do wives; expectations regarding marriage are also important correlates of marital satisfaction. Research on changes in marital satisfaction over the life cycle most often documents a "U-shaped curve" of marital satisfaction. Alternatives to marriage became more visible in the 1970s, 1980s, and 1990s. These alternatives include remaining single, cohabitation, and homosexuality.

Emotional reactions to divorce include anger, depression, disequilibrium, continuing attachment to the former spouse, relief, and feeling that one has a new chance in life. Partly because it is a less common experience, the breakup of marriage in the middle and later years can be more trying and complex than it is earlier in adulthood. Many divorced people eventually remarry, although the rate of remarriage following divorce has decreased in recent years. Researchers have compared satisfaction with initial marriages and remarriages, and most evidence suggests that remarriages are not more successful than initial marriages.

KEY TERMS

Ambivalent
Asexual
Assortativeness
Balanced connection
Behavior exchange theory (BET)
Close-coupled
Cohabitation
Couple-centered connection
Dysfunctional
Exchange theories
Family-centered connection
Functional
Loose connection

Marital noncohabitation
Marital well-being
Open-coupled
Postparental phase
Regretful
Resolved
Role compatibility stage
Stimulus stage
Stimulus-value-role (SVR) theory
U-shaped curve
Value comparison stage
Wishful

SUGGESTIONS FOR FURTHER READING

Brubaker, T. H. (1985). *Later Life Families*. Beverly Hills: Sage Publications.

Brubaker, T. H. (1990). *Family Relationships in Later Life* (2nd Edition). Beverly Hills: Sage Publications.

Cargan, L., & Melko, M. (1982). *Singles: Myths and Realities*. Beverly Hills: Sage Publications.

Goodman, G., Lakey, G., Lashof, J., & Thorne, E. (1983). *No Turning Back: Lesbian and Gay Liberation for the '80s*. Philadelphia: New Society Publishers.

Hunter, S., & Sundel, M. (Eds.). (1989). *Midlife Myths: Issues, Findings, and Practice Implications*. Newbury Park, CA: Sage Publications.

Troll, L. E. (1986). *Family Issues in Current Gerontology*. New York: Springer

CHAPTER ELEVEN

RELATIONSHIPS BETWEEN GENERATIONS: AFFECTION AND INTERACTION

Does being a good parent come naturally? Do most marriages break up when the children grow up and leave home? Are most grandparents today like elderly, nurturing ones pictured on television? This chapter examines reasons that people have children, the transition to parenthood, single parenting and stepparenting, and relationships between older parents and grown-up children. Voluntary childlessness, and some of the reasons that people do not wish to have children, are also considered. Finally, we survey grandparenthood and its impact on mental health, and the increasingly common experience of being a great-grandparent.

Questions to consider in reading the chapter include:

Why do people have children? What are motivations for not having children? What stresses and satisfactions do new parents confront?

How do parents react to the "empty nest"?

What is the extent of geographic proximity, interaction, and affection between elderly parents and adult children?

How does grandparenthood vary according to grandparents' age, gender, race, and ethnicity? What is it like to be a great-grandparent?

PARENTHOOD

Why do people have children?
Cross-cultural variation in motivations

Although American couples express common reasons for childbearing, there is variety across cultures in motivations for having children. The *Diversity in Adulthood* box explores reasons for having children from a cross-cultural perspective.

Historically, Americans' reasons for having children were largely pragmatic. In preindustrial America, the family was a unit of production and children provided physical labor. Since infant mortality rates were high prior to the twentieth century, families were large to insure a sufficient labor supply. Today, however, very few American parents mention utilitarian reasons for having children (Hoffman, 1987). In recent surveys, the reasons that people give for having children included establishing a close relationship, having a "real" family life, and taking part in training a young person (Campbell, Townes, & Beach, 1982; Neal, Groat, & Wicks, 1989).

Remaining child-free

Recall from Chapter Three that infertility can be emotionally devastating for those who want to have children. What is known, though, about people who choose not to parent? What considerations lead to such a decision, and what impact does the choice have?

Some suggest that the choice to remain childless has become more popular since the 1960s (e.g., Faux, 1984; Veevers, 1979). However, census data actually reveal little change in the frequency of this decision. According to Houseknecht (1987), the percentage of married women of childbearing age who expect to remain childless has remained at approximately 5 percent since the 1960s. That figure, of course, does not reflect the numbers of unmarried women and of men who choose to remain child-free.

Most often, the wife initiates the decision not to have children, although husband-initiated, mutual, and independent decision making also occur (Houseknecht, 1987). Veevers (1980) distinguished two patterns through which individuals or couples reach a decision to remain child-free. Some are **early articulators**, who know from youth (often before marriage) that they will never want children. Early articulators' choice is a central aspect of their personality, entirely independent of the spouse or other life circumstances. Others are **postponers** who initially believe that they will have children "someday" (Veevers, 1980). As they repeatedly postpone parenthood, however, these individuals and couples gradually realize that they do not ever want to have children.

Child-free couples and individuals offer several rationales for their decision (Houseknecht, 1987). Most explain that they want to remain free from

---

BOX 11.1 *DIVERSITY IN ADULTHOOD*

Why have children? It depends on culture!

Contemporary Americans express varied motivations for having children. What about people in other cultures? Do they have similar notions, or are their ideas dramatically different from those voiced in America today?

Cross-cultural research sheds some light on these questions. One particularly important research program was the Cross-National Value of Children study conducted by Lois Hoffman and her colleagues (e.g., Hoffman, 1987). Hoffman's work was guided by the notion that children fulfill parents' needs. In any culture, the needs that children satisfy depend on the importance of those needs in that culture, the availability of alternative means of need satisfaction, and the extent to which having children actually can satisfy those needs. In the Cross-National Value of Children study, investigators from eight countries—Indonesia, Korea, the Philippines, Singapore, Taiwan, Thailand, Turkey, and the United States—interviewed young married women, and sometimes their husbands. In each country, parents identified the advantages of having children, as opposed to remaining childless.

There were eight needs that children apparently satisfy. Women in several countries (Turkey, Indonesia, Thailand) stressed the economic value of children. These women believed that children would be a reliable source of help and support, both now and when the children reached adulthood. Women in other non-Western countries (Philippines, Korea, Taiwan, Singapore) most often mentioned the stimulation and fun that children provide; American women also referred to this advantage, but more often said that the opportunities for affection that children provide were important. Women in the other seven countries mentioned children as a source of affection less often than the American women, and much less often than they mentioned other advantages of childrearing.

Women identified still other advantages to having children. Particularly in Taiwan and Indonesia, some women felt that having children was an expansion of self. Some women in the United States and Turkey asserted that one attains adult status when one becomes a mother. Some women, particularly the Korean women, viewed having children as an opportunity for achievement. A few women in each country cited moral reasons or the desire for power as motivations for childrearing.

Certainly, this project reveals a wide variety of reasons that women, at least, wish to have children. Although the study did include participants from an impressive array of cultural backgrounds, we should also recognize that this single study did not represent the full range of human cultures. Indeed, no single piece of work possibly could reflect that degree of diversity! While one can comfortably assert, then, that culture has a strong impact upon the way that adults feel about parenthood, there is still much to learn about the many ways in which that impact is experienced in a broad array of societies.

---

child-care responsibility and to enjoy greater opportunities for self-fulfillment and growth than they could expect as parents. Other reasons are the desire for a more satisfactory marriage, women's career considerations, financial issues, concern about overpopulation, and dislike of children.

Whatever the motivation, most people who choose to remain child-free find that other people react negatively to their choice. Men and women who forego parenthood are often believed to be selfish, immature, or cold (e.g., Bernard, 1974; Faux, 1984; Houseknecht, 1987). However, personal well-being is actually quite similar for mothers and child-free wives, and child-free wives may

Child-free marriages may provide greater intimacy and intellectual stimulation than marriages with children.

enjoy more time with their husbands and more intellectual stimulation in their marriages than mothers (Callen, 1987).

Remaining child-free is not associated with long-term negative consequences. Compared to elderly parents, older individuals without children do not differ in psychological well-being, happiness, morale, loneliness, or life satisfaction (Bengtson, Rosenthal, & Burton, 1990). In later life, individuals without children may establish satisfying bonds with extended kin, such as nephews or nieces, or with unrelated individuals who are "as close as family" (Bengtson et al., 1990). However, these networks may be less viable than networks including children and grandchildren for older individuals who are frail and need long-term care (Bengtson et al., 1990).

Pregnancy and birth: Women's and men's unique experiences

The physiological and psychological events of pregnancy and childbirth profoundly affect women. Despite the moment of these consequences, there has been relatively little published research on women's reactions to pregnancy per se. There has been even less work exploring men's reactions to impending fatherhood, although most would agree that this transition is surely important for men as well.

In one study of first-time mothers, Leifer (1977) found that most reported mixed and shifting emotional reactions to pregnancy and the postpartum period. Overall reactions were related to the symbolic meaning of the pregnancy: women who viewed pregnancy as an opportunity for growth had more positive responses than those who considered it a symbol of security. Among the most common negative feelings were anxiety about the health of the fetus and embarrassment about the sexual implications of pregnancy (Leifer, 1977; Osofsky & Osofsky, 1984).

The last few weeks of pregnancy were marked by still further emotional changes (Leifer, 1977). Many women found that their interest and emotions focused increasingly on the fetus. Some were emotionally fragile, experiencing mood swings, anxiety, and irritability. But many also reported feelings of well-being and security.

Most women reacted to birth itself with elation (Leifer, 1977). For most, however, the postpartum period was colored by negative emotions. Some women felt irritated, isolated, and depressed. Initially, child care was overwhelming. After a few months, however, many confessed to boredom with feeding, diapering, bathing the baby, and the like. Most were also concerned about the impact of parenthood on their marriage, their household, and their lifestyle.

More recently, Gloger-Tippelt (1983) proposed that pregnancy be viewed as a sequence of four phases (see below) proceeding along three levels: the biological level (e.g., fetal development and related hormonal and physiological changes in the mother), the psychological level (e.g., the woman's perceptions and evaluations of her pregnancy), and the social level (e.g., impacts of the pregnancy on close family relationships and social roles). Of course, these levels are not entirely distinct: events on one level trigger and influence events on the other levels.

The biological changes of pregnancy probably influence the woman's psychological reaction to childbearing, for example. The way that the woman's partner, family, and friends react to the pregnancy will almost certainly reflect and influence her own psychological response to her condition. Also, the woman's status prior to the pregnancy on the biological level (e.g., age, general health, previous pregnancies and miscarriages), the psychological level (e.g., motivation for pregnancy, extent to which the pregnancy is welcome), and the social level (e.g., marital status, economic status, attitudes of husband and parents, general social norms) can affect the pregnancy (Gloger-Tippelt, 1983).

The first phase in Gloger-Tippelt's (1983) model is **disruption**. This phase lasts from conception to 12 weeks; during this time, radical change occurs on all levels. With dramatic hormonal and physiological shifts as well as the prospect of changing identity and social roles, this stage may be stressful. The phase of **adaptation** (12 to 20 weeks), however, is calmer. Distressing physical symptoms, such as morning sickness, have usually subsided; identity changes become more comfortable; and the woman makes plans regarding changes in her lifestyle. During the **centering** phase (20 to 32 weeks), the woman becomes more aware of her body and more introspective, and her energies are concentrated on the developing fetus. As the pregnancy becomes increasingly visible, others may respond to the woman as simply "pregnant" rather than as an individual. Her partner and coworkers, for example, may dismiss any irritation or anxiety that the woman expresses as simply the result of her pregnancy.

The final phase of **anticipation and preparation** (32 weeks to birth) is characterized by the woman's growing orientation toward the future. According to Gloger-Tippelt (1983) and other scholars (e.g., Osofsky & Osofsky, 1984), the more anticipatory socialization and coping the woman experiences, the more positive her birth and postpartum period are likely to be. In other words, the more things that the woman does to learn about and prepare for parenthood before the birth, the smoother her transition to parenting will probably be. Gathering information about Lamaze and other prepared childbirth methods, the effects of medication on labor and the fetus, breathing and relaxation techniques, and infant care are possible means of anticipatory socialization.

In addition to preparation and education, the quality of the marriage can affect the pregnancy. Low levels of marital satisfaction are associated with pregnancy complications (e.g., Snowden, Schott, Awalt, & Gillis-Knox, 1988), whereas support from the husband is associated with low levels of distress (Liese, Snowden, & Ford, 1989). Interestingly, support from a partner (even the father of the fetus) is not related to unmarried pregnant women's levels of distress (Liese et al., 1989). Perhaps because these unmarried women's expectations for support from the partner are different from those of a pregnant wife, the association between support and distress are correspondingly different for married and unmarried pregnant women.

Pregnancy and birth are of tremendous significance for fathers-to-be, as well as for future mothers. However, men's reactions to pregnancy and birth have been studied less extensively than women's reactions. Furthermore, problems of self-selected, and possibly biased, samples loom large in the study of impending fatherhood. Probably, men interested in participating in this sort of research are also unusually concerned about being good fathers.

Like women, most men experience mixed and shifting emotional reactions to their wife's or partner's pregnancy (May & Perrin, 1985; Osofsky & Osofsky, 1984). These reactions include ambivalence and confusion, wonder and excitement, nurturance and tenderness, worry and anxiety, and jealousy and rivalry. In addition, most expectant fathers are concerned with practical issues such as financial matters, plans for labor and delivery, the role that they will play in the child's birth, and how the baby's birth will affect the relationship with their wife or partner (May & Perrin, 1985). Some fathers experience a **couvade syndrome** involving physical distress in reaction to the pregnancy (May & Perrin, 1985). These men sometimes gain or lose weight, notice changes in appetite (including food cravings), feel unusually tired, or have backaches.

Advance preparation for birth and parenting is just as important for expectant fathers as for expectant mothers. Not being well-informed about parenting makes adjustment to fatherhood more difficult, and programs and courses that prepare a couple for postpartum changes in their relationship are especially helpful to new fathers (Osofsky & Osofsky, 1984).

The transition to parenthood

Both classic and recent work portrays the transition to parenthood as a stressful experience. Family sociologist Alice Rossi (1968) was among the first to identify aspects of parenthood that make this passage difficult. Rossi points out that there is cultural pressure to become a parent. Women more than men may feel that others do not think of them as "real adults" until they have a baby.

Furthermore, parenthood is a unique adult role since it may be assumed involuntarily, as the result of an unplanned and unwanted pregnancy (Rossi, 1968). Once one becomes a parent, there is no turning back: there is no equivalent to divorce for individuals who are dissatisfied with parenthood. In contrast, the roles of husband or wife and of worker (other major adult roles) are ones that most people enter more or less voluntarily and can terminate if they are dissatisfied.

Rossi (1968) also argues that few adults are adequately prepared to become parents. Schools provide few opportunities to learn effective parenting skills, and the opportunities to prepare for parenthood during pregnancy are limited. Expectant parents can certainly learn to feed, bathe, and diaper a baby, and those concrete skills are important. But parents cannot know in advance what their child's temperament will be like, and that factor—among other unknowns—can drastically affect their experience as parents.

In addition, preparation for parenthood is inadequate because the transition is so abrupt. As Rossi (1968) describes, taking on responsibility for a completely dependent and demanding infant is much like making an overnight career jump from college freshman to full professor and department chair. It is also difficult to prepare to be a good parent because there are so many notions of what a good parent is like: friends, family, neighbors, and nearly everyone else under the sun might offer a different definition.

Rossi (1968), then, paints a discouraging portrait of the transition to parenthood. Recent research also suggests that the early years of parenthood, at least, are stressful. One sample of first-time parents reported problems that they experienced when their infants were 3, 6, 9, and 12 months old (McKim, 1987). Working mothers and parents of difficult infants reported the most problems, although virtually all parents experienced some strain. Infant illness was the most frequent problem at each age (see Figure 11.1). Other problems were concerns about infant nutrition; crying; needs for information; problems with role conflict, the marriage, or depression; or congenital anomalies (e.g., physical handicaps, chronic illnesses) of their infants. In other research, many of the same concerns have been reported, as well as problems related to relationships with in-laws, other children, and stepchildren (Ventura, 1987).

Other work suggests that fathers' levels of stress reflect both the infant's characteristics and the father's involvement with the infant (Hawkins & Belsky, 1989). Men who have daughters may experience a boost to their self-esteem during the first few months of their baby's life. In contrast, fathers of sons—who are often more involved in child care—may find that their self-esteem declines, perhaps because they are struggling with unfamiliar duties.

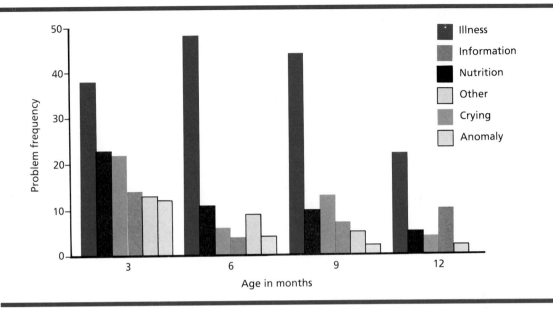

Figure 11.1
Problems reported by new parents. (Source: McKim, "Transition to What? New Parents' Problems in the First Year," *Journal on Marriage and Family Relations, 36* (1): 22–25. Copyrighted 1987 by the National Council on Family Relations, 3989 Central Ave. N.E., Suite #550, Minneapolis, MN 55421. Reprinted by permission.)

Recall from the last chapter that marital satisfaction typically declines during the childrearing years; this pattern may reflect the hard work entailed in being a parent. MacDermid, Huston, and McHale (1990) found that spouses' activities became more child-centered and less couple-centered, and that they divided household tasks more along traditional gender lines, following children's birth. Couples in their research also reported decreased marital satisfaction. Other research shows, though, that such a decline is by no means inevitable. In one study, some parents did experience diminished marital quality, but others reported either no change or enhanced satisfaction with their marriage (Belsky & Rovine, 1990).

Although the transition to parenthood can be difficult, professionals have found ways to minimize this stress. Remember that preparatory education concerning childbirth and parenting is often helpful (e.g., Gloger-Tippelt, 1983; Osofsky & Osofsky, 1984). Parent training programs are offered in many communities through hospitals, community mental health centers, YWCAs and YMCAs, and university extension or outreach services. Support from extended family members (particularly parents and grandparents) also reduces the stresses of parenting, particularly for African-American parents (e.g., Harrison, Serafica, & McAdoo, 1984).

We should also recognize the more positive aspects of the transition to parenthood. Most new parents enjoy their babies, despite the stress. Sources of enjoyment include pride in the baby's development, the fun of playing with the baby, the absence of boredom in one's life, and discovery of a new purpose in life (Russell, 1974).

Parenting under special circumstances

Single mothers and fathers   Demographers estimated in the mid-1980s that nearly two-thirds of the nation's children would spend some time in a single-parent household before reaching adulthood (e.g., Norton & Glick, 1986). Single parents are a diverse group. One may become a single parent as a result of divorce, separation, desertion, or the choice to have children as a single person. One may also be a single parent temporarily, if the spouse is incarcerated or serving in the military. Some single parents have sole custody of their children, while others share custody; and, some noncustodial single parents have virtually no opportunities to see their children. Finally, some single parents are homosexuals; the *Open Questions* box identifies some of the issues surrounding homosexual parenting.

Given this variety, it is perilous to generalize about stresses of single parenting. However, scholars have reached some tentative conclusions about single mothers' experiences; unfortunately, much less is known about single fathers. Most single mothers face a financial struggle (e.g., McLanahan & Booth, 1989; Norton & Glick, 1986), although a strong informal support network may mediate that stress (e.g., Gladow & Ray, 1986). A less common problem is when intergenerational boundaries blur, and the single mother and her young adolescent develop a quasipeer relationship (e.g., Glenwick & Mowrey, 1986). Many single mothers and virtually all single fathers work outside of the home, and these parents are often burdened as they strive to manage work and parenthood (e.g., Burden, 1986; Sanik & Mauldin, 1986). Again, a strong informal support network can be critically important (e.g., Hanson, 1986; Ihinger-Tallman, 1986).

The support network, however, can itself create still other problems. Grandparents are central figures in many single mothers' support networks (e.g., Cherlin & Furstenberg, 1985; Johnson, 1985). In one recent study, single mothers emphasized the value of grandparents' support but also stressed that grandparents' interference in childrearing could cause problems (Thomas, 1990a).

Noncustodial fathers may encounter difficulties when they attempt to implement court-ordered visitation arrangements: some custodial mothers actively resist fathers' visitation. These single fathers may face prolonged, frustrating, and costly legal battles to have court-ordered visitation agreements enforced; some never succeed. However, courts have shown increased willingness to award custody to single fathers, and recent research shows that gender of the custodial parent is unrelated to intimacy in the parent-child bond, the

Should homosexuals be allowed to rear children?

Some assert that Americans' traditionally pejorative attitudes toward homosexuality have mellowed since the mid-1950s (e.g., Bozett, 1988). Admittedly, the Gay Liberation Movement coalesced in the late 1960s, homosexuality has been removed from the ranks of psychiatric disorders, and homosexual communities and networks are visible presences in many American cities today. Nonetheless, discrimination against homosexuals continues, and many homosexual men and women keep their sexual preference hidden out of fear of discrimination.

Family life is one area in which homosexuals may confront discriminatory actions. Homosexuals who have been married may lose custody—or even visitation access—to their children. Those who have never been married and who want to have children are likely to find adoption difficult, if not impossible. On what bases are such actions rationalized? To what extent does evidence support these rationalizations?

Marciano (1985) summarized three arguments frequently leveled against homosexual parenting. Such family forms, she asserts, are seen as unnatural and thus inherently deviant. Homosexuality is often condemned on religious grounds, as these unions are nowhere sanctioned in the scriptures. Finally, some assert that children growing up under the guidance of homosexual parents will probably become homosexual themselves.

Marciano's first two arguments are not open to evaluation by empirical methods, and will not be addressed here. However, there is scientific evidence

bearing on homosexual parents' impact on their children. Although long-term longitudinal studies have not been published, there is no compelling evidence that children reared by homosexual parents are disproportionately likely to develop problems of sexual identity—or to become homosexual (e.g., Bozett, 1988; Richardson, 1981). Nor do these children suffer from social isolation (Richardson, 1981), or differ from children reared by heterosexual parents in overall adjustment (Parrot & Ellis, 1985).

Some evidence suggests that children reared by homosexual parents may actually reap certain advantages. Homosexual men, at least, are often especially anxious to be superlative fathers, and to raise children who hold nonsexist, egalitarian attitudes (Bozett, 1988). These fathers may also be more nurturing than other fathers, and have more positive feelings about fatherhood than other fathers.

While the evidence currently suggests that growing up in a household headed by a homosexual is unlikely to damage children psychologically, this issue is far from resolved. There is woefully little evidence of any kind bearing upon this issue, and the available evidence fails to examine long-term consequences of being reared by a homosexual parent. Furthermore, as attitudes toward homosexuality continue to evolve toward greater acceptance—or, perhaps, decreased intolerance—the consequences of growing up in such a family setting are likely to change as well. Whether or not homosexuals should rear children, then, will be an open question for some time to come.

child's physical, cognitive, or emotional development, or division of household duties in single-parent homes (e.g., Risman & Park, 1988).

Clearly, single parenthood is an imposing challenge. As the numbers of single parents have grown, however, the resources available for them have expanded. These resources include agencies and organizations charged with assisting parents and children. Table 11.1 lists some of these organizations.

Stepparents   Many single parents eventually marry or remarry (see Chapter Ten, pp. 274–276), and become members of a "blended family." Nearly 1.5

Table 11.1
Agencies and organizations serving the needs of single parents

---

Women's Legal Defense Fund. Child Custody Project, Suite 400, 2000 P St., N.W., Washington, DC 20036. Publishes a guide to child custody disputes for single mothers, and provides technical assistance to attorneys.

Joint Custody Association. 10606 Wilkins Ave., Los Angeles, CA 90024. Provides information on joint custody and lobbies in support of legislation relating to joint custody.

National Congress for Men. Al Lebow, c/o Fathers for Equal Rights of Michigan, P. O. Box 2272, Southfield, MI 48037. Works on legal issues confronting divorced parents and sexism in family law.

---

million Americans remarry each year, and approximately 60 percent of these individuals have custody of at least one child (Ganong & Coleman, 1989). Unfortunately, negative stereotypes of stepparents abound, and stepparents' self-esteem may suffer from the impact of these images (e.g., Giles-Sims & Crosbie-Burnett, 1989). Stepparents are more likely than biological parents to encounter disagreements over childrearing, perhaps because they have a relatively short family history and must blend their expectations of family life (Ganong & Coleman, 1989).

Stepparents also face troubling legal issues. Stepparents share many of biological parents' responsibilities (e.g., financial support). However, stepparents lack some of biological parents' rights, such as the right to authorize medical treatment, or visitation rights after divorce (Giles-Sims & Crosbie-Burnett, 1989). Clearly, being a stepparent means confronting an ambiguous, contradictory set of expectations.

Some couples actively prepare for remarriage and stepparenting. Cohabitation is one strategy; while cohabitation may benefit the marital relationship, however, it has little effect on relationships between stepparents and stepchildren (e.g., Ganong & Coleman, 1989). Other steps to ease the adjustment to "blended" family life are reading about stepfamily issues, seeking advice from friends or professionals, and entering a support group or counseling program. Of these approaches, remarried individuals most often report that reading was helpful (Ganong & Coleman, 1989).

Older parents and older children

Parents and adolescents   Adolescence stands out as one of the most momentous periods in the life span. The teenager confronts seemingly unpredictable changes in physical appearance, sexuality, and identity—at about the same time that middle-aged parents are experiencing change in many of the same areas. What are the implications for the family at midlife?

Although stressful for both generations, some parent-adolescent conflict is normal (Montemayor, 1982). In early adolescence, most arguments with parents concern household rules and chores, or schoolwork (e.g., Boxer, Solomon, Offer, Petersen, & Halprin, 1984). Later, conflict may center on dating, jobs, money, curfews and other rules.

Despite conflict over everyday matters, parents and adolescents agree on many social values such as the importance of world peace, and share attitudes toward politics and religion (e.g. Troll & Bengtson, 1982). Parents often find positive changes in their relationships with teenagers as their children mature. These parents see their children growing more understanding, tolerant, and helpful (Boxer et al., 1984).

The "empty nest"   Parents who are certain that their children's adolescence will drive them to an early grave can look forward to the product of normal development—their children's departure from the home in late adolescence or early adulthood. This period has traditionally been termed the **"empty nest,"** and is the subject of both popular misconception and empirical research. Although many assume that mothers react to the empty nest with depression and a sense of meaninglessness, and that this transition can reveal emotional barrenness in the midlife marriage, most research contradicts these notions.

The timing of a young adult's departure from her parents' home reflects characteristics of the young person, her family, and the setting in which they live. The departure may come with the young adult's entry into college, the military, the labor force, or marriage. In American families, most young people expect to establish their own households before getting married; their parents do not always share that expectation, however (Goldscheider & Goldscheider, 1989). Stepparents and single mothers are more likely than parents in intact families to expect children to leave home before marriage (Goldscheider & Goldscheider, 1989; Mitchell, Wister, & Burch, 1989). Researchers suggest that these trends reflect emotional distance in stepparent-stepchild relationships and a later expected age at marriage for young adults in single-mother families. Other research shows that region of the country is also associated with the timing of departure from the parents' home (Mitchell et al., 1989).

When the nest does empty, how do parents feel about the change? Folk wisdom suggests that parents, especially mothers, cannot figure out how to fill the hours no longer devoted to nurturing. This image does not apply to many parents, however. Overall, mothers report more extreme reactions than fathers do (Troll, 1989), perhaps because women are more attuned to the rhythms of the family life cycle. Nonetheless, some men experience more distress at the emptying of the nest than stereotypes of work-preoccupied fathers would suggest (e.g., Mancini & Blieszner, 1989).

Most parents find far more pleasure than pain in the empty nest transition. Few consider children's departure from the home a major transformation of their own lives (e.g., Lowenthal & Chiriboga, 1972). However, most anticipate and psychologically rehearse the event, and feel well-prepared to make the transition with ease (Greene & Boxer, 1986). Although most research on the empty nest has involved non-Hispanic Caucasian, middle class samples, one study of Mexican-American women's well-being in the postparental years showed that the empty nest has no negative consequences for psychological or physical well-being (Rogers & Markides, 1989).

Usually, the empty nest provides an opportunity to develop new and pleasurable dimensions in relationships with young adult children. Middle-aged parents and their children can now become friends, as they share continued affection and attachment (Greene & Boxer, 1986; Lehr, 1984; Mancini & Blieszner, 1989; Troll, 1989). This trend continues as young adult children marry and have children. Middle-aged adults in a qualitative study found that grandchildren's birth drew them closer to their children: the grandchildren provided a new focus for shared interest and affection, and new occasions for family gatherings (Thomas, 1985a).

The young adult's entry into independence is an achievement for parents. Many parents see this transition as a mark of their own success as parents; in fact, children's failure to empty the nest at an expected age may lead to a sense of failure (Greene & Boxer, 1986; Spence & Lonner, 1971). The children's departure from the home gives parents the freedom and opportunity to pursue new interests (Hagestad, 1982; Lehr, 1984).

The popular image of the mother who is devastated by her children's newfound independence does have a kernel of truth, however. Women who centered their lives around childrearing—those with few other interests and sources of social involvement—sometimes suffer depression, believe that their health worsens after the children's departure, feel that life has become meaningless, or express negative views of their own aging (Lehr, 1984; Spence & Lonner, 1971; Troll, 1989). These "child-centered" women, ironically, may also find that they have less contact, but more conflict, with their children after the children establish their own households (Lehr, 1984).

Another popular notion surrounding the empty nest transition is that its impact on the middle-aged parents' marriage is inevitably negative. Parents, it is believed, find that they have nothing in common when children at home no longer bind them. This image has little basis in reality, however.

Parents anticipating the empty nest expect their marriages to become less conflicted and more enjoyable when their children leave home (e.g., Lowenthal & Chiriboga, 1972; Lowenthal, Thurnher, & Chiriboga, 1976). Happily, these expectations are realistic for most parents. Parents who have already experienced the empty nest report greater marital satisfaction after children's departure than before—and they attribute the improvement to their children's absence (e.g., Deutscher, 1969). Without children at home, there are fewer sources of conflict, there is less housework of all kinds, and there are more opportunities for the husband and wife to spend time together.

The "refilled nest"   In the 1980s, researchers turned their attention toward an increasingly common phenomenon: nests which empty only temporarily or do not empty at all. Demographers reported that by the mid-1980s nearly one-third of young adults lived with their parents (e.g., Glick & Lin, 1986). The most frequent reasons for this arrangement are the child's unemployment or other economic problems and the child's divorce and consequent needs for support (Clemons & Axelson, 1985; Glick & Lin, 1986; Mancini & Blieszner, 1989).

Which young adults are most likely to live with their parents? Marital status is by far the strongest predictor. Only parents of unmarried or divorced children are likely to have an adult child living at home (Aquilino, 1990). Adult children live with parents more frequently in African-American families than in non-Hispanic Caucasian families, but this racial difference reflects racial differences in young adults' marital status rather than a cultural preference for shared living arrangements (Aquilino, 1990). Among parents aged 55 and older who have unmarried or divorced adult children, Hispanics are more likely than non-Hispanic Caucasians or African-Americans to have these children living with them (Aquilino, 1990).

The positive reactions to the empty nest might suggest that the refilled nest is fraught with conflict. However, Suitor and Pillemer's (1988) study of a random sample of older parents who shared their home with an adult child revealed that conflict was surprisingly rare. In this sample, the extent of parent-child conflict was lowest for dyads in which the child was relatively old and for dyads in which the parent and child had similar marital statuses, such as a widowed mother living with her unmarried or divorced daughter. Not all research paints such an optimistic picture, however. Clemons and Axelson (1985) studied parent-adult child coresidence among a small sample of parents participating in a workshop on parenting the young adult. In that sample, nearly half of the parents reported serious conflict with resident adult children. Of course, such a workshop might have attracted members of families that were unusually troubled by conflict.

ELDERLY PARENTS AND ADULT CHILDREN

Are elderly people abandoned and neglected by their children and grandchildren? Many people think so. Supposedly, geographic mobility has put great distance between older people and their offspring, and prevents them from seeing one another often. This impression is in contrast to the warmer image of the "good old days," when **multigenerational households** (in which three or more generations of the family reside) were common and the elderly consequently were an integral part of the everyday lives of their children and grandchildren. Similarly benevolent images exist of elderly people's family relationships in contemporary nonindustrial societies, in which modernization has supposedly not yet disrupted traditions of family closeness (e.g., Nydegger, 1983).

These images are surprisingly tenacious, given the amount of data that soundly contradicts them. For over three decades, family gerontologists have demonstrated that older people are by no means abandoned by their families:

Most older adults enjoy warm, satisfying relationships with their children and grandchildren.

most enjoy warm, satisfying relationships with children and grandchildren. The image of the "good old days" is also inaccurate, since historical research reveals that multigenerational households have never been typical in America. A closer look at evidence concerning geographic proximity, frequency of contact, and affect between the aged and their sons and daughters provides an optimistic picture of family life in old age.

Geographic proximity

Among the best-documented findings in family gerontology is that older people and their adult children generally prefer to live near one another but not with one another, and that most families are successful in implementing that preference (e.g., Bengtson et al., 1990). About three out of four elderly parents live within a half-hour of at least one of their children (e.g., Shanas, 1979), although many also have other children living at greater distances (Moss, Moss, & Moles, 1985). Since the early 1960s, there has been a slight decrease in the percentage of older parents who live very close—within 10 minutes—to one of their children, but the percentage living within a half-hour of an adult child has not changed (Crimmins & Ingegneri, 1990). Although this close intergenerational proximity applies to older people of all ethnic backgrounds, older Hispanic–Americans generally live closer to kin than do non-Hispanic older people (Markides & Mindel, 1987).

Multigenerational households   Few older adults today live with an adult son or daughter. Although multigenerational households have never been common, they have grown even more infrequent in recent decades. Whereas only about a third of older parents lived with a child in the early 1960s, the figure had dropped to 18 percent by 1975 and did not change over the following nine years (Crimmins & Ingegneri, 1990). When multigenerational living was adopted in the past, it was typically for only a brief period between the time that an aged father surrendered control of the farm to his offspring and the parents' deaths (Treas & Bengtson, 1987). In fact, older Americans in the nineteenth century preferred to take in boarders or lodgers to maintain economic independence rather than to share a home with one of their adult children (Moddell & Hareven, 1973).

Then, as now, a member of the oldest generation was usually the head of a multigenerational household (Treas & Bengtson, 1987). In other words, it has always been more common for adult children to live in an aged parent's home than for an elderly parent to move in with a son or daughter. Although some assume that multigenerational living is nearly always undertaken to meet the needs of frail or impoverished parents, the arrangement may well stem from the needs of adult children as well as the elderly parent (Crimmins & Ingegneri, 1990; Silverstone & Hyman, 1976).

Sometimes, a multigenerational household is formed to give companionship to an older parent who is too fearful or emotionally dependent to live alone; other times, the arrangement reflects a mutual decision to pool finances so that all can live more comfortably. In some families, an elderly parent helps with childcare and housework so that adult children can pursue careers or special interests. Divorce, widowhood, or ill health of *either* the elderly parent or the adult child may also prompt multigenerational living.

The likelihood of multigenerational living varies according to race, gender, age, and place of residence. Older African-Americans, Hispanic-Americans, and Asian-Americans more often live with adult children than do non-Hispanic Caucasians (Treas & Bengtson, 1987; Koh & Bell, 1987; Markides & Mindel, 1987; Taylor, 1988). Women are more likely to live in a multigenerational household than are men, perhaps reflecting gender differences in mean longevity (Coward, Cutler, & Schmidt, 1989). Census data show that whereas only about one person in five aged 65 to 69 lived with one of their children, nearly half (46.6 percent) of people in their nineties lived in multigenerational households (Coward et al., 1989). In contrast to the United States, most older people in six Latin American nations (the Dominican Republic, Columbia, Costa Rica, Panama, Peru, Mexico) live in a multigenerational household (De Vos, 1990).

Contact between the elderly and adult children: Gender, race, and class differences

As the data on geographic proximity suggest, older adults generally see their sons and daughters frequently. Most older people see at least one of their adult children on a weekly basis, and many see an adult child nearly every day (Bengtson et al., 1990; Treas & Bengtson, 1987; Crimmins & Ingegneri, 1990; Shanas, 1979). What factors determine just *how* often an elderly mother or father is likely to see an adult child? Roberts and Bengtson (1990) proposed that frequency of contact between an older parent and adult child reflects their mutual feelings of affection, the beliefs of each about appropriate family closeness, and the extent to which parent and child can maintain a balanced exchange of resources. This model is illustrated in Figure 11.2.

According to the model (see Figure 11.2), the extent to which a parent and child believe that they *should* remain close, the extent to which they help one another (and thus attain a balanced exchange of resources), and their affection for one another all influence how often they get together (their association). In addition, the balanced exchange of resources itself influences affection between parent and child, and contributes to their frequency of contact. There is a reciprocal relationship between the parent's and child's levels of affection for one another, and both the parent's affection for the child and the child's affection for the parent also influence frequency of contact. According to this model,

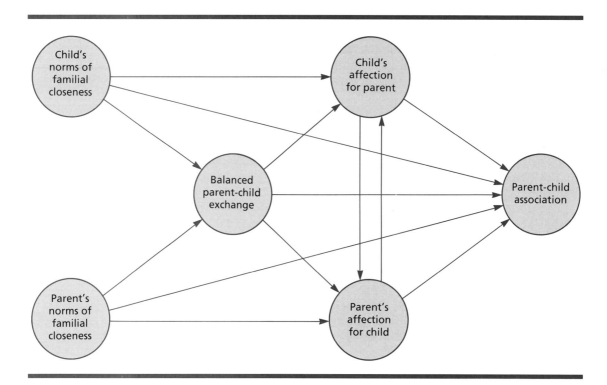

Figure 11.2
Model of elderly parent-adult child contact. (Source: Roberts & Bengtson, 1990. "Is Intergenerational Solidarity a Unidimensional Construct?" *Journal of Gerontology: Social Sciences, 45:* S12–S20. Copyright © The Gerontological Society of America. Reprinted by permission.)

then, older parents and adult children get together because they think they should (norms of family closeness), because they need to (balanced exchange of resources), and because they want to (mutual feelings of affection).

Other approaches to describing frequency of contact between older parents and adult children point not to feelings and beliefs, but to demographic characteristics. In addition to the relatively intangible factors included in Roberts and Bengtson's model, four social characteristics are associated with frequency of contact between the elderly and their adult children (e.g., Bengtson et al., 1990; Treas & Bengtson, 1987). First, older people have more frequent contact with their daughters than with their sons; partly for this reason, middle-aged women have been labeled **kinkeepers** who maintain contact among relatives. Second, marital status is related to contact frequency: widows see their children more often than older married couples, and unmarried adult children maintain closer ties to their parents, at least in terms of the likelihood of sharing a household (see the "refilled nest," above).

Third, there are social class differences in contact frequency: working class families see each other more often than do white-collar families (Treas & Bengtson, 1987). Occupational mobility also plays a part. When adult children are upwardly mobile, frequency of contact with parents may increase; downward mobility, however, is associated with decreased contact with kin (Schoenholz, 1978).

Finally, race and ethnicity are associated with the frequency of seeing adult children. Older Hispanic-Americans have more frequent contact with their sons and daughters than non-Hispanics do (Treas & Bengtson, 1987; Cantor, 1975; Dowd & Bengtson, 1978). The findings concerning African-Americans are inconsistent. Some report that older African-Americans see their adult children slightly more often than do older non-Hispanic Caucasians, whereas others find no difference between African-Americans and non-Hispanic Caucasians in frequency of contact with children (Markides & Mindel, 1987; Taylor, 1988).

Of course, what older people and their children do when they get together is at least as important as how often they see one another. Vern Bengtson and his colleagues identified three clusters of occasions for family contact: informal activities when parents and children get together for conversation or recreation; ceremonial or family ritual activities such as reunions, anniversaries, and birthdays; and exchanges of assistance between elderly parents and adult children (Treas & Bengtson, 1987).

Feelings between older parents and their children

How older people and their sons and daughters feel about one another is potentially the most important part of their relationship, but probably also the least tangible aspect. Data describing affect between the aged and their children, like the data on proximity and contact, point to warm, close relationships as the norm.

Typically, both elderly parents and adult children report strong feelings of affection for one another (e.g., Bengtson et al., 1990; Treas & Bengtson, 1987). Older African-Americans and Hispanic-Americans are particularly likely to describe their relationships with adult children as close, warm, and affectionate (Bengtson et al., 1990; Taylor, 1988). Older parents sometimes describe their relationships with children as embodying greater affection and attitudinal similarity than the children themselves do; this tendency reflects the **developmental stake** that each generation has in their relationship (Bengtson & Kuypers, 1971). According to Bengtson & Kuypers (1971), the older parent's developmental needs to express generativity and deal with awareness of mortality lead her to minimize evidence of distance or differences between herself and her children. However, the adult child's developmental needs to achieve a personal identity may prompt her to exaggerate distances.

The level of affection between older parents and adult children does not depend on how often they see each other. Elderly parents describe their relationships with geographically distant, infrequently seen children as close and satisfying, much like their relationships with children living nearby that they see more often (Mercier, Paulson, & Morris, 1989; Moss et al., 1985).

In emphasizing the fact that most older people have warm, affectionate relationships with adult children, we must not overlook the possibility of conflicted relationships between the aged and their children. Probably the most extreme hostility is acted out in **elder abuse**, the physical and/or psychological maltreatment of the aged or theft of an older person's material resources. As with other forms of family violence, it is difficult to know how often elder abuse occurs; reported cases probably only represent a fraction of all instances, although several states have enacted mandatory reporting laws for suspected cases of elder abuse. One recent study of a random sample of over 2000 community-dwelling elderly people indicated a prevalence rate of 32 instances of abuse for every 1000 persons (Phillemer & Finkelhor, 1988). The "typical victim" is often vulnerable because of advanced age and physical frailty, chronic disease, or mental impairment (e.g., Phillemer & Finkelhor, 1988; Rathbone-McCuan, 1986). The abuser may be the victim's spouse, an adult child, another family member, or a nonrelative.

Several explanations have been proposed for elder abuse (e.g., Rathbone-McCuan, 1986). Some believe that the abuser was (or believes that he was) mistreated by the elderly victim in the past, or that family violence has been transmitted through the generations as a learned response to stress. Occasionally, a family caregiver abuses the elderly relative under her care; in these instances, the abuse may stem from the stress of caregiving (see Chapter Twelve, pp. 306–316), inadequate community supports to relieve caregiver burden, or from the caregiver's incapacity to meet overwhelming needs for care. Others propose that a personality disorder or substance abuse problem causes the abuser's behavior. In a few instances, abuse may be a reaction to a dependent elder who attempts to control others in maladaptive ways such as pitting family members against one another, imposing guilt on family caregivers, or manipulating family members.

GRANDPARENTHOOD AND GREAT-GRANDPARENTHOOD

Grandparents

The media conveys a sentimental image of grandparents. Grandmothers are portrayed as plump, gray-haired, bespectacled bundles of nurturing thoughts and deeds; supposedly, they tirelessly bake cookies and Thanksgiving turkeys, read stories, and treat grandchildren's cuts and scrapes with band-aids, kisses, and hugs. Grandfathers, too, have the girth, gray hair, and glasses of age. Some grandfathers teach grandchildren fishing and carpentry, some are mischievous companions who indulge grandchildren with treats and outings, and all tell fascinating stories of the "good old days."

Although these images may have once had a realistic basis, they do not describe many contemporary grandparents. Today, grandparents better fit a far more youthful image, as the transition to grandparenthood now typically occurs in the forties. A 45-year-old grandmother today probably devotes more time to her career than to baking cookies; her husband may be more concerned with his own parents' and grandparents' increasing frailty than with his granddaughter's interest in woodworking.

Scholars describe grandparenthood as a tenuous role, a social status lacking clear, agreed-on norms for behavior (Rosow, 1985). Unlike institutional roles incorporating both a status (e.g., student) and behavioral norms (e.g., attends classes, completes assignments, etc.), tenuous roles such as grandparenthood lack specific guidelines for acting out the role. Grandparents' legal status reflects this ambiguity. The extent to which grandparents can be held financially responsible for grandchildren's support varies from one state to another, as do grandparents' legal basis for visitation rights following parents' divorce (Wilson & DeShane, 1982).

Although this role ambiguity may be frustrating, it may also have benefits. The very absence of well-defined norms allows each grandparent the flexibility to be a grandparent in a unique way. Research documents tremendous variety in how the grandparent role is acted out.

Diversity in grandparenthood

Age differences   Age is one dimension differentiating the ways in which people grandparent. In a classic study, Neugarten and Weinstein (1968) identified distinct styles of grandparenting. Among Neugarten and Weinstein's (1968) most important findings was an association between grandparents' ages and the most frequently adopted styles of grandparenting. Formal grandparents, who made clear distinctions between parenting and grandparenting, were usually older than age 65. However, fun-seekers (who had informal, playful relationships with grandchildren) and distant figures (who had benevolent but remote relationships with grandchildren) were typically younger than age 65. As Neugarten and Weinstein (1968) suggested, these age differences might reflect maturational changes on the part of grandparents and grandchildren, or cohort differences in notions of appropriate family roles.

More recent research also reveals age differences in grandparenting. Grandparents in their forties, fifties, and sixties express greater readiness to offer childrearing advice to parents than do grandparents in their seventies and eighties (Thomas, 1986a). Not all young grandparents want this type of involvement, though. Some African-American grandmothers in their twenties and thirties reject grandparent role behaviors, as they associate grandparenthood with old age and are already burdened with other responsibilities (Burton & Bengtson, 1985; see below).

Gender differences   Men and women react to grandparenthood differently. Grandmothers enjoy grandparenthood more than grandfathers do, and grandmothers express less obligation to offer childrearing advice and take care of grandchildren than grandfathers do (Thomas, 1986a; 1986b; 1989). Grandfathers find the extension of their family through a new generation, and the opportunities to indulge grandchildren, more personally meaningful than grandmothers do (Thomas, 1989).

Gender also makes a difference in the relationships from the grandchild's perspective. In a survey of young adult college students, women stressed the value of close intergenerational relationships more than men did (Kennedy, 1990). However, grandparents' feelings of satisfaction and meaningfulness in relationships with grandchildren do not depend on whether the child is a grandson or a granddaughter (Thomas, 1989).

Race, ethnicity, and grandparenthood   Historically, African-American grandmothers have been depicted as central family figures fulfilling a well-defined role as "guardians of generations" (Frazier, 1939). For these women, grandmotherhood was by no means a tenuous role; becoming a grandmother meant assuming a definite set of rights and duties. For example, Taylor (1988) reports that African-American grandmothers more often act as parent surrogates for grandchildren than non-Hispanic Caucasian grandmothers do, and that some African-American grandparents informally adopt grandchildren by assuming primary care of them until adulthood.

Some research suggests that the role of the African-American grandmother may be in transition, however. Burton (Burton & Bengtson, 1985) studied extremely young African-American grandmothers; many had been teenaged mothers themselves, and became grandmothers in their twenties or thirties when their teenaged daughters had children. These atypically young grandmothers reacted negatively to their role. They considered grandparenthood a mark of old age (for which they were by no means ready); many were committed to other responsibilities within and outside the family. Some were either preoccupied with raising their own young children or were content to be free of the everyday tasks of childcare.

Like the traditional African-American grandmother, grandparents in Hispanic families play important parts in their grandchildren's upbringing

Historically, African-American grandmothers have been central figures in their families.

(Markides & Mindel, 1987). These grandparents pass along family history and ethnic heritage, are often sources of support in times of crisis, and influence family decisions. Within Hispanic groups, Mexican-American grandparents are most likely to be involved with grandchildren on an everyday basis; Cuban-American grandparents are least likely to have such involvement (Bengtson, 1985).

Unfortunately, we know very little about Native American grandparents. Native American culture represents a collection of such highly diverse systems and historical traditions that generalizing on the basis of the data that are available is perilous. These data suggest, however, that Native American grandparents fulfill important roles. About one-fourth of Native American grandparents regularly care for at least one grandchild, and two-thirds live within a few minutes of kin with whom they regularly exchange support (National Indian Council on Aging, 1981).

Grandparenthood and mental health

Is it true, as bumper stickers proclaim, that "happiness is being a grandparent"? Does having grandchildren benefit the grandparent's mental health? Recent research suggests that it does.

Kivnick (1982a; 1982b; 1985) identified associations between the symbolic meaning attributed to grandparenthood and grandparents' mental health. For grandmothers, emphasis on the symbolic meaning of grandparenthood was associated with low levels of morale and life satisfaction. Grandmothers may stress symbolic aspects of relationships with grandchildren in the face of age-related pressures; if so, grandparenthood may compensate for the impacts of age-related deprivations on life satisfaction and morale. As an elderly woman confronts such things as chronic illness, limited finances, and the death of her husband, bonds with her grandchildren may minimize her distress. For grand-fathers, emphasis on grandparenthood was positively related to life satisfaction and morale: men who found grandparenting pleasant and important enjoyed life in general.

Is the concrete relationship with a specific grandchild (as opposed to the symbolic meaning of being a grandparent) linked to mental health? J. Thomas (1990b) examined associations between the relationship with the oldest grand-child in the two-parent household geographically closest to a grandparent and the grandparent's mental health. The grandparent's feelings of satisfaction and nurturance in that relationship were positively associated with mental health, although the extent to which the grandparent wielded authority in the relation-ship (by disciplining the grandchild, for example) was not. Both on a symbolic and a concrete level, then, being a grandparent offers psychological benefits in middle and later adulthood.

Great-grandparents

Prior to the twentieth century, great-grandparents were a rarity. However, in-creased life expectancy (see Chapters One, p. 3, and Three, p. 22) has changed that situation. Today, nearly everyone age 65 and older who has living children also has grandchildren; nearly half of all grandparents are also great-grandpar-ents (Shanas, 1980).

In an exploratory study, nineteen older women (ages 66 to 92) shared their view of great-grandparenthood (Wentowski, 1985). These women often com-mented initially that being a great-grandmother was "just like being a grand-mother." On further reflection, however, most added that age and geographic distance prevented them from having the same kind of involvement with great-grandchildren that they had enjoyed with their grandchildren.

Consequently, being a great-grandmother was important more for sym-bolic reasons than because of personal relationships with great-grandchildren (Wentowski, 1985). To these women, great-grandchildren were symbols of fam-ily success and vitality. In another study, respondents said that being a great-grandparent reflected personal and family renewal and was a mark of longevity, and that great-grandchildren provided diversion (Doka & Mertz, 1988).

This overview of intergenerational relationships leads to three conclu-sions. First, these bonds are of critical importance throughout adulthood: for most people, relationships with children, grandchildren, and great-grandchil-dren endure until death. Second, these relationships unfold in diverse ways in contemporary America; relationships with children and grandchildren vary according to such characteristics as age, gender, race and ethnicity, and social class. Finally, these relationships entail some stress, at least occasionally, and are characterized by high levels of affection in most families most of the time. These characteristics remain apparent as we examine family caregiving in the next chapter.

SUMMARY

Reasons for having children vary both in contemporary America and cross-culturally. Motivations for remaining child-free include freedom from child-care responsibility, self-fulfillment and growth, the desire for a more satisfactory marriage, career consider- ations and finances, concern about overpopulation, and dislike of children. Most expec- tant parents report mixed emotional reactions to pregnancy, and shifting reactions over the course of the pregnancy. Generally, the more anticipatory socialization expectant parents experience, the more positive the postpartum period is likely to be. However, research on the transition to parenthood portrays the experience as a stressful one.

Among the best-documented findings in family gerontology is that elderly people and their adult children generally prefer to live near one another but not with one another, and that most families are successful in implementing that preference. Survey data show that most older people see at least one of their adult children on a weekly basis, and that many see adult children nearly every day. Data describing affect between the aged and their children, like the data on proximity and contact, point to warm, close relationships as the norm.

Grandparenting varies according to age, gender, and race. Recent research shows that grandparenthood is associated with psychological well-being. Being a great-grand- parent is often important more for symbolic reasons than because of the personal relationships with great-grandchildren. Great-grandchildren can be symbols of family success and vitality.

KEY TERMS

Adaptation	Early articulators
Anticipation and preparation	Elder abuse
Centering	Empty nest
Couvade syndrome	Kinkeepers
Developmental stake	Multigenerational household
Disruption	Postponers

SUGGESTIONS FOR FURTHER READING

Bengtson, V. L., & Robertson, J. F. (1985). *Grandpar- enthood*. Beverly Hills: Sage Publications.

Brubaker, T. H. (1985). *Later Life Families*. Beverly Hills: Sage Publications.

Brubaker, T. H. (1990). *Family Relationships in Later Life*, 2nd Ed. Beverly Hills: Sage Publications.

Cherlin, A. J., & Furstenberg, F. F. (1986). *The New American Grandparent*. New York: Basic Books.

Troll, L. E. (1986). *Family Issues in Current Gerontology*. New York: Springer

CHAPTER TWELVE

FAMILY RELATIONSHIPS: HELPING OLDER RELATIVES

Do younger relatives ignore older people's needs for care? If younger relatives do help older adults, do they do so with resentment or with pleasure? The previous two chapters described feelings of affection within families and the things that family members do together. The family is also important as a helping network, however, particularly in old age. That facet of the family is the focus of this chapter.

The chapter begins with a description of lifelong patterns through which generations in the family exchange help. The second section focuses on how relatives cooperate in caring for frail elderly members, and addresses issues of the stresses and satisfactions of family caregiving, interventions designed to ease the burdens of caregiving, and ways in which caregiving differs depending on the status of the caregiver. Finally, we describe ways in which family support is coordinated with use of community-based long-term care services and is affected by institutionalization.

Questions to consider in reading the chapter include:

In what respects are middle-aged adults pivotal in family support networks?

What kinds of care do family members provide to frail elderly relatives? What kinds of services can minimize caregiver burden?

How are family caregiving networks linked to sources of community long-term care? How does a frail elderly person's institutionalization affect their family's caregiving?

FAMILY TRADITIONS OF MUTUAL SUPPORT

The last chapter demonstrated that the image of older people who are isolated from their families has little basis in contemporary America. This chapter shows that a related notion—that most older adults in need are neglected by their families—is also a myth. Although there is increasing recognition of family caregiving for frail elderly relatives, there is less explicit notice that this support builds on a long-term foundation of helping within families.

Long-term reciprocal support patterns

R. Hill's (1968) classic study of interdependence in three-generation families illustrates typical patterns of exchanging help. Hill interviewed grandparents in their sixties and seventies, parents in their forties and fifties, and young adult children in their twenties and thirties. Much of the interview focused on ways in which members of each generation gave help to and received help from the other generations over a year's time.

Hill's results, illustrated in Figure 12.1, highlight two features of **intergenerational support networks**. First, these networks show a high degree of **reciprocity**: members of each generation both give and receive help. Although these data are not longitudinal, it is reasonable to infer that they reflect long-term patterns in which individuals give to and receive help from other generations in the family throughout their adult lives.

Antonucci (1985; 1990) suggests that intergenerational reciprocity can be likened to a **"support bank."** One makes "deposits" into the support bank by providing help to parents, grandparents, and great-grandparents during early

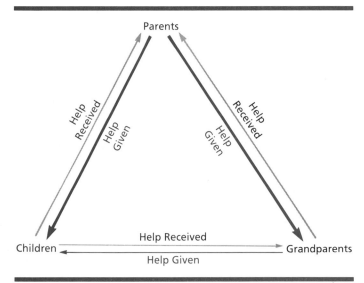

Figure 12.1
Family help exchanges. (Source: Hill, 1968. "Decision Making and the Family Life Cycle," in *Social Structure and the Family: Generational Relations*, Shanas and Streib, eds. © 1965, pp. 123–126. Adapted by permission of Prentice Hall, Englewood Cliffs, NJ.)

and middle adulthood and the early years of old age. One can then anticipate "withdrawing" help from children, grandchildren, and great-grandchildren when one is older and in greater need of help. Of course, the types of help given and received, and the balance between giving and receiving help (see below), shift over the life cycle, as needs and resources change.

A second feature of intergenerational support networks is the pivotal position of the middle-aged parent generation (see Figure 12.1). The breadth of the arrows in Figure 12.1 corresponds to the extent of help given and received by each generation. Notice that the arrows denoting help that the middle-aged parents provide are broader than those denoting help that the parents receive, and are broader than the arrows denoting the help that the children and grandparents exchange with one another. As Hill (1968) notes, the parent generation provides more help to both the young adult grandchild and the elderly adult grandparent generations than these generations exchange with one another. Furthermore, the parents give more help to the other two generations than it receives from them; Hill described the parent generation as having a **patron-type status** relative to the other two generations.

Recent research shows that Hill's (1968) data still provide an accurate picture of family interdependence today, more than two decades later. As in Hill's study, contemporary scholars find that young, middle-aged, and elderly adult relatives exchange help in the forms of child care, care during illness, emotional support and advice, help with household tasks or home repairs, and financial support and advice (e.g., Bengtson, Rosenthal, & Burton, 1990; Brubaker, 1985; Nakao, Okabe, & Bengtson, 1988). Remember, though, that families with four and five adult generations are increasingly common (see Chapter Eleven, p. 300); correspondingly, the patterns of exchanging help among generations are likely to be more complex than shown in Figure 12.1.

Still, the middle generations in these networks maintain a patron-type status, as they provide more help to the oldest and youngest adult generations than they receive from them (e.g., Bengtson et al., 1990; Brody, 1981). Some suggest that young and middle-aged people enact this patron-type status on a society-wide level as well as within the family, referring to the so-called dependency ratio of working-age people to young children and retired adults. Neugarten and Neugarten (1989) provide a critical discussion of the dependency ratio concept.

Men and women generally provide different types of help to family members. Women most often help by providing care during illness, emotional support, and help with housekeeping, whereas men are more likely to help by giving money, maintaining financial records, or help with home repairs, home maintenance, and yard work (Chappell, 1990; Coward & Dwyer, 1990). These gender distinctions are flexible, however. If an older person needs help with housework and a female relative is not available, then a male relative will probably rise to the occasion.

How important is reciprocity in family support? Scholars have considered associations between the extent of reciprocity in family help exchanges and elderly adults' reactions to the exchanges, in the belief that the older person's ability to "repay" younger relatives' help may be important to her morale. Although common sense suggests such a relationship, research has failed to substantiate it (Lee & Ellithorpe, 1982; McColloch, 1990). However, the degree of reciprocity in exchanging help is related to elderly parents' satisfaction with the help that they receive from adult children (Thomas, 1988). Parents aged 60 to 74 reporting an even balance between the amounts of help that they gave to children and help that they received from children were more satisfied with children's help than were parents reporting less balanced exchanges.

Race and class variation in support patterns

Details in the picture of lifelong, reciprocal patterns of helping vary with the race and social class of the families involved. Compared to non-Hispanic Caucasian families, African-American families exchange more help between generations and report a greater degree of reciprocity in these exchanges (Antonucci & Jackson, 1989; Mitchell & Register, 1984; Markides & Mindel, 1987; Mutran, 1985). Although some scholars caution against portraying Hispanic families in an overly-romanticized fashion, Mexican-American and other Hispanic families exchange more support than do non-Hispanic Caucasian families (Markides & Mindel, 1987).

The predominant direction in which help flows varies with social class. In an early study, Shanas (1968) reported that most help in white-collar families goes from older parents to adult children, and that children in those families provide less help to their parents than they receive. However, adult children in working-class families gave more help to their parents than they received from them (Shanas, 1968). In African-American samples, social class is related to help exchanges in a different way. Mitchell and Register (1984) found that older African-Americans of lower social class gave more help to children and grandchildren than did more affluent elderly African-Americans.

FAMILY CAREGIVING FOR THE FRAIL ELDERLY

Remember that the fastest growing segment of America's population are people aged 85 and older. Although advanced age does not inevitably bring frailty and dependence, some extremely old people need regular help to continue to live in the community. Some rely on others to accomplish basic tasks of everyday living such as shopping and cooking, health maintenance, or even bathing and dressing. Still others require virtually full-time care that may be provided in an institution or in the community.

Many people assume that most frail elderly people who need regular assistance with **instrumental activities of daily living (IADL)** such as housework and shopping or with **activities of daily living (ADL)** such as bathing and toileting receive help from formal sources—a home health aide, a visiting nurse, or health care professionals in a nursing home. Actually, though, the family provides such long-term care far more often (Chappell, 1990; Penning, 1990; World Health Organization, 1980). Some estimate that as much as 80 percent of all care provided to elderly adults comes from informal sources—primarily family members (e.g., Brody, 1981). What is being a caregiver like?

Caregiving experience

Generalizing about family caregivers is perilous, because there is enormous diversity among caregivers, caregiving situations, and caregivers' experiences. Many caregivers themselves are elderly people, since a caregiver may be the aged spouse or sibling of the person receiving care. In other instances, a caregiver may be a middle-aged child, a more distant relative, or even a friend or neighbor. Although most caregivers are women, men take on caregiving responsibilities as well. The need to provide care may arise from an elderly person's physical incapacity, dementia or other mental impairment, or a combination of frailties. The course of physical aging is so variable (see Chapter Three, p. 75) that very old parents may need to provide care for their aged children. And, of course, family caregiving occurs in all racial and ethnic groups, and all social classes.

Given these caveats, what general description of family caregiving is possible? Although the concrete duties of caregiving obviously depend on the specific needs of each care-recipient, reviewers identify tasks that family caregivers most often perform. These tasks include providing emotional support, companionship, and advice; providing direct assistance with such things as cooking, housecleaning, laundry, shopping, and transportation; providing personal care (e.g., bathing, dressing, help with medications or injections, colostomy care, help transferring from bed to wheelchair and so forth, toileting); providing help in managing money; providing direct financial assistance; and providing linkage to formal services by arranging for and supervising services in the home (e.g., Chappell, 1990; Gatz, Bengtson, & Blum, 1990).

CAREGIVER BURDEN: A STRESS AND COPING MODEL

Scholars agree that stress, or **caregiver burden**, is associated with providing support to elderly relatives. When caregivers are compared to population norms or to appropriate control groups, the caregivers report higher levels of depression, demoralization, grief, despair, and hopelessness as well as higher rates of physical illness and impaired immune responses (Schulz, Visintainer, & Williamson, 1990). At least for wives, providing care to husbands suffering from Alzheimer's Disease is associated with depression, which in turn leads to physical health problems and subjective feelings of being burdened, stressed, or overwhelmed (Pruchno, Kleban, Michaels, & Dempsey, 1990).

Family caregivers help older relatives with tasks such as shopping, transportation, finances, and linkage to formal services.

How does caregiver burden unfold as the family provides support to frail elderly members? Researchers often take a stress and coping model as their framework; one such model (Gatz et al., 1990) is illustrated in Figure 12.2. This model provides a framework for our overview of the tremendous amount of research on caregiver burden. As Figure 12.2 shows, a caregiver's feelings of burden reflect the impacts of (1) an objective event (the elderly person's incapacitating illness), (2) stressors that are consequences of that event (the older person's symptoms, tasks that the caregiver performs, changes in the caregiver's life), (3) the caregiver's perception of these consequences, and (4) the resources available to her.

Thus, it is not only the concrete problems to be managed—such as the areas in which the older person needs care, and ways in which the caregiver must change her life in order to provide care—that are important. Just as significant is the caregiver's *appraisal* of the situation, and the skills and sources of support that she can draw upon. What kinds of stressors, appraisals, and mediators are most critical?

The stressors of caregiving

Given the diversity of caregivers and caregiving situations (see above), it is not surprising that a wide variety of sources of burden have been identified. Some find that providing nursing care and meeting the older person's needs for companionship are upsetting (Treas & Bengtson, 1987). Others specify dementia patients' problematic behaviors such as wandering, aggression, repetitive questioning, and incontinence as stressors (Niederehe & Funk, 1987).

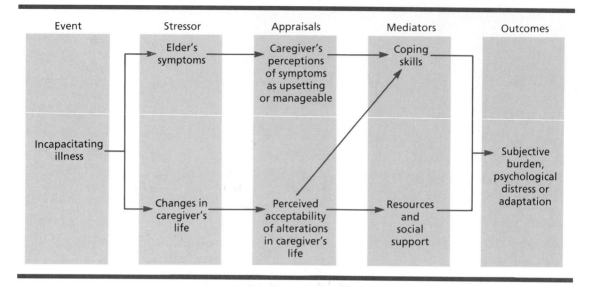

Figure 12.2

Stress and coping model of caregiver burden. (Source: Gatz et al., 1990. Reprinted by permission.)

Caregivers may be burdened by interruptions in family activities and vacation plans, diminished time with their spouse, and—when the care recipient lives with the caregiver—restrictions in the family's privacy and alterations in the family's preferred use of space (e.g., Kleban, Brody, Schoonover, & Hoffman, 1989; Zarit, Orr, & Zarit, 1985). Caregivers for dementia patients are further burdened by their sense of loss as they witness the victim's gradual decline (Gatz et al., 1990; Zarit et al., 1985).

It seems logical to expect that caregiving becomes more burdensome the longer that care is provided. However, that pessimistic picture does not inevitably develop. In a longitudinal study, adult children caring for elderly parents varied tremendously in the extent to which they were able to adapt to caregiving (Townsend, Noelker, Deimling, & Bass, 1989). For these caregivers, mental health more often improved than worsened with time: caregivers reported less stress, and more feelings of effectiveness as caregivers, as they continued to care for their parents.

Caregiving and role conflict: "Women in the middle"   Middle-aged women have traditionally been caregivers for older people (e.g., Brody, 1985). Given women's increased labor force participation, what conflicts challenge women who have both work and caregiving responsibilities? Is caregiving curtailed when the caregiver works? Does job performance suffer when the employee is a caregiver?

Paid employment apparently has little impact on women's caregiving, but fulfilling both roles may exact a heavy cost from the caregiver. Comparisons of women who do and who do not work outside the home typically reveal few differences in the amounts of care provided to elderly parents (e.g., Brody, 1985; Stoller, 1983), although some researchers do find that employed women spend less time caregiving than do full-time homemakers (e.g., Steuve & O'Donnell, 1989). However, most research shows that employed women provide substantial amounts of care by maintaining rigid personal schedules and by giving up time for their own rest and enjoyment (Chappell, 1990). Women with paid work may share caregiving with siblings, their husbands, their children, or other people. Matthews, Werkner, and Delaney (1989) reported that nonemployed women helped parents with medical appointments and daytime emergencies and care, whereas their employed sisters helped with tasks that could be fit around their work schedules.

Women do not, then, neglect their parents in order to pursue careers. However, being a caregiver apparently does affect women's work. Elaine Brody (1985) compared working and nonworking women caring for their elderly mothers, and found that nearly a third of the nonworking women had left their jobs to meet their mothers' needs; similar numbers of working women were considering giving up their jobs, and many had already reduced their work hours. More recently, Scharlach and Boyd (1989) reported that employees with caregiving responsibilities were more likely than other employees to miss work or to take time off because of caregiving. These employees also admitted that they were sometimes so exhausted from caregiving that it was difficult for them to do their jobs.

Role conflict does not arise solely because of the competing demands of work and caregiving, however. Brody (1981) proposes a broader notion of role conflict in her discussion of "**women in the middle.**" These middle-aged women provide support to their husbands; they may have children (even preschool-aged children) still living at home; and they also are often pursuing careers while caring for their elderly parents and/or parents-in-law. Clearly, these women are caught in the middle of a complex set of demanding roles within the family and outside it.

Given the extreme stress that these individuals must experience, it is reassuring to learn that being "caught in the middle" of this role complex is an unusual experience (Spitze & Logan, 1990; Rosenthal, Matthews, & Marshall, 1989). Some caregivers with other roles—particularly nonfamily roles—enjoy greater psychological well-being than caregivers subject to lower levels of role conflict (Stoller & Pugliesi, 1989). Recall that some women thrive on a challenging mix of responsibilities (see Chapter Eight, p. 210).

Appraisals: Attitudes toward providing care

Many family caregivers are daughters and sons of frail elderly people. **Filial responsibility** is an adult child's feeling that she should provide care for her aged parents if the need arises. Some believe that these feelings of obligation are a mark of the adult child's maturity. **Filial maturity** is the adult child's recognition that her parents have frailties and needs, *and* that she—the adult child—can and should meet those needs (Blenkner, 1965).

To the extent that people do what they think they should do, filial responsibility and filial maturity are appraisals that affect caregiving behavior. Feeling that one is fulfilling an important and expected duty can be a source of satisfaction in caregiving. Those who reject the notion of filial responsibility may be less willing to provide care for a frail older relative, and may experience greater stress if they do become caregivers.

Furthermore, differences between adult children's and aged parents' views of filial responsibility could lead to family conflict. Parents may feel neglected—and children may feel unreasonably burdened—if the parents' notions of filial responsibility imply more intensive caregiving than their children's notion does. On the other hand, parents may resent overzealous caregiving if they place less value on filial responsibility than their children do.

Some research identifies generational differences in filial responsibility norms. Young adults generally endorse these norms more enthusiastically than elderly adults do (e.g., Brody, Johnson, & Fulcomer, 1984), although other work points to a moderate level of agreement between generations on the value of filial responsibility (Hamon & Blieszner, 1990). Even though most young adults do endorse filial responsibility, some also express anxiety about the prospect of caregiving (Horne, Lowe, & Murray, 1990).

Feelings of filial responsibility vary by gender and ethnicity, as well as by generation. Women express stronger feelings of filial responsibility than men do (Martin, 1988), and Mexican-Americans in one study expressed higher levels of filial responsibility than African-Americans or non-Hispanic Caucasians did (Becerra, 1983). There are also cross-cultural differences in these norms. The *Diversity in Adulthood* box summarizes some of these differences.

Mediators: Steps to minimize caregiver burden

Just as gerontologists have documented the extent of caregiver burden, they have also identified means through which professionals can minimize burden. Family counseling is often helpful (e.g., Gatz et al., 1990; Toseland & Smith, 1990). In this case, however, the counselor's goal is not the traditional effort to enhance personality and behavior, but rather to help the family deal with a situational problem (Pruchno & Smyer, 1984).

Other approaches are more innovative. For example, Goodman and Pynoos (1990) described a telephone information and support program for caregivers of Alzheimer's Disease patients. In this program, caregivers could either participate in a peer network that engaged in regular telephone conversations about caregiving, or they could listen to informational minilectures delivered by telephone. Both telephone-based interventions increased caregivers' knowledge about the disease, as well as their satisfaction with their social supports.

Another common intervention is a **caregiver support group**. In these groups, caregivers can receive information about specific disorders, share social support, and exchange ideas about how to manage problematic behaviors. Although members typically give support groups high praise, objective evidence that the groups reduce burden is sparse (Chappell, 1990; Gatz et al., 1990; Toseland & Rossiter, 1989).

Respite care (see Chapter Four, p. 101) is one of the services that caregivers request most often (Chappell, 1990; Gatz et al., 1990). Like support groups, respite care typically elicits caregivers' enthusiastic approval but does not necessarily reduce scores on objective measures of burden (e.g., Lawton, Brody, & Sapirstein, 1989). Given limited resources, these findings present a dilemma for those planning services for caregivers. Should service providers concentrate on providing the kinds of services that caregivers request or on services with clearly documented benefits for caregivers, if the two are not the same? If services are provided according to caregivers' preferences (rather than according to the demonstrated benefits of those services), then how should those services be evaluated?

Mediation through caregiving networks   Nationally, only about one-third of caregivers are the *only* person providing care to an impaired elderly person; most sole caregivers are spouses (Stone, Cafferata, & Sangl, 1987). Most of the remaining caregivers are **primary caregivers**, who give most of the necessary help but also coordinate their efforts with those of other family members or friends (Stone et al., 1987). Who are the **secondary caregivers** providing this assistance? What kinds of help do they usually provide? How do they react to their role?

Whereas primary caregivers are usually the spouse or daughter of the impaired older person, secondary caregivers are typically sons-in-law, grandchildren, siblings, or nonrelatives (Tennstedt, McKinlay, & Sullivan, 1989). Caregiving daughters, then, often enlist family help in providing care. Nonrelatives (e.g., friends or neighbors of the impaired person) most often become secondary caregivers when the primary caregiver is either the spouse of the impaired person or a more distant relative (Tennstedt et al., 1989).

Secondary caregivers share in most tasks that the primary caregiver performs. But primary caregivers do the lion's share of personal care, housekeeping, and meal preparation—tasks that demand regular involvement (Tennstedt et al., 1989). Secondary caregivers usually take on tasks such as transportation and home repairs that come up intermittently (Tennstedt et al., 1989). As secondary caregivers, women generally provide more help than men do (Brody, Hoffman, Kleban, & Schoonover, 1989; Coward & Dwyer, 1990).

Secondary caregivers experience burden, just as primary caregivers do. Townsend et al. (1989) found no differences between primary and secondary caregivers' feelings of stress, depression, and effectiveness in the caregiving role. Other research suggests that siblings who are secondary caregivers for a frail elderly parent may be distressed by the relatively low level of their own involve-

BOX 12.1   DIVERSITY IN ADULTHOOD

What should adult children do for aged parents? Answers from American and Japanese women

According to folk wisdom, the aged are accorded a higher level of respect in non-Western than in Western societies. Asian families are assumed to be more willing to meet the needs of elderly relatives than families in Western nations. How accurate are these beliefs? Recent research suggests that folk wisdom may not do justice to the high level of filial responsibility that characterizes American as well as Asian families.

Like the United States, Japan has a rapidly growing population of elderly people. Both countries are witnessing greater proportions of middle-aged women (traditionally, the principal caregivers for elderly relatives) entering the work force. Japan, however, has a long tradition of providing care for the aged within three-generational households (Maeda, 1983). Furthermore, Japanese social interaction is bound by

Japan has a long tradition of providing care to older relatives within three-generation households.

ment in caregiving. Men—and to an even greater extent women—who live at a distance from their mothers and are secondary caregivers partly for that reason often feel helpless, guilty, and emotionally strained (Brody et al., 1989; Schoonover, Brody, Hoffman, & Kleban, 1988). Less often, these individuals find that conflict with the primary caregiver sibling is distressing (Brody et al., 1989; Schoonover et al., 1988).

ties of social obligation; children expect to reciprocate the sacrifices that their parents made for them by providing care to their parents in old age (Lebra, 1976).

Thus, both countries confront patterns of social change that could strain norms of filial responsibility. But, given Japan's traditions of family care and obligation, it would be logical to expect the contemporary Japanese to express a greater sense of filial responsibility than would their American counterparts. Parallel surveys of three generations of women in both countries allows us to test the accuracy of this supposition.

In the early 1980s, Elaine Brody and her colleagues conducted a three-generation study of women's attitudes toward providing care for frail elderly relatives (e.g., Brody et al., 1984). The Tokyo Metropolitan Institute of Gerontology replicated this study with a sample of three generations of Japanese women, allowing comparison of American and Japanese women's attitudes toward care of elderly relatives (Campbell & Brody, 1985).

These parallel surveys revealed both similarities and differences in the American and Japanese women's outlook on providing care to the aged. In both countries, women expressed neither great enthusiasm for nor strong rejection of formal services for elderly relatives. In both countries the youngest women expressed the most positive attitudes toward family caregiving; the oldest women expressed the most favorable attitudes toward formal services

There were cultural differences—more in degree than in direction—in beliefs about family responsibility toward aged parents. Contrary to folk wisdom, the American women expressed a stronger sense of family responsibility than the Japanese women did. For example, the American women agreed more strongly than the Japanese women did with the idea that older people should be able to depend on their grown children for help. Similarly, the American women disagreed more strongly than the Japanese women did with the notion that adult children with families of their own should not be expected to help their parents with household tasks.

As Campbell and Brody (1985) suggested, these differences in attitudes may reflect cultural differences in the ways in which family caregiving is implemented in the two countries. In the United States, daughters tend to care for aged parents whereas daughters-in-law take on those responsibilities in Japan. Family caregiving more often occurs in a multigenerational household (typically, the home of the aged parent's oldest son) in Japan than in the United States. Negative experiences arising in these households (crowding, for example, or conflict between mothers- and daughters-in-law) may have colored the Japanese women's attitudes. Thus, caregiving occurs in a different context in the two countries: Campbell & Brody's (1985) data illustrate ways in which common social trends interact with distinct cultural traditions.

Other reactions to caregiving

Although most caregivers experience some degree of burden, many also identify ways in which providing care is a positive experience. Some find that caregiving draws them closer to the elderly person receiving care, or that the family as a whole becomes closer as a result of caregiving (Kinney & Stephens, 1989; Motenko, 1989; Stoller & Pugliesi, 1989a; 1989b). Others take comfort in the

Some people find that caregiving draws them closer to an elderly relative.

assurance that their elderly relative is receiving good care (Kinney & Stephens, 1989). For some, providing care brings pride in managing a difficult challenge, or an opportunity to learn new skills and experience personal growth (Brody, 1985; Davies, Priddy, & Tinklenberg, 1986; Schulz et al., 1990; Stoller & Pugliesi, 1989a; 1989b).

Others have considered ways in which aged care recipients react to family caregiving. Treas and Bengtson (1987) note that "the family caregiving literature appears generally to assume that impaired aged persons, expect, willingly accept, and react positively to assistance from their families . . ." (p. 643). Not all care recipients have such positive reactions, however. Well-intentioned relatives may provide inappropriate amounts or types of care, and thereby undermine an elderly person's wish to remain as independent as possible (e.g., Arling, Parham, & Teitleman, 1978; Cicirelli, 1990; Thomas, 1987).

Variation in caregiving: Gender, relationship, and racial differences

Individual differences among caregivers are associated with the types of care provided and with reactions to caregiving. Most researchers have studied gender differences in caregiving, as well as differences between elderly spouses and adult children as caregivers. Some data identify race and class differences in caregiving, and differences related to the type of impairment necessitating family care. Variation in caregiving stressors, appraisals, and mediators are associated with differences in reactions to caregiving (see Figure 12.2).

Men's and women's caregiving experiences differ in the types of care typically provided, in how much help others provide with caregiving, and in the extent of burden experienced. Most studies contrast husbands and wives as caregivers *or* sons and daughters as caregivers. Unfortunately, this approach precludes simultaneously examining the importance of both gender and relationship to the impaired person as influences of caregiving experience (see the studies by Miller and Montgomery (1990) and by Young and Kahana (1989) below for exceptions).

In some ways, men fare better than women do as caregivers. Women— particularly adult daughters (Young & Kahana, 1989)—take responsibility for a wider variety of caregiving tasks than men do, and receive less help from other family members and friends in carrying out these responsibilities than men do (Horowitz, 1985; Pruchno & Resch, 1989; Stoller, 1990; Zarit, Orr, & Zarit, 1985). However, some research presents a different picture. Using a nationally representative sample of caregivers, B. Miller (1990) found no differences between men and women in the numbers of caregiving tasks performed or in the extent of help received.

Since women do more caregiving with less help than men do, it is not surprising that women experience more negative consequences of caregiving. Wives and daughters, as compared to husbands and sons, experience greater restrictions in social activities as a result of caregiving (Miller & Montgomery, 1990). Given that women may curtail their careers (and thus lose employee benefits such as pensions and health insurance) as a result of caregiving, these women can become particularly dependent on publically-funded sources of support such as Social Security and Medicare.

Wives are more likely than husbands to report that caregiving causes their health to worsen (Miller, 1990). Also, women experience a higher level of caregiver burden than men do (Barusch & Spaid, 1989; Gallagher, Rose, Rivera, Lovett, & Thompson, 1989; Horowitz, 1985; Pruchno & Resch, 1989; Young & Kahana, 1989). Husbands caring for wives suffering from dementia, however report concerns about their sexual relationship (Davies et al., 1986; Litz, Zeiss & Davies, 1990); researchers have not discussed caregiving wives' sexual concerns.

Other research contrasts spouses and adult children as caregivers. Spouses, in general, provide care to younger and more impaired elderly people (e.g., Montgomery & Borgatta, 1989). Furthermore, spouses and children report different caregiving-related concerns. For spouses caring for dementia patients, one source of distress is missing the way the victim "used to be" (Barusch, 1988). Since spouses enter caregiving with greater age and physical frailty than adult children do, they find caregiving more physically straining and they more often worry about becoming ill or otherwise unable to provide care (Barusch, 1988). Adult children, in contrast, more often experience conflict between caregiving and their other responsibilities (Brody, 1985). Compared to spouses, adult children report greater restrictions in social activities (Miller & Montgomery, 1990) and higher levels of burden (Young & Kahana, 1989).

Racial differences in caregiving parallel the racial differences in family support discussed earlier in the chapter. Compared to non-Hispanic Caucasians, African-American families, Hispanic-American families, Asian-American families, and Native American families are characterized by broader networks of extended relatives providing care to impaired elderly members (Chappell, 1990; Markides & Mindel, 1987). It is difficult to determine, of course, the extent to which these differences reflect cultural preferences as opposed to racial differences in socioeconomic status.

Finally, caregiving will obviously vary as a function of the type of impairment from which the elderly care recipient suffers. The types of assistance that the individual needs, the time and physical effort needed to provide that help, and the sources of support for the caregiver may be dramatically different depending on whether the older person suffers from cognitive impairments, physical frailties, or some combination of mental and physical problems. Compared to caregivers for the physically impaired, those caring for dementia victims report higher levels of emotional, physical, and financial strain (Birkel & Jones, 1989; Scharlach, 1989). Caregivers of dementia victims also receive less help with caregiving and more often find that caregiving interferes with their work responsibilities (Birkel & Jones, 1989; Scharlach, 1989).

FAMILY CAREGIVING AND FORMAL SOURCES OF LONG-TERM CARE

In addition to the help that secondary caregivers provide, family caregivers sometimes also rely on formal sources of long-term care for assistance. Recall that long-term care may be provided by many community sources (e.g., paid helpers, government-funded services, etc.), or may take place in a nursing home (see Chapter Four, pp. 100–108). Policy makers and social planners attempt to find the ideal mix between formal and family long-term care; the *Open Questions* box considers the appropriate balance between the obligation of the family and the state to care for frail elderly people.

How does family care mesh with care available from formal sources? Noelker and Bass (1989) describe four means through which family care is united with help from formal sources. There may be **kin independence**, in which the family cares for the older individual without any formal help; this, in fact, is the most frequent caregiving situation (Montgomery & Borgatta, 1989; Noelker & Bass, 1989; Tennstedt et al., 1989). Another model is **formal service specialization**, in which family members and formal service providers share some caregiving tasks but formal service providers alone perform other tasks. For example, a visiting nurse may take charge of the older person's injections (a task that the family caregiver does not have the skill to carry out), and help the primary caregiver bathe the patient.

OPEN QUESTIONS   BOX 12.2

Should the family or the state be responsible for older people's long-term care?

This chapter shows that family members take center stage in meeting older individuals' needs for support. Most families take on caregiving out of feelings of love and duty. However, family caregiving also has a foundation in statute. At the close of the 1980s, thirty states had some type of **filial responsibility law** specifying family obligations for support of older people in need, and most of the other states had such laws in the past (Bulcroft, Leynseele, & Borgatta, 1989). Such laws, however, are rarely invoked, partly because most are vague in defining need on the part of the older individual, in specifying the type of support that family members are bound to provide, and identifying the jurisdiction procedures involved (Bulcroft et al., 1989). The laws may also be rarely enforced because there is little need to do so, since most families willingly provide support.

Some gerontologists question whether this situation can continue into the twenty-first century. We have already noted the rapid growth of the oldest segments of the population—those most likely to need long-term care (see Chapter One, pp. 3–4). Coupled with this trend is a shrinking pool of potential family caregivers. Family size has decreased throughout most of the twentieth century, and women's labor force participation has increased. All of these patterns of social change prompt questions concerning the ability of the family to continue to care for the frail elderly—particularly as the "baby boom" cohorts age.

Perhaps in the future, the state will have to take a much more active role in providing care to elderly people. Many would argue that the state *should* do so. Exhorting families to take responsibility for the aged can be construed as social irresponsibility toward those who helped to build our nation through their paid employment, childrearing, and citizenship (e.g., Brody, 1985).

Unfortunately, the 1980s also witnessed a trend toward curtailed public involvement in providing long-term care. Rising costs of long-term care, coupled with political conservatism and the desire to save public funds, have diminished the availability of publically-funded long-term care both in the community and in institutions. Some raise questions of "**generational equity**," charging that older people receive a large share of public resources at the same time that the numbers of children living in poverty is skyrocketing (e.g., Neugarten & Neugarten, 1989). These trends suggest that families must be prepared to continue to be the primary caregivers for the frail aged.

The ideal source of long-term care—whether the family or the state—is likely to remain an open question. Unexpected historical events, technological and medical advances, and social change could undoubtedly change the need for long-term care and the resources available to provide it. Perhaps the most certain answer is that the family and the state should be prepared to cooperate in providing care to frail elderly people in the future.

In **dual specialization**, the family caregivers and formal service providers each carry out different caregiving tasks. Here, a home health aide alone might be responsible for changing dressings and colostomy care, whereas the family takes full responsibility for shopping, housework, and meal preparation. **Supplementation** occurs when formal service providers and family members share responsibility for certain kinds of assistance, and family caregivers alone help the older person in additional ways. For example, both the family caregivers and a visiting nurse might change dressings and bathe the older person, and the family (but not the visiting nurse) might also provide companionship, transportation, and help with housework and meal preparation.

Family caregiving and institutionalization

Although it may seem that family caregiving ends when an elderly person enters a nursing home, rarely is that the case. The family typically continues to provide care even after institutionalization. However, the kinds of care that family members provide and the burdens that they encounter change.

Gerontologists agree that the decision to institutionalize an older person is rarely taken lightly, but is an agonizing process that often encompasses years of overwhelming family burden (Brody, Dempsey, & Pruchno, 1990; Pruchno, Michaels, & Potashnik, 1990). After an elderly person enters a nursing home, the family can provide care by taking part in such tasks as keeping the room clean; doing laundry; and helping with money, shopping, and transportation (Brody et al., 1990). Of course, the family also provides affection and companionship. For daughters of nursing home residents, taking part in these duties is associated with relatively low levels of depression following nursing home placement (Brody et al., 1990).

Just as the types of family-provided care change, the sources of caregiver burden alter with nursing home placement. Kinney, Stephens, Ogrocki, and Bridges (1989) compared the sources of stress most often reported by in-home caregivers and caregivers of nursing home residents. Both groups were troubled by the care recipient's confusion, forgetfulness, mental decline, agitation, and lack of interest in things. However, the in-home caregivers also experienced stress due to the need to provide personal care, the older person's lack of cooperation, and her repetitive questions; the caregivers of nursing home residents complained of the care recipient's failure to recognize familiar people. Other research identifies competing demands on the caregiver's time, worry over the quality of care in the institution, numbers and availability of staff and the staff's attitudes toward the resident and her family as sources of stress for family caregivers to nursing home residents (Brody et al., 1990).

CONCLUDING THOUGHTS

This overview of intergenerational support networks leads to three general conclusions. First, exchanging help is a tradition within most families, and one in which middle-aged adults play pivotal roles. Second, family members exchange help in a reciprocal fashion over the long run. Even though parents or grandparents may receive more help from younger relatives than they provide in advanced old age, they may have previously given far more help to their children and grandchildren than they received from them. Third, the increasingly common experience of family caregiving must be considered using a contextual perspective. Only by considering the stressors that a caregiver confronts, her appraisals of those stressors, and the mediators available to help her to deal with the stressors does her reaction to caregiving make sense.

SUMMARY

Young, middle-aged, and elderly adult relatives exchange help in the forms of child care, care during illness, emotional support and advice, help with household tasks or home repairs, and financial support and advice. The middle generations in these intergenerational networks provide more help to the oldest and youngest adult generations than they receive from them.

Caregivers' feelings of burden reflect the impact of (1) an objective event (the elderly person's incapacitating illness), (2) consequences of that event (the older person's symptoms, tasks that the caregiver performs, changes in the caregiver's life), (3) the caregiver's perception of these consequences, and (4) the resources available to her. Family caregivers perform a wide variety of tasks for frail elderly relatives. Women carry out more caregiving tasks than men do, and receive less help from other family members and friends in carrying out these responsibilities than men do. Potential resources include family counseling, caregiver support groups, respite care, other types of long-term care available in the community, and telephone support programs.

KEY TERMS

Activities of daily living (ADL)
Caregiver burden
Caregiver support group
Dual specialization
Filial maturity
Filial responsibility
Filial responsibility law
Formal service specialization
Generational equity
Instrumental activities of daily living (IADL)

Intergenerational support networks
Kin independence
Patron-type status
Primary caregiver
Reciprocity
Respite care
Secondary caregiver
Supplementation
Support bank
"Women in the middle"

SUGGESTIONS FOR FURTHER READING

Biegel, D. E., & Blum, A. (1990). *Aging and Caregiving: Theory, Research, and Policy*. Newbury Park, CA: Sage Publications.

Biegel, D. E., Sales, E., & Schulz, R. (1990). *Family Caregiving in Chronic Illness*. Newbury Park, CA: Sage Publications.

Brody, E. M. (1990). *Women in the Middle: Their Parent-care Years*. New York: Springer.

Mace, N. L., & Rabins, P. V. (1991). *The 36-hour Day*, 2nd Ed. Baltimore: Johns Hopkins University Press.

Troll, L. E. (1986). *Family Issues in Current Gerontology*. New York: Springer.

Zarit, S. H., Orr, N. K., & Zarit, J. M. (1985). *The Hidden Victims of Alzheimer's Disease: Families Under Stress*. New York: New York University Press.

CHAPTER THIRTEEN

BONDS WITH SIBLINGS, FRIENDS, AND THE COMMUNITY

Do people have different kinds of relationships with brothers, sisters, and friends as they get older? Are old people more religious than younger people? Are age-segregated apartment complexes and communities beneficial to older adults, or are they ghettos in disguise? This chapter begins with an examination of relationships with siblings, and continues with a consideration of friendship. The final topic of the chapter is how people contribute to their communities throughout adulthood. In that context, we survey involvement in politics and in voluntary organizations, the importance of volunteer work, age differences in spirituality and religious involvement, and the benefits and problems of specialized communities for older adults.

Questions to consider in reading the chapter include:

How do relationships with siblings change during adulthood? What is the importance of friends and confidants in old age? How do men's and women's perspectives on friendship differ?

What age differences in political interest, involvement, and orientations have been identified?

What age, gender, and racial differences in religious involvement have been identified?

How do age-segregated housing and communities benefit the old? What are problems associated with specialized housing and communities for older people?

SIBLING RELATIONSHIPS THROUGHOUT ADULTHOOD

The importance of brothers and sisters

Most adults have at least one sibling, although older people have fewer surviving siblings than do younger adults (Bengtson, Rosenthal, & Burton, 1990). Only about one in ten Americans today are only children (Cicirelli, 1982), but the increasing frequency of one-child families predicts that future cohorts will include more individuals who do not have brothers or sisters. Will these people miss anything substantial?

Sibling relationships are unique (Cicirelli, 1982). People have the longest lasting relationships of their lifetimes with brothers and sisters, and share things with them—such as early experiences with parents—that they share with no one else. Sibling relationships are also more egalitarian than many other relationships. Unlike parent-child relationships, relationships in the workplace, and some marriages, there is rarely a marked difference in the power that siblings wield in their relationships. These relationships can have tremendous symbolic importance, particularly in old age. Bonds with brothers and sisters can provide a sense of identity and security, as well as a connection to the personal past (Bengtson et al., 1990).

Sibling relationships are governed in part by norms. These are ascribed relationships: one becomes a sibling automatically when a brother or sister is born, and no personal action can alter that fact. However, in American culture norms dictate some measure of affection between brothers and sisters. People who are not emotionally close to their siblings typically express some guilt or pain about the distance in their relationship (Cicirelli, 1989; Ross, Dalton, & Milgram, 1980).

Contact, feelings, and exchanging help
between adult brothers and sisters

Many young adults see a sibling about once a month or even once a week, although most people see brothers and sisters less often after they get married than before marriage (Leigh, 1982). Middle-aged and older adults generally see or talk to a sibling several times a year (Bengtson et al., 1990; Cicirelli, 1982; Scott, 1983). Generally, older adults who do not have living children are in more frequent contact with their brothers and sisters than are older people with children (Bengtson et al., 1990; Scott, 1983).

Frequency of contact with siblings depends on the feelings that they have for one another, geographic proximity, and gender (Lee, Mancini, & Maxwell, 1990). Not surprisingly, siblings who live relatively close to one another see each other more often than those who live farther away. In addition, sisters usually see each other more often than brothers or brother-sister pairs. Finally, individuals who express relatively high levels of emotional closeness to their siblings and who feel responsible for their siblings' welfare get together more often with brothers and sisters than those who report lower levels of these feelings.

Most people have close relationships with their brothers and sisters (Cicirelli, 1982). Older adults, particularly widowed elderly people, may describe their siblings as close friends or confidants (Bengtson et al., 1990; Connidis & Davies, 1990; Kendig, Coles, Pittelkow, & Wilson, 1988). Sisters are usually closer emotionally than are brothers or brother-sister pairs (Cicirelli, 1982).

Those who have the closest sibling relationships were quite close to their brothers and sisters as children; very few people become close to their brothers and sisters for the first time when they are adults (Ross & Milgram, 1982). Adults who feel especially close to their brothers and sisters usually cite childhood experiences as explanations (Ross & Milgram, 1982). These individuals recall their parents' emphasis on family unity while they were growing up, and democratic childrearing practices that stressed family harmony, avoidance of favoritism, and recognition of individual talents and accomplishments. On the other hand, family circumstances can also prevent siblings from developing close relationships (Ross & Milgram, 1982). For example, when siblings are far apart in age, or when divorce or other disruptive events separate siblings during childhood, they may not have the opportunity to become close.

A few adults have enduring feelings of rivalry toward siblings; such rivalry is more common between brothers than between sisters or brother-sister dyads (Ross & Milgram, 1982). Rivalry usually centers on siblings' achievements, intelligence, physical attractiveness, social competence, and maturity (Ross & Milgram, 1982). Not all sibling rivalry (either in childhood or adulthood) is marked by antagonism; for some, the vying for approval is tinged with affection and humor (Ross & Milgram, 1982).

Still other adults report having little or no feelings toward their siblings (Cicirelli, 1982; Ross & Milgram, 1982). These individuals may only see brothers and sisters at family rituals and holidays, and even less often than that after their parents' death. However, it is quite unusual for someone to have no contact at all with their brothers and sisters (Bengtson et al., 1990; Cicirelli, 1982; Ross & Milgram, 1982). Distance in sibling relationships may arise after a parent's death, if siblings disagree about the extent to which the parent's estate was divided equitably (see Chapter Fifteen, page 387).

Given that most adults have regular contact with siblings, what is the nature of that contact? What do adult brothers and sisters do together? Relatively few young adults regularly exchange help with brothers and sisters, or discuss intimate matters and important decisions with siblings (Cicirelli, 1982). Throughout adulthood, siblings rely on one another for help to a lesser extent than they rely on children or grandchildren (Scott, 1983). However, exchanging help may maintain closeness in the relationships: a propensity to help siblings is associated with more frequent contact between brothers and sisters (Lee et al., 1990).

Later in adulthood, siblings may collaborate to care for frail elderly parents (see Chapter Twelve, pp. 311–312). The way in which caregiving tasks are divided depends on the quality of the relationship, as well as on such pragmatic concerns as the siblings' geographic proximity to the parent and their employ-ment status. M. A. Matthews (1987) reported that, not surprisingly, siblings who prize their relationship take greater care to insure an equitable division of tasks and responsibilities than siblings who value their relationship less. Caring for an aged parent can affect the quality of bonds between siblings. When these relationships are marked by long-term feelings of rivalry, caregiving may further strain the relationships (Ross & Milgram, 1982).

Although exchanging help is not a typical feature of sibling relationships in old age (e.g., Bengtson et al., 1990; Depner & Ingersoll-Dayton, 1988), brothers and sisters are important sources of support for some older people. Elderly people without living spouses or children may look to siblings when they need assistance (e.g., O'Bryant, 1988). Even if siblings are rarely called on for help, knowing that they are available and willing to help if needed can provide a sense of security in old age (Cicirelli, 1985).

Finally, not all researchers agree that siblings are unimportant sources of support in old age. For elderly men and women participating in a qualitative study of sibling relationships, helping one another was very important (Ross & Milgram, 1982). The older people in this study exchanged help with their brothers and sisters more than did the young adult and middle-aged partici-pants. In old age, these individuals and their siblings helped each other by giving physical assistance (e.g., home repairs, care during illness), emotional support and companionship, and—when necessary—financial support.

In old age, differences between individuals increase for virtually all char-acteristics; the kind of relationship that people have with brothers and sisters is no exception. Deborah Gold (1989; Gold, Woodbury, & George, 1990) recently examined relatively well-educated and affluent older adults' descriptions of their relationships with siblings. On the basis of these descriptions, she offered a typology of sibling relationships in later life. Gold characterized the relation-ships in terms of the levels of closeness, instrumental support, emotional sup-port, acceptance, psychological involvement, contact, envy, and resentment that respondents expressed for their siblings.

Gold (1989; Gold et al., 1990) distinguished five types of sibling relation-ships among her elderly respondents; the relative frequencies of these relation-ships in her sample are illustrated in Figure 13.1. Those who had **intimate sibling relationships** reported relatively high levels of closeness, support, acceptance, involvement, and contact, but relatively low levels of envy and resentment; those who had **congenial sibling relationships** also had rela-tively high levels of closeness, support, acceptance and involvement, average levels of contact, and relatively low levels of envy and resentment. **Loyal sibling relationships** were characterized by average levels of closeness, involvement, and contact as well as relatively low levels of support, envy, and resentment.

The remaining two patterns of sibling relationships did not share the benign character of the first three. In **apathetic sibling relationships**, levels of all of the dimensions (e.g., closeness, support, etc.) were relatively low. **Hostile sibling relationships**, however, were characterized by relatively high levels of

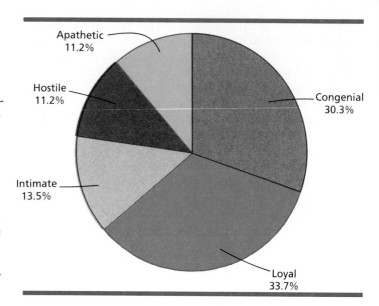

Figure 13.1
Frequencies of sibling relationships. (Source: Gold, 1989; Gold et al., 1990. "Relationship Classification Using Grade of Membership Analysis," *Journal of Gerontology: Social Sciences,* 45: S43–S52. Copyright © The Gerontological Society of America. Reprinted by permission.)

involvement and resentment and relatively low levels of closeness, support, acceptance, contact, and envy. Gold (Gold et al., 1990) notes that these two types may be more alike than they are different. In practical terms, it probably matters little whether one feels indifference or antipathy for a brother or sister. In further research, Gold (1990) found that older African-Americans described apathetic and hostile relationships with their siblings far less often than older Caucasians did (4.5 percent for African-Americans versus 22 percent for Caucasians).

Gold's (1989; Gold et al., 1990) research is particularly valuable in raising an important question. There is no information about the history of these relationship types. Whether one has, for example, a congenial or a loyal relationship with siblings throughout adulthood—or whether these types crystallize in old age—remains to be demonstrated.

FRIENDSHIP

Age differences in friendship

Scholars have considered the structure of **friendship networks** (e.g., number of friends, frequency of contact with friends), the qualities attributed to friends, and the qualities of hypothetical "ideal friends." Most cross-sectional studies show that both the number of friends and the frequency of getting together with friends decrease throughout adulthood. People generally have more friends, and see more of their friends, when they are young adults than in middle or later adulthood (e.g., Farrell & Rosenberg, 1981; Fiebert & Wright, 1989; Weiss & Lowenthal, 1975).

For adults of all ages, friends tend to be close to one's own age (e.g., Weiss & Lowenthal, 1975). Middle-aged and older adults are less likely than young adults to have cross-sex friendships (Adams, 1985; Huyck, 1982). Perhaps young people have more opportunities (e.g., on college campuses and other educational settings) to develop cross-sex friendships than middle-aged and older people do.

Furthermore, contemporary middle-aged and older people may assume that friendships between men and women include a sexual component (Adams, 1985; Huyck, 1982). Since most middle-aged people are married, this assumption typically precludes developing cross-sex friendships (Huyck, 1982). Because there are few unmarried elderly men relative to the numbers of widows, and because of norms proscribing romantic involvements for elderly people, elderly women are often hesitant to pursue cross-sex friendships (Adams, 1985). With changing notions of men's and women's roles and relationships, however, today's young adults will probably feel more free to develop cross-sex relationships as they get older than current cohorts of older people do.

Why do older people typically have fewer friends than younger adults? Both cohort differences and maturational changes probably contribute. Morgan (1988) found that age differences in social networks—including age differences in numbers of friends and frequency of contact with friends—were predicted by age differences in income, level of education, and health. Having adequate finances, some measure of cognitive sophistication, and good health makes it easier to maintain relationships with friends. Older cohorts, on the average, have lower levels of education than do younger cohorts; with age, both income and health tend to decline. Thus, older people have less extensive resources for maintaining friendship networks than do younger adults. Also one becomes increasingly likely to lose same-aged friends through death as one gets older. Since friends tend to be close to one's own age (see above), a shrinking friendship network is almost inevitable in old age.

Another possibility, though, is that a shrinking friendship network reflects the preferences of aging individuals. **Selectivity theory** (Carstensen, 1987; 1989; Fredrickson & Carstensen, 1990) posits that people grow increasingly "choosey" about their social partners throughout the life cycle. For some people, old age brings the opportunity to cherish a few intimate friendships and to withdraw from more peripheral ones (Adams, 1987). Compared to children, adolescents, and young adults, older individuals maximize their contact with and investment in their closest, most familiar and predictable relationships—as opposed to less intimate, less meaningful, and less predictable relationships. According to selectivity theory, this process allows elderly people to conserve their physical energy, a goal that becomes particularly important in later life, and to regulate their emotional experience. Because older people have a lifetime of social experience on which to draw, they have a firmer foundation than younger people do for being selective in choosing social partners.

Do adults of different ages seek different things in their friends? Weiss and Lowenthal's (1975) classic study points to few age differences in qualities prized in friends. For adults of all ages, **similarity** (e.g., shared experiences, ease of communication), **reciprocity** (e.g., mutual help and support), and **compatibility** (e.g., comfort and ease of relationship, likability) were critical qualities in friends. People of all ages also described friendships in terms of **structural dimensions**, such as the duration of the relationship, the friend's geographic proximity, or the convenience of being with the friend. Some, finally, described friends as **role models** who possessed qualities that the respondent particularly admired or respected.

However, other work suggests that women of different ages do identify different qualities in their friends. Candy, Troll, and Levy (1981) asked women in six age groups to describe their five best friends; the age groups spanned adolescence through old age. Intimacy (being able to share personal feelings with friends) and assistance (exchanging help with friends) in friendship were equally important to women of all ages. However, status (deriving prestige or esteem from association with friends) was less important to women in their twenties, thirties, forties, and fifties than to adolescent women or older women. Similarly, power (having authority over friends) was a less important dimension of friendship to young adult women, middle-aged women, and older women than to teenagers.

In other research, middle-aged adults described their friends more positively than younger people did. These descriptions include greater intimacy and tenderness (Haan, 1976; Fieber & Wright, 1989) and greater enjoyment and satisfaction (Gould, 1978) in the relationships. The contrasts do not all favor middle-aged adults' friendships, however. In one study, middle-aged respondents rated close friendships as less stimulating and intense than younger adults, but also as providing greater security than younger adults (Reinhardt, 1987). For older adults, friendships are most satisfying when the relationship is marked by concern for the friend's needs and by absence of conflict (Jones & Vaughn, 1990).

Class, race, and gender differences in friendship

Working-class adults generally have fewer close friends than do middle-class people (e.g., Bell, 1981b; Farrell & Rosenberg, 1981; Lowenthal & Haven, 1968). Working- and lower-class individuals are more likely than middle-class people to have sex-segregated friendship networks, to prefer to spend time with family rather than with friends, and to engage in less self-disclosure with friends (George, 1988).

Racial differences have also been explored. For African-Americans, the church is often a center of friendship networks (e.g., Taylor, 1988; Taylor & Chatters, 1986). African-Americans generally have fewer friends than Caucasians, although there are no racial differences in satisfaction with friendships or in frequency of contact with friends (George, 1988). Native Americans' networks of social relationships, including their friendship networks, depend on whether the individuals live on or off reservations. Reservation-dwelling older Native Americans have fewer social contacts and are relatively socially isolated (John, 1985).

Gender is by far the most frequently studied source of individual differences in friendship. The *Diversity in Adulthood* box summarizes some of this work. It may be easy to draw the conclusion from that research that women are better at having and being friends than men are, and that women are correspondingly advantaged in psychological well-being. That conclusion, however, is an oversimplification (see Box 13.1).

R. R. Bell (1981a), in a series of interviews with men and women, explored friendship networks and qualities that stood out in friendships. In addition to comparing men's and women's views, Bell compared participants that he described as "nonconventional" and as "conventional" with regard to their evaluations and feelings about their lives. The nonconventional men and women were those who sought to enact change, to enhance their levels of happiness and life satisfaction, to take gambles in their lives, and to increase the amount of control that they had in their lives. Bell described the conventional men and women as expressing an opposite character on these dimensions.

Like most researchers in this area (see Box 13.1), Bell (1981a; 1981b) found that women described more personal and emotionally-based friendships than did men. In addition, the nonconventional and conventional groups differed in their friendships. Nonconventional men and women reported more cross-sex friendships and friendships of greater emotional depth and openness than did conventional men and women. Clearly, then, one's outlook on life and the world may have just as much to do with friendship as one's gender.

Confidants in old age

Earlier chapters identified a spectrum of characteristics and circumstances associated with life satisfaction in old age. Relationships with **confidants**—intimate friends with whom one can discuss personal feelings and concerns—can be added to that list. Of course, having such intimate and trusted friends is beneficial throughout the life cycle, not only in old age. Women are more likely to have confidants than are men, and married older people are more likely than unmarried, widowed, or divorced elderly people to have confidants (e.g., Lowenthal & Haven, 1968). Confidants are usually a spouse, an adult son or daughter, or a friend; however, women rarely name their husbands as confidants, whereas men usually cite their wives as confidants (e.g., Lowenthal & Haven, 1968).

In a classic study, Lowenthal and Haven (1968) considered associations between older adults' level of social interaction and their level of morale. One of

BOX 13.1 *DIVERSITY IN ADULTHOOD*

What is a friend? The contrasting perspectives of men and women

Virtually all researchers who compare men's and women's notions of friendship report that women have deeper friendships than men. More often than men, women describe friendships as forums for mutual self-disclosure, psychological intimacy, and support (e.g., Bell, 1981b; Depner & Ingersoll-Dayton, 1988; Fiebert & Wright, 1989; Huyck, 1982; Lowenthal & Haven, 1968; Stein, 1986). When men describe their friends, they usually concentrate on the things they do together rather than on the intimacy of their relationships (Huyck, 1982).

There is less certainty about the sources of this gender difference, however. **Homophobia** is probably one reason that men describe friendship in less intimate terms than women do; some men may hesitate to express intimacy toward other men out of fear of arousing sexual feelings or of being considered homosexual (Huyck, 1982; Stein, 1986). It may also be that men stress intimacy in friendship less than women do because of our society's emphasis on male competitiveness (e.g., Huyck, 1982; Stein, 1986). If that is the case, future cohorts of men and women may have more similar friendships as women take on more competitive roles at work.

Do women, then, have an advantage over men in their relationships with friends? Not necessarily. For one thing, it would be wrong to conclude that men do not value friendship. Young men in one recent study found that their friendships with other men were very important, and they felt a deep commitment to developing and maintaining these bonds—even though many found it difficult to discuss these feelings (Stein, 1986). Many of these men had belonged to a men's group at some time. Men's groups, like women's consciousness-raising groups of the 1970s, provide an opportunity to explore gender roles, to discuss social and cultural issues, and to develop a support network.

A substantial minority of older men in another study similarly stated that they placed great value on their friendships (Reisman, 1988). Although friendships were less important to most of these men than their families or careers, many regarded friends as an important and satisfying part of their lives. Men may express friendship differently than women do, then, but that difference should not be equated with a difference in the quality or value of the relationship.

Furthermore, the more intimate friendships that women typically report can bring stress as well as pleasure. While noting that women typically have larger networks of intimate relationships, Antonucci and Akiyama (1988) also reported that this circumstance sometimes leads to unhappiness. They explained that friends expect help and support from these women, and that meeting those expectations could occasionally be difficult. Women may also be burdened by conflict between network members (Leffler, Kranich, & Gillespie, 1986). Thus, for some women the demands of being a friend may offset some of the pleasure in having a friend.

the measures of social interaction was whether or not the individual had a confidant, and those who had such an intimate friend had higher morale than those who did not. Furthermore, having a confidant was a "buffer" against the stresses of such age-related social losses as bereavement and retirement. Having a confidant was of little help when these older people confronted serious physical illness, however. Perhaps the dependency that serious illness brings threatens close relationships.

Relationships with confidants can be an important source of life satisfaction in old age.

More recent research continues to document the association between presence of friends and/or a confidant and relatively high morale among elderly adults (e.g., Antonucci, 1990; Chappell & Badger, 1989; Lee & Shehan, 1989; Mullins & Dugan, 1990; Reinhardt & Fisher, 1989). However, it is hard to say what kinds of causal patterns produce that association. It may be that having friends and confidants lead to relatively high levels of morale. But it is also possible that people who are characteristically in good spirits are more capable of maintaining close relationships than more somber individuals are.

ADULTS IN THE COMMUNITY

There is little empirical information describing ways in which adults of different ages are involved in their communities—either through political activities, participation in voluntary organizations, volunteer work, church work, or other avenues of involvement. Nonetheless, these kinds of activities may be personally meaningful for adults of all ages, and may be of practical importance for their communities.

Political involvement

In theory, all adults are involved in their communities through political participation; unfortunately, many people pass up this opportunity. Recall that Havighurst (1952) includes community involvement in his developmental tasks of young adulthood (see Chapter Eight, p. 194). However, he also acknowledges the difficulty that many young adults face in establishing civic roles. Most young adults are preoccupied with careers, education, and families, and many experience the greatest geographic mobility of their lifetimes.

H. S. Maas (1989) points out that middle-aged people confront unique opportunities for civic leadership. Contemporary personality theorists (e.g., Erikson, Levinson) assert that these opportunities are important settings for personal growth in middle adulthood. Not only may these individuals be at a point in their personal growth when such involvement can be uniquely satisfying (see Chapter Eight, pp. 190–193), but they also face a set of family and work responsibilities that permit such involvement. With release from the demanding family responsibilities and extreme career pressures of young adulthood, many are now able to devote themselves to issues of social responsibility.

What about in old age? Many believe that people become more conservative as they get older. However, there is little evidence that age is related to political orientation in a systematic way (e.g., Jacobs, 1990). Older people, then, are no more likely as a group to endorse reactionary political positions than are young or middle-aged people. In fact, the extent to which elderly people are now—or are likely to become—a cohesive political force remains to be seen (e.g., Hudson, 1987).

The Gray Panthers is among the most active political organizations of older adults.

Several politically-oriented organizations lobbying on behalf of older people germinated in the 1960s, 1970s and 1980s; these associations include the **National Council of Senior Citizens (NCSC)**, the **American Association of Retired Persons (AARP)**, and the **Gray Panthers**. The groups vary in the extent to which they attempt to represent the interests of older people exclusively. The Gray Panthers, for example, advocate on behalf of legislation that would benefit people of all ages. In the past, the Gray Panthers have supported legislation that would provide better public transportation, and that which would create national health care insurance. The NCSC and AARP, by comparison, focus much more specifically on issues of particular concern to older citizens, such as the futures of Medicare and Social Security benefits.

Interest in politics increases with age; older people are more likely to vote than younger people are, controlling for cohort differences in such factors as education and marital status (George, 1988; Jacobs, 1990). Many who assume positions of political leadership—whether by election or appointment—are in their fifties, sixties, or seventies. Other kinds of political involvement (e.g., helping with political campaigns, contributing money to campaigns) are more frequent among middle-aged people than among elderly adults; these differences probably reflect cohort differences in education and income.

Voluntary organizations and volunteer work

Other avenues of community involvement include membership in civic organizations and volunteer work. Volunteer work, in particular, offers benefits to both the individual and the community. Although textbook definitions and economic indicators fail to recognize it, volunteer work—as a major category of productive activity—is an important national resource (e.g., Ager, 1986; Herzog, Kahn, Morgan, Jackson, & Antonucci, 1989; Morrow-Howell & Ozawa, 1987). This work, though unpaid, produces goods or services that would otherwise have to be bought or hired.

For young and middle-aged women, volunteer work can mean several things (Jenner, 1982). Some women see this activity as consciously-chosen primary work: rather than having a paid job, a woman considers her volunteer work with the local museum or literacy council a "surrogate career." For others, volunteer work is a supplement to primary work; a job and/or homemaking is the primary work for these women. Still other women view their volunteer work as a stepping stone to enter or reenter the labor force. Doing clerical work for a neighborhood school or church, for example, could be an opportunity to acquire and demonstrate skills in word processing or accounting.

Whatever volunteer work represents to young and middle-aged women, most volunteers devote a substantial amount of time to these activities and feel a serious commitment to continue them (Jenner, 1982). Even for those who think of volunteer work as primary work, however, that undertaking typically takes a backseat to family responsibilities. The amount of time that married women with children devote to volunteer activities is significantly related to the age of the youngest child, and these women report that their children's needs set limits on their own opportunities for volunteer involvement (Jenner, 1983).

Participation in voluntary organizations and volunteer work continues to be an important means of community involvement in old age. Some data suggest that voluntary organization participation decreases with age (Morgan, 1988), and some studies show that older people volunteer less often than younger adults do (Chambre, 1984). However, other work documents remarkable stability in organization participation (Costa, Zonderman, & McCrae, 1985) and in the percentage of people participating in volunteer work through old age (Herzog et al., 1989). In fact, helping others and unpaid work (including volunteer work) represents an increasing percentage of productive activity with increasing age, as illustrated in Figure 13.2 (Herzog et al., 1989).

What are the motivations for doing volunteer work in old age? Activity theory (see Chapter Two, pp. 36–37, and Chapter Eight, pp. 203–208) posits that men and women may volunteer to compensate for the loss of other roles in old age, although empirical support for this proposition is equivocal (e.g., Chambre,

Figure 13.2
Annual hours of productive activities, by age and sex. (Source: Herzog et al., 1989. "Age Differences in Productive Activities," *Journal of Gerontology: Social Sciences, 44:* S129–S138. Copyright © The Gerontological Society of America. Reprinted by permission.)

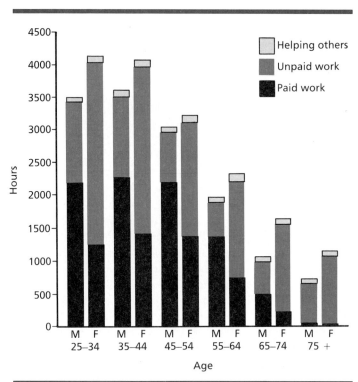

1984; also see Chapters Two and Eight). Surveys of older individuals and professionals who work with elderly people more commonly identify other motivations, including the need to cope with life transitions such as widowhood (Adlersberg & Thorne, 1990; Ager, 1986; Vinokur-Kaplan & Bergman, 1986), the desire for social contact and interaction (Morrow-Howell & Mui, 1989), and the desire to improve the community (Morrow-Howell & Mui, 1989). Older individuals who volunteer benefit not only by fulfilling these needs but also in terms of enhanced self-esteem (Lee & Shehan, 1989) and self-confidence (Berkman, 1984).

Religious involvement

Age, gender, and racial differences in religious involvement Religious involvement can refer to many things. In a classic article, Moberg (1968) points out that one might consider the emotions aroused by one's religion (**experiential religiosity**), the particular religious beliefs that one holds (**ideological religiosity**), the type of religious rituals that one observes and the frequency of observing these rituals (**ritualistic religiosity**), one's knowledge of the tenets and sacred texts of one's religion (**intellectual religiosity**), or the ways in which one's religion affects one's behavior (**consequential religiosity**). Thus, the question of how age is associated with religious involvement is more complex than it might initially appear. Most research has focused on the ritualistic dimension, examining age differences in church membership, frequency of

For many older people, the church is a particularly important means of community involvement.

attending religious services, and frequency of private religious activities such as prayer.

The church assumes unique importance among voluntary associations for older adults. Moberg (1968) reports that people of all ages are more likely to be church members than to be members of any other kind of organization. Simply being a member of a church, however, is potentially a rather "empty" indicator of religious involvement. One could conceivably be a member of a church without ever attending services or in any other way being involved in religion. How is age associated with religious involvement when we consider more active means of involvement?

Some studies show that frequency of church attendance is lower for elderly adults than for younger people (e.g., Ainlay & Smith, 1984; Koenig, Kvale, & Ferrel, 1988; Markides, Levin, & Ray, 1987; Moberg, 1968). However, these differences are slight, and probably reflect age differences in health, income, and availability of transportation. In most respects, older adults are more actively involved in religion than are younger adults. Because most of the research in this area is cross-sectional, however, it would be inaccurate to conclude that people become more religious as they get older. Although such age changes may occur, it is also possible that cohort differences account for age differences in religious involvement. If that is the case, older people in the future may be no more religious than future cohorts of young adults.

Compared to younger adults, contemporary elderly men and women engage in private religious activities more often. For example, older people listen to religious radio or television programs more often than younger adults (Moberg, 1968; Nielsen, 1985), and read the Bible and other devotional literature more frequently than do younger adults (Princeton Religion Research Center, 1982; Profile of *Guideposts* Reader, 1984). In national surveys, most older adults report that they pray at least daily (Princeton Religion Research Center, 1982). Older people are more likely than young adults to believe that religion can provide a solution to national and world problems (Glenn, 1980).

Religious involvement is associated with other characteristics, in addition to age. Throughout adulthood, women engage in virtually all kinds of religious activities—attending religious services, praying, reading devotional literature, and so on—more often than men do (Chatters & Taylor, 1989; Koenig et al., 1988; Princeton Religion Research Center, 1982; 1985). Ethnicity and race are also important. Elderly Mexican-Americans and non-Hispanic Caucasian women showed an increase in strength of religious feelings over a four-year period, although non-Hispanic Caucasian men showed no such increase (Markides, 1983).

Throughout adulthood, the church plays a more central role in the lives of African-Americans than of Caucasians (e.g., Chatters & Taylor, 1989; George, 1988). This contrast may reflect geographic influences in part (George, 1988). The African-American population is more concentrated than the Caucasian population in the southeastern United States, and levels of religious participation are generally higher in the southeastern "Bible Belt" than in other parts of the country. In addition, however, African-Americans have traditionally considered the church to be an institution second in importance only to the family (Taylor, 1986). Historically, the church has been virtually the only institution in the African-American community that was built, funded, and controlled by African-Americans (Nelson & Nelson, 1975).

What age differences in religious involvement have been documented among African-Americans? In a recent national survey of African-Americans, older respondents reported higher levels of organizational religious participation, such as church membership and church attendance (Chatters & Taylor, 1989). These older African-Americans also reported more frequent non-organizational religious involvement than did their younger counterparts; these kinds of involvement included reading religious materials, watching or listening to religious programs, praying, asking others to pray on their behalf, and experiencing religious feelings.

Religion as a resource in old age Older adults apparently derive psychological and practical support from religion. Classic as well as more recent research identifies religious involvement as a positive correlate of adjustment (Harvey, Barnes, & Greenwood, 1987; Koenig, George, & Siegler, 1988; Krause & Van Tran, 1989; Markides et al., 1987; Moberg, 1968). Some researchers have concluded that religious involvement provides a strategy for coping with stresses of aging (Bearon & Koenig, 1990; Koenig, George, & Siegler, 1988), and older adults experiencing personal crises are far more likely to seek counsel from a member of the clergy than from a mental health professional (Krause & Van Tran, 1989). However, the latter tendency may be cohort-specific: older people in the future may prefer to consult a psychologist or psychiatrist rather than the clergy during times of crisis (see Chapter Nine, p. 244). On a more concrete level, church-based networks of volunteers sometimes provide support services (e.g., respite care, transportation) for frail elderly people and their families (Filinson, 1988; Sheehan, Wilson, & Marella, 1989).

Specialized housing and communities for elderly people

For people of all ages, the match between individual abilities, needs, and preferences, on the one hand, and the challenges and resources that the environment presents, on the other hand, can influence quality of life. As the individual develops, therefore, the environments that promote optimal functioning change as well. Lawton and Nahemow (1973) capture this dynamic match in their model of individual **competence** vis-a-vis **environmental press** in old age; this model is illustrated in Figure 13.3.

In Lawton and Nahemow's (1973) model, competence is the individual's overall maximum capacity to function; competence reflects the individual's physical health, sensory capacities, motor skills, cognitive skills, and psychological integrity. As an aging person encounters chronic illness, sensory declines, or changes in intellectual functioning, competence decreases. Environmental

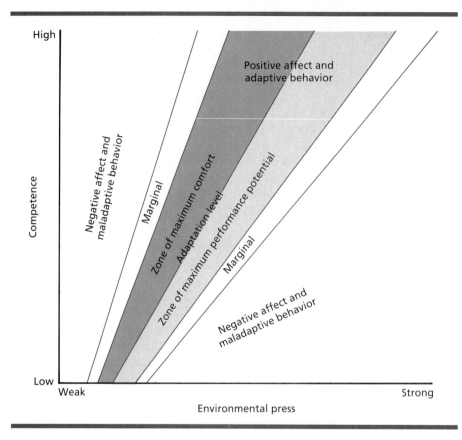

Figure 13.3

Interface between individual competence and environmental press.

(Source: Lawton & Nahemow, "Ecology of the Aging Process," *The Psychology of Adult Development and Aging*, Eisdorger and Lawton, eds., 1973, pp. 619–674. Copyright 1973 by the American Psychological Association. Reprinted by permission of the APA.)

press is the set of demands that the environment places on the individual. The demands may be physical, such as the number of stairs and rooms in one's home. Other demands are social or interpersonal, such as the number of nearby friends.

According to Lawton and Nahemow's (1973) model, the likelihood that one's behavior and emotions are adaptive depends on the congruence between competence and environment. At any age, environments that are too demanding *or not demanding enough* (e.g., those falling in the areas labeled "negative affect and maladaptive behavior" in Figure 13.3) detract from quality of life. People of all ages are most comfortable and behave most effectively in environments that are moderately challenging (e.g., those falling in the areas labeled "positive affect and adaptive behavior" in Figure 13.3).

As competence declines, a narrower range of environments will present the ideal moderate level of challenge (see Figure 13.3). Individuals with a high level of competence can generally function well in environments representing a wide range of press levels, including environments making strong physical and/or social demands. However, should these individuals experience failing health, diminished visual acuity and hearing sensitivity, or decreased strength and stamina, they will be able to function adaptively in a much narrower range of settings. The environments that are best for the individual at that point will present relatively low levels of environmental press.

Because individual differences in nearly all characteristics increase with age, an important message of Lawton and Nahemow's (1973) model is the value of a range of environmental options for the aged. The settings in which elderly people of the 1990s reside form a spectrum of environments, some shared by people of all ages and others designed especially for older adults. Many people assume that most older adults live either in institutions or in retirement communities. However, only about 5 percent of people over age 65 live in institutions at any one time (although nearly a quarter of people in that age group spend some time in a nursing home before death—see Chapter Four, p. 104), and less than 5 percent live in planned retirement communities (Hunt & Ross, 1990; Lawton, 1980).

Most elderly people live in their own homes, which are typically single-family detached houses. Although older adults' homes tend to be older, in poorer condition, and in more dilapidated neighborhoods than those of young and middle-aged homeowners (Kendig, 1990), they still offer important advantages. Most elderly homeowners have paid off their mortgages, so that housing is a minor portion of their total living expenses.

Furthermore, the high value that an aged widow places on her home undoubtedly reflects psychological and symbolic factors, as well as monetary considerations (Rowles, 1987; 1978; Rubenstein, 1989). Her home and neighborhood are familiar; because of that familiarity, this setting probably presents a lower press level (see Figure 13.3) than an environment that might objectively seem easier to manage. In addition, the woman's home of many years may also provide access to lifelong friends and neighbors, social resources that can further mitigate the environment's press level. Her home may be a symbol of physical and financial independence, and certainly abounds in concrete reminders of the years during which she shared the home with her husband and children.

A minority of elderly adults live in some form of housing that was designed for older people and that is restricted to the aged. The extent to which such **age-segregated housing** is beneficial to older people, to younger people, and to society in general is a matter of debate. Both sides of this issue are examined in the *Open Questions* box.

What kinds of age-segregated housing are available? Since 1956, there have been federally-subsidized age-segregated apartment complexes in the United States (Kendig, 1990); most residents of these complexes are women who are

---

BOX 13.2   *OPEN QUESTIONS*

Is age-segregated housing best for young and old?

Of the possible questions concerning housing for older adults, some attracting the greatest attention are the potential benefits of age-segregated housing. Do elderly men and women benefit or suffer when they live primarily with age-peers, as opposed to living with people of all ages? What is the impact of age-segregated living on children, adolescents, and younger adults? How is society affected when older adults reside in age-segregated facilities?

Some might think that these questions are ageist. The implication is that a community comprised exclusively or primarily of older people cannot possibly be a desirable setting for the older residents themselves or for the town or city that houses it. In contrast, few people question the desirability of young adults living on age-segregated college campuses, of housing subdivisions that cater to young families, or of condominium complexes that attract primarily middle-aged residents.

Most gerontological research shows that many elderly people prefer age-segregated living and benefit from the situation. When older adults live in facilities that have a high concentration of elderly residents, they generally have more friends, more contact with friends, higher morale, and more satisfaction with their housing than when they live in settings with a greater mix of age groups (e.g., Berkowiz, Waxman, & Yaffe, 1988; Carp, 1968; 1976; Kendig, 1990; Lawton, 1980; Lawton & Cohen, 1974; Rosow, 1967; Ward, LaGory, & Sherman, 1985). A strong sense of community develops among the elderly residents of some age-segregated housing facilities (e.g., Keith, 1982).

One could also argue that elderly people are not the only beneficiaries of age-segregated housing. Most age-segregated housing (whether it be federally-subsidized apartments, retirement communities, life-care communities, or congregate housing) is newer, in better condition, and inherently easier to care for than housing not designed for older adults. Thus, the residents of these facilities experience lower levels of environmental press, and probably need less assistance from younger family members in order to live independently. Putting it more concretely, when 85-year-old Mrs. Jones moves from her three-story, five bedroom home into a congregate housing facility for older adults, neither she nor her son and daughter-in-law (both in their 60s) need to be concerned with such

---

either single, widowed, or divorced (Lawton, 1980). This form of housing does not include supportive services, such as medical assistance or communal meals; however, such services are provided in **congregate housing**. Occasionally, congregate housing also provides resource coordinators who help residents find out about and use supportive services in the broader community (Blandford, Chappell, & Marshall, 1989). Congregate housing can be an ideal choice for an older person who can no longer live independently but does not need the extent of long-term care that a nursing home would provide.

Planned retirement communities are a form of age-segregated housing usually open only to healthy and affluent older people. These communities are restricted to individuals and couples aged 50 and older with no children younger than age 18 in the household. Most are located in the Sun Belt states and are nearly self-contained: these communities usually offer churches, stores, clubs, and recreational facilities of all kinds. In addition, many cities have **naturally-occurring retirement communities (NORCs)**, housing develop-

tasks as mowing the lawn, shoveling snow, mounting storm windows, or regularly cleaning a large house.

Although some communities resist plans to build age-segregated living facilities, this resistance seems to be based on fears concerning group housing in general rather than an aversion toward high concentrations of elderly people in the neighborhood. Community attitudes toward age-segregated housing are much more favorable than attitudes toward ordinary apartment complexes, public housing in general, or group homes for juvenile delinquents (Mangum, 1988). Landlords in NORCs describe their elderly tenants as stable residents who pay their rent reliably and cause less wear-and-tear on the facilities than younger residents (Hunt & Ross, 1990). Neighborhoods in which age-segregated facilities are located tend to experience positive changes in levels of home maintenance, numbers of local stores, traffic, and levels of neighborhood crime (Lawton & Hoffman, 1984).

These data suggest that age-segregated housing is best not only for its aged residents but also for younger people and for society in general. However, one can mount an opposing argument. Age-segregation, like racial segregation, can potentially support negative stereotypes. If children and young people encounter few elderly adults in their neighborhoods, then these young people have few opportunities for positive experiences with older men and women. By the same token, elderly adults who have little contact with young people could all too easily stereotype young people as irresponsible, drug-crazed radicals. Age-segregated housing is also perceived as a threat to property values and local tax bases (Kendig, 1990; Mangum, 1988).

There may be no absolute answer to questions concerning the desirability of age-segregated living. Perhaps the best answer is that both age-segregated and age-integrated living situations should be options for people of all ages. For the large numbers of elderly adults that prefer it, age-segregated housing should allow respite from the noise and clutter of young children and should provide support for independent living. But for the old and younger adults who believe that variety is the spice of life, housing and long-term care policies are needed that promote independent living for older adults in neighborhoods that include people of all ages.

ments that were not deliberately planned for older residents but that attract a preponderance of older residents (Hunt & Ross, 1990).

Life care communities are relatively new to the spectrum of age-segregated housing; these facilities provide both housing and long-term care. Residents pay a substantial one-time entrance charge and monthly fees after entrance into the community. In return, the community provides the assurance of a place to live for the rest of the resident's life, as well as whatever nursing care she might need in the future. Some life care communities also offer transportation and housekeeping services, libraries, beauty and barber shops, recreational activities, and religious services. Although these communities can be an ideal alternative for the well-to-do older person, one must select a life care community cautiously. The financial stability of life care communities varies, so that some present a questionable picture as to their future ability to deliver the care for which residents have contracted (Communities for the elderly, 1990).

SUMMARY

Throughout adulthood, contact with siblings decreases, although most adults are emotionally close to their brothers and sisters. Relationships with siblings in old age may be intimate, congenial, loyal, apathetic, or hostile.

More often than men, women describe friendship as a forum for mutual self-disclosure, psychological intimacy, and support. Most cross-sectional studies show that both the number of friends and the frequency of contact with friends decrease throughout adulthood. In old age, having a confidant is associated with high levels of morale.

Interest in politics increases with age; older people are more likely to vote than are younger people. Surveys of older individuals and professionals who work with elderly people identify several motivations for volunteer work. The church assumes unique importance among voluntary associations for older adults. Throughout adulthood, women engage in virtually all kinds of religious activities more often than men do, and the church plays a more central role in the lives of African-Americans than of Caucasians.

The likelihood that one's behavior and emotions are adaptive depends on the congruence between competence and environment. The settings in which elderly people of the 1990s reside form a spectrum of environments, some shared by people of all ages and others designed especially for older adults. Most research shows that many elderly people prefer age-segregated living and benefit from the situation.

KEY TERMS

Age-segregated housing
American Association of Retired Persons (AARP)
Apathetic sibling relationships
Compatibility
Competence
Confidant
Congenial sibling relationships
Congregate housing
Consequential religiosity
Environmental press
Experiential religiosity
Friendship networks
Gray Panthers
Homophobia
Hostile sibling relationships

Ideological religiosity
Intellectual religiosity
Intimate sibling relationships
Life care community
Loyal sibling relationships
National Council of Senior Citizens (NCSC)
Naturally-occurring retirement communities (NORC's)
Planned retirement communities
Reciprocity
Ritualistic religiosity
Role models
Selectivity theory
Similarity
Structural dimensions

SUGGESTIONS FOR FURTHER READING

Clements, W. M. (1989). *Religion, Aging, and Health*. Binghamton, NY: Haworth Press.

Jacobs, J. (1974). *Fun City: An Ethnographic Study of a Retirement Community*. New York: Holt, Rinehart, & Winston.

Lawton, M. P. (1980). *Environment and Aging*. Monterey, CA: Brooks/Cole.

Pastalan, L. A. (1990). *Aging in Place: The Role of Housing and Social Supports*. Binghamton, NY: Haworth Press.

Reisman, J. M. (1979). *Anatomy of Friendship*. New York: Irvington Publishers.

Rowles, G. D. (1978). *Prisoners of Space? Exploring the Geographical Experience of Older People*. Boulder, CO: Westview Press.

CHAPTER FOURTEEN

WORK AND RETIREMENT

Besides the need for income, why do people work? Does retirement cause health problems? Will Social Security be around when you are old enough to collect benefits? All of these questions concern work in one way or another. This chapter examines work as a critical dimension of adult experience. There is an overview of the processes of career choice and development, and of age differences in job satisfaction. Unusual work experiences—such as unemployment, employment discrimination, and sexual harassment—are also considered. Finally, the chapter reviews the history of retirement in the United States, and issues related to early retirement, retirement preparation, and retirement income.

Questions to consider in reading the chapter include:

How do differentialist and developmental theories of career choice differ?

What motivations do older adults cite for working? To what extent does age discrimination exist in the workplace?

What racial differences in careers have been identified? What actions have been taken on behalf of workers facing job discrimination? What is sexual harassment?

How do workers prepare for retirement? What factors are related to adjusting to retirement? How do people finance retirement?

CAREERS

Many people think of work as a topic of interest to sociologists, rather than developmental psychologists. However, work structures the life cycle, particularly during adulthood (e.g., Havighurst, 1982). One way of "dividing up" the life course is to distinguish periods of career preparation, career entry, career advancement, and retirement.

Furthermore, your occupation affects the way in which you spend time even when you are not at work. Jobs influence friendships, values, interests, hobbies, attitudes, and choice of residential location. Work affects one's financial well-being, social class, and social status. For example, a concert pianist will almost certainly have a different lifestyle from an auto mechanic; part of the difference can be traced directly or indirectly to the differences in occupations.

Clinicians have recently documented emotional problems that are especially common among certain occupational groups (Sandroff, 1989; Sauter, Murphy, & Hurrell, 1990). For example, health professionals have higher-than-expected suicide and substance-abuse rates; human service and teaching professionals experience unusually high rates of burnout. Such occupational mental health hazards reflect the nature of the work itself, the types of individuals attracted to certain occupations, and the interaction between the work and those who are attracted to it.

Theories of career choice

Differentialist views   John Holland (1973) has provided the most extensive and well-known **differentialist theory** of occupational choice. In that theory, Holland proposes that workers can be classified—or differentiated—on the basis of their interests. Altogether, Holland identifies six types: the realistic, investigative, artistic, social, enterprising, and conventional.

Holland (1973) describes realistic types as individuals who excel in mechanical and technical skills, but are weak in social and educational skills; in contrast, social types have strong "people" skills and teaching talents, but weak mechanical skills. Investigative types do well with scientific and mathematical tasks, but not when they must persuade other people; enterprising people, however, are good leaders and persuaders but are not skilled in handling scientific tasks. Artistic types prefer unstructured activities in which they can create original products; these individuals are not good at clerical and business tasks. Conventional types manage clerical and computational tasks with ease, but are uncomfortable when confronting unstructured activities.

Most people see themselves in more than one of these types. In actually classifying people, Holland (1973) examines tendencies and capacities in all six areas, looking for areas of strength and weakness. This pattern of high and low capacities constitutes an individual's **personality pattern**.

Holland (1973) also categorizes work settings into the same six types. Settings are categorized on the basis of the people drawn to them, so that a setting such as a theater, in which most workers are artists, would be classified as an artistic setting. Like people, work settings are rarely "pure types." In a theater, for example, most of the workers probably are artists, but there would also be conventional employees who keep business records for the company, enterprising individuals concerned with advertising performances and soliciting donations, and realistic people charged with maintenance and repair of the facilities.

Holland (1973) believes that career choice reflects pressure toward congruence between people and work settings. People are happiest when they work in settings that fit their personality pattern, and occupations recruit employees—through both formal and informal channels—who have personalities that match the character of the workplace. In essence, this theory proposes that "birds of a feather flock together."

Holland's (1973) theory is reasonably well supported by research (e.g., Neff, 1985). However, defining work environments on the basis of the relative frequencies of types of individuals working in those settings seems circular, since person types are defined partially on the basis of preferred activities. Furthermore, Holland gives little attention to ways in which work affects personality. This theory, nonetheless, is important in vocational guidance and has contributed to the development of career interest inventories.

Developmentalist views   Still another criticism of differentialist approaches to career choice is that these theories are static. **Developmentalist theories**, in contrast, portray career choice as a process spanning much of the life cycle. Developmentalist approaches include those of Super and Ginsberg.

Donald Super (Super et al., 1963; Neff, 1985) developed one of the best known and most elaborate developmental theories of careers. Super believed that vocational development is a lifelong process linked to the developing self-concept. As the individual builds a coherent picture of herself, her skills, her habits, and the sorts of activities that are appropriate for her, her career plans are correspondingly channeled.

Super distinguished several stages through which the individual develops more and more refined notions of her career as her self-concept unfolds. In early adolescence one is in a **crystallization** stage: ideas about careers are vague. The **specification** stage of later adolescence is when thinking centers on a more or less specific occupation. Early adulthood is a period of **implementation**, during which one acquires the education, training, and experience needed for the chosen field. Depending on the career that an individual has selected, the implementation stage might involve attending college, pursuing graduate degrees, carrying out an apprenticeship, or entering a vocational or technical school (see Chapter Seven, pp. 177–184, for a discussion of education as it affects adults of different ages). In the twenties or thirties, most people enter their chosen careers, and a stage of **establishment** begins.

The forties and fifties are a **maintenance stage.** By this time, many have achieved their major occupational goals; they usually find further accomplishments less important than maintaining the level of authority and responsibility that they have achieved. The **deceleration stage** begins in the late fifties for most workers, when they begin to prepare for retirement; "workaholics" may experience difficulty with this process. The **retirement stage** begins when the individual formally retires.

There are problems with Super's theory. First and foremost, career development is rarely as orderly as Super portrays. According to Super (Super et al., 1963), people must make increasingly strong commitments to a single field in order to have a satisfying career. However, research fails to support this assertion (e.g., Philips, 1982). Second, the notion that career choice primarily reflects self-concept rests on the assumptions that individuals have complete freedom in their choices of career, that they have clear insight into their self-concepts, and that they will use that insight rationally (e.g., Neff, 1985). In reality, these assumptions may often be untenable.

Eli Ginzberg and his colleagues offer a second developmental approach. Originally, Ginzberg (Ginzberg, Ginzberg, Alexrod, & Herma, 1951) described career choice as a decision-making process spanning adolescence and the early twenties. This process had a facet of irrevocability, since decisions made at one time determined which alternatives would be available later. Furthermore, the process inevitably involved compromise to achieve the best possible fit between interests and opportunities. That description applied reasonably well to the relatively privileged group of young people—predominantly white male college students—that Ginzberg and his colleagues originally studied.

However, subsequent study involving women, minorities, and individuals from more varied social backgrounds prompted Ginzberg (1972) to offer a revised account. At that point, Ginzberg (1972) asserted that decision making is an open-ended process extending throughout working life, and is not limited to a single decade. While it is true that decisions made early in life may constrain later options, an important career challenge is to make choices that maximize future options. Early decisions need not have a truly irrevocable impact on one's lifelong prospects. Finally, Ginzberg described the process of career selection as one of optimization rather than compromise.

This reformulation takes Ginzberg's model of career development from one that, like Super's model, emphasizes universal, orderly processes to one that allows for ongoing change. Ginzberg (1972) noted that many workers make more or less substantial career changes over the course of working life. And, contemporary women's careers often defy orderly, stagelike descriptions. Given that American women today may interrupt or postpone their careers for marriage and motherhood, and that some married women give their husband's careers precedence over their own, the challenge of charting women's careers remains open. The special nature of women's careers are examined in the *Diversity in Adulthood* box.

Career entry

Generally, contemporary Americans usually spend between 12 and 16 weeks carrying out a job search, depending upon their age and experience, the type of job that they are seeking, where they live, and the general economic climate at

---

BOX 14.1 DIVERSITY IN ADULTHOOD

Women and work: Are their experiences unique?

Contemporary American women are entering an ever-widening array of occupations. It is much more common today than in the past to find women working as computer programmers and technicians, police officers and firefighters, and business executives and college administrators. Nonetheless, the overall occupational distributions of men and women continue to differ noticeably (U. S. Department of Labor, 1985). As in the past, most women work in clerical or sales positions, and in managerial or professional (primarily teaching) fields. Men's most commonly selected occupations, in contrast, are more evenly distributed among managerial and professional work; technical, sales, and administrative/clerical jobs; skilled crafts and construction; and work as operators, fabricators, and laborers.

These differences have important long-term implications for women. Men's average annual salaries continue to exceed women's, and men are more likely than women to work in jobs covered by pension plans. Retired women (particularly single, divorced, and widowed women) can face financial jeopardy as a result.

There are also gender differences in the tempo of career involvement. Recall that one of the criticisms of developmental theories of career choice was that these models provide a picture of careers that is too orderly to apply to most people. These models probably describe men's careers better than women's, however. Although many men do indeed change careers one or more times during their working life, and although some experience career inter-

ruptions through layoffs or unemployment, most men work for pay more or less continuously throughout adulthood.

The situation is different in at least two ways for women. First, women's career development has a "step" or decision-point that does not arise for men (e.g., Fitzgerald & Betz, 1983). Unless he has the good fortune to be born to immense wealth, a boy will assume that paid employment will be a continual part of his life. His major decision will be what type of occupation he will pursue. However, a girl traditionally has had to consider both *whether or not* she would work, as well as what type of career she might enter. Perhaps as work becomes a normative part of adulthood for American women, girls will begin to assume that a career will be part of their lives as well.

In addition, women's career patterns are more varied than men's. Even today, relatively few women are in the labor force continuously from early adulthood until old age. Rather, many women move in and out of the labor force as their family responsibilities expand and contract. To describe this phenomenon, scholars have offered several typologies of women's career involvement. In one of the earliest formulations, Super (1957) distinguished the *stable homemaking* pattern (marriage shortly after completing school, no significant work experience), the *stable working* pattern (continuous work throughout adulthood, no significant family roles), and the *interrupted* pattern (entering or reentering the work force in middle adulthood or later). More recently, Stroud

the time of their job search (e.g., Bolles, 1988). What *should* happen during that time, according to experts, and what actually *does* happen for most people? According to Bolles (1988), successful job searches start with a thorough self-evaluation. This process includes determining *what* job skills one possesses and wants to exploit, *where* one would like to use these skills, and *how* to best secure such a job.

For example, self-evaluation might convince you that you are good at advising others. You might further decide that you would like to work in an

(1981) distinguished career patterns both on the basis of women's work history and their psychological involvement in their jobs. Working women with high job involvement were *work committed*, whereas working women with lower levels of job involvement were *double track* workers.

On the basis of these data, one might conclude that women's work experiences are fundamentally distinct from those of men. However, Helen Astin (1984) argues that men's and women's career choice and work motives are similar. Men and women alike, according to Astin, work to fulfill needs for physical survival, for pleasure, and for feeling that one has made a contribution to the general welfare. Both men and women choose careers on the basis of their expectations about the availability of different kinds of work and the likelihood that different kinds of work can meet their needs.

Men's and women's expectations about work are shaped by two general forces. First, early socialization—the reactions of parents, siblings, friends, and teachers—influence expectations. In addition, work expectations are affected by the "structure of opportunity" in one's society. The structure of opportunity includes the kinds of jobs available and the extent to which jobs are formally or informally sex-typed, the level of employment discrimination in the society, the nature of the economy at a given time, the family structure of the society, and the level of reproductive technology in the society.

Astin (1984) proposes, finally, that socialization and the structure of opportunity influence one another and that both affect work expectations. As our society changes, then, the structure of opportunity and early socialization processes evolve. In this way, generational changes in work and careers can be explained.

According to Astin, then, the processes leading up to John's and Susan's decisions about which careers to pursue are quite similar. Astin would explain John's decision to become an attorney and Susan's decision to become a teacher as the outcome of their childhood experiences and the general tenor of their society when they reached adulthood. In addition, Astin would explain many of the differences in John's and Susan's childhood experiences in terms of the structure of opportunity at that time. Finally, Astin would predict that John's and Susan's children—because they experience a new structure of opportunity and changed socialization messages—might make different career choices and have different expectations about work than their parents did.

The overall picture of women's careers as compared to men's is best described as one of contrast as well as similarity. Men and women generally do different kinds of work and have different career patterns in contemporary America. However, Astin's (1984) model of work and careers provides a basis for hope that future cohorts of men and women might enjoy greater similarity of occupational experience.

educational setting, such as a high school guidance department or a regional staff development center for teachers. Your next task would be to determine how to obtain that type of work. You would need to identify the titles of specific jobs, the names of schools or school boards that offer these jobs, the names of specific individuals who would have the authority to hire you for that position, and how to approach these individuals and convince them to hire you.

Most people, unfortunately, are not as systematic or rational as Bolles (1988) would suggest. Often, jobs are selected less on the basis of planning than on the basis of luck, circumstances, and opportunities; these factors may themselves be shaped by the social and economic climate at the time of a job search—or even social and economic events occurring years earlier (e.g., Miller, 1983; Vondracek & Lerner, 1982). Among the more commonly used job-seeking methods are asking friends or relatives for information about jobs; responding to newspaper advertisements; using employment agencies, state employment services, or school placement offices; and taking Civil Service tests. Using these methods, between 7 and 24 percent of job seekers report finding work (Bolles, 1988).

The latter figures suggest that most people are not very effective at finding jobs. One might draw the same conclusion by examining job turnover rates for new workers. One scholar reports that over half of new employees in a wide variety of organizations leave their jobs within seven months of being hired (Wanous, 1980). Some believe that if individuals gave greater consideration to **organizational culture** during job searches, they would make decisions that provided more stable employment (e.g., Bolles, 1988; Sathe, 1985).

Organizational culture includes assumptions shared by a group of workers that, even if unwritten or unstated, influence the group's activities (Sathe, 1985). These assumptions include beliefs about the appropriate pace of work and the importance of punctuality and meeting deadlines; the best uses of space and objects; the most effective means of communication; and the appropriate level of formality in the workplace. Thus, organizational culture affects such everyday decisions as whether you wear jeans or a suit to work, whether or not you keep personal photographs or plants on your desk, and whether or not you address supervisors on a first-name basis.

Job satisfaction

Some report that young adults are less satisfied overall with their jobs than are older adults (e.g., Havighurst, 1982; Rhodes, 1983). Furthermore, young adults are less satisfied with their work per se, as opposed to their jobs, than are older adults, and young adults express less satisfaction with their pay, promotions, supervisors, and coworkers than do older workers (Rhodes, 1983). However, it is difficult to identify the source of these age differences. Since most research in this area is cross-sectional, some or all of these age differences may reflect cohort differences in work values or experiences. Perhaps, too, young adults are less able to cope with problems, including job-related problems, than are middle-aged and older adults (Rhodes, 1983). Because younger workers also express less involvement in their jobs and less commitment to their organizations than do older workers (Rhodes, 1983), the age difference in job satisfaction may simply reflect young adults' greater willingness to admit unhappiness with their jobs.

Although some believe that individuals performing repetitive and tedious work (e.g., assembly line workers) are most likely to express dissatisfaction with their jobs (Miernyk, 1975), others disagree. In *Working*, journalist Studs Terkel (1972) describes his conversations with hundreds of Americans in a wide variety of occupations. Nearly all—from the auto plant worker to the receptionist to the model—expressed alienation from and disappointment with their jobs.

Professionals such as physicians and scholars may encounter unique sources of job dissatisfaction (Wrightsman, 1988). One problem is feeling overwhelmed by a work schedule that provides many opportunities for achievement, but few opportunities for leisure. Many professionals feel conflicted because clients or students view them as infallible, whereas they themselves are only too aware of their own fallibility. Still other professionals experience a gradual loss of challenge from professional activities.

Career changes

Perhaps your grandfather worked at the same type of job, and even for the same employer, throughout his life. It is unlikely that you can expect that degree of career stability. Today, most people change jobs at least five times during their working life; job changes usually occur within the first few years in the labor force.

Sometimes people make **horizontal career changes** that involve shifting from one field to another (e.g., a former salesperson becomes a clerical worker), whereas others make **vertical career changes** in which they attain a higher level of authority and responsibility (e.g., a former salesperson becomes a district sales manager) (Osipow, 1983). Although job changes occur at all socioeconomic levels, top executives and professionals in one longitudinal study were more likely than blue collar workers to change jobs (Clausen, 1981).

What prompts career changes? The match between the person and the job may be one factor, as Holland (1973) would predict. Some people also change jobs not because they are seeking more satisfying work, but because they have little choice. With technology advancing at an unprecedented pace, some occupations become obsolete and others are newly created each year.

Career changes can be beneficial, but are often costly as well. To the extent that one manages to find a better fit between job opportunities and personal talents, changing jobs can promote personal growth. Recall that Levinson asserts that changing the life structure—which can involve changing occupations—is a process of adult development (see Chapter Eight, p. 197). Similarly, Peck advocates flexibility in interests and involvements as an adaptive dimension of middle and later adulthood (see Chapter Eight, p. 195).

However, the financial impact of changing jobs can be substantial for workers who are covered by pension plans (Allen, Clark, & McDermed, 1988; Clark & McDermed, 1988). Under many pension plans, the worker must remain with her employer for a minimum number of years (usually, five to ten years) before her pension rights are "vested." Individuals who leave a pension-covered job before being vested may forfeit their pension; those who change jobs after their pension rights are vested often do not participate in pension plan improvements (e.g., cost-of-living adjustments, expanded benefits) so that the value of their pension diminishes as a result of inflation (Bernstein & Bernstein, 1988).

Older adults in the labor force

Many people are content to retire in their sixties or seventies. In fact, early retirement is becoming more and more popular. There is also, however, a substantial minority of older people who do not want to retire at all or who return to work following retirement. In one national survey, most people aged 55 or older said that they intended to work until age 65, if not longer (Harris et al., 1981). Most said that they would like to work part time after retirement, and most retired people in this survey said that they would like to work.

The bleak economic picture of the late 1980s and early 1990s might suggest that younger people would be opposed to older adults remaining in or returning to the work force. However, that is not the case. Recent surveys show that more recently-born cohorts express greater support for working in old age than earlier-born cohorts do (Ferraro, 1990b; 1989). Perhaps, then, more elderly adults will work in the future.

Some older people successfully implement their preference to work. One common pattern is reentering the labor force with a part-time job following retirement (Ruhm, 1989); between 10 percent and 25 percent of retirees follow this path. Most of the time, these retirees take jobs involving wage cuts, changes in industry or occupation, or self-employment (Ruhm, 1989). Those who return to work after retirement are relatively young—usually people who retired early or on time; late retirees rarely return to the labor force (Palmore, Burchett, Fillenbaum, George, & Wallman, 1985).

Undoubtedly, elderly adults who want to work are motivated by many impulses. For some, work has been a lifelong source of fulfillment that they are reluctant to abandon. Others value the intrinsic challenge of work, the social stimulation of coworkers, and the structure and activity that work adds to their lives. Financial pressures motivate many who reenter the work force after retirement (Boaz, 1987b). Compared to retirees who do not work, those who return to work after retirement generally have lower levels of education and occupational status and more dependents (Palmore et al., 1985).

Stereotypes of older workers and age discrimination   Individuals who want to reenter the labor force after retirement, and middle-aged and older employees,

Older adults may return to the labor force after retirement in order to gain personal fulfillment, intellectual stimulation, or financial rewards.

may confront negative stereotypes regarding older workers and age discrimination. Gerontologists have documented negative stereotypes of older workers for nearly 40 years (for a review, see Stagner, 1985). Older employees are believed to be slower, less able to learn new skills, more prone to accidents, less able to get along with coworkers and customers, more rigid, more resistant to supervision, and more likely to miss work than younger employees (Stagner, 1985). Tragically, older workers themselves may accept these ideas, which can then function as self-fulfilling prophecies (Avolio & Waldman, 1989). These stereotypes—like most stereotyped beliefs—are inaccurate for the most part.

Recall that older adults are capable of learning, that they experience relatively few accidents at work, and that they generally do not undergo dramatic personality changes leading to rigidity or irritability. Age does, of course, bring a gradual slowing of behavior (see Chapter Five, pp. 125–128); but, then, speed is not important for many jobs. Other research shows that there are few consistent age differences in job performance across a wide variety of occupations, that there are lower job turnover rates for older workers, and that older workers have better attendance records than younger workers (Martocchio, 1989; Stagner, 1985; Streufert, Pogash, Piasecki, & Post, 1990).

Despite their inaccuracy, negative stereotypes of older workers are tenacious and are probably one source of age discrimination in employment. The federal **Age Discrimination in Employment Act (ADEA)** is designed to protect workers between the ages of 40 and 70 from negative personnel decisions based on age. Thus, employers cannot legally refuse to hire an applicant, discharge an employee, or segregate or classify workers in a detrimental manner on the basis of their age. There are some exceptions to these provisions. Small employers are exempt from the ADEA; jobs in which age is a bona fide occupational qualification are also exempt. Public safety jobs (e.g., firefighter, police officer) are examples of the latter category.

Although age discrimination is illegal, it continues. Statistics suggest that age discrimination is anything but rare (e.g., Snyder & Barrett, 1988). Age discrimination cases filed with the Equal Employment Opportunity Commission increased through most of the 1980s. Older people who are unemployed typically have to look for work longer than younger workers (Love & Torrence, 1989; U. S. Senate Special Committee on Aging, 1987), and some firms do not retrain older employees for work involving new technology (Stagner, 1985). Finally, older workers receive lower wages than younger workers, controlling for age differences in factors related to earnings such as education (Mueller, Mutran, & Boyle, 1989).

SPECIAL CAREER ISSUES

The issues considered in this section potentially affect workers of all ages and in all fields. Like women, African-Americans and members of other minority groups often have careers that follow different paths than is the case for Caucasian men. This section examines these differences, and related issues of discrimination and Affirmative Action. Two nonnormative career events—unemployment and harassment—are also considered.

Race, ethnicity, and careers

F. Smith (1983) notes that much research on the vocational experiences of racial minorities confounds race with other potentially important variables, such as socioeconomic status and family background. These confounds could lead to inaccurate stereotypes concerning the career potential and career needs of racial minorities. She also points out that there has been very little longitudinal research on the careers of minority group members: models of minority group career development are needed, as well as data describing age differences in job satisfaction among minority group members. Finally, most of the research that does exist describes the career experiences of African-Americans and Hispanic-Americans; there is less empirical information about Native Americans' and Asian-Americans' careers.

Despite these problems, it is clear that African-Americans, Hispanic-Americans, and Native Americans are at a disadvantage relative to Caucasians in the job market. According to Smith (1983), individuals in these groups typically have access to less information and less adequate information about careers than do Caucasians, and are exposed to a more restricted range of career role models than are Caucasians. Members of these minority groups are

African-Americans and other minority group members face barriers to their career development stemming, in part, from inadequate information about jobs.

more likely to face unemployment than are Caucasians, and their incomes are, on the average, substantially lower than Caucasians' incomes (e.g., Pavalko, 1988; Smith, 1983). Perhaps most frustrating from the standpoint of individual African-Americans, Hispanic-Americans, and Native Americans, education offers less of a career benefit—in terms of employment rates and occupational prestige—to minority group members than to Caucasians (Smith, 1983).

The situation is different for some Asian-Americans. Asian-Americans comprise a diverse group of national, ethnic, and linguistic backgrounds and generalizations regarding these groups are therefore particularly difficult. With this caveat in mind, note that Asian-Americans—especially Chinese-Americans and Japanese-Americans—in some respects enjoy high levels of success (Pavalko, 1988). Educational levels are high for these groups, and many Asian-Americans work in professional and technical occupations. However, Asian-Americans (again, especially Chinese-Americans and Japanese-Americans) have a bimodal occupational distribution. In other words, many are employed in service positions and unskilled jobs, but about as many work in professional and technical areas.

Not only do the vocational experiences of Caucasians and non-whites differ, but beliefs concerning work also vary by race (Smith, 1983). Reflecting historical and cultural experiences, African-Americans and Native Americans in many studies express more "extrinsic motivation" for work: work is a means of providing security rather than of attaining self-fulfillment (Lipsman, 1967; Richardson, 1981). The family is unusually important in Hispanic culture, and Hispanic-Americans may value work less than Caucasians do for that reason

(Chandler, 1974). However, African-American and Hispanic adolescents (particularly young women) express high career aspirations in some samples (Howell & Frese, 1982; Smith, 1983), although the findings are quite mixed (Pavalko, 1988).

Neither the differentialist nor the developmentalist approach fits the experiences of contemporary African-Americans, Hispanic-Americans, or Native Americans (Smith, 1983). External constraints, while playing a part in nearly everyone's career development, are especially likely to have an effect on racial minorities' experiences in the job market (LoCasio, 1967). Despite good intentions and legislative efforts, it would be naive to suppose that non-Caucasians' job opportunities are not substantially limited by discrimination.

Discrimination in employment   At least since the Second World War, American legislators and business officials have been concerned with **employment discrimination** on the basis of race, sex, national origin, or handicap. Initially, discrimination in employment was defined as "prejudicial treatment" in the workplace. However, demonstrating that unfavorable personnel decisions were motivated by prejudice toward a particular group was nearly impossible (Jain & Sloane, 1981).

A later definition of employment discrimination as "unequal treatment" of applicants or employees according to race, gender, national origin, or handicap was not much better. Using this definition, employers were free to institute virtually any job requirements or conditions, provided that these standards were applied to all applicants or employees in the same way. This approach could be equitable, but could also allow employers to specify testing, education, or training requirements that, in effect, would systematically exclude women and minorities from job pools. Today, such practices—through which women and minorities are disproportionately excluded from jobs on the basis of requirements that are *unrelated to the job in question*—are considered **indirect discrimination**, and are illegal.

What would have to be demonstrated to show that employment discrimination has occurred? Current guidelines include documentation of **adverse impact** and the potential for **alternative procedures** (Jain & Sloane, 1981). Both on the basis of a desire not to discriminate and good business sense, employers seek personnel selection procedures that are valid (e.g., that reliably predict job performance). A valid personnel selection procedure, such as a test that must be passed to be hired or qualified for promotion, has adverse impact if it results in a selection rate for any group less than 80 percent of the group with the highest selection rate (usually Caucasian men). For example, an employment test that results in hiring 100 out of 100 Caucasian men, but only 50 out of 100 African-American women, would have adverse impact. The test screens out a higher percentage of African-American women (half who take the test are not hired) than of Caucasian men (all who take the test are hired).

In such cases, it is critical that the employer search for and use alternative procedures to make personnel decisions (Jain & Sloane, 1981). The goal in this search would be to find different ways of identifying individuals best qualified for hiring or promotion. The new personnel procedures should be at least as useful in predicting job performance as the old procedures *and* should be free from adverse impact.

What actions have been taken on behalf of workers who have suffered from employment discrimination? Unfortunately, resources for enforcing anti-discrimination laws are limited; consequently, efforts have focused on large, visible targets—massive employers such as AT&T or entire industries such as the steel industry (Jain & Sloane, 1981). Court actions have included awarding back pay, reinstating employees who were fired, abolishing testing programs, and creating special employee recruitment and training programs targeted at groups experiencing discrimination.

These steps sometimes arouse mixed or negative feelings. Some believe that these actions constitute **reverse discrimination** against men and Caucasians. However, courts have generally upheld these kinds of Affirmative Action plans—provided that employees are not terminated in order to meet numerical goals for hiring and advancing women and minorities, that Caucasians and men are not barred from advancement opportunities, and that the plans are temporary strategies for reducing or eliminating traditional patterns of discrimination (Jain & Sloane, 1981). Affirmative Action is examined further in the *Open Questions* box.

Unemployment

What are the consequences of unemployment—both for society and for unemployed individuals? There are positive correlations between the nation's unemployment rate and the suicide rate, the homicide rate, the rate of admissions to mental hospitals, rates of substance abuse, and the numbers of substantiated reports of child abuse and neglect (Riegle, 1982). Of course, these correlational data do not demonstrate that increases in unemployment cause the extent of these social problems to increase. It is more likely that both unemployment rates and at least some of these social problems are outcomes of other social influences.

Without a doubt, however, unemployment does have profound personal impacts. Remember that work plays a central role in structuring adult life and identity. It is not surprising, then, that an involuntary job loss—whether expected or unexpected—is traumatic. Research documents a myriad of ways in which unemployment affects individual physical and psychological well-being (Keefe, 1984). Unemployment can lead to stress-related health problems, such as elevated blood pressure, pulse rate, and cholesterol levels. Psychologically, unemployment is associated with feelings of anger, guilt, grief, loss, anxiety, reduced self-esteem, and depression. Since health insurance benefits are linked to the job for many people, these physical and psychological problems arise just when health care resources are at a low ebb.

Not only does the individual worker suffer from the job loss, but the family is likely to struggle as well. In one study, women whose husbands experienced

| BOX 14.2 | *OPEN QUESTIONS* |

Affirmative action: Social justice or reverse discrimination?

Affirmative action plans are one step that government agencies and businesses have taken to correct the long-term impact of discrimination in education, training, and employment. Few would argue that these efforts are directed toward a worthy goal. However, in the actual implementation of affirmative action plans, hard feelings have often arisen; some feel that these plans are in themselves discriminatory.

In 1978, the *Uniform Guidelines on Employee Selection Procedures* was adopted by the EEOC, the U.S. Office of Personnel Management, and the Departments of Justice and Labor. Affirmative action, as discussed in the *Guidelines*, is much more than simply refraining from employment discrimination. Instead, employers may take positive steps (hence the term "affirmative action") by explicitly encouraging women and minority candidates to apply for jobs and by advertising job openings through media most likely to reach women and minorities. Affirmative action plans could also include special training opportunities that women and minorities can use to obtain job qualifications that would otherwise be unattainable.

One of the strongest inducements to develop effective affirmative action plans is the threat of losing federal contracts. Organizations can lose these contracts if the workforce does not include numbers of women and minorities commensurate with their availability for employment. The *Guidelines* state that individuals need not be hired on the basis of their race, sex, religion, or national origin. Further, affirmative action plans by no means mandate hiring individuals

who are unqualified, or hiring individuals that a company does not need merely to employ more women or minorities. However, many employers have been expected to establish voluntary affirmative action plans that include numerical goals for the employment of women and minorities and timetables according to which these goals will be met (e.g., Pottinger, 1977; Sowell, 1977).

If the intentions behind affirmative action plans are generally endorsed, then on what basis have objections been raised? One set of objections concerns the use of numerical goals and timetables. Some react to these features of affirmative action plans as the establishment of a quota system. With the unpleasant reality of a limited number of job openings, a rigid quota system could potentially lead to discrimination against Caucasians and men. However, goals and timetables are not, according to proponents of affirmative action, fixed quotas for the hiring of women and minorities (e.g., Pottinger, 1977). Rather, these aspects of affirmative action plans are merely measurement guidelines with which an organization can evaluate the success of their efforts.

Goals and timetables may not provide the most useful template for measuring success, however. Such an approach would condemn to failure the affirmative action plans of some well-intentioned employers, given the numbers of qualified women and minorities that are available. In an early essay on affirmative action plans, Sowell (1977) discussed the difficulties faced by administrators in higher education who

---

continual or intermittent unemployment over a two-year period reported greater stress than women whose husbands were continuously employed (Penkower, Bromet, & Dew, 1988). Not surprisingly, this effect was particularly marked for women who were most psychologically or socially vulnerable (e.g., had a personal or family history of psychiatric disorder, limited financial resources) at the outset of the study (Penkower, Bromet, & Dew, 1988). More generally, the families of unemployed workers are characterized by more interpersonal problems than the families of employed individuals (Shelton, 1985).

Just as feelings of job satisfaction are associated with age, reactions to unemployment also vary with age. Men in their thirties and forties in one

attempt to recruit African-American Ph.D.'s for their faculties. Sowell estimated then that if American colleges and universities hired every African-American Ph.D. in the country at that time (including all retired individuals, and all those who were currently employed by government, the military, and business), there would be two to three African-American faculty members per institution, on the average. Few would expect that such a feat could be accomplished, and fewer still would be willing to deem the outcome a success.

Other objections to affirmative action are sometimes made. For example, some would describe the hiring of a woman with mediocre qualifications rather than a man with outstanding qualifications as reverse discrimination. Jones (1977) more kindly describes this situation as one in which a "counterfactual meritocracy" operates. Jones points out that the logic behind the situation is that, although the woman's qualifications are in fact less noteworthy than the man's, had the woman not suffered the effects of sexism in the past—and, perhaps, if the man had not benefitted from sexism in the past—then the woman might have had the more admirable qualifications. If so, then hiring the woman is not discriminatory at all.

Jones (1977) goes on to summarize objections to this reasoning. First, it rests on the assumption that one knows the extent to which the woman experienced discrimination in the past, and the extent to which the man benefitted from past discrimination.

Rarely is such information available. Second, the universal adoption of a counterfactual meritocracy would probably result in reduced job efficiency and productivity, since the *best* qualified applicants would not always be hired. Finally, knowing that one was hired not on the basis of merit but on the basis of race or gender could be a blow to self-esteem.

Each of these objections can be answered (Jones, 1977). Although we rarely know the degree to which job applicants have suffered or benefitted from discrimination, it is usually a safe bet that many women and minorities have suffered, and that many Caucasian men have gained, from racism and sexism. Although selecting a qualified applicant who is not the *best* qualified applicant for a position may reduce efficiency or productivity, it may be possible to establish minimal job qualifications—or maximal differences in job qualifications—that are acceptable. The damage to self-esteem that results from being hired as an Affirmative Action step may be overestimated. Such an experience may be far less traumatic than that of being denied a position on the basis of race or gender.

Clearly, there are many perspectives on Affirmative Action and the situations under which this approach represents justice. It is also clear that this is an area in which easy answers do not exist, and are not likely to emerge in the foreseeable future. Rather, this issue is one in which questions are likely to remain open, and answers are best seen as evolving products and not final solutions.

---

sample expressed greater distress concerning job loss than did youths in their teens or early twenties (Rowley & Feather, 1987). The older men in this study also expressed more employment commitment than did the younger men, so their greater distress might have reflected their stronger feelings of commitment to work; the impact of unemployment is related to employment commitment (Jackson, Stafford, Bands, & Warr, 1983).

Although unemployed workers' spouses share the trauma of unemployment, the marital relationship is also an important stress buffer for many unemployed people (Liem & Liem, 1988). Some therapists, recognizing the extent to which spouses and children share the stress of unemployment and can buffer that stress, recommend family therapy following unemployment (e.g., Fleuridas, 1987). Others highlight the potential contribution of traditional forms of psychotherapy in which issues of depression, low self-esteem, coping techniques, stress management, and needs for supportive interpersonal relationships are stressed (e.g., Keefe, 1984; Shelton, 1985). Finally, Gordus (1986) describes the Employment Transition Program, in which relatively specific practical and psychological needs (e.g., needs for labor market information, inappropriate wage expectations, inexperience in job seeking, low self-esteem, high feelings of guilt and self-blame) of the unemployed are addressed.

Harassment in the workplace

In the 1970s and 1980s women's experiences in the workplace received increased attention from all quarters. Partly as a result, awareness of the problems that women experience on the job grew. One of the most serious problems—although one not only experienced by working women—is **sexual harassment**.

Sexual harassment is any unwanted, uninvited, or unwelcome sexual attention or expression which makes the recipient uncomfortable in the workplace. Clearly, this definition encompasses a wide range of actions, including sexual innuendos, humor and jokes about sex or gender-specific traits, leering, whistling, obscene gestures, touching, forced sexual intercourse, and assault.

Sexual harassment affects everyone. Some are affected as victims who suffer financial, psychological, or physical health problems. Others are affected as employees, customers, or clients of organizations and businesses in which sexual harassment occurs. Sexual harassment is harmful to these employers in terms of employee turnover and diminished productivity—and is potentially expensive, since sexual harassment lawsuits can be extremely costly.

It is difficult to obtain precise figures on the frequency of sexual harassment, partly because the definition is so broad and partly because victims are often reluctant to report these incidents. Several estimates are available, however, and these figures show that sexual harassment is anything but rare. In a survey of a representative sample of working men and women in Los Angeles county, researchers found that 21–53 percent of the women and 9–37 percent of the men had been sexually harassed during their working lives (Gutek, 1985).

How should one respond to sexual harassment? Many victims do not report incidents of sexual harassment, for a variety of reasons (Backhouse & Cohen, 1981; Gutek, 1985). Some are afraid that they themselves will be held responsible for the incident, whereas others believe that their report would only create a strained atmosphere among coworkers. Some are concerned about the consequences that their report could have for the harasser, and still others are simply embarrassed. Unfortunately, harassers usually do not stop of their own accord; victims have quit jobs rather than continue to tolerate harassment or report the incidents.

Victims of sexual harassment can take several steps. The first step is to confront the harasser, explaining that his or her behavior is offensive; the victim should keep dated notes of this conversation. If that action is not sufficient, there are further options. The victim can file a grievance through whatever formal channels exist in the workplace, and can take legal action; union members can file union grievances.

Taking legal action can be a complex and confusing process, involving a state or federal agency and perhaps a court system. Usually victims who successfully pursue action through the EEOC (Equal Employment Opportunity Commission) are compensated for their losses resulting from the harassment. A woman who was denied a promotion for failing to comply with a supervisor's sexual demands, for example, would receive the promotion and lost wages, and could be compensated for her attorney's fees. She probably would not receive any monetary award for pain and suffering, and she could not force her employer to fire the harasser. She might, however, be able to file a civil or criminal suit against the harasser, in addition to the EEOC suit.

RETIREMENT

Retirement has a short tradition in America. At the turn of the century, very few people retired. Today, however, most workers retire, and many people live 20 years or more following retirement.

Why has retirement become commonplace? At least three trends have contributed. First, industrialization reduced the number of workers required to produce needed goods and services, and resulted in occupational skills growing outdated with increasing speed. With industrialization, more people are employed by large corporations and fewer are self-employed. Entry into and exit from the labor force are thereby increasingly governed by corporate or governmental policy rather than by individual preferences.

Second, retirement has become financially possible for more people. Early in this century, most people worked as long as they could partly because they had to: there were few private pensions and no government-funded pension systems. The establishment of the Social Security system in the 1930s, and the proliferation of private pension plans later in the century, enabled people to stop working in old age and expect some measure of financial security.

Finally, remember that life expectancy has increased throughout most of the twentieth century (see Chapter One, p. 8). At the turn of the century, relatively few people lived into their sixties or beyond; those who did were generally in relatively good health and thus were physically able to work. More people are living longer today, including some whose health would not permit continued employment. This trend, coupled with the shift to an industrial economy and the emergence of sources of retirement income, has led to the establishment of retirement as a normative event of later life.

Early retirement

"Retirement age" is commonly defined as the age at which one becomes eligible for full Social Security benefits. That age has been 65 since the establish-

Retirement has become a social institution in contemporary America.

ment of the system, but will gradually rise to 67 by the early twenty-first century. Increasing numbers of workers, however, are retiring early and choosing to accept reduced Social Security benefits at age 62. As Figure 14.1 illustrates, men in their late fifties and early sixties have retired with increasing frequency since the 1950s, although no such trend is apparent for women (Clark, 1988).

Likelihood of early retirement varies by occupation. In general, blue-collar workers retire earlier than white-collar workers; and, employees in the manufacturing, transportation, and construction industries retire earlier than those in the service and trade industries (Mitchell, Levine, & Pozzebon, 1988). Professionals at the highest occupational strata (e.g., physicians, top executives, attorneys) rarely retire early; in fact, individuals at this level often work at least part-time as consultants or in some other capacity following retirement (Palmore, George, & Fillenbaum, 1982).

Reasons for retiring early are varied; some of these reasons suggest that early retirement is hardly voluntary. Some retire early because of poor health (Ekerdt, Vinick, & Bosse, 1989; Quinn & Burkhauser, 1990), some to escape risks of work-related injuries (Mitchell et al., 1988), and some older industrial workers feel pressure from younger coworkers to retire (Stagner, 1985). Some people retire early because they believe that they are less productive than when they were younger (Mitchell et al., 1988); and some retire early because they lose their job and then cannot find other work (Boaz, 1987a).

Other motivations for early retirement reflect a greater measure of voluntary choice. Some early retirees report that, although their occupation was of immense personal importance, they had been dissatisfied with their jobs (e.g., employer policies, working conditions) and were happy to retire for that reason (McConnell, 1983). For others, the pension and Social Security benefits available at age 62—though smaller than if the workers wait until age 65 to retire—

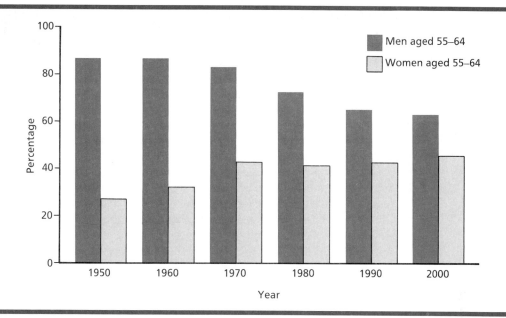

Figure 14.1
Civilian labor force participation rates. (Source: U.S. Dept. of Labor, 1980 and R. L. Clark, 1988: "The Future of Work and Retirement," *Research on Aging*, 10: 169–193. Copyright © 1988 by Sage Publications. Reprinted by permission of Sage Publications, Inc.)

provide an adequate income and an incentive to retire (Quinn & Burkhauser, 1990; Ekerdt et al., 1989).

Workers in some fields retire far earlier than age 62. Professional athletes, for example, may end their careers in their thirties. Some retire even earlier: Olympic gymnasts may retire from competition by their late teens. Similarly, police officers, firefighters, and members of the armed forces may become eligible to retire with a full pension in their forties. Unfortunately, we know very little about the events that follow "off-time" retirement of this sort. Do these individuals enter second careers? How are these second careers related to initial careers? How do these individuals cope with age discrimination as they attempt to enter second careers? Do some very early retirees devote themselves to leisure or learning? The answers to these questions await future research.

Preparing for retirement

Research suggests that retirement does not represent a major life crisis for many men and women (Matthews & Brown, 1987). But retiring undoubtedly changes the individual's financial status, social relationships, and lifestyle. Preparing for retirement, then, is probably to the individual's benefit.

Some employers offer **preretirement programs**, courses or workshops designed to help employees develop their retirement plans. Virtually all of these programs cover financial issues such as Social Security benefits, Medicare and other health insurance plans, pension benefits, investments, tax issues germane to retirees, and policies governing work and earnings following retirement. Some programs are broader, addressing psychological and health changes that occur in old age, adaption to a leisure-oriented lifestyle, and legal issues.

Unfortunately, fewer than 10 percent of workers take part in these programs (Ferraro, 1990a). Workers who most need assistance in planning are particularly unlikely to participate. In a national sample, married men who had families, were in good health, had moderate incomes, and had attained higher occupational levels were those most likely to attend a preretirement program (Campione, 1988). Because health and income adequacy are associated with retirement satisfaction (see below), it is troubling that individuals in poor health and those with low incomes rarely take part in preretirement programs.

A preretirement program is not the only way to prepare for retirement, though. One can prepare informally by discussing retirement with one's spouse, children, and retired friends; reading about retirement; building up savings and investments; buying a home; learning about pension and Social Security benefits; developing hobbies; deciding whether or not to relocate after retirement; preparing a will; and making provisions for long-term care. When researchers ask workers whether they have taken these kinds of steps, they find that most either have or plan to do so (Ferraro, 1990a; Karp, 1989). Although older workers are more involved in these kinds of informal preparation (Kilty & Behling, 1986; Richardson & Kilty, 1989), even those not expecting to retire for 15 years have usually done some informal preparing (Evans, Ekerdt, & Bosse, 1985). Among professionals, income is positively associated with the extent of informal preparation (e.g., Kilty & Behling, 1986; Richardson & Kilty, 1989). Racial minorities and individuals with relatively little education generally do little to prepare informally for retirement (Ferraro, 1990a). As is the case with preretirement programs, then, workers who might be expected to particularly benefit from retirement preparation are less likely than others to prepare.

Furthermore, it is not only characteristics of the person who is retiring—such as race, education, and income—that are associated with the extent of informal retirement preparation. Ferraro (1990a) found a time of measurement effect (see Chapter One, p. 20) in informal preparation. Fewer workers prepared for retirement by saving or learning about pensions in the economic downturn of the early 1980s, as compared to the more affluent years of the mid-1970s.

Partial retirement, in which a worker gradually decreases her work hours as retirement approaches, is another means of preparing for retirement. Although American workers have expressed great interest in partial retirement, few employers make it available (Quinn & Burkhauser, 1990). Partial retirement has been available throughout Sweden since 1976, and Swedish workers (particularly men) have welcomed this option (Wise, 1990).

Adjusting to retirement

Although retirement is rarely a major life crisis, few would argue that it is an important transition. The retiree must develop new avenues of active involvement, and a sense of health maintenance; she must also reevaluate her achievements and commitments, and her outlook on the world in light of the changes in her roles and lifestyle (Antonovsky & Sagy, 1990). Which retirees adapt most successfully? Having a comfortable retirement income and good health are the most consistent predictors of satisfaction with retirement (e.g., Barfield & Morgan, 1978; McConnell, 1983; Matthews & Brown, 1987). In addition, the individual's feelings about work are important. Men for whom the work role is not as important as other roles (e.g., husband, civic leader) have higher morale in retirement, although saliency of the work role is not related to retired women's morale (Matthews & Brown, 1987).

In earlier chapters, we considered marriage in old age (see Chapter Ten, pp. 266–267) and how community involvement changes in old age (see Chapter Thirteen, pp. 329–335). Researchers have also examined retirement as a correlate of health and patterns of social support. Folk wisdom maintains that retirement can be practically lethal: anecdotes describing retirees who receive their gold watches one day and drop dead the next abound. Folk wisdom notwithstanding, there is no evidence that retiring has a negative impact on health (Ekerdt, 1987).

Retirement has little relationship to men's patterns of social support (Bosse, Aldwin, Levenson, Workman-Daniels, & Ekerdt, 1990). Although retirees may discuss personal and financial problems with former coworkers less often than working men do, many retirees still think of their former coworkers as their friends. Furthermore, retirees and working men do not differ in numbers of confidants and in perceptions that they can count on family and friends.

Gender and racial differences   Most research on retirement has involved samples of Caucasian men; however, researchers today give increasing attention to women's and racial minorities' experiences of retirement. Because married women are likely to have interrupted or delayed their entry into the labor force, their retirement may occur at a different career phase—within a relatively short time after beginning work—than is the case for men. Also, because women generally live longer than men and experience greater comorbidity (see Chapter Four, p. 94), retirement may encompass fundamentally different life experiences for men and women.

Generally, the timing of a married woman's retirement is closely linked to the time of her husband's retirement (George, Fillenbaum, & Palmore, 1984; Hayward, Grady, & McLaughlin, 1988; Matthews & Brown, 1987). For married retired women, financial adequacy and the frequency and certainty of support from friends predict satisfaction with retirement; maintenance of preretirement friendships and frequency of contact with friends predict retirement satisfaction for widowed women (Dorfman & Moffett, 1987).

It is difficult to make general statements about retirement among African-Americans: research thus far has addressed a diverse set of issues. In a study of African-American as compared to Caucasian professionals, similarities in retirement planning predominated over differences. African-Americans were less likely than Caucasians to invest in stocks, bonds, and bank certificates, but age and income—rather than race—were the most important factors distinguishing patterns of retirement preparation (Richardson & Kilty, 1989). African-American women are less likely than Caucasian women to retire early, possibly because African-American women are more likely than Caucasian women to have worked throughout adulthood (Belgrave, 1988).

Discussing findings from one of the few nationally representative samples of African-Americans, Gibson (1988) described a new type of African-American retiree: the "unretired retired." These individuals are aged 55 and older; they do not work, but they do not call themselves retired. Their ambiguous retirement status reflects continuity with their earlier patterns of labor force involvement. Many have never had a full-time job, but instead worked part-time throughout adulthood; they continue to work sporadically in old age. The "unretired retired" are often poor and poorly educated; given the high unemployment rates of African-American adolescents and youths today, it is possible that the ranks of the "unretired retired" will swell in the future. Furthermore, Mexican-Americans share many of the labor market experiences that channel African-Americans into the ranks of the "unretired retired" (Zsembik & Singer, 1990); thus, the "unretired retired" may emerge in Mexican-American communities as well.

Retirement income

The economic status of elderly Americans has improved tremendously since World War II, particularly since the 1970s. Although the range of income is quite broad, most older Americans are not poor; as is the case for younger age groups, more women and minority group older people (especially aged African-Americans) live in or near poverty. On the average, elderly people have lower cash incomes than do younger people, but elderly adults also receive government-subsidized in-kind transfers not available to younger people (e.g., Medicare) and many older individuals have assets accumulated over their working years (Neugarten & Neugarten, 1989).

Most retirement income, for most people, is derived from three general sources: Social Security, an employer or union pension, and savings and other assets. In addition, some retired individuals supplement these sources with earned income and public assistance. Persons who receive Social Security benefits can receive other income, but Social Security benefits are reduced if earned income exceeds a maximum amount.[1] As Figure 14.2 illustrates, the relative proportions of income sources varies with income levels. Among older people with low incomes, Social Security is the major source of income, whereas earnings and assets account for most income for affluent elderly people (Clark, 1990; Gohmann, 1990).

Bernice Neugarten (Neugarten & Neugarten, 1989) recently summarized issues of concern as our society ages. Many of these issues concern the economic viability of an aging society, and much of that concern derives from uneasiness regarding the Social Security system. But because of ongoing adjustments in the system, much of that uneasiness is unfounded.

Initiated in 1935, Social Security operates on a "pay-as-you-go" system. Nearly all workers are covered by Social Security, and the retirement benefits received do not depend on the retiree's level of financial need. An individual's Social Security retirement benefits are determined by applying a legislated formula to their earnings history in Social Security-covered employment; these benefit levels increase regularly. Each year, there is an approximate balance between the amounts being paid into the system by workers and employers, as compared to the amounts being paid out to older people receiving retirement benefits.

To ensure that this balance can be maintained, Congress passes amendments every few years to adjust the Social Security tax and benefit levels in light of economic and demographic projections. Since 1983, these adjustments have been made so as to gradually build up surplus funds for the upcoming needs of the large baby-boom cohorts. R. L. Clark (1990) notes, however, that Congress' ability to resist the temptation to use this surplus to finance ongoing government deficits is an emerging concern.

Together with income and assets, pensions provided by an employer or union complement Social Security benefits for some retirees. Few workers were covered by pensions before 1940, and only half of all American workers were covered by 1984 (Clark, 1990). Those most likely to be covered by a pension are union workers, employees of large companies, those with relatively high salaries, older workers, men, and married workers (Clark, 1990). Virtually all pension plans include provisions that provide older workers with strong incentives to retire, usually by reducing the amount of pension compensation to be gained by staying on the job (Clark, 1990).

There are two basic types of pension plans. In a **defined-benefit pension plan**, the employer promises to pay a specified retirement benefit when employees meet length-of-service requirements and reach a certain age. Most employees are covered by these plans, and these plans are government-insured. **Defined-contribution pension plans** are ones in which the em-

---

1. Social Security benefits are not reduced for people over age 70 with earned income above the maximum amount.

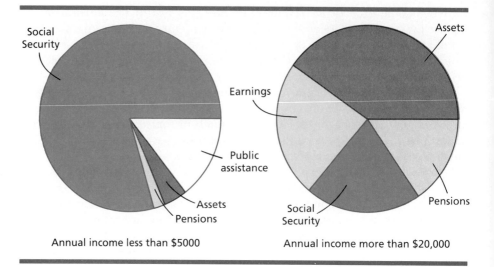

Figure 14.2
Percentage of household income for aged households, 1984. (Source: Yeas & Grad, 1987. Reprinted by permission.)

ployer contributes a fixed amount to an employee's pension account each pay period; these funds are invested and accumulate throughout the employee's tenure with the employer. When the employee retires, their retirement benefits are determined by the size of the individual's pension account, which in turn depends on how profitably the funds were invested.

A general conclusion at this point is that each individual's experience of retirement—including the timing of retirement and the extent of financial stability that one enjoys—reflect the long term impact of work-related choices and opportunities that occurred years earlier. Furthermore, those choices and opportunities themselves often stem from developmental trends in personality, intellectual abilities, and physical functioning. Work and retirement, then, are issues for which the importance of a life-span perspective is particularly clear.

SUMMARY

Differentialist theory proposes that career choice reflects pressure toward congruence between people and work settings. Developmentalist theories, in contrast, portray career choice as a process which spans much of the life cycle and which is enmeshed in individual maturation. Young adults are less satisfied overall with their jobs than are older adults, and are less satisfied with their work per se, as opposed to their jobs, than are older adults.

Elderly adults who work are motivated by the fulfillment or challenge of work, the social stimulation of coworkers, the structure that work adds to their lives, and financial pressures. These older workers, however, may confront age discrimination in employment. Similarly, members of minority groups are at a disadvantage in the job market.

Nonnormative work experiences include unemployment and sexual harassment. Research documents a myriad of ways in which unemployment affects physical and psychological well-being. Although substantial numbers of workers are victims of sexual harassment, many do not report the incidents.

Some employers offer preretirement programs, but fewer than 10 percent of workers take part in these programs, and workers who most need assistance in planning are less likely than more advantaged workers to take part in these programs. Having a comfortable retirement income and good health are the most consistent predictors of satisfaction with retirement. Retirement income, for most people, is derived from Social Security, pensions, and assets.

KEY TERMS

Adverse impact
Age Discrimination in Employment Act (ADEA)
Alternative procedures
Crystallization stage
Deceleration stage
Defined-benefit pension plan
Defined-contribution pension plan
Developmentalist theories
Differentialist theories
Employment discrimination
Establishment stage
Horizontal career change

Implementation
Indirect discrimination
Maintenance stage
Organizational culture
Partial retirement
Personality pattern
Preretirement program
Retirement stage
Reverse discrimination
Sexual harassment
Specification stage
Vertical career change

SUGGESTIONS FOR FURTHER READING

Dennis, H. (1984). *Retirement Preparation*. Lexington, MA: Lexington Books.

Fyock, C. (1990). *America's Work Force is Coming of Age*. Lexington, MA: Lexington Books.

Gutek, B. A. (1985). *Sex and the Workplace*. San Francisco: Jossey-Bass Publishers.

Myles, J. (1984). *Old Age in the Welfare State: The Political Economy of Public Pensions*. Boston: Little, Brown & Co.

Palmore, E. B., Burchett, B., Fillenbaum, G. G., George, L. K., & Wallman, L. M. (1985). *Retirement: Causes and Consequences*. New York: Springer.

Pavalko, R. M. (1988). *Sociology of Occupations and Professions*. Itasca, IL: F. E. Peacock, Publishers.

CHAPTER FIFTEEN

DEATH AND DYING

Although it is tempting to end the book with the statement that "they all lived happily ever after," that closing is fittingly reserved for fairy tales. Death, of course, is one of the two certainties of life. Unlike taxes (the other certainty), awareness of death affects perceptions of life and the world, and thus—directly or indirectly—influences behavior through much of the life span.

This chapter considers death, the process of dying, and grief and mourning. Initially, medical, psychological, and social aspects of death are examined. Next, there is an overview of research on attitudes toward death, and of Erikson's concept of ego integrity and Butler's notion of the life review. The chapter closes with a discussion of social and legal issues pertinent to death and dying.

Questions to consider in reading the chapter include:

How has the institutionalization of death affected the care of terminally-ill patients? How do hospices differ from other types of settings in which terminally ill patients might be cared for?

What kinds of attitudes toward death are expressed by relatively healthy adults? How did Elizabeth Kübler-Ross portray the psychological process of confronting life-threatening illness?

How do men and women differ in their reaction to death of a spouse?

What are the purposes of funerals?

What are common inheritance patterns?

DEFINING DEATH

Throughout most of the 1980s, America was embroiled in a controversy over the moral and legal acceptability of abortion; much of the debate centered on when human life begins. Pinpointing the end of life is no easier. Physicians and scientists, as well as psychologists, philosophers, and theologians, all offer definitions.

In this chapter, death is seen as a multifaceted phenomenon occurring on several interrelated but distinct levels. **Physiological death** occurs when all of the physical processes sustaining life cease. At one time, that point was the cessation of respiration and cardiac functioning. Today, however, medical technology allows detection of more subtle signs of life, and both heartbeat and breathing can be mechanically sustained almost indefinitely—even when other physiological processes have stopped. The signals of physiological death have changed correspondingly.

Today, the Harvard criteria of **total brain death** define physiological death. These criteria emphasize the sustained absence of brain activity. For example, reflexes must be absent, and an EEG must show no activity in both cortical lobes and the brainstem for at least ten minutes. In addition, conditions other than death that can produce these signs (e.g., deep coma, hypothermia) must not be present. For total brain death to be declared, all of the Harvard criteria must be met not just once, but also a second time 24 hours later.

Some suggest that the Harvard criteria are too broad. Consider the case of Karen Ann Quinlan, a young woman whose mixture of alcohol and barbiturates placed her in a deep, irreversible coma. Ms. Quinlan was able to breathe independently and showed brainstem activity for approximately ten years after mechanical life support measures were disconnected. She had, however, no evidence of higher brain activity during that time. Cases such as hers have prompted some to suggest that **cerebral death**—the cessation of activity in the cortex—is a more appropriate criterion than a completely flat EEG (Schulz, 1978).

On what other levels does death occur? **Psychological death** is the loss of "personhood," an integrated personality capable of interacting with others (e.g., Veatch, 1981). That loss usually follows physiological death, but does not always. One could argue that dementia or a coma produce psychological death before physiological death.

Social death is the process during which other people relinquish their relationships with the deceased. The death is marked by a funeral and/or other rituals, and eventually survivors cease interacting with, talking about, or even thinking about the deceased. As is the case for psychological death, social death usually follows physiological death but can precede it. For example, an individual meeting the definition of cerebral death might be institutionalized and abandoned by the family and community. Or, a person who violates social norms (e.g., marrying outside of one's faith or race) might be outcast by the family, congregation, and community.

Funerals and other rituals are components of social death.

Perhaps more important than distinguishing physiological, psychological, and social death is the notion of death as a process. Robert Kastenbaum (1985) describes dying as a psychosocial process that begins when a life-threatening medical situation is detected and the victim is informed of the situation. From that point, both the dying individual and health care professionals shape the dying process through their response to the individual's condition.

MEDICAL AND ETHICAL ISSUES

Some assert that death has become institutionalized. At one time, most people died at home; still, most people of all ages say that they would prefer to die at home (Kalish & Reynolds, 1976). The vast majority of people today, however, die in health care institutions—usually, a general hospital or a nursing home (Kalish, 1985). Hospices (see below) are an alternative for specialized care of terminally ill patients.

The institutionalization of death has had at least two consequences for dying people. First, the dying individual and her family are affected far more by the attitudes of health care professionals and institutional regimes than is the case when death occurs at home. Many people are uncomfortable confronting death; unfortunately, nurses, physicians, and other health care professionals are no exception. Some physicians, for example, avoid patients when they conclude that there is nothing more that can be done to restore health (e.g., Glaser & Strauss, 1965).

Some researchers suggest that individuals are attracted to medical professions because of their precision and predictability; these people are frustrated in medical situations in which predictability and precision break down, such as the care of dying patients (Rossman, 1977). However, many medical and nursing schools have incorporated courses on **thanatology** (the study of death and dying) and on terminal care into their curricula over the past twenty years (e.g.,

Kalish, 1985; Marshall & Levy, 1990). Hopefully, these steps will prepare nurses and physicians to work more comfortably with the terminally ill.

Not only the attitudes of doctors and nurses but also institutional rules and schedules affect those dying in hospitals and nursing homes. Dying patients and their families may be distressed by the impersonality and lack of privacy in these settings, or by the feeling that they have given up control over their life and their daily routines. Restrictions on visiting hours and on who is allowed to visit may also be frustrating (e.g., Marshall & Levy, 1990).

A second consequence of the institutionalization of death is the availability of measures maintaining life in the presence of terminal conditions. Current technology provides a range of **life support measures** that can be used to prolong the lives of individuals suffering from life-threatening illness. CPR can restore a heartbeat, a respirator can maintain breathing, nasogastric tube feeding can provide nourishment, and fluids can be provided intravenously. Minor illnesses and infections can often be treated effectively, even when a patient is in a coma and unlikely to regain consciousness. Treatments such as surgery and chemotherapy can extend life even when it is virtually impossible to restore health and vigor. Some people find these medical approaches reassuring.

Euthanasia and living wills

Not everyone, however, wants such steps to be taken. Some say that they do not fear death itself, but are afraid of an emotionally and financially draining, artificially prolonged process of dying. These individuals would oppose the use of many life support measures if they confronted a terminal illness, and would probably welcome some approach to euthanasia in that event.

Euthanasia, derived from the Greek phrase for "good death," can be practiced in two ways. **Active euthanasia** is taking deliberate action to end a patient's life; a physician who administers a lethal overdose commits active

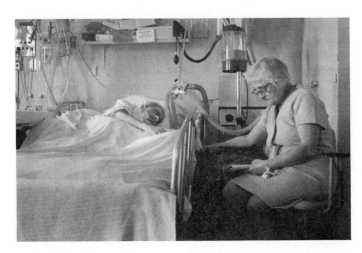

Some people express greater fear of an artificially prolonged process of dying than of death itself.

euthanasia. **Passive euthanasia**, on the other hand, is refraining from treatment that would prolong a person's life (e.g., chemotherapy, surgery, antibiotic therapy, nasogastric feeding tube) but taking no steps to end her life. Many people are undecided about the moral acceptability of euthanasia; some of the moral dilemmas surrounding this practice are examined in the *Open Questions* box.

BOX 15.1   *OPEN QUESTIONS*

Euthanasia: Mercy or murder?

Euthanasia is popularly termed "mercy killing." Some people, in contemplating the fate of a loved one suffering an irreversible coma or life-threatening illness, feel strongly that either active or passive euthanasia is indeed a merciful act. Others are comfortable with the notion of letting nature take its course through passive euthanasia, but shrink from giving nature a prod by committing active euthanasia. Still others condemn any approach to ending human life, under any circumstances, as murder.

What kinds of considerations enter into decisions regarding the acceptability of euthanasia? Respondents in a recent survey of patients and their potential proxies for health care decisions considered hypothetical cases (see Table 15.1) of gravely ill people whose lives could be sustained by various treatment approaches, offered their views of whether or not these treatments were well-advised, and reported the factors that they had considered in making their decisions (Zweibel & Cassel, 1989). The hypothetical cases required judgments of whether or not passive euthanasia would be justified.

In this context, the critical findings are not the recommendations that the patients and their potential proxies offered, nor the extent of disagreement between patients and potential proxies. Instead, the major issue is the basis of these recommendations. What factors did these individuals believe were relevant to their decisions?

Most patients and most potential proxies said that they considered the cognitive status of the person described and the likelihood that the individual would become a burden to the family (Zweibel & Cassel, 1989). Other factors that over half of both groups

deemed important were the patient's age and survival potential, the cost of treatment, and the amount of pain that the individual experienced. For these individuals and their relatives, then, the acceptability of even passive euthanasia depended on individual circumstances.

Making a decision to commit active euthanasia is undoubtedly even more agonizing. As well as judging the quality of a patient's life and likelihood of recovery, physicians and family members choosing this course of action must be prepared to face public outcry and possible legal prosecution. Although active euthanasia is not legally sanctioned, some believe that it can be the most humane choice for an individual facing months of suffering and little hope of restored vigor.

But others maintain that practicing active euthanasia on the comatose or terminally ill could be the first step toward using these techniques on physically healthy but disoriented victims of dementia, mentally retarded individuals, or anyone deemed an unproductive member of society. And, of course, the decision to commit active euthanasia requires the patient and her survivors to abandon all hope of either a medical breakthrough or a miracle. Some would argue that neither medical science nor life itself are predictable enough to justify that decision.

The acceptability of euthanasia, like the acceptability of abortion, is an issue unlikely to be resolved soon or easily. Perhaps neither issue should have a final resolution. Both abortion and euthanasia call into question the nature of life and its quality, an issue that may best be considered in the concrete context of an individual life rather than in the abstract.

Unfortunately, relatively few people provide formal notice of their opinions regarding terminal care. There are at least two means of providing such notice. In many states, individuals can establish a Durable Power of Attorney for Health Care, in which they appoint a proxy[1] charged with making their health care decisions if they are incapacitated; this alternative covers a wide variety of health care decisions. An alternative that applies specifically to individuals facing life-threatening illness is to make a **living will** (see below), a declaration to physicians that outlines wishes regarding the use of life support measures.

Unfortunately, relatively few people take either of these steps (Zweibel & Cassel, 1989). Fewer than one out of five people report that they have written a living will (e.g., High, 1988; Zweibel & Cassel, 1989), and still fewer have given family members specific instructions about their future medical care (Cassel & Zweibel, 1987). When a patient cannot express her own wishes (if she is in a coma, for example) and has neither made a living will nor established a Durable Power of Attorney for Health Care, her physician must identify one or more proxies (usually a close relative such as a spouse, child, or parent) who attempt to determine the best course for the patient's care.

Treatment choices made by proxy are certainly not a desirable situation. Inevitably, both the proxy and the physician must wonder whether they are making decisions as the incapacitated patient would wish. Recent evidence suggests that they often do not.

One group of researchers presented four hypothetical case vignettes (see Table 15.1) to elderly outpatients and to relatives who were their potential proxies, and asked the patient and the proxy separately what directions they would give regarding life-sustaining care. These patient-proxy pairs gave discrepant directions between 24 percent (in the case of tube feeding) and 50 percent (in the case of chemotherapy) of the time, with the proxies sometimes authorizing care that the patient would not want and other times directing the physician to withhold care that the patient would want (Zweibel & Cassel, 1989).

A living will (see above) is a written, witnessed declaration to physicians of the individual's wishes regarding life-sustaining care in the face of terminal illness. While these documents can assist physicians and proxies, living wills do not solve all of the problems. Living wills are themselves surrounded by practical dilemmas, including who is cognitively capable of making a living will; when and how to make a living will and be sure that physicians and relatives are aware of its existence[2]; the ability and willingness of hospitals,

---

1. A proxy can be anyone over age 18 who is of sound mind. The proxy should also be someone with whom the individual feels comfortable discussing their health care wishes, and can trust to see that their wishes are carried out if she does become inacapacitated.

2. Professionals advise that individuals who have made living wills should carry a copy of it at all times, keep another copy with their important papers, see that their primary care physician has a copy, and also see that close family members and friends and their attorney all have copies. A copy should also be brought to the hospital any time that the individual is admitted.

Table 15.1
Hypothetical case vignettes (proxy versions).

1. **Ventilation**

   Mrs. K is an elderly widow who has recently suffered a major stroke leaving her in a coma and unable to breathe without a machine. After a few months, the doctor tells her daughter that it is unlikely that Mrs. K will come out of the coma and that no one can be certain what her level of functioning would be if she ever did come out of the coma. What if this were (Patient) and the doctor asked you whether or not the breathing machine should be removed?

2. **Resuscitation**

   (This vignette includes the above scenario about Mrs. K and ends with the question: Now suppose the doctor wanted to know whether to try to revive [Patient] if her/his heart stopped beating?)

3. **Chemotherapy**

   Mr. L is an elderly widower who has been diagnosed as having a type of cancer that probably can't be cured. His doctor recommends to Mr. L's daughter that chemotherapy be started. The doctor explains that the chances of curing Mr. L are very small but that the chemotherapy may help him live longer. Mr. L's daughter is also told about the side effects of chemotherapy, which can make you very ill.

4. **Amputation**

   Mr. S is a widower who is unable to make medical decisions for himself because he has become mentally confused. Because of diabetes, he has developed gangrene, or blood poisoning, in his leg. The doctor recommends to Mr. S's daughter that unless Mr. S has his leg removed, he will almost certainly die in a very short time.

5. **Tube Feeding**

   Mrs. M is an older woman who has broken her hip and is recuperating from an operation to repair it. Since the operation, she has become very withdrawn and will not speak to any of the nurses or doctors. She refuses to eat and after several days, the doctor wants to feed Mrs. M using a feeding tube placed into her stomach.

Source: Zweibel & Cassel, 1989. "Treatment Choices at the End of Life," *The Gerontologist, 29:* 615–621. Copyright © The Gerontological Society of America. Reprinted by permission.

nursing homes, and physicians to respect the wishes outlined in a living will; and the legal status of living wills (Diamond, Jernigan, Moseley, Messina, & McKeown, 1989).

Currently, laws regarding living wills differ from one state to another. An individual could have no assurance that her living will would be respected if she were hospitalized outside of the state in which she made her living will. Even though many physicians support the concept of living wills, some doctors feel ethically obligated to do everything possible to fight disease. Anyone making a living will should discuss the matter with her physician. If her physician cannot support her wishes, then her care can be transferred to another doctor.

Some argue, too, that the wording of living wills is often too vague to provide useful guidance (e.g., Henderson, 1990). For example, if a patient's living will requests that "no extraordinary means" be used to prolong life in the face of a terminal illness, others are left to decide what the patient would view as extraordinary means—cardiopulmonary resuscitation, chemotherapy or surgery, antibiotic treatment for infections, providing food and fluids?

Hospice care

For some who face a terminal illness, a hospice is a desirable alternative to hospital care and the use of life support measures. **Hospices** are designed to provide patients and their families with the conditions promoting an **appropriate death**, one that conforms to the patient's wishes and expectations (Weisman, 1972). In a hospice, the goal is not to attempt to cure the patient's illness nor to prolong her life artificially. Rather, efforts are aimed at keeping the patient as comfortable and alert as possible, supporting the patient and her family as they prepare for death, and helping the family to grieve when death occurs (e.g., Rossman, 1977).

Since the establishment of the first American hospices in the early 1970s, hospices have flourished throughout the United States. Hospices exist in different forms in different communities, but most can be classified as either inpatient or outpatient. Inpatient hospices are located within a hospital, usually as a distinct ward or floor. Outpatient hospices, which are becoming increasingly popular, are a support network of professionals and volunteers assisting families as they care for a terminally ill patient in her home. Many outpatient hospices are formally affiliated with a hospital: patients spend as much time at home as possible, but enter the hospital if their condition must be restabilized or if their caregiver needs temporary respite. Medicare provides some coverage for hospice care.

Most hospice patients are relatively young, and most are cancer patients (Kalish, 1985). Not every patient facing a terminal illness, and not every family, is a good candidate for hospice treatment. Most hospices develop admission criteria designed to identify patients and families most likely to benefit from hospice care. For example, one outpatient hospice will accept only patients who have a designated caregiver, who have a diagnosis of a life-threatening illness, who choose **palliative care** aimed at relieving pain and other symptoms rather than active cure treatments, who realize that life support measures will not be used, and who are aware of their condition and have been informed of treatment alternatives.

Whether an inpatient or an outpatient setting, hospices differ from hospitals and nursing homes in several ways. There is usually a more multidisciplinary, team-oriented approach to patient care than is typical of most hospital settings (Rossman, 1977). In a hospice, the chaplain, social worker, and nurses are at least as involved in patient care as are physicians. Volunteers are an important component of most hospice staffs; Kastenbaum (1985) notes that elderly volunteers, in particular, are valued staff components in many hospices.

Another unique aspect of hospice is that the ill person *and her family*, rather than the ill person alone, are the focus of care. Family members, in fact, are centrally involved in caring for the patient. Professionals and volunteers provide family caregivers with the practical and moral support that they need to maintain that involvement. When death occurs, the hospice continues to support the family by providing bereavement counseling and support groups (Rando, 1984).

Finally, inpatient hospices differ from hospitals and nursing homes in the general absence of restrictions. Most achieve a homelike atmosphere. Patients have private rooms and private baths, and there are cheerfully-decorated rooms for visiting with family and friends. Usually hospice patients and their loved ones enjoy 24-hour visiting privileges, and hospices welcome visitors of all ages. Even well-behaved pets are allowed to visit in many hospices! Visitors are encouraged to bring favorite foods and beverages (including alcoholic beverages), and patients may be permitted to smoke. Pain-relief medication is administered regularly without concern over possible addiction; the goal is to keep patients alert and free not only of pain but free also of the fear of pain (e.g., Rossman, 1977).

Unfortunately, there has been little empirical work evaluating hospice impacts on patients and families. Kalish (1985) summarizes two early studies showing that hospice patients expressed less anxiety, depression, and hostility than control patients who were cared for in hospitals; these hospice patients' families were also more satisfied than were the families of hospital patients. Again, however, hospice is not the answer for every terminally ill patient and family. According to Parkes (1980), patients who are especially concerned about burdening their families may experience greater stress from hospice care than they would in a hospital or nursing home. Similarly, family members who are—for whatever reason—unprepared for terminal caregiving may not be helped by hospice.

ATTITUDES TOWARD DEATH

What attitudes do people express toward the prospect of death and dying? This question is examined from three perspectives. First, developmental theory provides a vantage point: Erikson's concept of ego integrity and Butler's discussion of the life review are considered. Second, survey research describes the ways in which adults of different ages express their thoughts and feelings about death. Because the participants in these surveys were not, to their knowledge, suffering from life-threatening illness, this body of research identifies attitudes toward death in the abstract. Finally, we look at research examining terminally ill patients' reactions to their own impending death.

Facing death: Theoretical perspectives

Erikson's (1963) theory of psychosocial development proposes that your outlook on death reflects your perspective on your life. The eighth, and final, challenge in Erikson's life-span theory is that of balancing a sense of **ego integrity** with a sense of **despair**. Older people become increasingly aware that their lives are finite, and that awareness prompts them to look back at how they have spent their lives. Those who can derive satisfaction from their commitments and accomplishments, and who can accept their disappointments and failures, have attained a predominance of ego integrity. According to Erikson, these individuals will accept impending death without fear. On the other hand, those who are overcome with regrets about the past will experience a predominance of despair. These individuals, Erikson believes, will fear death.

Some research supports Erikson's (1963) contentions. Death anxiety is negatively associated with such traits as self-esteem and a sense of competence (Gesser, Wong, & Reker, 1987-1988; Kastenbaum & Costa, 1977). However, studies in which older adults completed measures of both ego integrity and death anxiety do not identify consistent relationships between the two constructs (Hayslip & Stewart-Bussey, 1986-1987; Nehrke, Belluci, & Gabriel, 1977-1978).

Robert Butler (1968) offers a similar notion. Butler notes that many older people are prone to reminisce, a process that he terms the **life review**. He proposes that the life review is prompted by the realization of impending death—and, often, by other kinds of personal crises. A new job, a serious illness, death of a close relative, or even something as mundane as a high school or college reunion may prompt a life review. According to Butler, the life review provides an opportunity to confront unresolved conflicts and—ideally—achieve integration regarding those issues. By reviewing the past, the individual can gain a deeper understanding of her life; that insight may mitigate fears of death.

Facing death: Survey research on age, gender, and racial differences

Surveys in which adults of different ages are asked about their reactions to death and dying offer a second viewpoint on attitudes toward death. Much of this research has concentrated on assessing fear of death or death anxiety, often distinguishing various aspects of these reactions (e.g., fear of personal death, reluctance to interact with the dying, fear of pain, reaction to reminders of death, fear of isolation, fear of dependence, etc.) and identifying correlates of these reactions. However, as Kalish (1985) points out, the most important conceptual problem in this approach—as in all attitude research—is the need to assume that research participants say what they mean and mean what they say.

Depth of religious feeling bears an inconsistent relationship to level of death anxiety. Some find that deeply religious older individuals express less fear of death; others, however, report that fear of death is lower among the deeply religious *and* the deeply irreligious than among those who are uncertain about their faith (e.g., Kalish, 1985). Other psychological characteristics have also been linked to levels of death anxiety. **Awareness of finitude**, the tendency to estimate the amount of time left until death (Marshall, 1975), is associated with relatively positive attitudes toward death (Keith, 1982).

There are ethnic differences in levels of death anxiety, although these differences are generally small and—as with religious and psychological outlooks—findings are inconsistent. In one of the most extensive studies, Kalish and Reynolds (1976) questioned over 400 adults concerning their fear of death; their study included African-American, Japanese-American, Mexican-American, and Caucasian men and women. The African-Americans and Caucasians expressed less fear of death than did the Japanese-Americans and the Mexican-Americans, although most respondents in all ethnic groups said that they were not afraid to die. Other survey research involving multiethnic samples has not identified race as a significant predictor of death anxiety (e.g., Bengtson, Cueller, & Ragan, 1977).

In some studies, women have higher scores on measures of death anxiety than men do (e.g., Immarino, 1975; Templer, Ruff, & Franks, 1971). However, other investigators report no gender differences in levels of death anxiety (e.g., Bengtson et al., 1977; Dickstein, 1972; Kalish & Reynolds, 1976). One researcher found that women expressed both greater death anxiety and greater acceptance of their own death than men do (Keith, 1979).

One group of researchers approached the matter differently, and asked over 4000 respondents what they had been thinking about in the past five minutes; their goal was to see how often death was a focal concern and how often it was a matter of fleeting consideration (Cameron, Stewart, & Biber, 1973). In this study, women were more likely than men to report that death had crossed their minds during the five minute period. Very few (less than 5 percent) men or women, however, said that death had been the main thing on their minds during the time under question.

Age differences in attitudes toward death have been documented more consistently. In general, older adults think more about death than younger people do, but express less anxiety about death than young and middle-aged adults do. In Cameron et al.'s (1973) study of the frequency of thoughts of death, elderly adults (as well as young adolescents and young adults) reported that death had crossed their minds in the five-minute period more often than middle-aged adults did. Other researchers also report that older adults think and talk more about death than do younger people (e.g., Kalish & Reynolds, 1976; Riley, 1970).

Even though elderly adults have more frequent thoughts about death, they express less death anxiety than younger adults do (e.g., Bengtson et al., 1977; Kalish & Reynolds, 1976). That is not to say that older adults express no concern over the prospect of death. Although elderly adults express less anxiety than younger people about death per se, they also express greater concern than younger adults over such dying-related events as losing others, experiencing pain and suffering, losing goals or achievements, and losing control over their bodies and actions (Pinder & Hayslip, 1981).

Why do older people think about death more but fear it less than younger people? Such an outlook can be adaptive for people who realistically expect that death is not far off. Being able to think about death without fear allows one to take such practical steps as planning a funeral, preparing a will, and designating a proxy for health care decisions. In addition, Kalish (1985) suggests that older people may be less anxious about death because many desirable social roles (e.g., worker, spouse) have already been lost, or because they may already have lived longer than they expected. Most older people, too, have experienced the deaths of their parents and spouse, friends, and possibly siblings and children. These experiences may give some familiarity with death, and—for those who believe in an afterlife—may even make death a welcome prospect.

Facing death: Research on the terminally ill

Probably the most widely known work on the emotional needs of dying people is that of Elizabeth Kübler-Ross. In her work as a consulting psychiatrist in a large teaching hospital, Kübler-Ross regularly dealt with patients facing life-threatening illnesses. At that time (the 1960s), medical professionals often did not clearly inform such patients about their prognosis. Kübler-Ross became convinced that this practice deprived the terminally ill individual of the opportunity to discuss their situation and their emotional reaction to it, and that such discussions could be critically important.

Despite resistance on the part of some members of the hospital staff, Kübler-Ross began to talk with these patients about death. She found that, whether their physician had informed them of their prognosis or not, most patients knew that they were dying. Furthermore, her interviews with over 200 such patients led to her assertion that patients suffering from terminal illnesses experience five emotional stages culminating in acceptance of death. Her work, described in *On Death and Dying* (Kübler-Ross, 1969), has had a profound impact on the treatment of terminally-ill patients.

Kübler-Ross' stages   The initial reaction to a terminal diagnosis is **denial**. The patient is sure that the doctor has made a mistake: perhaps a mixup occurred in the laboratory, or the doctors misinterpreted complex medical information. Some seek third or fourth opinions in this stage.

For most patients, however, reality sinks in eventually and denial is replaced by **anger**. Now the individual turns hostility and resentment toward doctors, nurses, family, and friends. She searches for a reason that she, of all people, is about to be struck down—when so many others can go on living. As anger diminishes, though, the patient enters a stage of **bargaining**. As in the stage of denial, the patient is not convinced that her illness is terminal; now she wonders if she can deal with God or fate so as to postpone death. She may, for example, promise to devote herself to church or charity work if only a miracle reverses her condition.

When efforts to bargain have been exhausted, the patient enters a stage of **depression**. At this point, the individual may withdraw from others and express deep sadness. The patient, in effect, is grieving for the losses that death will bring—the loss of all loving relationships, of all interests and activities, and of all goals and hopes. This grieving process ideally leads to **acceptance**. The patient now seems to be at peace, open to the inevitability of death.

Although it is virtually impossible not to present Kübler-Ross' model as a rigid sequence of stages that all terminally ill patients experience in the same order, Kübler-Ross (1974) maintains that this is not the case. She feels instead that some patients do not have all five of these reactions, and that some experience these emotions in different orders.

Despite its value in heightening awareness of terminally ill patients' emotional needs, Kübler-Ross' (1969) work has been criticized on several grounds. First, Marshall (1980) questions the generality of her model. He notes that many of the patients that Kübler-Ross interviewed were relatively young, and that expressions of denial, anger, and bargaining may be rational reactions to impending death for young people in particular. Elderly patients, looking back on a long life with satisfying accomplishments, might react differently to life-threatening illness. Marshall also suggests that the expressions of denial on the part of Kübler-Ross' patients might have been better labeled statements of uncertainty, since some of the patients had not been clearly informed of their prognosis.

It is important, too, that relatives and professionals caring for terminally ill patients not attempt to apply Kübler-Ross' (1969) model too rigidly. Although her framework implies that all patients *should* progress beyond denial and eventually accept their impending death, that course of events may not be best for everyone. For some patients, and some families, denial may be an adaptive defense mechanism or a means of maintaining hope. Similarly, one should not be too quick to dismiss a patient's protestations about the quality of care or relatives' reactions to their illness as a simple reflection of "being in the anger stage;" the patient may well have legitimate reason to complain (e.g., Hayslip & Martin, 1988).

Researchers who have attempted to confirm Kübler-Ross' model have had little success. Antonoff and Spilka (1984–1985) videotaped terminally ill patients at various points in the course of their illness, and examined the patients' facial expressions for signs of denial, anger, bargaining, depression, and acceptance. There was neither an increase in happy expressions (that might reflect acceptance), nor a decrease in angry expressions, as the patients' illnesses progressed; sad expressions became increasingly frequent as time passed. In other studies, individuals facing life-threatening illnesses were found to be predominantly hopeful (Metzger, 1979-1980) or depressed (Schulz & Adelman, 1974).

Other research on terminal illness   Other approaches to understanding reactions to terminal illness also emphasize the notion of a relatively long-term process of emotionally preparing for death. Weisman (1972) views dying as a sequence of three phases. The first, **acute phase**, begins when the patient initially learns of her diagnosis. During this period of adapting to the reality of being terminally ill, most patients experience anxiety and anger. In the **chronic living-dying phase**, patients have a range of emotional reactions: many are fearful—of loneliness and loss of control, if not of death itself— and many also feel grief as well as hope and acceptance. Finally, in the **terminal phase**, the patient withdraws emotionally from the world prior to dying.

Another approach is that of distinguishing **dying trajectories**, processes of dying which differ in their length and predictability (Glaser & Strauss, 1965; 1968; Strauss & Glaser, 1970). One may have a relatively short and predictable dying trajectory. For example, the physician estimates that the patient has six months to live, and the patient does, in fact, die after approximately six months. Others have less predictable dying trajectories, however. For example, an individual who has been exposed to the AIDS virus cannot predict how long the disease may remain dormant, when symptoms might erupt, or when death might occur. For both terminally ill patients and health care professionals, the less predictable dying trajectories are associated with higher levels of anxiety (Marshall & Levy, 1990).

SOCIAL AND LEGAL ISSUES

Survivors' reactions to death

Death of a loved one calls forth both emotional and behavioral reactions. Survivors experience **grief**, a collection of emotions including sadness, anger, guilt, and other reactions varying from one person to another. In all societies, survi-

Few events are as traumatic as the death of a spouse, when one loses an intimate companion, a social role, and a part of one's personal identity.

vors undergo **mourning** as they share in culturally-developed rituals to recognize the departure and allow expression of grief.

Conjugal bereavement

Few events are as traumatic as the death of a husband or wife (Holmes & Rahe, 1976). Like many stressful events, conjugal bereavement is associated with increased health problems and mortality rates (e.g., Thompson, Breckenridge, Gallagher, & Peterson, 1984; Wisocki & Averill, 1987). Not only does one lose an intimate companion, but one also loses the social role of husband or wife (Norris & Murrell, 1990; Wisocki & Averill, 1987).

Like dying, grieving is a process; for most, that process spans months or years. Normal grieving is generally divided into at least four stages (e.g., Kalish, 1985; Wisocki & Averill, 1987). The initial reaction to a spouse's (or other loved one's) death is usually **shock**. During this stage, the bereaved person feels numb and often isolated from the world and reality; this stage typically lasts for several hours, or even several days.

The next stage, usually lasting for several months, is that of **protest and yearning**. Now the bereaved individual has greater recognition of her loss, and feels intense emotional pain and longing for the deceased. Many are agitated and restless during this time, dream and think about the deceased, and are preoccupied with places and activities that were associated with past pleasures involving the deceased. Some people even fantasize or hallucinate that they "find" the departed individual in familiar places.

The third stage, **disorganization and despair**, often lasts for a year or more (e.g., Kalish, 1985; Wisocki & Averill, 1987). Although the bereaved person now has greater acceptance of her loss, a bitter pining remains. Common reactions during this stage are apathy, withdrawal, loss of energy, despondency, loss of sexual interest, loss of appetite, sleep disturbances, and shifting emotions such as despair, hostility, shame, guilt, anger, and irritability. Some bereaved individuals (particularly women) engage in **sanctification** of their departed spouse, recalling the spouse and their marriage in idealized terms (e.g., Futterman, Gallagher, Thompson, Lovett, & Gelewski, 1990; Kalish, 1985; Lopata, 1979). This process may provide a sense of having been an important person to an important man or woman, and relieves pressure to risk establishing new relationships.

Normal grieving is concluded (sometimes after several years) with a stage of **detachment, reorganization, and recovery** (Wisocki & Averill, 1987). The characteristics of the third stage recede. The individual develops a new outlook on her life and the world, establishes new roles, and regains a sense of purpose in life. Even after reaching this point, however, many bereaved men and women experience **anniversary reactions**, feelings of relatively intense grief triggered by holidays and dates marking meaningful events (Wisocki & Averill, 1987).

Sometimes grieving begins before the spouse actually dies; a woman may begin grieving, for example, when her husband receives a terminal diagnosis or enters a coma. Such **anticipatory grief** may help the bereaved to cope with her loss (Carey, 1979–1980). However, that is not always the case. Often, anticipatory grief is possible because the spouse suffers from chronic illness; recall that family members may be primary caregivers in such situations. Caregivers may experience such physical and mental strain that they have little energy to deal with their own emotional concerns and little time to reach out to others for emotional support (e.g., Balkwell, 1981; Bass & Bowman, 1990; Wisocki & Averill, 1987).

Distressing though they might be, all of the reactions that comprise the stages of grieving are normal. Some bereaved men and women, however, experience a pathological reaction. These individuals do not necessarily experience different emotions than those who undergo normal grief, but their emotional distress becomes such a central aspect of their lives that they cannot reorganize and recover—even after years (Schulz, 1985). One longitudinal study suggests that people who have low self-esteem prior to their spouse's death are particularly likely to experience pathological grief (Lund et al., 1985–1986).

What circumstances help bereaved individuals to eventually resolve their grief and reorganize their lives? Social support is critically important. The quality of the bereaved individual's support network (e.g., perceived closeness of relationships, amount of helping and confiding with network members) is more important than how many people are available to provide support (Dimond, Lund, & Caserta, 1987).

Who provides support makes a difference. Children are often helpful, although some researchers emphasize widows' self-sufficiency rather than their reliance on children for emotional or practical support (e.g., Goldberg, Comstock, & Harlow, 1988; Lopata, 1979; O'Bryant & Morgan, 1990). Furthermore, relationships with children—and other relatives—can be stressful as well as supportive. Widows in a recent study described their interactions with family members negatively as often as in positive terms (Morgan, 1989). These widows said that family relationships often involved commitments and obligations that the women found physically or emotionally draining. The widows in that study described relationships with friends more positively, noting that they were free to deepen friendships that were supportive and to relinquish those that were not.

For widows who have living parents, parental support can be the single most important kind of assistance (Bankoff, 1984). Parents are unparalleled sources of nurturance, and long-term ties such as these can help the widow to maintain a stable sense of identity in the face of bereavement. A widowed mother is a unique source of empathy for a recent widow, and may be a role model.

Gender and age are associated with the kinds of adjustments that bereaved individuals find most challenging. Although some investigators conclude that men and women face a universal set of problems following the death of their spouse (e.g., Lund, Caserta, & Dimond, 1986), others distinguish the problems that widows and widowers encounter. Most researchers report that widows rank financial problems, loneliness, and unfamiliar duties such as home repairs and automobile maintenance among their greatest problems (e.g., Connidis, 1989; Kalish, 1985). Contemporary elderly widows sometimes suffer not only from having an insufficient income after their husband's death, but also because they had been unfamiliar with the family finances and unaccustomed to managing money while their husbands were alive (O'Bryant & Morgan, 1989).

Widowers experience difficulties with loneliness and homemaking duties (Connidis, 1989). Loneliness may, in fact, be a greater problem for widowers than it is for widows. Because widows outnumber widowers (particularly in older age groups), widowers face a relative scarcity of same-sex widowed peers (Connidis, 1989); perhaps this situation is one of the reasons that men are more likely than women to remarry. In contrast, some women are integrated into a "society of widows" after their husband's death; this "society" is an informal group of widows, most of them elderly, who form a social network (e.g., Kalish, 1985).

Compared to older people, young adults have more intense grief reactions immediately after the spouse's death; older people, however, report stronger feelings of grief a few months later (Sanders, 1980–1981; Wisocki & Averill, 1987). Young widowed women are more likely than older widows to experience problems relating to men, dating, and—not surprisingly—parenting and child care (Lopata, 1979). Some widows find that "couple friendships" become strained after their husband's death, as wives may jealously regard the new widow as a threat to their marriages.

Older widows, more often than young bereaved women, experience somatic complaints (Wisocki & Averill, 1987), and concerns about isolation, housing, and safety (Connidis, 1989; Lopata, 1979). Older individuals are also more likely than younger people to experience **bereavement overload**, the need to deal with the deaths of several close friends and/or relatives within a short time. Lacking the opportunity to adequately mourn all of these deaths, those suffering from bereavement overload may become depressed or physically ill (Kastenbaum, 1978).

Death of a parent

Although most research on bereavement has focused on reactions to death of a spouse, that is obviously not the only situation in which adults encounter loss. Most adults experience the deaths of their parents, many encounter the deaths of siblings, and a few lose children to death. Elderly parents' deaths are less disruptive and emotionally debilitating than is the death of a spouse, perhaps because the former deaths are more predictable events that adult children may rehearse as their parents grow increasingly old and frail (e.g., Moss & Moss, 1980b; Norris & Murrell, 1990; Owen, Fulton, & Markusen, 1983).

Most people do feel distress when their parents die, of course; some may even feel irrational anger at the departed parent's "abandonment." Moss and

Moss (1983–1984) reported that some young and middle-aged adult children whose parents had died felt that their parents had died too young, or they were upset about suffering that their parents experienced while dying. Others regretted lost opportunities to resolve conflicts or otherwise improve their relationships, and still others felt that their parents' passing had brought them closer to death themselves.

Funerals

In virtually all societies, death sets into motion a set of rituals and customs comprising social death; funerals are a central event in this sequence. Funerals' major functions are to ensure a socially accepted and hygienic means of preparing the body for disposal, to provide a symbolic rite of passage from life to death, and to provide psychological support and recognition of loss for the survivors (Pine, 1975; Schulz, 1978).

Kalish (1985) distinguishes five major phases of funerals. First, the body is removed from the place of death, effecting a separation of the dead from the living. The second phase is a visitation period, during which mourners might attend a wake or scripture service, or sit shiva. The funeral rite itself marks the third phase, and the fourth phase is the procession from the funeral to the place of burial of the body. The final phase is the committal of the body to its final disposal. The specific way in which these phases are enacted differs considerably from society to society, and even within societies. Some variations in funeral practices are explored in the *Diversity in Adulthood* box.

Criticisms have been leveled against American funeral practices. Some assert that funerals are needlessly expensive, and that unscrupulous funeral directors sometimes exploit bereaved family members to purchase more elaborate services than they can afford (e.g., Mitford, 1983). Paradoxically, though, others charge that American funerals are too simple and brief to give mourners adequate opportunity to grieve and receive comfort (e.g., Gorer, 1965).

There is little doubt that American funeral practices are changing. As a reaction against marketing of highly elaborate funerals, there is a countermovement toward simple, inexpensive funerals and a shift from burial to cremation (Bowman, 1971). Even these smaller funerals are ritualistic, but the rituals are carried out on a smaller scale (Marshall & Levy, 1990).

Funerals are not, of course, the only way in which death is socially recognized. Every society prescribes certain behaviors and proscribes other behaviors for the bereaved (Kalish, 1985). For example, a recent widow in the United States might be expected to dress conservatively, to absent herself from parties and other celebratory occasions, to remain home from work, to express happiness only in moderation, and to avoid open expression of sexuality. Although such expectations vary by society, and by subculture and social class within societies, all societies have some expectations for people in mourning, and all punish infringements of these expectations by disapproval or even ostracism (Kalish, 1985).

BOX 15.2   *DIVERSITY IN ADULTHOOD*

Racial differences in funeral practices

Although death is a universal experience, the way in which death is socially recognized displays remarkable diversity. Among the Kalai of the South Pacific, for example, a dying person gathers kinsmen in order to distribute his possessions, repay his obligations, and forgive the obligations owed to him. Funerals are not held in this society, because the Kalai believe that essential social tasks are accomplished prior to death (Marshall & Levy, 1990). Certainly, this practice differs from American customs.

It is virtually impossible to generalize about funerals even within American society, however, because these customs vary so much by social class, by religious denomination, by geographic region, and by ethnicity. In *Aging and Ethnicity*, Markides and Mindel (1987) profile funeral practices for African-Americans, Mexican-Americans, and Native Americans.

African-American funeral customs reflect the heritage of slavery (Markides & Mindel, 1987). Because family ties were severed by slavery, mourners often lacked family support and turned to the church instead. Correspondingly, funeral rituals historically assumed great importance in the African-American community. In small southern towns, it is not uncommon for African-Americans to designate prior to their death the pastor that they want to officiate at their funeral, and one of the motivations for maintaining church membership is the desire for a church funeral. Funeral services are often marked by emotional expression, the incorporation of religious songs into the ceremony, and eloquent eulogies.

For African-Americans, as for many other groups, prestige and class distinctions in funeral ceremonies are important (Markides & Mindel, 1987). Among the benefits of membership in African-American lodges and fraternal organizations are death-benefit plans permitting even those of modest means to have funerals marked by style and status. In fact, death may be the only occasion of real luxury for poor African-Americans.

In Mexican-American communities, funeral practices show the strong value placed on family ties in Hispanic groups (Markides & Mindel, 1987). Compared to non-Hispanic Caucasians, Mexican-Americans mark death by a greater outpouring of emotion from a larger kin network. Relatives may remain at the funeral parlor long into the night during the visitation period, and return to view the body one last time prior to the funeral itself.

Markides and Mindel (1987) point out that it is difficult to generalize about death-related customs among Native Americans because these rituals vary tremendously from one tribe to another, and because the oral traditions of these societies mean that relatively few written accounts exist. Members of some tribes (e.g., Apache, Mescalero) evidence little fear regarding death, whereas members of other tribes traditionally express a great deal of anxiety about death and an intense fear of ghosts.

For example, traditional Navajos bury their dead quickly and with little ceremony away from their village, as the dead are thought to be dangerous to the living. Fear of death extends to the dying. Traditionally, terminally ill Navajos were kept in shelters away from the home; even today, Navajos usually let the terminally ill spend their last days in a hospital. When death occurs, the Indian Health Service or a missionary sometimes handle funeral arrangements, so that the family is spared contact with the body.

Even this brief overview of death-related customs in selected groups shows that these practices generally reflect broader values regarding life, the family, and religious or spiritual matters. In this respect, funeral practices are but one thread in an intricately-woven cultural fabric. However, as a means of fulfilling the basic functions of providing comfort to the bereaved and bringing symbolic closure to the life of the deceased, these customs and rituals are indeed universal.

Wills and inheritance patterns

Just as virtually every culture includes funeral rituals of some kind, nearly all societies have conceptualizations of proper and improper ways to die. Among the most common expectations of the dying are that they should ensure a smooth transfer of their financial and material resources to survivors (Marshall & Levy, 1990). In most societies, individuals accomplish this transfer through wills that legally specify how their wealth is to be distributed.

Rarely is the deceased person's estate distributed evenly among survivors. Sussman (1985) notes that the normal pattern is for the deceased to leave the estate to the spouse, if the spouse is still living. In fact, that pattern is so widely accepted that it usually occurs even when an individual dies **intestate**, without leaving a will (Sussman, 1965).

Sometimes remarried individuals make prenuptial agreements under which they agree not to claim their allowable share of the estate, should their spouse die without a will. These agreements permit children of the first marriage to inherit the estate if there is no will, but do not prevent an individual from designating a second (or subsequent) spouse, and offspring of second and subsequent marriages, as beneficiaries (Sussman, 1985).

When the deceased is a widow or widower, the bulk of the estate is distributed among his or her children. Usually, this distribution follows a pattern of **serial reciprocity** (Sussman, 1985). In that case, the adult child who has rendered the greatest service to the parent over the years receives the greatest share of the estate. Adult children generally accept the notion that bequests should be proportional to the amount of assistance provided to the aged parent; when disagreements about bequests arise among siblings, they usually stem from discrepant views of who actually provided the most help to the parent (Sussman, 1985).

Like funeral practices, the patterns according to which Americans distribute their estates are changing. Marshall and Levy (1990) note that it is becoming increasingly common for bequests to skip one or more generations, so that the deceased wills resources to grandchildren or great-grandchildren rather than to children. It is also becoming more common for wealth to be transferred to children in various forms while the older person is still alive (Cheal, 1983). For example, such transfers may be made in an effort to avoid "Medicaid spend-down" when an elderly person requires long-term care (see Chapter Four, p. 102). Some speculate that, as lifelong singlehood and childfree marriages become more common, more bequests in the future will be to friends, cohabitants, charities, and relatives such as siblings, nephews, and nieces (Sussman, 1985).

In looking back, we find that death and dying—like most processes of life-span development—reflect social and historical context. These processes unfold differently in different parts of the world, and even in different social classes and ethnic groups within a single society. With historical change, processes of growth (including the confrontation with death) take on new characteristics.

SUMMARY

Physiological death occurs when the processes sustaining life cease. Psychological death is the loss of "personhood," and social death is a long-term process during which other people relinquish their relationships with the deceased person.

An array of measures can be used to maintain life in the presence of terminal conditions; designating a Durable Power of Attorney for Health Care and preparing a living will may ensure that one's wishes regarding such measures are respected. Euthanasia, derived from the Greek phrase for "good death," can be practiced actively or passively. Hospices provide conditions promoting an appropriate death. Efforts are aimed at keeping the patient as comfortable and alert as possible, supporting the patient and her family as they prepare for death, and helping the family to grieve when death occurs.

Elizabeth Kübler-Ross concluded that patients suffering from terminal illnesses experience denial, anger, bargaining, depression, and acceptance. Despite its undeniable value in heightening awareness of the emotional needs of terminally ill patients, Kübler-Ross' work has been criticized.

Widows rank financial problems, loneliness, and unfamiliar duties such as home repairs and automobile maintenance among their greatest problems. Widowers experience difficulties with loneliness and homemaking duties. Death of a parent is less disruptive and emotionally debilitating than is the death of a spouse.

Funerals' major functions are to ensure a socially accepted and hygienic means of preparing the body for disposal, to provide a symbolic rite of passage from life to death, and to provide psychological support and recognition of loss for the survivors. In virtually all societies, dying people are supposed to ensure a smooth transfer of resources to survivors; usually individuals accomplish this transfer through wills.

KEY TERMS

Acceptance

Active euthanasia

Acute phase

Anger

Anniversary reaction

Anticipatory grief

Appropriate death

Awareness of finitude

Bargaining

Bereavement overload

Cerebral death

Chronic living-dying phase

Denial

Depression

Despair

Detachment, reorganization, and recovery

Disorganization and despair

Dying trajectories

Ego integrity

Grief

Hospice

Intestate

Life review

Life support measures

Living wills

Mourning

Palliative care

Passive euthanasia

Physiological death

Protest and yearning

Psychological death

Sanctification

Serial reciprocity

Shock

Social death

Terminal phase

Thanatology

Total brain death

*S*UGGESTIONS *FOR FURTHER READING*

Kübler-Ross, E. (1975). *Death: The Final Stage of Growth*. Englewood Cliffs, NJ: Prentice Hall.

Kübler-Ross, E. (1969). *On Death and Dying*. New York: Macmillan.

Lopata, H. Z. (1979). *Women as Widows: Support Systems*. New York: Elsevier.

Marshall, V. W. (1980). *Last Chapters: A Sociology of Aging and Dying*. Monterey, CA: Brooks/Cole.

Mitford, J. (1978). *The American Way of Death*. New York: Simon & Schuster.

Rossman, P. (1977). *Hospice*. New York: Fawcett Columbine.

*A*PPENDIX: *STATISTICAL TOOLS COMMONLY USED IN DEVELOPMENTAL RESEARCH*

Overview

This appendix is not intended to provide complete explanations of statistical principles or techniques. It was prepared because of the likelihood that readers will vary in their familiarity with psychological or sociological research approaches and statistics. While a detailed understanding of statistics is by no means necessary to appreciate the material covered in this book, readers with some awareness of widely used techniques can examine the material more critically, are better prepared to read a wider range of primary source material, and are prepared to draw more soundly-based inferences regarding that material.

This appendix can be used in several ways. Individuals who have no background in statistics are advised to read the appendix first. The appendix should give these readers a foundation for understanding the measurement and methodological issues presented in the initial chapter and for evaluating the research described throughout the book. The appendix is also a resource for more sophisticated readers who are planning research projects dealing with adult development. In that case, the appendix could provide a brief review of techniques covered in a statistics course and might provide preparation for more advanced reading.

No formulas or computational examples are presented here, and only a very narrow selection of statistical tests are discussed. The goal is to provide an overview of some of the most commonly encountered statistical techniques in the research literature on adult development and aging. In presenting these techniques, the emphasis is on the logic underlying their use.

In other words, statistics are discussed as tools that researchers use to answer questions. Each group of tools is presented with regard to the kinds of questions that it might be used to answer, and—in very general conceptual terms—how these tools provide information bearing on the questions. Readers wishing more detailed information are advised to consult one of the many statistical texts that are available.

Answering any substantive question through empirical means begins with the formulation of a hypothesis, the design of a study to test the hypothesis, and the collection of data according to the study design. The choice of statistical techniques is guided by the hypothesis formulated, the study design, and the nature of the data collected. Thus, the researcher needs to begin thinking about how her data will be analyzed when she initially decides what her hypothesis will be and what kind of study she will conduct to test it.

Regardless of the specific hypothesis and research design, researchers will draw on two general categories of statistical tools: descriptive statistics and inferential statistics.

DESCRIPTIVE STATISTICS

Descriptive statistics, as the label implies, are tools that a researcher uses to describe the performance of a sample of subjects who actually participated in her research. For example, if a scientist has conducted a study to see if elderly Caucasians and elderly African-Americans differ in levels of life satisfaction, she would have scores on one or more reliable and valid measures (see Chapter One, pp. 13–18) of life satisfaction provided by a large sample of elderly Caucasians and African-Americans. Although she could describe their performance (in this case, their scores on the life satisfaction measures) by simply listing the scores for each participant, such a description would probably not be very useful. It would be difficult for the researcher or anyone else to examine a large set of individual scores and gain any insight into racial differences in life satisfaction. The problem is in not being able to see the forest for the trees.

A better approach would be to use descriptive statistics providing two kinds of information about these data. Measures of central tendency identify typical performance within a group. Measures of variability show the extent to which performance differs from one individual to another within a group.

Measures of central tendency

There are three commonly used measures of central tendency; each describes typical performance in a different sense. The mean, or arithmetic average, is probably the most commonly used measure. If the researcher described above used the mean as her measure of central tendency, she would describe typical levels of life satisfaction by presenting the average scores on the life satisfaction measures for Caucasians, for African-Americans, and for the entire sample.

The mean is a straightforward measure of central tendency, but it is not always the best. If there are a few extreme scores in a small sample, the mean can give a misleading picture of average performance. For example, if there were only four scores to be averaged (0, 17, 18, 17) the average score of 13 would not give an accurate view of typical performance. And, it does not make sense to compute an average for some kinds of data: the notion of "average race," for example, is meaningless.

Another measure of central tendency is the median. If a set of scores is rank-ordered, the median is the score that divides the distribution in half. Suppose a researcher ranked all the subjects in an experiment according to the subjects' ages: the oldest subject was ranked first and the youngest was ranked last. The median would be the age of the subject who was older than half of her peers and younger than the remaining peers. Here, typical performance is the score that is "in the middle." When there are a few extreme scores in a small sample, the median is often a better choice than the mean. In the example of life satisfaction scores above, the median of 17 gives a more accurate sense of typical performance than does the mean.

The mode is the third measure of central tendency, and is the most frequently occurring score in a set. The mode, like the median, can be a better choice than the mean when a group of scores includes a few extreme scores. The mode can be used to indicate typical performance for kinds of data for which the mean does not make sense. If one had collected demographic data as well as scores on life satisfaction measures, and wanted to describe the typical demographic characteristics for the sample, it would not make sense to compute average scores for such variables as race and gender. But reporting the mode on those characteristics would tell you whether most of the subjects were Caucasian or African-American, and whether most were women or men.

Measures of variability

Knowing the typical performance within a group does not give a full picture; one also needs to know how much or how little individual subjects' performances differed from one another. The extent of individual differences within groups can be described in at least two ways. One could present the range of scores, or the difference between the highest and the lowest scores in a distribution. If a researcher conducted a study in which the youngest subject was 18 and the oldest subject was 88, then the range of ages would be 70.

More commonly used measures of variability are the standard deviation and the variance. The standard deviation is the average distance between the mean of a set of scores and individual scores in the set. This measure of variability, then, tells how much individual subjects' scores typically differ from the mean score of a sample. The variance is the square of the standard deviation, so this measure also describes the extent to which scores in a sample are closely clustered around the mean or are widely dispersed. The variance is an important computational element of some of the more widely used inferential statistics (see below).

INFERENTIAL STATISTICS

Once a researcher has computed descriptive statistics for a set of data, she has an overall picture of her sample's performance. If she has collected data on Caucasians' and African-Americans' levels of life satisfaction, she now knows what the typical levels of life satisfaction are for members of both races, and for her entire sample; she knows how much variation in life satisfaction there is in both races and in the sample overall. As another example, if a researcher conducted a cross-sectional study of young, middle-aged, and elderly adults' recall performance, then descriptive statistics would show typical levels of recall performance for subjects in each age group in the sample, and how much variation in recall performance existed within each age group in the sample.

If the researcher were only interested in life satisfaction or recall performance among the samples of individuals who actually participated in the research, then statistical analysis could stop at that point. The researcher could examine the descriptive statistics and readily report whether Caucasians and African-Americans in the sample differed in their typical levels of life satisfaction. Similarly, there would be no question as to whether the young, middle-aged, and elderly adults' typical recall performances differed in this sample: the researcher would need only to look at the mean recall performance for the three age groups and see whether the means were the same or different.

But researchers are almost always interested in using their observations of their specific sample to draw conclusions about the performances of a more general population. The researcher studying racial differences in levels of life satisfaction probably wants to make statements applying to Caucasians and African-Americans in general, not just to those who actually took part in the study. The researcher comparing young, middle-aged, and elderly participants' recall performances probably wants to learn about such performance differences among contemporary adults in general, rather than only among the sample of people who were actually in the study.

In other words, researchers usually want to know whether the things that they have observed in their sample (e.g., racial differences in life satisfaction scores, age differences in recall performance) would be likely to reappear if they repeated their study an infinite number of times using new samples from the same population. The question is whether or not the outcome of their study is statistically reliable (e.g., likely to occur again in different samples) or is simply a chance outcome occurring in one sample but unlikely to occur in other samples from the same population. Conceivably, a researcher could actually repeat a study time after time to determine the reliability of the results. Inferential statistics, however, provide an alternative means of evaluating the statistical reliability of a study's results.

Whereas descriptive statistics provide information about a specific sample's performance, inferential statistics evaluate the likelihood that the specific sample's performance reflect performance that could be observed in the general population from which the sample was drawn. These tools are labeled inferential statistics because they are used to draw inferences about a population (that was not observed) on the basis of performance in an observed sample from that population. Types of inferential statistics commonly used in developmental research include those that make comparisons among group means and those that evaluate patterns of association among variables.

Comparing group means

One "family" of inferential statistical tools allows a researcher to determine whether the differences between group means observed in her sample reflect differences in population group means. For example, if a researcher finds that the Caucasians in her sample have an average life satisfaction score of 17 and the African-Americans in her sample have an average score of 15, she could use inferential statistics to determine the likelihood that Caucasians *in general* have higher levels of life satisfaction than African-Americans *in general*. If a researcher finds that mean recall scores for the young, middle-aged, and elderly adults in his sample are 30 items, 25 items, and 15 items respectively, then applying inferential statistics would be necessary to know whether or not young, middle-aged, and elderly people *in general* differ in recall performance.

In very broad terms, the same logic underlies most of the tools testing the reliability of differences between group means. The extent of variation *between* groups (e.g., the differences between Caucasians' and African-Americans' means; differences between young, middle-aged, and elderly adults' means) is compared with the extent of variation *within* groups (e.g., the variances in life satisfaction scores within races; the variances in recall scores within age groups). This comparison tells the researcher whether or not the groups being compared are more different from one another than individual members within each group are from one another. If so, then the differences between the groups are considered statistically reliable and could be expected to appear in other samples from the same population.

The specific statistical tool selected to compare group means depends primarily on the number of groups being compared and on the number of variables for which comparisons are being made. When only two groups are being compared, the tools most often used are the t-test (for comparing the groups on a single variable) or Hotelling's T^2 (for comparing the groups on several variables). The researcher comparing Caucasians' and African-Americans' levels of life satisfaction could use a t-test to determine whether racial differences in mean levels of a single measure of life satisfaction were reliable. She could use Hotelling's T^2 to simultaneously determine whether racial differences in levels of a measure of life satisfaction, a measure of morale, a measure of psychological adjustment, and a measure of self-esteem were reliable.

When more than two groups are being compared, tools that are commonly used include the Analysis of Variance (ANOVA) and Multivariate Analysis of Variance (MANOVA). The researcher comparing young, middle-aged, and elderly adults' recall performance could use ANOVA to determine whether the differences in the age groups' mean recall scores were statistically reliable if he had only one measure of recall (e.g., the number of items recalled). If the ANOVA told him that the differences in the age groups' recall performances were statistically reliable, he would need to conduct further analyses to determine exactly *which* groups differed (e.g., the young versus the elderly, the middle-aged versus the elderly, the young versus the middle-aged).

If the researcher had several measures of recall (e.g., the number of items recalled, time required to recall the items, number of errors, etc.), then he could use MANOVA to simultaneously determine whether the age group differences in any or all of these measures were statistically reliable. As with the ANOVA, further analysis would be needed to pinpoint exactly which age groups differed on which recall measures if the MANOVA indicated that reliable group differences existed.

Examining patterns of association between variables

Scientists often have research questions that do not concern differences between groups, but instead concern how different characteristics are associated with one another. For example, a researcher may want to know what characteristics are associated with adults' problem solving performance: does performance reliably vary according to individuals' age, general level of intelligence, years of formal education, or memory performance? Such information might provide insight into some of the processes underlying problem solving (e.g., the extent to which problem solving depends on intelligence, memory, or drawing on learned knowledge).

Furthermore, identifying reliable patterns of associations can provide a basis for making predictions. Suppose you wanted to predict which kinds of people were likely to have difficulty solving problems, so you could provide these individuals with training that would make them more effective problem-solvers in the workplace or the home. You would need to be able to predict which kinds of people are most likely to have difficulty solving problems to know who would derive the greatest benefit from your program. Knowing that a relatively low level of formal education is associated with poor problem-solving performance would allow you to target your program at poorly educated individuals.

Correlational analyses allow researchers to identify statistically reliable associations among variables. Among the most common correlational techniques are bivariate correlation and multiple regression. A bivariate correlation evaluates the strength of association between two variables. For example, a researcher could use a bivariate correlation to measure the strength of association between problem-solving performance and IQ, or problem-solving performance and memory performance. The correlation would indicate whether, for example, people who have high IQs also tend to be effective problem solvers, or whether people with good memories are also good at solving problems.

Bivariate correlations can range from –1 to 1. The larger the correlation (e.g., the closer it is to –1 or 1), the more important the association between the two variables. Further, the greater the magnitude of the correlation, the more accurate predictions concerning one variable (e.g., problem-solving performance) on the basis of the other variable (e.g., IQ or memory performance) are likely to be.

Multiple regression evaluates the association between a set of several predictor variables and a single criterion variable. A researcher could use multiple regression to evaluate the association between the predictors of age, IQ, years of formal education, and memory performance on the one hand and the criterion of problem-solving performance on the other hand. This analysis can tell the researcher whether the predictors as a group are reliably associated with the criterion, and which of the individual predictor variables are the most reliable ones.

Causal analysis

Many important research questions concern cause-effect relationships among variables. Examples of such questions are whether having a low income and poor health causes life satisfaction to decline in old age; whether having high levels of education and of social interaction causes physical health to be maintained in old age; and whether high levels of stress and low levels of social support cause individuals to develop psychological disorders. Although an experiment is a conventionally accepted means of answering cause-effect questions empirically, none of the research questions above could be answered using an experiment. Both ethical and practical constraints would preclude experimentation in each case.

Does that mean that these important questions cannot be addressed at all? Not necessarily. Recently-developed techniques can shed some light on questions such as these. One approach that is becoming widely used is structural equation modeling. Structural equation modeling is sometimes referred to as LISREL, after the name of the statistical program most often used to conduct this analysis.

Although carrying out this kind of analysis is an extremely complex statistical process, the logic underlying structural equation modeling is fairly simple. A researcher begins with a model describing the causal relationships that she believes exist among a set of variables; she would base her model primarily on her understanding of the results of prior research. For example, the researcher might formulate a model in which having a low income causes individuals to receive little formal health care, the paucity of health care in turn causes health to worsen, and deteriorating health as well as poverty itself cause low levels of life satisfaction. Next, the researcher would obtain measures of the variables included in the model (e.g., income, use of formal health care, health status, life satisfaction) from a sample of subjects, and would measure the associations among all of the variables in the model.

Next, statistical software generates the patterns of association that would exist among the variables if the researcher's model were an accurate picture of reality. The software then compares the patterns of association that the researcher actually observed in her sample with those that would exist if the model were true. The extent to which the actual pattern of association matches the one that would exist under the model determines the extent to which the researcher's data support her model. If data support the model, the researcher cannot claim definitive proof that her model is accurate, but can claim that the data are consistent with her proposed pattern of causal relationships.

GLOSSARY

Absolute threshold: Smallest amount of a sensory stimulus (e.g., light, sound) that can be detected; amount of light needed for comfortable reading or close work

Acceptance: In Kübler-Ross' (1969) formulation, the stage of confronting death in which the patient is at peace

Acetylcholine: Neurotransmitter important in learning and memory; found in decreased amounts in brains of Alzheimer's disease victims

Achieving stage: Stage in intellectual development in which the individual attempts to use knowledge to establish independence, competence, and credibility

Acquired immunodeficiency syndrome (AIDS): Sexually transmitted disease spread through body fluids; not curable as of 1991

Acquisitive stage: Stage in intellectual development in which the individual gathers information to prepare for adult roles

Active: View of the organism in the organismic model; individual (rather than the environment) is the source of behavior

Active euthanasia: Taking deliberate action to end a patient's life

Activities of daily living (ADL): Actions needed for basic health and hygiene (e.g., bathing, toileting)

Activity theory: View that life satisfaction in old age results from continued social involvement

Acute phase: Phase of dying in which one adapts to being terminally ill

Adaptation: In Gloger-Tippelt's (1983) model of pregnancy, phase in which initial physiological, psychological, and social disruption subside

Adult day care: Center at which rehabilitative services and/or social activities are provided during the day for frail or confused elderly people

Adverse impact: Personnel selection procedure resulting in a selection rate for any group less than 80 percent of the group with the highest selection rate

Age: Chronological age, an index of maturational status

Age Discrimination in Employment Act (ADEA): Federal law protecting workers aged 40 to 70 from negative personnel decisions based on age

Age-segregated housing: Housing designed for older people and restricted to aged residents

Aging spots: Dark spots on the skin appearing in later adulthood; formed by clusters of pigment cells in the epidermis

Alienated achievement: Adolescent identity status in which one does not make a commitment to an ideology or occupation, but has a rationale for doing so

Alleviative optimization: Efforts to minimize the impact of a negative influence

Alternate forms reliability: The extent to which alternative forms of the test administered concurrently yield consistent scores

Alternative procedures: Personnel selection procedures replacing those with adverse impact

Alzheimer's disease: Form of primary undifferentiated dementia; most frequently diagnosed source of dementia symptoms

Ambivalent: In Shostak's (1987) typology, individuals who are voluntarily but temporarily single

American Association of Retired Persons (AARP):   Politically-oriented organization lobbying on behalf of older people

Amyloid: Protein forming the core of senile plaques characteristic of Alzheimer's disease

Anger: In Kübler-Ross' (1969) formulation, the stage in which a dying patient expresses hostility and resentment toward doctors, nurses, family members, and friends

Anima: Man's archetype of femininity

Animus: Woman's archetype of masculinity

Anniversary reaction: Aspect of bereavement in which one experiences relatively intense grief triggered by dates marking meaningful events involving the deceased

Antecedent-consequent: Analysis of behavior in terms of preceding cues and subsequent consequences

Anticipation and preparation: In Gloger-Tippelt's (1983) model of pregnancy, phase characterized by growing orientation toward the future

Anticipatory grief: Grieving that begins before a spouse or loved one dies

Antipsychotic medication: Medications aimed at normalizing the action of neurotransmitters in the central nervous system

Apathetic sibling relationship: Relationships marked by low levels of closeness, support, acceptance, involvement, contact, envy, and resentment

Appropriate death: Death that conforms to a patient's and her family's expectations

Archetypes: Universal ideas with a strong emotional component

Arcus senilis: White or yellowish ring forming on the outer circumference of the cornea of older adults

Armored-defended: Personality type including ambition and achievement orientation, as well as strong impulse control

Arousal hypothesis: Notion that older adults perform relatively poorly on tasks requiring sustained attention because they are less aroused than young adults

Arteriosclerosis: Increase of connective tissue, and decrease of elastin, in blood vessel walls

Artificial embryonation: Female donor is inseminated with sperm from the partner of a woman with ovulation or tubal problems; embryo is flushed from donor's uterus and transferred to social mother's uterus

Artificial insemination by donor: Woman is inseminated with sperm from an anonymous donor

Asexual: In Bell and Weinberg's (1978) study, homosexuals who were generally uninvolved with others and reported sexual problems

Assortativeness: Tendency for an individual to marry someone similar to herself

Athersclerosis: Gradual accumulation of lipids in blood vessel walls, resulting in narrowed diameter of blood vessels

Attachment/separateness: Polarity integrated during mid-life crisis, according to Levinson

Attention switching: Tasks in which individuals must alternately monitor two or more sources of information

Autoimmune responses: Immune responses are directed against one's own body tissue

Autoimmune theories: Theories of physical aging which posit that aging results from immune responses directed against one's own body tissue

Automatic processing: Information processing that occurs rapidly, accurately, and without effort

Awareness of finitude: Tendency to estimate the amount of time left until death

Balanced connection: Marriage in which partners have even balance between shared undertakings and privacy

Baltimore Longitudinal Study: Ongoing examination of physical and psychological aging among healthy community residents

Bargaining: Stage in which a dying patient attempts to deal with fate or God to reverse her condition

Basal metabolism rate: Rate at which the body uses oxygen

Behavior exchange theory (BET): Notion that marital satisfaction reflects the way that the spouses behave toward one another

Behavior therapy: Treatment aimed at changing a patient's pathological behaviors by altering their consequences

Bereavement overload: Confronting the deaths of several close friends and/or relatives within a short time

Biological growth orientation: View that maturation and growth continue only up to the point of maturity and that any subsequent changes represent deterioration

California Personality Inventory (CPI): Self-report measure of personality

Cardiac output: Amount of blood pumped per minute

Cardiac reserve: Heart's ability to increase output under stress and exercise

Cardinal trait: Characteristics having such a pervasive influence that they color everything that a person does

Caregiver burden: Common emotional consequence of caring for a dementia victim

Caregiver support group: Groups in which caregivers can receive information about specific disorders, share social support, and exchange ideas

Cataracts: Clouding of the lens to the point that vision is impaired

Centering: In Gloger-Tippelt's (1983) model of pregnancy, phase in which the woman's energies are concentrated on the developing fetus

Central nervous system: Brain and spinal cord

Cerebral death: Cessation of activity in the cortex

Chronic diseases: Long-term, progressive diseases that are not currently curable and without a readily identifiable external cause

Chronic living-dying phase: Stage of dying in which a range of emotional reactions are experienced

Ciliary body: Muscles, connective tissue, and blood vessels connected to the lens; cause the lens to become thicker or thinner to focus images on the retina

Classic aging pattern: Tendency for older adults' scores on the WAIS verbal scale to exceed their scores on the performance scale

Climacteric: Period of several years in midlife during which the functioning of the reproductive system gradually changes

Clinical threshold: Point in the process of physical aging at which pathological symptoms appear

Close-coupled: In Bell & Weinberg's (1978) study, homosexuals involved in enduring monogamous relationships

Cochlear implant: Small microphone acting as an "artificial ear" for those with nerve deafness

Cognitive therapy: Treatment aimed at changing maladaptive thought patterns

Cohabitation: Status of individuals sharing a household and sexual relations

Cohort: Group of individuals born at or about the same time

Cohort-sequential design: Measuring two or more cohorts at two or more ages

Collective unconscious: Inherited foundation of personality including memories of experiences repeated with each generation

Comorbidity: Suffering from two or more chronic illnesses

Comparative developmental approach: Systematic, theory-guided examination of developmental change in varied populations

Compatibility: Ease and comfort in friendships

Competence: Individual's maximum capacity to function, reflecting physical health, sensory capacities, motor skills, cognitive skills, and psychological integrity

Compliance: Maximum amount of air that can be moved in and out of the lungs during forced voluntary breathing within a fixed period of time

Conductive deafness: Impaired transmission of sound waves through the external or middle ear; sensory receptor cells are not damaged; hearing aids can help

Confidant: Intimate friend with whom one can discuss personal feelings and concerns

Confound: Design flaw preventing a researcher from distinguishing between alternative explanations for the outcome of research

Congenial sibling relationship: Relationship marked by high levels of closeness, support, acceptance, and involvement; average levels of contact; and relatively low levels of envy and resentment

Congregate housing: Age-segregated housing in which supportive services are provided

Consequential religiosity: Ways in which religion affects one's behavior

Construct validity: Extent to which a measurement instrument assesses the intended quality

Constructed knowledge: Perspective in which one recognizes the individual as a creator of knowledge

Continuity: Development proceeds as new behaviors appear that are predictable outgrowths of earlier behaviors

Contrast sensitivity: Ability to discriminate alternating light and dark bars of a test pattern

Cortex: Outer covering of the brain

Couple-centered connection: Marriage in which the husband-wife relationship is more important to both than individual concerns are to either

Couvade syndrome: A prospective father's reaction to his partner's pregnancy in which he experiences physical distress

Cross-linkage theory: Theory of physical aging proposing that stable bonds continually form between molecules in body cells and adversely affect cell functioning

Cross-linked: Process through which cells become attached to one another as part of the aging process

Cross-sectional design: Measuring two or more cohorts on one occasion

Cross-sequential design: Measuring two or more cohorts at two or more times of measurement

Crystallization stage: Stage of early adolescence in which ideas about careers are vague

Crystallized intelligence: Capacity to draw on learned information to make decisions and solve problems

Cued recall: Assessing memory by providing information to guide and support recollection at the time of assessment

Dark adaptation: Process through which the eye adapts to lowered lighting

Debilitating anxiety: Anxiety that interferes with test performance

Deceleration stage: Career stage of later middle adulthood during which preparation for retirement begins

Defined-benefit pension plan: Pension plan in which the employer pledges to pay a specified retirement benefit when employees meet length of service requirements and reach a certain age

Defined-contribution pension plan: Pension plan in which the employer contributes a fixed amount to an employee's pension fund account every pay period; funds are invested and accumulate throughout the employee's tenure

Deinstitutionalize: Providing treatment for psychotic patients outside of in-patient psychiatric hospitals whenever possible

Dementia: Progressive and sometimes irreversible deterioration of cognitive functioning

Denial: In Kübler-Ross' (1969) formulation, the initial reaction to learning of a terminal illness; the patient is convinced that the diagnosis is wrong

Depression: In Kübler-Ross' (1969) formulation, the stage in which a dying patient withdraws from others and grieves for the losses that death will bring

Dermis: Inner layer of connective tissue in the skin

Description: Objective of life-span developmental research in which one attempts to characterize behavioral change with age

Despair: Feelings of regret about the past in old age, according to Erikson; the source of fear of death

Destruction/creation: Polarity integrated during mid-life crisis, according to Levinson

Detachment, reorganization, and recovery: Conclusion of normal grieving in which a new outlook on life and the world, new roles, and a sense of purpose in life are regained

Developmental stake: Tendency for elderly parents to report greater affection in their relationships with adult children than the adult children do themselves

Developmental tasks: Challenge arising at a certain period in the life cycle; success or failure influences future development

Developmentalist theories: Theories portraying career choice spanning much of the life cycle

Diabetic retinopathy: Damage to vessels supplying blood to the retina, resulting in the formation of scar tissue on the retina and subsequent blindness

Dialectical: Most recently constructed model of development, in which humans are viewed as both reactive and active; change is quantitative and qualitative; and development is explained as a result of person-environment interactions, intrapersonal conflict, and incidental causes

Dichotic listening task: Individual hears two different, simultaneous recordings played to the right and the left ear; listener must repeat a designated portion of the information

Differentialist theories: Theories proposing that workers and work settings can be classified and that career choice reflects pressure toward congruence between the worker and the setting

Directionality: Characteristic of developmental change, in that these changes are not easily reversed

Discontinuity: Development proceeds as new behaviors emerge that are fundamentally different from earlier behaviors

Discourse: Spoken language or written passages

Disengagement theory: View that life satisfaction in old age results from mutual withdrawal on the part of the older individual and society

Disorganization and despair: Stage of normal grieving in which acceptance of loss is combined with yearning for the deceased

Disruption: In Gloger-Tippelt's (1983) model of pregnancy, phase in which radical change occurs on the physiological, psychological, and social levels

Diverticulosis: Condition in which small pockets develop in the intestinal wall

Divided attention: Process through which attention is controlled to carry out two tasks simultaneously

Dream: Sense of oneself and one's potential in the world

Dual specialization: Caregiving pattern in which family caregivers and formal service providers each carry out different caregiving tasks

Dying trajectories: Processes of dying that differ in their length and predictability

Dynamic visual acuity (DVA): Ability to detect features of moving targets

Dysfunctional: In Bell and Weinberg's (1978) study, homosexuals who are troubled and often report sexual problems and legal difficulties

Dysphoria: Persistent mood disturbance characteristic of depression

Early articulators: Individuals who know from youth that they will never want children

Early onset: Pattern of pathological alcohol use beginning in early adulthood

Echoic memory: Sensory memory for auditory information

Efficient cause: External or environmental influence of behavior

Effortful processing: Processing of information that involves active, conscious control; may be affected by task complexity and competing demands

Egg donation: Anonymous female donor provides an ovum to be implanted in a woman who does not ovulate or whose fallopian tubes are blocked

Ego: Rational capacity for coping with reality

Ego integrity: Feeling in old age that one has lived a meaningful, worthwhile life

Elder abuse: Physical and/or psychological maltreatment of the aged or theft of an older person's material resources

Elderhostel: Continuing education program for elderly adults

Electroconvulsive therapy (ECT): Treatment for major depression in which a brief current of electricity is passed between the patient's temples to cause a convulsion

Electroencephalogram (EEG): Measurement of brain wave activity

Elementarism: Analysis in which individual behaviors are studied in isolation from other behaviors

Embryo adoption: Female donor is inseminated with sperm from a male donor; embryo is flushed from donor's uterus and implanted in uterus of the social mother

Emergency response systems: Automated system using the telephone, an alarm device, and cooperation of family, neighbors, and local emergency medical services

Employment discrimination: Negative personnel decisions on the basis of race, sex, national origin, or handicap

Empty nest: Adolescent or young adult children's departure from their parents' home in order to pursue education, careers, and/or marriage

Encapsulation model: Description of components of adult intelligence in which the emergence and growth of domain-ordered knowledge is emphasized

Encoding deficit: Ineffective means of processing new information for later recall

Environmental press: Demands that the environment makes on the individual

Epidermis: Outer layer of the skin

Establishment stage: Stage of early adulthood in which the individual enters her chosen career

Exchange theories: Theories of mate selection proposing that both parties in a relationship attempt to make their interaction as rewarding as possible

Excitation: Initial stage of sexual response cycle

Executive processes of the personality: Qualities such as self-awareness, mastery, and competence that become prominent in middle adulthood

Executive stage: Stage in intellectual development in which the individual becomes skilled at integrating complex relationships

Experiential religiosity: Emotions aroused by one's religion

Explanation: Objective of life-span developmental research in which one attempts to identify causes of behavioral change with age

External validity: Extent to which research findings can be generalized across subjects, measures, and settings

False assumptions: Unfounded ideas about onself, the world, and life that are progressively relinquished throughout adulthood, according to Gould

Family-centered connection: Marriage in which shared undertakings are more important to the husband and wife than are their individual concerns

Family therapy: Treatment approach aimed at evaluating family interactions and replacing problematic patterns with more adaptive ones

Filial maturity: Adult child's recognition that her parents have needs and that she can and should meet those needs

Filial responsibility: Adult child's feeling that she should provide care for her elderly parents should the need arise

Filial responsibility law: Laws specifying family obligations for support of older people in need

Final cause: View that developmental changes are necessary steps toward an end state of absolute maturity

Five-factor model: Notion that adult personality reflects stable levels of neuroticism, extraversion, openness to experience, agreeableness, and conscientiousness

Fixation: Lifelong imprint of early experience on the personality

Fluid intelligence: Capacities to form concepts, identify similarities, and reason; believed to reflect neurological health and to be fairly invulnerable to cultural influence

Foreclosure: Adolescent identity status in which one accepts an ideology and occupation without personally chosing them

Formal cause: View that behavior is the result of the underlying organization of the individual's skills, traits, and capacities

Formal health care: Physicians and other health care professionals and institutions

Formal service specialization: Caregiving pattern in which family members and formal service providers share some caregiving tasks but formal service providers alone perform other tasks

Free radical theory: Notion that unstable chemical compounds are constantly produced by body metabolism and aid in the cross-linkage process; cell operation and eventually organ functioning are thus impaired

Free recall: Assessing memory by requiring individuals to reproduce what has been learned

Freedom from coercion: Research participants' right to discontinue participation in an experiment without fear of negative consequences

Friendly visiting: Service in which regular visits are paid to older people who are lonely

Friendship networks: Numbers of friends and frequency with which they are seen

Functional: In Bell and Weinberg's (1978) study, homosexuals who were not involved in an exclusive relationship but who expressed little discomfort over their sexual orientation

Functional disorders: Psychiatric problems with primarily psychological (as opposed to physical) origins

Gene mutation theory: Theory of physical aging proposing that genetic mutations occur throughout the lifespan in most body cells, and that their long-term consequence is impaired cell functioning

Gene theory: Theory of physical aging proposing that the organism carries genes that are activated in old age; the action of these genes causes physical aging

Generational equity: Charge that older adults receive a large share of public resources when the numbers of children living in poverty is increasing

Generativity: Concern for establishing and guiding the next generation

Geriatric medicine: Medical speciality devoted to physical aging and diseases of old age

Glaucoma: Build-up of pressure within the eye as a result of insufficient drainage of fluid within the eye

Gray Panthers: Politically-oriented organization lobbying on behalf of older people

Grief: A collection of emotions including sadness, guilt, anger, and other idiosyncratic reactions

Group therapy: Treatment approach in which several patients work simultaneously with one therapist or facilitator

G. Stanley Hall: Early American psychologist who published one of the first studies of aging

Hayflick limit: Species-specific number of times that body cells undergo division

Heterocyclic antidepressants (HCAs):   Medication often used to treat depression

Hippocampus: Brain region associated with memory functioning

History: Influence of events that coincide with an experiment and exert an influence on the experimental results

Historiometric approach: Approach to studying developmental trends in creativity in which associations between age and the rate of creative productions is examined

Holism: Analysis in which individual behaviors are studied in the context of other behaviors

Holtzman inkblot technique (HIT):   Projective measure of personality

Home care: Array of services that may include nursing care at home and/or assistance with housework

Homeostasis: Processes of physical self-regulation

Homophobia: Unreasonable fear of homosexuals, of arousing homosexual feelings, or of being considered homosexual

Horizontal career change: Shift from one field to another with no substantial change in authority or responsibility

Hospice: Organizations designed to provide dying patients and their families with the conditions promoting an appropriate death

Hostile sibling relationships: Relationships characterized by high levels of involvement and resentment, and low levels of closeness, support, acceptance, contact, and envy

Hot flashes: Occasional symptom of the climacteric during which a woman experiences a brief feeling of intense heat

Human factors: Field that provides optimal designs for the conditions under which people live and work

Huntington's disease: Form of primary differentiated dementia

Hypodermis: Tissue immediately beneath the skin in which subcutaneous fat is stored

Hypothalamus: Master timekeeper of the body that directs the production of hormones regulating growth and development

Hypothesis: Prediction based on a theory

Iconic memory: Sensory memory for visual information

Id: Irrational set of instinctive impulses

Identity achievement: Adolescent identity status in which one makes a commitment to an ideology and occupation after considering alternatives

Identity diffusion: Adolescent identity status in which one fails to make a commitment to an ideology and occupation

Ideological religiosity: Religious beliefs that one holds

Implementation: Career stage of early adulthood in which one acquires the education and training needed for a chosen career

Incidental cause: Chance or accidental happening that influences development in unpredictable ways

Incidental memory: Memory for information that was learned unintentionally

Indirect discrimination: Practices through which women, minorities, or others are disproportionately excluded from jobs on the basis of requirements that are unrelated to the job in question

Individuation: Mid-life process of integrating polarities, according to Levinson

Industrial gerontology: Study of the older worker

Infertility: Inability to conceive after 12 to 18 months of unprotected sexual activity, or inability to carry a pregnancy to term

Informal care: Health care provided by family, friends, and neighbors

Information processing theory: Contemporary approach to examining intelligence, learning, and memory; information is traced through stages of encoding, storage, and retrieval

Informed consent: Research participants' agreement to take part in an experiment, having been given all information that could reasonably be expected to influence willingness to participate

Inhibited sexual desire: Lack of interest in sex causing concern for the individual or problems in the relationship with the sexual partner

Inhibited sexual excitement: Inability to become sexually aroused when an individual wants to have sex

Instrumental activities of daily living (IADL):   Tasks necessary for independent living in the community (e.g., shopping, housekeeping)

Integrated: Personality type in old age marked by cognitive and emotional integrity

Integumentary system: Body system including the skin, hair, and nails

Intellectual religiosity: Knowledge of the tenets and sacred texts of one's religion

Intentional memory: Memory for information known to be needed later; deliberate steps are taken to commit the information to memory

Interactions with treatment variable: Effects of an independent variable cannot be distinguished from the effects of a potential threat to internal validity

Intergenerational support networks: Patterns through which generations in a family exchange help with one another

Interindividual differences: Differences in maturational processes between individuals

Interiority: Increased self-reflection in middle adulthood

Intermediate nursing care facilities: Facilities for older people who do not need continual skilled nursing care but who are unable to live alone

Internal consistency: Extent to which all items of a test or scale assess the same quality

Internal validity: Extent to which an experiment can provide a test of its hypothesis

Interscorer reliability: Extent to which different observers or scorers agree in evaluating an examinee's behavior

Intestate: Status of dying without leaving a will

Intimacy: Tendency toward interpersonal closeness

Intimate: Level of intimacy in which individuals have close friends and a satisfying sexual relationship

Intimate sibling relationships: Relationships marked by high levels of closeness, support, acceptance, involvement, and contact but low levels of envy and resentment

Intra-individual change: Changes in behavior occuring within a person

***In-vitro* fertilization**: Ovum is removed from a woman's ovary and fertilized with her partner's sperm in a shallow dish filled with a nourishing medium; embryo is implanted in woman's uterus

Involutional psychosis: A unipolar depression appearing for the first time in middle age

Iris: Round, pigmented muscular diaphragm of the eye

Isolate: Level of intimacy in which one lacks enduring personal relationships and rarely initiates social contacts

Isolation: Tendency to avoid relationships that might lead to commitment

Jakob-Creutzfeldt disease: Form of dementia

Kin independence: Caregiving pattern in which the family cares for an older individual without any help from formal service providers

Kinesthesis: Capacity to sense the position of various parts of the body, and movement of the limbs and other body parts

Kinkeepers: Middle-aged women who maintain contact among relatives in their families

Late onset: Pattern of pathological alcohol use beginning in middle adulthood or old age

Learning: Acquisition of new skill or knowledge through study, practice, or experience

Lens: Curved structure near the front of the eye that focuses images on the retina

Libido: Psychic energy

Life care community: Age-segregated facilities providing both housing and long-term care

Life review: Process of reminiscence prompted by realization of impending death, or sometimes by other kinds of personal crises

Life satisfaction: Older individual's contentment with her current life circumstances, her perspectives on her past, and her outlook on the future

Life-span perspective: Orientation regarding the study of development

Life structure: Underlying pattern of one's life at any particular time

Life support measures: Medical techniques that can prolong life in the face of life-threatening illness

Living wills: A declaration to physicians that outlines an individual's wishes regarding the use of life support measures

Long-term care: Ongoing medical and social services provided to frail elderly people

Longevity: Length of life

Longitudinal design: Measuring a single cohort at two or more times of measurement

Loose connection: Marriage in which both partners concentrate energy on their individual concerns rather than on shared concerns or the relationship

Low statistical power: Study in which a relationship between variables cannot be detected because of a small sample, use of rigorous statistical tests, or a rigorous significance level

Loyal sibling relationships: Relationships characterized by average levels of closeness, involvement, and contact as well as low levels of support, envy, and resentment

Maintenance stage: Career stage of middle adulthood in which workers prepare to decrease their career involvement, and concentrate on maintaining the authority and responsibility that they have achieved

Major depression: Functional disorder characterized by dysphoria and persistent behavioral changes

MAO inhibitors: Family of drugs used to treat depression

Marital noncohabitation: Marriage style in which the husband and wife live apart

Marital well-being: Quality of the marital relationship

Masculine/feminine: Polarity integrated during mid-life crisis, according to Levinson

Mastery: Extent to which a woman feels in control of her life

Material cause: View that behavior changes result from changes in an individual's physical make-up

Maturation: Naturally-occurring changes within the individual that can masquerade as effects of an independent variable

Maximum longevity: Longest recorded lifespan for a species

Maximum oxygen consumption: Amount of oxygen that can be delivered to working muscles within a given period of time

Mean longevity: Average life span for a species or subspecies; age at which half the members of the population have died

Mechanistic: Model in which humans are assumed to be reactive, and development involves quantitative change resulting from material and efficient causes

Mediator: Strategy used in an effort to enhance learning and memory

Medicaid: Federal health insurance program for low-income people of all ages

Medicare: Federal health insurance program for people age 65 and older, regardless of income

Memory: Retrieval of information or skills that have previously been learned

Menopause: Cessation of the menses; point at which one year has elapsed since the last menstrual period

Metamemory: Knowledge about memory

Metasystematic reasoning: Style of postformal reasoning in which thinking is directed toward a collection of diverse systems and their interrelationships

Midlife transition: Structure-changing period of the early forties, according to Levinson

Minnesota Multiphasic Personality Inventory (MMPI):   Self-report measure of personality

Model: Set of assumptions about human nature and human development forming the foundation for a family of theories

Moratorium: Adolescent identity status in which the individual is seeking a commitment to an ideology and occupation

Mortality: Biasing loss of research participants over the course of a study

Mourning: Culturally-developed rituals to recognize death and allow expression of grief

Multigenerational household: Household in which members of three or more generations reside

Multi-infarct dementia (MID):   Form of primary undifferentiated dementia caused by multiple small strokes

Multiple intelligences theory: Notion that humans possess seven distinct intelligences, each with neurological underpinnings

Multiple treatment interference: Simultaneously testing the effects of several treatments on the same participants; precludes generalizing the effects of these variables to situations in which they are used alone

Myotonia: Process marking sexual arousal; series of involuntary muscular contractions

National Council of Senior Citizens (NCSC):   Politically-oriented organization lobbying on behalf of older people

Naturally-occurring retirement communities (NORCs):   Housing developments not planned for elderly people but that attract a preponderance of older residents

Nerve deafness: Hearing loss resulting from damage to auditory sensory receptor cells or the cells which transmit auditory information to the central nervous system

Neuritic plaque: Abnormal formations between neurons developing in the hippocampus in old age; more prominant in the brains of AD victims than in the brains of healthy, alert older adults

Neuroendocrine theory: Theory positing that aging results from the hypothalamus' diminished ability to effectively direct the production and transmission of hormones regulating growth and development

Neurofibrillary tangle: Abnormal masses within neurons developing in the hippocampus in old age; more prominant in the brains of AD victims than in the brains of healthy, alert older adults

Neuron: Nerve cell

Neurotransmitter: Chemical substances accomplishing communication between neurons

Normative age-graded event: Experience affecting most individuals at about the same age, within any particular culture

Normative history-graded event: Historical events and processes having a universal or near-universal impact

Nonnormative life event: Unusual or atypical experience having a dramatic impact on individual development

Nutrition services: Provision of inexpensive and nutritious meals in communal settings or in the home

Open-coupled: In Bell and Weinberg's (1978) study, homosexuals who lived with a lover but were interested in other sexual contacts

Optimization: Goal of life-span developmental science; attempting to apply research findings to ensure that development and aging are as "problem-free" as possible for as many people as possible

Organismic: Model in which humans are assumed to be active, and development involves qualitative change resulting from formal and final causes

Organizational culture: Shared assumptions that influence a group of workers' activities

Orgasm: Third stage of sexual arousal during which three to five rhythmic contractions of the pelvic muscles produce intensely pleasurable sensations

Osteoarthritis: Chronic inflammation of the joints eventually causing joints to degenerate

Osteoporosis: Condition in which bones become extremely brittle and vulnerable to fractures

Oval window: Boundary of the inner ear

Paired associate: Task in which individuals must learn pairs of words

Palliative care: Treatment aimed at relieving pain and other symptoms, as opposed to active cure treatment approaches

Parkinson's disease: Condition sometimes producing dementia symptoms; form of primary differentiated dementia

Partial retirement: Pattern in which a worker gradually decreases her work hours as retirement approaches

Passive/dependent: Polarity integrated during mid-life crisis, according to Levinson

Passive euthanasia: Refraining from treatment that would prolong a patient's life but taking no deliberate action to end the patient's life

Patron-type status: Role of middle generations in intergenerational support networks; middle generations provide more help to the older and younger generations than they receive from those generations

Perception: Processes through which sensory information is interpreted

Peripheral nervous system: Nerves connecting the central nervous system with other body structures

Personal unconscious: Experiences which were once conscious but that have been forgotten, repressed, or ignored according to Jung

Personality pattern: Pattern of high and low capacities in the realistic, investigative, artistic, social, enterprising, and conventional areas

Pet therapy: Providing pets in a community or institutional setting to address feelings of isolation, loneliness, and uselessness

Pharmacotherapy: Treatment with psychoactive drugs

Physiological death: Point at which the physical processes sustaining life cease

Pick's disease: Form of primary undifferentiated dementia

Planned retirement community: Age-segregated housing open to people aged 50 and older with no children younger than age 18 in the household; usually offer churches, stores, clubs, and recreational facilities

Plateau: Second phase of sexual arousal

Pleasure: Feelings of happiness and optimism

Postparental phase: Phase of married life in which children are no longer living in the home

Postponers: Individuals who believe that they will want children someday, but eventually realize that they do not want children at all

Preintimate: Intimacy status in which individuals date and have some notion of intimacy but have not established an intimate relationship

Premenstrual syndrome (PMS):   Relatively common set of symptoms preceding menstrual periods

Preretirement program: Courses or workshops designed to help employees develop their retirement plans

Presbycusis: Age-related hearing loss

Presbyopia: Farsightedness

Presbystasis: Diminished equilibrium in old age

Preventative optimization: Applying knowledge of development to prevent maladaptive maturational changes from occurring

Prework: Confronting a psychosocial crisis prior to its time of primary importance

Primary aging: Inevitable and universal physical changes

Primary caregiver: Caregiver who provides most needed help to an older person but who also coordinates efforts with other family members and friends

Primary differentiated dementia: Conditions affecting brain tissue and producing dementia symptoms as well as other unique symptoms

Primary memory: Information in current consciousness

Primary Mental Abilities Test (PMA): Widely used measure of adult intelligence

Primary undifferentiated dementia: Diseases affecting brain tissue to produce a common set of dementia symptoms; can be distinguished from one another only by direct examination of brain tissue

Private long-term care insurance: Insurance policies covering the cost of long-term care in nursing homes or the community

Problem finding: Hypothetical stage of adult intellectual development in which individuals can identify new problems in ambiguous situations

Procedural knowledge: Perspective in which one learns and uses accepted procedures for gathering and communicating information

Professional obsolescence: Use of knowledge or skills that are less effective in solving problems than other types of currently available knowledge or skills

Projective measures: Personality assessment tools requiring an examinee to react to an ambiguous stimulus

Prospective memory: Remembering to perform an action in the future

Prostate gland: Gland producing secretions contributing to semen formation

Protest and yearning: Stage of normal grieving in which the survivor feels intense emotional pain and longing for the deceased

Pseudodementia: Collection of diseases and circumstances not attacking brain tissue but yielding characteristic dementia symptoms

Pseudointimate: Intimacy status in which individuals have superficial friendships and have made a commitment to a dating partner

Psychological death: Loss of personhood

Psychometric approach: Approach to studying developmental trends in creativity in which age differences in performance on standardized measures of creativity are examined

Psychomotor skills: Actions that require dexterity and improve with practice

Psychosexual dysfunction: Recurrent disinclination to engage in sexual activity, inability to become sexually aroused, or inability to attain orgasm; episodes do not have a physiological basis

Psychotherapy: Treatment based on discussion of problems with a professional

Pupil: Round opening in the center of the eye through which light enters

Qualitative change: New behaviors emerge which are fundamentally different from earlier behaviors; change to a new stage of development

Quantitative change: Apparently new behaviors are actually increases or decreases of older behaviors, or recombinations of earlier behaviors

Quetelet: Early European scholar writing about adult development and aging

Racial mortality crossover phenomenon: Greater life expectancy for African-Americans, Native Americans, and Hispanic-Americans who survive to old age, as compared to Caucasians

Random sample: Sample in which each member of a population is equally likely to be included and the selection of one member does not influence the selection of other members

Reaction time: Time required for an individual to respond to a stimulus

Reactive: View of humans in the mechanistic model; behavior is the result of environmental influence

Reactive effects: Influence of a study's setting on the outcome

Reactive effects of testing: An event irrelevant to the purposes of a study occurs and influences the relationship between the variables being examined in the study

Reality orientation: Psychotherapy aimed at enhancing dementia patients' functioning by strengthening previously unused capacities

Recall: Reconstruction of previously learned material

Received knowledge: Perspective in which one can reproduce information but not create new information

Reciprocal causation: Cause-effect relationships are bidirectional; the cause influences the effect, but the effect also influences the cause

Reciprocity: Feature of intergenerational support networks; members of each generation both give and receive help

Recognition: Assessing memory by requiring an individual to distinguish previously learned information from new, unlearned information

Refractory period: Period following orgasm during which a man cannot have another orgasm

Regretful: In Shostak's (1987) typology, unmarried individuals who are involuntarily single but expect to remain unmarried

Reintegrative stage: Stage in adult intellectual development in which the individual attempts to identify meaning and purpose in knowledge

Reliability: Extent to which a measurement instrument produces consistent results

Representative sample: Sample in which variation in important characteristics is proportional to variation in those characteristics in the population

Resolution: Final stage of sexual arousal during which the body returns to the pre-aroused state

Resolved: In Shostak's (1987) typology, unmarried individuals who are voluntarily single and expect to remain unmarried

Respite care: Provision of long-term care by professionals or volunteers when a family caregiver is temporarily unavailable

Responsible stage: Stage in adult intellectual development in which knowledge is used to solve practical problems related to family and career responsibilities

Retina: Innermost layer of the eye, in which visual sensory cells are located

Retirement stage: Stage in career development in which the worker formally retires

Retrieval deficit: Ineffective means of searching memory to access encoded and stored information

Reverse discrimination: Employment discrimination against men and Caucasians

Rework: Confronting a psychosocial crisis after its time of primary importance

Ribot's law: Proposition that information is forgotten in the reverse order from which it was acquired

Ritualistic religiosity: Type of religious rituals that one observes and frequency of observing them

Role compatibility stage: Stage in mate selection in which partners evaluate how well they function as a couple

Role models: Individuals possessing qualities that one admires or respects

Rorschach: Projective measure of personality

Sanctification: Tendency to remember one's departed spouse and marriage in idealized terms

Secondary aging: Age-related changes resulting from disease, disuse, or abuse

Secondary caregiver: Family member or friend who assists a primary caregiver

Secondary dementia: Collection of diseases and circumstances not attacking brain tissue but yielding characteristic dementia symptoms

Secondary memory: Permanent storage of virtually unlimited capacity; repository for information not currently being used or thought about

Selection: Internal validity threat in which comparison groups in an experiment differ in important ways at the outset of the study

Selective attention: Capacity to ignore irrelevant information while completing a task

Selectivity theory: Notion that people become increasingly selective about their social partners

Self: Archetype representing the human striving for total unity

Self-care: Steps that an individual takes to prevent illness, restore health, or relieve symptoms

Self-realization: State in which all aspects of the personality are fully developed and blended into a balanced whole

Self-report measures: Personality assessments in which an examinee describes her own personality

Senior citizen's centers: Community centers providing educational, recreational, and sometimes health and/or nutritional programs for elderly people

Sensation: Physical stimulation of sensory cells and transmission of that stimulation throughout the nervous system

Sensory memory: Stage at which new information is initially registered

Serial reciprocity: Common inheritance pattern in which the survivor who rendered the greatest service to the deceased over the years inherits the bulk of the estate

Sexual harassment: Any unwanted, uninvited, or unwelcome sexual attention or expression which makes the recipient uncomfortable in the workplace

Sexually transmitted diseases (STD's):   Diseases transmitted through sexual contact

Shock: Initial reaction to a loved one's death in which the survivor feels numb and isolated from reality

Silence: Perspective in which a learner is unaware of her cognitive resources

Similarity: Shared experiences between friends

Sixteen Personality Factor Questionnaire (16-PF):   Self-report measure of personality

Skilled nursing care facilities: Most sophistocated level of nursing home care, involving daily medical records for each patient, round-the-clock nursing, and a spectrum of medically-related services

Social death: Process during which other people relinquish their relationships with the deceased

Specification stage: Career stage of later adolescence in which thinking centers on a more or less specific occupation

Spiral organ: Inner ear structure activated as sound waves are transmitted; causes nerve impulses to be transmitted to the central nervous system via the vestibulocochlear nerve

Split Dream: Women's senses of themselves that include equal attention to careers and relationships

Stage: Distinct era of development in which behavior is fundamentally different from that in earlier and later stages

Stagnation: Obsessive self-indulgence that may emerge in middle adulthood, according to Erikson

Stereotyped relationships: Intimacy status in which individuals have superficial friendships

Stimulus stage: Stage in mate selection in which partners evaluate first impressions of one another

Stimulus-value-role (SVR) theory: Theory of mate selection proposing that partners evaluate different qualities in one another during different stages of their relationship

Stress: Body's reaction to a threat

Structural dimensions: Characteristics of friendship networks including duration of friendships, friends' geographic proximity, and convenience of contact with friends

Structure-function: Analysis in which the purpose of behavior and ways in which the characteristics of the behavior reflect that purpose are identified

Subjective knowledge: Perspective in which knowledge and truth are viewed as entities that can only be reached through personal experience and intuition

Superego: Personality component comprised of moral principles

Supplementation: Caregiving pattern in which formal service providers and family members share responsibility for certain tasks, and family caregivers also help the elderly person in other ways

Support bank: Pattern in which reciprocity is established in intergenerational support networks on a long-term basis

Surrogate motherhood: A woman is inseminated with sperm from a man whose partner cannot conceive or carry a pregnancy to term; surrogate gives birth and social parents adopt the infant

Sustained attention: Capacity to maintain concentration on a task for an extended period

Synapse: Connections between neurons

Task content: Material to be learned in a learning/memory task

Task pacing: Speed with which material must be studied and remembered

Telephone reassurance: Daily telephone calls made at a prearranged time to older people living alone

Temporality: Characteristic of developmental change, in that these changes require relatively substantial amounts of time

Terminal drop: Deterioration in intellectual functioning preceding death by 2–5 years

Terminal phase: Phase of dying in which the patient withdraws from the world emotionally

Tertiary memory: Repository for information stored for very long periods

Test-retest reliability: Correlation between scores on the same test administered on two occasions

Testing: Influence of an initial evaluation on later evaluations

Thanatology: Study of death and dying

Thematic apperception test (TAT): Projective measure of personality

Theory: Set of statements including laws and definitions of terms

E. L. Thorndike: Early American psychologist studying associations between age and interests

Time of measurement: When in historical time a study is conducted; also, the number of occasions on which participants are evaluated

Time-lag design: Study in which participants of a selected age are studied on two or more times of measurement

Time-sequential design: Comparing two or more age groups at two or more times of measurement

Total brain death: Sustained absence of brain activity

Triarchic theory: Sternberg's theory that intelligence includes a componential element, an experiential element, and a contextual element

Tympanic membrane: Eardrum; a boundary of the middle ear

Type "A" behavior pattern: Pattern in which an individual is characteristically impatient, competitive, aggressive, and hostile

Type "B" behavior pattern: Pattern in which an individual is characteristically relaxed, easygoing, and benevolent in outlook

Unidirectional causation: Cause influences an effect, but the effect has no influence on the cause

Unintegrated: Personality type of later life characterized by impaired cognitive or emotional functioning

U-shaped curve: Most frequently reported pattern of changes over time in marital satisfaction

Value comparison stage: Stage in mate selection in which partners evaluate the match between their interests, attitudes, and beliefs

Vasocongestion: Aspect of sexual arousal in which blood vessels near the surface of the body become engorged

Vertical career change: Career change involving greater authority or responsibility

Vestibular system: System of organs, primarily in the inner ear, providing the sense of balance and spatial orientation

Vestibulocochlear nerve: Nerve transmitting auditory nerve impulses from the spiral organ to the central nervous system

Visual acuity: Ability to detect details in viewed objects

Vital capacity: Difference between a normal inhalation and a deep maximum breath plus the amount that can still be exhaled following a normal exhalation

Vitreous humor: Fluid inside the posterior chamber of the eye

Wechsler Adult Intelligence Scale—Revised (WAIS–R):   Widely used measure of adult intelligence

Wishful: In Shostak's (1987) typology, unmarried individuals who are involuntarily and temporarily single

Women in the middle: Middle-aged women caring for an elderly relative, as well as fulfilling other demanding roles in the family and workplace

Working memory: Processes through which information stored in primary memory is actively manipulated or reorganized

Young/old: Polarity integrated during mid-life crisis, according to Levinson

REFERENCES

Adam, J. (1978). Sequential strategies and the separation of age, cohort, and time-of-measurement contributions to developmental data. *Psychological Bulletin, 85,* 1309–1316.

Adams, C., Labouvie-Vief, G., Hobart, C. J., & Dorosz, M. (1990). Adult age group differences in story recall style. *Journal of Gerontology: Psychological Sciences, 45,* P17–P27.

Adams, D. (1983). *The psychosocial development of professional black women's lives and the consequences of their careers for their personal happiness.* Unpublished doctoral dissertation, Wright Institute, Berkeley, CA.

Adams, R. G. (1985). People would talk: Normative barriers to cross-sex friendships for elderly women. *The Gerontologist, 25,* 605–611.

Adams, R. G. (1987). Patterns of network change: A longitudinal study of friendships of elderly women. *The Gerontologist, 27,* 222–227.

Adlersberg, M., & Thorne, S. (1990). Emerging from the chrysalis: Older women in transition. *Journal of Gerontological Social Work, 16,* 4–8.

Ager, C. L. (1986). Therapeutic aspects of volunteer and advocacy activities. *Physical and Occupational Therapy in Geriatrics, 5,* 3–11.

Agnew, N. M., & Pike, S. W. (1987). *The Science Game.* Englewood Cliffs, NJ: Prentice Hall.

Ainlay, S. C., & Smith, D. R. (1984). Aging and religious participation. *Journal of Gerontology, 39,* 357–363.

Allen, S. G., Clark, R. L., & McDermed, A. A. (1988). The pension cost of changing jobs. *Research on Aging, 10,* 459–471.

Allport, G. W. (1961). *Patterns and Growth in Personality.* New York: Holt Rinehart & Winston.

American Association of Retired Persons (AARP). (1985). *The Right Place at the Right Time: A Guide to Long-term Care Choices.* Washington, DC: AARP.

American Association of Retired Persons (AARP). (1988). *A Profile of Older Americans.* Washington, DC: AARP.

American Cancer Society. (1984). *Cancer Facts for Men.* Atlanta: American Cancer Society.

American Psychological Association. (1982). *Ethical Principles in the Conduct of Research with Human Participants.* Washington, DC: American Psychological Association.

Anderson, S. A., Russell, C. S., & Schumm, W. R. (1983). Perceived marital quality and family life-cycle categories: A further analysis. *Journal of Marriage and the Family, 45,* 127–139.

Andrews, L. B. (1984). *New Conceptions.* New York: St. Martin's Press.

Anschutz, L., Camp, C. J., Markley, R. P., & Kramer, J. J. (1985). Maintenance and generalization of mnemonics for grocery shopping by older adults. *Experimental Aging Research, 11,* 157–160.

Anschutz, L., Camp, C. J., Markley, R. P., & Kramer, J. J. (1987). Remembering mnemonics: A three-year follow-up on the effects of mnemonic training in elderly adults. *Experimental Aging Research, 13,* 141–143.

Antonoff, S. R., & Spilka, B. (1984–1985). Patterning of facial expressions among terminal cancer patients. *Omega, 15,* 101–108.

Antonovsky, A., & Sagy, S. (1990). Confronting developmental tasks in the retirement transition. *The Gerontologist, 30,* 362–368.

Antonucci, T. C. (1985). Personal characteristics, social support, and social behavior. In R. H. Binstock & E. Shanas (Eds.), *Handbook of Aging and the Social Sciences* (2nd ed.). (pp. 94–128). New York: Van Nostrand Reinhold.

Antonucci, T. C. (1990). Social supports and social relationships. In R. H. Binstock & L. K. George (Eds.), *Handbook of Aging and the Social Sciences* (3rd ed.). (pp. 205–226). San Diego: Academic Press.

Antonucci, T C., & Akiyama, H. (1988, November). *The negative effects of intimate social networks among older women as compared with men.* Paper presented at the annual meeting of the Gerontological Society of America, San Francisco, CA.

Antonucci, T. C., & Jackson, J. S. (1989). Successful aging and life course reciprocity. In A. Warnes (Ed.), *Human Ageing and Later Life: Multidisciplinary Perspectives* (pp. 83–95). London: Hodder & Stoughton.

Aquilino, W. S. (1990). The likelihood of parent-adult child coresidence: Effects of family structure and parental characteristics. *Journal of Marriage and the Family*, 52, 405–419.

Arenberg, D., & Robertson-Tchabo, E. (1977). Learning and aging. In J. E. Bir·en & K. W. Schaie (Eds.), *Handbook of the Psychology of Aging* (pp. 421–449). New York: Van Nostrand Reinhold.

Arlin, P. K. (1975). Cognitive development in adulthood: A fifth stage? *Developmental Psychology*, 11, 602–606.

Arling, G., Parham, I., & Teitleman, J. (1978, November). *Learned Helplessness and Social Exchanges: Convergence and Application of Theories.* Paper presented at the 31st annual meeting of the Gerontological Society, Dallas, TX.

Aronson, M. K. (1988). *Understanding Alzheimer's Disease.* New York: Scribner.

Astin, H. S. (1984). The meaning of work in women's lives: A sociopsychological model of career choice and work behavior. *The Counseling Psychologist*, 12, 117–126.

Atchley, R. C. (1989). A continuity theory of normal aging. *The Gerontologist*, 29, 183–190.

Atchley, R. C., & Miller, S. J. (1983). Types of elderly couples. In T. H. Brubaker (Ed.), *Family Relationships in Later Life* (pp. 77–90). Beverly Hills, CA: Sage Publications.

Atwater, L. (1985). Long-term cohabitation without a legal ceremony is equally valid and desirable. In H. Feldman & M. Feldman (Eds.), *Current Controversies in Marriage and Family* (pp. 243–252). Beverly Hills, CA: Sage Publications.

Ausman, L. M., & Russell, R. M. (1990). Nutrition and aging. In E. L. Schneider & J. W. Rowe (Eds.), *Handbook of the Biology of Aging*, 3rd Ed. (pp. 384–406). San Diego: Academic Press.

Avolio, B. J., & Waldman, D. A. (1989). Ratings of managerial skill requirements: Comparison of age- and job-related factors. *Psychology and Aging*, 4, 464–470.

Babcock, R. L., & Salthouse, T. A. (1990). Effects of increased processing demands on age differences in working memory. *Psychology and Aging*, 5, 421–428.

Backhouse, C., & Cohen, L. (1981). *Sexual Harassment on the Job.* Englewood Cliffs, NJ: Prentice Hall.

Baddeley, A. (1986). *Working Memory.* Oxford, England: Clarendon Press.

Baer, D. M. (1973). The control of developmental processes: Why wait? In J. R. Nesselroade & H. W. Reese (Eds.), *Life-span Developmental Psychology: Methodological Issues* (pp. 187–196). New York: Academic Press.

Bahrick, H. P. (1979). Maintenance of knowledge: Questions about memory we forgot to ask. *Journal of Experimental Psychology: General*, 108, 296–308.

Bahrick, H. P., Bahrick, P. P., & Wittlinger, R. P. (1975). Fifty years of memory for names and faces: A cross-sectional approach. *Journal of Experimental Psychology*, 104, 54–75.

Baker, F. M. (1988). Dementing illness and black Americans. In J. S. Jackson (Ed.), *The Black American Elderly: Research on Physical and Psychosocial Health* (pp. 215–233). New York: Springer.

Balding, M., & DeBlassie, R. R. (1983). Separated, divorced, or widowed women and career choice: The displaced homemaker. *Journal of Employment Counseling*, 20, 19–25.

Balkwell, C. (1981). Transition to widowhood: A review of the literature. *Family Relations*, 30, 117–125.

Baltes, P. B. (1979). Life-span developmental psychology: Some converging observations on history and theory. In *Life-span Development and Behavior*, Vol. 2 (pp. 255–279). New York: Academic Press.

Baltes, P. B., Cornelius, S. W., & Nesselroade, J. R. (1980). Cohort effects in developmental psychology. In J. R. Nesselroade & P. B. Baltes (Eds.), *Lon-*

gitudinal Research in the Study of Behavior and Development. New York: Academic Press.

Baltes, P. B., Dittmann-Kohli, F., & Kliegl, R. (1986). Reserve capacity of the elderly in aging-sensitive tests of fluid intelligence: Replication and extension. *Psychology and Aging*, 1, 172–177.

Baltes, P. B., Reese, H. W., & Lipsitt, L. P. (1980). Life-span developmental psychology. In *Annual Review of Psychology* (pp. 65–110). New York: Annual Reviews, Inc.

Baltes, P. B., Reese, H. W., & Nesselroade, J. (1977). *Life Span Developmental Psychology: Introduction to Research Methods*. Monterey, CA: Brooks/Cole.

Baltes, P. B., & Schaie, K. W. (1974, March 5). The myth of the twilight years. *Psychology Today*, pp. 35–40.

Baltes, P. B., & Schaie, K. W. (1976). On the plasticity of intelligence in adulthood and old age: Where Horn and Donaldson fail. *American Psychologist*, 31, 720–725.

Baltes, P. B., Sowarka, D., & Kliegl, R. (1989). Cognitive training research on fluid intelligence in old age: What can older adults achieve by themselves? *Psychology and Aging*, 4, 217–221.

Baltes, P. B., & Willis, S. L. (1982). Plasticity and enhancement of intellectual functioning in old age: Penn State's Adult Development and Enrichment Program (ADEPT). In F. I. M. Craik & S. E. Trehub (Eds.), *Aging and Cognitive Processes* (pp. 353–389). New York: Plenum Press.

Bandura, A. (1977). *Social Learning Theory*. Englewood Cliffs, NJ: Prentice Hall.

Bankoff, E. A. (1984). Aged parents and their widowed daughters: A support relationship. *Journal of Gerontology*, 39, 230–239.

Barfield, R. E., & Morgan, J. N. (1978). Trends in satisfaction with retirement. *The Gerontologist*, 18, 19–23.

Baron, A., & Journey, J. W. (1989). Age differences in manual versus vocal reaction times: Further evidence. *Journal of Gerontology: Psychological Sciences*, P157–P159.

Baron, A., & Mattila, W. R. (1989). Response slowing of older adults: Effects of time-limit contingencies on single- and dual-task performances. *Psychology and Aging*, 4, 66–72.

Barrett, G. V., Alexander, R. A., & Forbes, J. B. (1977). Analysis of performance measurement and training requirements for driving decision making in emergency situations. *JSAS Catalogue of Selected Documents in Psychology*, 7 (Ms. No. 1623), 126.

Barrett, T. R., & Wright, M. (1981). Age-related facilitation in recall following semantic processing. *Journal of Gerontology*, 36, 194–199.

Baruch, G. (1984). The psychological well-being of women in the middle years. In G. Baruch & J. Brooks-Gunn (Ed.), *Women in Midlife* (pp. 161–180). New York: Plenum Press.

Baruch, G., Barnett, R., & Rivers, C. (1983). *Lifeprints*. New York: McGraw-Hill.

Barusch, A. S. (1988). Problems and coping strategies of elderly spouse caregivers. *The Gerontologist*, 28, 677–685.

Barusch, A. S., & Spaid, W. M. (1989). Gender differences in caregiving: Why do wives report greater burden? *The Gerontologist*, 29, 667–676.

Bass, D. M., & Bowman, K. (1990). The transition from caregiving to bereavement: The relationship of care-related strain and adjustment to death. *The Gerontologist*, 30, 35–42.

Bayer, L. M., Whissell-Buechy, D., & Honzik, M. P. (1981). Health in the middle years. In D. H. Eichorn, J. A. Clausen, N. Haan, M. P. Honzik, & P. H. Mussen (Eds.), *Present and Past in Middle Life* (pp. 55–88). New York: Academic Press.

Bean, J. P., & Metzner, B. S. (1985). A conceptual model of nontraditional undergraduate student attrition. *Review of Educational Research*, 55, 485–540.

Bearon, L. B., & Koenig, H. G. (1990). Religious cognitions and use of prayer in health and illness. *The Gerontologist*, 30, 249–253.

Becerra, R. M. (1983). The Mexican American; Aging in a changing culture. In R. L. McNeely & J. L. Colen (Eds.), *Aging Minority Groups* (pp. 108–118). Beverly Hills: Sage Publications.

Beck, A. T. (1967). *Depression: Clinical, Experimental, and Therapeutic Aspects*. New York: Harper & Row.

Belenkey, M. F., Clinchy, B. M., Goldberger, N. R., & Tarule, J. M. (1986). *Women's Ways of Knowing: The Development of Self, Voice, and Mind*. New York: Basic Books.

Belgrave, L. L. (1988). The effects of race differences in work history, work attitudes, economic resources, and health on women's retirement. *Research on Aging*, 10, 383–398.

Bell, A. P., & Weinberg, M. S. (1978). *Homosexualities: A Study of Diversity among Men and Women*. New York: Simon & Schuster.

Bell, R. R. (1981a). Friendships of women and of men. *Psychology of Women Quarterly*, 5, 402–417.

Bell, R. R. (1981b). *Worlds of Friendship*. Beverly Hills, CA: Sage Publications.

Belloc, N. B. (1973). Relationship of health practices and mortality. *Preventative Medicine*, 2, 67–81.

Belloc, N. B., & Breslow, L. (1972). Relationship of physical health status and health practices. *Preventative Medicine*, 1, 409–421.

Belsky, J., & Rovine, M. (1990). Patterns of marital change across the transition to parenthood: Pregnancy to three years postpartum. *Journal of Marriage and the Family*, 52, 5–19.

Benet, S. (1976). *How to Live to be 100: The Life-style of the People of the Caucasus*. New York: Dial Press.

Bengtson, V. L. (1985). Diversity and symbolism in grandparental roles. In V. L. Bengtson & J. F. Robertson (Eds.), *Grandparenthood* (pp. 11–25). Beverly Hills: Sage.

Bengtson, V. L., Cueller, J. B., & Ragan, P. K. (1977). Stratum contrasts and similarities in attitudes toward death. *Journal of Gerontology*, 32, 76–88.

Bengtson, V. L., & Kuypers, J. A. (1971). Generational differences and the developmental stake. *Aging and Human Development*, 2, 249–260.

Bengtson, V., Rosenthal, C., & Burton, L. (1990). Families and aging: Diversity and heterogeneity. In R. H. Binstock & L. K. George (Eds.), *Handbook of Aging and the Social Sciences* (3rd ed.). (pp. 263–287). San Diego: Academic Press.

Bennett, N. G., & Garson, L. K. (1986). Extraordinary longevity in the Soviet Union: Fact or artifact? *The Gerontologist*, 26, 358–361.

Bennett, W. I., Goldfinger, S. E., & Johnson, G. T. (Eds.). (1987). *Your Good Health: How to Stay Well and What to Do When You're Not*. Cambridge, MA: Harvard University Press.

Berkman, S. C. (1984). Community service by visually impaired older adults. *Journal of Visual Impairment and Blindness*, 78, 10–12.

Berkowitz, M. W., Waxman, R., & Yaffe, L. (1988). The effects of a resident self-help model on control, social involvement, and self-esteem among the elderly. *The Gerontologist*, 28, 620–624.

Bernard, J. (1972). *The Future of Marriage*. New York: Bantam Books.

Bernard, J. (1974). *The Future of Motherhood*. New York: Penguin Books.

Bernstein, M. C., & Bernstein, J. B. (1988). *Social Security: The System That Works*. New York: Basic Books.

Best, F. (1989, June). *Flexible Life Scheduling: Does the Idea Have a Future?* Paper presented at the Fourteenth International Congress of Gerontology, Acapulco, Mexico.

Bhanthumnavin, K., & Schuster, M. M. (1977). Aging and gastrointestinal function. In C. E. Finch & L. Hayflick (Eds.), *Handbook of the Biology of Aging* (pp. 709–723). New York: Van Nostrand Reinhold.

Birkel, R. C., & Jones, C. J. (1989). A comparison of the caregiving networks of dependent elderly individuals who are lucid and those who are demented. *The Gerontologist*, 29, 114–119.

Birkhill, W. R., & Schaie, K. W. (1975). The effect of differential reinforcement of cautiousness in intellectual performance among the elderly. *Journal of Gerontology*, 30, 578–583.

Birren, J. E. (1964). *The psychology of aging*. Englewood Cliffs, NJ: Prentice Hall.

Birren, J. E., & Renner, V. J. (1980). Concepts and issues of mental health and aging. In J. E. Birren & R. B. Sloane (Eds.), *Handbook of Mental Health and Aging* (pp. 3–33). Englewood Cliffs, NJ: Prentice Hall.

Bitzan, J. E., & Kruzich, J. M. (1990). Interpersonal relationships of nursing home residents. *The Gerontologist*, 30, 385–390.

Blackburn, J. A., Papalia-Finlay, D., Foye, B. F., & Serlin, R. C. (1988). Modifiability of figural relations performance: A combination of two training approaches. *Journal of Gerontology*, 43, 87–89.

Blanchard-Fields, F. (1986). Reasoning on social dilemmas varying in emotional saliency: An adult developmental perspective. *Psychology and Aging*, 1, 325–332.

Blandford, A., Chappell, N., & Marshall, S. (1989). Tenant resource coordinators: An experiment in supportive housing. *The Gerontologist*, 29, 826–829.

Blazer, D., George, L. K., & Hughes, D. C. (1988). Schizophrenic symptoms in an elderly community. In J. A. Brody & G. L. Maddox (Eds.), *Epidemiology and Aging: An International Perspective* (pp. 134–149). New York: Springer.

Blazer, D., Hughes, D. C., & George, L. K. (1987). The epidemiology of depression in an elderly community population. *The Gerontologist, 27*, 281–287.

Blenkner, M. (1965). Social work and family relationships in later life with some thoughts on filial maturity. In E. Shanas & G. Streib (Ed.), *Social Structure and the Family: Generational Relations* (pp. 46–59). Englewood Cliffs, NJ: Prentice Hall.

Blieszner, R. (1986). Trends in family gerontology research. *Family Relations, 35*, 555–562.

Block, J. (1971). *Lives Through Time*. Berkeley, CA: Bancroft Books.

Block, M. R., Davidson, J. L., & Grambs, J. D. (1981). *Women Over Forty: Visions and Realities*. New York: Springer.

Bloom, A. (1987). *The Closing of the American Mind*. New York: Simon & Schuster.

Blumenstein, P., & Schwartz, P. (1983). *American Couples*. New York: Morrow.

Boaz, R. F. (1987a). Early withdrawal from the labor force: A response only to pension pull or also to labor market push? *Research on Aging, 9*, 530–547.

Boaz, R. F. (1987b). Work as a response to low and decreasing real income during retirement. *Research on Aging, 9*, 428–440.

Bolles, R. N. (1978). *The Three Boxes of Life and How to Get Out of Them*. Berkeley, CA: Ten Speed Press.

Bolles, R. N. (1988). *What Color Is Your Parachute?* Berkeley, CA: Ten Speed Press.

Borgatta, E. F., Montgomery, R. J. V., & Borgatta, M. L. (1982). Alcohol use and abuse, life crises events, and the elderly. *Research on Aging, 4*, 378–408.

Bosse, R., Aldwin, C. M., Levenson, M. R., Workman-Daniels, K., & Ekerdt, D. J. (1990). Differences in social support among retirees and workers: Findings from the Normative Aging Study. *Psychology and Aging, 5*, 41–47.

Botwinick, J. (1977). Intellectual abilities. In J. E. Birren & K. W. Schaie (Eds.), *Handbook of the Psychology of Aging* (pp. 580–605). New York: Van Nostrand Reinhold.

Botwinick, J. (1978). *Aging and Behavior* (2nd ed.). New York: Springer.

Botwinick, J., & Thompson, L. W. (1966). Components of reaction time in relation to age and sex. *Journal of Genetic Psychology, 108*, 175–183.

Bowman, L. (1971). The effects of city civilization. In C. A. Jackson (Ed.), *Passing: The Vision of Death in America* (pp. 153–173). Westport, CT: Greenwood.

Boxer, A. M., Solomon, B., Offer, D., Petersen, A. C., & Halprin, F. (1984). Parents' perceptions of young adolescents. In R. S. Cohen, B. J. Cohler, & S. H. Weissman (Eds.), *Parenthood: A Psychodynamic Perspective* (pp. 64–84). New York: Guilford Press.

Boyer, E. L. (1987). *College: The Undergraduate Experience in America*. New York: Harper & Row.

Bozett, F. W. (1988). Gay fatherhood. In P. Bronstein & C. P. Cowan (Eds.), *Fatherhood Today: Men's Changing Role in the Family* (pp. 214–235). New York: Wiley.

Braun, K. L., & Rose, C. L. (1987). Geriatric patient outcomes and costs in three settings: Nursing home, foster family, and own home. *Journal of the American Geriatrics Society, 35*, 387–397.

Brickel, C. M. (1979). The therapeutic roles of cat mascots with a hospital-based geriatric population: A staff survey. *The Gerontologist, 19*, 368–372.

Brickel, C. M. (1984). The clinical use of pets with the aged. *Clinical Gerontologist, 2*, 72–74.

Broderick, C. B. (1982). Adult sexual development. In B. B. Wolman (Ed.), *Handbook of Developmental Psychology* (pp. 726–733). Englewood Cliffs, NJ: Prentice Hall.

Brody, E. (1981). Women in the middle and family help to older people. *The Gerontologist, 21*, 471–480.

Brody, E. M. (1985). Parent care as a normative family stress. *The Gerontologist, 25*, 19–29.

Brody, E. M., Dempsey, N. P., & Pruchno, R. A. (1990). Mental health of sons and daughters of the institutionalized aged. *The Gerontologist, 30*, 212–219.

Brody, E. M., Hoffman, C., Kleban, M. H., & Schoonover, C. B. (1989). Caregiving daughters and their local siblings: Perceptions, strains, and interactions. *The Gerontologist, 29*, 529–538.

Brody, E. M., Johnson, P. T., & Fulcomer, M. C. (1984). What should adult children do for elderly parents? Opinions and preferences of three generations of women. *Journal of Gerontology, 39*, 736–746.

Brody, J. A. (1982). Aging and alcohol abuse. *Journal of the American Geriatrics Society, 30*, 123–126.

Bromley, D. B. (1974). *The psychology of human ageing*. Middlesex, England: Penguin Books.

Brookfield, S. (1985). A critical definition of adult education. *Adult Education Quarterly, 36*, 44–49.

Broverman, J. K., Broverman, D. M., & Clarkson, F. E. (1970). Sexual stereotypes and clinical judgement. *Journal of Consulting and Clinical Psychology, 34*, 1–7.

Brown, B. B. (1982). Professionals' perceptions of drug and alcohol abuse among the elderly. *The Gerontologist, 22*, 519–525.

Brubaker, T. H. (1990). *Later life families* (2nd ed.). Beverly Hills, CA: Sage Publications.

Buchsbaum, H. J. (1983). *The Menopause*. New York: Springer-Verlag.

Buck-Morss, S. (1975). Socio-economic bias in Piaget's theory and its implications for cross-culture studies. *Human Development, 18*, 35–49.

Bulcroft, K., Leynseele, J. V., & Borgatta, E. F. (1989). Filial responsibility laws: Issues and state statutes. *Research on Aging, 11*, 374–393.

Bulcroft, K., & O'Conner-Roden, M. (1986). Never too late. *Psychology Today*, pp. 66–70.

Burden, D. S. (1986). Single parents and the work setting: The impact of multiple job and homelife responsibilities. *Family Relations, 35*, 37–44.

Burr, W. R. (1970). Satisfaction with various aspects of marriage over the life cycle: A random middle class sample. *Journal of Marriage and the Family, 32*, 29–37.

Burton, L. M., & Bengtson, V. L. (1985). Black grandmothers: Issues of timing and continuity of roles. In V. L. Bengtson & J. M. Robertson (Eds.), *Grandparenthood* (pp. 61–77). Beverly Hills, CA: Sage.

Buskirk, E. R. (1985). Health maintenance and longevity: Exercise. In C. E. Finch & E. L. Schneider (Eds.), *Handbook of the Biology of Aging*. New York: Van Nostrand Reinhold.

Butler, R. N. (1968). The life review: An interpretation of reminiscence in the aged. In B. L. Neugarten (Ed.), *Middle Age and Aging* (pp. 486–496). Chicago: University of Chicago Press.

Callen, V. J. (1987). The personal and marital adjustment of mothers and of voluntarily and involuntarily childless wives. *Journal of Marriage and the Family, 49*, 847–856.

Cameron, P., Stewart, L., & Biber, H. (1973). Consciousness of death across the life span. *Journal of Gerontology, 28*, 92–95.

Campbell, R., & Brody, E. M. (1985). Women's changing roles and help to the elderly: Attitudes of women in the United States and Japan. *The Gerontologist, 25*, 584–592.

Campbell, D. T., & Stanley, J. C. (1963). Experimental and quasi-experimental designs for research on teaching. In N. L. Gage (Ed.), *Handbook of Research on Teaching*. Chicago: Rand McNally.

Campbell, F. L., Townes, B. D., & Beach, L. R. (1982). Motivational bases of childbearing decisions. In G. L. Fox (Ed.), *The Childbearing Decision: Fertility Attitudes and Behavior*. Beverly Hills, CA: Sage Publications.

Campione, W. A. (1988). Predicting participation in retirement preparation programs. *Journal of Gerontology: Social Sciences, 43*, S91–95.

Candy, S. G., Troll, L. E., & Levy, S. G. (1981). A developmental exploration of friendship functions in women. *Psychology of Women Quarterly, 5*, 456–472.

Canestrari, R. E. (1963). Paced and self-paced learning in young and elderly adults. *Journal of Gerontology, 18*, 165–168.

Canestrari, R. E. (1968). Age changes in acquisition. In G. A. Talland (Ed.), *Human Aging and Behavior* (pp. 168–187). New York: Academic Press.

Cantor, M. H. (1975). Life space and the social support system of the inner city elderly of New York city. *The Gerontologist, 15*, 23–27.

Carey, R. G. (1979–1980). Weathering widowhood: Problems and adjustment of the widowed during the first year. *Omega, 10*, 135–145.

Carlson, N. R. (1988). *Foundations of Physiological Psychology*. Needham Heights, MA: Allyn & Bacon.

Carp, F. M. (1968). Effects of improved housing on the lives of older people. In B. L. Neugarten (Ed.), *Middle Age and Aging* (pp. 409–416). Chicago: University of Chicago Press.

Carp, F. M. (1976). Housing and living environments of older people. In R. H. Binstock & E. Shanas (Eds.), *Handbook of Aging and the Social Sciences* (pp. 244–271). New York: Van Nostrand Reinhold.

Carstensen, L. L. (1987). Age-related changes in social activity. In L. L. Carstensen & B. A. Edelstein

(Eds.), *Handbook of Clinical Gerontology* (pp. 222–237). New York: Pergammon Press.

Carstensen, L. L. (1989, November). *A longitudinal analysis of social and emotional dimensions of interpersonal relationships*. Paper presented at the annual meeting of the Gerontological Society of America, Minneapolis, MN.

Carstensen, L. L., & Fremouw, W. J. (1981). The demonstration of a behavioral intervention for late life paranoia. *The Gerontologist, 21,* 329–333.

Caserta, M. S., Lund, D. A., Wright, S. D., & Redburn, D. E. (1987). Caregivers to dementia patients: The utilization of community services. *The Gerontologist, 27,* 209–214.

Cassel, C. K., & Zweibel, N. R. (1987). Attitudes regarding life-extending medical care among the elderly and their children. *The Gerontologist* (Special Issue), *27,* 229(a).

Cate, R. M., Lloyd, S. A., & Long, E. (1988). The role of rewards and fairness in developing premarital relationships. *Journal of Marriage and the Family, 50,* 443–452.

Cavanaugh, J. C. (1983). Comprehension and retention of television programs by 20- and 60-year olds. *Journal of Gerontology, 38,* 190–196.

Cavanaugh, J. C. (1984). Effects of presentation format on adults' retention of television programs. *Experimental Aging Research, 10,* 51–53.

Cavanaugh, J. C., Grady, J. G., & Perlmutter, M. (1983). Forgetting and use of memory aids in 20 to 70 year olds' everyday life. *International Journal of Aging and Human Development, 17,* 113–122.

Cavanaugh, J. C., & Poon, L. W. (1989). Metamemorial predictors of memory performance in young and older adults. *Psychology and Aging, 4,* 365–368.

Cerella, J. (1985). Information processing rates in the elderly. *Psychological Bulletin, 98,* 67–83.

Cerella, J. (1990). Aging and information-processing rate. In J. E. Birren & K. W. Schaie (Eds.), *Handbook of the Psychology of Aging* (3rd ed.) (pp. 201–221). San Diego: Academic Press.

Chambre, S. M. (1984). Is volunteering a substitute for role loss in old age? An empirical test of activity theory. *The Gerontologist, 24,* 292–298.

Chandler, C. R. (1974). Value orientations among Mexican Americans in a southwestern city. *Sociology and Social Research, 58,* 262–271.

Chappell, N. L. (1990). Aging and social care. In R. H. Binstock & L. K. George (Eds.), *Handbook of Aging and the Social Sciences* (3rd ed.). (pp. 438–454). San Diego: Academic Press.

Chappell, N. L., & Badger, M. (1989). Social isolation and well-being. *Journal of Gerontology: Social Sciences, 44,* S169–176.

Charles, D. C. (1970). Historical antecedents of life-span developmental psychology. In L. R. Goulet & P. B. Baltes (Eds.), *Life-span Developmental Psychology: Research and Theory* (pp. 24–53). New York: Academic Press.

Charness, N. (1989). Age and expertise: Responding to Talland's challenge. In L. W. Poon, D. C. Rubin, & B. A. Wilson (Eds.), *Everyday Cognition in Adulthood and Old Age*. New York: Cambridge University Press.

Charness, N., & Bosman, E. A. (1990). Human factors and design for older adults. In J. E. Birren & K. W. Schaie (Eds.), *Handbook of the Psychology of Aging* (3rd ed.). (pp. 446–463). San Diego: Academic Press.

Chatters, L. M., & Taylor, R. J. (1989). Age differences in religious participation among Black adults. *Journal of Gerontology: Social Sciences, 44,* S183–189.

Cheal, D. (1983). Intergenerational family transfers. *Journal of Marriage and the Family, 45,* 805–813.

Cherlin, A. (1978). Remarriage as an incomplete institution. *American Journal of Sociology, 84,* 634–650.

Cherlin, A., & Furstenberg, F. F. (1985). Styles and strategies of grandparenting. In V. L. Bengtson & J. F. Robertson (Eds.), *Grandparenthood* (pp. 97–116). Beverly Hills: Sage Publications.

Chiriboga, D. A. (1982). Adaptation to marital separation in later and earlier life. *Journal of Gerontology, 37,* 109–114.

Chiriboga, D., & Cutler, L. (1980). Stress and adaptation: Life-span perspectives. In L. W. Poon (Ed.), *Aging in the 1980's: Psychological issues* (pp. 347–362). Washington, DC: American Psychological Association.

Chown, S. M. (1968). Personality and aging. In K. W. Schaie (Ed.), *Theory and Methods of Research on Aging* (pp. 134–157). Morgantown, WV: West Virginia University.

Cicirelli, V. G. (1982). Sibling influence throughout the lifespan. In M. E. Lamb & B. Sutton-Smith

(Eds.), *Sibling Relationships: Their Nature and Significance across the Lifespan* (pp. 267–284). Hillsdale, NJ: Lawrence Erlbaum.

Cicirelli, V. G. (1985). The role of siblings as family caregivers. In W. J. Sauer & R. T. Coward (Eds.), *Social Support Networks and the Care of the Elderly* (pp. 93–107). New York: Springer.

Cicirelli, V. G. (1989). Feelings of attachment to siblings and well-being in later life. *Psychology and Aging, 4,* 211–216.

Cicirelli, V. G. (1990). Relationship of personal-social variables to belief in paternalism in parent caregiving situations. *Psychology and Aging, 5,* 458–466.

Clark, R. L. (1988). The future of work and retirement. *Research on Aging, 10,* 169–193.

Clark, R. L. (1990). Income maintenance policies in the United States. In R. H. Binstock & L. K. George (Eds.), *Handbook of Aging and the Social Sciences* (3rd ed.). (pp. 382–397). San Diego: Academic Press.

Clark, R. L., & McDermed, A. A. (1988). Pension wealth and job changes: The effects of vesting, portability and lump-sum distributions. *The Gerontologist, 28,* 524–532.

Clark, W. B., & Midanik, L. (1982). Alcohol use and alcohol problems among U. S. adults: Results of the l979 national survey. In National Institute on Alcohol Abuse and Alcoholism, *Alcohol Consumption and Related Problems.* Alcohol and Health Monograph No. l. Rockville, MD: NIAAA.

Clausen, J. A. (1981). Men's occupational careers in the middle years. In D. H. Eichorn, J. A. Clausen, N. Haan, M. P. Honzik, & P. Mussen (Eds.), *Present and Past in Middle Life* (pp. 321–351). New York: Academic Press.

Clayton, V. P., & Birren, J. P. (1980). The development of wisdom across the life span: A reexamination of an ancient topic. In P. B. Baltes & O. G. Brim (Eds.), *Life-span Development and Behavior,* Vol. 3 (pp. 103–135). New York: Academic Press.

Clemens, A. W., & Axelson, L. J. (1985). The not-so-empty nest: The return of the fledgling adult. *Family Relations, 34,* 259–264.

Cockrum, J., & White, P. (1985). Influences on the life satisfaction of never-married men and women. *Family Relations, 34,* 551–556.

Cohen, G. D. (1990). Psychopathology and mental health in the mature and elderly adult. In J. E. Birren & K. W. Schaie (Eds.), *Handbook of the Psychology of Aging* (3rd ed.). (pp. 359–371). San Diego: Academic Press.

Cohen, G. (1979). Language comprehension in old age. *Cognitive Psychology, 11,* 412–429.

Cohen, R. J., Montague, P., Nathanson, L. S., & Swerdik, M. E. (1988). *Psychological Testing: An Introduction to Tests and Measurement.* Mountain View, CA: Mayfield Publishing.

Cohen, S. (1980). Aftereffects of stress on human performance and social behavior: A review of research and theory. *Psychological Bulletin, 88,* 82–108.

Cohen-Mansfield, J., Marx, M. S., & Rosenthal, A. S. (1990). Dementia and agitation in nursing home residents: How are they related? *Psychology and Aging, 5,* 3–8.

Colby, A., Kohlberg, L., Gibbs, J., & Lieberman, M. (1983). A longitudinal study of moral judgment. *Monographs of the Society for Research in Child Development, 48* (1–2).

Comalli, P. E., Jr. (1970). Life-span changes in visual perception. In L. R. Goulet & P. B. Baltes (Eds.), *Life-span Developmental Psychology: Research and Theory* (pp. 211–227). New York: Academic Press.

Comalli, P. E., Jr., Wapner, S., & Werner, H. (1959). Perception of verticality in middle and old age. *Journal of Psychology, 47,* 259–266.

Commons, M. L., Richards, F. A., & Kuhn, D. (1982). Systematic, metasystematic, and cross paradigmatic reasoning: A case for stages of reasoning beyond Piaget's stage of formal operations. *Child Development, 53,* 1058–1068.

Communities for the elderly. (1990). *Consumer Reports,* pp. 123–131.

Connidis, I. A. (1989). *Family Ties and Aging.* Toronto: Butterworths.

Connidis, I. A., & Davies, L. (1990). Confidants and companions in later life: The place of family and friends. *Journal of Gerontology: Social Sciences, 45,* S141–149.

Cook, T. D., & Campbell, D. T. (1979). *Quasi-experimentation: Design and Analysis Issues for Field Settings.* Chicago: Rand McNally.

Cornelius, S. W., & Caspi, A. (1987). Everyday problem solving in adulthood and old age. *Psychology and Aging, 2,* 144–153.

Cornett, C. W., & Hudson, R. W. (1987). Middle adulthood and the theories of Erikson, Gould, and

Vaillant: Where does the gay man fit? *Journal of Gerontological Social Work, 10*, 61–73.

Correa, P., Pickle, L. W., Fontham, E., Lin, Y., & Haenszel, W. (1983). Passive smoking and lung cancer. *The Lancet*, 595–597.

Corso, J. F. (1977). Auditory perception and communication. In J. E. Birren & K. W. Schaie (Eds.), *Handbook of the Psychology of Aging* (pp. 535–553). New York: Van Nostrand Reinhold.

Costa, P. T. (1989). Personality continuity and the changes of adult life. In M. Storandt & G. R. VandenBos (Eds.), *The Adult Years: Continuity and Change* (pp. 41–77). Washington, DC: American Psychological Association.

Costa, P. T., & McCrae, R. R. (1988). Personality in adulthood: A six-year longitudinal study of self-reports and spouse ratings on the NEO personality inventory. *Journal of Personality and Social Psychology, 54*, 853–863.

Costa, P. T., McCrae, R. R., & Arenberg, D. (1980). Enduring dispositions in adult males. *Journal of Personality and Social Psychology, 38*, 793–800.

Costa, P. T., McCrae, R. R., Zonderman, A. B., Barbano, H. E., Lebowitz, B., & Larson, D. M. (1986). Cross-sectional studies of personality in a national sample: 2. Stability in neuroticism, extraversion, and openness. *Psychology and Aging, 1*, 144–149.

Costa, P. T., Zonderman, A. B., & McCrae, R. R. (1985). Longitudinal course of social support among men in the Baltimore Longitudinal study of aging. In I. Sarason & B. R. Sarason (Eds.), *Social support: Theory, Research, and Applications* (pp. 137–154). The Hague: Nijhoff.

Coward, R. T., Cutler, S. J., & Schmidt, F. E. (1989). Differences in the household composition of elders by age, gender, and area of residence. *The Gerontologist, 29*, 814–821.

Coward, R. T., & Dwyer, J. W. (1990). The association of gender, sibling network composition, and patterns of parent care by adult children. *Research on Aging, 12*, 158–181.

Cozby, P. C., Worden, P. E., & Kee, D. W. (1989). *Research Methods in Human Development*. Mountain View, CA: Mayfield Publishing.

Craik, F. I. M. (1968). Two components in free recall. *Journal of Verbal Learning and Verbal Behavior, 7*, 996–1004.

Craik, F. I. M. (1977). Age differences in human memory. In J. E. Birren & K. W. Schaie (Eds.), *Handbook*

of the Psychology of Aging* (pp. 384–420). New York: Van Nostrand Reinhold.

Craik, F. I. M., & Lockhart, R. S. (1972). Levels of processing: A framework for memory research. *Journal of Verbal Learning and Verbal Behavior, 11*, 671–684.

Craik, F. I. M., Morris, R. G., & Gick, M. L. (1989). Adult age differences in working memory. In G. Vallar & T. Shallice (Eds.), *Neuropsychological Impairments of Short-term Memory*. New York: Cambridge University Press.

Crimmins, E. M., & Ingegneri, D. G. (1990). Interaction and living arrangements of older parents and their children: Past trends, present determinants, future implications. *Research on Aging, 12*, 3–35.

Cristofalo, V. J. (1988). An overview of the theories of biological aging. In J. E. Birren & V. L. Bengtson (Ed.), *Emergent Theories of Aging* (pp. 118–127). New York: Springer.

Crohan, S. J., & Veroff, J. (1989). Dimensions of marital well-being among white and black newlyweds. *Journal of Marriage and the Family, 51*, 373–383.

Crook, T. (1987). Dementia. In L. L. Carstensen & B. A. Edelstein (Eds.), *Handbook of Clinical Gerontology* (pp. 96–111). New York: Pergammon Press.

Crosbie-Burnett, M. (1989). Application of family stress theory to remarriage: A model for assessing and helping stepfamilies. *Family Relations, 38*, 323–331.

Cuber, J. F., & Harroff, P. (1965). *The Significant Americans: A Study of Sexual Behavior among the Affluent*. New York: Appleton-Century.

Cumming, E., & Henry, E. W. (1961). *Growing Old*. New York: Basic Books.

Cutler, R. G. (1981). Life-span extension. In J. L. McGaugh & S. B. Kiesler (Eds.), *Aging: Biology and Behavior* (pp. 31–76). New York: Academic Press.

Dan, A. J., & Bernhard, L. A. (1989). Menopause and other health issues for midlife women. In S. Hunter & M. Sundel (Eds.), *Midlife Myths: Issues, Findings, and Practice Implications* (pp. 51–66). Newbury Park, CA: Sage Publications.

Danish, S. J. (1983). Musings about personal competence: The contributions of sport, health, and fitness. *American Journal of Community Psychology, 11*, 221–240.

Danner, D. B., & Holbrook, N. J. (1990). Alterations in gene expression with aging. In E. L. Schneider & J. W. Rowe (Eds.), *Handbook of the Biology of Aging* (3rd ed.) (pp. 97–115). San Diego: Academic Press.

Darbonne, A. R. (1969). Suicide and age: A suicide note analysis. *Journal of Clinical Psychology, 33,* 46–50.

Darling-Fisher, C. S., & Leidy, N. K. (1988). Measuring Eriksonian development in the adult: The modified Eriksonian psychosocial stage inventory. *Psychological Reports, 62,* 747–754.

Datan, N., Antonovsky, A., & Maoz, B. (1984). Love, war, and the life cycle of the family. In K. A. McCluskey & H. W. Reese (Eds.), *Life-span Developmental Psychology: Historical and Generational Effects* (pp. 143–159). New York: Academic Press.

Datan, N., & Reese, H. W. (1977). *Life-span Developmental Psychology: Dialectical Perspectives on Experimental Research.* New York: Academic Press.

Davies, H., Priddy, J. M., & Tinklenberg, J. R. (1986). Support groups for male caregivers of Alzheimer's patients. In T. L. Brink (Ed.), *Handbook of Clinical Gerontology* (pp. 385–395). New York: Haworth Press.

Denney, N. W., & Denney, D. R. (1974). Modeling effects on the questioning strategies of the elderly. *Developmental Psychology, 10,* 458.

Denney, N. W., & Heidrich, S. M. (1990). Training effects on Raven's Progressive Matrices in young, middle-aged, and elderly adults. *Psychology and Aging, 5,* 144–145.

Denney, N. W., & Palmer, A. M. (1981). Adult age differences on traditional and practical problem-solving measures. *Journal of Gerontology, 36,* 323–328.

Denney, N. W., & Pearce, K. A. (1989). A developmental study of practical problem solving in adults. *Psychology and Aging, 4,* 438–442.

Denney, N. W., Pearce, K. A., & Palmer, A. M. (1982). A developmental study of adults' performance on traditional and practical problem-solving tasks. *Experimental Aging Research, 8,* 115–118.

Dennis, W. (1956). Age and achievement: A critique. *Journal of Gerontology, 11,* 331–337.

Dennis, W. (1958). The age decrement in outstanding scientific contributions: Fact or artifact? *American Psychologist, 13,* 457–460.

Dennis, W. (1966). Creative productivity between the ages of 20 and 80 years. *Journal of Gerontology, 21,* 1–8.

Depner, C. E., & Ingersoll-Dayton, B. (1985). Conjugal social support: Patterns in later life. *Journal of Gerontology, 40,* 761–766.

Depner, C. E., & Ingersoll-Dayton, B. (1988). Supportive relationships in later life. *Psychology and Aging, 3,* 348–357.

Deutscher, I. (1969). From parental to post-parental life. *Sociological Symposium, 3,* 47–60.

De Vos, S. (1990). Extended family living among older people in six Latin American countries. *Journal of Gerontology: Social Sciences, 45,* S87–94.

Diagnostic and statistical manual of mental disorders (3rd Ed.—Revised) (DSM-III-R). (1987). Washington, DC: American Psychiatric Association.

Diamond, E. L., Jernigan, J. A., Moseley, R. A., Messina, V., & McKeown, R. A. (1989). Decision-making ability and advance directive preferences in nursing home patients and proxies. *The Gerontologist, 29,* 622–626.

Dickstein, L. S. (1972). Death concern: Measurement and correlates. *Psychological Reports, 30,* 563–571.

Digman, J. M., & Inouye, J. (1986). Further specification of the five robust factors of personality. *Journal of Personality and Social Psychology, 50,* 116–123.

Dimond, M., Lund, D. A., & Caserta, M. S. (1987). The role of social support in the first two years of bereavement in an elderly sample. *The Gerontologist, 27,* 599–604.

Dobbs, A. R., & Rule, B. G. (1989). Adult age differences in working memory. *Psychology and Aging, 4,* 500–503.

Doherty, W. J., & Jacobson, N. S. (1982). Marriage and the family. In B. B. Wolman (Ed.), *Handbook of Developmental Psychology* (pp. 667–680). Englewood Cliffs, NJ: Prentice Hall.

Doka, K. J., & Mertz, M. E. (1988). The meaning and significance of great-grandparenthood. *The Gerontologist, 28,* 192–197.

Domino, G., & Hannah, M. T. (1989). Measuring effective functioning in the elderly: An application of Erikson's theory. *Journal of Personality Assessment, 53,* 319–328.

Doppelt, J. E., & Wallace, W. L. (1955). Standardization of the Wechsler Adult Intelligence Scale for older persons. *Journal of Abnormal and Social Psychology, 51,* 312–330.

Dorfman, L. T., & Moffett, M. M. (1987). Retirement satisfaction in married and widowed rural women. *The Gerontologist, 27,* 215–221.

Dowd, J. J., & Bengtson, V. L. (1978). Aging in minority populations: An examination of the double jeopardy hypothesis. *Journal of Gerontology, 33,* 427–436.

Downes, J. J., Davies, A. D. M., & Copeland, J. R. M. (1988). Organization of depressive symptoms in the elderly population: Hierarchical patterns and Guttman scales. *Psychology and Aging, 3,* 367–374.

Droege, R. (1982). *A psychosocial study of the formation of the middle adult life structure in women.* Unpublished doctoral dissertation, California School of Professional Psychology, Berkeley, CA.

Dunham, R. G. (1981). Aging and changing patterns of alcohol use. *Journal of Psychoactive Drugs, 13,* 33–41.

Eames, E., & Eames, T. (1990). Partners in independence. *Dog World, 75,* 30, 162–163, 172.

Eckensberger, L. H. (1973). Methodological issues of cross-cultural research in developmental psychology. In J. R. Nesselroade & H. W. Reese (Eds.), *Life-span Developmental Psychology: Methodological Issues* (pp. 43–64). New York: Academic Press.

Edwards, C. P. (1980). The comparative study of the development of moral judgement and reasoning. In R. H. Munroe, R. L. Munroe, & B. B. Whiting (Eds.), *Handbook of Cross-cultural Human Development.* New York: Garland STM Press.

Eichorn, D. H., Clausen, J. A., Haan, N., Honzik, M. P., & Mussen, P. H. (Eds.). (1981). *Present and Past in Middle Life.* New York: Academic Press.

Eichorn, D. H., Hunt, J. V., & Honzik, M. P. (1981). Experience, personality, and IQ: Adolescence to middle age. In D. H. Eichorn, J. A. Clausen, N. Haan, M. P. Honzik, & P. H. Mussen (Eds.), *Present and Past in Middle Life* (pp. 89–116). New York: Academic Press.

Eisdorfer, C., Nowlin, J., & Wilkie, F. (1970). Improvement of learning in the aged by modification of autonomic nervous system activity. *Science, 170,* 1327–1329.

Ekerdt, D. J. (1987). Why the notion persists that retirement harms health. *The Gerontologist, 27,* 454–457.

Ekerdt, D. J., Vinick, B. H., & Bosse, R. (1989). Orderly endings: Do men know when they will retire? *Journal of Gerontology: Social Sciences, 44,* S28–35.

Elias, M. F., Elias, J. W., & Elias, P. K. (1990). Biological and health influences on behavior. In J. E. Birren & K. W. Schaie (Eds.), *Handbook of the Psychology of Aging* (3rd ed.). (pp. 80–102). San Diego: Academic Press.

Elias, M. F., Robbins, M. A., Schultz, N. R., & Pierce, T. W. (1990). Is blood pressure an important variable in research on aging and neuropsychological test performance? *Journal of Gerontology: Psychological Sciences, 45,* P128–P135.

Emery, C. F., & Blumenthal, J. A. (1990). Perceived change among participants in an exercise program for older adults. *The Gerontologist, 30,* 516–521.

Epstein, L. J. (1978). Depression in the elderly. *Journal of Gerontology, 31,* 278–282.

Erber, J. T. (1981). Remote memory and age: A review. *Experimental Aging Research, 1,* 189–199.

Erber, J. T. (1989). Younger and older adults' appraisal of memory failures in young and older adult target persons. *Journal of Gerontology: Psychological Sciences, 44,* P170–P175.

Erber, J. T., Szuchman, L. T., & Rothberg, S. T. (1990). Everyday memory failure: Age differences in appraisal and attribution. *Psychology and Aging, 5,* 236–241.

Erikson, E. H. (1950). *Childhood and Society.* New York: W. W. Norton & Co.

Erikson, E. H. (1963). *Childhood and Society* (2nd ed.) New York: W. W. Norton & Co.

Erikson, E. H. (1982). *The Life Cycle Completed.* New York: W. W. Norton & Co.

Erikson, E. H., Erikson, J. M., & Kivnick, H. Q. (1986). *Vital Involvement in Old Age.* New York: W. W. Norton and Co.

Evans, L., Ekerdt, D. J., & Bosse, R. (1985). Proximity to retirement and anticipatory involvement: Findings from the normative aging study. *Journal of Gerontology, 40,* 368–374.

Farrell, M. P., & Rosenberg, S. D. (1981). *Men at Mid-life*. Dover, MA: Auburn House.

Faux, M. (1984). *Childless by Choice: Choosing Childlessness in the Eighties*. Garden City, NY: Anchor Press.

Ferraro, K. F. (1989). The ADEA amendment and public support for older workers. *Research on Aging*, *11*, 53–81.

Ferraro, K. F. (1990a). Cohort analysis of retirement preparation, 1974–1981. *Journal of Gerontology: Social Sciences*, *43*, S21–31.

Ferraro, K. F. (1990b). Group benefit orientation toward older adults at work? A comparison of cohort analytic methods. *Journal of Gerontology: Social Sciences*, *45*, S220–227.

Fethke, C. C. (1989). Life-cycle models of savings and the effect of the timing of divorce on retirement economic well-being. *Journal of Gerontology: Social Sciences*, *44*, S121–128.

Fiebert, M. S., & Wright, K. S. (1989). Midlife friendships in an American faculty sample. *Psychological Reports*, *64*, 1127–1130.

Field, D., Schaie, K. W., & Leino, E. V. (1988). Continuity in intellectual functioning: The role of self-reported health. *Psychology and Aging*, *3*, 385–392.

Filinson, R. (1988). A model for church-based services for frail elderly persons and their families. *The Gerontologist*, *28*, 483–486.

Fisk, A. D., McGee, N. D., & Giambra, L. M. (1988). The influence of age on consistent and varied semantic-category search performance. *Psychology and Aging*, *3*, 323–333.

Fitting, M., Rabins, P., Lucas, M. J., & Eastham, J. (1986). Caring for dementia patients: A comparison of husbands and wives. *The Gerontologist*, *26*, 248–252.

Fitzgerald, L. F., & Betz, N. E. (1983). Issues in the vocational psychology of women. In W. B. Walsh & S. H. Osipow (Eds.), *Handbook of Vocational Psychology*. Hillsdale, NJ: Erlbaum.

Flavell, J. H. (1963). *The Developmental Psychology of Jean Piaget*. Princeton, NJ: Van Nostrand Reinhold.

Fleuridas, C. (1987). The stress of unemployment: Its effects on the family. *Family Therapy Collections*, *22*, 111–122.

Folsom, G. S. (1985). Reality orientation: Full circle. *Bulletin of the NY Academy of Medicine*, *61*, 343–350.

Foos, P. W. (1989). Adult age differences in working memory. *Psychology and Aging*, *4*, 269–275.

Fozard, J. L. (1990). Vision and hearing in aging. In J. E. Birren & K. W. Schaie (Eds.), *Handbook of the Psychology of Aging* (3rd ed.). (pp. 150–171). San Diego: Academic Press.

Frazier, E. F. (1939). *The Negro Family in the United States*. Chicago: University of Chicago Press.

Fredrickson, B. L., & Carstensen, L. L. (1990). Choosing social partners: How old age and anticipated endings make people more selective. *Psychology and Aging*, *5*, 335–347.

Freedman, M. B., & Bereiter, C. A. (1963). A longitudinal study of personality development in college alumnae. *Merrill-Palmer Quarterly*, *9*, 295–302.

Friedman, M., & Rosenman, R. H. (1974). *Type A Behavior and Your Heart*. New York: Knopf.

Fries, J. E., & Crapo, L. M. (1981). *Vitality and Aging*. San Francisco: W. H. Freeman.

Frisbie, W. P. (1986). Variation in patterns of marital instability among Hispanics. *Journal of Marriage and the Family*, *48*, 99–106.

Fry, P. S. (1986). *Depression, Stress, and Adaptation in the Elderly*. Rockville, MD: Aspen.

Furst, D. (1983). *Origins and Evolution of Women's Dreams in Early Adulthood*. Unpublished doctoral dissertation, California School of Professional Psychology, Berkeley, CA.

Futterman, A., Gallagher, D., Thompson, L. W., Lovett, S., & Gilewski, M. (1990). Retrospective assessment of marital adjustment and depression during the first two years of spousal bereavement. *Psychology and Aging*, *5*, 277–283.

Gallagher, D., Rose, J., Rivera, P., Lovett, S., & Thompson, L. W. (1989). Prevalence of depression in family caregivers. *The Gerontologist*, *29*, 449–456.

Gallagher, D., & Thompson, L. (1983). Depression. In P. Lewinsohn & L. Teri (Eds.), *Clinical Geropsychology: New Directions in Assessment and Treatment* (pp. 7–37). New York: Pergammon Press.

Ganong, L. H., & Coleman, M. (1989). Preparing for remarriage: Anticipating the issues, seeking solutions. *Family Relations*, *38*, 28–33.

Gardner, H. (1985). *Frames of Mind*. New York: Basic Books.

Gardner, J. N., & Jeweler, A. J. (1985). *College Is Only the Beginning: A Student's Guide to Higher Education*. Belmont, CA: Wadsworth.

Gatz, M. (1989). Clinical psychology and aging. In M. Storandt & G. R. VandenBos (Eds.), *The Adult Years: Continuity and Change* (pp. 83–114). Washington, DC: American Psychological Association.

Gatz, M., Bengtson, V. L., & Blum, M. J. (1990). Caregiving families. In J. E. Birren & K. W. Schaie (Eds.), *Handbook of the Psychology of Aging* (3rd ed.). (pp. 404–426). San Diego: Academic Press.

Gatz, M., & Hurwicz, M. (1990). Are old people more depressed? Cross-sectional data on Center for Epidemiological Studies Depression Scale factors. *Psychology and Aging, 5*, 284–290.

Gatz, M., & Pearson, C. G. (1988). Ageism revised and the provision of psychological services. *American Psychologist, 43*, 184–188.

Gatz, M., Popkin, S. J., Pino, C. D., & VandenBos, G. R. (1985). Psychological interventions with older adults. In J. E. Birren & K. W. Schaie (Eds.), *Handbook of the Psychology of Aging* (2nd ed.). (pp. 755–785). New York: Van Nostrand Reinhold.

Gaylord, S. A., & Zung, W. W. K. (1987). Affective disorders among the aging. In L. L. Carstensen & B. A. Edelstein (Eds.), *Handbook of Clinical Gerontology* (pp. 76–95). New York: Pergammon Press.

Gentry, M., & Shulman, A. D. (1989). Remarriage as a coping response for widowhood. *Psychology and Aging, 3*, 191–196.

George, L. K. (1988). Social participation in later life: Black-white differences. In J. S. Jackson (Ed.), *The Black American Elderly: Research on Physical and Psychosocial Health* (pp. 99–126). New York: Springer.

George, L. K., Fillenbaum, G. G., & Palmore, E. (1984). Sex differences in the antecedents and consequences of retirement. *Journal of Gerontology, 39*, 364–371.

Gergen, K. J. (1977). Stability, change and chance in understanding human development. In N. Datan & H. W. Reese (Eds.), *Life-span Developmental Psychology: Dialectical Perspectives on Experimental Research* (pp. 136–158). New York: Academic Press.

Gerner, R. H., & Jarvik, L. F. (1984). Antidepressant drug treatment in the elderly. In E. Friedman, F. Mann, & S. Gerson (Eds.), *Depression and Antidepressants: Implications for Consideration and Treatment*. New York: Raven.

Gesser, G., Wong, P. T., & Reker, G. T. (1987–1988). Death attitudes across the life-span: The development and validation of the Death Attitude Profile (DAP). *Omega, 18*, 113–128.

Gibson, R. C. (1988). The work, retirement, and disability of older Black Americans. In J. S. Jackson (Ed.), *The Black American Elderly: Research on Physical and Psychosocial Health* (pp. 304–324). New York: Springer.

Giles-Sims, J., & Crosbie-Burnett, M. (1989). Stepfamily research: Implications for policy, clinical interventions, and further research. *Family Relations, 38*, 19–23.

Gilford, R. (1984). Contrasts in marital satisfaction throughout old age: An exchange theory analysis. *Journal of Gerontology, 39*, 325–333.

Gilford, R., & Bengtson, V. L. (1979). Measuring marital satisfaction in three generations: Positive and negative dimensions. *Journal of Marriage and the Family, 41*, 387–398.

Gilligan, C. (1982). *In a Different Voice: Psychological Theory and Women's Development*. Cambridge, MA: Harvard University Press.

Ginzberg, E. (1972). Toward a theory of occupational choice: A restatement. *Vocational Guidance Quarterly, 20*, 169–176.

Ginzberg, E., Ginsberg, S. W., Axelrad, S., & Herma, J. L. (1951). *Occupational Choice: An Approach to a General Theory*. New York: Columbia University Press.

Gladow, N. W., & Ray, M. P. (1986). The impact of information support systems on the well-being of low-income single parents. *Family Relations, 35*, 113–124.

Glaser, B. G., & Strauss, A. L. (1965). *Awareness of Dying*. Chicago: Aldine.

Glaser, B. G., & Strauss, A. L. (1968). *Time for Dying*. Chicago: Aldine.

Glenn, N. D. (1980). Values, attitudes, and beliefs. In O. G. Brim & J. Kagan (Eds.), *Constancy and Change in Human Development* (pp. 596–640). Cambridge, MA: Harvard University Press.

Glenwick, D. S., & Mowrey, J. D. (1986). When parent becomes peer: Loss of intergenerational boundaries in single parent families. *Family Relations, 35*, 57–62.

Glick, P. C., & Lin, S. L. (1986). Recent changes in divorce and remarriage. *Journal of Marriage and the Family, 48*, 737–748.

Gloger-Tippelt, G. (1983). A process model of the pregnancy course. *Human Development, 26*, 134–149.

Gohmann, S. F. (1990). Retirement differences among the respondents to the retirement history survey. *Journal of Gerontology: Social Sciences, 45,* S120–127.

Gold, D. T. (1990). Late-life sibling relationships: Does race affect typological distribution? *The Gerontologist, 30,* 741–748.

Gold, D. T. (1989). Sibling relations in old age: A typology. *International Journal of Aging and Human Development, 28,* 37–51.

Gold, D. T., Woodbury, M. A., & George, L. K. (1990). Relationship classification using grade of membership analysis: A typology of sibling relationships in later life. *Journal of Gerontology: Social Sciences, 45,* S43–51.

Goldberg, A. P., & Hagberg, J. M. (1990). Physical exercise in the elderly. In E. L. Schneider & J. W. Rowe (Eds.), *Handbook of the Biology of Aging* (3rd ed.). (pp. 407–426). San Diego: Academic Press.

Goldberg, E. L., Comstock, G. W., & Harlow, S. D. (1988). Emotional problems and widowhood. *Journal of Gerontology: Social Sciences, 43,* S206–208.

Goldman, R. (1977). Aging in the excretory system: Kidney and bladder. In C. E. Finch & L. Hayflick (Eds.), *Handbook of the Biology of Aging* (pp. 409–431). New York: Van Nostrand Reinhold.

Goldscheider, F. K., & Goldscheider, C. (1989). Family structure and conflict: Nest-leaving expectations of young adults and their parents. *Journal of Marriage and the Family, 51,* 87–97.

Goldstein, M. S. (1951). Physical status of men rejected through selective service in World War II. *Public Health Reports, 66,* 587–609.

Goldstrom, I. D., Burns, B. J., Kessler, L. G., Feuerberg, M. A., Larson, D. B., Miller, N. E., & Cromer, W. J. (1987). Mental health services use by elderly adults in a primary care setting. *Journal of Gerontology, 42,* 147–153.

Gomberg, E. L. (1982). Patterns of alcohol use and abuse among the elderly. In National Institute on Alcohol Abuse and Alcoholism. *Special Population Issues.* Alcohol and Health Monograph No. 4. Rockville, MD: NIAAA.

Goodman, G., Lakey, G., Lashof, J., & Thorne, E. (1983). *No Turning Back: Lesbian and Gay Liberation for the '80's.* Philadelphia: New Society Publishers.

Goodman, C. C., & Pynoos, J. (1990). A model telephone information and support program for caregivers of Alzheimer's patients. *The Gerontologist, 45,* 399–404.

Goodnow, J. J. (1969). Problems in research on culture and thought. In D. Elkind & J. H. Flavell (Eds.), *Studies in Cognitive Development: Essays in Honor of Jean Piaget* (pp. 439–464). New York: Oxford University Press.

Goodwin, D. W. (1988). *Is Alcoholism Hereditary?* New York: Ballantine Books.

Gordus, J. P. (1986). Coping with involuntary job loss and building a new career: Workers' problems and career professionals' challenges. *Journal of Career Development, 12,* 316–326.

Gorer, G. (1965). *Death, Grief, and Mourning.* Garden City, NY: Doubleday.

Gottesman, I. (1979). Schizophrenia and genetics: Toward understanding uncertainty. *Psychiatric Annals, 9,* 54–78.

Gould, R. L. (1972). The phases of adult life: A study in developmental psychology. *American Journal of Psychiatry, 129,* 521–531.

Gould, R. L. (1978). *Transformations: Growth and Change in Adult Life.* New York: Simon & Schuster.

Green, M. (1989). *Theories of Development: A Comparative Approach.* Englewood Cliffs, NJ: Prentice Hall.

Greene, A. L., & Boxer, A. M. (1986). Daughters and sons as young adults: Restructuring the ties that bind. In N. Datan, A. L. Greene, & H. W. Reese (Eds.), *Life-span Developmental Psychology: Intergenerational Relations* (pp. 125–150). Hillsdale, NJ: Lawrence Erlbaum.

Greene, M. G., Hoffman, S., Charon, R., & Adelman, R. (1987). Psychosocial concerns in the medical encounter: A comparison of the interactions of doctors with their young and old patients. *The Gerontologist, 27,* 164–168.

Greenfield, P. M. (1976). Cross-cultural research and Piagetian theory: Paradox and progress. In K. Riegel & J. Meacham (Eds.), *The Developing Individual in a Changing World,* Vol. 1 (pp. 322–333). Chicago: Aldine.

Greenfield, S., Blanco, D. M., Elashoff, R. M., & Ganz, P. A. (1987). Patterns of care related to age of breast cancer patients. *Journal of the American Medical Association, 257,* 2766–2770.

Gruber, H. W. (1977). Geriatrics—Physician attitudes and medical school training. *Journal of the American Geriatrics Society, 25*, 494–499.

Gubrium, J. (1975). Being single in old age. *Aging and Human Development, 6*, 29–41.

Gutek, B. A. (1985). *Sex and the Workplace*. San Francisco: Jossey-Bass Publishers.

Gutmann, D. (1975). Parenthood: A key to the comparative psychology of the life cycle. In N. Datan & L. H. Ginsberg (Eds.), *Life-span Developmental Psychology: Normative Life Crises* (pp. 167–184). New York: Academic Press.

Gutmann, D. (1977). The cross-cultural perspective: Notes toward a comparative psychology of aging. In J. E. Birren & K. W. Schaie (Eds.), *Handbook of the Psychology of Aging* (pp. 302–326). New York: Van Nostrand Reinhold.

Gutmann, D. (1985). The parental imperative revisited: Towards a developmental psychology of adulthood and later life. *Contributions to Human Development, 14*, 31–60.

Haan, N. (1976). Personality organizations of well-functioning younger people and older adults. *International Journal of Aging and Human Development, 7*, 117–127.

Haan, N. (1981). Common dimensions of personality development: Early adolescence to middle life. In D. Eichorn, J. Clausen, N. Haan, M. Honzik, & P. Mussen (Eds.), *Present and Past in Middle Life* (pp. 117–151). New York: Academic Press.

Haan, N. (1989). Personality at midlife. In S. Hunter & M. Sundel (Eds.), *Midlife Myths: Issues, Findings, and Practice Implications* (pp. 116–144). Newbury Park: Sage Publications.

Haan, N., Millsap, R., & Hartka, E. (1986). As time goes by: Change and stability in personality over fifty years. *Psychology and Aging, 1*, 220–232.

Hagestad, G. O. (1982). Parent and child: Generations in the family. In T. M. Field, A. Huston, H. C. Quay, L. Troll, & G. E. Finley (Eds.), *Review of Human Development* (pp. 485–499). New York: Wiley.

Hagestad, G. O., & Neugarten, B. L. (1985). Age and the Life Course. In R. H. Binstock & E. Shanas (Eds.), *Handbook of Aging and the Individual* (pp. 35–61). New York: Van Nostrand Reinhold.

Hagestad, G. O., Smyer, M. A., & Stierman, K. (1984). The impact of divorce in middle age. In R. S.

Cohen, B. J. Cohler, & S. H. Weissman (Eds.), *Parenthood: A Psychodynamic Perspective* (pp. 247–262). New York: Guilford Press.

Haley, W. E. (1983). A family-behavioral approach to the treatment of the cognitively impaired elderly. *The Gerontologist, 23*, 18–20.

Hall, C. S., & Lindzey, G. (1978). *Theories of Personality* (3rd ed.). New York: Wiley.

Hall, G. S. (1922). *Senescence: The Last Half of Life*. New York: Appleton.

Hamon, R. R., & Blieszner, R. (1990). Filial responsibility expectations among adult child–older parent pairs. *Journal of Gerontology: Social Sciences, 45*, S110–112.

Hamscher, J. H., & Farina, A. (1967). "Openness" as a dimension of projective test responses. *Journal of Consulting Psychology, 31*, 525–528.

Hanson, S. M. H. (1986). Healthy single parent families. *Family Relations, 35*, 125–132.

Harbin, T. J., & Blumenthal, J. A. (1985). Relationship among age, sex, the Type A behavior pattern, and cardiovascular reactivity. *Journal of Gerontology, 40*, 714–720.

Harris, L., & Associates. (1981). *Aging in the Eighties: America in Transition*. Washington, DC: National Council on Aging.

Harris, R. L., Ellicott, A. M., & Holmes, D. S. (1986). The timing of psychosocial transitions and changes in women's lives: An examination of women aged 45 to 60. *Journal of Personality and Social Psychology, 51*, 409–416.

Harrison, A., Serafica, F., & McAdoo, H. (1984). Ethnic families of color. In R. D. Parke (Ed.), *Review of Child Development Research: The Family* (pp. 329–371). Chicago: University of Chicago Press.

Hartley, J. T. (1986). Reader and text variables as determinants of discourse memory in adulthood. *Psychology and Aging, 1*, 150–158.

Harvey, C. D., Barnes, G. E., & Greenwood, L. (1987). Correlates of morale among Canadian widowed persons. *Social Psychiatry, 22*, 65–72.

Hasher, L., & Zacks, R. (1979). Automatic and effortful processes in memory. *Journal of Experimental Psychology: General, 108*, 356–388.

Haskell, W. L., Camargo, C., Williams, P. T., Vranizan, K. M., Krauss, R. M., Lindgren, F. T., & Wood, P. D. (1984). The effect of cessation and resumption of moderate alcohol intake on serum high-density-lipoprotein subfractions. *New England Journal of Medicine, 310,* 805–810.

Havighurst, R. J. (1952). *Developmental Tasks and Education.* New York: David McKay Company, Inc.

Havighurst, R. J. (1982). The world of work. In B. B. Wolman (Ed.), *Handbook of Developmental Psychology* (pp. 771–787). Englewood Cliffs, NJ: Prentice Hall.

Havighurst, R. J., Neugarten, B. L., & Tobin, S. S. (1968). Disengagement and patterns of aging. In B. L. Neugarten (Ed.), *Middle Age and Aging* (pp. 161–172). Chicago: University of Chicago Press.

Hawkins, A. J., & Belsky, J. (1989). The role of father involvement in personality change in men across the transition to parenthood. *Family Relations, 38,* 378–384.

Hayes, M. P., Stinnett, N., & DeFrain, J. (1980). Learning about marriage from the divorced. *Journal of Divorce, 4,* 23–29.

Hayflick, L. (1975). Why grow old? *The Stanford Magazine, 3,* 36–43.

Hayslip, B. (1989). Alternative mechanisms for improvements in fluid ability performance among older adults. *Psychology and Aging, 4,* 122–124.

Hayslip, B., & Kennelly, K. J. (1985). Cognitive and noncognitive factors affecting learning among older adults. In D. B. Lumsden (Ed.), *The Older Adult as Learner: Aspects of Educational Gerontology* (pp. 73–98). New York: Hemisphere.

Hayslip, B., & Martin, C. (1988). Approaching death. In K. Esberger & S. Hughs (Eds.), *Nursing Care of the Aged.* Bowie, MD: Brady.

Hayslip, B., Schneider, L. J., & Bryant, K. (1989). Older women's perceptions of female counselors: The influence of therapist age and problem intimacy. *The Gerontologist, 29,* 239–244.

Hayslip, B., & Stewart-Bussey, D. (1986–1987). Locus of control—levels of death anxiety relationships. *Omega, 17,* 41–48.

Hayward, M. D., Grady, W. R., & McLaughlin, S. D. (1988). The retirement process among older women in the United States: Changes in the 1970's. *Research on Aging, 10,* 358–382.

Heckheimer, E. F. (1989). *Health Promotion of the Elderly in the Community.* Philadelphia: W. B. Saunders.

Heinemann, G. D. (1985). Negative health outcomes among the elderly: Predictors and profiles. *Research on Aging, 7,* 363–382.

Helson, R., & Moane, G. (1987). Personality change in women from college to midlife. *Journal of Personality and Social Psychology, 53,* 176–186.

Henderson, M. (1990). Beyond the living will. *The Gerontologist, 30,* 480–485.

Hendrick, S. S., Hendrick, C., & Adler, N. L. (1988). Romantic relationships: Love, satisfaction, and staying together. *Journal of Personality and Social Psychology, 54,* 980–988.

Herpel, S., & Straube, E. (1988). Assessment of occupational factors of influence on pregnancy. *Zentralbl-Gynakol, 110,* 516–522.

Herr, J. J., & Weakland, J. H. (1979). *Counseling Elders and their Families: Practical Techniques for Applied Gerontology.* New York: Springer.

Hershey, D. (1974). *Life-span and Factors Affecting It.* Springfield, IL: Charles C. Thomas.

Hertzog, C. (1989). Influences of cognitive slowing on age differences in intelligence. *Developmental Psychology, 25,* 636–651.

Hertzog, C., Dixon, R. A., & Hultsch, D. F. (1990). Relationships between metamemory, memory predictions, and memory task performance in adults. *Psychology and Aging, 5,* 215–227.

Hertzog, C., & Schaie, K. W. (1986). Stability and change in adult intelligence: 1. Analysis of longitudinal covariance structures. *Psychology and Aging, 1,* 159–171.

Hertzog, C., & Schaie, K. W. (1988). Stability and change in adult intelligence: 2. Simultaneous analysis of longitudinal means. *Psychology and Aging, 3,* 122–130.

Herzog, A. R., Kahn, R. L., Morgan, J. N., Jackson, J. S., & Antonucci, T. C. (1989). Age differences in productive activities. *Journal of Gerontology: Social Sciences, 44,* S129–138.

Herzog, A. R., & Rodgers, W. L. (1989). Age differences in memory performance and memory ratings as measured in a sample survey. *Psychology and Aging, 4,* 173–182.

Heston, L. L., & White, J. A. (1983). *Dementia: A Practical Guide to Alzheimer's Disease and Related Illnesses.* New York: W. H. Freeman.

Hickey, T. (1980). *Health and Aging.* Monterey, CA: Brooks/Cole Publishing Co.

High, D. M. (1988). All in the family: Extended autonomy and expectations in surrogate health care decision-making. *The Gerontologist, 28,* 46–52.

Hill, C. T., Peplau, L. A., & Rubin, Z. (1981). Differing perceptions in dating couples: Sex roles versus alternative explanations. *Psychology of Women Quarterly, 5*, 418–434.

Hill, R. (1968). Decision making and the family life cycle. In B. L. Neugarten (Ed.), *Middle Age and Aging* (pp. 286–295). Chicago: University of Chicago Press.

Hill, R. D., Evankovich, K. D., Sheikh, J. I., & Yesavage, J. A. (1987). Imagery mnemonic training in a patient with primary degenerative dementia. *Psychology and Aging, 2*, 204–205.

Hirsch, E. D., Jr. (1987). *Cultural Literacy: What Every American Needs to Know.* Boston: Houghton Mifflin.

Hochhausser, M. (1982). Learned helplessness and substance abuse in the elderly. In D. M. Petersen & F. J. Whittington (Eds.), *Drugs, Alcohol, and Aging.* Dubuque: Kendall/Hunt.

Hochman, L. O., Storandt, M., & Rosenberg, A. M. (1986). Age and its effect on psychopathology. *Psychology and Aging, 1*, 337–338.

Hoffman, L. W. (1987). The value of children to parents and childrearing patterns. In C. Kagitcibasi (Ed.), *Growth and Progress in Cross-cultural Psychology* (pp. 159–170). Lisse: Swets & Zeitlinger.

Holahan, C. K. (1988). Relation of life goals at age 70 to activity participation and health and psychological well-being among Terman's gifted men and women. *Psychology and Aging, 3*, 286–291.

Holden, C. (1981). Human-animal relationship under scrutiny. *Science, 214*, 418–420.

Holland, J. L. (1973). *Making Vocational Choices: A Theory of Careers.* Englewood Cliffs, NJ: Prentice Hall.

Holmes, T. H., & Rahe, R. H. (1976). The social readjustment rating scale. *Journal of Psychosomatic Research, 11*, 213.

Hooper, F. H., Fitzgerald, J., & Papalia, D. (1971). Piagetian theory and the aging process: Extensions and speculations. *Aging and Human Development, 2*, 3–20.

Hooper, F. H., & Sheehan, N. W. (1977). Logical concept attainment during the aging years: Issues in the neo-Piagetian research literature. In W. F. Overton & J. Gallagher (Eds.), *Knowledge and Development. Vol 1: Advances in Research and Theory* (pp. 205–253). New York: Plenum.

Horn, J. L. (1970). Organization of data on life-span development of human abilities. In L. R. Goulet & P. B. Baltes (Eds.), *Life Span Developmental Psychology: Research and Theory* (pp. 424–467). New York: Academic Press.

Horn, J. L. (1982). The aging of human abilities. In B. B. Wolman (Ed.), *Handbook of Developmental Psychology* (pp. 847–870). Englewood Cliffs, NJ: Prentice Hall.

Horn, J. L., & Cattell, R. B. (1966). Refinement and test of the theory of fluid and crystallized intelligences. *Journal of Educational Psychology, 57*, 253–270.

Horn, J. L., & Cattell, R. B. (1967). Age differences in fluid and crystallized intelligence. *Acta Psychologica, 26*, 107–129.

Horn, J. L., & Donaldson, G. (1976). On the myth of intellectual decline in adulthood. *American Psychologist, 31*, 701–719.

Horn, J. L., & Donaldson, G. (1977). Faith is not enough: A response to the Baltes-Schaie claim that intelligence does not wane. *American Psychologist, 32*, 369–373.

Hornblum, J. N., & Overton, W. F. (1976). Area and volume conservation among the elderly: Assessment and training. *Developmental Psychology, 12*, 68–74.

Horne, H. L., Lowe, J. D., & Murray, P. D. (1990, August). *Anxiety of young adults over expected caregiver role.* Paper presented at the annual meeting of the American Psychological Association, Boston, MA.

Horner, K. J., Rushton, P., & Vernon, P. A. (1986). Relation between age and research productivity of academic psychologists. *Psychology and Aging, 1*, 319–324.

Horowitz, A. (1985). Sons and daughters as caregivers to older parents: Differences in role performance and consequences. *The Gerontologist, 25*, 612–617.

Houseknecht, S. K. (1987). Voluntary childlessness. In M. B. Sussman & S. K. Steinmetz (Eds.), *Handbook of Marriage and the Family* (pp. 369–395). New York: Plenum Press.

Howell, F. M., & Frese, W. (1982). *Making Life Plans: Race, Gender and Career Decisions.* Washington, DC: University Press of America.

Howes, J. L., & Katz, A. N. (1988). Assessing remote memory with an improved public events questionnaire. *Psychology and Aging, 3*, 142–151.

Hudson, R. B. (1987). Tomorrow's able elders: Implications for the state. *The Gerontologist, 27*, 405–409.

Hulicka, I. M. (1967). Age differences in retention as a function of interference. *Journal of Gerontology, 22*, 180–184.

Hulicka, I., & Grossman, J. (1967). Age group comparisons for the use of mediators in paired-associate learning. *Journal of Gerontology, 22*, 46–51.

Hultsch, D. (1969). Adult age differences in the organization of free recall. *Developmental Psychology, 1*, 673–678.

Hultsch, D. F., & Dixon, R. A. (1990). Learning and memory in aging. In J. E. Birren & K. W. Schaie (Eds.), *Handbook of the Psychology of Aging* (3rd ed.). (pp. 259–274). San Diego: Academic Press.

Hultsch, D. F., Hertzog, C., & Dixon, R. A. (1990). Ability correlates of memory performance in adulthood and aging. *Psychology and Aging, 5*, 356–368.

Hunt, M. E., & Ross, L. E. (1990). Naturally occurring retirement communities: A multiattribute examination of desirability factors. *The Gerontologist, 30*, 667–674.

Huyck, M. H. (1982). From gregariousness to intimacy: Marriage and friendship over the adult years. In T. M. Field, A. Huston, H. C. Quay, L. Troll, & G. E. Finley (Eds.), *Review of Human Development* (pp. 471–484). New York: Wiley.

Ihinger-Tallman, M. (1986). Member adjustment in single parent families: Theory building. *Family Relations, 35*, 215–221.

Immarino, N. K. (1975). Relationship between death anxiety and demographic variables. *Psychological Reports, 17*, 262.

Ivancevich, J. M., & Matteson, M. T. (1988). Type A behavior and the healthy individual. *British Journal of Medical Psychology, 61*, 37–56.

Jackson, J. S., Antonucci, T. C., & Gibson, R. C. (1990). Cultural, racial, and ethnic minority influences on aging. In J. E. Birren & K. W. Schaie (Eds.), *Handbook of the Psychology of Aging* (3rd ed.). (pp. 103–123). San Diego: Academic Press.

Jackson, J. J., & Perry, C. (1989). Physical health conditions of middle-aged and aged blacks. In K. S. Markides (Ed.), *Aging and Health: Perspectives on Gender, Race, Ethnicity, and Class* (pp. 111–176). Newbury Park, CA: Sage Publications.

Jackson, P. R., Stafford, E. M., Bands, M. H., & Warr, P. B. (1983). Unemployment and psychological distress among young people: The moderating role of employment commitment. *Journal of Applied Psychology, 68*, 525–535.

Jacobs, B. (1990). Aging and politics. In R. H. Binstock & L. K. George (Eds.), *Handbook of Aging and the Social Sciences* (3rd ed.). (pp. 349–361). San Diego: Academic Press.

Jacobs, D., Ancoli-Israel, S., Parker, L., & Kripke, D. F. (1989). Twenty-four hour sleep-wake patterns in a nursing home population. *Psychology and Aging, 4*, 352–357.

Jacobson, N. S., & Martin, B. (1976). Behavioral marriage therapy: Current status. *Psychological Bulletin, 83*, 540–566.

Jain, H. C., & Sloane, P. J. (1981). *Equal Employment Issues: Race and Sex Discrimination in the United States, Canada, and Britain*. New York: Praeger.

Jarvik, L. F., & Perl, M. (1981). Overview of physiologic dysfunction and the production of psychiatric problems in the elderly. In A. Levenson & R. C. W. Hall (Eds.), *Psychiatric Management of Physical Disease in the Elderly* (pp. 1–15). New York: Raven.

Jenner, J. R. (1983). Correlates of career choices of women volunteers. *Psychological Reports, 53*, 1135–1142.

Jenner, J. R. (1982). Participation, leadership, and the role of volunteerism among selected women volunteers. *Journal of Voluntary Action Research, 11*, 27–38.

Jin, H., Zhang, M., Qu, O., Wang, Z., Salmon, D. P., Katzman, R., Grant, I., Liu, W. T., & Yu, E. S. H. (1989). Cross-cultural studies of dementia: Use of a Chinese version of the Blessed-Roth Information-Memory-Concentration test in a Shanghai dementia survey. *Psychology and Aging, 4*, 471–479.

John, R. (1985). Service needs and support networks of elderly native Americans: Family, friends, and social service agencies. In W. A. Peterson & J. Quadagno (Eds.), *Social Bonds in Later Life* (pp. 229–247). Beverly Hills, CA: Sage Publications.

Johnson, C. L. (1985). The impact of illness on late-life marriages. *Journal of Marriage and the Family, 47*, 165–172.

Johnson, D. (1990). Animal rights and human lives: Time for scientists to right the balance. *Psychological Science, 1*, 213–214.

Johnson, D. R., & Booth, A. (1990). Rural economic decline and marital quality: A panel study of farm marriages. *Family Relations, 39*, 159–165.

Jones, D. C., & Vaughn, K. (1990). Close friendships among senior adults. *Psychology and aging, 5,* 451–457.

Jones, H. E. (1977). On the justifiability of reverse discrimination. In B. R. Gross (Ed.), *Reverse Discrimination* (pp. 348–357). Buffalo: Prometheus Books.

Kahn, R. L. (1975). The mental health system and the future aged. *The Gerontologist, 15,* 24–31.

Kalish, R. A. (1985). The social context of death and dying. In R. H. Binstock & E. Shanas (Eds.), *Handbook of Aging and the Social Sciences* (2nd ed.). (pp. 149–170). New York: Van Nostrand Reinhold.

Kalish, R. A., & Reynolds, D. (1976). *Death and Ethnicity: A Psychocultural Study.* Los Angeles: University of Southern California Press.

Kane, R. L., & Kane, R. A. (1990). Health care for older people: Organizational and policy issues. In R. H. Binstock & L. K. George (Eds.), *Handbook of Aging and the Social Sciences* (3rd ed.). (pp. 415–437). San Diego: Academic Press.

Kane, R. L, Solomon, D. H., Beck, J. C., Keeler, E., & Kane, R. A. (1981). *Geriatrics in the United States: Manpower Projections and Training Considerations.* Lexington, MA: Heath.

Kaplan, M. (1983a). The issue of sex bias in DSM-III. *American Psychologist, 38,* 802–803.

Kaplan, M. (1983b). A woman's view of DSM-III. *American Psychologist, 38,* 786–792.

Karp, D. A. (1989). The social construction of retirement among professionals 50–60 years old. *The Gerontologist, 29,* 750–760.

Kastenbaum, R. (1978). Death, dying and bereavement in old age: New developments and their possible implications for psychosocial care. *Aged Care and Services Review, 1,* 1–10.

Kastenbaum, R. (1985). Dying and death: A life-span approach. In J. E. Birren & K. W. Schaie (Eds.), *Handbook of the Psychology of Aging* (2nd ed.). (pp. 619–643). New York: Van Nostrand Reinhold.

Kastenbaum, R., & Costa, P. (1977). Psychological perspectives on death. *Annual review of psychology, 28,* 225–249.

Kausler, D. H. (1989). Impairments in normal memory aging: Implications of laboratory evidence. In G. C. Gilmore (Ed.), *Memory, Aging, and Dementia: Theory, Assessment, and Treatment.* New York: Springer.

Keefe, T. (1984). The stresses of unemployment. *Social Work, 29,* 264–268.

Keith, J. (1982). *Old People as People: Social and Cultural Influences on Aging and Old Age.* Boston: Little, Brown & Co.

Keith, J. (1990). Age in social and cultural context: Anthropological perspectives. In R. H. Binstock & L. K. George (Eds.), *Handbook of Aging and the Social Sciences* (3rd ed.). (pp. 91–111). San Diego: Academic Press.

Keith, P. M. (1979). Life changes and perceptions of life and death among older men and women. *Journal of Gerontology, 34,* 870–878.

Keith, P. M. (1986). The social context and resources of the unmarried in old age. *International Journal of Aging and Human Development, 23,* 81–96.

Kelly, E. L. (1955). Consistency of the adult personality. *American Psychologist, 10,* 659–681.

Kelly, J. B. (1982). Divorce: The adult perspective. In B. B. Wolman (Ed.), *Handbook of Developmental Psychology* (pp. 734–750). Englewood Cliffs, NJ: Prentice Hall.

Kendig, H. L. (1990). Comparative perspectives on housing, aging, and social structure. In R. H. Binstock & L. K. George (Eds.), *Handbook of Aging and the Social Sciences* (pp. 288–306). San Diego: Academic Press.

Kendig, H. L., Coles, R., Pittelkow, Y., & Wilson, S. (1988). Confidants and family structure in old age. *Journal of Gerontology: Social Sciences, 43,* S31–40.

Kennedy, G. E. (1990). College students' expectations of grandparent and grandchild role behaviors. *The Gerontologist, 30,* 43–48.

Kenshalo, D. R. (1977). Age changes in touch, vibration, temperature, kinesthesis, and pain sensitivity. In J. E. Birren & K. W. Schaie (Eds.), *Handbook of the Psychology of Aging* (pp. 562–579). New York: Academic Press.

Kermis, M. D. (1986). The epidemiology of mental disorder in the elderly: A response to the Senate/AARP report. *The Gerontologist, 26,* 482–487.

Kilty, K. M., & Behling, J. M. (1986). Retirement financial planning among professional workers. *The Gerontologist, 26,* 525–530.

Kinney, J. M., & Stephens, M. A. P. (1989). Hassles and uplifts of giving care to a family member with dementia. *Psychology and Aging, 4,* 402–408.

Kinney, J. M., Stephens, M. A. P., Ogrocki, P. K., & Bridges, A. M. (1989, November). *Daily hassles and well-being among caregivers to older adults with dementia: The in-home versus nursing home experience.* Paper presented at the annual meeting of the Gerontological Society of America, Minneapolis, MN.

Kitson, G. C., & Raschke, H. J. (1981). Divorce research: What we know, what we need to know. *Journal of Divorce, 4,* 1–38.

Kivnick, H. Q. (1982a). Grandparenthood: An overview of meaning and mental health. *The Gerontologist, 22,* 59–66.

Kivnick, H. Q. (1982b). *The Meaning of Grandparenthood.* Ann Arbor: UMI Research Press.

Kivnick, H. Q. (1985). Grandparenthood and mental health: Meaning, behavior, and satisfaction. In V. L. Bengtson & J. F. Robertson (Eds.), *Grandparenthood* (pp. 151–158). Beverly Hills, CA: Sage.

Kleban, M. H., Brody, E. M., Schoonover, C. B., & Hoffman, C. (1989). Family help to the elderly: Perceptions of sons-in-law regarding parent care. *Journal of Marriage and the Family, 51,* 303–312.

Kleemeier, R. W. (1962). Intellectual change in the senium. *Proceedings of the Social Statistics Section of the American Statistical Association,* 290–295.

Kline, D. W., & Scheiber, F. (1985). Vision and aging. In J. E. Birren & K. W. Schaie (Eds.), *Handbook of the Psychology of Aging* (2nd ed.). (pp. 296–331). New York: Van Nostrand Reinhold.

Koenig, H. G., George, L. K., & Siegler, I. C. (1988). The use of religion and other emotion-regulating coping strategies among older adults. *The Gerontologist, 28,* 303–310.

Koenig, H. G., Kvale, J. N., & Ferrel, C. (1988). Religion and well-being in later life. *The Gerontologist, 28,* 18–28.

Koh, J. Y., & Bell, W. G. (1987). Korean elders in the United States: Intergenerational relations and living arrangements. *The Gerontologist, 27,* 66–71.

Kohlberg, L. (1963). The development of children's orientation toward a moral order: A sequence in the development of moral thought. *Vita Humana, 6,* 11–33.

Kohlberg, L. (1970). Continuities in childhood and adult moral development revisited. In P. B. Baltes & K. W. Schaie (Eds.), *Life-span Developmental Psychology: Personality and Socialization* (pp. 179–204). New York: Academic Press.

Kohlberg, L., Levine, C., & Hewer, A. (1983). Moral stages: A current formulation and a response to critics. *Contributions to Human Development, 10.*

Kosnik, W., Winslow, L., Kline, D., Rasinski, K., & Sekuler, R. (1988). Visual changes in daily life throughout adulthood. *Journal of Gerontology: Psychological Sciences, 43,* P63–P70.

Kotlikoff, L. J., & Sumners, L. H. (1981). The role of intergenerational transfers in aggregate capital accumulation. *Journal of Political Economy, 89,* 706–732.

Krause, N. (1990). Illness behavior in later life. In R. H. Binstock & L. K. George (Eds.), *Handbook of Aging and the Social Sciences* (3rd ed.). (pp. 227–244). San Diego: Academic Press.

Krause, N., & Van Tran, T. (1989). Stress and religious involvement among older Blacks. *Journal of Gerontology: Social Sciences, 44,* S4–13.

Krauss, I., Poon, L. W., Gilewski, M., & Schaie, K. W. (1982). Effects of biased sampling on cognitive performances. *The Gerontologist, 22,* 104.

Kübler-Ross, E. (1969). *On Death and Dying.* New York Macmillan.

Kübler-Ross, E. (1974). *Questions and Answers on Death and Dying.* New York: Macmillan.

Kunitz, S. J., & Levy, J. E. (1989). Aging and health among Navaho Indians. In K. S. Markides (Ed.), *Aging and Health: Perspectives on Gender, Race, Ethnicity, and Class* (pp. 211–246). Newbury Park, CA: Sage Publications.

Labouvie-Vief, G. (1980). Adaptive dimensions of adult cognition. In N. Datan & N. Lohmann (Eds.), *Transitions of Aging* (pp. 3–26). New York: Academic Press.

Labouvie-Vief, G. (1982). Discontinuities in development from childhood to adulthood: A cognitive-developmental view. In T. M. Field, A. Huston, H. C. Quay, L. Troll, & G. E. Finley (Eds.), *Review of Human Development* (pp. 447–455). New York: Wiley.

Labouvie-Vief, G. (1985). Intelligence and cognition. In J. E. Birren & K. W. Schaie (Eds.), *Handbook of the Psychology of Aging* (2nd ed.). (pp. 500–530). New York: Van Nostrand Reinhold.

Labouvie-Vief, G., & Hakim-Larson, J. (1989). Developmental shifts in adult thought. In S. Hunter & M. Sundel (Eds.), *Midlife Myths: Issues, Findings, and Practice Implications* (pp. 69–96). Newbury Park: Sage Publications.

Lago, D., Connell, C. M., & Knight, B. (1983). Initial evaluation of PACT (People and Animals Coming Together): A companion animal program for community-dwelling older persons. In M. Smyer & M. Gatz (Eds.), *Mental Health and Aging: Programs and Evaluations*. Beverly Hills, CA: Sage.

LaGreca, A. J., Akers, R. L., & Dwyer, J. W. (1988). Life events and alcohol behavior among older adults. *The Gerontologist, 28*, 552–558.

Lamy, P. P. (1988). Actions of alcohol and drugs in older people. *Generations, 7*, 9–13.

Landers, S. (1989, April). Scientists take stand for animal research. *The APA Monitor*, pp. 1, 4.

LaRue, A., Dessonville, C., & Jarvik, L. F. (1985). Aging and mental disorders. In J. E. Birren & K. W. Schaie (Eds.), *Handbook of the Psychology of Aging* (2nd ed.). (pp. 664–702). New York: Van Nostrand Reinhold.

Lasoski, M. C., & Thelen, M. H. (1987). Attitudes of older and middle-aged persons toward mental health intervention. *The Gerontologist, 27*, 288–292.

Lauerson, N., & Whitney, S. (1977). *It's Your Body: A Woman's Guide to Gynecology*. New York: Grosset & Dunlap.

Lawton, M. P. (1980). *Environment and Aging*. Monterey, CA: Brooks/Cole.

Lawton, M. P., Brody, E. M., & Sapirstein, A. R. (1989). A controlled study of respite service for caregivers of Alzheimer's patients. *The Gerontologist, 29*, 8–16.

Lawton, M. P., & Cohen, J. (1974). The generality of housing impact on the well-being of older people. *Journal of Gerontology, 29*, 194–204.

Lawton, M. P., & Hoffman, C. (1984). Neighborhood reactions to elderly housing. *The Gerontologist, 24*, 41–53.

Lawton, M. P., & Nahemow, L. (1973). Ecology of the aging process. In C. Eisdorfer & M. P. Lawton (Eds.), *The Psychology of Adult Development and Aging* (pp. 619–674). Washington, DC: American Psychological Association.

Lazarus, R. S. (1981). Little hassles can be hazardous to your health. *Psychology Today, 15*, 58–62.

Leaf, P. J., Berkman, C. S., Weissman, M. M., Holzer, C. E., Tischler, G. L., & Myers, J. K. (1988). The epidemiology of late-life depression. In J. A. Brody & G. L. Maddox (Eds.), *Epidemiology and Aging: An International Perspective* (pp. 117–133). New York: Springer.

Lebowitz, B. D. (1987). Correlates of success in community mental health programs for the elderly. *Hospital and Community Psychiatry, 39*, 721–722.

Lebowitz, B. D., Light, E., & Bailey, F. (1988). Mental health center services for the elderly: The impact of coordination with area agencies on aging. *The Gerontologist, 27*, 699–702.

Lebra, T. S. (1976). *Japanese Patterns of Behavior*. Honolulu: The University Press of Hawaii.

Lee, A. T., & Cerami, A. (1990). Modifications of proteins and nucleic acids by reducing sugars: Possible role in aging. In E. L. Schneider & J. W. Rowe (Eds.), *Handbook of the Biology of Aging* (3rd ed.). (pp. 116–130). San Diego: Academic Press.

Lee, G. R. (1988). Marital satisfaction in later life: The effects of nonmarital roles. *Journal of Marriage and the Family, 50*, 775–783.

Lee, G. R., & Ellithorpe, E. (1982). Intergenerational exchange and subjective well-being among the elderly. *Journal of Marriage and the Family, 44*, 217–224.

Lee, G. R., & Shehan, C. L. (1989). Social relations and the self-esteem of older persons. *Research on Aging, 11*, 427–442.

Lee, T. R., Mancini, J. A., & Maxwell, J. W. (1990). Sibling relationships in adulthood: Contact patterns and motivations. *Journal of Marriage and the Family, 52*, 431–440.

Leffler, A., Krannich, R. S., & Gillespie, D. L. (1986). Contact, support, and friction: Three faces of networks in community life. *Sociological Perspectives, 29*, 337–355.

Lehman, H. C. (1953). *Age and Achievement*. Philadelphia: American Philosophical Society.

Lehmann, H. E. (1982). Affective disorders in the aged. In L. F. Jarvik & G. W. Small (Eds.), *The Psychiatric Clinics of North America* (pp. 27–44). Philadelphia: W. B. Saunders.

Lehr, U. (1984). The role of women in the family generation context. In V. Garms-Homolova, E. M. Hoerning, & D. Schaeffer (Eds.), *Intergenerational Relationships* (pp. 125–132). Lewiston, NY: C. J. Hogrefe.

Leifer, M. (1977). Psychological changes accompanying pregnancy and motherhood. *Genetic Psychology Monographs, 95*, 55–96.

Leigh, G. K. (1982). Kinship interaction over the family life span. *Journal of Marriage and the Family, 44*, 197–208.

Lerner, R. M. (1990). Plasticity, person-context relations, and cognitive training in the aged years: A developmental contextual perspective. *Developmental Psychology, 26*, 911–915.

Levine, C., Kohlberg, L., & Hewer, A. (1985). The current formulation of Kohlberg's theory and a response to critics. *Human Development, 28*, 94–100.

Levinson, D. J. (1986). A conception of adult development. *American Psychologist, 41*, 3–13.

Levinson, D. J., Darrow, C. N., Klein, E. B., Levinson, M. H., & McKee, B. (1978). *The Seasons of a Man's Life*. New York: Knopf.

Lewirsohn, P. M. (1975). The behavioral study and treatment of depression. In M. Herson, R. M. Eisler, & P. M. Miller (Eds.), *Progress in Behavior Modification, Vol. 1* (pp. 19–64). New York: Academic Press.

Lewinsohn, P. M., Fenn, D. S., Stanton, A. K., & Franklin, J. (1986). Relation of age of onset to duration of episode in unipolar depression. *Psychology and Aging, 1*, 63–68.

Lewis, M. A., Cretin, S., & Kane, R. L. (1985). The natural history of nursing home patients. *The Gerontologist, 25*, 382–388.

Liem, R., & Liem, J. H. (1988). The psychological effects of unemployment on workers and their families. *Journal of Social Issues, 44*, 87–105.

Liese, L. H., Snowden, L. R., & Ford, L. K. (1989). Partner status, social support, & psychological adjustment during pregnancy. *Family Relations, 38*, 311–316.

Lipsman, C. K. (1967). Maslow's theory of needs in relation to vocational choice for lower socioeconomic levels. *Vocational Guidance Quarterly, 15*, 283–288.

Litz, B. T., Zeiss, A. M., & Davies, H. D. (1990). Sexual concerns of male spouses of female Alzheimer's Disease patients. *The Gerontologist, 30*, 113–116.

Liu, K., Doty, P., & Manton, K. (1990). Medicaid spenddown in nursing homes. *The Gerontologist, 30*, 7–15.

LoCasio, R. (1967). Continuity and discontinuity in vocational development theory. *Personnel and Guidance Journal, 46*, 32–36.

Logan, R. D. (1986). A reconceptualization of Erikson's theory: The repetition of existential and instrumental themes. *Human Development, 29*, 125–136.

Long, G. M., & Crambert, R. F. (1990). The nature and basis of age-related change in dynamic visual acuity. *Psychology and Aging, 5*, 138–143.

Lopata, H. Z. (1979). *Women as Widows: Support Systems*. New York: Elsevier.

Love, D. O., & Torrence, W. D. (1989). The impact of worker age on unemployment and earnings after plant closings. *Journal of Gerontology: Social Sciences, 44*, S190–195.

Lowenthal, M. F., & Chiriboga, D. (1972). Transition to the empty nest. *Archives of General Psychiatry, 26*, 8–14.

Lowenthal, M. F., & Haven, C. (1968). Interaction and adaptation: Intimacy as a critical variable. In B. L. Neugarten (Ed.), *Middle Age and Aging* (pp. 390–400). Chicago: University of Chicago Press.

Lowenthal, M. F., Thurnher, J., Chiriboga, D., & Associates. (1975). *Four Stages of Life*. San Francisco: Jossey-Bass.

Lown, J. M., McFadden, J. R., & Crossman, S. M. (1989). Family life education for remarriage focus on financial management. *Family Relations, 38*, 40–45.

Lubin, B., Larsen, R. M., & Mattarazzo, J. D. (1984). Patterns of psychological tests usage in the United States: 1935–1982. *American Psychologist, 39*, 451–454.

Lund, D., Caserta, M. S., & Dimond, M. F. (1986). Gender differences through two years of bereavement among the elderly. *The Gerontologist, 26*, 314–320.

Lund, D. A., Dimond, M. S., Caserta, M. F., Johnson, R. J., Poulton, J. L., & Connelly, J. R. (1985–1986). Identifying elderly with coping difficulties after two years of bereavement. *Omega, 16*, 213–224.

Maas, H. S. (1989). Social responsibility in middle age: Prospects and preconditions. In S. Hunter & M. Sundel (Eds.), *Midlife Myths: Issues, Findings, and Practice Implications* (pp. 253–271). Newbury Park, CA: Sage Publications.

Maas, J. W. (1978). Clinical and biochemical heterogeneity of depressive disorders. *Annals of Internal Medicine, 88*, 556–563.

MacDermid, S. M., Huston, T. L., & McHale, S. M. (1990). Changes in marriage associated with the transition to parenthood: Individual differences as a function of sex-role attitudes and changes in the division of household labor. *Journal of Marriage and the Family, 52*, 475–486.

Mace, N. L., & Rabins, P. V. (1981). *The 36-hour Day*. Baltimore: Johns Hopkins University Press.

Macklin, E. D. (1978). Non-marital heterosexual cohabitation: A review of research. *Marriage and Family Review, 1*, 1–12.

Macklin, E. D. (1980). Nontraditional family forms: A decade of research. *Journal of Marriage and the Family, 42*, 175–192.

Macklin, E. D. (1982). Nonmarital heterosexual cohabitation. *Marriage and Family Review, 1*, 1–12.

Macklin, E. D. (1987). Nontraditional family forms. In M. B. Sussman & S. K. Steinmetz (Eds.), *Handbook of Marriage and the Family* (pp. 317–353). New York: Plenum Press.

Madden, D. J. (1990). Adult age differences in the time course of visual attention. *Journal of Gerontology: Psychological Sciences, 45*, P9–P17.

Maddox, G. L. (1963). Activity and morale: A longitudinal study of selected elderly subjects. *Social Forces, 42*, 195–204.

Maddox, G. L. (1965). Fact and artifact: Evidence bearing on disengagement theory from the Duke geriatric project. *Human Development, 8*, 117–130.

Maeda, D. (1983). Family care in Japan. *The Gerontologist, 23*, 579–583.

Mancini, J. A., & Blieszner, R. (1989). Aging parents and adult children: Research themes in intergenerational relations. *Journal of Marriage and the Family, 51*, 275–290.

Mandel, R. G., & Johnson, N. S. (1984). A developmental analysis of story recall and comprehension in adulthood. *Journal of Verbal Learning and Verbal Behavior, 23*, 643–659.

Mangum, W. P. (1988). Community resistance to planned housing for the elderly: Ageism or general antipathy to group housing? *The Gerontologist, 28*, 325–329.

Manning, C. A., Hall, J. L., & Gold, P. E. (1990). Glucose effects on memory and other neuropsychological tests in elderly humans. *Psychological Science, 1*, 307–311.

Manton, K. G., Blazer, D. G., & Woodbury, M. A. (1987). Suicide in middle and later life: Sex and race specific life table and cohort analyses. *Journal of Gerontology, 42*, 219–227.

Many doctors favor end of life-support gear in some cases. (1988, June). *Wall Street Journal*, p. 95.

Marciano, T. D. (1985). Homosexual marriage and parenthood should not be allowed. In H. Feldman & M. Feldman (Eds.), *Current Controversies in Marriage and Family* (pp. 293–302). Beverly Hills: Sage Publications.

Markides, K. S. (1983). Age, religiosity, and adjustment: A longitudinal analysis. *Journal of Gerontology, 38*, 621–625.

Markides, K. S. (Ed.). (1989). *Aging and Health: Perspectives on Gender, Race, Ethnicity, and Class*. Newbury Park, CA: Sage Publications.

Markides, K. S., Coreil, J., & Rogers, L. P. (1989). Aging and health among Southwestern Hispanics. In K. S. Markides (Ed.), *Aging and Health: Perspectives on Gender, Race, Ethnicity, and Class* (pp. 177–210). Newbury Park, CA: Sage Publications.

Markides, K. S., Levin, J. S., & Ray, L. A. (1987). Religion, aging, and life satisfaction: An eight-year, three-wave longitudinal study. *The Gerontologist, 27*, 660–665.

Markides, K. S., & Mindel, C. H. (1987). *Aging and Ethnicity*. Newbury Park, CA: Sage Publications.

Marks, S. R. (1989). Toward a systems theory of marital quality. *Journal of Marriage and the Family, 51*, 15–26.

Marsh, G. R., & Thompson, L. W. (1977). Psychophysiology of aging. In J. E. Birren & K. W. Schaie (Eds.), *Handbook of the Psychology of Aging* (pp. 219–248). New York: Van Nostrand Reinhold.

Marshall, V. W. (1975). Age and awareness of finitude in developmental gerontology. *Omega, 6*, 113–129.

Marshall, V. W. (1980). *Last Chapters: A Sociology of Aging and Dying*. Monterey, CA: Brooks/Cole.

Marshall, V. W., & Levy, J. A. (1990). Aging and dying. In R. H. Binstock & L. K. George (Eds.), *Handbook of Aging and the Social Sciences* (3rd ed.). (pp. 245–260). San Diego: Academic Press.

Martin, M. (1988). *Filial Responsibility in Three Generation Families: The Influence of Gender and*

Generation. Unpublished doctoral dissertation, University of Southern California, Los Angeles.

Martocchio, J. J. (1989). Age-related differences in employee absenteeism: A meta-analysis. *Psychology and Aging, 4,* 409–414.

Masters, W. H., & Johnson, V. E. (1966). *Human Sexual Response*. Boston: Little, Brown & Co.

Masters, W. H., & Johnson, V. E. (1970). *Human Sexual Inadequacy*. Boston: Little, Brown & Co.

Masters, W. H., Johnson, V. E., & Kolodny, R. C. (1985). *Human Sexuality*. Boston: Little, Brown & Co.

Matarazzo, J. D. (1972). *Wechsler's Measurement and Appraisal of Adult Intelligence* (5th ed.). New York: Oxford University Press.

Matlin, M. W. (1988). *Sensation and Perception*. Boston: Allyn & Bacon.

Matthews, M. A. (1987). Widowhood as an expectable life event. In V. W. Marshall (Ed.), *Aging in Canada: Social Perspectives* (2nd ed.). (pp. 343–366). Markham, ON: Fitzhenry & Whiteside.

Matthews, A. M., & Brown, K. H. (1987). Retirement as a critical life event: The differential experiences of men and women. *Research on Aging, 9,* 548–571.

Matthews, S. H., Werkner, J. E., & Delaney, P. J. (1989). Relative contributions of help by employed and nonemployed sisters to their elderly parents. *Journal of Gerontology: Social Sciences, 44,* S36–44.

May, K. A., & Perrin, S. P. (1985). Prelude: Pregnancy and birth. In S. M. H. Hanson & F. W. Bozett (Eds.), *Dimensions of Fatherhood* (pp. 64–91). Beverly Hills: Sage Publications.

Mazess, R. B., & Forman, S. H. (1979). Longevity and age exaggeration in Vilacamba, Ecuador. *Journal of Gerontology, 34,* 94–98.

McAdams, D. P., Ruetzel, K., & Foley, J. M. (1986). Complexity and generativity at mid-life: Relations among social motives, ego development, and adults' plans for the future. *Journal of Personality and Social Psychology, 50,* 800–807.

McCann, I. L., & Holmes, D. S. (1984). Influence of aerobic exercise on depression. *Journal of Personality and Social Psychology, 46,* 1142–1147.

McColloch, B. J. (1990). The relationship of intergenerational reciprocity of aid to the morale of older parents: Equity and exchange theory comparisons. *Journal of Gerontology: Social Sciences, 45,* S150–155.

McConnell, S. R. (1983). Retirement and employment. In D. S. Woodruff & J. E. Birren (Eds.), *Aging: Scientific Perspectives and Social Issues* (2nd ed.). (pp. 333–350). Monterey, CA: Brooks/Cole.

McCrae, R. R., & Costa, P. T. (1984). *Emerging Lives, Enduring Dispositions: Personality in Adulthood*. Boston: Little, Brown & Co.

McCrae, R. R., Costa, P. T., & Arenberg, D. (1980). Constancy of adult personality structure in males: Longitudinal, cross-sectional, and time-of-measurement analyses. *Journal of Gerontology, 35,* 877–883.

McDowd, J. M., & Birren, J. E. (1990). Aging and attentional processes. In J. E. Birren & K. W. Schaie (Eds.), *Handbook of the Psychology of Aging* (3rd ed.). (pp. 222–233). San Diego: Academic Press.

McEvoy, C. L., & Patterson, R. L. (1986). Behavioral treatment of deficit skills in dementia patients. *The Gerontologist, 26,* 475–478.

McFarland, R. A. (1968). The sensory and perceptual processes in aging. In K. W. Schaie (Ed.), *Theory and Methods of Research on Aging* (pp. 9–52). Morgantown, WV: West Virginia University Press.

McKim, M. K. (1987). Transition to what? New parents' problems in the first year. *Family Relations, 36,* 22–25.

McLanahan, S., & Booth, K. (1989). Mother-only families: Problems, prospects, and politics. *Journal of Marriage and the Family, 51,* 557–580.

Medvedev, Z. A. (1974). Caucasus and Altay longevity: A biological or social problem. *The Gerontologist, 14,* 381–387.

Meeks, S., Carstensen, L. L., Stafford, P. B., Brenner, L. L., Weathers, F., Welch, R., & Oltmanns, T. F. (1990). Mental health needs of the chronically mentally ill. *Psychology and Aging, 5,* 163–171.

Menaghan, E. (1983). Marital stress and family transitions: A panel analysis. *Journal of Marriage and the Family, 45,* 371–386.

Menninger, K. A. (1953). *The Human Mind*. New York: Knopf.

Mercier, J. M., Paulson, L., & Morris, E. W. (1989). Proximity as a mediating influence on the perceived aging parent-adult child relationship. *The Gerontologist, 29,* 785–791.

Metzger, A. M. (1979–1980). A Q-methodological study of the Kübler-Ross stage theory. *Omega, 10,* 291–301.

Meyer, B. J. F., & Rice, G. E. (1981). Information recalled from prose by young, middle, and old adults. *Experimental Aging Research, 7,* 253–268.

Miernyk, W. H. (1975). The changing life cycle of work. In N. Datan & L. H. Ginsberg (Eds.), *Lifespan Developmental Psychology: Normative Life Crises* (pp. 279–286). New York: Academic Press.

Miller, B. (1990). Gender differences in spouse caregiver strain: Socialization and role explanations. *Journal of Marriage and the Family, 52,* 311–321.

Miller, B., & Montgomery, A. (1990). Family caregivers and limitations in social activities. *Research on Aging, 12,* 72–93.

Miller, D. B., Lowenstein, R., & Winston, R. (1976). Physicians' attitudes toward the ill aged and nursing homes. *Journal of the American Geriatrics Society, 24,* 498–505.

Miller, M. J. (1983). The role of happenstance in career choice. *Vocational Guidance Quarterly, 32,* 16–20.

Miller, P. H. (1983). *Theories of Developmental Psychology.* San Francisco: W. H. Freeman.

Mishara, B. L., & Kastenbaum, R. (1980). *Alcohol and Old Age.* New York: Grune & Stratton.

Mitchell, B. A., Wister, A. V., & Burch, T. K. (1989). The family environment and leaving the parental home. *Journal of Marriage and the Family, 51,* 605–613.

Mitchell, J., & Register, J. C. (1984). An exploration of family interaction with the elderly by race, socioeconomic status, and residence. *The Gerontologist, 24,* 48–54.

Mitchell, O. S., Levine, P. B., & Pozzebon, S. (1988). Retirement differences by industry and occupation. *The Gerontologist, 28,* 545–551.

Mitford, J. (1983). *The American Way of Death.* New York: Simon & Schuster.

Moberg, D. O. (1968). Religiosity in old age. In B. L. Neugarten (Ed.), *Middle Age and Aging* (pp. 497–508). Chicago: University of Chicago Press.

Modell, J., & Hareven, T. K. (1973). Urbanization and the malleable household: An examination of boarding and lodging in American families. *Journal of Marriage and the Family, 35,* 467–479.

Molander, B., & Backman, L. (1989). Age differences in heart rate patterns during concentration in a precision sport: Implications for attentional functioning. *Journal of Gerontology: Psychological Sciences, 44,* P80–P87.

Montemayor, R. (1982). The relationship between parent-adolescent conflict and the amount of time adolescents spend with their parents, peers, and alone. *Child Development, 53,* 1512–1519.

Montgomery, R. J. V., & Borgatta, E. F. (1989). The effects of alternative support strategies on family caregiving. *The Gerontologist, 29,* 457–464.

Moos, R. H., Brennan, P. L., Fondacaro, M. R., & Moos, B. S. (1990). Approach and avoidance coping responses among older problem and nonproblem drinkers. *Psychology and Aging, 5,* 31–40.

Morgan, D. L. (1988). Age differences in social network participation. *Journal of Gerontology: Social Sciences, 43,* S129–137.

Morgan, D. L. (1989). Adjusting to widowhood: Do social networks really make it easier? *The Gerontologist, 29,* 101–107.

Morrell, R. W., Park, D. C., & Poon, L. W. (1990). Effects of labeling techniques on memory and comprehension of prescription information in young and old adults. *Journal of Gerontology: Psychological Sciences, 45,* P166–P172.

Morrow-Howell, N., & Mui, A. (1989). Elderly volunteers: Reasons for initiating and terminating service. *Journal of Gerontological Social Work, 13,* 21–34.

Morrow-Howell, N., & Ozawa, M. N. (1987). Helping networks: Seniors to seniors. *The Gerontologist, 27,* 17–20.

Moses, S. A. (1990). The fallacy of impoverishment. *The Gerontologist, 30,* 21–25.

Moss, M. S., & Moss, S. Z. (1980a). The image of the deceased spouse in remarriage of elderly widow(er)s. *Journal of Gerontological Social Work, 3,* 59–70.

Moss, M. S., & Moss, S. Z. (1980b, November). *The Impact of Parental Death on Middle-aged Children.* Paper presented at the 38th Annual Meeting of the American Association of Marriage and Family Therapy, Toronto, Canada.

Moss, M. S., & Moss, S. Z. (1983–1984). The impact of parental death on middle-aged children. *Omega, 12,* 74–80.

Moss, M. S., Moss, S. Z., & Moles, E. L. (1985). The quality of relationships between elderly parents and their out-of-town children. *The Gerontologist, 25,* 134–140.

Motenko, A. K. (1989). The frustrations, gratifications, and well-being of dementia caregivers. *The Gerontologist, 29,* 166–172.

Mueller, C. W., Mutran, E., & Boyle, E. H. (1989). Age discrimination in earnings in a dual-economy market. *Research on Aging, 11,* 492–507.

Mullins, L. C., & Dugan, E. (1990). The influence of depression, and family and friendship relations, on residents' loneliness in congregate housing. *The Gerontologist, 30,* 377–384.

Murphy, M. D., Schmitt, F. A., Caruso, M. J., & Sanders, R. E. (1987). Metamemory in older adults: The role of monitoring in serial recall. *Psychology and Aging, 2,* 331–339.

Murstein, B. I. (1976). *Who Will Marry Whom? Theories and Research in Marriage Choice.* New York: Springer.

Murstein, B. I. (1980). Mate selection in the 1970's. *Journal of Marriage and the Family, 42,* 51–66.

Murstein, B. I. (1982). Marital choice. In B. B. Wolman (Ed.), *Handbook of Developmental Psychology* (pp. 652–666). Englewood Cliffs, NJ: Prentice Hall.

Mutran, E. (1985). Intergenerational family support among blacks and whites: A response to culture or to socioeconomic difference? *Journal of Gerontology, 40,* 382–389.

Nakao, K., Okabe, T., & Bengtson, V. L. (1988, February). *Reciprocity across generations in social support.* Paper presented at the annual meeting of the International Network for Social Network Analysis, Sunbelt Social Network Conference, San Diego, CA.

National Center for Health Statistics. (1980). Monthly vital statistics reports: Advance report of final marriage statistics, 1978. DHHS Publication No. (PHS) 80–1120, Vol 29, No. 6, September 12.

National Center for Health Statistics. (1984). *Annual summary of births, deaths, marriages, and divorces: U.S., 1983.* (DHHS Publication No. PHS 84–1120). Hyattsville, MD: Public Health Service.

National Center for Health Statistics. (1985). *Vital statistics of the United States, 1980. Vol. II—Mortality, Part B.* Hyattsville, MD: USDHHS, PHS.

National Indian Council on Aging. (1981). 1981 White House Conference on Aging: The Indian issues. *National Indian Council on Aging Quarterly, 4,* 1.

National Institute on Aging. (1987). *Health resources for older women.* (NIH Publication No. 87–2899). Bethesda, MD: National Institutes of Health.

Neal, A. G., Groat, H. T., & Wicks, J. W. (1989). Attitudes about having children: A study of 600 couples in the early years of marriage. *Journal of Marriage and the Family, 51,* 313–328.

Neff, W. S. (1985). *Work and Human Behavior.* New York: Aldine.

Nehrke, M. F., Bellucci, G., & Gabriel, S. J. (1977–1978). Death anxiety, locus of control, and life satisfaction in the elderly: Toward a definition of ego integrity. *Omega, 8,* 359–368.

Nelson, H. M., & Nelson, A. K. (1975). *Black Church in the Sixties.* Lexington, KY: University Press of Kentucky.

Neugarten, B. L. (1968a). The awareness of middle age. In B. L. Neugarten (Ed.), *Middle Age and Aging* (pp. 93–98). Chicago: University of Chicago Press.

Neugarten, B. L. (1968b). *Middle Age and Aging.* Chicago: University of Chicago Press.

Neugarten, B. L. (1977). Personality and aging. In J. E. Birren & K. W. Schaie (Eds.), *Handbook of the Psychology of Aging* (pp. 626–649). New York: Van Nostrand Reinhold.

Neugarten, B. L., & Datan, N. (1973). Sociological perspectives on the life cycle. In P. B. Baltes & K. W. Schaie (Eds.), *Life-span Developmental Psychology: Personality and Socialization* (pp. 53–71). New York: Academic Press.

Neugarten, B. L., & Gutmann, D. L. (1964). Age-sex roles and personality in middle age: A thematic apperception study. In B. L. Neugarten and associates, *Personality in Middle and Late Life* (pp. 44–89). New York: Atherton Press.

Neugarten, B. L., Havighurst, R. J., & Tobin, S. S. (1968). Personality and patterns of aging. In B. L. Neugarten (Ed.), *Middle Age and Aging* (pp. 173–177). Chicago: University of Chicago Press.

Neugarten, B. L., Moore, J. W., & Lowe, J. C. (1965). Age norms, age constraints, and adult socialization. *American Journal of Sociology, 70,* 710–717.

Neugarten, B. L., & Neugarten, D. A. (1989). Policy issues in an aging society. In M. Storandt & G. R. VandenBos (Eds.), *The Adult Years: Continuity and Change* (pp. 147–167). Washington, DC: American Psychological Association.

Neugarten, B. L., & Peterson, W. A. (1957). A study of the American age grading system. *Proceedings of the Fourth Congress of the International Association of Gerontology*, Vol. 3.

Neugarten, B. L., & Weinstein, K. K. (1968). The changing American grandparent. In B. L. Neugarten (Ed.), *Middle Age and Aging* (pp. 280–285). Chicago: University of Chicago Press.

Neugarten, B. L., Wood, V., Kraines, R. J., & Loomis, B. (1968). Women's attitudes toward the menopause. In B. L. Neugarten (Ed.), *Middle Age and Aging* (pp. 195–200). Chicago: University of Chicago Press.

Newman, J. P. (1989). Aging and depression. *Psychology and Aging, 4*, 150–165.

Niederehe, G., & Funk, J. (1987, August). *Family Interaction with Dementia Patients: Caregiver Styles and Their Correlates*. Paper presented at the annual meeting of the American Psychological Association, New York, NY.

Nielsen, A. C. (1985). *Report on Devotional Programs: February 1985*. New York: A. C. Nielsen.

Noelker, L. S., & Bass, D. M. (1989). Home care for elderly persons: Linkages between formal and informal caregivers. *Journal of Gerontology: Social Sciences, 44*, S63–70.

Nolen-Hoeksema, S. (1988). Life-span views on depression. In P. B. Baltes & R. M. Lerner (Eds.), *Life-span Development and Behavior*, Vol. 9 (pp. 203–241). Hillsdale, NJ: Lawrence Erlbaum.

Norris, F. H., & Murrell, S. A. (1990). Social support, life events, and stress as modifiers of adjustment to bereavement by older adults. *Psychology and Aging, 5*, 429–436.

Norton, A. J., & Glick, P. C. (1986). One parent families: A social and economic profile. *Family Relations, 35*, 9–18.

Norton, A. J., & Moorman, A. J. (1987). Current trends in marriage and divorce among American women. *Journal of Marriage and the Family, 49*, 3–14.

Nydegger, C. N. (1983). Family ties of the aged in cross-cultural perspective. *The Gerontologist, 23*, 26–32.

O'Boyle, M., Amadeo, M., & Self, D. (1990). Cognitive complaints in elderly depressed and pseudodemented patients. *Psychology and Aging, 5*, 467–468.

O'Bryant, S. L. (1988). Sibling support and older widows' well-being. *Journal of Marriage and the Family, 50*, 173–183.

O'Bryant, S. L., & Morgan, L. A. (1989). Financial experience and well-being among mature widowed women. *The Gerontologist, 29*, 245–251.

O'Bryant, S. L., & Morgan, L. A. (1990). Recent widows' kin support and orientations to self-sufficiency. *The Gerontologist, 30*, 391–398.

Ochs, A. L., Newbury, J., Lenhardt, M. L., & Harkins, S. W. (1985). Neural and vestibular aging associated with falls. In J. E. Birren & K. W. Schaie (Eds.), *Handbook of the Psychology of Aging* (2nd ed.). (pp. 378–399). New York: Academic Press.

Ogilvie, D. M. (1987). Life satisfaction and identity structure in late middle-aged men and women. *Psychology and Aging, 2*, 217–224.

Oliver, R., & Bock, F. A. (1987). *Coping with Alzheimer's: A Caregiver's Emotional Survival Guide*. North Hollywood: Wilshire Book Co.

Olsho, L. W., Harkins, S. W., & Lenhardt, M. L. (1985). Aging and the auditory system. In J. E. Birren & K. W. Schaie (Eds.), *Handbook of the Psychology of Aging* (2nd ed.). (pp. 332–377). New York: Van Nostrand Reinhold.

Orlofsky, J. L., Marcia, J. E., & Lesser, I. M. (1973). Ego identity status and the intimacy versus isolation crisis of young adulthood. *Journal of Personality and Social Psychology, 27*, 211–219.

Osgood, N. (1985). *Suicide in the Elderly*. Rockville, MD: Aspen.

Osipow, S. H. (1983). *Theories of Career Development*. Englewood Cliffs, NJ: Prentice Hall.

Osofsky, J. D., & Osofsky, H. J. (1984). Psychological and developmental perspectives on expectant and new parenthood. In R. D. Parke (Ed.), *Review of Child Development Research* (Vol. 7). (pp. 372–397). Chicago: University of Chicago Press.

Ouslander, J. G. (1982). Illness and psychopathology in the elderly. In L. Jarvik & G. W. Small (Eds.), *The Psychiatric Clinics of North America* (pp. 145–158). Philadelphia: W. B. Saunders.

Over, R. (1989). Age and scholarly impact. *Psychology and Aging, 4*, 222–225.

Overton, W. F., & Reese, H. W. (1973). Models of development: Methodological implications. In J. R. Nesselroade & H. W. Reese (Eds.), *Life-span Developmental Psychology: Methodological Issues* (pp. 65–86). New York: Academic Press.

Owen, G., Fulton, R., & Markusen, E. (1983–1984). Death at a distance: A study of family survivors. *Omega, 12*, 191–226.

Owens, W. A. (1966). Age and mental abilities: A second adult follow-up. *Journal of Educational Psychology, 57*, 311–325.

Owlsley, C., & Sloane, M. E. (1987). Contrast sensitivity, acuity, and the perception of "real world" targets. *British Journal of Ophthalmology, 71*, 791–796.

Palmore, E. B. (1984). Longevity in Abkhasia: A reevaluation. *The Gerontologist, 24*, 95–96.

Palmore, E. B., Burchett, B., Fillenbaum, G. G., George, L. K., & Wallman, L. M. (1985). *Retirement: Causes and Consequences*. New York: Springer.

Palmore, E. B., George, L. K., & Fillenbaum, G. G. (1982). Predictors of retirement. *Journal of Gerontology, 37*, 733–742.

Panek, P. E., Barrett, G. V., Sterns, H. L., & Alexander, R. A. (1977). A review of age changes in perceptual information processing ability with regard to driving. *Experimental Aging Research, 3*, 387–449.

Papalia, D. E. (1972). The status of several conservation abilities across the life-span. *Human Development, 15*, 229–243.

Papalia, D. E., & Bielby, D. D. V. (1974). Cognitive functioning in middle and old age adults: A review of research based on Piaget's theory. *Human Development, 17*, 424–443.

Papalia, D. E., & Olds, S. W. (1988). *Psychology*. New York: McGraw-Hill.

Parasuraman, R., Nestor, P., & Greenwood, P. (1989). Sustained-attention capacity in young and older adults. *Psychology and Aging, 4*, 339–345.

Parkes, C. M. (1980). Terminal care: Evaluation of an advisory domiciary service at St. Christopher's Hospice. *Postgraduate Medical Journal, 56*, 685–689.

Parrot, A., & Ellis, M. J. (1985). Homosexuals should be allowed to marry and adopt or rear children (pp. 303–312). In H. Feldman & M. Feldman (Eds.), *Current Controversies in Marriage and Family*. Beverly Hills: Sage Publications.

Pavalko, R. M. (1988). *Sociology of Occupations and Professions*. Itasca, IL: F. E. Peacock.

Peck, R. C. (1968). Psychological developments in the second half of life. In B. L. Neugarten (Ed.), *Middle Age and Aging* (pp. 88–92). Chicago: University of Chicago Press.

Penkower, L., Bromet, E., & Dew, M. A. (1988). Husbands' layoff and wives' mental health: A prospective analysis. *Archives of General Psychiatry, 45*, 994–1000.

Penning, M. J. (1990). Receipt of assistance by elderly people: Hierarchical selection and task specificity. *The Gerontologist, 30*, 220–227.

Pepper, S. C. (1942). *World Hypotheses*. Berkeley, CA: University of California Press.

Perlmutter, M., & Hall, E. (1985). *Adult Development and Aging*. New York: John Wiley & Sons.

Perlmutter, M., & Nyquist, L. (1990). Relationship between self-reported physical and mental health and intelligence performance across adulthood. *Journal of Gerontology: Psychological Sciences, 45*, P145–P155.

Perry, W. G. (1970). *Forms of Intellectual and Ethical Development in the College Years*. New York: Holt, Rinehart, & Winston, Inc.

Peterson, B. E., & Stewart, A. J. (1990). Using personal and fictional documents to assess psychosocial development: A case study of Vera Brittain's generativity. *Psychology and Aging, 5*, 400–411.

Philips, S. D. (1982). The development of career choices: The relationship between patterns of commitment and career outcomes in adulthood. *Journal of Vocational Behavior, 20*, 141–152.

Phillemer, K., & Finkelhor, D. (1988). The prevalence of elder abuse: A random sample curve. *The Gerontologist, 28*, 51–57.

Piaget, J. (1972). Intellectual evolution from adolescence through adulthood. *Human Development, 15*, 1–12.

Piaget, J. (1970). Piaget's theory. In P. H. Mussen (Ed.), *Carmichael's Manual of Child Psychology*, Vol. 1. New York: Wiley.

Pinder, M., & Hayslip, B. (1981). Cognitive, attitudinal, and affective aspects of death and dying in adulthood: Implications for care providers. *Educational Gerontology, 6*, 107–123.

Pine, V. R. (1975). *Caretaker of the Dead: The American Funeral Director*. New York: Irvington.

Pineo, P. (1961). Disenchantment in the later years of marriage. *Marriage and Family Living, 23*, 3–11.

Plude, D. J. (In press). Attention and memory improvement. In D. Herrmann, H. Weingartner, A. Searleman, & C. McEvoy (Eds.), *Memory Improvement: Implications for Memory Theory*. New York: Springer-Verlag.

Plude, D. J., & Doussard-Roosevelt, J. A. (1989). Aging, selective attention, and feature integration. *Psychology and Aging, 4*, 98–105.

Plude, D. J., & Murphy, L. J. (In press). Aging, selective attention, and everyday memory. In R. L. West & J. D. Sinnott (Eds.), *Everyday Memory and Aging: Current Research and Methodology.* New York: Springer-Verlag.

Poon, L. W. (1985). Differences in human memory with aging: Nature, causes, and clinical implications. In J. E. Birren & K. W. Schaie (Eds.), *Handbook of the Psychology of Aging* (2nd ed.). (pp. 427–462). New York: Van Nostrand Reinhold.

Poon, L., & Fozard, J. L. (1980). Age and word frequency effects in continuous recognition memory. *Journal of Gerontology, 35,* 77–86.

Poon, L. W., Fozard, J. L., Paulshock, D. R., & Thomas, J. C. (1979). A questionnaire assessment of age differences in retention of recent and remote events. *Experimental Aging Research, 5,* 401–411.

Popper, K. R. (1961). *The Logic of Scientific Discovery.* New York: Basic Books.

Post, F. (1987). Paranoid and schizophrenic disorders among the aging. In L. L. Carstensen & B. A. Edelstein (Eds.), *Handbook of Clinical Gerontology* (pp. 43–56). New York: Pergammon Press.

Pottinger, J. S. (1977). The drive toward equality. In B. R. Gross (Ed.), *Reverse Discrimination* (pp. 41–49). Buffalo: Prometheus Books.

Powell, D. J., & Fuller, R. W. (1983). Marijuana and sex: Strange bedpartners. *Journal of Psychoactive Drugs, 15,* 269–280.

Prevention Research Center. (1986). *Prevention Index 1986: A Report Card on the Nation's Health.* Emmaus, PA: Rodale.

Princeton Religion Research Center. (1982). *Religion in America.* Princeton, NJ: The Gallup Poll.

Princeton Religion Research Center. (1985). *Religion in America.* Princeton, NJ: The Gallup Poll.

Prinz, P. N., Dustman, R. E., & Emmerson, R. (1990). Electrophysiology and aging. In J. E. Birren & K. W. Schaie (Eds.), *Handbook of the Psychology of Aging* (3rd ed.). (pp. 135–149). San Diego: Academic Press.

Profile of the *Guideposts* Reader. (1984). *Daily Guideposts.* Carmel, CA: Trost Associates.

Pruchno, R. A., Kleban, M. H., Michaels, J. E., & Dempsey, N. P. (1990). Mental and physical health of caregiving spouses: Development of a causal model. *Journal of Gerontology: Psychological Sciences, 45,* P192–199.

Pruchno, R. A., Michaels, J. E., & Potashnik, S. L. (1990). Predictors of institutionalization among Alzheimer disease victims with caregiving spouses. *Journal of Gerontology: Social Sciences, 45,* S259–266.

Pruchno, R. A., & Resch, N. L. (1989). Husbands and wives as caregivers: Antecedents of depression and burden. *The Gerontologist, 29,* 159–165.

Pruchno, R. A., & Smyer, M. A. (1984, April). *Therapeutic Interventions with Adult Caregivers.* Paper presented at the Future of Natural Caregiving Networks in Later Life: Policy, Planning, Research and Intervention Workshop, Buffalo, NY.

Quayhagen, M. P., & Quayhagen, M. (1989). Differential effects of family-based strategies on Alzheimer's Disease. *The Gerontologist, 29,* 150–155.

Quetelet, A. (1842). *A Treatise on Man and the Development of His Faculties.* Edinburgh: Chambers.

Quinn, J. F., & Burkhauser, R. V. (1990). Work and retirement. In R. H. Binstock & L. K. George (Eds.), *Handbook of Aging and the Social Sciences* (3rd ed.). (pp. 307–327). San Diego: Academic Press.

Rabbitt, P. (1977). Changes in problem solving ability with age. In J. E. Birren & K. W. Schaie (Eds.), *Handbook of the Psychology of Aging* (pp. 606–621). New York: Van Nostrand Reinhold.

Rabinowitz, J. C. (1989). Age deficits in recall under optimal study conditions. *Psychology and Aging, 4,* 378–380.

Radecki, S. E., Kane, R. L., Solomon, D. H., Mendenhall, R. C., & Beck, J. C. (1988). Do physicians spend less time with older patients? *Journal of the American Geriatrics Society, 36,* 713–718.

Ragland, O. R., & Brand, R. J. (1988). Type A behavior and mortality from coronary heart disease. *New England Journal of Medicine, 318,* 65–69.

Rando, T. A. (1984). *Grief, Dying, and Death: Clinical Interventions for Caregivers.* Champaign, IL: Research Press.

Rapp, S. R., & Davis, K. M. (1989). Geriatric depression: Physicians' knowledge, perceptions, and diagnostic practices. *The Gerontologist, 29,* 252–257.

Raschke, H. J. (1987). Divorce. In M. B. Sussman & S. K. Steinmetz (Eds.), *Handbook of Marriage and the Family* (pp. 597–624). New York: Plenum Press.

Rathbone-McCuan, E. (1986). Elder abuse resulting from caregiving overload in older families. In N. Datan, A. L. Greene, & H. W. Reese (Eds.), *Life-span Developmental Psychology: Intergenerational Relations* (pp. 245–264). Hillsdale, NJ: Erlbaum.

Ray, D. C., McKinney, K. A., & Ford, C. V. (1987). Differences in psychologists' ratings of older and younger clients. *The Gerontologist, 27,* 82–86.

Rebecca, M. (1975). *A Dialectical Approach to Sex-role Socialization.* Unpublished manuscript, University of Michigan, Ann Arbor, MI.

Rebok, G. W., & Balcerak, L. J. (1989). Memory self-efficacy and performance differences in young and old adults: The effect of mnemonic training. *Developmental Psychology, 25,* 714–721.

Reedy, M. N. Birren, J. E., & Schaie, K. W. (1981). Age and sex differences in satisfying love relationships across the adult life span. *Human Development, 24,* 52–66.

Reese, H. W., & Overton, W. F. (1970). Models of development and theories of development. In L. R. Goulet & P. B. Baltes (Eds.), *Life-span Developmental Psychology: Research and Theory* (pp. 116–149). New York: Academic Press.

Reese, H. W., & Rodeheaver, D. (1985). Problem solving and complex decision making. In J. E. Birren & K. W. Schaie (Eds.), *Handbook of the Psychology of Aging* (2nd ed.). (pp. 474–499). New York: Van Nostrand Reinhold.

Reinhardt, J. P. (1987, August). *The strength and rewardingness of friendship across adulthood.* Paper presented at the Annual Meeting of the American Psychological Association, New York, NY.

Reinhardt, J. P., & Fisher, C. B. (1989). Kinship versus friendship: Social adaptation in married and widowed elderly women. In L. Grau (Ed.), *Women in the Later Years: Health, Social, and Cultural Perspectives* (pp. 191–211). New York: Haworth Press.

Reinke, B. J., Ellicott, A. M., Harris, R. L., & Hancock, E. (1985). Timing of psychosocial changes in women's lives. *Human Development, 28,* 259–280.

Reisberg, B., Ferris, S. H., deLeon, M. J., & Crook, T. (1982). The Global Deterioration Scale for assessment of primary degenerative dementia. *American Journal of Psychiatry, 139,* 1136–1139.

Reisman, J. M. (1988). An indirect measure of the value of friendship for aging men. *Journal of Gerontology: Psychological Sciences, 43,* P109–110.

Restak, R. (1984). *The Brain.* Toronto: Bantam Books.

Rexroat, C., & Shehan, C. (1987). The family life cycle and spouses' time in housework. *Journal of Marriage and the Family, 49,* 737–751.

Rhodes, S. R. (1983). Age-related differences in work attitudes and behaviors: A review and conceptual analysis. *Psychological Bulletin, 93,* 328–367.

Ribot, T. (1882). *Diseases of Memory.* New York: Appleton.

Rice, G. E., & Meyer, B. J. F. (1985). Reading behavior and prose recall performance of young and older adults with high and average verbal ability. *Educational Gerontology, 11,* 57–72.

Richardson, D. (1981). Lesbian mothers. In J. Hart & D. Richardson (Eds.), *The Theory and Practice of Homosexuality* (pp. 149–158). London: Routledge & Kegan Paul.

Richardson, E. H. (1981). Cultural and historical perspectives in counseling American Indians. In D. W. Sue (Ed.), *Counseling the Culturally Different.* New York: Wiley.

Richardson, V., & Kilty, K. M. (1989). Retirement financial planning among black professionals. *The Gerontologist, 29,* 32–37.

Riegel, K. F. (1975). Toward a dialectical theory of development. *Human Development, 18,* 50–64.

Riegel, K. F., & Riegel, R. M. (1972). Development, drop, and death. *Developmental Psychology, 6,* 309–316.

Riegel, K. F., Riegel, R. M., & Meyer, G. (1967). A study of the dropout rates in longitudinal research on aging and the prediction of death. *Journal of Personality and Social Psychology, 5,* 342–348.

Riegle, D. W. (1982). The psychological and social effects of unemployment. *American Psychologist, 37,* 1113–1115.

Riley, J. W. (1970). What people think about death. In O. G. Brim, H. E. Freeman, S. Levine, & N. A. Scotch (Eds.), *The Dying Patient* (pp. 30–41). New York: Russell Sage Foundation.

Rindfuss, R. R., & Stephen, E. H. (1990). Marital non-cohabitation: Separation does not make the heart grow fonder. *Journal of Marriage and the Family, 52,* 259–270.

Risman, B. J., & Park, K. (1988). Just the two of us: Parent-child relationships in single-parent homes. *Journal of Marriage and the Family, 50,* 1049–1062.

Roberts, L. J., & Krokoff, L. J. (1990). A time-series analysis of withdrawal, hostility, and displeasure in satisfied and dissatisfied marriages. *Journal of Marriage and the Family, 52,* 95–105.

Roberts, P., & Newton, P. M. (1987). Levinsonian studies of women's adult development. *Psychology and Aging, 2,* 154–163.

Roberts, R. L., & Bengtson, V. L. (1990). Is intergenerational solidarity a unidimensional construct? A second test of a formal model. *Journal of Gerontology: Social Sciences, 45,* S12–20.

Robertson-Tchabo, E., Hausman, C., & Arenberg, D. (1976). A classical mnemonic for older learners: A trick that works! *Educational Gerontology, 1,* 215–226.

Rockstein, M., & Sussman, M. (1979). *Biology of Aging.* Belmont, CA: Wadsworth.

Rodin, J., & Langer, E. (1977). Long-term effects of a control-relevant intervention with the institutionalized aged. *Journal of Personality and Social Psychology, 35,* 897–902.

Rogers, L. P., & Markides, K. S. (1989). Well-being in the postparental stage in Mexican-American women. *Research on Aging, 11,* 508–516.

Rollins, B. C. (1989). Marital quality at midlife. In S. Hunter & M. Sundel (Eds.), *Midlife Myths: Issues, Findings, and Practice Implications* (pp. 184–194). Newbury Park, CA: Sage Publications.

Rollins, B. C., & Cannon, K. L. (1974). Marital satisfaction over the family life cycle: A reevaluation. *Journal of Marriage and the Family, 36,* 271–283.

Rollins, B. C., & Feldman, H. (1970). Marital satisfaction over the family life cycle. *Journal of Marriage and the Family, 32,* 20–28.

Root, N. (1981). Injuries at work are fewer among older employees. *Monthly Labor Review, 104,* 30–34.

Rosenthal, C. J., Matthews, S. H., & Marshall, V. W. (1989). Is parent care normative? The experiences of a sample of middle-aged women. *Research on Aging, 11,* 244–260.

Rosow, I. (1967). *Social Integration of the Aged.* New York: Free Press.

Rosow, I. (1985). Status and role change throughout the life cycle. In R. H. Binstock & E. Shanas (Eds.), *Handbook of Aging and the Social Sciences* (2nd ed.). (pp. 62–93). New York: Van Nostrand Reinhold.

Ross, H. G., Dalton, M. J., & Milgram, J. I. (1980, November). *Older adults' perceptions of closeness in sibling relationships.* Paper presented at the annual meeting of the Gerontological Society of America, San Diego, CA.

Ross, H. G., & Milgram, J. I. (1982). Important variables in adult sibling relationships: A qualitative study. In M. E. Lamb & B. Sutton-Smith (Eds.), *Sibling Relationships: Their Nature and Significance Across the Lifespan* (pp. 225–249). Hillsdale, NJ: Lawrence Erlbaum.

Rossi, A. S. (1968). Transition to parenthood. *Journal of Marriage and the Family, 30,* 26–39.

Rossman, P. (1977). *Hospice.* New York: Fawcett Columbine.

Rowles, G. D. (1978). *Prisoners of Space? Exploring the Geographical Experience of Older People.* Boulder, CO: Westview Press.

Rowles, G. D. (1987). A place to call home. In L. L. Carstensen & B. A. Edelstein (Eds.), *Handbook of Clinical Gerontology* (pp. 335–353). New York: Pergammon Press.

Rowley, K. M., & Feather, N. T. (1987). The impact of unemployment in relation to age and length of unemployment. *Journal of Occupational Psychology, 60,* 323–332.

Roy, P. G., & Storandt, M. (1989). Older adults' perceptions of psychopathology. *Psychology and Aging, 4,* 369–371.

Roy, S. W. (1986). Programming for returning women students. *Journal of College Student Personnel, 27,* 75–76.

Roybal, E. R. (1988). Mental health and aging: The need for an expanded federal response. *American Psychologist, 43,* 189–194.

Rubenstein, R. L. (1987). Never married elderly as a social type: Re-evaluating some images. *The Gerontologist, 27,* 108–113.

Rubenstein, R. L. (1989). The home environments of older people: A description of the psychosocial processes linking person to place. *Journal of Gerontology: Social Sciences, 44,* S45–53.

Ruhm, C. J. (1989). Why older Americans stop working. *The Gerontologist, 29,* 294–299.

Russell, C. S. (1974). Transition to parenthood: Problems and gratification. *Journal of Marriage and the Family, 36,* 294–301.

Ruvolo, A., & Veroff, J. (1989, August). *Relationship between marital happiness and general happiness of newlyweds.* Presented at the 97th Annual Convention of the American Psychological Association, New Orleans, LA.

Rybash, J. M., Hoyer, W. J., & Roodin, P. A. (1986). *Adult Cognition and Aging: Developmental Changes in Processing, Knowing, and Thinking*. New York: Pergammon Press.

Ryff, C. D. (1982). Successful aging: A developmental approach. *The Gerontologist, 22*, 209–214.

Ryff, C. D. (1986, November). *The failure of successful aging research*. Paper presented at the annual meeting of the Gerontological Society of America, Chicago, IL.

Ryff, C. D. (1989). In the eye of the beholder: Views of psychological well-being among middle-aged and older adults. *Psychology and Aging, 4*, 195–210.

Ryff, C. D., & Migdal, S. (1984). Intimacy and generativity: Self-perceived transitions. *Signs, 9*, 470–481.

Sabatini, P., & Labouvie-Vief, G. (1979, November). *Age and professional specialization: Formal reasoning*. Paper presented at the Annual Meeting of the Gerontological Society of America, Washington, DC.

Sacher, G. A. (1977). Life table modification and life prolongation. In C. E. Fince & L. Hayflick (Eds.), *Handbook of the Biology of Aging* (pp. 582–638). New York: Van Nostrand Reinhold.

Salthouse, T. A. (1984). Effects of age and skill in typing. *Journal of Gerontology, 39*, 345–371.

Salthouse, T. A. (1985). Speed of behavior and its implications for cognition. In J. E. Birren & K. W. Schaie (Eds.), *Handbook of the Psychology of Aging* (2nd ed.). (pp. 400–426). New York: Van Nostrand Reinhold.

Sanders, C. M. (1980–1981). Comparison of younger and older spouses in bereavement outcome. *Omega, 11*, 217–232.

Sandroff, R. (1989). Is your job driving you crazy? *Psychology Today*, pp. 41–45.

Sands, L. P., Terry, H., & Meredith, W. (1989). Change and stability in adult intellectual functioning assessed by Wechsler item responses. *Psychology and Aging, 4*, 79–87.

Sanick, M. M., & Mauldin, T. (1986). Single versus two parent families: A comparison of mothers' time. *Family Relations, 35*, 53–56.

Sathe, V. (1985). *Culture and Related Corporate Realities*. Homewood, IL: Richard D. Irwin.

Sauter, S. L., Murphy, L. R., & Hurrell, J. J. (1990). Prevention of work-related psychological disorders: A national strategy proposed by the National Institute for Occupational Safety and Health. *American Psychologist, 45*, 1146–1158.

Scailfa, C. T., Kline, D. W., & Lyman, B. J. (1987). Age differences in target identification as a function of retinal location and noise level: Examination of the useful field of view. *Psychology and Aging, 2*, 14–19.

Scannell, E., & Petrich, B. (1987). Displaced homemakers' financial problems: Curriculum implications. *Journal of Vocational Home Economics Education, 6*, 67–77.

Scanzoni, L., & Scanzoni, J. (1976). *Men, Women, and Change: A Sociology of Marriage and the Family*. New York: McGraw-Hill.

Schaie, K. W. (1965). A general model for the study of developmental problems. *Psychological Bulletin, 64*, 92–107.

Schaie, K. W. (1974). Translations in gerontology—from lab to life: Intellectual functioning. *American Psychologist, 29*, 802–807.

Schaie, K. W. (1977–1978). Toward a stage theory of adult cognitive development. *International Journal of Aging and Human Development, 8*, 129–138.

Schaie, K. W. (1979). The primary mental abilities in adulthood: An exploration in the development of psychometric intelligence. In P. B. Baltes & O. G. Brim (Eds.), *Life-span Development and Behavior* (Vol. 2). New York: Academic Press.

Schaie, K. W. (1983a). *Longitudinal Studies of Adult Psychological Development*. New York: The Guilford Press.

Schaie, K. W. (1983b). The Seattle longitudinal study: A twenty-one year investigation of psychometric intelligence. In K. W. Schaie (Ed.), *Longitudinal Studies of Adult Personality Development* (pp. 64–135). New York: Guilford.

Schaie, K. W. (1990). Intellectual development in adulthood. In J. E. Birren & K. W. Schaie (Eds.), *Handbook of the Psychology of Aging* (3rd ed.). (pp. 291–309). New York: Van Nostrand Reinhold.

Schaie, K. W., & Baltes, P. B. (1977). Some faith helps to see the forest: A final comment on the Horn and Donaldson myth of the Baltes-Schaie position on adult intelligence. *American Psychologist, 32*, 1118–1120.

Schaie, K. W., & Labouvie-Vief, G. (1974). Generational versus ontogenetic components of change in adult cognitive behavior: A fourteen year cross sequential study. *Developmental Psychology, 10,* 305–320.

Scharlach, A. E. (1989). A comparison of employed caregivers of cognitively impaired and physically impaired elderly persons. *Research on Aging, 11,* 225–243.

Scharlach, A. E., & Boyd, S. L. (1989). Caregiving and employment: Results of an employee survey. *The Gerontologist, 29,* 382–387.

Schoenholz, K. (1978, November). *Occupational Mobility and Kin Interaction: A Reconceptualization.* Paper presented at the annual meeting of the American Sociological Association, San Francisco, CA.

Schoonover, C. B., Brody, E. M., Hoffman, C., & Kleban, M. (1988). Parent care and geographically distant children. *Research on Aging, 10,* 472–492.

Schuckit, M. A. (1977). Geriatric alcoholism and drug abuse. *The Gerontologist, 17,* 168–174.

Schuckit, M. A. (1984). Prospective markers for alcoholism. In D. W. Goodwin, K. T. Van Dusen, & S. A. Mednick (Eds.), *Longitudinal Research in Alcoholism.* Boston: Kluwer-Nijhoff.

Schuckit, M. A., & Miller, P. L. (1975). Alcoholism in elderly men: A survey of a general medical ward. *Annals of the New York Academy of Sciences, 37,* 558–571.

Schulz, R. (1978). *The Psychology of Death, Dying, and Bereavement.* Reading, MA: Addison-Wesley.

Schulz, R. (1985). Emotion and affect. In J. E. Birren & K. W. Schaie (Eds.), *Handbook of the Psychology of Aging* (2nd ed.). (pp. 531–543). New York: Van Nostrand Reinhold.

Schulz, R., & Adelman, D. (1974). Clinical research and the stages of dying. *Omega, 5,* 137–143.

Schultz, N. R., & Hoyer, W. J. (1976). Feedback effects on spatial egocentrism in old age. *Journal of Gerontology, 31,* 72–75.

Schulz, R., Visintainer, P., & Williamson, G. M. (1990). Psychiatric and physical morbidity effects of caregiving. *Journal of Gerontology: Psychological Sciences, 45,* P181–P191.

Schumm, W. R., & Bugaighis, M. A. (1986). Marital quality over the marital career: Alternative explanations. *Journal of Marriage and the Family, 48,* 165–168.

Schurman, R. A., Kramer, P. D., & Mitchell, J. B. (1985). The hidden mental health network. *Archives of General Psychiatry, 42,* 89–94.

Scialfa, C. T., Kline, D. W., & Lyman, B. J. (1990). Age differences in target identification as a function of retinal location and noise level: Examination of the useful field of view. *Psychology and Aging, 2,* 14–19.

Scogin, F., & Bienias, J. L. (1988). A three-year follow-up of older adult participants in a memory-skills training program. *Psychology and Aging, 3,* 334–337.

Scott, J. P. (1983). Siblings and other kin. In T. H. Brubaker (Ed.), *Family Relationships in Later Life* (pp. 47–62). Beverly Hills, CA: Sage Publications.

Sears, R. R. (1979). Mid-life development. *Contemporary Psychology, 24,* 97–98.

Sekuler, R., Owlsley, C., & Hukman, L. (1982). Assessing spatial vision of older people. *American Journal of Optometry and Physiological Optics, 59,* 961–968.

Sendbeuhler, J. M., & Goldstein, S. (1977). Attempted suicide among the aged. *Journal of the American Geriatrics Society, 25,* 245–248.

Shanas, E. (1968). Family help patterns and social class in three countries. In B. L. Neugarten (Ed.), *Middle Age and Aging* (pp. 296–305). Chicago: University of Chicago Press.

Shanas, E. (1979). Social myth as hypothesis: The case of the family relations of old people. *The Gerontologist, 19,* 3–9.

Shanas, E. (1980). Older people and their families: The new pioneers. *Journal of Marriage and the Family, 42,* 9–15.

Sheehan, N. W., Wilson, R., & Marella, L. M. (1989). The role of the church in providing services for the aging. *Journal of Applied Gerontology,* in press.

Shelton, B. K. (1985). The social and psychological impact of unemployment. *Journal of Employment Counseling, 22,* 18–22.

Shock, N. W., Greulich, R. C., Andres, R., Arenberg, D., Costa, P. T., Lakatta, E. G., & Tobin, J. D. (1984). *Normal Human Aging: The Baltimore Longitudinal Study of Aging.* NIH Publication No. 84–2450. Bethesda, MD: National Institutes of Health.

Shostak, A. B. (1987). Singlehood. In M. B. Sussman & S. K. Steinmetz (Eds.), *Handbook of Marriage and the Family* (pp. 355–367). New York: Plenum Press.

Siegler, I. C. (1989). Developmental health psychology. In M. Storandt & G. R. VandenBos (Eds.), *The Adult Years: Continuity and Change* (pp. 119–142). Washington, DC: American Psychological Association.

Silverstone, B., & Hyman, H. (1976). *You and Your Aging Parent.* New York: Pantheon Books.

Simonton, D. K. (1989). The swan-song phenomenon: Last-works effects for 172 classical composers. *Psychology and Aging, 4,* 42–47.

Simonton, D. K. (1990). Creativity and wisdom in aging. In J. E. Birren & K. W. Schaie (Eds.), *Handbook of the Psychology of Aging* (3rd ed.). (pp. 320–329). San Diego: Academic Press.

Sinnott, J. D. (1984). Postformal reasoning: The relativistic stage. In M. L. Commons, F. A. Richards, & C. Armon (Eds.), *Beyond Formal Operations.* New York: Praeger.

Sinnott, J. D. (1986). Prospective/intentional and incidental everyday memory: Effects of age and passage of time. *Psychology and Aging, 1,* 110–116.

Sinnott, J. D. (1989a). Changing the known; knowing the changing: The general systems theory metatheory as a conceptual framework to study complex change and complex thoughts. In D. A. Kramer & M. J. Bopp (Eds.), *Transformations in Clinical and Developmental Psychology.* New York: Springer-Verlag.

Sinnott, J. D. (1989b). General systems theory: A rationale for the study of everyday memory. In L. W. Poon, D. C. Rubin, & B. A. Wilson (Eds.), *Everyday Cognition in Adult and Late Life.* New York: Cambridge University Press.

Skinner, B. F. (1953). *Science and Human Behavior.* New York: Free Press.

Skinner, B. F. (1974). *About Behaviorism.* New York: Knopf.

Skolnick, A. (1981). Married lives: Longitudinal perspectives on marriage. In D. H. Eichorn, J. A. Clausen, N. Haan, M. P. Honzik, & P. H. Mussen (Eds.), *Present and Past in Middle Life* (pp. 269–298). New York: Academic Press.

Smallegan, M. (1989). Level of depressive symptoms and life stresses for culturally diverse older adults. *The Gerontologist, 29,* 45–50.

Smith, A. D. (1980). Age differences in encoding, storage, and retrieval. In L. W. Poon, J. L. Fozard, L. S. Cermack, D. Arenberg, & L. W. Thompson (Eds.), *New Directions in Memory and Aging: Proceedings of the George A. Talland Memorial Conference.* Hillsdale, NJ: Lawrence Erlbaum.

Smith, E. (1983). Issues in racial minorities' career behavior. In W. B. Walsh & S. H. Osipow (Eds.), *Handbook of Vocational Psychology. Vol 1: Foundations* (pp. 161–222). Hillsdale, NJ: Lawrence Erlbaum.

Smith, J., & Baltes, P. B. (1990). Wisdom-related knowledge: Age/cohort differences in response to life-planning problems. *Developmental Psychology, 26,* 494–505.

Smyer, M. A., Zarit, S. H., & Qualls, S. H. (1990). Psychological intervention with the aging individual. In J. E. Birren & K. W. Schaie (Eds.), *Handbook of the Psychology of Aging* (3rd ed.). (pp. 375–404). San Diego: Academic Press.

Snowden, L. R., Schott, T. L., Awalt, S. J., & Gillis-Knox, J. (1988). Marital satisfaction in pregnancy: Stability and change. *Journal of Marriage and the Family, 50,* 325–333.

Snyder, C. J., & Barrett, G. V. (1988). The Age Discrimination in Employment Act: A review of court decisions. *Experimental Aging Research, 14,* 3–47.

Sontag, S. (1972). The double standard of aging. *Saturday Review, 55,* 29–38.

Sorkin, B. A., Rudy, T. E., Hanlon, R. B., Turk, D. C., & Stieg, R. L. (1990). Chronic pain in old and young patients: Differences appear less important than similarities. *Journal of Gerontology: Psychological Sciences, 45,* P64–P68.

Sowell, T. (1977). "Affirmative action" reconsidered. In B. R. Gross (Ed.), *Reverse Discrimination* (pp. 113–131). Buffalo: Prometheus Books.

Spanier, G. B., & Furstenberg, F. F. (1987). Remarriage and reconstituted families. In M. B. Sussman & S. K. Steinmetz (Eds.), *Handbook of Marriage and the Family* (pp. 419–434). New York: Plenum Press.

Spence, A. P. (1989). *Biology of Human Aging.* Englewood Cliffs, NJ: Prentice Hall.

Spence, D., & Lonner, T. (1971). The "empty nest": A transition within motherhood. *Family Coordinator, 20,* 369–375.

Spirduso, W. W., & MacRae, P. G. (1990). Motor performance and aging. In J. E. Birren & K. W. Schaie (Eds.), *Handbook of the Psychology of Aging* (3rd ed.). (pp. 184–200). San Diego: Academic Press.

Spitze, G., & Logan, J. (1990). More evidence on women (and men) in the middle. *Research on Aging, 12*, 182–198.

Spitzer, R. L., Endicott, J., & Robins, E. (1978). Research diagnostic criteria: Rationale and reliability. *Archives of General Psychiatry, 35*, 773–782.

Stagner, R. (1985). Aging in industry. In J. E. Birren & K. W. Schaie (Eds.), *Handbook of the Psychology of Aging* (2nd ed.). (pp. 789–817). New York: Van Nostrand Reinhold Co.

Stankov, L. (1988). Aging, attention, and intelligence. *Psychology and Aging, 3*, 59–74.

Stearns, H. L., Barrett, G. V., & Alexander, R. A. (1985). Accidents and the aging individual. In J. E. Birren & K. W. Schaie (Eds.), *Handbook of the Psychology of Aging* (2nd ed.). (pp. 703–724). New York: Van Nostrand Reinhold Co.

Stearns, H. L., & Sanders, R. E. (1980). Training and education of the elderly. In R. R. Turner & H. W. Reese (Eds.), *Life-span Developmental Psychology: Intervention* (pp. 307–330). New York: Academic Press.

Stein, P. J. (1981). *Single Life: Unmarried Adults in Social Context.* New York: St. Martin's Press.

Stein, P. J. (1986). Men and their friendships. In R. A. Lewis & R. E. Salt (Eds.), *Men in Families* (pp. 261–269). Beverly Hills, CA: Sage Publications.

Steinberg, L., & Silverberg, S. B. (1987). Influences on marital satisfaction during the middle stages of the family life cycle. *Journal of Marriage and the Family, 49*, 751–760.

Stenback, A. (1980). Depression and suicidal behavior in old age. In J. E. Birren & R. B. Sloane (Eds.), *Handbook of Mental Health and Aging* (pp. 616–652). Englewood Cliffs, NJ: Prentice Hall.

Sternberg, R. J. (1985). *Beyond IQ.* Cambridge: Cambridge University Press.

Steuve, A., & O'Donnell, L. (1989). Interactions between women and their elderly parents: Constraints of daughters' employment. *Research on Aging, 11*, 331–353.

Stevens, J. C., & Crain, W. S. (1987). Old-age deficits in the sense of smell as gauged by thresholds, magnitude matching, and odor identification. *Psychology and Aging, 2*, 36–42.

Stevens-Long, J. (1988). *Adult life* (3rd ed.). Belmont, CA: Mayfield.

Stewart, W. (1977). *A psychosocial study of the formation of the early adult life structure in women.* Unpublished doctoral dissertation, Columbia University, New York, NY.

Stine, E. A. L., & Wingfield, A. (1987). Process and strategy in memory for speech among younger and older adults. *Psychology and Aging, 2*, 272–279.

Stine, E. A. L., & Wingfield, A. (1988). Memorability functions as an indicator of qualitative age differences in text recall. *Psychology and Aging, 3*, 179–183.

Stoller, E. P. (1983). Parent caregiving by adult children. *Journal of Marriage and the Family, 45*, 851–858.

Stoller, E. P. (1990). Males as helpers: The role of sons, relatives, and friends. *The Gerontologist, 30*, 228–235.

Stoller, E. P., & Pugliesi, K. L. (1989a). Other roles of caregivers: Competing responsibilities or supportive resources. *Journal of Gerontology: Social Sciences, 44*, S231–238.

Stoller, E. P., & Pugliesi, K. L. (1989b). The transition to the caregiving role: A panel study of helpers of elderly people. *Research on Aging, 11*, 312–330.

Stone, R., Cafferata, G. L., & Sangl, J. (1987). Caregivers of the frail elderly: A national profile. *The Gerontologist, 27*, 616–626.

Storandt, M. (1983). *Counseling and Therapy with Older Adults.* Boston: Little, Brown & Co.

Strauss, A. L., & Glaser, B. G. (1970). *Anguish.* Mill Valley, CA: Sociology Press.

Streufert, S., Pogash, R., Piasecki, M., & Post, G. M. (1990). Age and management team performance. *Psychology and Aging, 5*, 551–559.

Strickland, B. R. (1988). Menopause. In E. A. Blechman & K. D. Brownell (Eds.), *Handbook of Behavioral Medicine for Women* (pp. 41–47). New York: Pergammon Press.

Strom, R., & Strom, S. (1987). Preparing grandparents for a new role. *Journal of Applied Gerontology, 6*, 476–486.

Stroop, J. R. (1935). Studies of interference in serial verbal reactions. *Journal of Experimental Psychology, 18*, 643–662.

Stroud, J. G. (1981). Women's careers: Work, family, and personality. In D. H. Eichorn, J. A. Clausen, N. Haan, M. P. Honzik, & P. H. Mussen (Eds.), *Present and Past in Middle Life* (pp. 356–392). New York: Academic Press.

Stull, D. E. (1989). Never married elderly: A reassessment with implications for long-term care policy. *Research on Aging, 11*, 124–139.

Stull, D. E., & Scarisbrick-Hauser, A. (1989). Never married elderly: A reassessment with implications for long-term care policy. *Research on Aging, 11*, 124–139.

Suitor, J. J., & Pillemer, K. (1988). Explaining intergenerational conflict when adult children and elderly parents live together. *Journal of Marriage and the Family, 50*, 1037–1047.

Sullivan, H. S. (1953). *The Interpersonal Theory of Psychiatry*. New York: Norton.

Super, D. E. (1957). *The Psychology of Careers*. New York: Harper & Row.

Super, D. E., Starishevsky, R., Matlin, N., & Jordaan, J. P. (1963). *Career Development: Self Concept Theory*. New York: College Entrance Examination Board.

Sussman, M. B. (1985). The family life of old people. In R. H. Binstock & E. Shanas (Eds.), *Handbook of Aging and the Social Sciences* (2nd ed.). (pp. 415–449). New York: Van Nostrand Reinhold.

Taylor, R. J. (1986). Religious participation among elderly Blacks. *The Gerontologist, 26*, 630–636.

Taylor, R. J. (1988). Aging and supportive relationships among black Americans. In J. S. Jackson (Ed.), *The Black American Elderly: Research on Physical and Psychosocial Health* (pp. 259–281). New York: Springer.

Taylor, R. J., & Chatters, L. M. (1986). Patterns of informal support to elderly black adults: Family, friends, and church members. *Social Work, 31*, 432–438.

Tellis-Nayak, V., & Tellis-Nayak, M. (1989). Quality of care and the burden of two cultures: When the world of the nurse's aide enters the world of the nursing home. *The Gerontologist, 29*, 307–313.

Templer, D., Ruff, C., & Franks, C. (1971). Death anxiety: Age, sex, and parental resemblance in diverse populations. *Developmental Psychology, 4*, 108–114.

Tennstedt, S. L., McKinlay, J. B., & Sullivan, L. M. (1989). Informal care for frail elders: The role of secondary caregivers. *The Gerontologist, 29*, 677–683.

Teri, L., Hughes, J. P., & Larson, E. B. (1990). Cognitive deterioration in Alzheimer's Disease: Behavioral and health factors. *Journal of Gerontology: Psychological Sciences, 45*, P58–63.

Terkel, S. (1972). *Working*. New York: Avon.

Thomas, J. L. (1985a). Grandchildren's impact on adult child-elderly parent relationships. *Academic Psychology Bulletin, 7*, 27–37.

Thomas, J. L. (1985b). Visual memory: Adult age differences in map recall and learning strategies. *Experimental Aging Research, 11*, 93–95.

Thomas, J. L. (1986a). Age and sex differences in perceptions of grandparenting. *Journal of Gerontology, 41*, 417–423.

Thomas, J. L. (1986b). Gender differences in satisfaction with grandparenting. *Psychology and Aging, 1*, 215–219.

Thomas, J. L. (1987). Adult children's assistance as a health care resource: The older parent's perspective. *Family and Community Health, 9*, 34–42.

Thomas, J. L. (1988). Predictors of satisfaction with children's help for younger and older elderly parents. *Journal of Gerontology: Social Sciences, 43*, S9–14.

Thomas, J. L. (1989). Gender and perceptions of grandparenthood. *International Journal of Aging and Human Development, 29*, 269–282.

Thomas, J. L. (1990a). Grandparenthood and mental health: Implications for the practitioner. *Journal of Applied Gerontology, 9*, 464–479.

Thomas, J. L. (1990b). The grandparent role: A double bind. *International Journal of Aging and Human Development, 31*, 169–177.

Thomas, V. G. (1990). Determinants of global life happiness and marital happiness in dual-career black couples. *Family Relations, 39*, 174–178.

Thomas, R. K., Miller, T. M., & Karsko, J. E. (1989, August). *Satisfaction and commitment in dating couples: Personality and relationship effects*. Paper presented at the 97th Annual Convention of the American Psychological Association, New Orleans, LA.

Thompson, H. L. (1985). The ready-for-prime-time players: Colleges cater to the adult schedule. *Educational Record, 66*, 33–37.

Thompson, L., Breckenridge, J. N., Gallagher, D., & Peterson, J. (1984). Effects of bereavement on self-perceptions of physical health in elderly widows and widowers. *Journal of Gerontology, 39*, 309–314.

Thompson, L., & Walker, A. J. (1989). Gender in families: Women and men in marriage, work, and parenthood. *Journal of Marriage and the Family,* *51*, 845–871.

Tomlinson-Keasey, C. (1972). Formal operations in females from eleven to fifty-four years of age. *Developmental Psychology, 6,* 364.

Toseland, R. W., & Rossiter, C. M. (1989). Group interventions to support family caregivers: A review and analysis. *The Gerontologist, 29,* 438–448.

Toseland, R. W., & Smith, G. C. (1990). Effectiveness of individual counseling by professional and peer helpers for family caregivers of the elderly. *Psychology and Aging, 5,* 256–263.

Tourigny-Rivard, M. F., & Drury, M. (1987). The effects of monthly psychiatric consultation in a nursing home. *The Gerontologist, 27,* 363–366.

Townsend, A., Noelker, L., Deimling, G., & Bass, D. (1989). Longitudinal impact of interhousehold caregiving on adult children's mental health. *Psychology and Aging, 4,* 393–401.

Treas, J., & Bengtson, V. L. (1987). The family in later years. In M. B. Sussman & S. K. Steinmetz (Eds.), *Handbook of Marriage and the Family* (pp. 625–648). New York: Plenum Press.

Treat, N. J., & Reese, H. W. (1976). Age, imagery, and pacing in paired-associate learning. *Developmental Psychology, 12,* 119–124.

Troll, L. E. (1989). Myths of midlife intergenerational relationships. In S. Hunter & M. Sundel (Eds.), *Midlife Myths: Issues, Findings, and Practice Implications* (pp. 210–232). Newbury Park, CA: Sage Publications.

Troll, L. E., & Bengtson, V. L. (1982). Intergenerational relations throughout the life span. In B. B. Wolman (Ed.), *Handbook of Developmental Psychology* (pp. 890–911). Englewood Cliffs, NJ: Prentice Hall.

Tschann, J. M., Johnston, J. R., & Wallerstein, J. S. (1989). Resources, stressors, and attachment as predictors of adult adjustment after divorce: A longitudinal study. *Journal of Marriage and the Family, 51,* 1033–1046.

Turner, N. W. (1980). Divorce in mid-life: Clinical implications and applications. In W. H. Norman & T. J. Scaramella (Eds.), *Mid-life: Developmental and Clinical Issues* (pp. 149–177). New York: Bruner/Mazel, Publishers.

Turner, B. F., & Adams, C. (1983). The sexuality of older women. In E. W. Markson (Ed.), *Older Women* (pp. 55–72). Lexington, MA: Lexington Books.

Turner, B. F., & Turner, C. B. (1982). Mental health in the adult years. In T. M. Field, A. Huston, H. C. Quay, L. Troll, & G. E. Finley (Eds.), *Review of Human Development* (pp. 456–470). New York: Wiley.

Uhlenberg, P., Cooney, T., & Boyd, R. (1990). Divorce for women after midlife. *Journal of Gerontology: Social Sciences, 45,* S3–11.

Uniform Guidelines on Employee Selection Procedures. (1978). *Federal Register, 43,* 38296–38309.

U. S. Bureau of the Census. (1984). *National Data Book and Guide to Sources: Statistical Abstract of the United States, 1985.* (105th Ed.). Washington, DC: U. S. Government Printing Office.

U. S. Department of Education. (1987). *Enrollment in colleges and universities, Fall 1985.* (Office of Educational Research and Improvement Bulletin CS 87–311B). Washington, DC: Center for Educational Statistics.

U. S. Department of Health and Human Services (USDHHS). (1982). *Breast cancer: We're making progress every day* (NIH Publication No. 82–2409). Washington, DC: U. S. Government Printing Office.

U. S. Department of Health and Human Services (USDHHS). (1985). *Health, United States, 1985* (DDH Publication No. PHS 86–1232). Washington, DC: U. S. Government Printing Office.

U. S. Department of Health and Human Services (USDHHS). (1986a). *Health statistics on older persons: United States, 1986* (DHHS Publication No. PHS 87–1409). Washington, DC: U. S. Government Printing Office.

U. S. Department of Health and Human Services (USDHHS). (1986b). *Health, United States, 1986 and prevention profile* (DDH Publication No. PHS 87–1232). Washington, DC: U. S. Government Printing Office.

U. S. Department of Health and Human Services (USDHHS). (1986c). *Surgeon General's report on Acquired Immune Deficiency Syndrome.* Washington, DC: U. S. Government Printing Office.

U. S. Department of Health and Human Services (USDHHS). (1987a). *Health statistics on older persons: United States, 1986.* Hyattsville, MD: National Center for Health Statistics.

U. S. Department of Health and Human Services (USDHHS). (1987b). *Smoking and health: A national status report.* (HHS/PHS/CDC Publication No. 87–8396). Washington, DC: U. S. Government Printing Office.

U. S. Department of Health and Human Services (USDHHS). (1989). *Aging in the eighties: The prevalence of comorbidity and its association with disability.* (DHHS Publication No. PHS 89–1250). Washington, DC: U. S. Government Printing Office.

U. S. Department of Labor. (1985). *Employed persons by major occupational group and sex.* Statistics. Washington, DC: U. S. Government Printing Office.

U. S. Public Health Service. National Center for Health Statistics. (1981). Current estimates from the National Health Interview Survey: United States, 1980. *Vital Health Statistics* (Series 10, No. 139). Washington, DC: U. S. Government Printing Office.

U. S. Senate Special Committee on Aging. (1987). *Aging America: Trends and projections* (1987–1988 ed.). Washington, DC: U. S. Department of Health and Human Services.

Usher, R. S. (1986). Reflection and prior work experience: Some problematic issues in relation to adult students in university studies. *Studies in Higher Education, 11*, 245–256.

Valimaki, M., & Ylikahri, R. (1983). The effect of alcohol on male and female sexual function. *Alcohol and Alcoholism, 18*, 313–320.

Veatch, R. M. (1981). *A Theory of Medical Ethics.* New York: Basic Books.

Veevers, J. E. (1979). Voluntary Childlessness: A Review of Issues and Evidence. *Marriage and Family Review, 2*, 3–26.

Veevers, J. E. (1980). *Childless by Choice.* Toronto: Butterworth.

Vemer, E., Coleman, M., Ganong, L. H., & Cooper, H. (1989). Marital satisfaction in remarriage: A meta-analysis. *Journal of Marriage and the Family, 51*, 713–725.

Ventura, J. N. (1987). The stresses of parenthood reexamined. *Family Relations, 36*, 26–29.

Verbrugge, L. M. (1989). Gender, aging, and health. In K. S. Markides (Ed.), *Aging and Health: Perspectives on Gender, Race, Ethnicity, and Class* (pp. 23–78). Newbury Park, CA: Sage Publications.

Vestal, R. E., & Crusack, B. J. (1990). Pharmacology and aging. In E. L. Schneider & J. W. Rowe (Eds.), *Handbook of the Biology of Aging* (3rd ed.). (pp. 349–383). San Diego: Academic Press.

Veterans Health Service and Research Administration (VHSRA). (1989). *Dementia: Guidelines for diagnosis and treatment.* Washington, DC.

Viney, L. L. (1987). A sociophenomenological approach to life-span development complementing Erikson's sociodynamic approach. *Human Development, 30*, 125–136.

Vinokur-Kaplan, D., & Bergman, S. (1986). Retired Israeli social workers: Work, volunteer activities, and satisfaction among retired professionals. *Journal of Gerontological Social Work, 9*, 73–86.

Voda, A. M., & Eliasson, M. (1983). Menopause: The closure of menstrual life. In S. Golub (Ed.), *Lifting the Curse of Menstruation* (pp. 137–156). New York: The Haworth Press.

Vondracek, F. W., & Lerner, R. M. (1982). Vocational role development during adolescence. In B. B. Wolman (Ed.), *Handbook of Developmental Psychology* (pp. 602–614). Englewood Cliffs, NJ: Prentice Hall.

Wacks, V. Q. (1987). A case for self-transcendence as a purpose of adult education. *Adult Education Quarterly, 38*, 46–55.

Walford, R. L. (1983). *Maximum Life Span.* New York: Norton.

Wallace, S. P. (1990). The no-care zone: Availability, accessibility, and acceptability in community-based long-term care. *The Gerontologist, 30*, 254–261.

Wallerstein, J. S., & Kelly, J. B. (1980). *Surviving the Breakup: How Children Actually Cope with Divorce.* New York: Basic Books.

Wanous, J. P. (1980). *Organizational Entry.* Reading, MA: Addison-Wesley.

Ward, R. A., LaGory, M., & Sherman, S. R. (1985). Neighborhood and network age concentration: Does age homogeneity matter for older people? *Social Psychology Quarterly, 48*, 138–149.

Waugh, N. C., Thomas, J. C., & Fozard, J. L. (1978). Retrieval time from different memory stores. *Journal of Gerontology, 33*, 718–724.

Weg, R. B. (1989). Sensuality/sexuality of the middle years. In S. Hunter & M. Sundel (Eds.), *Midlife*

Myths: Issues, Findings and Practice Implications (pp. 31–50). Newbury Park, CA: Sage Publications.

Weidman, J. C., & White, R. N. (1985). Postsecondary "high tech" training for women on welfare: Correlates of program completion. *Journal of Higher Education, 56*, 555–568.

Weiner, R. D. (1979). The psychiatric use of electrically-induced seizures. *American Journal of Psychiatry, 136*, 1507–1517.

Weisman, A. T. (1972). *On Dying and Denying: A Psychiatric Study of Terminality*. New York: Behavioral Publications.

Weiss, L., & Lowenthal, M. F. (1975). Life-course perspectives on friendship. In M. F. Lowenthal, M. Thurnher, D. Chiriboga, & Assoc. (Eds.), *The Four Stages of Life* (pp. 48–61). San Francisco: Jossey-Bass Publishers.

Weisskopf, E. A., & Dieppa, J. J. (1951). Experimentally induced faking of TAT responses. *Journal of Consulting Psychology, 15*, 469–474.

Welford, A. T. (1977). Motor performance. In J. E. Birren & K. W. Schaie (Eds.), *Handbook of the Psychology of Aging* (pp. 450–496). New York: Van Nostrand Reinhold Co.

Wentowski, G. J. (1985). Older women's perceptions of great-grandmotherhood: A research note. *The Gerontologist, 25*, 593–596.

West, R. L. (1984, August). *An analysis of prospective everyday memory*. Paper presented at the annual meeting of the American Psychological Association, Toronto, Canada.

Whitbourne, S. K. (1976). Test anxiety in elderly and young adults. *International Journal of Aging and Human Development, 7*, 201–210.

Whitbourne, S. K. (1985). *The Aging Body: Physiological Changes and Psychological Consequences*. New York: Springer-Verlag.

White, N., & Cunningham, W. R. (1988). Is terminal drop pervasive or specific? *Journal of Gerontology: Psychological Sciences, 43*, P141–P144.

Who can afford a nursing home? (1988, May). *Consumer Reports*, pp. 300–311.

Wilkinson, R. T., & Allison, S. (1989). Age and simple reaction time: Decade differences for 5,325 subjects. *Journal of Gerontology: Psychological Sciences, 44*, P29–P36.

Williams, M. (1984). Alcohol and the elderly: An overview. *Alcohol Health and Research World, 8*, 3–10.

Williams, G., Stinson, F., Parker, D., Harford, T., & Noble, J. (1987). Demographic trends, alcohol abuse, and alcoholism. *Alcohol Health and Research World, 11*, 80–83, 91.

Williams, S. A., Denney, N. W., & Schadler, M. (1983). Elderly adults' perceptions of their own cognitive development during the adult years. *International Journal of Aging and Human Development, 16*, 147–158.

Willis, S. L. (1985). Towards an educational psychology of the older adult learner: Intellectual and cognitive bases. In J. E. Birren & K. W. Schaie (Eds.), *Handbook of the Psychology of Aging* (2nd ed.). (pp. 818–847). New York: Van Nostrand Reinhold.

Willis, S. L. (1989). Adult intelligence. In S. Hunter & M. Sundel (Eds.), *Midlife Myths: Issues, Findings, and Practical Implications* (pp. 97–111). Newbury Park: Sage Publications.

Willis, S. L., & Nesselroade, C. S. (1990). Long-term effects of fluid ability training in old-old age. *Developmental Psychology, 26*, 905–910.

Wilson, V. (1989, June). *Health protective behaviors of the rural black elderly woman*. Paper presented at the XIV International Congress of Gerontology, Acapulco, Mexico.

Wilson, K. B., & DeShane, M. R. (1982). The legal rights of grandparents: A preliminary discussion. *The Gerontologist, 22*, 67–71.

Winkler, A., Fairnie, H., Gericevich, F., & Long, M. (1989). The impact of a resident dog on an institution for the elderly: Effects on perceptions and social interactions. *The Gerontologist, 29*, 216–223.

Wise, L. R. (1990). Partial and flexible retirement: The Swedish system. *The Gerontologist, 30*, 355–361.

Wisniewski, K., Wisniewski, H., & Wen, G. Y. (1983). Plaques, tangles, and dementia in Down's syndrome. *Journal of Neuropathology and Experimental Neurology, 42*, 340–346.

Wisocki, P. A., & Averill, J. R. (1987). The challenge of bereavement. In L. L. Carstensen & B. A. Edelstein (Eds.), *Handbook of Clinical Gerontology* (pp. 312–321). New York: Pergammon Press.

Wohlwill, J. F. (1970). Methodology and research strategy in the study of developmental change. In L. R. Goulet & P. B. Baltes (Eds.), *Life-span Developmental Psychology: Research and Theory* (pp. 150–193). New York: Academic Press.

Wohlwill, J. F. (1973). The concept of experience: S or R? *Human Development, 16*, 90–107.

Woll, S. B., & Young, P. (1989). Looking for Mr. or Ms. Right: Self-presentation in videodating. *Journal of Marriage and the Family, 51*, 483–488.

Wong, H. (1981). Typologies of intimacy. *Psychology of Women Quarterly, 5*, 435–443.

Woodruff, D. (1985). Arousal, sleep, and aging. In J. E. Birren & K. W. Schaie (Eds.), *Handbook of the Psychology of Aging* (2nd ed.). (pp. 261–295). New York: Van Nostrand Reinhold.

Woodruff, D. S., & Birren, J. E. (1972). Age changes and cohort differences in personality. *Developmental Psychology, 6*, 252–259.

Woodward, N. J., & Wallston, B. S. (1987). Age and health care beliefs: Self-efficacy as a mediator of low desire for control. *Psychology and Aging, 2*, 3–9.

World Health Organization, Regional Office for Europe. (1980). *Appropriate Levels For Continuing Care of the Elderly*. Report of a WHO Working Group, Berlin ICP/ADR o26 4566B.

Wrightsman, L. S. (1988). *Personality Development in Adulthood*. Newbury Park: Sage Publications.

Yeas, M., & Grad, S. (1987). Income of retirement-aged persons in the United States. *Social Security Bulletin, 50*, 5–14.

Yesavage, J. A. (1983). Imagery pretraining and memory training in the elderly. *Gerontology, 29*, 271–275.

Yesavage, J. A., Sheikh, J. I., Friedman, L., & Tanke, E. (1990). Learning mnemonics: Roles of age and subtle cognitive impairment. *Psychology and Aging, 5*, 133–137.

Young, R. F., & Kahana, E. (1989). Specifying caregiver outcomes: Gender and relationship aspects of caregiving strain. *The Gerontologist, 29*, 660–666.

Zaks, P. M., & Labouvie-Vief, G. (1980). Spatial perspective taking and referential communication skills in the elderly: A training study. *Journal of Gerontology, 35*, 217–224.

Zarit, S. H., Cole, K. D., & Guider, R. L. (1981). Memory training strategies and subjective complaints of memory in the aged. *The Gerontologist, 21*, 158–164.

Zarit, S. H., Orr, N. K., & Zarit, J. M. (1985). *The Hidden Victims of Alzheimer's Disease: Families under Stress*. New York: New York University Press.

Zelinski, E. M., Gilewski, M. J., & Anthony-Bergstone, C. R. (1990). Memory functioning questionnaire: Concurrent validity with memory performance and self-reported memory failures. *Psychology and Aging, 5*, 388–399.

Zelinski, E. M., & Miura, S. A. (1988). Effects of thematic information on script memory in young and old adults. *Psychology and Aging, 3*, 292–299.

Zimberg, S. (1974). The elderly alcoholic. *The Gerontologist, 14*, 221–224.

Zsembik, B. A., & Singer, A. (1990). The problem of defining retirement among minorities: The Mexican Americans. *The Gerontologist, 30*, 749.

Zweibel, N. R., & Cassel, C. K. (1989). Treatment choices at the end of life: A comparison of decisions by older patients and their physician-selected proxies. *The Gerontologist, 29*, 615–621.

INDEX

Note: The letter *b* following a page number refers to boxed text; *n* refers to a footnote.

AARP. *See* American Association of Retired Persons
Absolute threshold, of vision, 115
 definition of, 398
Acceptance, stage of dying, 380
 definition of, 398
Acetylcholine, 237
 definition of, 398
Achieving stage, of intellectual development, 141
 definition of, 398
Acquired immunodeficiency syndrome, 89–91, 235–236
 definition of, 398
 impact on homosexual lifestyles, 270
Acquisitive stage, of intellectual development, 141
 definition of, 398
Active, definition of, 43, 398
Active euthanasia, 371–372, 372*b*
 definition of, 398
Activities of daily living
 definition of, 398
 help with, source of, 305–306
 impairments of, in old age, 96
Activity theory, of aging, 35, 36*b*–37*b*, 39, 205–207
 definition of, 398
Acute phase, of preparation for dying, 381
 definition of, 398
AD. *See* Alzheimer's disease
Adaptation, definition of, 398
Adaptation phase, of pregnancy, 282
Adjustment, views of, by age group, 222
Adolescent(s), and parents, 288–289

Adult day care, 101
 definition of, 398
Adult development and aging
 professional interest in, 5
 study of
  development of, 4–6
  life-span perspective, 6–13
  significance of, 3–6
  theories in, 32–50
Adulthood
 developmental periods of, 198
 developmental tasks of, 193–194
 middle years of, 212*b*. *See also* Midlife crisis; Midlife transition
 themes of, 200
Adult intelligence. *See* Intelligence
Adult personality. *See* Personality
Adults, in community, 329–339
Adverse impact, of employment discrimination, 354
 definition of, 398
Affirmative action, 355, 356*b*–357*b*
Age
 definition of, 398
 as variable in research design, 20
Age differences
 in cross-sectional study, versus age changes, 21
 identification of, 21–22
Age discrimination, 350–352
Age Discrimination in Employment Act, 351–352, 398
Age-segregated housing, 337, 338*b*–339*b*
 definition of, 398
Aging
 biological theories of, 35, 75–76
 demographics of, 3, 77–78
 double standard of, 55, 56*b*
 genetic theories of, 75–76

 as gradual process, 75
 as individual process, 75
 patterns of, 207
 physical, 75
 successful, definition of, 36*b*–37*b*
 wear and tear theories of, 76
Aging spots, 54
 definition of, 399
Agreeableness, 203
AIDS. *See* Acquired immunodeficiency syndrome
Air pollution, 60–61
Alcohol, effects of
 on fertility, 72
 on health, 88–89
Alcohol abuse, in old age, 231–233
 assessment of, 233
 reasons for concern, 231–232
 treatment of, 232–233
Alienated achievement, 191
 definition of, 399
Alleviative optimization, 8
 definition of, 399
Alternate forms reliability, 18
 definition of, 399
Alternative procedures, for personnel selection, 354
 definition of, 399
Alzheimer's disease (AD), 58, 233
 course of, 237–238
 definition of, 399
 diagnosis of, 238–242
 distinguishing features of, 236–237
 incidence of, 236
 possible causes of, 238
 treatment of, 242–243
Ambivalent singles, 267
 definition of, 399

American Association of Retired Persons, 331, 399
American Psychological Association, 5
    guidelines for developmental research, 26–30, 28b–29b
Amyloid, 237
    definition of, 399
Analysis of Variance (ANOVA), 395
Anger
    definition of, 399
    in reaction to divorce, 271
    stage of dying, 379
Anima, 189
    definition of, 399
Animal rights, 28b–29b
Animus, 189
    definition of, 399
Anniversary reaction, 382
    definition of, 399
ANOVA. See Analysis of Variance
Antecedent-consequent analysis, 34
    definition of, 399
Anticipation and preparation phase, of pregnancy, 283
    definition of, 399
Anticipatory grief, 383
    definition of, 399
Antidepressants
    for Alzheimer's disease, 242
    for depression, 225
Antipsychotic medication
    for Alzheimer's disease, 242
    definition of, 399
APA. See American Psychological Association
Apathetic sibling relationship, 323
    definition of, 399
Appearance, changes in, with aging, 53–55
Appropriate death, 375
    definition of, 399
Archetypes, definition of, 189, 399
Arcus senilis, 114
    definition of, 399
Armored-defended personality type, 207
    definition of, 399
Arousal, age differences in, 122–125
Arousal hypothesis, 124–125
    definition of, 399
Arteriosclerosis, 59
    definition of, 400

Artificial embryonation, 73–74
    definition of, 400
Artificial insemination by donor, 72–74
    definition of, 400
Asexual homosexuals, 270
    definition of, 400
Assortativeness, 254
    definition of, 400
Asynchronies, in Riegel's developmental theory, 46–47, 50
Atherosclerosis, 59
    definition of, 400
Attachment/separateness polarity, 199
    definition of, 400
Attention, age differences in, 122–125
Attention switching, 123
    definition of, 400
Autoimmune responses, 64
    definition of, 400
Autoimmune theories
    of aging, 76
    definition of, 400
Automatic processing, 142
    definition of, 400
Autonomy, personal, 18–19
Awareness of finitude, 377–378
    definition of, 400

Baby Boom generation, and divorce rates, 271
Balanced connection marriage, 262b–263b
    definition of, 400
Baltimore Longitudinal Study of Aging, 5, 95, 203–204, 400
Bargaining
    definition of, 400
    stage of dying, 379
Basal metabolic rate, 61
    definition of, 400
Behavior, measures of, age equivalence of, 18–19
Behavior exchange theory (BET)
    definition of, 400
    and marital satisfaction, 258
Behaviorism, 42–43
Behavior modification, 43
Behavior therapy
    definition of, 400
    for depression, 226
Bereavement overload, 384
    definition of, 400
Berkeley Growth Studies, 92

BET. See Behavior exchange theory
Biological growth orientation, 9
    definition of, 400
Bivariate correlation, 395–396
Bladder, changes in, with aging, 63–64
Blended families, 287–288
Blindness, incidence of, and age, 117
BLSA. See Baltimore Longitudinal Study of Aging
Body temperature, and longevity, 78–79
Body transcendence, vs. body preoccupation, 195
Bolles, Richard, 183b

California Personality Inventory (CPI), 201–202, 400
Cancer, of reproductive system, 91
Cardiac output, 58
    definition of, 400
Cardiac reserve, 60
    definition of, 401
Cardinal trait, 187
    definition of, 401
Cardiovascular system, changes in, with aging, 58–60
Career changes, 349–350
Career choice, theories of, 343–346
    developmentalist, 344–346
    differentialist, 343–344
Careers
    and ethnicity, 352–355
    and race, 352–355
Caregiver burden, 243, 306–307
    definition of, 401
    mediators, 310–312
    minimizing, 310–312
Caregiver support group, 311
    definition of, 401
Cataracts, 118
    definition of, 401
Cathectic flexibility, 195
Causal analysis, 396–397
Centering phase, of pregnancy, 282–283
    definition of, 401
Central nervous system, 57
    definition of, 401
Central tendency, measures of, 391–392
Cerebral death, 369
    definition of, 401

Children
  motivations for not having,
    279–281
  reasons for having, 279, 280*b*
Chronic diseases
  definition of, 401
  frequencies of, in middle age and
    older adulthood, 92–96
Chronic living-dying phase, 381
  definition of, 401
Ciliary body, 112–114
  definition of, 401
Classic aging pattern, in intelligence,
    149
  definition of, 401
Climacteric, 65–66
  definition of, 64, 401
  effects on health, 91–92
  effects on sexuality, 66–67
  psychological effects of, cultural
    differences in, 67, 68*b*–69*b*
Clinical threshold of symptoms, 60
  definition of, 401
Close-coupled homosexuals, 269–
    270
  definition of, 401
Cocaine abuse, 89
Cochlear implant, 120
  definition of, 401
Cognitive development, adult,
    150–151
Cognitive functioning
  age differences in, 122–132
  and aging, 45–46
  changes in, with aging, 110–134
  effect of chronic illness and com-
    orbidity on, 96
Cognitive regression, with aging,
    153–154
Cognitive therapy
  definition of, 401
  for depression, 226–227
Cohabitation, 268–269
  definition of, 401
Cohort
  definition of, 401
  as variable in research design,
    20
Cohort-sequential research design,
    23–25
  definition of, 401
Collective unconscious, definition
    of, 189, 401
College(s), 177–180
  American, 180

College students, diversity among,
    180
Communities, specialized, for el-
    derly, 335–339
Comorbidity, 93–96
  definition of, 401
Comparative developmental ap-
    proach, 12*b*
  definition of, 401
Compatibility, 326
  definition of, 401
Competence
  definition of, 401
  and environmental press,
    335–337
Compliance, respiratory, 60
  definition of, 401
Conductive deafness, 120
  definition of, 402
Confidants
  definition of, 402
  in old age, 327–329
Conflict, and change, 47
Conflict-habituated marriage, 262*b*
Confound, definition of, 402
Confounding, of variables, in re-
    search, 21
Congenial sibling relationship, 323
  definition of, 402
Congregate housing, 338
  definition of, 402
Conjugal bereavement, 382–384
Conscientiousness, 203
Consequential religiosity, 333
  definition of, 402
Constructed knowledge, 179*b*
  definition of, 402
Construct validity, 17
  definition of, 402
Contentment, in old age, paths to,
    205–208
Continuing education, 181–183, 184
  job-related, 182
Continuity, 34
  definition of, 402
Contrast sensitivity, 115–116
  definition of, 402
Control, perception of, effect on
    health, 86–87
Correlational analyses, 395–396
Cortex, 58
  definition of, 402
Couple-centered connection mar-
    riage, 263*b*
  definition of, 402

Couvade syndrome, 283
  definition of, 402
CPI. *See* California Personality Inven-
    tory
Creation. *See* Destruction/creation
Creativity, developmental trends in,
    research on, 158–160
Crises, psychosocial, in Erikson's
    theory, 48*b*–49*b*, 190–193
Cross-cultural research, 11, 12*b*
Cross-linkage theory, of aging, 76
  definition of, 402
Cross-linked, definition of, 402
Cross-linking, of proteins, 54
Cross-sectional research design,
    20–22
  definition of, 402
Cross-sequential research design,
    24–26
  definition of, 402
Crystallization stage, 344
  definition of, 402
Crystallized intelligence, 96,
    144–145
  definition of, 402
  stability or age-related improve-
    ments of, 149–152
Cued recall, 171
  definition of, 402
Culture
  and definition of mental health,
    220*b*
  and development, 49*b*
  effects on age-related hearing loss,
    114*b*–115*b*
  effects on age-related vision
    changes, 114*b*–115*b*
  and menopause, 67, 68*b*–69*b*

Dark adaptation, 115
  definition of, 402
Dating relationships, age and gender
    differences in, 251–254
Deafness, 120
Death
  attitudes toward, 376–381
    age differences in, 378–379
    ethnic differences in, 378
    gender differences in, 378
    and religion, 377–378
    in terminally ill, 379–381
  causes of
    in early adulthood, 83
    in old age, 96–97
  definition of, 369–370

Death *(continued)*
  medical and ethical issues related to, 370–376
  of parent, 384–385
  as process, 370
  social and legal issues related to, 381–387
  survivors' reactions to, 381–382
Debilitating anxiety, 148
  definition of, 402
Deceleration stage, 345
  definition of, 402
Defined-benefit pension plan, 365
  definition of, 403
Defined-contribution pension plan, 365–366
  definition of, 403
Deinstitutionalizing, 229
  definition of, 403
Dementia, 63, 233–243
  definition of, 58*n*, 403
  and depression, symptoms that distinguish, 236
  prevalence of, age-specific, 237
  stages of, 240–241
  symptoms of, 234–236
Demographic trends, 3–4
Denial
  definition of, 403
  stage of dying, 379
Depression, 221–227
  causes of, 224–225
  definition of, 403
  and dementia, symptoms that distinguish, 236
  diagnosis of, 221–224
  in elderly, treatment of, 225–227
  in reaction to divorce, 271–272
  stage of dying, 380
Dermis, 54
  definition of, 403
Description, in life-span developmental research, 7
  definition of, 403
Descriptive statistics, 391–393
Despair, 192–193, 377
  definition of, 403
Destruction/creation polarity, 199
  definition of, 403
Detachment, reorganization, and recovery, as stage of bereavement, 382
  definition of, 403
Development
  cultural context of, 11

definition of, 38
historical context of, 11
as life-long process, 9
models of, 33–34, 39–50
pluralism of, 9
structural versus behavioral change in, 34
Developmentalist theories, of career choice, 344–346
  definition of, 403
Developmental research, ethical issues in, 26–30. *See also* Research methodology
Developmental research design(s), 20–26
  basic designs, 20–23
  central variables of, 20
  sequential designs, 23–26
Developmental stake, 296
  definition of, 403
Developmental tasks, 193
  of adulthood, 193–194
  definition of, 403
Developmental theories, 32–50
  and research, 38–39
  variety of, 35–38
Devitalized marriage, 262*b*
Diabetic retinopathy, 118
  definition of, 403
Dialectical model, of development, 39–40, 46–50
  definition of, 403
Dichotic listening task, 123
  definition of, 403
Diet
  effect on health, 85–86
  and longevity, 78–79
Differentialist theories, of career choice, 343–344
  definition of, 403
Differentiation model, 138–139
Digestive system, changes in, with aging, 62–63
Directionality, of developmental changes, 38
  definition of, 404
Discontinuity, 34
  definition of, 404
Discourse
  age differences in memory of, 175
  definition of, 404
Discrimination, in employment, 354–355

Disengaged personality type, 207
Disengagement theory, of aging, 35, 36*b*–37*b*, 39, 205–207
  definition of, 404
Disequilibrium, in reaction to divorce, 272
Disorganization and despair, as stage of bereavement, 382
  definition of, 404
Disruption phase, of pregnancy, 282
  definition of, 404
Diverticulosis, 63
  definition of, 404
Divided attention, 123
  definition of, 404
Divorce, 271–274
  emotional reactions to, 271–272
  financial impact of, 272–274
  in middle and later adulthood, 272–274
Divorce rates, 271
  for remarriages, 276*b*
Dream, as sense of oneself, 209
  definition of, 404
Driving, in old age, 130, 131*b*
Drug abuse, effect on health, 89
Dual specialization, in caregiving, 316–317
  definition of, 404
DVA. *See* Dynamic visual acuity
Dying, stages of, 379–380
Dying trajectories, 381
  definition of, 404
Dynamic visual acuity, 115–116, 133
  definition of, 404
Dysfunctional homosexuals, 270
  definition of, 404
Dysphoria, definition of, 223, 404

Ear, structures of, 118–119
Early articulators, 279
  definition of, 404
Early onset of drinking, 232
  definition of, 404
Early retirement, 359–361
Echoic memory, 166
  definition of, 404
ECT. *See* Electroconvulsive therapy
Education
  as box of life, 183*b*
  throughout adulthood, 177–185
Educational programs, older adults in, 129–130
EEG. *See* Electroencephalogram

Efficient causes, 41
  definition of, 404
Effortful processing, 142
  definition of, 404
Egg donation, 73–74
  definition of, 404
Ego, definition of, 188–189, 404
Ego differentiation, vs. work-role pre-
    occupation, 195
Ego integrity, 192, 377
  definition of, 404
Ego transcendence, vs. ego preoccu-
    pation, 195
Elder abuse, 296
  definition of, 404
Elderhostel, 184, 404
Electroconvulsive therapy (ECT)
  definition of, 404
  for major depression, 225–226
Electroencephalogram, 124
  definition of, 404
Elementarism, 33–34
  definition of, 405
Embryo adoption, 73–74
  definition of, 405
Emergency response systems, 101
  definition of, 405
Emotional flexibility, 195
Employment discrimination, 354–355
  definition of, 405
Empty nest, 289–290
  definition of, 405
Encapsulation model, of adult intelli-
    gence, 142–143
  definition of, 405
Encoding deficits
  age differences in, 170
  definition of, 405
  vs. retrieval deficits, 169–171
Engagement, 36b–37b
Environment
  and development, 36–37
  interventions in, to optimize per-
    formance and mobility in
    later life, 132–133
Environmental press, 335–337
  definition of, 405
Epidermis, 54
  definition of, 405
Erectile dysfunction, 70n, 71
Erikson, Erik, 5
  developmental theory of, 46, 48b–
    49b, 157, 190–193, 376–377
Establishment stage, 345
  definition of, 405

Ethical guidelines, for research, 26–
    30, 28b–29b
Euthanasia, 371–372, 372b
Exchange theories, of mate selec-
    tion, 255–256
  definition of, 405
Excitation stage, of sexual arousal, 65
  definition of, 405
Executive processes of the personal-
    ity, 195
  definition of, 405
Executive stage, of intellectual devel-
    opment, 141
  definition of, 405
Exercise, effects of
  on health, 86
  on reaction time, 126
Experiential religiosity, 333
  definition of, 405
Explanation, in life-span develop-
    mental research, 7
  definition of, 405
External validity, in research, 15
  definition of, 405
  threats to, 15–16
Eye, structures of, 112–113

Falls, incidence of, and age, 122,
    130
False assumptions, 199
  definition of, 405
Family caregiving
  caregivers, 306
  and formal sources of long-term
    care, 316–318
  for frail elderly, 305–306
  gender differences in, 315
  and institutionalization, 318
  and needs of elderly recipient, 316
  positive responses to, 313–314
  racial differences in, 316
  relationship differences in, 315
  and role conflict, 308–309
  sibling relationships in, 322–323
  stressors of, 307–308
  tasks of, 306
  variation in, 314–316
Family-centered connection mar-
    riage, 263b
  definition of, 405
Family life cycle, mythical, 196
Family support networks, 302–319
  long-term reciprocal patterns in,
    303–305

Family therapy, 246
  definition of, 405
Feminine. See Masculine/feminine
    polarity
Filial maturity, 310
  definition of, 405
Filial responsibility, 309–310
  cultural differences in, 312b–313b
  definition of, 406
Filial responsibility law, 317b
  definition of, 406
Final cause, 44
  definition of, 406
Five-factor model of personality,
    204
  definition of, 406
Fixation, 188
  definition of, 406
Fluid intelligence, 96n, 144–145
  age-related changes in, 149–151
  definition of, 406
Foreclosure, 191
  definition of, 406
Formal cause, 44
  definition of, 406
Formal health care, 97–99
  definition of, 406
Formal models of thought, 139–
    140
Formal operations, 44–45, 138,
    152–155
Formal service specialization, in car-
    egiving, 316
  definition of, 406
Frail elderly, family caregiving for,
    305–306
Framingham Study, 5
Freedom from coercion, 29–30
  definition of, 406
Free radical theory, of aging, 76
  definition of, 406
Free recall, 171
  definition of, 406
Freud, Sigmund
  psychoanalytic theory of adult per-
    sonality, 188
  theory of personality development,
    44
Friendly visiting, 101
  definition of, 406
Friendship
  age differences in, 324–326
  class differences in, 326
  gender differences in, 327, 328b
  racial differences in, 326–327

Friendship networks, 324–326
  definition of, 406
Frigidity, 70*n*
Functional disorders, 221–233. *See also* Mental disorders
  definition of, 406
Functional homosexuals, 270
  definition of, 406
Funerals, 385
  racial differences in, 386*b*

Gastrointestinal tract, 62
Gay couples, 270
Gene mutation theory of aging, 76
  definition of, 406
Generational equity, 317*b*
  definition of, 407
Generativity, 192
  definition of, 407
Gene theory of aging, 75–76
  definition of, 406
Geriatric medicine, 100
  definition of, 407
Gerontological Society of America, 5
The Gerontologist, 5
Gilligan, Carol, theory of women's moral reasoning, 214–215
Glaucoma, 117–118
  definition of, 407
Good boy/nice girl orientation to moral reasoning, 213
Gould, Roger
  description of personality development, 199–201
  themes of adult periods, 200
Grandparents/grandparenthood, 297
  age differences in, 297–298
  diversity in, 297–299
  ethnic differences in, 298–299
  gender differences in, 298
  and mental health, 299–300
  racial differences in, 298–299
Gray Panthers, 331, 407
Great-grandparents, 300–301
Grief, 381–382
  definition of, 407
Group means, comparing, 394–395
Group therapy, 246
  definition of, 407
Guidance Study, 5, 92

Hair, changes in, with aging, 54
Hall, G. Stanley, 5, 407
Harassment, in workplace, 358–359

Havighurst, Robert, developmental tasks theory of, 193–194
Hayflick limit, 76
  definition of, 407
HCAs. *See* Heterocyclic antidepressants
Health
  changes in, in adulthood, 91–97
    gender differences in, 92–96
    racial differences in, 92–96
  definition of, 83
  in early adulthood, 83–84
    and gender, 83–84
    and race, 83–84
  and lifestyle, 84–91
  in old age, 84*b*
    and race, 84*b*–85*b*
  self-ratings of, in older adults, 95–96
  threats to, in early adulthood, 83–84
Health care, and aged, 97–108
  physicians' attitudes toward, 100
Health care services, older adults' use of, 97–99
Healthy adult personality, 220*b*
Hearing
  age-related changes in. *See also* Presbycusis
    normal, 118–120
    pathological, 120
    variations in, 112, 114*b*–115*b*
  in early adulthood, 111–112
Hearing aids, 133
Hearing dogs, 133
Height, changes in, with aging, 55
Heredity, and development, 36–37
Heterocyclic antidepressants (HCAs), 225
  definition of, 407
Heterosexual assumption, 270
Hippocampus, 58
  definition of, 407
Historiometric approach, in research on creativity, 158–160
  definition of, 407
History
  definition of, 407
  as threat to internal validity of research, 13–14
HIT. *See* Holtzman Inkblot Technique
Holism, 33–34
  definition of, 407

Holtzman Inkblot Technique (HIT), 202
  definition of, 407
Home care, 101
  definition of, 407
Homeostasis, 61
  definition of, 407
Homogamy, 254
Homophobia, 328*b*
  definition of, 407
Homosexuality, 269–271
Homosexuals, as parents, 287*b*
Horizontal career change, 349
  definition of, 407
Hormone replacement therapy, 92
Hospice, definition of, 407
Hospice care, 375–376
Hostile sibling relationships, 323–324
  definition of, 407
Hotelling's T^2, 394
Hot flashes, 66
  definition of, 407
Housing, for elderly, 335–339
Human factors, 132
  definition of, 407
Huntington's disease, 234–235
  definition of, 408
Hydrocephalus. *See* Normal-pressure hydrocephalus
Hypodermis, 54
  definition of, 408
Hypothalamus, 75
  definition of, 408
Hypothesis, 38
  definition of, 408

IADL. *See* Instrumental activities of daily living
Iconic memory, 166
  definition of, 408
Id, definition of, 188, 408
Identity achievement, 191
  definition of, 408
Identity diffusion, 191
  definition of, 408
Identity matrices, 207–208
Ideological religiosity, 333
  definition of, 408
Immune system, changes in, with aging, 64
Implementation, 344
  definition of, 408
Impotence, 70*n*

Incidental causes, 47–48
    definition of, 408
Incidental memory, 174
    definition of, 408
Indirect discrimination, 354
    definition of, 408
Individuation, 199
    definition of, 408
Industrial gerontology, 128–129
    definition of, 408
Inferential statistics, 393–397
Infertility, 71–75
    definition of, 408
Informal care, 97, 99
    definition of, 408
Information processing theory, 142
    definition of, 408
Informed consent, from research
        subjects, 27–29
    definition of, 408
Inheritance, 387
Inhibited sexual desire, 70
    definition of, 408
Inhibited sexual excitement, 70–71
    definition of, 408
Institutionalization, family caregiv-
        ing and, 318
Instrumental activities of daily living
    definition of, 408
    help with, source of, 305–306
Instrumental-relativist orientation,
        to moral reasoning, 213
Integrated personality type, 207
    definition of, 408
Integumentary system
    changes in, with aging, 54
    definition of, 408
Intellectual development, stages of,
        138–142
Intellectual religiosity, 333
    definition of, 409
Intelligence, 44–45. *See also* Intellec-
        tual development
    age-related changes in
        controversy about, 161*b*
        explanations for, 151–152
        psychometric research on,
            148–151
    components of, 142–145
    definition of, 137–138
    measures of, 146
        problems with, 147–148
    psychometric studies of, 146–152
    views of, 137–145

Intelligence tests, problems with,
        147–148
Intentional memory, 174
    definition of, 409
Interactions with treatment variable,
        15–16
    definition of, 409
Interdisciplinary approach, to study
        of development, 11–13
Intergenerational support networks,
        303–305
    definition of, 409
    racial and social class differences
        in, 305
Interindividual differences, in devel-
        opment, 6–7
    definition of, 409
Interiority, 195
    definition of, 409
Intermediate nursing care facilities,
        104
    definition of, 409
Internal consistency, 18
    definition of, 409
Internal validity, 13–14
    definition of, 409
Interscorer reliability, 18
    definition of, 409
Interventions, for enhancement of
        performance and mobility in
        later life, 132–133
Intestate, 387
    definition of, 409
Intimacy
    components of, 190–191
    definition of, 409
    before marriage, age and gender
        differences in, 251
Intimate sibling relationships,
        323
    definition of, 409
Intimate status, 191
    definition of, 409
Intra-individual change, 6, 22
    definition of, 409
Intrinsic marriage, 262*b*
In-vitro fertilization, 72–73
    definition of, 409
Involutional psychosis, 68*b*
    definition of, 409
Iris, 112–113
    definition of, 409
Isolate status, 191
    definition of, 409

Isolation, 191
    definition of, 409

Jakob-Creutzfeldt disease, 235
    definition of, 409
Job performance, age differences in,
        128
Job satisfaction, 348–349
Journal of Gerontology, 5
Jung, Carl
    analytic theory of personality de-
        velopment, 188–190
    cross-cultural research on paren-
        tal imperative, 188–190

Kansas City Study of Adult Life, 37*b*
Kegel exercises, 67
Kidneys, changes in, with aging, 64
Kinesthesis
    age-related changes in, normal,
        121–122
    definition of, 409
Kin independence, 316
    definition of, 409
Kinkeepers, 295
    definition of, 410
Knowledge. *See* Ways of knowing
Kohlberg, Lawrence, stages of moral
        development, 210–214
Kubler-Ross, Elizabeth, 379–380

Labor force, older adults in, 350–352
Late onset drinking, 232
    definition of, 410
Law and order orientation, to moral
        reasoning, 213
Learning
    age differences in, 125, 184–185
    definition of, 165, 410
    differentiated from performance,
        165–166
    and memory, inseparability of, 165
Lens, of eye, 112–114
    definition of, 410
Lesbian couples, 270
Levinson, Daniel, life structure the-
        ory, 197–199
Libido, definition of, 188, 410
Life care communities, 339
    definition of, 410
Life expectancy, 4. *See also* Longevity
Lifelong isolates, 268
Life-planning problems, 158–159

Life review, 377
definition of, 410
Life satisfaction, 205
correlates of, 205–208
definition of, 410
Life-span developmental science, 11
definition of, 6
Life-span perspective, 6–13
assumptions of, 9–13
definition of, 410
goals of, 6–9
topics of, 6–9
Life structure
definition of, 410
Levinson's theory of, 197–199
Lifestyle
effect on health, 84–91
and longevity, 78
Life support measures, 371
definition of, 410
Lighting, for optimal performance in later life, 132–133
Liver, changes in, with aging, 63
Living will, 373–375
definition of, 410
Longevity, 77–79
definition of, 410
exceptional, claims of, 79
extrinsic factors and, 77
gender differences in, 77
influences on, 77–79
intrinsic factors and, 77
racial differences in, 77
Longitudinal design, definition of, 410
Longitudinal research, 5, 20–23
Long-term care
in community, 100–104
definition of, 97, 410
financing of, 101, 102b–103b, 106–108
formal sources of, family caregiving and, 316–318
in nursing homes, 104–108
state versus family responsibility for, 317b
Loose connection marriage, 263b
definition of, 410
Love relationships. See Dating relationships; Marriage
Low statistical power, 16
definition of, 410
Loyal sibling relationships, 323
definition of, 410

Maintenance stage, 345
definition of, 410
Major depression
definition of, 410
diagnosis of, 221
signs of, 222–223
MANOVA. See Multivariate Analysis of Variance
MAO inhibitors, 225
definition of, 410
Marijuana, 89
effect on fertility, 72
Marital noncohabitation, 262b
definition of, 410
Marital satisfaction
behavior exchange theory (BET) of, 258
changes over time in, 260–267
characteristics associated with, 259–260
gender differences in, 266
research on, 257–260
U-shaped curve of, 264–265
Marital status, and longevity, 78
Marital well-being
competence component of, 258
components of, 258–259
control component of, 258
for couples who did and who did not live together before marriage, 269
definition of, 410
dimensions of, 258
equity component of, 258
happiness component of, 258
Marriage. See also Remarriage
adjustment to, 257
alternatives to, 267–271
American ways of, 262b–263b
expectations regarding, 259
first, relative success of, as compared to remarriages, 276b
high-quality, types of, 262b–263b
impact of, 260
mate selection, 254–257
postparental phase of, 266
variability in, 261, 262b–263b
Marriage cohort, 275
Masculine/feminine polarity, 199
definition of, 411
Mastery
definition of, 411
feelings of, 195
for women, 210–211

Material cause, 41
definition of, 411
Mate selection, 254–257
exchange theories of, 255–256
influences of, 256
stimulus-value-role theory (SVR) of, 255–256
Maturation
definition of, 411
as threat to internal validity of research, 14
Maximum longevity, 77
definition of, 411
Maximum oxygen consumption, 59
definition of, 411
Mean longevity, 77
definition of, 411
Mechanical presbycusis, 119
Mechanistic model, of development, 39–43
definition of, 411
Mediators, 173
definition of, 411
Medicaid, 102b, 106–108
definition of, 411
Medicare, 99n, 101
definition of, 411
Medications, problems with, in older adults, 63, 93
Memory
age differences in, 125, 166–177, 184–185
definition of, 165, 411
differentiated from performance, 165–166
in everyday life, 173–175
information-processing model of, 166–169, 184
and learning, inseparability of, 165
nonability influences of, 171–173
of older adults, interventions to improve, 176–177
optimal study conditions, 173
Men
experience of pregnancy and birth, 283
in family support networks, 304
as friends, 327, 328b
Menopause, 65–66
definition of, 411
psychological effects of, 67–70
Mental disorders, 245–247. See also Functional disorders
Mental flexibility, vs. mental rigidity, 195

Mental health
  definition of, 219–221
  of women, in middle years of adult-
    hood, 212*b*
Mental health services
  for elderly, 243–247
  older adults' use of, 244–245
Metamemory, 176
  definition of, 411
Metasystematic reasoning, 140–141
  definition of, 411
MID. *See* Multi-infarct dementia
Midlife crisis, 205, 206*b*
Midlife transition, 197–198
  definition of, 411
Minnesota Multiphasic Personality
    Inventory (MMPI), 201–202
  definition of, 411
MMPI. *See* Minnesota Multiphasic
    Personality Inventory
Mobility
  age-related changes in, 122
  interventions to optimize, 132–133
Models, 33–34
  definition of, 411
  of development, 35, 39–50
  functions of, 33–34
Moral development, Kohlberg's
    stages of, 210–214
Moral reasoning, 210–215
  conventional, 213
  postconventional, 213
  preconventional, 213
  of women, Gilligan's theory of,
    214–215
Moratorium, 191
  definition of, 411
Mortality
  definition of, 411
  and interpretation of longitudinal
    results, 22
  as threat to internal validity of re-
    search, 14
Mourning, 382
  definition of, 411
Multigenerational households,
    291–293
  definition of, 411
Multi-infarct dementia (MID), 235
  definition of, 411
Multiple intelligences theory, 143
  definition of, 411
Multiple regression, 395–396
Multiple treatment interference, 16
  definition of, 411

Multivariate Analysis of Variance
    (MANOVA), 395
Muscular system, changes in, with
    aging, 61–62
Myotonia, 65
  definition of, 412
Mythical family life cycle, 196

National Council of Senior Citizens
    (NCSC), 331, 412
Naturally occurring retirement com-
    munities, 338–339
  definition of, 412
NEO model, of personality, 203
Nerve deafness, 120
  definition of, 412
Nervous system, changes in, with
    aging, 57–58
Neugarten, Bernice, description of
    personality development,
    195–196
Neural presbycusis, 118–119
Neuritic plaques, 58
  definition of, 412
Neuroendocrine theory of aging, 75
  definition of, 412
Neurofibrillary tangles, 58
  definition of, 412
Neuron, 57
  definition of, 412
Neuroticism, extraversion, and open-
    ness to experience (NEO)
    model, of personality, 203
Neurotransmitters, 224
  definition of, 412
Nonnormative life events, 10–11
  definition of, 412
NORCs. *See* Naturally occurring re-
    tirement communities
Normal-pressure hydrocephalus,
    234–235
Normative age-graded events, 9–10
  definition of, 412
Normative history-graded events, 10
  definition of, 412
Nurse's aides, 105–106
Nursing home
  adjustment to, 104–106
  evaluation of, 106–107
  staff, importance of, 105–106
Nursing home care, 104–108
  financing of, 102*b*–103*b*, 106–108
Nutrition services, 101
  definition of, 412

Oakland Growth Studies, 92
Obesity, and longevity, 78
Old. *See* Young/old polarity
Older workers, 350–352
Open-coupled homosexuals, 270
  definition of, 412
Optimization, 7. *See also* Alleviative
    optimization; Preventative op-
    timization
  definition of, 412
Organismic model, of development,
    39–40, 43–46
  definition of, 412
Organizational culture, 348
  definition of, 412
Orgasm, 65
  definition of, 412
Osteoarthritis, 62
  definition of, 413
Osteoporosis, 61–63, 91
  definition of, 413
Oval window, 118–119
  definition of, 413
Oxygen consumption, maximum,
    59
  definition of, 441

Pain perception, age-related
    changes in, 121
Paired associate learning task,
    171–172
  definition of, 413
Palliative care, 375
  definition of, 413
Papalia, Diane, research on cognitive
    functioning, 45
Parent(s)
  and adolescents, 288–289
  death of, 384–385
  elderly, and adult children, 291–
    297
    contacts between: gender, race,
      and class differences, 293–
      295
    feelings between, 295–297
    geographic proximity of, 292
  homosexual, 287*b*
  single, 286–287
    agencies and organizations serv-
      ing, 288
Parental imperative, Jung's cross-cul-
    tural research on, 188–190
Parenthood, 279–291
  transition to, 284–286

Parkinson's disease, 234–235
 definition of, 413
Partial retirement, 362
 definition of, 413
Part-whole discrimination, 112
Passive-congenial marriage, 262b
Passive-dependent personality type,
  207
 definition of, 413
Passive euthanasia, 372
 definition of, 413
Patron-type status, 304
 definition of, 413
Peck, Robert, description of personality development, 194–195
Pedestrian accidents, and age, 130
Perception
 age-related changes in, 111–122
 definition of, 111, 413
Perceptual closure, 112
Performance, interventions to optimize, 132–133
Peripheral nervous system, 57
 definition of, 413
Personal autonomy, 18–19
Personality Chicago researchers' descriptions of, 193–196
 definition of, 187–188
 effect on health, 87
 five-factor model of, 204
 of healthy adult, 220b
 measurement of, 201–205
 NEO (neuroticism, extraversion,
  and openness to experience)
  model of, 203
 qualitative descriptions of, classic
  stage theories, 188–201
 quantitative research on, 203–
  205
 recent approaches to, 196–201
Personality development
 early formation theories of, 188
 Erikson's theory of, 46, 48b–49b,
  190–193
 Freud's theory of, 44, 188
 Gould's description of, 199–201
 Havighurst's theory of, 193–194
 Jung's theory of, 188–190
 Neugarten's description of, 195–
  196
 Peck's description of, 194–195
 in women, 208–210
Personality pattern
 and career choice, 343–344
 definition of, 413

Personality types, 207
Personal unconscious, definition of,
  189, 413
Pet therapy, 246–247
 definition of, 413
16-PF. See Sixteen Personality Factor
  Questionnaire
Pharmacotherapy
 definition of, 413
 for depression, 225
Physical powers, value of, vs. value of
  wisdom, 195
Physiological death, 369
 definition of, 413
Piaget, Jean, theory of intellectual development, 44–46, 138, 139b,
  152–153
Pick's disease, 235
 definition of, 413
Planned retirement communities,
  338
 definition of, 413
Plateau stage, of sexual arousal, 65
 definition of, 413
Pleasure
 definition of, 413
 for women, 210–211
PMA. See Primary Mental Abilities
  Test
PMS. See Premenstrual syndrome
Political involvement, of adults,
  329–331
Postformal models of thought,
  139–141
Postparental phase, of marriage, 266
 definition of, 413
Postponers, 279
 definition of, 413
Pregnancy and birth, experience of,
  sex differences in, 281–283
Preintimate status, 191
 definition of, 413
Premenstrual syndrome (PMS),
  220b
 definition of, 413
Preretirement program, 362
 definition of, 414
Presbycusis, 118–120
 definition of, 414
 social effects of, 120
Presbyopia, 114
 definition of, 414
Presbystasis, 122
 definition of, 414
Preventative health care, 91–92

Preventative optimization, 8
 definition of, 414
Prework, 190
 definition of, 414
Primary aging, 55
 definition of, 414
Primary caregivers, 311
 definition of, 414
Primary differentiated dementias,
  234–235
 definition of, 414
Primary memory
 age differences in, 167, 184
 definition of, 414
Primary Mental Abilities Test, 146–
  148, 414
Primary undifferentiated dementias,
  234
 definition of, 414
Private long-term care insurance,
  108
 definition of, 414
Problem finding, 140
 definition of, 414
Problem solving
 cultural differences in, 139b
 logical, in adulthood, research on,
  152–155
 practical, in adulthood, research
  on, 155–156
 strategies for, 195
Procedural knowledge, 179b
 definition of, 414
Professional obsolescence, 181
 definition of, 414
Projective measures, of personality,
  201–203
 definition of, 414
Prospective memory, 174
 definition of, 414
Prostate gland
 changes in, with aging, 66
 definition of, 414
Prosthetic devices, for enhancement
  of perception in later life, 133
Protest and yearning, stage of bereavement, 382
 definition of, 414
Pseudodementia, 235
 definition of, 414
Pseudointimate status, 191–192
 definition of, 414
Psychoactive drugs, for Alzheimer's
  disease, 242
Psychohistory, 49b

Psychological death, 369
  definition of, 414
Psychological well-being, of women,
  aspects of, 210
Psychometric approach, in research
  on creativity, 158
  definition of, 414
Psychometric studies, of adult intelligence, 146–152
Psychomotor skills
  age differences in, 126–128
  definition of, 415
Psychosexual dysfunction, 69–71
  definition of, 415
Psychotherapy
  definition of, 415
  for depression, 226
Punishment and obedience orientation, to moral reasoning, 213
Pupil, of eye, 112–113
  definition of, 415

Qualitative changes, 44, 46–47
  definition of, 415
Quantitative changes, 40–41, 46–47
  definition of, 415
Quetelet, 4, 415

Racial mortality crossover phenomenon, 84b–85b
  definition of, 415
Random sample, 19
  definition of, 415
Raven Progressive Matrices, 144
Reaction time
  age differences in, 125–128
  definition of, 415
Reactive, definition of, 40, 415
Reactive effects, 16
  definition of, 415
Reactive effects of testing, 15
  definition of, 415
Reality orientation, and dementia,
  242–243
  definition of, 415
Reasoning, logical, in adulthood, research on, 152–155
Recall
  age differences in, 168–169, 184
  definition of, 415
Received knowledge, 178b–179b
  definition of, 415
Reciprocal causation, 33
  definition of, 415

Reciprocity
  definition of, 415
  in family support networks,
    303–305
  of friendships, 326
  serial, 387, 417
Recognition
  in memory research, 168–169, 184
    definition of, 415
  in perception, 112
Refilled nest, 290–291
Reflexes, changes in, with aging, 58
Refractory period, 65
  definition of, 415
Regretful singles, 268
  definition of, 415
Reintegrative stage, of intellectual development, 142, 157
  definition of, 415
Reliability, of measurements, 16–18
  definition of, 416
Relief, in reaction to divorce, 272
Religious involvement
  of adults, 333–335
  age differences in, 334
  definition of, 333–334
  gender differences in, 334
  racial differences in, 334–335
  as resource in old age, 335
Remarriage(s), 274–275
  divorce rates for, 276b
  in old age, 275
  relative success of, as compared to
    first marriage, 276b
Reorganizers, 207
Representative sample, 19–20
  definition of, 416
Reproductive system
  changes in, with aging, 64–75
  female, 64
  male, 64
Research methodology, 13–20
  sampling considerations, 19–
    20
Research participants, rights of,
  28b–29b
Resolution stage, of sexual arousal,
  65
  definition of, 416
Resolved singles, 268
  definition of, 416
Respiratory system, changes in, with
  aging, 60–61
Respite care, 101, 311
  definition of, 416

Responsible stage, of intellectual development, 141
  definition of, 416
Retina, 112–113
  definition of, 416
Retirement, 359–366
  adjustment to, 363
  as box of life, 183b
  gender differences in, 363–364
  preparing for, 361–362
  racial differences in, 363–364
Retirement income, 364–366
Retirement stage, 345
  definition of, 416
Retrieval deficits
  age differences in, 171
  definition of, 416
  vs. encoding deficits, 169–171
Reverse discrimination, 355
  definition of, 416
Rework, 190
  definition of, 416
Ribot's law, 169
  definition of, 416
Riegel, Klaus, developmental theory,
  46–47, 50
Ritualistic religiosity, 333
  definition of, 416
Role compatibility stage, 255
  definition of, 416
Role models
  definition of, 416
  friends as, 326
Rorschach, 202
  definition of, 416

Sanctification stage, of bereavement,
  382
  definition of, 416
Schizophrenia, 228–231
  cause of, nature-nuture contro-
    versy, 230b
  in elderly, treatment of, 229–231
  symptoms of, 228–229
  treatment of, 229
Seattle Longitudinal Study, 150
Secondary aging, 55
  definition of, 416
Secondary caregivers, 311–312
  definition of, 416
Secondary dementia, 235
  definition of, 416
Secondary memory
  age differences in, 167–168,
    184

Secondary memory *(continued)*
definition of, 416
Selection effect, as threat to internal
validity of research, 14, 16
definition of, 416
Selective attention, 122–123
definition of, 416
Selectivity theory, of friendship,
325–326
definition of, 417
Self, definition of, 189, 417
Self-awareness, 195
Self-care, 97, 99
definition of, 417
Self-examination, in cancer detection, 91–92
Self-realization, 189
definition of, 417
Self-report measures, 201–202
definition of, 417
Senior citizen's centers, 101
definition of, 417
Sensation
age-related changes in, 111–122
definition of, 111, 417
versus perception, 111
Sensitizing effect, of testing, 15
Sensory memory
age differences in, 166–167, 184
definition of, 417
Sensory presbycusis, 118
Separateness. *See* Attachment/sepa-
rateness polarity
Serial reciprocity, 387
definition of, 417
Sex-role socialization, Rebecca's
study of, 48–50
Sexual dysfunction, 69–71
Sexual functioning and physiology,
64–65
Sexual harassment, in workplace,
358–359
definition of, 417
Sexually transmitted diseases, 89–91
definition of, 417
Shock stage, of bereavement, 382
definition of, 417
Sibling relationships, in adulthood,
321–324
Silence, as perspective, 178*b*
definition of, 417
Similarity, of friends, 326
definition of, 417

Singles
as parents, 286–287
types of, 267–268
Sixteen Personality Factor Question-
naire (16-PF), 201–202, 417
Skeletal system, changes in, with
aging, 61–62
Skilled nursing care facilities, 104
definition of, 417
Skin, changes in, with aging, 54
Sleep patterns, age differences in, 124
Smell, age-related changes in,
120–121
Smoking, 60–61
effect on health, 88
and longevity, 78
Social clock, 11
Social contract orientation, to moral
reasoning, 213
Social death, 369
definition of, 417
Socialization, for older alcoholics,
232
Social learning theory, 42–43
Social therapy, for older alcoholics,
232
Spatial orientation, 112
Specification stage, 344
definition of, 417
Speech comprehension, age-related
changes in, 119–120
Spiral organ, 118–119
definition of, 417
Split Dreams, of women, 209
definition of, 417
Stages, of development, 44
definition of, 417
Stagnation, 192
definition of, 417
Standard deviation, 392–393
Statistical conclusion validity, 16–17
Statistical techniques, 390–397
Statistical tests, in developmental re-
search, 19
STD. *See* Sexually transmitted dis-
eases
Stepparents, 287–288
Stereotyped relationships, 191–192
definition of, 418
Stereotypes, of older workers,
350–352
Stimulus stage, 255
definition of, 418

Stimulus-value-role (SVR) theory, of
mate selection, 255–256
definition of, 418
Stress
adaptive management of, 87
definition of, 86, 418
effect on health, 86–87
perceptions of, age differences in,
88
Strial presbycusis, 119
Stroop effect, 126
Structural dimensions, of friendships, 326
definition of, 418
Structure-function analysis, 34
definition of, 418
Students
at college, diversity among, 180
nontraditional, 181–183
Subjective knowledge, 179*b*
definition of, 418
Suicide rates, age, gender, and racial
differences in, 227–228
Superego, definition of, 188, 418
Supplementation, in caregiving, 317
definition of, 418
Support bank, 303–304
definition of, 418
Surrogate motherhood, 73–74
definition of, 418
Sustained attention, 123–125
definition of, 418
Synapses, 57
definition of, 418

Task content
definition of, 418
and memory performance, 171
Task pacing
definition of, 418
and memory performance, 171, 175
Taste, age-related changes in,
120–121
TAT. *See* Thematic Apperception
Test
Telephone reassurance, 101
definition of, 418
Temporality, of developmental
changes, 38
definition of, 418
Terminal drop, in intellectual performance, 151–152
definition of, 418

Terminal illness, and attitudes toward death, 379–381
Terminal phase, of dying, 381
  definition of, 418
Tertiary memory
  age differences in, 167–169, 184
  definition of, 418
  in old age, 170
Testing, definition of, 418
Testing effect, as threat to internal validity of research, 14
Test-retest reliability, 17
  definition of, 418
Thanatology, 370–371
  definition of, 418
Thematic Apperception Test (TAT), 197, 202
  definition of, 418
Theories, 34–39. *See also* Developmental theories
  definition of, 34, 419
  evaluation of, 35
  family of, 35
  functions of, 34–35
Thorndike, E. L., 5, 419
Three boxes of life, 183*b*
Time-lag research design, 21, 23
  definition of, 419
Time of measurement, as variable in research design, 20
  definition of, 419
Time-sequential research design, 24–25
  definition of, 419
Total brain death, 369
  definition of, 419
Total marriage, 262*b*
Traffic accidents, and age, 130, 131*b*
Triarchic theory, of intelligence, 143
  definition of, 419
T^2, Hotelling's, 394
t-test, 394
Tympanic membrane, 118–119
  definition of, 419
Type A behavior pattern, 87
  definition of, 419
Type B behavior pattern, 87
  definition of, 419

Unconscious
  collective, 189, 401
  personal, 189, 413
Unemployment, 355–358
Unidirectional causation, 33
  definition of, 419
Unintegrated personality type, 207
  definition of, 419
Universal ethical principle orientation, to moral reasoning, 213
Urinary system, changes in, with aging, 63–64
U-shaped curve, of marital satisfaction, 264–265
  definition of, 419

Validity, in research, 13–17
Value comparison stage, 255
  definition of, 419
Variability, measures of, 392–393
Variables
  cause-effect relationships among, 396–397
  patterns of association between, 395–396
Variance, 392–393
Vasocongestion, in sexual arousal, 65
  definition of, 419
Vertical career change, 349
  definition of, 419
Vestibular system
  age-related changes in, normal, 121–122
  definition of, 419
Vestibulocochlear nerve, 118–119
  definition of, 419
Vigilance, 123
Vigilance decrement, 123
Vision
  age-related changes in
    normal, 112–117
    pathological, 117–118
  in early adulthood, 111–112
Visual acuity, 115–116
  definition of, 419
Vital capacity, 60
  definition of, 419
Vital marriage, 262*b*
Vitamin B-12, 63

Vitreous humor, 113–114
  definition of, 419
Voluntary organizations, 331–333
Volunteer work, 331–333

WAIS–R. *See* Wechsler Adult Intelligence Scale—Revised
Ways of knowing, of women, 178*b*–179*b*
Wechsler Adult Intelligence Scale—Revised (WAIS–R), 146–148
  definition of, 419
Weight, changes in, with aging, 55
Wills, 387
Wisdom, 156–158
  value of, vs. value of physical powers, 195
Wishful singles, 268
  definition of, 419
Women
  careers of, 345, 346*b*–347*b*
  Dreams of, 209
  experience of pregnancy and birth, 281–283
  in family support networks, 304
  as friends, 327, 328*b*
  in middle years of adulthood, mental health of, 212*b*
  moral reasoning of, Gilligan's theory of, 214–215
  personality development in, 208–210
  psychological well-being of, aspects of, 210
  split Dreams of, 209
  ways of knowing of, 178*b*–179*b*
Women in the middle, 308–309
  definition of, 420
Work
  as box of life, 183*b*
  older adults and, 350–352
Working memory, 167. *See also* Primary memory
  definition of, 420
Work-role preoccupation, vs. ego differentiation, 195

Young/old polarity, 199
  definition of, 420